INTRODUCTION TO

Criminal Justice

INTRODUCTION TO

Criminal Justice

A BRIEF EDITION

SECOND EDITION

John Randolph Fuller
University of West Georgia

New York   Oxford
Oxford University Press

Oxford University Press is a department of the University of Oxford.
It furthers the University's objective of excellence in research, scholarship,
and education by publishing worldwide. Oxford is a registered trade mark of
Oxford University Press in the UK and certain other countries.

Published in the United States of America by Oxford University Press
198 Madison Avenue, New York, NY 10016, United States of America.

Cataloging-in-Publication Data is on file with the Library of Congress.
ISBN: 978-0-19-750404-8

9 8 7 6 5 4 3 2 1
Printed by Quad/Graphics, Inc., Mexico

For Amy
For everything

Brief Contents

Contents

Chapter 3   **Criminal Law**   63

PART II   ENFORCING THE LAW   95

FEATURES

Chapter 6 Policing: Innovations and Controversies 159

FEATURES

PART IV FROM PENOLOGY TO CORRECTIONS AND BACK 291

Chapter 12   Community Corrections   359

⚖️ PART V   CONTEMPORARY ISSUES   389

Chapter 13   Juvenile Justice   391

Preface

The field of criminal justice is constantly changing. As new laws are enacted and new technology is developed, criminal justice professionals must constantly adapt. *Introduction to Criminal Justice: A Brief Edition* has kept abreast of these changes. This second edition features a renewed emphasis on policing, police militarization, victimology, white-collar crime, and the political considerations that shape criminal justice policies.

The fundamental job of the criminal justice system is to protect individuals and property within the rule of law. This has always been a difficult mission, one that requires ensuring public safety while protecting individual rights and liberties. Quests to improve the system's institutions—police, courts, and corrections—focus on making them more equitable and decent for everyone.

The criminal justice system is not as neat and orderly as it is often portrayed. Many factors, issues, and controversies must be put in context if we are to understand how the system functions. This book is written with a somewhat critical perspective that recognizes the profound influences of economic inequality, race, and gender on criminal justice outcomes. In light of these contexts, this book is designed to spark and deepen interest in the field while conveying the immense responsibility and challenges involved in serving the country and community. The main narrative provides foundational knowledge while helping students separate fact from fiction and gain insight into the complexities of ethical decision-making. It articulates the important issues of the field and supplies students with the basics necessary to work in this arena.

Introduction to Criminal Justice: A Brief Edition is designed as a standard text that covers the canon in the first course for criminal justice majors. Additionally, the book serves as an introduction to the discipline for students who have not yet chosen a major. The history and contemporary concerns of criminal justice are among the most interesting and necessary fields of study offered at universities. However, students often embark with myths they have absorbed from television shows, movies, and media coverage of sensational cases. Debunking these myths by engaging in critical thinking is thus essential to fully understanding the field. This text is unique in its robust pedagogical framework that encourages critical thinking, not merely memorization of facts and figures. Students must appreciate the history of social control and the limits of science and government to respond to antisocial behavior. Most important, students should be open to the many ways in which the criminal justice system might be effectively reformed.

Features of the Second Edition

This second edition of *Introduction to Criminal Justice: A Brief Edition* presents the latest available research, statistics, and developments in a comprehensive yet concise format. The text walks students through scenarios that reflect high-pressure, on-the-job circumstances, preparing them to meet such challenges in both the classroom and the real world. Throughout, the learning design emphasizes the critical thinking and ethical decision-making skills required to work in the criminal justice system.

> Each chapter begins with a **chapter-opening vignette**, which introduces a controversial case and/or event in the news that illuminates the chapter's major themes. All 14 vignettes, one of the most popular features of the first edition, are new to this edition. The scenarios are based on news stories, current events, and cases that capture the attention of students and highlight important issues addressed in the chapter. Each opening vignette ends with a critical thinking question that instructors can use as a conversation starter in class and that students can reconsider after reading the entire chapter.

> **Updated examples.** To ensure the text is contemporary and captivating, we have revisited and updated examples to reflect criminal justice issues that have recently gained prominence.

> **Updated with the most current statistics available.** The second edition includes the latest available statistics on crime and the criminal justice system, as per the *Uniform Crime Reports*.

> **New and updated figures and tables.** Each figure and table has been carefully analyzed to ensure that it presents current and clear information. Included with each figure is a critical thinking question to help students understand the material.

> **Updated supplements package written by the author.** Each supplement available on the Oxford Learning Link (including the instructor's manual, test bank, PowerPoints, and all student resources) was not only written by the author but has been reviewed and revised to ensure clarity, accuracy, and consistency with the text.

> **New video package.** For the second edition, there are 14 new videos (one per chapter) that help illustrate chapter issues and concepts. Additionally, all Focus on Ethics videos have been re-examined, and several have been replaced with more contemporary and more targeted videos that help relate chapter concepts to students.

> **New Fast-Class Mini-Lectures.** This feature presents a short, 5-minute lecture narrated by the author and supported by four to six PowerPoint slides. These mini-lectures will be valuable conversation-starters, addressing current criminal justice events that reflect issues presented in the text. New mini-lectures will be provided throughout the semester via the Instructor Resources section of Oxford Learning Link.

> **Learning objectives** describe the educational goals for each chapter and are keyed to each chapter-ending summary, as well as the major headings within the chapters.

> **Pause and Review** questions are knowledge-based review questions that appear at the end of each major section to test students' memory and understanding of the material as it is presented.

> The new **Getting It Right** feature in several chapters highlights instances in which criminal justice practitioners have successfully implemented solutions. This feature is accompanied by video clips and critical thinking questions.

> The feature **A Closer Look** has been popular with students and instructors because it digs deeply into specific criminal justice issues. Some of the feature topics have been retained because reviewers identified them as particularly important, but several new topics have been added to address recent issues and controversies. Each box includes one or two critical thinking questions.

> **Case in Point** boxes summarize landmark court cases relevant to the chapter discussion.

> › **Criminal Justice Reference** boxes provide pertinent information for students to refer to throughout their studies.

> › **Focus on Ethics** boxes at the end of each chapter place students in on-the-job scenarios and ask them to respond to ethical dilemmas. The feature is accompanied by a set of questions to help students understand the consequences of a potential decision (these also can be used to encourage in-class discussion). This feature also connects to Oxford Learning Link, where students can watch videos about related real-world situations.

> › Each **Chapter Summary** is linked to the learning objectives and outlines the main concepts covered in each chapter.

> › **Critical Reflection** questions are located at the end of each chapter. These questions are open-ended, and some may require further research.

> › **Key terms** appear in the chapter margins where terms are first used (or pop up in the ebook), as well as in a chapter-ending list to help students recall the important concepts covered in the chapter.

> › A rich **graphics program** of photographs and figures that illustrate the latest statistics helps students explore essential chapter themes.

Introduction to Criminal Justice: A Brief Edition has been substantially revised to reflect both changes in the law and the patterns of crime in the United States. This edition has been completely updated with the latest available research, statistics, and developments in the field of criminal justice. Chapter-specific revisions include the following:

Chapter 2
– New A Closer Look 2.1: Crime Apps: Reporting Crime or Reporting Fear?

Chapter 3
– New A Closer Look 3.1: Watson Murder
– New Getting It Right 3.1: Restoring the Vote to Felons

Chapter 4
– Updated A Closer Look 4.1: Who Polices the Police?

Chapter 5
– New Getting It Right 5.1: Problem-Solving Policing
– New Case in Point 5.1: *Miranda v. Arizona*

Chapter 6
– New Case in Point 6.1: *Graham v. Connor*
– New A Closer Look 6.1: Policing Is Getting Safer

Chapter 7
– New Getting It Right 7.1: Marijuana Convictions Going Up in Smoke
– New Figure 7.2: Outcome of Cases Handled in U.S. District Court

Chapter 8
– New A Closer Look 8.1: Public Defender Salaries are Indefensible

Chapter 9
– New Getting It Right 9.1: The Role of the Prosecutor and Conviction Review Units

Chapter 10
– New A Closer Look 10.1: Closing Rikers
– New Figure 10.4: Death Penalty and Race

Chapter 11
– New Case in Point 11.1: *Ross v. Blake*
– New Figure 11.2: Federal Prison Security Levels
– New Getting It Right 11.1: Learning a Lesson

Chapter 12
– New Getting It Right 12.1: To Bee: Reintegration Programs and Preparing for Life after Prison

Chapter 13
– New Getting It Right 13.1: Reading as Punishment

Chapter 14
– New A Closer Look 14.1: Of Prisons and Pandemics
– New Focus on Ethics 14.1: Future Cop

Appendix material on Theories of Crime
– For instructors who wish to cover theory, former Chapter 3 Theories of Crime has been streamlined to offer coverage of the most essential theories of crime in appendix format.

Oxford Learning Link

Oxford Learning Link at www.oup.com/he/fuller2e is your hub for a wealth of engaging digital learning tools and resources. Material hosted there includes the instructor's manual, test bank, PowerPoints, videos, and all student resources. In addition, Oxford Learning Link Direct brings the high-quality digital teaching and learning tools for *Introduction to Criminal Justice: A Brief Edition* right to your local learning management system.

Oxford Insight Study Guide

All new print and digital copies of the second edition of *Introduction to Criminal Justice: A Brief Edition* include access to the Oxford Insight Study Guide. This data-driven, personalized digital learning tool reinforces key concepts from the text and encourages effective reading and study habits. Developed with a learning-science-based design, Oxford Insight Study Guide engages students in an active and highly dynamic review of chapter content, empowering them to critically assess their understanding. Real-time, actionable data generated by student activity in the tool helps instructors ensure that each student is best supported along a unique learning path. Learn more at oxfordinsight.oup.com.

Acknowledgments

The professionals at Oxford University Press have been delightful to work with. My editor, Steve Helba, has been instrumental in helping me to refine the focus of this text to appeal to a broad range of students and professors. His wise counsel and sound judgment mean a lot to me, and I will forever be indebted for his commitment to this project. Senior Production Editor William Murray expertly shepherded the manuscript through copy editing and paging. I am also indebted to Tony Mathias for his many helpful suggestions in developing and marketing this edition. I am especially indebted to Maegan Sherlock and Lauren Mine, my development editors who made countless insightful contributions to this book. Kora Fillet is also acknowledged for her contributions and responsiveness to my many questions and concerns. Finally, Amy Hembree is so very much appreciated for her hard work, wise counsel, sense of humor, and tolerance over these many years of working with me.

I was lucky to have a set of reviewers who were not afraid to suggest ways that this edition could be improved. The following reviewers gave generously of their time and expertise, and I am grateful for their many wise suggestions:

Gary Copus, University of Alaska, Fairbanks
Shana Maier, Widener University
Jeff Schwartz, Rowan University
Abigail Novak, University of Florida
Jonathan Kremser, Kutztown University
Michelle L. Foster, Kent State University
Mary G. Wilson, Kent State University
Nicole Lasky, Northeastern State University
Doug Klutz, University of Alabama
Brad Reyns, Weber State University
Patricia Riley, University of West Georgia
Allison Crowson, Norwich University
Melissa Bemiller, Augusta University
Allan Barnes, University of Alaska Anchorage
Cassie White, University of West Georgia
Hasmik Arakelyan, California State University Los Angeles
Haley Slade, Mott Community College
Steven Scibelli, STCC
Pamela Newell, University of North Georgia
Sebahattin Gultekin, Odessa College
Ben Stickle, Middle Tennessee State University
Whitney Nickels, Northwest Mississippi Community College
Kimberly Renteria, Arkansas Tech University
Kevin Flemens, College of Southern Maryland
Brittany Rodriguez, Tarleton State University
Louis Martine, Harper College

About the Author

John Randolph Fuller is Professor Emeritus at the University of West Georgia where he taught in the Department of Criminology for 33 years. He brings both an applied and theoretical background to his scholarship and has been recognized by his students and peers as an outstanding teacher and scholar. In addition, he served as the university's Ombuds, where his knowledge of conflict resolution helped settle disputes among and between students, faculty, staff, and administrators.

Dr. Fuller served as a probation and parole officer for the Florida Probation and Parole Commission in Broward County, Florida, where he managed a caseload of more than 100 felons. In addition, he served as a criminal justice planner for the Palm Beach County metropolitan criminal justice planning unit. In this capacity, he worked with every criminal justice agency in a three-county area and wrote grants for the Law Enforcement Assistance Administration that funneled more than $1 million into local criminal justice agencies. By working directly with offenders as a probation and parole officer and with criminal justice administrators as a criminal justice planner, Dr. Fuller gained significant insights that inform his writing about the criminal justice system.

Dr. Fuller has authored and edited numerous journal articles, chapters, and books on criminal justice, criminology, global crime, courts, and juvenile delinquency.

PART I

Crime: Problems, Measurement, and Law

Chapter 1

Crime and Criminal Justice

Tyler Barriss in court during a preliminary hearing. What is meant by the term *swatting*?

On December 28, 2017, police in Wichita, Kansas, received a call from

a man who claimed he had just shot his father, was holding his mother and sister at gunpoint, and wanted to burn down his house and commit suicide. Officers were dispatched to the address, but before they could contact the occupants, the front door opened and 28-year-old Andrew Finch stepped out onto the porch. The officers instructed him to raise his hands. When Finch lowered one hand to his waist, an officer shot and killed him.[1]

Police searching the house found no gun and no gasoline. They did find a family traumatized not by a suicidal maniac, but by the death of their innocent son. The police quickly realized something was wrong.[2]

Eventually, investigators learned that the initial call emerged from a dispute between online gamers. Casey Viner of Ohio and Shane Gaskill of Kansas had argued over a $1.50 wager on a videogame. Viner then hired Tyler Barriss of Los Angeles to "swat" Gaskill, that is, to call the police and falsely report a crime in progress so that police would dispatch a SWAT (special weapons and tactics) team.[3]

This was not Tyler Barriss's first swatting. He had previously called in bomb threats to schools in order to give friends a day off.[4] A gaming tournament in Dallas, Texas, was evacuated because of a bomb threat from Barriss. He even called in a threat to a Federal Communications Commission meeting about net neutrality.[5] Barriss also earned money by contracting his swatting skills to clients like Casey Viner. However, Shane Gaskill no longer lived at the address that Viner gave to Barriss. That address was occupied by the Finch family.

The police officer who killed Andrew Finch was cleared of any wrongdoing. Barriss was sentenced to 20 years in federal prison, and Viner was sentenced to 15 months in federal prison and restricted from gaming for two years after serving his term.[6] The judge ordered Gaskill to pay $1,000 in restitution and other costs and deferred further prosecution until December 31, 2020. If Gaskill fulfills all the conditions of the court agreement, charges against him will likely be dropped.[7]

THINK ABOUT IT > How did this interpersonal dispute become a violent crime?

Did law enforcement fulfill its role in enforcing the law and keeping the community safe?

LEARNING OBJECTIVE 1.1

Define social control.

LEARNING OBJECTIVE 1.2

Outline how the U.S. criminal justice system protects individual rights.

LEARNING OBJECTIVE 1.3

Define crime and criminal justice.

1.1 What Is Crime?

Social control consists of the rules, habits, and customs a society uses to enforce conformity to its norms. Imagine how chaotic society would be if there were no rules and everyone did whatever they wanted. Communities and countries are composed of the citizens who live in them. In a democracy, not only do citizens decide which laws they want to govern them, but sometimes citizens must also ensure that the laws are enforced. This is an important aspect of social control in a democracy. The feature that sets the U.S. criminal justice system apart from those of many other countries is the way individual rights are protected as an integral part of the functioning of law enforcement. The system must maintain a delicate balance between imposing order and preserving individual rights. This task, which is difficult in the best of times, becomes even more problematic in times of war and terrorism. Yet it would be a grave mistake to think of these issues as mutually exclusive. In other words, keeping people safe does not mean removing their constitutional rights. To successfully create and nurture meaningful communities, the government must control crime without turning the country into a police state. Achieving this balance is part of the Herculean task of the criminal justice system. Consider the opening case in which the police shot a man during a hoax gone wrong. If the report had not been a hoax, the police might have been lauded for doing their job. Instead, a citizen thought it would be appropriate revenge for a perceived slight to use law enforcement's crime-control function against another person.

The task that lies ahead of us is to appreciate the complexities and ambiguities of crime control in the 21st century. Although crime must be addressed within the rule of law, many practitioners recognize that more fundamental questions must be considered. These questions about the nature of justice in the United States include concerns of racial prejudice, the power of law enforcement to decide what to do with suspects, economic inequality, and the gaps in access to decision-making processes in all aspects of society.

Crime can be described as the violation of the laws of a society by a person or a group of people who are subject to the laws of that society. In this context, **justice** is the administration of a punishment or reward in accordance with morals that a given society considers correct. **Criminal justice** is a social institution that has the mission of controlling crime by detecting, detaining, adjudicating, and punishing and/or rehabilitating people who break the law. Most people envision crime as fairly straightforward, often sordid affairs, such as robbery, rape, and murder. For example:

> In August 2016, Kala Brown, 30, and her boyfriend, Charles David Carver, 32, went missing after going to a cleaning job near Woodruff, South Carolina. Following their disappearance, the couple's friends noted that messages posted to Carver's Facebook page seemed odd, as if someone else were using his account. In November, after tracing the couple's cell phone signals, police found Brown chained inside a metal storage container on the property of realtor Todd Christopher Kohlhepp. In a search of Kohlhepp's property, police found the body of Carver, as well as the bodies of a married couple who had been missing since December 2015. Kohlhepp had hired all of the victims to work on his property.[8] After his arrest, Kohlhepp also admitted to shooting to death four people at a motorcycle shop in Chesnee, South Carolina, in 2003. In a plea bargain that spared him from the death penalty, Kohlhepp pleaded guilty and was sentenced to seven consecutive life sentences without the possibility of parole.[9]

Many offenses involve the harm not of other people but of social order. Although order is a good thing to have in a society, sometimes the order itself is questionable.

> In January 2019, a federal judge found Oona Holcomb, Madeline Huse, Zaachila Orozco-McCormick, and Natalie Hoffman guilty of entering a wildlife refuge on the United States–Mexico border without a permit and leaving jugs of water, food, and other items for migrants crossing the desert. The women, who were activists with the humanitarian group No More Deaths, told the court their actions were motivated by religious convictions and a

Social control—The rules, habits, and customs a society uses to enforce conformity to its norms.

Crime—The violation of the laws of a society by a person or a group of people who are subject to the laws of that society.

Justice—The administering of a punishment or reward in accordance with morals that a given society considers to be correct.

Criminal justice—A social institution that has the mission of controlling crime by detecting, detaining, adjudicating, and punishing and/or rehabilitating people who break the law.

Sheriff's deputies search the home of Todd Christopher Kohlhepp. How were law enforcement officers able to solve this case?

belief that everyone should have their survival needs met.[10] The women were sentenced to 15 months of unsupervised probation, fined $250, and banned from the refuge.[11]

Other offenses, such as espionage (spying), threaten not only society's laws but also its political stability. How these offenses are dealt with, however, is usually a result of the political mood of the times. In the 1950s, Julius and Ethel Rosenberg were found guilty of providing classified military information to the Soviet Union and executed.[12] In the last 10 years, those who have committed offenses considered to be treasonous have been sent to prison.

In 2010, Chelsea Manning, a United States Army intelligence analyst, gave thousands of classified military and diplomatic documents to WikiLeaks, an Internet organization that publishes classified or controversial information from anonymous sources.[13] In 2013, Manning was found guilty of 17 out of the 22 charges against her and of amended versions of four others. She was acquitted of aiding the enemy.[14] Manning was sentenced to 35 years at the U.S. Disciplinary Barracks at Fort Leavenworth, the U.S. military's only maximum security prison. In 2017, President Barack Obama commuted Manning's sentence, and she was released.[15] Manning was jailed again in March 2019 for refusing to testify before a grand jury against Wikileaks founder Julian Assange but was released after 62 days.[16]

Incidents such as these make rational discussion about crime difficult. The personal nature of crime further compounds this problem. In a society as diverse as the United States, what is rational to one person might not be rational to another, and everyone has his or her own solution to crime based on what he or she considers rational.

Taking these factors into account, a student of criminal justice can begin to understand how the apparently simple progression of crime → **arrest** → trial → punishment really represents many subtleties and complications. Still, as individuals, we hold tightly to the perspectives that support our personal notions of fairness, justice, and goodness, even when we know those notions might be grounded

Arrest—When law enforcement detains and holds a criminal suspect or suspects.

in the privilege of middle-class values concerning race, class, sex, and gender. However, crime is a messy human problem that does not respond to simple, mechanical, or straightforward solutions.

The study of crime and the criminal justice system is not an exact science. In thinking about crime, we must use what sociologist C. Wright Mills called the **sociological imagination**, or the idea that we must look beyond the obvious to evaluate how our social location influences how we perceive society.[17] Mills encouraged us to step back from our personal experiences and examine issues apart from our social location. For example, could the father of a murdered daughter reasonably sit on a jury of the accused killer? Of course not. Likewise, according to Mills, each of us should attempt to look at crime and criminal justice policy from a neutral and objective position. The key word here is "attempt." It can be argued that no one can truly be neutral and objective when considering social issues. We must be honest and acknowledge that our social class, race, gender, sex, age, and other personal attributes affect our thinking. Only by explicitly stating our social location can we, and those we seek to convince, put our opinions in context and evaluate them.

Sociological imagination—The idea that we must look beyond the obvious to evaluate how our social location influences the way we perceive society.

PAUSE AND REVIEW

1. What feature sets the U.S. criminal justice system apart from those of other countries?
2. What is crime? What is criminal justice?
3. What is the relationship between crime and justice?

1.2 The Criminal Justice System and Process

When the law is broken, the criminal justice system must respond in the name of society. The criminal justice system comprises various agencies from different levels of government, each of which has a mission to deal with some aspect of crime. Although the duties of some of these agencies appear to overlap and the system seems to be inefficient and cumbersome, it chugs along, processing a vast number of cases. However, the criminal justice system is often criticized by the public for being ineffective and failing to produce the justice that many people expect. Why do so many people perceive the criminal justice system in this way?

First, the system is not confined to one level of government. The criminal justice system spans the range from local governments to the federal government. The lines of authority and distinction between agencies are not always clear and in some cases must be negotiated according to the politics of the case. For example, tension exists between federal agencies such as the FBI and local law enforcement agencies. Depending on the case, investigators must decide whether federal or state laws have been violated and which agency has the primary responsibility for investigation. Although interagency cooperation is the stated norm, conflict does arise. (See A Closer Look 1.1 to learn more about interagency cooperation.) In addition, problems between different components of the criminal justice system may exist. The goals and missions of law enforcement are not always viewed as identical to those of the judicial system or the corrections system. Individual criminal justice practitioners might believe that other agencies are working against them.

LEARNING OBJECTIVE **1.4**

List the steps of the criminal justice process.

LEARNING OBJECTIVE **1.5**

Explain the major difference between the due process and crime-control models.

LEARNING OBJECTIVE **1.6**

Describe the wedding-cake model of criminal justice.

The FBI often assist local and state law enforcement agencies. Why is interagency cooperation between criminal justice agencies sometimes problematic?

Probation—The suspension of all or part of a sentence, subject to certain conditions and supervision in the community.

For example, the police sometimes believe that district attorneys and judges are working against them by helping offenders get plea bargains, light sentences, and **probation**. On the other hand, prison officials might think that lawmakers who legislate tougher, longer sentences are overcrowding the prisons.

Now let's examine how the criminal justice system is set up.

The Criminal Justice Process: An Overview

The criminal justice process is covered in great detail in the following chapters. However, this brief overview will provide some orientation as to how each component of the system is related to the process.

Cases move through the criminal justice system in a consistent manner. They begin with contact with a law enforcement agency, and then they proceed to the courts, which determine guilt (if any) and prescribe a sentence for the guilty. The convicted then move to the correctional system where punishment and/or treatments are administered. At each step of the process, criminal justice officials decide whether the case should continue to the next stage.

LAW ENFORCEMENT

Police officers are typically the first responders to crime and thus make initial contact. Someone may report or alert them to the crime, or they may witness it themselves. Upon making contact, police officers seek to determine the causes and perpetrators of the crime through investigation. They gather evidence, preserve the crime scene, and interview victims and witnesses. Individuals suspected of breaking the law are arrested and taken into custody. They are advised of their constitutional rights, questioned, and subjected to limited freedom until further processing. Once an individual is arrested, the booking process takes place. This process involves several activities, including fingerprinting, taking photographs (mugshots), and in some cases collecting DNA evidence from the suspect.

Role of law enforcement: initial contact → investigation → arrest → booking

A CLOSER LOOK 1.1
A Comparison of Federal, State, and Local Law Enforcement

One of the most stubborn problems in U.S. law enforcement is getting agencies to work together. Although we call it a criminal justice "system," historic, structural, personal, and jurisdictional issues prevent or impede criminal justice agencies from freely exchanging information and resources. Local, state, and federal law enforcement agencies are all subject to individual agency cultures rather than one national law enforcement culture affecting individual law enforcement agencies.

This philosophy had an especially tragic effect on September 11, 2001. Following the attacks, the National Commission on Terrorist Attacks Upon the United States, known as the 9/11 Commission, was created to investigate the circumstances surrounding the attacks. The Commission discovered that many major federal law enforcement and investigation agencies held separate pieces of information regarding the terrorist plot but had not communicated them to one another.[18] The Commission concluded that had various agencies acted together, the attacks might have been prevented.

A solution to this problem would be to create a large, federally mandated law enforcement agency, but this is unlikely to happen. Although other countries have this type of law enforcement structure, one of the intrinsic values of the United States is the idea that, when possible, government control should be vested at the level closest to the people. According to Sunil B. Desai, a U.S. Marine Corps major who served on the Council on Foreign Relations, four factors challenge the transition to greater interagency cooperation:

1. There is no formal, comprehensive concept of coordination for either routine or crisis situations.
2. There is no independent authority to develop and train personnel in interagency cooperation.
3. Individual agencies organize their policies and operations differently.
4. Personnel policies focus on developing personnel who are primarily dedicated to the individual agency rather than the community of agencies.[19]

Table 1.1 illustrates how the various federal, state, and local agencies are organized and funded and what they do. Law enforcement agencies at different levels of government have different resources, funding authorities, and mandates. Cooperation between these agencies is always a goal, but their differences are grounded in legal mandates. Also, agency cultures dictate that there will always be some degree of conflict, competition, and distrust between law enforcement agencies operating at different levels of government. Until the culture changes, our law enforcement system will be challenged to find ways to get federal, state, and local agencies to work together.

THINK ABOUT IT

1. What would you do to encourage law enforcement agencies to work together?
2. Should there be a national police force? Explain your answer.

TABLE 1.1   Comparison of Law Enforcement Levels of Jurisdiction

	FEDERAL	**STATE**	**LOCAL**
Agencies	• FBI • Immigration and Customs Enforcement • Secret Service	• State highway patrol • State investigative agencies	• Municipal police departments • County sheriff's offices
Mandate for Enforcing Laws	• Offenses on federal property and military reservations • Interstate crime	• Interstate highway systems • Offenses of local and state government officials	• State statutes within local jurisdictions
Funding	• Federal income tax	• State income tax • Sales tax • User taxes (driver's license, license plate fees, etc.)	• Sales tax • Property tax

COURTS

If the prosecutor's office decides that there is enough evidence to proceed with the case, it will charge the suspect with a specific crime. At this major decision-making point, the prosecutor may decide to dismiss the case. If the prosecutor decides to charge the suspect, however, a preliminary hearing is held. This process is designed to determine whether there is reason to think that a law has been broken. In some states and in the federal system, a grand jury makes this determination. At this stage, the defendant is brought before the court, and the formal charges are read. The defendant is also informed of his or her constitutional right to be represented by legal counsel. A plea of guilty or not guilty is entered, and a trial date is set. Bail may also be considered at this point. Following **arraignment**, plea bargaining occurs. Here, the prosecutor and defense attorney discuss the case and attempt to agree on a resolution. Typically, prosecutors seek a guilty plea in exchange for a reduced sentence. Defense attorneys who believe that the case against their client is weak or that their client is innocent may reject a plea bargain and demand a jury trial.

If the case proceeds to trial, the prosecution and defense present their cases before a jury, which decides whether the prosecution has presented enough evidence to convict the defendant. A verdict of guilty or not guilty is returned. This is called **adjudication**. In cases in which a jury cannot decide on a verdict, the prosecutor must choose between releasing the defendant or requesting a new trial. If a guilty verdict is reached, the judge sentences the convicted party to a punishment, usually a fine, a treatment program, probation, incarceration, or some combination of these. In some serious cases, the sentence may be death.

Role of courts: charging → preliminary hearing → arraignment → plea bargaining → adjudication → sentencing

CORRECTIONS

An offender may have to pay a sum of money as part of his or her punishment. In addition, an offender may be able to serve all or part of the sentence outside of prison or jail. The offender must agree to a set of conditions by which he or she will

Arraignment—Court appearance in which the defendant is formally charged with a crime and asked to respond by pleading guilty, not guilty, or *nolo contendere* (I do not wish to contend).

Adjudication—The action of administering a legal process of judging and pronouncing a judgment.

Parkland school shooting suspect Nikolas Cruz appears in court for a motion filed by the Public Defender's Office to withdraw from the case due to Cruz receiving an inheritance that can be used to pay for a private attorney. Defense attorneys Melisa McNeill (L) and Diane Cuddihy (R) speak with their client. Who represents the state in the court's process?

remain free and report to a probation officer. The offender may have to wear an electronic device that tracks his or her location.

Offenders serve sentences of less than a year in a local jail and sentences of longer than a year in prison. After release from incarceration, the corrections system attempts to ease the reintegration of the offender into the community. This process is typically carried out through **parole** in which the rights and liberties of the former convict are restricted and requirements such as drug-testing, job counseling, and educational requirements may be imposed.

Role of corrections: fines and probation and/or incarceration → re-entry

The Due Process and Crime-Control Models

The criminal justice system has a complicated mission. People expect the system to operate efficiently and move cases through the system as expeditiously as possible, but also to protect the innocent, convict and punish the guilty, and deliver justice. Not only are these two expectations difficult to achieve consistently, but they are sometimes at odds. In the 1960s, legal scholar Herbert L. Packer created models to describe these two expectations: the **due process model** and the **crime-control model**. The crime-control model describes the expectation of an efficient criminal justice system. The due process model describes the expectation of a just and fair system. The tension between these two models can be described as a competition between two sets of values: one that seeks to control crime and one that seeks to protect the legal rights of individuals accused of violating the law. In truth, the criminal justice system exemplifies both of these value systems and seeks to create a balance in which crime is controlled while individual rights are protected.[20]

The crime-control model is based on the idea that the repression of crime is the most important function of the criminal process. According to this model, crime control is important to individual freedom. It is difficult to be truly free in a society that does not enforce laws, apprehend offenders, and convict the guilty. If individuals are always living in fear of being victimized, they cannot behave in a free manner, thus threatening the social order. So, under the crime-control model, the justice process moves like an assembly line. Suspects are apprehended; the most likely suspects are charged and their guilt is ascertained; and the guilty receive an appropriate disposition. A free society depends on the criminal justice system carrying out this process efficiently and well. In contrast to the crime-control model's assembly line, the due process model operates more like an "obstacle course." Each stage of the due process model is designed to obstruct the movement of suspects further along the justice process. This is because the due process model recognizes the role of human error. People make mistakes, or they can be corrupt. Thus, the due process model pursues informal, non-judgmental fact-finding that recognizes the right of a suspect or defendant to receive the most correct and just judicial process possible.[21] Some major distinctions between the two models are outlined in Table 1.2.

The application of these models is affected by the political climate at any given time. Two good examples are illustrated by the efforts of the Warren Court (the U.S. Supreme Court between 1953 and 1969 named for its Chief Justice Earl Warren) and the passage of the USA PATRIOT ACT in response to the terrorist attacks of September 11, 2001. Friendly to the due process model, the Warren Court left a lasting mark on U.S. criminal procedure with its decisions. Notable cases include *Gideon v. Wainwright* (1963), which established that states must provide impoverished defendants with an attorney in felony cases (see Chapter 9) and *Miranda v. Arizona* (1966), which established that police must inform arrestees

Parole—The conditional release of a prison inmate who has served part of a sentence and who remains under the court's control.

Due process model—A model proposed by legal scholar Herbert L. Packer to describe the public's expectation of a just and fair criminal justice system.

Crime-control model—A model proposed by legal scholar Herbert L. Packer to describe the public's expectation of an efficient criminal justice system.

TABLE 1.2   The Crime-Control Model versus the Due Process Model

ASPECT OF THE CRIMINAL JUSTICE SYSTEM	CRIME-CONTROL MODEL	DUE PROCESS MODEL
Most Important Function	To repress crime: a necessary condition for meaningful communities and a free society	To deliver fundamental fairness of the law and due process
Ideal Concentration	Victim's rights before the defendant's rights	Defendant's rights, protected expressly by the Bill of Rights, before victim's rights
Police Power	Expanded powers to investigate, arrest, and search suspects	Limited to prevent oppression of individuals by the state
Legal Limits	Legal technicalities that obstruct the police should be eliminated	Criminal justice authority should be held accountable to the rules, procedures, and guidelines embedded in the Constitution
Emphasis on Efficiency versus Technical Correctness	The criminal justice system should operate like an assembly line that moves cases efficiently toward disposition	A person should be found guilty only if the government has followed legal procedures in its processing of the case.
Main Objective	To discover the truth and establish the factual guilt of the accused	To correctly follow legal procedure in establishing the factual guilt of the accused

that they do not have to answer questions and may have an attorney present during questioning (see Chapter 5). On the other hand, the USA PATRIOT ACT is an example of the crime-control model. USA PATRIOT stands for Uniting and Strengthening America by Providing Appropriate Tools Required to Intercept and Obstruct Terrorism. This legislation greatly expanded the government's powers to

The U.S. Supreme Court in 1957. Seated from left are Felix Frankfurter; Hugo Black; Earl Warren, chief justice; Stanley Reed; and William O. Douglas. Standing from left are, John M. Harlan; Harold Burton; Tom Clark; and William J. Brennan. In which cases did the Warren Court support the due process model of criminal justice?

investigate and process cases of terrorism, while curtailing the legal protections not only of criminal suspects, but also, to a large extent, the general public.[22]

How Cases Move through the System

With an appreciation of how complex the criminal justice system is, we now turn to how cases are processed. Only a small percentage of offenses result in someone going to prison. This is because the system is close to being overloaded. An even slightly larger percentage of cases would be nearly impossible for the system to process in a fair and legal manner given the resources currently available. Therefore, police officers, prosecutors, judges, and corrections officials use their judgment to decide which cases are pushed further into the criminal justice system and which ones are kicked out. It is useful to envision the criminal justice system as a large funnel in which cases move downward toward their final disposition (see Figure 1.1). The problem with the funnel, however, is that it is too small to hold all the cases, so a considerable amount of leakage occurs.

The criminal justice system is much more complex than suggested by the funnel analogy, and this complexity will be revealed in subsequent chapters that cover the system's components in greater detail. The analogy's goal is to indicate how the numbers dwindle drastically when we move down the funnel from offense to sentencing. This funnel analogy illustrates the relatively low number of offenders who are actually incarcerated. Many offenses that enter the system are excluded for several reasons. Briefly, these reasons include, but are not limited to, the following:

1. Cost. As a society, we simply cannot afford to spend the money and resources necessary to have a totally crime-free society. Although crime is a serious social problem, many other worthy items compete for our tax dollars. Increased spending on crime means that health care, national defense, education, highways, and many other legitimate and desirable services do not get enough of the resources they require to function effectively. For example, decisions must be made on which military aircraft are built because we cannot afford all of them. Similarly, most students must take out loans to pay for a college education because the government can fund only so many scholarships. The criminal justice system, by some estimates, could bankrupt the country if funded for all its legitimate needs. This is especially true at the local level: Local governments spend far more on criminal justice than state governments or the federal government. Therefore, only a relatively small percentage of offenses ever receive what the public believes to be "full justice."

2. Discretion. Criminal justice practitioners exercise a considerable amount of **discretion**—that is, the power to make decisions—in deciding what happens to individual cases. Although this discretion is constrained by resources, a good amount of personal philosophy and judgment also goes into deciding what happens to cases. This discretion is sometimes deemed problematic, and the influence of individual decision-makers is curbed. For example, there can be wide disparity in sentencing across jurisdictions or even between judges in the same city. In an effort to ensure that similar cases are treated more equally, legislatures have passed laws mandating fixed sentences. Mandatory-minimum statutes and three-strikes laws greatly limit the discretion judges have in sentencing offenders. Similarly, some police departments are required to make arrests in domestic assault

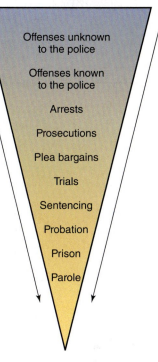

Offenses unknown to the police

Offenses known to the police

Arrests

Prosecutions

Plea bargains

Trials

Sentencing

Probation

Prison

Parole

FIGURE 1.1 The Funnel Effect This figure represents the pattern of how cases move through the criminal justice system. The actual number of cases varies by jurisdiction, severity, and annual occurrence. At each point along the way, cases drop out of the system. Charges may be dropped; cases may be dismissed; offenders may abscond; or defendants may plea bargain. Relative to the number of suspects arrested, only a small percentage of offenders actually go to prison. Does the funnel illustrate the total number of offenses that catch the full implications of the public's perception of justice?

Discretion—The power of a criminal justice official to make decisions on issues within legal guidelines.

cases in which there is clear evidence of physical abuse. Some discretion is inherent in the criminal justice system, but its use is contested.

3. Errors. Sometimes cases simply fall through the cracks. Criminal justice practitioners are human and can make mistakes. They are often overworked and underpaid, and they experience a considerable amount of stress in doing a difficult job. Most jurisdictions do not have sophisticated computer systems that link all the components of the criminal justice system that would help ensure that cases are handled efficiently. Also, criminal justice practitioners might make errors in judgment. The police officer who gives a suspect a second chance or the judge who places a sex offender on probation might be betrayed by offenders who do not or cannot appreciate the break they have been given.

The Perception of Crime and the Wedding-Cake Model of Criminal Justice

Not all crime is the same. Many offenses go undetected, and their harm to society is not generally perceived. Some offenses are just a step across the line of good, effective business practices and are considered the price we pay for a market economy. An example of this offense is insider trading (using confidential information about an investment instrument to buy and sell on the stock exchange). Other offenses, such as some murders, are sensationalized by the media and given such vast resources in their detection and prosecution that they distort the perception of the amount and seriousness of crime. Finally, there is the problem of **street crime**: small-scale, violent, and property offenses. These types of crime illustrate how complex and differentiated the issue really is. Making broad general statements about crime is difficult because so many behaviors are considered criminal offenses.

In the United States, both property crime (burglary, larceny-theft, motor-vehicle theft, and arson) and violent crime (murder, rape, robbery, and aggravated assault) have dropped for the last several years (see Figure 1.2).[23] This drop in crime reveals an interesting disconnect between the occurrence of crime and the perception of crime. Street crime is often what most people fear and what they consider as needing the strictest social control. As such, prisons continue to be built, zero-tolerance policies enforced, and the **war on drugs** fought.

The wedding-cake model of criminal justice differentiates types of cases based on the seriousness of the offense, the defendant/offender's criminal record, and the relationship between the victim and the defendant/offender.[24] This model also highlights the differences between types of cases based on how the media treats them and how the public considers them. The four layers of the model are as follows (see Figure 1.3).

1. The top layer. As on a wedding cake, the top layer is the smallest but receives the most attention. Referred to as "celebrated cases," the cases in this layer are the ones that fascinate the public the most: unusual or gruesome murders; serial murders and mass murders; mysterious missing-persons cases; and cases that involve famous people. These cases may also interest the public for additional reasons: They may involve children or terrorism, or they may have significant racial or gender dimensions. Examples of such cases include the 2015 shooting of nine people at a historic black church in Charleston, South Carolina, the 2016 Orlando nightclub shooting that killed 49 people and wounded 53 others, or the 2018 shooting at Marjory Stoneman Douglas High School in Parkland, Florida, that killed 17 students and staff members and injured 17 others. The participants in these cases

Street crime—Small-scale, personal offenses such as single-victim homicide, rape, robbery, assault, burglary, and vandalism.

War on drugs—Governmental policy aimed at reducing the sale and use of illegal drugs.

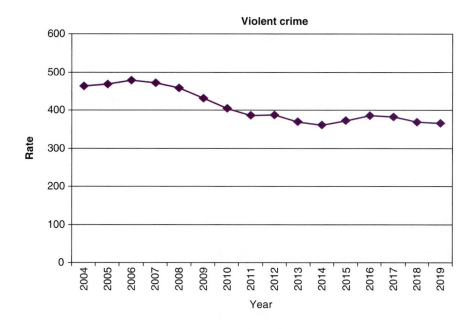

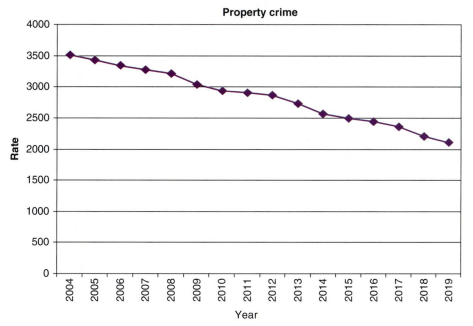

FIGURE 1.2 The Decrease in Violent and Property Crime Rates Although the rate of violent offending increased slightly in 2016, it continued to decline generally. The rate of property crime was down for the fifteenth year in a row. Give some possible reasons for the decreases in both types of crime.

Source: Federal Bureau of Investigation, Uniform Crime Reports: Crime in the United States 2019, Table 1, ucr.fbi.gov/crime-in-the-u.s/2019/crime-in-the-u.s.-2019/topic-pages/tables/table-1.

may also have defining qualities that are favorable to media coverage. For instance, in the O. J. Simpson murder case, Simpson, who was accused of murdering his wife and her friend, was a college and professional football star who had gone on to a successful career as a sportscaster and media personality. Top-layer cases differ from others in that they usually involve a criminal trial and extensive publicity. It is through these cases that many people develop their opinions of the criminal justice system and their perceptions of how it operates. Although these cases receive a great amount of attention, they are relatively rare.

2. The second layer. The second layer comprises serious felonies, such as rape, murder, manslaughter, and robberies that result in fatalities. As with the first layer, the cases in the second layer often

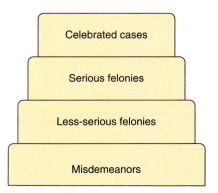

FIGURE 1.3 The Wedding-Cake Model How are celebrated cases different from the lower three layers?

Felicity Huffman leaves federal court with her husband, actor William H. Macy, left, after she was sentenced in a nationwide college admissions bribery scandal. Do celebrity cases deserve all the attention they get from the media?

involve a gruesome offense and a criminal trial. Second-layer cases may receive local media coverage and attention but do not reach first-layer status because they involve more ordinary offenses and participants. For example, the robbery of a small-town jewelry store by some local youths who shoot and kill its owner would qualify as such a case.

3. **The third layer.** Less-serious felonies that typically do not involve fatalities, such as burglary and larceny, compose the third layer. These cases are sometimes dismissed, or defendants may be allowed to plea bargain. Convicted defendants may be placed on probation (the suspension of all or part of a sentence subject to certain conditions). The outcomes for defendants in this layer are less predictable because the charges are not as serious. Trials become increasingly rare in this layer. Here, criminal justice proceedings are more routine and less dramatic, and usually the only people interested in them are those who are directly involved.

4. **The bottom layer.** The bottom layer consists of misdemeanors, or minor offenses, which include traffic violations, minor drug violations, shoplifting, and minor assault. Lower criminal courts usually deal with bottom-layer offenses, which are punishable by a fine or jail time up to a year, although there are so many of these offenses that they overwhelm some small courts. Defendants in these cases are not considered threats to public safety, and the typical outcome is a fine, probation, or jail.[25] Trials are rare: Some defendants consider the proceedings an annoyance and prefer to just pay the fine for, say, a speeding ticket, rather than go to court. A more troubling outcome in these cases is that, although the offenses are minor, they constitute a major problem for the offenders. Many offenders are too impoverished to pay the fine and/or any court fees, or to even challenge the case. Instead, many go to jail and lose their jobs, sending themselves and their families deeper into poverty. In an economically disadvantaged community, enough of these cases can endanger the entire community.

The cases in the top layer represent the most media interest, even though they are relatively rare. At the bottom layer, the number of cases expands greatly. Few cases are unusual enough to command media attention, and the vast number of routine cases remains unseen, unknown, and unappreciated by the public.

PAUSE AND REVIEW

1. What is the nature of the relationship between local, state, and federal levels of criminal justice?
2. What are the basic steps of the criminal justice process? Discuss the difference between the due process and crime-control models.
3. Describe the four layers of the wedding-cake model.

1.3 Types of Crime

Crime can be divided into different types. Sometimes it is categorized according to a specific characteristic of the offense. For instance, as you study crime, you will see references to gang crime, victimless crime, environmental crime, sex crime, urban crime, rural crime, drug crime, hate crime, cybercrime, and so on. In these cases, the differentiation is itself worth studying. For example, the phenomenon of young people banding together to sell drugs, commit murders, wear specific colors, and defend neighborhood turf is an important characteristic of gang crime that is worthy of study and differentiates it from, say, hate crime.

This section divides crime into two broad types: street crime and corporate/white-collar crime. As discussed in the previous section, street crime is what most people worry about when they think of crime, probably because it sometimes involves violence. However, **corporate crime** and **white-collar crime** are just as damaging, perhaps even more so, but these types of crime get less attention because no violence is involved. This is essential to the measurement of crime because measures of crime are what help to generate criminal justice funding, media attention, and public concern. If there is little or no official measurement of a type of crime—as with corporate and white-collar crime—then that type of crime will likely receive less social attention. It is significant, then, that the differences between street crime and corporate and white-collar crime are discussed.

Street Crime

Street crime includes a wide variety of acts in both public and private spaces, including interpersonal violence and property crime. These offenses, which include homicide, rape, assault, **larceny**, **arson**, breaking-and-entering, **burglary**, **robbery**, and motor-vehicle theft, are the ones most often included in official measurements of crime. (We discuss official measurements of crime further in Chapter 2.)

A healthy fear of street crime is wise. The effect of rape, assault, and especially homicide may alter how a person and his or her loved ones relate to others and may require many years of recovery. However, street crime is still relatively rare. Most of us go about our daily lives without encountering danger, and we do not need to carry a weapon or distrust people most of the time. Some studies have found that those with the least likelihood of being victimized fear crime the most. Elderly citizens demonstrate the greatest fear of street crime, yet they are the least likely to encounter it. Conversely, young males are the most victimized, but they do not have a great fear of crime. In some ways, this disjuncture is understandable, but it also illustrates how distorted our concept of crime is.[26]

LEARNING OBJECTIVE 1.7

Discuss why street crime receives more attention than corporate and white-collar crime.

Corporate crime— Offenses committed by a corporation's officers who pursue illegal activity in the corporation's name.

White-collar crime— A nonviolent criminal offense committed during the course of business for financial gain.

Larceny— A form of theft in which an offender takes possessions that do not belong to him or her, with the intent of keeping them.

Arson— Any willful or malicious burning or attempt to burn a dwelling, public building, motor vehicle, aircraft, or personal property of another.

Burglary— Breaking into and entering a structure or vehicle with intent to commit a felony or a theft.

Robbery— The taking or attempting to take anything of value from the care, custody, or control of a person or persons by force or threat of force or violence and/or by putting the victim in fear.

Larceny is the most common street crime reported to the police. Why is street crime more likely to be reported to the police than other types of crime?

The crime rate does not always correlate with the public perception of the level of crime. During the 1990s, even as the national crime rate was declining, people felt that crime was one of the most important social problems.[27] Because the public is so concerned about street crime, many criminal justice resources are devoted to its prevention and prosecution. This emphasis on street crime is both understandable and problematic. We need to believe that the criminal justice system is doing all that can be done to protect innocent people from predatory criminals. The public clearly demands that the police "do something" to prevent crime and apprehend lawbreakers.[28] According to some criminologists, for example, aggressive control of the homeless is necessary for meaningful, safe communities. People who feel safe on the streets are engaged in public interaction to a greater degree, and this, in turn, means that the streets are populated by more lawful citizens.[29]

The emphasis on street crime is problematic because it drains resources from the prevention of other types of crime. Scholar Jeffrey Reiman contends that corporate crime is much more harmful to society than street crime, stating that the preoccupation of the criminal justice system with street crime is fueled by a racist and class-conscious society. Although street crime is significant to individuals, corporate crime is much more damaging to society as a whole. Reiman argues that individuals with the most money and power define crime and use the criminal justice system to protect their own interests.[30]

Corporate Crime and White-Collar Crime

Sometimes lawbreakers are conventional in all other aspects of their lives, and it is difficult to envision them as lawbreakers. Because harmful behaviors are not always defined as crime, envisioning how otherwise honorable citizens can be considered criminals is sometimes difficult. So-called pillars of society known for their charity, public service, and conventional behavior are sometimes the biggest crooks.

Corporate crime involves breaking laws in the otherwise lawful pursuit of profit. For example, a company that does not follow safety standards in disposing of its industrial waste can do irreparable harm to the environment and to the health of many people. Although the intent of the company's officers may be simply to maximize profits and not to hurt anyone, the result can be devastating. The company's officers did not physically rob or assault the citizens, but the damage done to the community water supply may be much more harmful. Corporations can hurt individuals in a variety of ways. Yet when we look at the law and the response of the criminal justice system, we see that street crime is often met with greater penalties.[31]

Sometimes the terms *corporate crime* and *white-collar crime* are used interchangeably, but there are important distinctions between them.[32] Corporate crime involves the purposeful commission or omission of acts by individuals acting as representatives of a business. Their goal is to make money for the business, and the offenses they commit are related to making the company profitable. Corporate crime, then, may also include environmental crime if a corporation's criminal negligence results in an environmental disaster, such as an oil spill. White-collar crime, by contrast, usually involves employees harming the corporation. For example, the treasurer who embezzles money and the office manager who steals office supplies are harming the company. Sometimes corporate and white-collar crime may be present in the same offense. It may be argued that the financial offenses of investor Bernard Madoff, who defrauded his investors of at least $20 billion, were perpetrated by someone who was acting not only in his personal interest but also as the head of a company.[33]

There is no official program that measures corporate and white-collar crime. Without a thorough official measurement, it is difficult to estimate how much corporate and white-collar crime is being perpetrated and who the victims are. Unlike street crime, corporate and white-collar crimes are difficult to investigate and difficult for laypeople to understand. Not only may it take years for an offense to be perpetrated, the investigation of a complicated scheme may take years to complete. Bernard Madoff perpetrated fraud for nearly his entire working life and was not caught until he was 71 years old. In contrast, a liquor store robbery may take only a few minutes to plan and execute, and the police may be onto the perpetrators within hours.

U.S. Representative Chris Collins, R-N.Y., speaks to reporters as he leaves a New York City courthouse. Collins pleaded guilty to conspiracy to commit securities fraud and lying to an FBI agent. Why is this case considered white-collar crime and not corporate crime?

PAUSE AND REVIEW

1. What are some examples of street crime?

2. How is corporate crime different from white-collar crime?

3. Why does street crime receive more attention than corporate and white-collar crime?

LEARNING OBJECTIVE 1.8

Give examples of violent crime, property crime, and public-order crime.

1.4 Offenses and Offenders

The behaviors that offend our sensibilities can be categorized in many ways. We have rules, regulations, norms, folkways, and laws that dictate what is acceptable and what is punished. Laws attempt to define crime in a comprehensible manner, the most basic distinction being between misdemeanors and felonies. This distinction is a rather crude way to distinguish the seriousness of these actions, and it is not made until a police officer decides which law the action violated. The distinction between a **misdemeanor** (a minor criminal offense punishable by a fine and/or jail time for up to one year) and a **felony** (an offense punishable by a sentence of more than a year in state or federal prison and sometimes by death) might be blurred when the prosecutor decides on the formal charge. The process becomes even more complicated when, as a result of plea negotiations, the judge passes sentence.[34]

Misdemeanor—A minor criminal offense punishable by a fine and/or jail time for up to one year.

Felony—An offense punishable by a sentence of more than a year in state or federal prison and sometimes by death.

Therefore, a man who gets into a fistfight may believe he is acting in self-defense, but he might also find that because he severely hurt his opponent, a police officer has charged him with misdemeanor assault and battery. The prosecutor may decide to kick the charge up to a felony because of the use of a baseball bat, but after a plea negotiation the charge might once again become a misdemeanor. The relationship between a behavior and the legal designation ultimately attached to it is sometimes difficult to justify. Therefore, the legal categorizations of offenses are not the best indicators of the nature of crime.[35]

Another way to understand crime is to consider the victimization. Focusing on the victim or object of harm instead of the charge can provide a better measure of the level of crime. The following three-group typology elucidates the similarities and differences among the general classes of crime:

Sexual assault—Sexual contact that is committed without the other party's consent or with a party who is not capable of giving consent.

1. Violent crime. These offenses include the violent personal offenses of homicide, rape, **sexual assault**, robbery, and assault.
2. Property crime. These offenses include burglary, arson, embezzlement, larceny-theft, and auto theft.
3. Public-order crime. These offenses include drug use, disturbing the peace, drunkenness, prostitution, and some forms of gambling.

Considering crime in this manner gives us a better idea of the harm caused by unlawful actions than does the simple misdemeanor/felony dichotomy. Although each of these categories spans the range of seriousness from minor irritation to extreme disruption, they organize offenses in terms of who or what is harmed. Exploring this typology in greater detail reflects the type of harm done to victims. Each of these categories includes a continuum of offenses that differ in degree and may be either stringently punished or relatively neglected by the criminal justice system.

Rape—Sexual activity, usually sexual intercourse, that is forced on another person without his or her consent, usually under threat of harm. Also, sexual activity conducted with a person who is incapable of valid consent.

Violent Crime

The most severe penalties, including capital punishment, are reserved for those who commit violent crime. Personal violent offenses such as murder and **rape** are the most devastating and the most feared of all offenses and receive the most media coverage.[36] These serious offenses occur much less frequently than do property offenses, but they are of the most concern to law enforcement and victims. When considering homicide and assault cases, we can discern motivations that apparently compel offenders to engage in this serious antisocial behavior.

> Interpersonal disputes. Sources of dispute can include disagreements over money, charges of infidelity, challenges to masculinity, or insults to moral character. Often, the difference between offender and victim is who is fastest on the draw; that is, there is sometimes no clear relationship between who is responsible for starting the dispute and who emerges the winner.[37] In some segments of society, a subculture of violence emerges in which assault or murder is expected as a way of resolving conflict.[38]

> Instrumental violence. Violence is sometimes used as a means to another criminal end. Drug dealers may kill competitors; robbers sometimes shoot convenience-store clerks, and carjackers sometimes attack drivers to steal automobiles.[39] Some forms of instrumental violence are premeditated. Intimidating witnesses or "teaching a lesson" to an informant employs violence as an extreme form of communication when "a message" needs to be sent.[40] Often, the motivation or message of instrumental violence is difficult to discern, such as when a bank robber successfully takes the money and then shoots the clerk on the way out of the bank.

> Group violence. Another source of motivation to commit violence can be found in the dynamics of certain groups. Assaults or homicides often occur in situations in which groups of young people conflict. Violence is often used in instrumental ways when youth gangs clash over territory or symbolic concerns such as colors of clothing or other displays of gang affiliation. Youths often feel a greater sense of bravado when surrounded by friends and may feel a greater need to demonstrate their courage and rebellion. Group dynamics might encourage and facilitate, and, in some cases, even demand, members' use of violence to address some real or imagined insult. When alcohol or drugs enter the equation, violence is even more likely.[41]

> Serial murder and mass murder. Sometimes violence is instrumental as a part of a larger pattern of crime, as with **serial murder** (the murder of several individual victims in separate incidents), and sometimes it seems random and indiscriminate, as with **mass murder** (the murder of three or more victims in a single incident). Often, this type of offender is the hardest to understand because there is no apparent motivation. Although serial murderers are rare, they usually have some underlying personal logic regarding their targets. Some, such as Ted Bundy, might kill young women with a certain hair color. Others, such as John Gacy or Jeffrey Dahmer, might exclusively kill young men. Even though the motivation might be the result of a psychological problem, the serial murderer is often capable of committing many offenses and eluding detection and arrest. The typical mass murderer is not a chronic violent offender: his or her offense may be the only time the offender has ever broken the law. For example, in 2017, Stephen Paddock opened fire into a crowd of more than 20,000 people attending a country music festival in Las Vegas, killing 58 and injuring 851. Paddock, who perpetrated the deadliest mass shooting by a single shooter in U.S. history and then committed suicide by shooting himself, had no criminal history and had never even been arrested.[42] This is what makes mass murder so difficult for law enforcement to deal with; it is explosive, singular, and devastating, and it often makes little sense.

Serial murder—The murder of a series of victims during three or more separate events over an extended period of time.

Mass murder—The murder of three or more people in a single incident.

Terrorism—The use or threat of violence against a state or other political entity in order to coerce.

› Political violence. Some offenses are meant to send a message. This is the case with political violence, of which the most well-known type is **terrorism**. Terrorism can be domestic, as in the case of the 1995 bombing of the Murrah Federal Building in Oklahoma City, or it can be of the international variety, as in the suicide plane hijackings of September 11, 2001. Terrorism is often committed by intelligent, sincere people who believe violence is necessary for their voices to be heard.[43]

› Rape and sexual assault. Because the motivations for committing rape and sexual assault are often different from the motivations for committing other types of personal violent offenses, and because the effect on the victims can be so devastating, these offenses will be considered as unique forms of violence. Rape is just one of a number of sex offenses that has garnered more attention from criminologists in recent years. Although rape has been a consistent occurrence throughout recorded history, the past 40 years have seen an increased awareness of the definition of what types of behavior constitute rape and sexual assault, as well as greater legal protections for victims. Women and children, once considered as not having individual rights when the perpetrator was a husband or father, are now protected by the criminal justice system.[44] In 2011, the Department of Justice changed the definition of rape from "the carnal knowledge of a female, forcibly and against her will" to "the penetration, no matter how slight, of the vagina or anus with any body part or object, or oral penetration by a sex organ of another person, without the consent of the victim."[45] This new definition expanded how the government collects rape statistics. Additionally, child molestation, date rape, acquaintance rape, the rape of males, and sexual harassment are now recognized as serious types of antisocial behavior and are dealt with in a more humane and serious manner by law enforcement and the courts.[46]

› Robbery. The FBI defines robbery as the taking or attempting to take anything of value from the care, custody, or control of a person or persons by force or threat of force or violence and/or by putting the victim in fear. Robbery varies by location, whether on the street (such as a mugging) or

In February 2020, movie producer Harvey Weinstein was found guilty of criminal sexual assault in the first degree and rape in the third degree. Why are rape and sexual assault considered unique forms of violence?

within an institution (such as a bank or a convenience store). Finally, even though carjackings involve the theft of a motor vehicle, they are considered robberies because of the force involved.

Property Crime

The accumulation of wealth and possessions is an important cornerstone of individual and group well-being in the United States, and laws protect the rights of those who own and control property. These laws range from prohibitions against theft to the copyrights that protect intellectual and creative endeavors. The types of property crime that are best measured by the criminal justice system are those in which the offender is a stranger to the victim. Although many laws address differences in opinion while transacting business, these conflicts are usually covered by civil law. Burglary, larceny-theft, motor-vehicle theft, and arson are dealt with by criminal law and are measured by the FBI. The following points need to be understood when considering the measurement of property crime.

> Burglary is different from larceny-theft. When classifying the taking of another person's property, several distinctions determine whether the offense is larceny-theft or burglary. Burglary involves the unlawful entry of a structure to commit a felony. Larceny-theft involves the unlawful taking of another person's property. Larceny-theft includes theft from a person by stealth such as pocket-picking, purse-snatching (when only minimal force is used), shoplifting, thefts of articles from motor vehicles, and thefts from coin-operated machines.

> Motor-vehicle theft involves the theft of most self-propelled vehicles that run on land surfaces and not on rails. The theft of water craft, construction equipment, airplanes, and farming equipment is classified as larceny rather than motor-vehicle theft.

> Arson involves purposely set fires. It does not matter whether the fire was started with the intent to defraud, only that it was willfully or maliciously set. Fires of suspicious or unknown origin are not treated as arson.[47]

Public-Order Crime

Some criminal offenses involve no discernible victim. **Victimless crime** involves consensual interactions or behaviors that offend the powerful groups of society who have succeeded in having their concerns and sensibilities elevated to the level of the criminal law. Although broad consensus exists on some of these behaviors, there is also a good deal of controversy about offenses that are a matter of values.[48]

Behaviors that fit into the category of offenses against the public order include drug use and sales, loitering, gambling, prostitution, vagrancy, disorderly conduct, and liquor law violations. These are often considered to be nuisance offenses, reflecting quality-of-life concerns for many people. The laws concerning these offenses are vigorously enforced in some places and almost completely ignored in others.[49] For instance, when vagrants, street people, and the homeless are considered to be interfering with the tourism trade, shopkeepers, hotel owners, and restaurant managers might ask the police to clear the streets.[50] The police have broad decision-making powers in deciding how to enforce public-order laws. They might overlook the possession of small amounts of marijuana in one instance and decide to make an arrest in another if the suspect does not show respect.[51]

Victimless crime—
Behaviors that are deemed undesirable because they offend community standards rather than directly harm people or property.

PAUSE AND REVIEW

1. **Give some examples of violent crime, property crime, and public-order crime.**

Two women march during a May Day rally in New York City. Why is prostitution considered a public-order crime?

FOCUS ON ETHICS — A Balance of Interests

In your job as a probation officer, you are assigned the case of a rich and successful accountant who is on probation for driving under the influence of alcohol. As part of her community service, the accountant has spent Saturday mornings at a local nursing home where she has been helping the residents fill out their tax forms. This accountant has secured thousands of dollars in tax refunds for these elderly citizens. In fact, one of the residents, who happens to be your grandmother, reports that not only is this accountant helping the residents save money, but she also has been coming to the nursing home during the middle of the week, on her own time, to talk to lonely and depressed residents.

You feel a little guilty that this accountant has developed a close relationship with your grandmother and that you have not been to the nursing home in months. Being suspicious, you investigate to see whether the accountant knows that you have a relative in the home. You discover that not only does she not know, but she has volunteered to serve as a member of the board of directors of the home and help the residents deal with confusing social service agencies such as Medicare and Social Security.

Late one night you get a call from the accountant. She is obviously drunk and informs you that she has just crashed her car into a tree and that she needs a ride home before the police come and arrest her. You know that if she gets another DUI, she not only will lose her license

but will also have to spend 90 days in jail and might lose her job. Although you have little sympathy for people who cannot control their drinking, this young woman has been turning her life around and doing good works, especially for the elderly. You see potential in this client.

WHAT DO YOU DO?

1. Pick her up. You owe her for helping your grandmother, and this is one of the few things you can do to repay her help and kindness.
2. Call the police and report her. You are a court officer, and you cannot ethically do anything else. Also, you might get in trouble if you do not call.
3. Help her but make a deal stipulating that she will check herself into a clinic and get help for her drinking problem. Use this last incident as leverage to force her to confront her drinking.
4. Call your supervisor and ask to be relieved of the case because you can no longer be objective.

For more insight on how someone might respond to such an ethical dilemma, visit Oxford Learning Link at www.oup.com/he/Fuller2e to watch a video that connects this scenario to a real-world situation.

Summary

LEARNING OBJECTIVE 1.1 Define social control.	Social control refers to the rules, habits, and customs a society uses to enforce conformity to its norms.
LEARNING OBJECTIVE 1.2 Outline how the U.S. criminal justice system protects individual rights.	The protection of individual rights is an integral part of the functioning of law enforcement. The government serves citizens' interests by finding methods to control crime without allowing law enforcement agencies to turn the country into a police state.
LEARNING OBJECTIVE 1.3 Define crime and criminal justice.	Crime is as an action taken by a person or a group of people that violates the rules of society to the point that harm is done to an individual or to society's interests. Criminal justice is a social institution whose mission is to control crime by detecting, detaining, adjudicating, and punishing and/or rehabilitating people who break the law.
LEARNING OBJECTIVE 1.4 List the steps of the criminal justice process.	**Law enforcement:** Initial contact, investigation, arrest, booking **Courts:** Charging, preliminary hearing, arraignment, plea bargaining, adjudication, sentencing **Corrections:** Fines and probation, incarceration, reentry
LEARNING OBJECTIVE 1.5 Explain the major difference between the due process and crime-control models.	The crime-control model describes the expectation of an efficient criminal justice system. The due process model describes the expectation of a just and fair system.
LEARNING OBJECTIVE 1.6 Describe the wedding-cake model of criminal justice.	The wedding-cake model of criminal justice differentiates types of cases based on the seriousness of the offense, the defendant/offender's criminal record, and the relationship between the victim and the defendant/offender. This model also highlights the differences between types of cases based on how the media treats them and how the public considers them. The top layer consists of cases that receive the most attention; the middle layers comprise grave felonies; and the fourth layer comprises less serious offenses.
LEARNING OBJECTIVE 1.7 Discuss why street crime receives more attention than corporate and white-collar crime.	People are more afraid of street crime because it is sometimes violent. It also gets more media attention and is easier for the public to understand. Corporate and white-collar offenses may take years to perpetrate and investigate, whereas most street crime happens relatively quickly.
LEARNING OBJECTIVE 1.8 Give examples of violent crime, property crime, and public-order crime.	Violent crime offenses include homicide, rape, sexual assault, robbery, and assault. Property crime offenses include burglary, arson, embezzlement, larceny-theft, and auto theft. Public-order offenses include drug use, disturbing the peace, drunkenness, prostitution, and some forms of gambling.

Critical Reflections

1. What is the proper role of the criminal justice system in maintaining social control? How does the criminal justice system share this responsibility with other institutions such as the school, family, and religious institutions?

2. Explain how different individuals can have wildly different opinions on what the goals of the criminal justice system should be. How may a person's social location (age, sex, race, gender, economic situation) influence how a person feels about the role of the criminal justice system?

Key Terms

Adjudication **p. 10**
Arraignment **p. 10**
Arrest **p. 6**
Arson **p. 17**
Burglary **p. 17**
Corporate crime **p. 17**
Crime **p. 5**
Crime-control model **p. 11**
Criminal justice **p. 5**
Discretion **p. 13**

Due process model **p. 11**
Felony **p. 20**
Justice **p. 5**
Larceny **p. 17**
Mass murder **p. 21**
Misdemeanor **p. 20**
Parole **p. 11**
Probation **p. 8**
Rape **p. 20**
Robbery **p. 17**

Serial murder **p. 21**
Sexual assault **p. 20**
Social control **p. 4**
Sociological imagination **p. 7**
Street crime **p. 14**
Terrorism **p. 22**
Victimless crime **p. 23**
War on drugs **p. 14**
White-collar crime **p. 17**

Notes

1 Cameron Knight, "Local Gamer Pleads Guilty in Fatal 'Swatting' Case," *Enquirer*/Cincinnati.com, April 12, 2019. Kyle Swenson, "Two Rival Gamers Allegedly Involved in Kansas 'Swatting' Incident Plead Not Guilty in Federal Court," *Washington Post*, June 14, 2018.

2 Ibid.

3 Ibid.

4 Knight, "Local Gamer Pleads Guilty in Fatal 'Swatting' Case."

5 Brendan Koerner, "It Started as an Online Gaming Prank. Then It Turned Deadly," *Wired*, October 23, 2018.

6 Knight, "Local Gamer Pleads Guilty in Fatal 'Swatting' Case." Jason Hanna and Jamiel Lynch, "An Ohio Gamer Gets Prison Time over a 'Swatting' Call That Led to a Man's Death," *CNN*, September 14, 2019.

7 Kate Cox, "Instigator of Fatal Kansas Swatting Receives Prison Sentence," *Ars Technica*, September 17, 2019. Roxana Hegeman, "Kansas Online Gamer in Hoax Case May Have Charges Dropped," AP/*Daily Herald* (Arlington Heights, Ill.), May 24, 2019.

8 Michael Burns and Nathaniel Cary, "Spartanburg Husband, Wife Identified as Bodies on Todd Kohlhepp

Land," *Greenville News*, November 9, 2016. *Greenville News, Anderson Independent Mail*, "Todd Kohlhepp: Timeline of Events," May 25, 2017.

9 Noah Feit, "Famed Serial Killer Bragged of Murder, Sex Slaves," *The State*, May 24, 2018.

10 Kristine Phillips, "They Left Food and Water for Migrants in the Desert. Now They Might Go to Prison," *Washington Post*, January 20, 2019. Don Sweeney, "Four Women Left Water for Migrants in the Arizona Desert. Now They May Go to Prison," *Sacramento Bee*, January 20, 2019.

11 Curt Prendergast, "Border Aid Volunteers Sentenced to Probation in Tucson," *Arizona Daily Star*/Tucson.com, March 1, 2019.

12 Stephen Dippnall, "Hating America? Great Britain and the Execution of Julius and Ethel Rosenberg." *Cold War History* 18, no. 1 (2018): 55–71.

13 Charlie Savage, "Chelsea Manning to Be Released Early as Obama Commutes Sentence," *New York Times*, January 17, 2017.

14 Ed Pilkington, "Bradley Manning Verdict: Cleared of 'Aiding the Enemy' but Guilty of Other Charges," *Guardian*, July 3, 2013.

15 Charlie Savage, "Chelsea Manning to Be Released Early as Obama Commutes Sentence," *New York Times*, January 17, 2017.

16 Caroline Kelly, "Chelsea Manning Released from Virginia Jail after 62 Days," *CNN*, May 9, 2019.

17 C. Wright Mills, *The Sociological Imagination* (New York: Oxford University Press, 1959).

18 Sunil B. Desai, "Solving the Interagency Puzzle," *Policy Review* (February 1, 2005): 57–71.

19 Ibid.

20 Herbert L. Packer, *The Limits of the Criminal Sanction* (Stanford, Calif.: Stanford University Press, 1968).

21 Herbert L. Packer, "Two Models of the Criminal Process," *University of Pennsylvania Law Review* 113, no. 1 (1964): 1–68.

22 Walter M. Brasch, *America's Unpatriotic Acts: The Federal Government's Violation of Constitutional and Civil Rights* (New York: Peter Lang, 2005).

23 Federal Bureau of Investigation, *Uniform Crime Reports: Crime in the United States 2019*, Table 1, ucr.fbi.gov/crime-in-the-u.s/2019/crime-in-the-u.s.-2019/topic-pages/tables/table-1.

24 Lawrence M. Friedman and Robert V. Percival, *The Roots of Justice: Crime and Punishment in Alameda County, California, 1870–1910* (Chapel Hill: University of North Carolina Press, 1981). Samuel Walker, *Sense and Nonsense about Crime, Drugs, and Communities*, 8th ed. (Stamford, Conn.: Cengage Learning, 2015), 43–54. Don M. Gottfredson, *Decision-making in the Criminal Justice System: Reviews and Essays* (Rockville, Md.: National Institute of Mental Health, Center for Studies of Crime and Delinquency, 1975).

25 Walker, *Sense and Nonsense about Crime, Drugs, and Communities*.

26 William G. Doerner and Stephen P. Lab, *Victimology*, 5th ed. (Cincinnati, Ohio: Lexis-Nexis, 2008), 289–299.

27 Alfred Blumstein and Joel Wallman, *The Crime Drop in America* (New York: Cambridge University Press, 2005).

28 Ronald D. Hunter and Mark L. Dantzker, *Crime and Criminality: Causes and Consequences* (Upper Saddle River, N.J.: Prentice-Hall, 2002).

29 James Q. Wilson and George L. Kelling, "Broken Windows," in *Critical Issues in Policing: Contemporary Issues*, 2d ed., eds. Roger G. Durham and Geoffrey P. Alpert (Prospect Heights, Ill.: Waveland Press, 1993).

30 Jeffrey Reiman, *The Rich Get Richer and the Poor Get Prison*, 8th ed. (Boston: Allyn & Bacon, 2006).

31 Ibid.

32 Lewis R. Mizell Jr., *Masters of Deception: The Worldwide White-Collar Crime Crisis and Ways to Protect Yourself* (New York: Wiley, 1997).

33 "The Madoff Recovery Initiative," www.madofftrustee.com.

34 Ellen Hochstedler Steury and Nancy Frank, *Criminal Court Process* (Minneapolis/St. Paul, Minn.: West, 1996).

35 Maximo Langer, "Rethinking Plea Bargaining: Prosecutorial Adjudication in American Criminal Procedure," *American Journal of Criminal Law* 33, no. 3 (2006): 223–299.

36 Chris McCormick, ed., *Constructing Danger: The Mis/Representation of Crime in the News* (Halifax, Nova Scotia: Fernwood, 1995).

37 Lance Hannon, "Race, Victim Precipitated Homicide, and the Subculture of Violence Thesis," *Journal of Social Sciences* 41, no. 1 (2004): 115–121.

38 Albert K. Cohen, *Delinquent Boys: The Culture of the Gang* (New York: The Free Press, 1955).

39 Mitch Stacy, "Details Sketchy in Killing of Charlotte County Prison Guard," *Florida Times Union*, June 12, 2003.

40 Frederic G. Reamer, *Criminal Lessons: Case Studies and Commentary on Crime and Justice* (New York: Columbia University Press, 2003). See especially Chapter 5, "Crimes of Revenge and Retribution," 97–119.

41 Malcolm Klein, *The American Street Gang: Its Nature, Prevalence, and Control* (New York: Oxford University Press, 1997).

42 Sabrina Tavernise, Serge F. Kovaleski, and Julie Turkewitz, "Who Was Stephen Paddock? The Mystery of a Nondescript 'Numbers Guy'," *New York Times*, October 7, 2017.

43 Alex Schmid and Janny de Graaf, *Violence as Communication: Insurgent Terrorism and the Western News Media* (Newbury Park, Calif.: Sage, 1982).

44 David Finkelhor and Kersti Yllo, *License to Rape: Sexual Abuse of Wives* (New York: Holt, Rinehart, and Winston, 1985).

45 Federal Bureau of Investigation, Attorney General Eric Holder Announces Revisions to the Uniform Crime Report's Definition of Rape, January 6, 2012, www.fbi.gov/news/pressrel/press-releases/attorney-general-eric-holder-announces-revisions-to-the-uniform-crime-reports-definition-of-rape.

46 Dean G. Kilpatrick, David Beatty, and Susan Smith Hawley, "The Rights of Crime Victims: Does Legal Protection Make a Difference?" in *Victims and Victimization: Essential Readings*, eds. David Shichor and Stephen G. Tibbetts (Prospect Heights, Ill.: Waveland Press, 2000), 287–304.

47 Terence D. Miethe and Richard C. McCorkle, *Crime Profiles: The Anatomy of Dangerous Persons, Places, and Situations* (Los Angeles: Roxbury, 2001).

48 Robert F. Meier and Gilbert Geis, *Victimless Crime? Prostitution, Drugs, Homosexuality, Abortion* (Los Angeles: Roxbury, 1997).

49 William H. Daly, "Law Enforcement in Times Square, 1970s–1990s," in *Sex, Scams, and Street Life: The Sociology of New York City's Times Square*, ed. Robert P. McNamara (Westport, Conn.: Praeger, 1995), 97–106.

50 John A. Backstand, Don Gibbons, and Joseph F. Jones, "Who's in Jail? An Examination of the Rabble Hypothesis," *Crime and Delinquency* 38 (1992): 219–229.

51 Joseph Goldstein, "Police Discretion Not to Invoke the Criminal Process," in *The Invisible Justice System: Discretion and the Law*, eds. Burton Atkins and Mark Pogrebin (Cincinnati, Ohio: Anderson, 1978), 65–81.

Learn more with this chapter's digital tools, including the Oxford Insight Study Guide, at www.oup.com/he/Fuller2e.

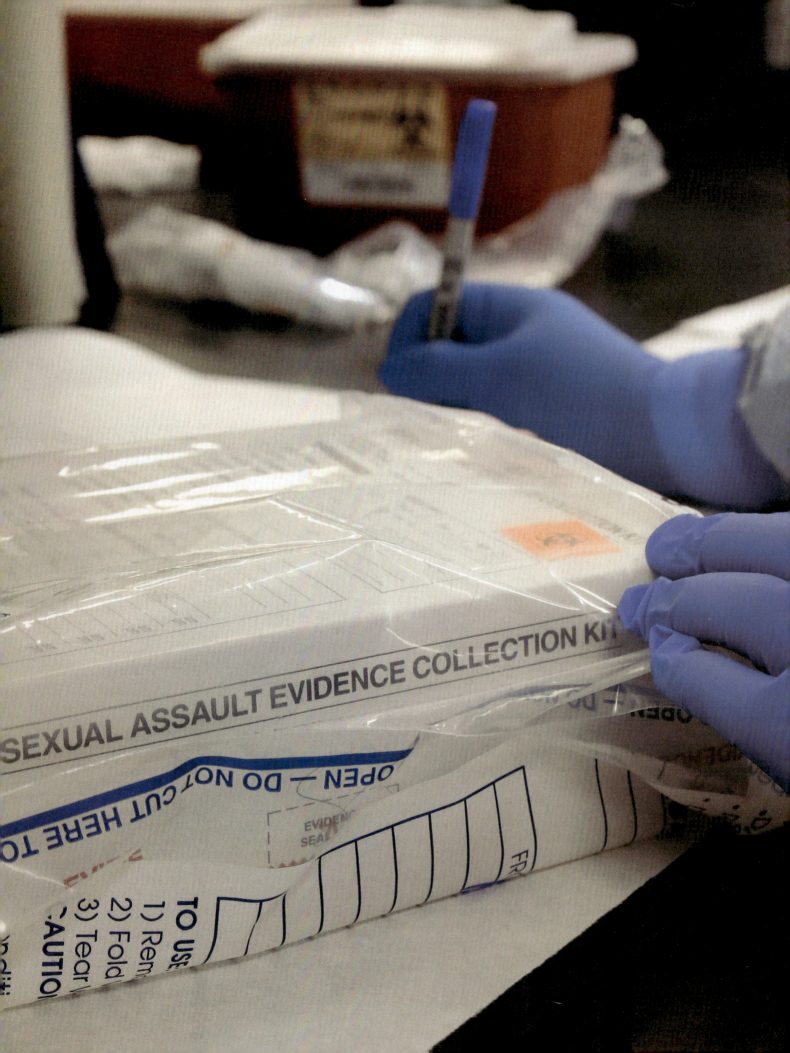

How Crime Is Measured and Who It Affects

A sexual assault evidence kit is logged in the biology lab at the Houston Forensic Science Center in Houston, Texas. In 2019, Texas Governor Greg Abbott signed a bill to eliminate the backlog of thousands of untested rape kits in Texas. How might the processing of these rape kits aid in the administration of justice in Texas?

In 2015,

Marina Conner, then a sophomore at the University of Texas at Austin, claimed that she was approached by a man in a parking garage who offered to sell her drugs. Conner stated that the man then bashed her head against a wall and raped her.[1]

Conner reported the incident to the police and got a sexual assault forensic examination. In an interview she said, "[I had] bruises on the back of my arms from being pinned against the wall and a gashed forehead from where he slammed it against the parking garage wall." She also called a friend during the rape and left a voicemail in which she is heard crying and telling the alleged assailant to stop.[2]

The police found her alleged assailant within a week. He said the encounter with Conner was consensual.[3] It then took two years for Conner's rape kit to be DNA tested. However, because Conner had showered before the medical exam, the rape kit contained no DNA, and the district attorney dropped the case. Conner's alleged attacker went free, and Conner dropped out of school for more than a year.[4]

In 2017, the Austin Police Department closed the case and reported it to the Federal Bureau of Investigation as "cleared by exceptional means." To anyone scanning Austin, Texas, rape statistics, it looks like the Austin Police Department solved Conner's case and others like it in the manner that most people likely associate with the police "clearing" a case: with a suspect being arrested and going to court.[5]

"It sounds like a good thing if you tell someone a case was cleared," Conner said. "It doesn't sound like I was violently raped and my rapist is still out there."[6]

THINK ABOUT IT > In what ways might the under-reporting of rape be subject to both intentional and unintentional sources of error?

In this case, how does "cleared by exceptional means" benefit the police department?

LEARNING OBJECTIVE 1.1

Describe three logistical obstacles to measuring crime effectively and efficiently.

2.1 The Problems of Measuring Crime

Measuring crime is tricky. Criminal justice scholars, government officials, and the public all have different motivations, interests, and ideologies that dictate why and how crime should be measured. Whereas scholars and the public want a realistic picture of crime so that they can make informed decisions, some police administrators may have an occupational perspective. For example, if a police chief wants to make the case that his or her department needs more financial resources, a crime wave could be used as justification. Conversely, if the police chief is in political trouble, that chief might determine that a drop in the crime rate would be evidence that he or she is doing a good job. The logistical obstacles to measuring crime effectively and efficiently are daunting. These logistical problems, which we will cover in detail later in the chapter, include:

> › Problems of definition: Although laws are written in a specific manner to minimize ambiguity, the interpretation of behaviors that seem to be criminal offenses can be problematic. For the legislator who writes the law in the safety of his or her office, the circumstances might seem clear-cut and easily defined. For the police officer, the information needed to determine whether a criminal offense is committed might be conflicting, absent, or even false.

> ❯ Problems of resources: Thousands of criminal justice jurisdictions report official criminal justice statistics. Some large metropolitan or state agencies have teams of well-trained personnel dedicated to tracking crime, whereas other, smaller agencies do not. Consequently, the priority of maintaining these records varies significantly across jurisdictions based on the available resources, in terms of both finances and personnel.

> ❯ Problems of politics: Public officials do not want their communities to be perceived as high-crime areas. The economic and social effects of the perception of crime can cause city officials to pressure law enforcement agencies to minimize the reporting of crime. For this reason, aggravated assaults might be reported as simple battery, and motor-vehicle theft might be deemed to be joyriding, depending on the political circumstances. Consider the introductory case. Police departments may report the clearance of cases to the Uniform Crime Reports in two ways: cleared by arrest and cleared by exceptional means. Cleared by arrest means that a suspect has been arrested, charged with the offense, and turned over to the court. To report a case as cleared by exceptional means, a police department must have, according to the FBI, "encountered a circumstance outside the control of law enforcement that prohibits the agency from arresting, charging, and prosecuting the offender."[7] Examples of this type of clearance are the suspect's death or the victim's refusal to cooperate with the prosecution. In the case of Marina Conner, the prosecution did not think the case would be well received by a jury because there was no DNA.[8] By using cleared by exceptional means, the Austin Police Department recorded some rape offenses so that it looked like the cases had been solved, giving the appearance to some that the police department was doing a better job than it really was.

To understand crime's effect on individuals and society, we must understand how crime is conceptualized and measured. There is a big difference between a homicide and some children throwing rocks through the windows of an abandoned house. Similarly, there is a big difference between massive corporate fraud and the motorist whose license is suspended after three drunken-driving convictions.[9] The total number of criminal offenses, or even the crime rate, fails to capture the variability and deleterious effects of crime. Although crime measures are useful in any comparison of the relative safety of cities, states, or regions, the way crime is measured can provide misleading and inaccurate pictures of how it is distributed and how it affects people, especially victims.[10]

The victim performs an important role in the criminal justice system. The victim of a criminal offense is one of a triad of important actors. The perpetrator commits the offense; the victim is on the receiving end of the behavior; and the criminal justice system responds to the offense in the name of the state. This is an important point. Once a criminal offense has been committed, the criminal justice system sets the victim aside, and the prosecutor acts in the name of society rather than the victim. Because of this structure, many claim that the victim is forgotten in the criminal justice process.[11] For example, the police may decide not to arrest a criminal suspect; the prosecutor may decide to accept a lenient plea bargain or not to press charges at all; a judge may dismiss the charges against a defendant or impose a lenient punishment on a convicted offender; or a death may not be counted as a homicide for political reasons. These actions often occur without any input from the victim or victim's family, which is not only frustrating for those parties, but also makes the public cynical about the quality of justice meted out by the criminal justice system.[12]

This chapter will explore the role and perspective of the victim in several ways. First, we will consider some typologies of victims. Next, we will look at categories of victims and how the criminal justice system responds to them, with a particular focus on programs aimed at alleviating harm.

PAUSE AND REVIEW

1. **What are three logistical obstacles to the effective and efficient measurement of crime?**

Explain what the Uniform Crime Reports program is, as well as its flaws.

Understand why the National Incident-Based Reporting System is an improvement over the Uniform Crime Reports program.

LEARNING OBJECTIVE 2.4
Compare and contrast the similarities and differences between the National Crime Victimization Survey and self-report studies.

Dark figure of crime—A term describing crime that is unreported and never quantified.

2.2 How Crime Is Measured

In this section, we will examine the various tools used for measuring crime and identify some of the issues and concerns raised by trying to measure the amount of crime in communities. Whenever there are variations in crime rates, care must be taken to ensure that these variations are the result of actual changes in crime and not measurement error. Besides definitional problems as to how to classify certain behaviors, there may also be perceptual problems about exactly when a behavior becomes a criminal offense. Kids who are fist fighting may think they are "just horsing around," but to the parent of the child with the bloody nose, it might look like bullying or an assault. To be included in the measurement of crime, the incident must be reported to law enforcement, which reports data to the Uniform Crime Reports and National Incident-Based Reporting System, or to researchers who collect data for the National Crime Victimization Survey and self-report studies.

One of the problems in attempting to measure crime is that not all offenses are reported. If an offense is not reported, it will not be counted in the indices that comprise the official measures of crime rates. Offenses that occur but do not get reported are called the "**dark figure of crime**" (see Figure 2.1). A victim might not want to report an offense to the police for several reasons.

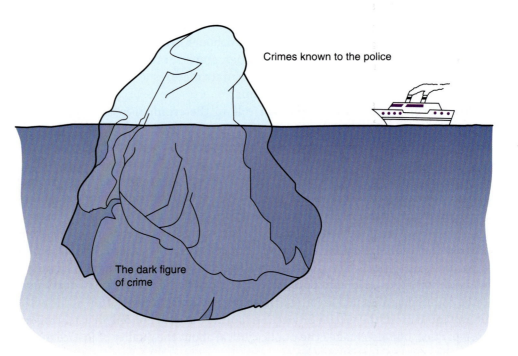

Crimes known to the police

The dark figure of crime

FIGURE 2.1   The Dark Figure of Crime Would efforts to shed light on the dark figure of crime infringe too much on individual civil rights?

> An offense might be so subtle that it is never known to have happened. Suppose that a person uses a passkey to break into an apartment with the intent to steal a television belonging to the resident, then changes his mind and leaves, disturbing nothing. This action constitutes **burglary**—which is the breaking into and entering of a structure or vehicle with intent to commit a felony or a theft—but no one but the offender would ever know it happened.

> An offense might not be perceived as such. Suppose that in the course of a hockey game, a defenseman for the Philadelphia Flyers were to slash a star center of the Montreal Canadiens with his hockey stick, opening a large cut over his eye. Such incidents occur in the heat of competition and are defined as major penalties within the context of the game. The incident described, of course, also constitutes a criminal offense that might be classified as an aggravated assault under the Uniform Crime Reports or as a wounding in the Canadian Crime Statistics. However, the event is unlikely to be perceived as a crime by either player, by either team, by the referees, or by the fans, and it is unlikely to be reported to the police. In the sport of boxing, a fighter who abides by the sport's rules might cause the death of the other fighter and face no sanctions from the criminal justice system, the referee, or the sport's ruling body.

> The offender is a family member, a friend, or an acquaintance.

> The victim believes that the offense was trivial or that the potential penalty is too grave for the harm done.

> The victim fears reprisal ("snitches get stitches").

> The victim feels antipathy toward the police.

> The victim may have broken the law as well or is embarrassed by the circumstances under which the offense occurred.

> The victim may not believe that the police can or will do anything about the offense.

> The victim or the perpetrator may be very young.

> In some cultures, victims, especially men, may consider it more masculine to pursue justice on their own. Calling the police may be considered a sign of weakness.[13]

Given these reasons for not reporting crime, does it make sense to try to measure crime and then base criminal justice system policy on these flawed numbers? The answer is yes, but with caution. Although the dark figure of crime will always be unknown, an idea of the extent of crime can be surmised with the development of precise definitions and uniform reporting standards. Because crime rates are calculated every year and show a pattern of stability, criminal justice experts can assume that unreported crime

Burglary (from Chapter 1)—Breaking into and entering a structure or vehicle with intent to commit a felony or a theft.

William Carrier, 28, of the Vegas Golden Knights and Brendan Lemieux, 48, of the New York Rangers fight during a National Hockey League game. Why is violence in professional sports seldom prosecuted in criminal court?

varies at about the same rates.[14] However, a change in reporting can be mistakenly interpreted as a change in the level of crime.

For example, suppose a community establishes a new rape crisis center. As part of their duties, the center's staff begins an educational prevention and awareness project in which they visit schools and community groups and encourage victims to report rape and sexual assaults. The staff members also support victims in the ordeal of reporting their experiences to the police. Although the number of rapes in the community might remain constant, the rape crisis center has stimulated an increase in victim reporting that results in more arrests, prosecutions, and incarcerations. Rape may appear to be on the rise in the community, when in reality, more of the dark figure of crime is becoming known and crime measurement is becoming more accurate.[15]

Imperfect as they are, crime measurements are used by criminal justice officials to make several types of decisions. For instance, law enforcement can use the frequency and seriousness of crime statistics in their jurisdictions as justifications for staffing patterns and tactical decisions. When law enforcement finds areas that have an unusual number of assaults, larcenies, or murders, they can use the statistics to commit more resources to these areas. Additionally, criminal justice officials can approach legislatures or city council members for additional funding based on measures of crime.

Researchers within both government agencies, such as the Bureau of Justice Statistics, and academia use official measures of crime to construct the crime picture. These pictures, in turn, are used by officials to make funding decisions and, to a large extent, develop the public's perception of the frequency and seriousness of crime in their jurisdictions. However, research has shown that these official measures of crime may be severely flawed.

Johnny Blymiller tries on his high-heeled shoes before the start of a "Walk a Mile in Her Shoes" event to raise awareness about violence against women. How might such events increase the reporting of rape and sexual assault?

Uniform Crime Reports

The FBI's **Uniform Crime Reports (UCR)** is the most extensive and useful measure of crime we have. The UCR's Summary Reporting System compiles the volume and rate of eight major criminal offenses—four violent crimes and four property crimes (see Table 2.1)—for the states and many jurisdictions (for an example of regional crime rates, see Figure 2.2). (The program collects only arrest data for another 20 offenses.)[16]

The UCR program is a cooperative statistical effort of law enforcement agencies that voluntarily report data on the offenses they know about. The program's main objective is to provide reliable information for use in law enforcement administration, operation, and management. Scholars, legislators, urban planners, and the media also use the UCR for research and decision-making purposes. Additionally, the UCR keeps citizens informed about the level and seriousness of crime in their communities.

Despite the numerous issues and concerns with how these records are compiled and used, they remain the best available picture of crime, even though that picture sometimes tends to be out of focus.[17] Generally, about 18,000 law enforcement agencies throughout the country voluntarily participate in the UCR program, representing about 98 percent of the U.S. population.[18]

Although the UCR provides a useful picture of crime in the United States, it is subject to both unintentional and intentional error.[19]

> Unintentional sources of error. The UCR represents a massive collection effort. Thousands of law enforcement officers and clerks enter data into the system, leaving plenty of opportunity for simple errors.[20] For instance, homicide would seem to be the most unambiguous category of crime. Someone is dead, which means the offense should be reported and coded as such. Yet, in some cases, the victim dies in the hospital weeks after the case has been entered into the system. Some jurisdictions are better than others when it comes to follow-up reporting of the subsequent death and the new homicide charge. Additionally, variations exist within and across jurisdictions in the categorization of rape if the parties involved are spouses or intimate partners.[21] Also, researchers have found that few rapes are committed along with other offenses, such as a robbery and a rape. However, rapes that do co-occur with other offenses are more likely to be reported to police than rapes that occur as single offenses. This means that the source of error is probably higher in rape statistics than in statistics for other violent offenses.[22]

> Intentional sources of error. The UCR is an important social indicator that reflects the quality of life in a jurisdiction. Police chiefs, sheriffs, mayors, and other public officials are judged by the efficacy of their policies, and the

Uniform Crime Reports (UCR)—An annual publication by the Federal Bureau of Investigation that uses data from all participating law enforcement agencies in the United States to summarize the incidence and rate of reported crime.

TABLE 2.1   Federal Bureau of Investigation Major Crime Classification

VIOLENT CRIMES	PROPERTY CRIMES
Murder and non-negligent manslaughter	Burglary
Rape	Larceny-theft
Robbery	Motor-vehicle theft
Aggravated assault	Arson

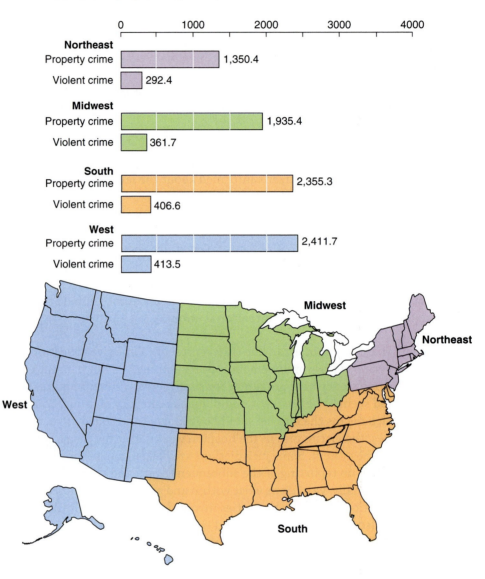

Regional Crime Rates, 2019
Violent and Property Crimes per 100,000 Inhabitants

Northeast
Property crime — 1,350.4
Violent crime — 292.4

Midwest
Property crime — 1,935.4
Violent crime — 361.7

South
Property crime — 2,355.3
Violent crime — 406.6

West
Property crime — 2,411.7
Violent crime — 413.5

FIGURE 2.2   Regional Crime Rates Examine the differences in regional crime rates. Why might the rates of some regions be so much higher than others?

Source: Federal Bureau of Investigation, Crime in the United States, 2019, *Crime Map, ucr.fbi. gov/crime-in-the-u.s/2019/crime-in-the-u.s.-2019/topic-pages/ offenses-known-browse-by/region.*

UCR presents objective criteria on which to base pay raises, promotions, and firings. Because careers are based on these numbers, and the opportunity exists to influence these numbers, it is not surprising that sometimes "the books get cooked."[23] This can happen in two ways. For example, perhaps a sheriff wants to modernize a fleet of squad cars and so instructs the deputies to change their crime-reporting behavior by counting every trivial infraction, inflating the level of crime and thus bringing in more money. By contrast, a police chief who is worried about reappointment instructs officers to overlook crime so that the reported crime rate seems to indicate that the chief's policies have been effective in reducing crime.

These examples should not be interpreted to suggest that law enforcement officials are corrupt or that their staffs are incompetent. Rather, these examples demonstrate that many possible sources of error exist in the reporting of crime and that the extent of this error is unknowable.

The FBI calculates the crime rates for individual offenses as well as the rates for violent offenses and property offenses. Why not just compare the total numbers of offenses within jurisdictions? The UCR shows the actual number of criminal offenses in each jurisdiction, but jurisdictions with more people will always have more crime. Consequently, to compare the rates for a specific offense across jurisdictions, the **crime rate** is calculated (see Figure 2.3). Comparing the rate of crime per 100,000 people is a much more accurate way to illustrate the true picture of crime.

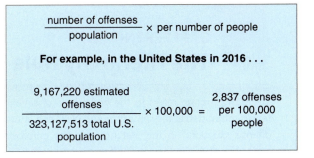

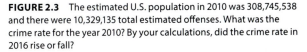

FIGURE 2.3 The estimated U.S. population in 2010 was 308,745,538 and there were 10,329,135 total estimated offenses. What was the crime rate for the year 2010? By your calculations, did the crime rate in 2016 rise or fall?

Source: Federal Bureau of Investigation, Crime in the United States: 2016, *Table 1, https://ucr.fbi.gov/crime-in-the-u.s/2016/crime-in-the-u.s.-2016/tables/table-1.*

When considering the categories the UCR uses to conceptualize types of crime, we must remember that these categories do not reflect the actual criminal statutes in each jurisdiction. For instance, a misdemeanor drug possession in Harvey, North Dakota, might qualify as a felony possession in the UCR. The reporting system collects data from thousands of jurisdictions, and the categories of crime are designed to quantify the criminal behavior in each jurisdiction, not to reflect which criminal laws have been violated. Because the UCR represents a limited agenda of counting offenses and comparing crime rates, it distorts the crime picture in the way it defines wrongdoing. This problem is most apparent when several offenses are committed in one incident.

Suppose someone breaks into your home, beats you up, steals your television, kicks your dog, and smokes marijuana while spray-painting obscene graffiti on your living room walls. You report the incident to the police, and after making the arrest, they charge the suspect with multiple offenses. What gets reported to the UCR system, however, is another matter. Because the UCR uses the **hierarchy rule** when dealing with multiple offenses, only the highest offense in the hierarchy is reported, and the rest are ignored.[24] In this case, the robbery of your television would be entered into the system, and the assault, vandalism, drug use, and abuse of your dog would not be counted. The offender may be prosecuted for each of the offenses (well, maybe not for kicking the dog), but only the robbery will be included in the official crime statistics. See CJ Reference 2.1 to understand how the hierarchy rule is applied.

Given the strengths and weaknesses of the UCR system, it should be evident that although the UCR provides a reasonably good picture of crime, it does not tell the whole crime story.[25] Fortunately, other measures supplement the UCR.

National Incident-Based Reporting System

The UCR's Summary Reporting System is over six decades old, and although it has improved greatly, it still has some problems in providing the types of information necessary for obtaining a clear picture of crime in the United States. Therefore, the federal government has embarked on a more comprehensive crime-reporting system designed to rectify some of the UCR's Summary Reporting System shortcomings. The **National Incident-Based Reporting System (NIBRS)**, which is part of the UCR, gathers data on each criminal offense even if several offenses are committed at one time. This system is an improvement over the Summary Reporting System because it compensates for the hierarchy rule.[26]

Developed in 1985, the NIBRS collects data on each single incident and arrest for 22 offense categories composed of 46 specific offenses in its Group A

Crime rate—The number of crime index offenses divided by the population of an area, usually given as a rate of crimes per 100,000 people.

Hierarchy rule—When more than one criminal offense is committed in a given incident, but only the offense that is highest on the hierarchy list is reported to the FBI's Uniform Crime Reports.

National Incident-Based Reporting System (NIBRS)—A crime-reporting system in which each separate offense in a crime is described, including data describing the offender(s), victim(s), and property.

CJ REFERENCE 2.1
The Hierarchy Rule

The UCR program refers to the occurrence of several offenses committed at the same time and place as a "multiple-offense situation." In this instance, the law enforcement agency must determine which offense occurs highest in the hierarchy and record that offense. The exceptions to the hierarchy rule are the offenses of justifiable homicide, motor-vehicle theft, and arson. In cases in which arson occurs along with another violent or property offense, both offenses, the arson and the additional offense, are reported. Otherwise, the offenses in order of hierarchy are as follows:

1. Criminal Homicide
   a. Murder and Non-negligent Manslaughter
   b. Manslaughter by Negligence
2. Rape
   a. Rape
   b. Attempts to Commit Rape
   c. Historical Rape
3. Robbery
   a. Firearm
   b. Knife or Cutting Instrument
   c. Other Dangerous Weapon
   d. Strong-arm—Hands, Fists, Feet, etc.
4. Aggravated Assault
   a. Firearm
   b. Knife or Cutting Instrument
   c. Other Dangerous Weapon
   d. Hands, Fists, Feet, etc.—Aggravated Injury
5. Burglary
   a. Forcible Entry
   b. Unlawful Entry—No Force
   c. Attempted Forcible Entry
6. Larceny-Theft (Except Motor-Vehicle Theft)
7. Motor-Vehicle Theft
   a. Autos
   b. Trucks and Buses
   c. Other Vehicles
8. Arson
   a. – g. Structural
   h. – i. Mobile
   j. Other[27]
9. Human Trafficking, Commercial Sex Acts
10. Human Trafficking, Involuntary Servitude

offenses. Additionally, arrest data are reported in 11 Group B offense categories (see Table 2.2). The advantage of the NIBRS over the UCR is that it allows law enforcement to identify precisely when and where an offense takes place, its form, and the characteristics of victims and perpetrators.

Participation in the NIBRS requires that a state restructure how it collects and reports crime data.[28] This system of recording crime may produce some unintended consequences. One issue is the complexity of reporting and coding procedures. Law enforcement must invest increased resources and personnel in crime data-collection efforts. In the past, police administrators did the job of collecting and analyzing data, but the NIBRS may require skilled civilians to make the program work.

Another issue connected with getting states to adopt the system is that it is optional.[29] States and jurisdictions have been slow to adopt the NIBRS because setting up the process is complicated and expensive. Another issue is the effect that the NIBRS may have on the duties of street-level police officers. NIBRS requires a much greater level of detail in the reporting of offenses than the UCR, and some critics are concerned that street-level officers will consider this requirement as interfering with "real" police work. Street-level officers might believe the NIBRS program to be more useful to researchers than to themselves. Finally, law enforcement officials might be concerned with what appears to be an increase in crime because the NIBRS reports each offense separately rather than reporting only one offense as does the UCR. The media and the public might not understand how changing the way crime is reported could result in the appearance of more crime.

TABLE 2.2 The National Incident-Based Reporting System Offense Categories

GROUP A OFFENSES

Extensive crime data for these offenses are collected in the National Incident-Based Reporting System.

Arson	Homicide offenses (murder and non-negligent manslaughter, negligent manslaughter, justifiable homicide)
Assault offenses (aggravated assault, simple assault, intimidation)	Human trafficking (commercial sex acts, involuntary servitude)
Bribery	Kidnapping/abduction
Burglary/breaking and entering	Larceny-theft offenses (pocket-picking, purse-snatching, shoplifting, theft from building, theft from coin-operated machine or device, theft from motor vehicle, theft of motor-vehicle parts or accessories, all other larceny)
Counterfeiting/forgery	Motor-vehicle theft
Destruction/damage/vandalism of property	Pornography/obscene material
Drug/narcotic offenses (drug/narcotic violations, drug equipment violations)	Prostitution offenses (prostitution, assisting or promoting prostitution, purchasing prostitution)
Embezzlement	Robbery
Extortion/blackmail	Sex offenses, forcible (rape, sodomy, sexual assault with an object, fondling)
Fraud offenses (false pretenses/swindle/confidence game, credit card/automatic teller machine fraud, impersonation, welfare fraud, wire fraud)	Sex offenses, non-forcible (incest, statutory rape)
Gambling offenses (betting/wagering, operating/promoting/assisting gambling, gambling equipment violations, sports tampering)	Stolen property offenses (receiving, etc.)
	Weapon law violations

GROUP B OFFENSES

Only arrest data are reported.

Bad checks	Liquor law violations
Curfew/loitering/vagrancy violations	Peeping tom
Disorderly conduct	Trespass of real property
Driving under the influence	Animal cruelty (data collection began in 2016)
Drunkenness	All other offenses
Family offenses, nonviolent	

This could be a public relations problem for police executives who are evaluated on their ability to control crime in their jurisdictions.[30]

White-collar and corporate crimes constitute special cases as far as the measurement of crime is concerned. In the long term, these types of crime may damage society as much as **street crime** does, but more of it is represented by the dark figure of crime than street crime. This is important because it is impossible for the criminal justice system to address crime that goes unreported and remains unknown. On a large scale, the financial offenses that usually occur within the framework of white-collar and corporate crime can damage the country's economy, and on an individual scale they can hurt thousands of people, particularly those who are impoverished and struggling to get by.[31] Therefore, it is important that white-collar and corporate crime be measured with the same rigor as street crime. The NIBRS is better equipped than the UCR to do this, but measuring white-collar and corporate crime remains a difficult task for several reasons:

> Like the UCR, the NIBRS primarily reflects street crime. This is because local and state agencies, not federal agencies, were originally surveyed during the development of the NIBRS. Because of their concern with immediate public safety, local and state agencies are more concerned with street crime and want street-crime statistics so that they can improve policing.

> White-collar and corporate crime typically fall within the federal jurisdiction, so offenses that are not fraud, embezzlement, counterfeiting, or bribery—which are already represented in the NIBRS—are not as thoroughly represented in the NIBRS as street offenses.

> Much of the investigation and regulation of corporate and white-collar crime is done by regulatory agencies and professional associations, not by law enforcement agencies and legislation. This means that corporate and white-collar offenses are reported to the UCR and NIBRS only if criminal charges are filed, which is not always the case in corporate crime.

> Common corporate offenses are typically classified as "All Other Offenses" in the NIBRS Group B offenses. Currently, there is no way to distinguish corporate offenses from the rest of the offenses in this category.

Street crime (from Chapter 1)—Small-scale, person offenses such as single-victim homicide, rape, robbery, assault, burglary, and vandalism.

Many white-collar crimes are handled administratively instead of in criminal court. Which government agencies deal with crime that may not be reflected in the Uniform Crime Reports?

> Corporations might not report white-collar offenses perpetrated against them because doing so might harm the company's reputation. Also, major corporate offenses are often too complicated and widespread for most people to understand that they have been victims of a corporate offense.

> The UCR was developed at about the same time—during the 1920s and 1930s—as the concept of white-collar crime. Therefore, many of the laws that criminalize white-collar and corporate offenses did not yet exist.

The FBI is working to improve the NIBRS. Because the NIBRS is being directed to include more information on white-collar and corporate offenses, a type of crime that was once thought to be relatively rare might be discovered to be quite common and widespread. The measurement of white-collar and corporate crime is a good example of the collection of statistics shining a light on the dark figure of crime.

National Crime Victimization Survey

The **National Crime Victimization Survey (NCVS)** is the primary source of information on criminal victimization in the United States. The survey is administered annually by the U.S. Census Bureau and gathers data on the frequency, characteristics, and consequences of criminal victimization from a representative sample of about 95,000 U.S. households comprising nearly 160,000 people.[32]

Previous discussions of the UCR and the NIBRS have highlighted flaws and issues that prevent each system from developing an accurate picture of the nature and extent of crime in the United States. Because both systems require people to report criminal offenses to law enforcement, they miss unreported crime. The NCVS differs from these means of reporting crime in important ways.[33] As the name implies, the survey asks crime victims about their experiences. As such, the survey does not attempt to create a comprehensive account of criminal offenses, but rather focuses on samples of the general public and specific types of crime.

Like the UCR and the NIBRS, the NCVS is imperfect. It cannot realistically account for every type of crime. Some types of offenses are not measured because the parties act in a consensual manner. For instance, the NCVS does not account for successfully completed drug transactions because buyers do not consider themselves crime victims, and thus they do not report these offenses in victimization surveys. The same could be said of gambling and prostitution.[34] In addition, the NCVS does not study murder victims (because they cannot report their experiences) or victims under 12 years of age.[35]

White-collar and corporate offenses are also difficult to measure using victimization surveys because people may be unaware that they have been victims of subtle corruption or fraud. Given the differences in the types of offenses that are measured, comparing the crime picture developed by the UCR with victimization surveys is problematic.[36] Rather than attempting to decide which method most accurately reports crime, it is more useful to think of them as measuring different aspects of crime. Used in conjunction, rather than in competition, these measures foster the development of a deeper appreciation of the types of crime that are committed and how crime affects communities.

Self-Report Studies

Another major technique for collecting data on unlawful behavior is the **self-report study**. In self-report studies, researchers, who are typically from universities, ask respondents to identify offenses they have committed. Such studies use questionnaires, which are relatively inexpensive and standardized, and do not

National Crime Victimization Survey (NCVS)—A survey that is the primary source of information on criminal victimization in the United States and attempts to measure the extent of crime by interviewing crime victims.

Self-report study—Research in which individuals are asked about criminal offenses they have committed, even those they have never been arrested for or charged with.

require personal contact. Studies may be conducted in person, by telephone, by mail, or online, although if the study is not conducted in person, the researcher can do little to ensure that the intended respondents are the ones actually answering the questions.[37] Often, the studies are conducted with high school and university students. However, some studies, particularly those concerned with juvenile delinquency, are conducted with correctional inmates or participants in rehabilitation programs.

Although some significant concerns about truthfulness arise when individuals are asked to admit to criminal behavior, there are also reasons to believe that these data provide a different and important picture of crime that is not supplied in government studies.[38] Self-report studies are important because they are not filtered through criminal justice agencies. The UCR provides better measures of what the police do than of the amount of crime being committed. Data from victimization surveys provide information on trends in violent crime, crime in schools, costs of crime, and the response of law enforcement to reports of victimization, but they fail to record offenses without a direct victim. Self-report studies, however, provide a relatively accurate picture of crime without having to view the behavior through the lens of law enforcement agencies or victims, both of which may introduce bias.

So that respondents will feel comfortable answering questions, researchers make several assurances. The first is confidentiality. No one other than the researchers knows who answers the questions. The other type of assurance is anonymity. The names of respondents are not recorded, so specific answers cannot be linked to specific respondents. Projects that promise anonymity presumably will elicit answers that are more truthful because respondents can safely report their offenses without fear that anyone will be able to connect specific offenses to them.

Researchers have attempted to determine whether respondents tell the truth in self-report studies.[39] For example, in one study of drug use, subjects underwent urinalysis to determine whether their answers to questions about drug use were accurate. Over two-thirds of those who used marijuana lied about it to the researchers, and over 85 percent of those who used cocaine lied.[40] However, over repeated surveys, the same approximate level of dishonesty can be expected, and researchers can assume that the measures are comparable and valid. If responses are consistent over repeated surveys, researchers then assume that any differences in self-reported crime measure actual offenses rather than signify errors that have been introduced by lying respondents.[41]

Another concern about using self-report studies to examine the amount and degree of crime has to do with the issue of representativeness. Many early self-report studies were done with samples of convenience: Researchers simply asked students in their classrooms to answer questionnaires. Generalizing to larger populations is difficult when the sample is constructed according to who shows up to class on a particular day. To correct for such a biased sample, researchers use probability theory to draw a sample that reflects the relevant characteristics of the population from which it is drawn. In this way, researchers can be reasonably confident that the findings derived from their study of a small number of respondents are applicable to the larger population.[42]

Finally, there are some types of crime that self-report studies simply cannot reach. For example, although self-report studies have had some success in getting individuals to talk about their drug-taking behaviors, efforts to get them to talk about their drug-selling behaviors have been less successful. The larger the drug dealer's business, the less likely the dealer is to self-identify as such for fear that a response could lead to arrest.[43] An additional problem in gathering information from drug dealers is that it is difficult to know who they are. Researchers have limited or no access to the subculture of drug dealers who are basically invisible to normal research techniques.[44]

Self-report studies and victimization surveys are powerful techniques for getting at the dark figure of crime, but these measures are not substitutes for the UCR or the NIBRS because they are not as comprehensive.[45] Taken together, however, these methods of collecting crime data give us the best picture we have ever had of crime. Although none presents the whole picture, each of these measures of crime concentrates on a different aspect of the problem.

The task of measuring crime with limited data-collection methods is daunting, but the findings are essential to the functioning of society. Legislators, criminal justice administrators, law enforcement, and the public all make decisions based on their perceptions of how much crime exists and how it affects victims. Although scholars and government officials provide a limited picture of crime, the quality of this picture is improving, and it is better than relying on the media or public opinion for the information on which public policy is made and criminal justice system budgets are based.

By employing systematically gathered UCR and NIBRS data with the snapshots provided by victimization surveys and self-report studies, we are able to get a reasonably accurate idea of the scope and severity of the crime problem. Because crime is a socially constructed concept—that is, society agrees that there is such a thing as behavior that harms others that must be controlled—some ambiguity will always exist about what behaviors constitute crime and whether particular incidents fit those definitions. Additionally, even when we agree on the definitions of crime, there will always be incentives and motivations for individuals not to report.

> **Victim**—"[A] person that has suffered direct physical, emotional, or pecuniary harm as a result of the commission of a crime."[49]

PAUSE AND REVIEW

1. **What are the Uniform Crime Reports?**

2. **How do the Uniform Crime Reports and the National Incident-Based Reporting System differ in their use of the hierarchy rule?**

3. **How are the National Crime Victimization Survey and self-report studies the same? How are they different?**

2.3 Victims of Crime

According to the Victims' Rights and Restitution Act, a **victim** is "a person that has suffered direct physical, emotional, or pecuniary [financial] harm as a result of the commission of a crime."[46] Typically, we think of a crime victim as someone who is completely innocent in an encounter with a predatory stranger. Much of the rhetoric that surrounds the pleas to elevate the victim's role in the criminal justice process offers a stereotypical view of the victim as innocent. However, victims sometimes play a much more complicated role in crime. Sometimes the victim is simply the person who lost a fight.[47] This means that our analysis of victims requires a more nuanced and comprehensive view of the crime victim's role. The "innocent victim" concept is at the heart of the stereotype of what attributes a victim should possess. Criminologist Nils Christie outlined six attributes that we typically associate with the idea of an innocent victim.[48]

1. The victim is weak in relation to the offender. The "ideal victim" is likely female, sick, weak, old, young, or some combination of these.

2. The victim is, if not acting virtuously, then at least going about his or her legitimate, everyday business.

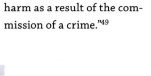

LEARNING OBJECTIVE 2.5

Define "victim."

LEARNING OBJECTIVE 2.6

Differentiate between the idea of victim precipitation and the idea of the innocent victim.

LEARNING OBJECTIVE 2.7

Debate the advantages and disadvantages of victim-impact statements.

3. The victim is blameless.

4. The victim is unrelated to and does not know the stranger who has committed the offense. This also implies that the offender is a person rather than a corporation and that the offense is a single incident.

5. The offender is unambiguously big and bad.

6. The victim has the right combination of power, influence, or sympathy to successfully elicit victim status without threatening (and thus risking opposition from) strong countervailing vested interests.

Examining this stereotype in more detail tells us a lot about how our society considers victims and how much sympathy to give them. Christie's description of the innocent victim is instructive for what it does not include. For instance, the most victimized group in American society comprises young black males, individuals who are often portrayed as the perpetrators rather than the victims.[50] However, the media tend to concentrate its victimization focus on young white females. This stereotypical view of crime victims does society and other crime victims a disservice because it diminishes the effects of crime on other types of victims.[51]

Typologies of Crime Victims

The two typologies discussed here are concerned primarily with the situational and personal characteristics of victims and the relationships of victims and offenders. One of the first scholars to develop a typology of victims was criminologist Benjamin Mendelsohn. His typology, developed in the 1950s, is controversial because Mendelsohn believed that most victims had an unconscious attitude that led to their victimization.[52] His typology included six types of victims (see Table 2.3).

TABLE 2.3	Mendelsohn's Typology of Victims
Innocent victim	This stereotypical victim detailed by Christie is viewed as someone who did not contribute to the conflict and is in the wrong place at the wrong time.
Victim with minor guilt	This victim does not actively participate in the victimization but contributes to it in some minor degree, such as frequenting high-crime areas.
Guilty victim, guilty offender	In this category, for example, the victim and the offender may have engaged in criminal activity together, after which one robs the other. The adage "there is no honor among thieves" applies here.
Guilty offender, guiltier victim	This victim may have been the attacker, and the offender was simply more successful in the conflict. A good example would be if the victim picked a fight with an offender who was a superior fighter.
Guilty victim	The victim has instigated a conflict and is killed by a party who acted in self-defense. The term *victim* is used carefully in this situation because the victim caused his or her own demise.
Imaginary victim	Some people pretend to be victims.

In 1948, criminologist Hans von Hentig studied homicide victims and developed a typology that differs significantly from Mendelsohn's. Whereas Mendelsohn considered situational factors, von Hentig considered biological, sociological, and psychological factors (see Table 2.4). Von Hentig's 12-point typology is the basis for later theories of **victim precipitation**.[53] According to this concept, many victims play a role in their victimization. Most definitions of victim precipitation assert two major points: first, that the victim acted first during the course of the offense, and second, that the victim instigated the commission of the offense.[54] Thus, the victim's actions "precipitated" the offense.

Victim precipitation— A situation in which a crime victim plays an active role in initiating a crime or escalating it.

Table 2.4's list of victim types illustrates why someone could be considered a victim. Of particular interest is the idea that some victims are responsible for precipitating their own victimization. One important point about this list is that it refers only to the victims' personal characteristics. It does not consider

TABLE 2.4   Von Hentig's Typology

The young	Young people are more susceptible to victimization because of their immaturity and vulnerability. Because young people are under adult supervision, adults are more likely to take advantage of them. Young people often lack the physical strength to protect themselves from assault, as well as the mental and emotional maturity to recognize when they are being sexually exploited.
Females	Females may not have the physical strength to ward off aggressive male attackers.
The elderly	The elderly are more likely to be crime victims because of their lack of strength. They may have low mental alertness, which makes them vulnerable to scam artists.
Mentally ill/ intellectually disabled	Those suffering from mental or intellectual problems are especially vulnerable to victimization. These individuals can easily be taken advantage of by bullies, scam artists, and sexual predators.
Immigrants	Immigrants to the United States may have problems understanding the English language and therefore may be easily taken advantage of. For those who are in the country illegally, the threat of deportation can become a leverage point for exploitation.
Minorities	Minorities are often marginalized individuals in a society. Many find themselves living in substandard housing and experiencing high unemployment.
Dull normals	In von Hentig's typology, "dull normals" are otherwise reasonably intelligent people who are naive or vulnerable in some way. This population has trouble recognizing deception by others and so is more prone to victimization.
The depressed	Depressed people are easily victimized because they are not on guard to the possibilities of being taken advantage of. They are often gullible, easily swayed, and not vigilant.
The acquisitive	These individuals tend to be greedy and can be targets for scammers who would take advantage of their desire for financial gain.
The lonesome and the heartbroken	These individuals are particularly prone to victimization by intimate partners. They desire to be with someone at any cost and are susceptible to manipulation by those who promise them companionship and intimacy.
Tormentors	These people are the primary abusers in relationships and become victims when those whom they assault finally turn on them.
Blocked, exempted, and fighting victims	These victims enter situations in which they are taken advantage of because of their own culpability. For example, people engaged in criminal activity may be victims of blackmail and be unable to report it because of their own vulnerabilities.

the structural conditions that are responsible for the development of patterns of victimization.[55] For instance, victims of white-collar crime and terrorism are not on von Hentig's list.[56]

The Incidence of Victimization

As mentioned earlier in the chapter, the National Crime Victimization Survey measures crime victimization of people age 12 and older. In 2018, the most recent statistics available, more than 1.2 million U.S. residents age 12 or older experienced serious violent victimizations, and more than 3.4 million experienced serious property victimizations. People age 24 or younger had higher rates of violent victimization than older people, and fewer than half of violent victimizations were reported to police.[57]

As we learned earlier in this chapter, victims have several reasons for not reporting criminal offenses. Many victims are unaware that when offenses go unreported, it affects how the system can assist them. Victims may not be able to obtain services to help them deal with the victimization, and the offender remains free to commit more offenses. Also, law enforcement resources may be misallocated or not allocated at all because the authorities do not have an accurate record of the total amount of crime.[58]

Categories of Victims

Anyone can be a crime victim, and victimhood can spread beyond the direct victim to indirect victims, such as family members, friends, neighbors, and the community. Here we will briefly consider some specific types of crime victims and the unique effects of their particular victimizations.

VICTIMS OF VIOLENT CRIME

Violent crime is perhaps the type of crime most people fear and what most people consider when thinking about crime. (See A Closer Look 2.1 to learn more about apps that purport to help their users avoid crime.) There are many types of violent crime, but all involve the injury or death of victims. Also, the "footprint" of violent crime—that is, the number of indirect victims or co-victims—can be quite large. Victims of murder, assault, and rape have family, friends, and neighbors who are affected by the loss or injury of the victim. Victims who survive violent crime may have trouble functioning afterward: They may be unable to remain employed, suffer post-traumatic stress, become dependent on drugs or alcohol, or become depressed. They may also have physical injuries that prevent normal functioning, such as traumatic brain injuries. Violent crime victims who survive the offense often need extensive care for the rest of their lives. In this section, we will consider three categories of violent victimization: the survivors of murder victims, or co-victims; domestic violence victims; and rape/sexual assault victims.

The families of murder victims lose not only a loved one but in some cases, a trusted parent, care provider, or breadwinner. The co-victims of murder victims often have several experiences unique to their status:

> › The intent to harm. Co-victims must deal with the anger, rage, and violence that have been inflicted upon someone they love.
> › Stigma. Society sometimes blames murder victims for their own deaths, which may extend to the victim's family when it is thought that they should have helped control the incident that led to the victim's murder.

A CLOSER LOOK 2.1
Crime Apps: Reporting Crime or Reporting Fear?

Although both violent and property crime have been decreasing for years, the average person using a mobile crime app probably would not think so. Crime apps, which use different methods to tell users how dangerous (or not) their local area is, come in different styles. Doorbell apps come packaged with front porch security cameras. Some apps, like traffic apps, use reports from app users about incidents in progress. Finally, some apps use official crime data to tell users which neighborhoods and areas are the most dangerous.[59]

Although many people say these apps make them feel safer by telling them which areas to avoid or by allowing them to submit incident alerts, some experts on crime statistics say that what such apps are best at is sowing fear. If people are more afraid of crime, the more they will turn to apps—and their advertisers—to find some sense of safety.[60]

The problem is that these apps are like police scanners that are always on, except not all the alerts represent actual crime, or they represent crime out of context. For example, a crime app that shows three homicides in a given neighborhood probably will not divulge that all the homicides stemmed from domestic violence, not robberies or random encounters, and that the neighborhood is generally safe. Also, app users often report incidents that may not be crime, thus needlessly heightening their neighbors' or bystanders' sense of danger. Apps that show an accumulation of reports, such as over a month, can make a relatively safe area look like it is in the middle of a crime wave. Furthermore, some apps have been criticized for encouraging racism, as some users submit reports involving people of color who are doing little more than being in the vicinity of the app user.[61]

THINK ABOUT IT

1. If you have a crime app on your phone, is it useful?
2. If your crime app takes user submissions, do you submit reports?

> Isolation. Co-victims may not want to discuss the offense or may feel that no one could understand their grief. Some co-victims may be unwillingly isolated when acquaintances stop calling because they do not want to trouble the co-victim.

> The media. Co-victims may become the subjects of media stories. The intrusion into co-victims' lives is different than media reportage of deaths from accidents or other causes.

> The justice system. The legal players, jargon, and process of the justice system may feel like yet another violation for co-victims. Co-victims may even be suspects and witnesses, and instead of grieving their loss, they must defend themselves or spend hours recounting what they witnessed. The justice system, which is designed to protect the rights of the accused and prosecute the offense in the name of the state, may appear unmoved by the plight of co-victims.[62]

The effect on co-victims can be widespread. For instance, in the December 2012 mass murder at Sandy Hook Elementary School in Newtown, Connecticut, where 26 people were killed, 20 of whom were 6-year-old children, the victimization includes not only those who were slain but also indirectly their family members, the community, and society at large.[63] This incident has given rise to new efforts to invoke more stringent gun-control policies.

Domestic violence, which includes intimate partner and family violence, encompasses physical, sexual, and financial abuse, neglect and maltreatment of children, and elder abuse. Domestic violence incidents are usually not sudden or

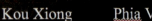

FRESNO POLICE DEPARTMENT

Deceased Victims
6 Additional Surviving Shooting Victims

Kou Xiong   Phia Vang   Kalaxang Thao   Xy Lee

These four men are the victims of a 2019 shooting rampage in Fresno, California's Hmong community. The victims were killed when attackers with semiautomatic weapons opened fire in the backyard of a Fresno home. According to police, the suspects are gang members who shot the men in retaliation for killing the brother of one of the shooters. In what ways are the families of murder victims considered co-victims?

A demonstrator holds a sign during a "March for Our Lives" rally for gun law reform in New York City. How have mass killings affected society's attitude toward firearms?

isolated but may involve years of emotional and physical abuse that increases in severity and frequency. A domestic violence victim is not only a crime victim but is in a difficult situation in that his or her offender may be a spouse and parent to his or her children. The offender may be the breadwinner, on whom the victim is completely dependent. Domestic violence incidents often go unreported because the victim cannot live without the offender and may be unable to escape. The victim may be afraid that the authorities will not take the offense seriously and that the result will be worse reprisals from the offender.

Rape is one of the most under-reported offenses in the United States. The stigma of being a victim of rape or sexual assault is still so strong that many victims do not want to go through the trauma of dealing with the criminal justice system. In fact, the criminal justice process is often called the "second victimization" of rape and sexual assault victims.[64] This is because the offense is sometimes difficult to prove in court, and until the advent of rape shield laws, the defense often used the victim's integrity and personal history against the victim. For example, a woman who was a prostitute, or had many boyfriends, or even wore a certain type of clothing might risk being accused of "asking for it." By calling the rape victim's character and integrity into question, law enforcement and medical personnel may re-victimize the victim.[65]

For males, the humiliation of admitting to being raped or sexually assaulted ensures that such cases rarely make it into the public eye, much less into a court of law. The idea of male rape was once considered so unlikely that it was not until 2012 that the U.S. Department of Justice changed its definition of rape to include males. FBI rape statistics counted only females; male victimizations were included in the sexual assault statistics. Today, the terms *rape* and *sexual assault* are almost interchangeable. However, some authorities consider sexual assault to constitute such activities as unwanted sexual touching, whereas rape includes penetration of the body.

In 2019, rape accounted for about 12 percent of violent offenses reported to the police and about 5 percent of arrests for all violent crime.[66] Victims of rape and sexual assault suffer significant mental health, medical, and social consequences. They have many concerns, including fears of being blamed by others, being found out by family and other people, becoming pregnant, contracting sexually transmitted diseases, and contracting HIV/AIDS.[67] Two general characteristics of rape victims' reactions are misunderstood, misinterpreted, and used to discredit them:

> Immediately after the attack, victims typically act in ways that people do not expect. Many victims experience shock, resulting in an appearance of calm or a flat affect. Victims often find it difficult to concentrate and may appear confused or inattentive.

> Later, as victims struggle to cope with the effects of the offense, they may have dramatic mood changes, which are often misinterpreted as indicators of inconsistencies in the victim's account of the offense. There is often a period of denial during which the victim may try to forget the incident. This may be evident in behaviors such as reporting the incident late, attempting to resume "a normal life," and avoiding anything that reminds the victim of the assault, including interacting with law enforcement, medical professionals, or other therapists.[68]

VICTIMS OF HATE CRIME

The 1990 Hate Crime Statistics Act defines hate crimes as "crimes that manifest evidence of prejudice based on race, religion, sexual orientation, or ethnicity." For the National Crime Victimization Survey to classify an offense as a hate crime, the victim must report one of two types of evidence: The offender used hate language or the offender left hate symbols. A third classification occurs if the police confirm that the incident was a hate crime through the presence of at least one bias motivation involving race/ethnicity/ancestry, religion, sexual orientation, gender identity, gender, or disability.[69] Although hate-crime legislation is sometimes criticized as being unnecessary, it has been found that a strong criminal justice reaction against hate crimes can stem riots and civil unrest that sometimes occur when a community perceives its members as being targeted.[70]

A man wears a yarmulke that reads "Stronger Than Hate" on the first anniversary of the shooting at the Tree of Life Synagogue in Pittsburgh, Pennsylvania, where 11 worshippers were killed. What groups of people are most at risk of being a target of hate crime in the United States?

The victim of a hate crime may be an individual, a business, an institution, or society as a whole. In 2018, the FBI recorded 8,819 victims of hate crime.[71] Of all victims:

> 60 percent were targeted because of race, ethnicity, or ancestry;
> 17 percent were targeted for their sexual orientation;
> 19 percent were targeted for their religious beliefs;
> 2 percent were targeted because of gender-identity bias;
> 2 percent were targeted for their disability.[72]

More than 5,500 were victims of crimes against persons, and nearly 3,000 were victims of crimes against property. Twenty-four people were murdered, and 22 were raped; about 70 percent were victims of property damage.[73] One study sorted hate-crime offenders into four categories:

> Thrill-seeking: 66 percent of offenders were looking for excitement.
> Defensive: 25 percent committed hate crimes in response to perceived outsiders in their neighborhoods.
> Retaliatory: 8 percent were retaliating for a real or perceived hate crime.
> Mission: Only 1 percent committed hate crimes out of a strong commitment to bigotry.[74]

Another study found that hate crimes are disproportionately directed "downward"; that is, the offenders typically belong to a majority or powerful social group, and the victims to a minority social group.[75]

Hate-crime victims suffer the same physical, emotional, and financial plights as victims of offenses that are not hate crimes, but they carry the additional burden of knowing that they were targeted for their skin color, religion, nationality, gender identification, or sexual orientation. People who fear hate-crime victimization may find themselves avoiding certain neighborhoods or situations in which they believe an attack is likely. Victimization may occur at any time and any place, however.

Because hate crimes ultimately seek to put fear into whole groups of people by attacking individuals, they are as damaging to society as to the individual.[76]

VICTIMS OF FINANCIAL CRIME

Financial crime encompasses many different offenses: identity theft, financial fraud, embezzlement, street scams, Internet scams, mail fraud, money laundering, Ponzi schemes, and so on. They may be committed by individuals or groups who come from all walks of life. There is no profile for a financial offender: He or she may be a white-collar worker who goes to the office every day in a suit, a young person hanging out on the street, or someone on the Internet whose face the victim never sees. As such, there is no typical victim either: the young, the elderly, the naïve, and even the financially savvy are all at risk.

Not all individuals who have experienced crime are direct victims. In many instances, the victim may never meet the offender and may never even realize that he or she is a crime victim. This is especially true for white-collar offenses in which price-fixing, embezzlement, and fraud go undetected.[77] There is considerable dissatisfaction with the criminal justice system because it often treats white-collar offenders more leniently than those accused of traditional street crime.[78] Because many victims of white-collar crime are unaware that they have been victimized or are unable to get the criminal justice system to take their victimization seriously, these victims often do not attempt to influence law enforcement to pursue white-collar offenders.

Unfortunately, the government does not keep statistics on the occurrence of financial crime and victimization to the extent that it does on street crime with the Uniform Crime Reports and the National Crime Victimization Survey. Because of the stigma of appearing "stupid," many victims likely never report the offense and just accept the financial loss and move on since they believe it is unlikely that they will ever recover their funds. Also, many financial offenses, especially those that occur in a white-collar or corporate environment, are difficult to investigate and prosecute because they are so complicated. It is often difficult to ascertain what the offense is, who is responsible, how much money is involved, and who the victims are.[79]

Victims of financial crime suffer different problems than victims of street crime, but this does not mean that their victimization is any less important or personally destructive. Victims of financial crimes can find their lifestyles, expectations, futures, and mental and physical health deeply affected. A good example of these consequences is the 2008 scandal in which trusted investor Bernard Madoff stole billions of dollars of his clients' funds. Unfortunately, it is common to paint victims of financial crime as greedy and thus deserving of their victimization. Some scam victims are taken in because they are presented with a prospect that is "too good to be true"; however, this does not make the offender any less criminal or the crime any less of a crime. Madoff presented himself as a careful and meticulous broker who offered his clients relatively small, steady returns. To inexperienced investors, the slim growth in their funds looked realistic, much like the interest on a bank statement. As a result, hundreds of people and charities deposited money with Madoff.[80]

Similar financial crimes occur but on a far less dramatic scale. Some occur on the street, when victims are approached by scammers perpetrating various types of cons. Many financial crimes occur online, such as advance-fee scams, in which scammers send out vast numbers of emails offering recipients money in exchange for assisting with a financial transaction. People posting items for sale online may also be the target for advance-fee scams. In such cases, sellers receive a response to

In 2009, Bernard Madoff was sentenced to 150 years in prison for carrying out the biggest financial fraud in Wall Street history. The financier cheated nearly 5,000 investors out of billions of dollars in a decades-long Ponzi scheme. Is financial crime any less serious if it victimizes those who have a great deal of money?

their ad from a buyer who offers to send a cashier's check for more than the asking price in return for sending the balance to the buyer. When the victim cashes the fake check and sends the balance to the buyer (who never shows to pick up the item), the bank holds the seller responsible for the entire amount.

Often, victims of such minor scams suffer little more than embarrassment and the loss of some money. Sometimes, however, as in the Madoff case, they suffer the loss of their life savings and become impoverished. If the financial offense is big enough, it can bring down entire institutions. Such major financial offenses may also cause unexpected collateral harm. In 2010, Bernard Madoff's son, Mark Madoff, who worked for his father as a broker, committed suicide.[81]

THE ELDERLY AND CHILDREN

The elderly and children are two particularly vulnerable classes of victims because they usually have little or no control over their caregivers and because they may not understand the nature of their victimization. These victims may be confused, naïve, mentally or physically ill, or simply unable to understand what is happening. Both types of victim are particularly vulnerable to unscrupulous caretakers—whether they are parents, children, spouses, or guardians—who take physical, emotional, and/or financial advantage of their charges.

Sometimes the victimization may not even be purposeful: The caregiver may simply be exhausted, frustrated, and unable to cope with the stress of dealing with the victim on a daily basis. The caregiver may not have the financial or physical ability to properly care for the victim. Another aspect of this type of victimization is that it often goes unreported because the victims cannot contact law enforcement. The victim may also be afraid to report the victimization because he or she is dependent on the offender. In addition, the victim may be unaware that the abuse is a criminal offense. We will briefly examine these forms of victimization.

The definition of elder abuse is inconsistent because there is no agreement on exactly what age constitutes "elderly" and what constitutes abuse. The term *elder abuse* may seem to apply to an independent 65-year-old man who is robbed, but not if the man's age was not a factor in the offense (for example, if the man would have been robbed if he were 25). Therefore, the typical definition of elder abuse involves a victim who is over the age of 60, is vulnerable, and is dependent on a caregiver, and the victimization involves violation of trust between the victim and someone known to the victim.

Like other victims, victims of elder abuse may feel shame, helplessness, and depression about their victimization. Unlike children or the mentally disabled, an elder-abuse victim may be fully aware that he or she is being victimized, yet be too frail, vulnerable, or fearful to do anything about it. Most elder abuse occurs in the victim's residence, which may be a private home (even his or her own home), nursing home, assisted-living facility, or retirement community.

Child abuse is a familiar topic. Countless state, jurisdiction, and community services, including the juvenile justice system, focus on the welfare of neglected and abused children. Although children are certainly harmed and bullied by other children, child abuse is considered to be perpetrated by adults. Children are extremely vulnerable to abuse because they have no control over their caregivers, living situations, homes, neighborhoods, where they go to school, peer groups, and so on. The younger the child, the more vulnerable he or she is. Children from birth to 3 years of age account for the highest percentage of child abuse and neglect victims.[82]

Although children may be victimized in any way conceivable through either abuse or neglect, sexual abuse is considered a particular problem. A child may be abducted by a stranger and subjected to sexual abuse or abused by a caregiver. The child may be forced into prostitution or pornography or forced to become the sexual partner of an adult. For example, in 1991, 11-year-old Jaycee Dugard was abducted from a school bus stop by a husband-and-wife pair of kidnappers. Repeatedly raped, Dugard spent the next 18 years living in the backyard of her kidnapper and bore two of his children. Dugard and her two daughters were rescued in 2009.

The effects of child abuse are of particular concern to the criminal justice system because most abused children grow up to become adults, and the effects of their victimization can plague their adult lives and even make them more likely to become criminal offenders themselves. Research has shown that children who are physically abused are at a greater risk for mental illness, homelessness, crime, and

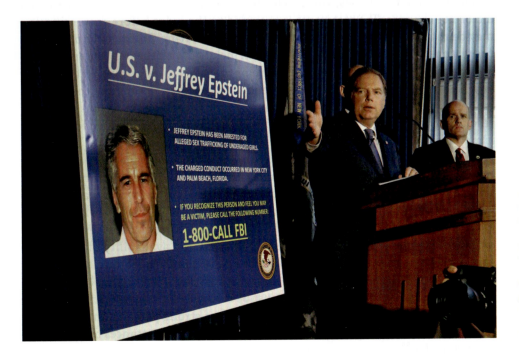

U.S. Attorney for the Southern District of New York Geoffrey Berman speaks during a news conference in which federal prosecutors announced sex-trafficking and conspiracy charges against financier Jeffrey Epstein. Epstein was found dead in his jail cell in August 2019, denying victims a trial. What avenues for seeking justice do his victims have?

Aside from establishing victims' rights, every state has some sort of victim-assistance program, and most have several. Some are public agencies, and some are community-based programs that receive federal and/or state funding. Victim-assistance programs ensure that victims are afforded their rights and provided with services. Assistance services include crisis intervention, emergency shelter and transportation, counseling, and criminal justice advocacy. For victims of federal crimes, the Federal Crime Victim Assistance Fund is available to assist victims with immediate services, such as transportation costs, emergency shelter, crisis intervention, and services to help victims participate in the criminal justice system.[89]

PAUSE AND REVIEW

1. What is the definition of "victim"?
2. How does the idea of victim precipitation differ from the idea of the innocent victim?

FOCUS ON ETHICS   To Report or Not to Report

You are a married man, and you have made your share of mistakes, but now you are in a dilemma that threatens to ruin your reputation, your career, and your marriage. If you do nothing, all will be saved in your life, but it will be at the expense of public safety and might result in a life-or-death situation.

While your wife went to Des Moines to take care of her ailing grandmother, you strayed off the path of monogamy, fidelity, and loyalty. You met a young woman who was walking her dog in the park, and after some shameless flirting you accepted her invitation to meet her at a downtown bar that night. Because this bar was a place you would never have gone to on your own, you were unconcerned that your friends might see you out with another woman.

The time at the bar was a blur of drinking, flirting, and suggestive dancing. At 2:00 a.m., you drove her back to her apartment and agreed to go inside with her. Once inside, however, after much soul-searching, you decided that you could not violate your marriage vows. The woman then became angry and demanded the $200 that she said you agreed to pay her at the bar. You were shocked. You did not remember offering her any money. When you tried to leave, a man jumped out of the closet with a baseball bat and beat you senseless.

After waking up in the hospital, you claimed that you were mugged in the park and did not get a good look at your assailant. Your wife flew home to take care of you, and as you began to heal, you renewed your determination to never again do anything that would hurt your wife.

Your unfortunate experience fades as the months pass, and you believe no one will ever discover your dalliance. Then one day as you are watching the local news, you see an exposé about how a number of men have been beaten with a baseball bat and dumped in the park. One man was beaten so badly he had permanent brain damage. The police chief tells the newscaster that it is only a matter of time before someone is killed by the man with the bat.

You remember the exact location of the apartment and the woman's name, and you can describe the man with the bat. You know you should tell the police what happened but realize that if you do so, your unfaithful behavior will be revealed. Because you are the vice president of your father-in-law's construction company, you may lose both your wife and your job. You are experiencing tremendous stress worrying that someone will be killed by this couple and that it is your moral responsibility to do something about it.

WHAT DO YOU DO?

1. Tell your wife the truth and hope she does not demand a divorce.
2. Go to the police and tell them what you know and beg them not to drag you into the case.
3. Write an anonymous letter to the police telling them what you know but protecting your identity.
4. Keep your mouth shut and let others worry about themselves.

For more insight as to how someone might respond to such an ethical dilemma, visit Oxford Learning Link at www.oup.com/he/Fuller2e to watch a video that connects this scenario to a real-world situation.

Summary

LEARNING OBJECTIVE 2.1 Describe three logistical obstacles to measuring crime effectively and efficiently.	**Definitional Problems:** Behaviors that seem to be criminal offenses are open to interpretation, thus skewing the definition of what constitutes a crime. **Resource Problems:** The priority of maintaining records of crime varies significantly across jurisdictions based on the available resources. **Political Problems:** The economic and social effects of the perception of crime can cause government officials to pressure law enforcement agencies to minimize the reporting of crime.
LEARNING OBJECTIVE 2.2 Explain what the Uniform Crime Reports program is, as well as its flaws.	The Federal Bureau of Investigation's Uniform Crime Reports (UCR) compiles the volume and rate of criminal offenses (four violent crimes and four property crimes) for the states and many jurisdictions. The UCR is a cooperative statistical effort of law enforcement agencies that voluntarily report data on the offenses they know about.
LEARNING OBJECTIVE 2.3 Understand why the National Incident-Based Reporting System is an improvement over the Uniform Crime Reports program.	The National Incident-Based Reporting System (NIBRS) gathers data on each criminal offense even if several offenses are committed at one time, thus compensating for the hierarchy rule. The NIBRS includes data describing the offender(s), victim(s), and property.
LEARNING OBJECTIVE 2.4 Compare and contrast the similarities and differences between the National Crime Victimization Survey and self-report studies.	The National Crime Victimization Survey (NCVS) is the primary source of information on criminal victimization in the United States and is administered annually by the U.S. Census Bureau. The NCVS attempts to measure the extent of crime by interviewing crime victims and gathers data on the frequency, characteristics, and consequences of criminal victimization from a large sample of people. Like the NCVS, self-report studies rely on respondents who are asked to identify offenses they have committed. Self-report studies provide a relatively accurate picture of crime without having to view the behavior through the lens of law enforcement agencies or victims, both of which might introduce bias.
LEARNING OBJECTIVE 2.5 Define "victim."	A victim is "a person that has suffered direct physical, emotional, or pecuniary [financial] harm as a result of the commission of a crime." [90]

LEARNING OBJECTIVE 2.6 Differentiate between the idea of victim precipitation and the idea of the innocent victim.	The innocent victim is weak in relation to the offender; going about his or her own business; blameless; does not know the stranger who has committed the offense. The offender is unambiguously bad; and the victim has the right combination of power, influence, or sympathy to successfully elicit victim status without threatening strong countervailing vested interests. Victim precipitation occurs when a crime victim plays an active role in initiating a criminal offense or escalating it.
LEARNING OBJECTIVE 2.7 Debate the advantages and disadvantages of victim-impact statements.	Victim-impact statements may provide information that help judges to determine restitution, if any. The victim-impact statement is intended to help give victims and co-victims a feeling of participation in the process and emotional release, as well as a sense of resolution and closure. Victim-impact statements can affect an offender's sentencing. Victim-impact statements may influence jurors to be more sympathetic toward the victim and the victim's family and may generate negative emotions toward the offender.

Critical Reflections

1. Is it possible to accurately measure the incidence and severity of crime? Do you have suggestions for improving how crime is measured in the United States?

2. Can we assume that crime victims are always innocent? Give an example of a situation in which victims might deserve what happens to them or in which they participate in their victimization.

Key Terms

Burglary **p. 33**
Crime rate **p. 37**
Dark figure of crime **p. 32**
Hierarchy rule **p. 37**
National Crime Victimization Survey (NCVS) **p. 41**

National Incident-Based Reporting System (NIBRS) **p. 37**
Self-report studies **p. 41**
Street crime **p. 40**

Uniform Crime Reports (UCR) **p. 35**
Victim **p. 43**
Victim-impact statement **p. 54**
Victim precipitation **p. 45**

Notes

1 Bernice Yeung, Mark Greenblatt, Mark Fahey, and Emily Harris, "When It Comes to Rape, Just Because a Case Is Cleared Doesn't Mean It's Solved," *ProPublica*, November 15, 2018. Emily Hernandez, "UT Senior, Sexual Assault Survivor Opens Up about Rape, Lawsuit Against Austin Police," *Daily Texan*, February 14, 2019.

2 Hernandez, "UT Senior, Sexual Assault Survivor Opens Up about Rape."

3 Ibid.

4 Yeung et al., "When It Comes to Rape, Just Because a Case Is Cleared Doesn't Mean It's Solved." Hernandez, "UT Senior, Sexual Assault Survivor Opens Up about Rape."

5 Ibid.

6 Yeung et al., "When It Comes to Rape, Just Because a Case Is Cleared Doesn't Mean It's Solved."

7 Federal Bureau of Investigation, *Crime in the United States 2017*, Clearances, https://ucr.fbi.gov/crime-in-the-u.s/2017/crime-in-the-u.s.-2017/topic-pages/clearances.

8 Hernandez, "UT Senior, Sexual Assault Survivor Opens Up about Rape."

9 Scott H. Decker, "Deviant Homicide: A New Look at the Role of Motives and Victim-Offender Relationships," in *Victims and Victimization: Essential Readings*, ed. David Shichor and

Stephen G. Tibbetts (Prospect Heights, Ill.: Waveland Press, 2002), 170–190.

10 Harvey Wallace, *Victimology: Legal, Psychological, and Social Perspectives* (Boston: Allyn and Bacon, 1998).

11 S. Shepherd Tate, "The Forgotten Victim," *American Bar Association Journal* 65, no. 4 (April 1979): 513.

12 Ben Bradford, "Voice, Neutrality and Respect: Use of Victim Support Services, Procedural Fairness and Confidence in the Criminal Justice System," *Criminology and Criminal Justice: An International Journal* 11, no. 4 (August 2011): 345–366.

13 Anna Rypi, Veronika Burcar, and Malin Åkerström, "Refraining from Reporting Crimes: Accounts from Young Male Crime Victims with an Immigrant Background," *Nordic Social Work Research* (July 2018): 131-146. Paul Brantingham and Patricia Brantingham, *Patterns in Crime* (New York: Macmillan, 1984), 49.

14 William A. Bonger, *Criminality and Economic Conditions* (Boston: Little, Brown, 1916).

15 Peggy Reeves Sanday, *Fraternity Gang Rape: Sex, Brotherhood, and Privilege on Campus* (New York: New York University Press, 2007).

16 Law Enforcement Support Section and Crime Statistics Management Unit, *Criminal Justice Information Services (CJIS) Division Uniform Crime Reporting (UCR) Program Summary Reporting System (SRS) User Manual* (Washington, D.C.: U. S. Department of Justice Federal Bureau of Investigation Criminal Justice Information Services Division, 2013), 21-22. Available at www.fbi.gov/file-repository/ucr/ucr-srs-user-manual-v1.pdf/view.

17 J. Kitsuse and A. V. Cicourel, "A Note on the Uses of Official Statistics," *Social Problems* 11 (1963): 131–139.

18 Federal Bureau of Investigation, *Crime in the United States 2019*, A Word about UCR Data, www.fbi.gov/file-repository/ucr/a-word-about-ucr-data.pdf/view.

19 Michael D. Maltz, "Crime Statistics: A Historical Perspective," *Crime and Delinquency* 23 (1977): 32–40.

20 James Nolan, Stephen Haas, and Jessica Napier, "Estimating the Impact of Classification Error on the 'Statistical Accuracy' of Uniform Crime Reports," *Journal of Quantitative Criminology* 27, no. 4 (December 2011): 497–519.

21 Julie Carr Smyth and Steve Karnowski, "Some States Seek to Close Loopholes in Marital Rape Laws," AP/*Chicago Tribune*, May 8, 2019. Briana Bierschbach, "This Woman Fought to End Minnesota's 'Marital Rape' Exception, and Won," National Public Radio, May 4, 2019.

22 Lynn A. Addington and Callie Marie Rennison, "Rape Co-occurrence: Do Additional Crimes Affect Victim Reporting and Police Clearance of Rape?" *Journal of Quantitative Criminology* 24, no. 2 (June 1, 2008): 205–226.

23 Ron Martin, "Crime Stats: Questions Linger after Atlanta Audit," *Atlanta Journal-Constitution*, January 28, 1999.

24 Clayton J. Mosher, Terence D. Miethe, and Dretha M. Phillips, *The Mismeasure of Crime* (Thousand Oaks, Calif.: Sage, 2002).

25 David Seidman and Michael Couzens, "Getting the Crime Rate Down: Political Pressure and Crime Reporting," *Law and Society Review* 8 (1974): 457–493.

26 Michael Maxfield, "The National Incident-Based Reporting System: Research and Policy Applications," *Journal of Quantitative Criminology* 15 (1999): 119–149.

27 Law Enforcement Support Section and Crime Statistics Management Unit, Criminal Justice Information Services (CJIS) Division Uniform Crime Reporting (UCR) Program Summary Reporting System (SRS) User Manual (Washington, D.C.: U. S. Department of Justice Federal Bureau of Investigation Criminal Justice Information Services Division, 2013), 23-24. Available at www.fbi.gov/file-repository/ucr/ucr-srs-user-manual-v1.pdf/view.

28 Cynthia Barnett-Ryan and Gregory Swanson, "The Role of State Programs in NIBRS Data Quality," *Journal of Contemporary Criminal Justice* 24, no. 1 (2008): 18–31.

29 David M. Bierie, "Enhancing the National Incident-Based Reporting System," *International Journal of Offender Therapy and Comparative Criminology* 59, no. 10 (September 2015): 1125–1143.

30 Mosher, Miethe, and Phillips, *Mismeasure of Crime*, 72.

31 Jeffery Reiman, *The Rich Get Richer and the Poor Get Prison*, 8th ed. (Boston: Allyn & Bacon, 2006).

32 Bureau of Justice Statistics, Data Collection: National Crime Victimization Survey (NCVS), www.bjs.gov/index.cfm?ty=dcdetail&iid=245. Accessed October 2020.

33 Douglas Eckberg, "Trends in Conflict: Uniform Crime Reports, the National Crime Victimization Surveys, and the Lethality of Violent Crime," *Homicide Studies* 19, no. 1 (February 2015): 58–87.

34 Robert F. Meier and Gilbert Geis, *Victimless Crime? Prostitution, Drugs, Homosexuality, Abortion* (Los Angeles: Roxbury, 1997).

35 Bureau of Justice Statistics, Research and Development (National Crime Victimization Survey), March 2016.

36 Brantingham and Brantingham, *Patterns in Crime*, 76–79.

37 David P. Farrington and Maria M. Ttofi, "Criminal Careers in Self-reports Compared with Official Records," *Criminal Behaviour and Mental Health* 24 (2014): 225–228; Marvin D. Krohn, Terence P Thornberry, Chris L Gibson, and Julie M Baldwin, "The Development and Impact of Self-Report Measures of Crime and Delinquency," *Quantitative Criminology* 26 (2010): 509–525; Zack Cernovsky, Gamal Sadek, and Simon Chiu, "Self-Reports of Illegal Activity SCL-90–R Personality Scales, and Urine Tests in Methadone Patients," *Psychological Reports: Disability and Trauma* 117, no. 3 (2015): 643–648; Alex R Piquero, Carol A Schubert, and Robert Brame, "Comparing Official and Self-report Records of Offending across Gender and Race/Ethnicity in a Longitudinal Study of Serious Youthful Offenders," *Journal of Research in Crime and Delinquency* 51, no. 4 (July 2014): 526–556; Francis L Huang and Dewey G Cornell, "The Impact of Definition and Question Order on the Prevalence of Bullying Victimization Using Student Self-Reports," *Psychological Assessment* 27, no. 4 (December 2015): 1484–1493; William S Aquilino, "Interview Mode Effects in Surveys of Drug and Alcohol Use," *Public Opinion Quarterly* 58 (1994): 210–240.

38 Terence Thornberry and Marvin D. Krohn, "The Self-Report Method for Measuring Delinquency and Crime," in *Criminal Justice 2000: Measurement and Analysis of Crime and Justice* (Washington, D.C.: U.S Department of Justice, 2000), 33–83.

39 Thomas Loughran, Ray Paternoster, and Kyle Thomas, "Incentivizing Responses to Self-report Questions in Perceptual Deterrence Studies: An Investigation of the Validity of Deterrence Theory Using Bayesian Truth Serum," *Journal of Quantitative Criminology* 30, no 4 (December 2014): 677–707.

40 Thomas Gray and Eric Walsh, *Maryland Youth at Risk: A Study of Drug Use in Juvenile Detainees* (College Park, Md.: Center for Substance Abuse Research, 1993).

41 Gary Kleck, "On the Use of Self-Report Data to Determine the Class Distribution of Criminal and Delinquent Behavior," *American Sociological Review* (1982): 427–433.

42 Delbert Elliott, David Huizinga, and Barbara Morse, "Self-Reported Violent

Offending: A Descriptive Analysis of Juvenile Violent Offenders and Their Offending Careers," *Journal of Interpersonal Violence* 1 (1986): 472–514.

43 Tom Mieczkowski, "Crack Dealing on the Street: Crew System and the Crack House," in *Drugs, Crime, and Justice: Contemporary Readings*, eds. Larry K. Gaines and Peter B. Kraska (Prospect Heights, Ill.: Waveland Press, 1997), 193–204.

44 Gary Potter and Larry Gaines, "Underworlds and Upperworlds: The Convergence of Organized and White Collar Crime," in *Readings in White-Collar Crime*, eds. David Shichor, Larry Gaines, and Richard Ball (Prospect Heights, Ill.: Waveland Press, 2002), 60–90.

45 David Huizinga and Delbert S Elliot, "Reassessing the Reliability and Validity of Self-Report Delinquency Measures," *Journal of Quantitative Criminology* 2 (1986): 293–327.

46 34 U.S. Code § 20141. Services to victims. See www.law.cornell.edu/uscode/text/34/20141. Accessed October 2020.

47 Kay B. Warren, "Troubling the Victim/Trafficker Dichotomy in Efforts to Combat Human Trafficking: The Unintended Consequences of Moralizing Labor Migration," *Indiana Journal of Global Legal Studies* 19, no. 1 (Winter 2012): 105–120.

48 Lance Hannon, "Race, Victim Precipitated Homicide, and the Subculture of Violence Thesis," *Social Science Journal* 41, no. 1 (January 2004): 115.

49 34 U.S. Code § 20141. Services to victims. See www.law.cornell.edu/uscode/text/34/20141. Accessed October 2020.

50 Dana L. Haynie and David P. Armstrong, "Race- and Gender-Disaggregated Homicide Offending Rates," *Homicide Studies* 10, no. 1 (February 2006): 3–32.

51 Sarah Stillman, "'The Missing White Girl Syndrome': Disappeared Women and Media Activism," *Gender and Development* 15, no. 3 (November 2007): 491–502.

52 Benjamin Mendelsohn, "The Origins of the Doctrine of Victimology," *Excerta Criminologicia* 3 (1963): 30.

53 Hans von Hentig, *The Criminal and His Victim: Studies in the Sociobiology of Crime* (New Haven, Conn.: Yale University Press, 1948).

54 Molly Smith and Leana A Bouffard, "Victim Precipitation," in *The*

Encyclopedia of Criminology and Criminal Justice, ed. Jay S. Albanese (Hoboken, N.J.: Wiley, 2014).

55 Toya Z. Like, "Urban Inequality and Racial Differences in Risk for Violent Victimization," *Crime and Delinquency* 57, no. 3 (May 2011): 432–457.

56 Elizabeth Moore and Michael Mills, "The Neglected Victims and Unexamined Costs of White-collar Crime," *Crime and Delinquency* 36, no. 3 (1990): 408–418.

57 Rachel E. Morgan and Barbara A. Oudekerk, *Criminal Victimization, 2018*, Tables 9, 19 (Washington, D.C.: U.S. Department of Justice Office of Justice Programs Bureau of Justice Statistics, 2019), 8, 10, 18. Available at www.bjs.gov/index.cfm?ty=pbdetail&iid=6686.

58 Lynn Langton, Marcus Berzofsky, Christopher Krebs, and Hope Smiley-McDonald, *Victimizations Not Reported to the Police, 2006–2010* (Washington, D.C.: U.S. Department of Justice Office of Justice Programs Bureau of Justice Statistics, 2012), 1–17. Available at www.bjs.gov/index.cfm?ty=pbdetail&iid=4393.

59 Brian X. Chen, "Apps That Blast Out Crime Alerts Don't Have to Rattle You," *New York Times*, May 29, 2019. Hank Tucker, "App Steers You Away from Local Crime; but Does It Magnify Fear, Social Divisions?" *Herald Sun* (Durham, N.C.), November 26, 2018.

60 Ibid.

61 Ibid.

62 Office for Victims of Crime Training and Technical Assistance Center, Resource Papers: Homicide, 2012, www.ovcttac.gov/views/TrainingMaterials/NVAA/dspNVAACurriculum.cfm. Accessed October 2020.

63 Elizabeth Williamson, "A Lesson of Sandy Hook: 'Err on the Side of the Victims'," *New York Times*, May 25, 2019. Reeves Wiedeman, "The Sandy Hook Hoax," *New York Intelligencer*, September 2016, nymag.com/intelligencer/2016/09/the-sandy-hook-hoax.html.

64 Rebecca Campbell, Sharon M. Wasco, Courtney E. Ahrens, Tracy Sefl, and Holly E. Barnes, "Preventing the 'Second Rape': Rape Survivors' Experiences with Community Service Providers," *Journal of Interpersonal Violence* 16, no. 12 (December 2001): 1239.

65 Shana L. Maier, "Sexual Assault Nurse Examiners' Perceptions of the

Revictimization of Rape Victims," *Journal of Interpersonal Violence* 27, no. 2 (January 15, 2012): 287–315.

66 Federal Bureau of Investigation, *Crime in the United States, 2019*, Table 1: Crime in the United States, Table 29: Estimated Number of Arrests, ucr.fbi.gov/crime-in-the-u.s/2019/crime-in-the-u.s.-2019/topic-pages/tables/table-29.

67 Dean G. Kilpatrick, Heidi S. Resnick, Kenneth J. Ruggiero, Lauren M. Conoscenti, and Jenna McCauley, *Drug Facilitated, Incapacitated and Forcible Rape: A National Study* (Charleston, S.C.: National Crime Victims Research and Treatment Center, Medical University of South Carolina, 2007). Available at www.ncjrs.gov/app/publications/abstract.aspx?ID=240972.

68 Anne Seymour and Linda Ledray, Office for Victims of Crime Training and Technical Assistance Center, Resources Papers: *Sexual Assault*, 2012, www.ovcttac.gov/views/TrainingMaterials/NVAA/dspNVAACurriculum.cfm.

69 Bureau of Justice Statistics, Hate Crime, www.bjs.gov/index.cfm?ty=tp&tid=37. Federal Bureau of Investigation, *2018 Hate Crime Statistics*, Victims, ucr.fbi.gov/hate-crime/2018/topic-pages/victims. Accessed May 2020.

70 Michael Lieberman, "Hate Crime Laws: Punishment to Fit the Crime," *Dissent* 57, no. 3 (Summer 2010): 81–84.

71 Federal Bureau of Investigation, *2018 Hate Crime Statistics*, ucr.fbi.gov/hate-crime/2018/topic-pages/victims.

72 Ibid.

73 Ibid.

74 J. McDevitt, J. Levin, and S. Bennett, "Hate Crime Offenders: An Expanded Typology," *Journal of Social Issues* 58, no. 2 (2002): 303–317.

75 Kathleen Deloughery, Ryan D. King, and Victor Asal, "Close Cousins or Distant Relatives? The Relationship Between Terrorism and Hate Crime," *Crime and Delinquency* 58, no. 5 (September 2012): 663–688.

76 Lieberman, "Hate Crime Laws."

77 E. Moore and M. Millsap, "The Neglected Victims and Unexamined Costs of White-collar Crime," *Crime and Delinquency* 36, no. 3 (July 1990): 408.

78 Shanna Van Slyke and William D Bales, "A Contemporary Study of the Decision to Incarcerate White-Collar

and Street Property Offenders," *Punishment and Society* 14, no. 2 (April 2012): 217–246.

79 Madoff Recovery Initiative, www. madofftrustee.com. Accessed October 2020.

80 Ibid.

81 Bob Van Voris, "Mark Madoff's Widow Blames His Suicide on Father Bernard Madoff in Book," *Bloomberg*, October 21, 2011.

82 Office of Juvenile Justice and Delinquency Prevention, Statistical Briefing Book, Juveniles as Victims: Child Maltreatment, 2017. Available at www.ojjdp.gov/ojstatbb/victims/ qa02102.asp.

83 Mario Gaboury, Angela McCown, and Scott Modell, Office for Victims of Crime Training and Technical Assistance Center, Resource Papers: *Child Abuse and Neglect*, 2012,

www.ovcttac.gov/views/ TrainingMaterials/NVAA/ dspNVAACurriculum.cfm.

84 Kristen Kracke, *Children Exposed to Violence: The Safe Start Initiative* (Washington, D.C.: Office of Juvenile Justice and Delinquency Prevention, 2001). Available at www.ncjrs.gov/app/publications/ abstract.aspx?id=187935. Alicia Summers, *Children's Exposure to Domestic Violence: A Guide to Research and Resources* (Reno, Nev.: National Council of Juvenile and Family Court Judges, 2006). Available at www. ncjfcj.org/advanced-cani-supplemental-materials.

85 Ray Paternoster and Jerome Deise, "A Heavy Thumb on the Scale: The Effect of Victim Impact Evidence on Capital Decision Making," *Criminology* 49, no. 1 (February 2011): 129–161.

86 Rubén Rosario, "Victims' Statements Can Affect Sentencing," *St. Paul Pioneer Press* (Minnesota), August 7, 2006.

87 Paternoster and Deise, "A Heavy Thumb on the Scale."

88 Susan Smith Howley, "Crime Victims and Offender Reentry," *Perspectives: The Journal of the American Parole and Probation Association*, Voice of the Victim issue, pp. 18–28. Available at www.appa-net.org/eweb/docs/appa/ pubs/Perspectives_2012_Spotlight. pdf. Accessed October 2020.

89 Offices of the United States Attorneys, Services to Crime Victims, www.justice. gov/usao-nh/programs/victim-witness-assistance-program. Accessed October 2020.

90 34 U.S. Code § 20141. Services to victims. See www.law.cornell.edu/uscode/ text/34/20141. Accessed June 2019.

Chapter 3

Criminal Law

FEATURES

Ronnie Bridgeman, now known as Kwame Ajamu, gets a hug from Judge Pamela A. Barker after charges against him were dismissed. How might have Ajamu's life been different if he had not been convicted?

force of the criminal justice system behind it, which can result in incarceration or even death. The continuum of proscribed behaviors is loosely matched by ever-increasing sanctions.

One of the principles behind social control, therefore, is proportionality. The more serious the infraction of society's rules and sensibilities, the more severe the sanction.[11] However, as we will see throughout this chapter, one of the main challenges of the criminal justice system is the variation in how similar cases are treated according to wealth, skin color, culture, sex, gender, and several other factors that demonstrate that justice is not always blind.[12]

Consider the opening case of Rickey Jackson, Ronnie Bridgeman, and Wiley Bridgeman. With no physical evidence, the case was built on the word of a 12-year-old boy who said the police threatened him for trying to recant. Police records also show that investigators had focused on two other men, one of whom had a history of robbery, owned a car that had license plates that matched the car fleeing the scene, and who later pled guilty to more than a dozen counts of aggravated robbery. Why did the police and prosecutors focus on three unlikely suspects instead of two who had more tangible evidence connecting them to the attack?

The imperfections of the criminal justice system are less the result of the criminal law and more the result of its application. There is a difference between the impartial law as it is written in the criminal code and the way that human beings enforce it. Law enforcement officers, prosecutors, judges, and probation officers may be sincere in their application of the law but flawed in other ways. They might have personal biases; they might make mistakes, and some of them might be corrupt, all of which results in discrepancies between how the law is meant to be applied and how it is actually applied.

A democratic society has the opportunity to ensure that the criminal law reflects the values of all citizens. This is relatively easy to do when a consensus exists about which behaviors should be outlawed. Certainly, homicide, rape, robbery, and embezzlement are behaviors we all wish to be protected from by the criminal law. We all agree that some dangerous individuals are best kept behind bars because of the harm they do. However, there are other behaviors for which there is no consensus, such as drug use, gambling, or pornography, and for which the criminal law is constantly in flux depending on which groups succeed in having their values addressed by the legislature and the courts.[13]

For example, several states make it difficult, if not nearly impossible, for people who have been convicted of certain offenses to vote (see Getting It Right 3.1).[14] The individuals who would most like to see these types of laws reversed are former convicts. However, because it is difficult for some former convicts to vote in many states, they are unable to support candidates who may be sympathetic to their desires. For example, those who have been convicted of some drug offenses may be ineligible to vote for candidates who advocate for the legalization or decriminalization of drugs.

Gambling laws are a good example of how economic and social values compete in the criminal law. In the past, Las Vegas and Atlantic City were the only places in the United States where gambling was legal. Now, many states permit various forms of gambling, and, in a turn of the criminal law that illustrates the differences between federal and state jurisdictions, many allow casinos only on federal lands controlled by American Indians. Citizens in many states have voted to allow lotteries that produce revenue to offset taxes. It is easy to see, then, that not all laws are equally grounded in the values of all citizens.

The process of developing the U.S. criminal law was and continues to be episodic, uneven, and political. Societies throughout history did not systematically build on the laws of previous cultures but instead chose elements consistent with

GETTING IT RIGHT 3.1
Restoring the Vote to Felons

Although most states have procedures to restore voting rights to former felons, more than 6 million Americans are not allowed to vote due to state laws that prevent citizens convicted of felony offenses from voting.[15] Every state has its own rules regarding this issue. Maine and Vermont allow felons to vote while in prison. Iowa requires offenders to apply to the governor or the president to have their voting rights restored. In Mississippi, people convicted of felonsies remain eligible to vote in presidential elections, but those convicted of certain offenses must convince their state representative to personally offer a bill restoring voting rights to that individual for state and local elections. Then the legislature must pass the bill. The governor can also directly grant enfranchisement.[16]

In an effort to fully reintegrate offenders into society, several states are granting voting privileges to former felons. In 2015, Kentucky's governor issued an executive order that granted the right to vote to 140,000 nonviolent offenders who had completed their sentences.[17] In California, the right to vote was restored to nearly 60,000 convicts in community supervision.[18] In 2018, Florida voters approved a ballot measure that restored voting rights for up to 1.5 million people with felony convictions. Shortly after, the Florida legislature passed a bill requiring former felons to fully pay any outstanding court costs or restitution before they can vote.[19] In May 2020, a federal judge struck down parts of that law, ruling that it is unconstitutional to prevent former felons from voting because they cannot afford to pay court fees, fines, and restitution.[20]

THINK ABOUT IT

1. Once former felons have served their sentences, should they be able to resume their lives as ordinary citizens with the same rights as everyone else? Why or why not?

2. Should all states adopt the policies of Maine and Vermont and allow all felons, even those currently in prison, to vote? Support your position.

Watch the related video on Oxford Learning Link at www.oup.com/he/Fuller2e.

their own values, religions, and economic structures and discarded elements that were not. Therefore, our own system is a hodgepodge of other societies' attempts to control conduct through the criminal law.[21] A brief look at some of the previous systems of law provides insight into how our laws came to be structured as they are.

The Choctaw Nation of Oklahoma owns the Choctaw Casino & Resort. Why is gambling allowed only on tribal properties in many states?

The Code of Hammurabi as inscribed on a basalt stele. These laws stand as one of the first written codes of law in recorded history. What is your interpretation of the "eye-for-an-eye" philosophy of this code?

Code of Hammurabi—An ancient code instituted by Hammurabi, a ruler of Babylonia, dealing with criminal and civil matters.

Magna Carta—"Great Charter"; a guarantee of liberties signed by King John of England in 1215 that influenced many modern legal and constitutional principles.

Habeas corpus—An order to have a prisoner/detainee brought before the court to determine if it is legal to hold the prisoner/detainee.

Common law—Laws that are based on customs and general principles and that may be used as precedent or for matters not addressed by statute.

Early Legal Codes

In 1901, a stone tablet was discovered that bore the laws of ancient Babylonia as written by its king, Hammurabi. The tablet chiseled in the Akkadian language dates to about 1780 BCE and includes laws relating to a wide range of behaviors. The laws followed, literally, the "eye-for-an-eye" or *lex talionis* philosophy, an indication that severe penalties have always been part of legal codes. However, Hammurabi used this philosophy as a way of introducing some proportionality into the law. The **Code of Hammurabi** contained more than 250 laws that covered many economic, social, and criminal issues that reflect the values of the times. For instance, some of the laws make the penalties for the death or injury of slaves less severe than those for the death and injury of free people.

The Code of Hammurabi is not the earliest known legal code, but it is quite similar to the legal code of Lipit-Ishtar, king of Isin, a Mesopotamian city-state in what is now Iraq. Lipit-Ishtar's code is 164 to 175 years older than Hammurabi's code and, like Hammurabi's code, introduces proportionality into the law. Unfortunately, archaeologists found only fragments of Lipit-Ishtar's code, so, unlike Hammurabi's code, it is largely incomplete.

Perhaps the most significant message to be learned from these codes has nothing to do with the actual laws—which, after all, apply to a society much different from ours—but rather, that legal codes existed more than 3,000 years ago. Archaeologists believe that the codes of Hammurabi and Lipit-Ishtar were likely only two of many that arose during that era and that there are other, possibly earlier, codes waiting to be found.[22] This tells us not only that the law has a long and fascinating history but that all complex human societies are likely to have some form of law.[23] Figure 3.1 provides a partial list of historical documents that have influenced the development of modern laws.

The Magna Carta

The English **Magna Carta**, a major document that contributed to U.S. law, limited the king's power and provided for the rights of citizens. King John signed the Magna Carta at Runnymede, England, on June 15, 1215, conceding a number of legal rights to the barons and the people. To finance his foreign wars, King John had taxed abusively. His barons threatened rebellion and coerced the king into committing to rudimentary judicial guarantees, such as freedom of the church, fair taxation, controls over imprisonment (**habeas corpus**), and the rights of all merchants to come and go freely, except in times of war. The Magna Carta has 61 clauses, the most important of which for our purposes is number 39: "No freeman shall be captured or imprisoned . . . except by lawful judgement of his peers or by the law of the land." This was the first time a king admitted that even he could be compelled to observe a law, with the barons allowed to "distrain and distress him in every possible way," which was just short of a legal right to rebellion.[24]

As the law developed over the centuries, it specified not only what rulers may do, but also what they may not do. The law limited the capricious decision-making powers of kings and dictated that people had certain protections from the government. The law set forth numerous behaviors that citizens were told not to engage in, while also granting them rights and protections. These dual functions of the law are important in the modern criminal justice system. A major factor in this system is the **common law**, which was first developed in England and brought to the North American colonies, where it was modified to fit the new culture.

Ur-Nammu's Code
The earliest known written legal code, from the Mesopotamian city of Ur, protects the poor, as well as deals with witchcraft, escaped slaves, and bodily injuries.

2100 BCE

c. 1750 BCE

The Code of Hammurabi
Babylonian King Hammurabi codifies a relatively sophisticated set of 282 case laws, including provisions for the regulation of commerce, slavery, marriage, theft, and debts. Its guiding principle is *lex talionis*, or the principle of "an eye for an eye, a tooth for a tooth."

The Ten Commandments
According to religious traditions, Moses receives these laws from God. Many commandments continue in the form of modern laws. Some scholars date the commandments between the 16th and 13th centuries BCE.

date unknown

621 BCE

Draco's Laws
Athenian politician Draco compiles the first comprehensive set of laws in Greece. The penalty for many offenses is death, and the code becomes infamous for its severity.

Solon's Laws
Solon makes important changes to the Athenian constitution and replaces Draco's laws with more humane codes. Solon's laws become the basis of the Athenian state

c. 570 BCE

451–450 BCE

Laws of the Twelve Tables
Magistrates create these laws to appease the plebes, who complained that the oral laws weren't fair. Often modified, the laws are used for almost a thousand years. The tablets are destroyed by the Gauls in 390 BCE.

Code of Justinian I
This collection of old Roman laws, which also incorporated some new laws, was compiled under the direction of the Byzantine emperor Justinian I.

527–565 CE

604

The Seventeen Article Constitution of Japan
Crown Prince Shotoku Taishi issues to the ruling class laws based on Confucian concepts, including that of a unified state governed by a single ruler and a virtuous government that practices justice, decorum, and diligence.

T'ang Dynasty Law
Chinese Emperor Kao-tsu codifies a set of laws and administrative procedures that is used for the next seven centuries. The Ming Dynasty models its code on it, and it's adopted later by the Japanese, Koreans, and Vietnamese. Considered the oldest complete Chinese legal code.

624

1085–1086

Domesday Book
On the order of William the Conqueror, a general census of England is taken in order to refine taxation. "Domesday" means "doomsday" or "day of judgment."

Revival of Roman Legal Studies
Italian legal scholar Irnerius and other teachers lecture on rediscovered portions of Emperor Justinian's Corpus Juris Civilis and found a law school at Bologna, which eventually becomes the foremost in Europe.

1088

1166

Assize of Clarendon
In order to improve criminal law procedures, Henry II issues a number of articles, one of which is the establishment of the grand jury.

Magna Carta (Great Charter)
King John concedes a number of legal rights and liberties to the people under threat of civil war. The charter is altered in 1216, 1217, and 1225.

1215

1689

The English Bill of Rights
This predecessor to the American Bill of Rights limits the crown's legal rights and assigns political supremacy to Parliament. It is supplemented in 1701 by the Act of Settlement.

The Salem Witch Trials
In a Massachusetts Bay Colony town, a group of young women accuses three other women of practicing witchcraft, sparking a legal hysteria. Nineteen people are hanged, and 150 are imprisoned.

1692

1765–1769

Blackstone's Commentaries on the Laws of England
English jurist Sir William Blackstone publishes his lectures in a work that clarifies English law.

The American Declaration of Independence
On July 4, the Continental Congress announces the separation of the American colonies from Great Britain.

1776

1787–1789

The Constitution of the United States of America
In the summer of 1787, 55 delegates meet in Philadelphia to write the law of the U.S. government. The resulting document defines the government's nature and the basic rights of the country's citizens.

The American Bill of Rights
The first 10 amendments to the Constitution guarantee individual rights and limit federal and state governments.

1791

1803

Marbury v. Madison
The Supreme Court establishes the power of judicial review, by which courts may declare statutes unconstitutional.

Napoleonic Code
Napoleon appoints a commission to write a code embodying French private law and ancient Roman law. The first modern legal code of France, it's still in force today.

1808

1865

Thirteenth Amendment
Slavery is abolished.

Fourteenth Amendment
Defines national citizenship and guarantees the basic rights of citizens.

1868

1896

Plessy v. Ferguson
The Supreme Court rules that the equal protection clause of the Fourteenth Amendment deals with political, not social equality, thus declaring racial segregation constitutional.

Harrison Narcotics Act
Opium and non-narcotic drugs such as cocaine are restricted. It is replaced in 1970 by the Controlled Substances Act.

1914

1919

Volstead Act
Also known as the National Prohibition Act, the Eighteenth Amendment enforces prohibition of alcohol. It was passed by Congress over the veto of President Woodrow Wilson.

Twenty-First Amendment
Prohibition is repealed.

1933

1937

Marijuana Tax Act
Possession of marijuana is restricted to those who pay an excise tax for specific medical and industrial uses.

Brown v. Board of Education of Topeka, Kansas
The Supreme Court unanimously overrules *Plessy v. Ferguson,* stating that segregation in the public schools violates the equal protection principles of the Fourteenth Amendment.

1954

1966

Miranda v. Arizona
The Supreme Court holds that individuals in police custody must be informed of their rights concerning statements they make while in custody.

The Racketeer Influenced and Corrupt Organizations Act (RICO)
Congress enacts this statute to combat organized crime. RICO defines racketeering activities and provides extended penalties for crimes committed by criminal organizations.

1970

1984

Comprehensive Crime Control Act
Federal criminal laws are substantially reformed, overhauling the federal sentencing system, permitting pretrial detention of suspects considered dangerous, restricting the legal definition of insanity, requiring mandatory minimum sentences for career criminals, increasing fines for drug offenses, broadening drug forfeiture laws, and establishing a victim compensation program.

FIGURE 3.1   A Partial List of Historical Documents That Have Influenced the Development of Modern Laws

Common Law

Statutory law—The type of law that is enacted by legislatures, as opposed to common law.

Common law is different from **statutory law**. Instead of being expressly specified by a constitution or a legislature, the common law is based on the judiciary's past decisions. The term *common law* comes from England during the reign of King Henry II (1154–1189). During this time, the king's judges abided by the common customs of the kingdom rather than the particular traditions of each village. The "common law" was so called because it was the law common to all of England.[25]

Precedent—A prior legal decision used as a basis for deciding a later, similar case.

Sometimes called case law, judiciary law, judge-made law, customary law, or unwritten law, common law is based largely on the doctrine of **precedent**.[26] This means that judges look to previous cases with similar circumstances to see how justice was meted out. The idea behind common law is that similar cases should be treated in a similar manner. Over the decades, thousands of cases came to form the foundation of common law. As precedents were set, lawyers and judges had to consider those precedents in the administration of cases. Today, four issues guide precedent:

1. Predictability. Predictability provides the concept of precedent with a certain level of order. By being consistent with the reasoning of previous cases and providing an outcome that fits with that reasoning, the common law gains legitimacy among people because they can understand how judgments are determined.

2. Reliability. Participants in the legal system expect the court to follow precedent. Even if some facts of the case are disputed, the court is obliged to consider how previous cases were decided. Reliability means that the court is using precedent as a guide.

3. Efficiency. Participants expect cases to be resolved in a reasonable time. Common law has created an expectation of how long cases should take to resolve. Although there are occasionally some extreme exceptions to the time it takes to try a sensational case, precedent defines when the time is becoming excessive.

4. Equality. Similar cases are expected to be treated in a similar fashion. This is the most important function of the concept of precedent. The concept of justice depends on the perception that the court treats individuals fairly. To have vast differences in outcomes of similar cases violates the concept of equality.[27]

Stare decisis—The doctrine under which courts adhere to legal precedent.

The doctrine of precedent means that courts are generally bound by the decisions of previous courts. This legal principle is known as **stare decisis**, whereby the precedent of a previous case becomes the standard by which subsequent cases are considered.[28] Part of the art of the practice of law is the attorney's skill in finding similar cases and convincing the court that the circumstances are so close to the present case that a similar decision should be imposed. The opposing attorney will dispute the similarity of the circumstances and find other similar cases with different outcomes to support a given position. Consequently, the law is not as cut and dried as is sometimes believed. The law is open to interpretation, and an attorney's legal reasoning, persuasive arguments, and reputation may play an important role in how a case is decided. Common law is important not only for the doctrine of precedent, but also because it has informed the development of other sources of law. As legislatures developed constitutions and statutes, they used the common law as a guide. In most areas, however, common law has been superseded by more formal and explicit sources of law. It is worth considering these in greater detail to gain a fuller understanding of how the criminal law operates.

3.2 Sources of Law

LEARNING OBJECTIVE **3.3**

Identify and define the sources of the criminal law.

The law is derived from no single source. Consequently, inconsistent principles, overlapping jurisdictions, and unclear nuances often appear in the criminal justice system. Ultimately, the U.S. Constitution defines the powers of the federal government. Conflicts between state and federal laws are dealt with by the Constitution's Supremacy Clause (Article VI, paragraph 2), which establishes the Constitution, federal statutes, and U.S. treaties as "the supreme law of the land." State constitutions and laws, then, are subject to federal law, and no laws may contradict the Constitution's principles.[29]

Considering the sources of the law can shed some light on this confusion. The primary sources of law are the U.S. Constitution and state constitutions; statutes enacted by legislative bodies (such as the U.S. Congress); court decisions (also known as case law); the rules of administrative agencies; and executive orders (see Figure 3.2).

Constitutions

In democracies, constitutions play a central and critical role in the development of criminal law. Constitutions express the will of the people. In a representative democracy, such as the United States, the Constitution binds elected legislators, the institutions of society, and the citizens to a system of government and laws. In the United States, the Constitution governs the country. Each state also has a constitution that pertains to the citizens and businesses of that state. State constitutions supplement but do not supersede the federal Constitution. This means that states cannot take away freedoms granted by the federal Constitution.

Although the U.S. Constitution does not proscribe many behaviors, it sets out some broad values that cannot be abridged by the criminal law. The Constitution specifies how the government is structured and the roles played by the various branches of government (see Figure 3.3). One of the first issues the framers of the Constitution dealt with was specifying how citizens were to be protected from the government. The first 10 amendments to the Constitution, also called the **Bill of Rights**, dictate the

Bill of Rights—The first 10 amendments to the U.S. Constitution, which guarantee fundamental rights and privileges to citizens.

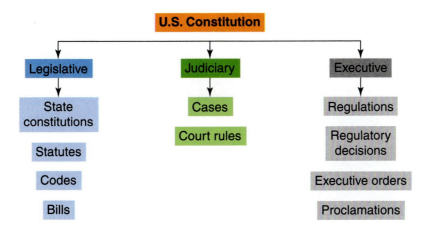

FIGURE 3.2 Sources of Law Which sources of law are you most familiar with? The least familiar with?

The Preamble to the Constitution. In what ways does the Bill of Rights serve as a foundation of the criminal law?

basic freedoms enjoyed by U.S. citizens (see CJ Reference 3.1). Later legislators did not stop there. The Constitution has been amended 27 times. Amending the Constitution is a cumbersome process, requiring the ratification of state legislatures, but the important point to remember is that the Constitution is a living and changing document, not an absolute one.

Statutes

Statute—A law enacted by a legislature.

Federal and state legislative bodies have developed the common law into specific **statutes** that prohibit criminal behavior. These laws are debated and voted on by the legislative bodies and presumably represent the will of the people. For many behaviors, such as homicide, a consensus exists as to what the law should cover. However, there are other offenses, such as drug use or gambling, that many citizens contend should not be illegal. Regardless of personal beliefs, however, all citizens are expected to obey the law or risk entering the criminal justice system.

Penal code—A code of laws that deals with crimes and the punishments for them.

The advantage of statutes over the common law is that statutes are published in **penal codes** and therefore fit the principles of predictability, reliability, efficiency, and equality better than the doctrine of precedent. Statutes are easier to change than the Constitution, but new laws cannot violate rights given in the

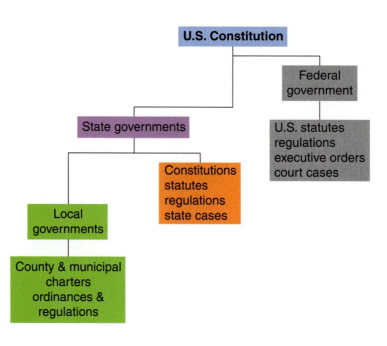

FIGURE 3.3 The Hierarchy of the U.S. Legal System Why might the hierarchy be structured this way? For example, why does the federal government rank higher than state governments?

CJ REFERENCE 3.1
The Bill of Rights

AMENDMENT I

Congress shall make no law respecting an establishment of religion, or prohibiting the free exercise thereof; or abridging the freedom of speech, or of the press; or the right of the people peaceably to assemble, and to petition the Government for a redress of grievances.

AMENDMENT II

A well regulated Militia, being necessary to the security of a free State, the right of the people to keep and bear Arms, shall not be infringed.

AMENDMENT III

No Soldier shall, in time of peace be quartered in any house, without the consent of the Owner, nor in time of war, but in a manner to be prescribed by law.

AMENDMENT IV

The right of the people to be secure in their persons, houses, papers, and effects, against unreasonable searches and seizures, shall not be violated, and no Warrants shall issue, but upon probable cause, supported by Oath or affirmation, and particularly describing the place to be searched, and the persons or things to be seized.

AMENDMENT V

No person shall be held to answer for a capital, or otherwise infamous crime, unless on a presentment or indictment of a Grand Jury, except in cases arising in the land or naval forces, or in the Militia, when in actual service in time of War or public danger; nor shall any person be subject for the same offence to be twice put in jeopardy of life or limb; nor shall be compelled in any criminal case to be a witness against himself, nor be deprived of life, liberty, or property, without due process of law; nor shall private property be taken for public use, without just compensation.

AMENDMENT VI

In all criminal prosecutions, the accused shall enjoy the right to a speedy and public trial, by an impartial jury of the State and district wherein the crime shall have been committed, which district shall have been previously ascertained by law, and to be informed of the nature and cause of the accusation; to be confronted with the witnesses against him; to have compulsory process for obtaining witnesses in his favor, and to have the Assistance of Counsel for his defence.

AMENDMENT VII

In Suits at common law, where the value in controversy shall exceed twenty dollars, the right of trial by jury shall be preserved, and no fact tried by a jury, shall be otherwise re-examined in any Court of the United States, than according to the rules of the common law.

AMENDMENT VIII

Excessive bail shall not be required, nor excessive fines imposed, nor cruel and unusual punishments inflicted.

AMENDMENT IX

The enumeration in the Constitution, of certain rights, shall not be construed to deny or disparage others retained by the people.

AMENDMENT X

The powers not delegated to the United States by the Constitution, nor prohibited by it to the States, are reserved to the States respectively, or to the people.

Constitution.[30] Consequently, new laws are often challenged on constitutional grounds. Laws may be challenged for constitutionality in two ways. The first is *unconstitutional* per se. In these cases, it is claimed that the law is unconstitutional under any and all circumstances. The other challenge is *unconstitutional as applied*, which is to claim that although the law may be valid, it is applied in a way that restricts or punishes the exercise of constitutional rights. This is an important distinction because a law that is found to be unconstitutional per se must be removed from the criminal code, whereas a law that is unconstitutional as applied requires only changes in the procedures of a criminal justice agency.

Case Law

Case law—The published decisions of courts that create new interpretations of the law and can be cited as precedent.

Cases decided by judges in state, local, and federal courts are all part of U.S. law. **Case law** operates under the principle of *stare decisis*; that is, similar cases are treated in a similar way. Case law enables the courts to prevent a vast disparity in judicial outcomes and ensure that a degree of uniformity exists across courts. Although case law depends on *stare decisis* to ensure that cases are in line with how past cases have been decided, it also evolves as new decisions are applied to new circumstances in each case. The legal reasoning of case law changes as appellate courts review the decisions of trial courts and note the reasons for their decisions that consequently guide future cases.

The issue of jurisdiction also heavily influences case law. Cases decided in one judicial circuit might not be as influential in other circuits. Although the decisions of the U.S. Supreme Court are important to every court, a decision of a court in Omaha might be less influential in a New York court than in a Nebraska court.[31]

Administrative Rules and Executive Orders

Federal, state, and local agencies have developed rules consistent with their responsibilities to oversee aspects of commerce and public protection. Health, environment, customs, and parole agencies all have the authority to enact rules that limit the freedoms of individuals operating within their spheres of influence. An example of an administrative rule in criminal justice would be rules specifying victim services. A rule set forth by the state of Utah, for instance, provides that emergency awards up to $1,000 can be granted to crime victims who need money for urgent expenses.[32] Another example, in the state of Georgia from the Georgia Bureau of Investigation, specifies the procedure for disclosing and viewing crime scene photographs and videos by members of the press.[33]

Sometimes administrative rules overlap with criminal statutes or constitutional rights and end up being contested in court. For instance, administrative rules about minority hiring practices or university admission policies have been found to be at odds with constitutional guarantees. In another example, parolees are subject to a host of conditions that require approval from one's parole officer, such as changing residences, traveling out of state, getting married, or drinking alcohol. These are all rules considered by the parole agency to be necessary to aid the parolee in making the transition from incarceration to the free world. Violation of these conditions can result in the parolee returning to prison. Because these issues are administrative rules rather than legal statutes, the parolee is not accorded the full range of constitutional rights, as is the criminal defendant.

Executive orders are directives that the president issues to government officials and agencies. Executive orders have the force and effect of law but usually only affect the general public indirectly. The president, or a subsequent president, may repeal or modify executive orders, or they may have an expiration date. An executive order may also become obsolete when the purpose for which it was issued no longer exists. Executive orders are used in several ways, including:

> to issue binding pronouncements to units of the executive branch;
> to make policy in fields such as security classification, governance of civil servants, foreign service and consular activities, and government contracting;
> to initiate or direct legislation;
> to delegate authority to other agencies or officers;
> to reorganize agencies, eliminate existing agencies, or create new ones;

> to manage federal personnel;
> to control the military; and
> to manage foreign policy.

State governors have authority similar to that of the U.S. president to issue executive orders concerning state administrative agencies and state military personnel.[34]

PAUSE AND REVIEW

1. **What are the sources of the criminal law?**

3.3 Types of Law

As a form of social control, the law performs many functions. In addition to defining socially unacceptable behaviors, it also regulates the rules of social conflict, dictates how authorities control behavior and maintain public order, and regulates how behavior is punished. Different types of laws accomplish these multiple functions. Here we will discuss the distinction between criminal law and civil law, followed by a discussion about substantive law and procedural law.

Criminal Law and Civil Law

The **criminal law** specifies the prosecution by the government of a person or people for an act that has been classified as a criminal offense. What criteria are used to determine that a behavior is so serious that it needs to be made a criminal offense and specified in the criminal law? Many objectionable behaviors are not covered by criminal law. Conversely, the criminal law covers some behaviors that many people believe it should not cover. Ideally, the criminal law is a mechanism of social control used only when other mechanisms (family, church, community) have failed and is used only for serious transgressions. Three criteria determine what behaviors are made criminal:

1. The enforceability of the law. Laws that cannot be enforced do little good. The prohibition of alcohol in the 1920s showed what happens when the law cannot be enforced. Alcohol continued to be manufactured and sold, and people continued to drink it, but the government received no revenue from alcohol sales that could be used to combat the negative effects of drinking. Many critics believe that the war on drugs is another example of laws that cannot be effectively enforced. Even as prison systems are overflowing with those convicted of drug-related offenses, illegal drugs continue to be bought and sold.

2. The effects of the law. Sometimes the cure is worse than the disease. During Prohibition, the consequences of attempting to enforce alcohol laws had a deleterious effect on society. Although alcohol was illegal, a great demand for it remained, bringing some unintended consequences in the form of organized crime and violence. Additionally, many otherwise law-abiding citizens were drawn into the criminal enterprise of alcohol production, transportation, and sales because of the lucrative alcohol trade. Perhaps even more harmful to society was the effect on the criminal justice system. Widespread corruption of judges and law enforcement officers seriously damaged the faith of citizens in the efficacy and fairness of government officials.

LEARNING OBJECTIVE 3.4

Compare and contrast the similarities and differences between criminal law and civil law.

LEARNING OBJECTIVE 3.5

Differentiate between substantive law and procedural law.

Criminal law—The law specifying the prosecution by the government of a person or people for an act that has been classified as a criminal offense.

3. The existence of other means to protect society against undesirable behavior. Many people argue that even though drug and alcohol use has some unattractive features, the criminal justice system is not the most efficient and effective institution to control this behavior. Instead of attempting to discourage addictive behavior by punishment and deterrence, some experts contend that medical and psychological treatment would be more effective and not cause the harmful side effects of the war on drugs. Instead of using the criminal law as a weapon against drugs, the medical and mental health community could be better funded and expanded to address the problem. The repeal of Prohibition did not eliminate the problems of alcohol, but most would agree that by legalizing alcohol, the United States dealt with its health and social problems more effectively.[35]

The criteria for deciding which behaviors should be made criminal are not always heeded by legislators. The making of criminal law is as much a political enterprise as it is a legal one. Most citizens try to obey the law, but all of us are guilty of choosing to disregard some laws. Think about the last time you exceeded the legal speed limit. Was it on your way to class today? Because of people like you, the government decided to repeal the once-universal 55-miles-per-hour speed limit on the interstate highway system. The trucking industry and those who traveled routinely broke the speeding laws, and ultimately, the federal and state governments were lobbied for a higher speed limit. From a safety perspective, the 55-miles-per-hour limit was useful, but it was ignored by too many citizens and was eventually modified.

Civil law—The law that governs private rights as opposed to the law that governs criminal issues.

There is an important difference between the criminal law and **civil law**. Both types of law try to control the behavior of people, and both can impose sanctions. Also, there is some considerable overlap in the types of behavior they address, such as personal assault or environmental pollution. The important difference between them, however, concerns the identity of the aggrieved party. In civil law, the case is between two individuals. In criminal law, the case concerns the defendant

State Senator Liz Krueger, co-sponsor of the Marijuana Regulation and Taxation Act (MRTA), speaks at a rally alongside the bill's supporters. The law would legalize and regulate the use of marijuana in New York State, ending disproportionate policing and providing millions of dollars in tax revenue. How would legalizing cannabis affect the crime rate?

and the government. In criminal law, when someone is charged with assault, the dispute becomes the property of the government. The government greatly reduces the victim's role and prosecutes the case in the name of the state.[36] This aspect of the criminal law confuses and frustrates many victims who still consider the case a problem between themselves and the accused.[37]

At this point, the victim can invoke the civil law for redress and sue the offender for compensation for damages. Private attorneys, as opposed to the state prosecutor, represent the victim and offender. The court sentence is concerned with monetary damages, not with the prospect of incarceration. Civil law covers contracts, personal property, maritime law, and commercial law. **Tort law**, a form of civil law, covers personal wrongs and damage and includes libel, slander, assault, trespass, and negligence.[38]

An often-misunderstood principle of law called **double jeopardy** states that a person cannot be tried for the same offense twice.[39] This concept applies to the criminal law but also allows for legal actions from multiple jurisdictions. Therefore, double jeopardy does not preclude a crime victim from suing for private damages after the criminal trial has concluded, nor does it protect a criminal defendant from being prosecuted by both state and federal jurisdictions. For example, because of the distinction between the criminal law and civil law, the families of Nicole Brown Simpson and Ronald Goldman were awarded monetary damages from O. J. Simpson after he was acquitted of criminal charges. The standards of proof in a civil trial (**preponderance of the evidence**) are not as stringent as those in a criminal trial (**beyond a reasonable doubt**), which explains how two juries can consider the same case and produce different verdicts.[40] In another example, a defendant accused of breaking both state and federal laws may be prosecuted in both jurisdictions. Roberto Miramontes Roman was acquitted by a state court jury of the 2010 killing of sheriff's deputy Josie Greathouse Fox during a traffic stop. In 2016, the federal government tried Roman on the charge of killing a law enforcement officer, as well as several federal drug and weapons violations. A federal jury convicted Roman.[41]

Substantive Law and Procedural Law

Substantive law tells us which behaviors have been defined as criminal offenses. The "thou shall nots" of the criminal law, substantive laws are found in the criminal codes of the state and federal governments and are the result of generations of political and social development. Homicide, rape, assault, money laundering, and all the other behaviors that are against the law are proscribed by the substantive law. The substantive law also sets the parameters on the punishment for each type of offense. Once a suspect has been convicted, the judge does not have unlimited discretion in imposing a sentence. For example, few offenses are eligible for the death penalty. In the case of minor offenses, the judge can choose a short period of incarceration or decide that society is better served by placing the offender on probation.

Whereas the substantive law specifies what individuals are not allowed to do, the **procedural law** specifies how the criminal justice system is allowed to deal with those who break the law. The procedural law sets the rules by which the police, courts, and corrections systems process cases. Based to a large degree on the rights granted to accused individuals by the Constitution, procedural law protects citizens from arbitrary decision-making by criminal justice professionals by dictating how cases are to be handled.[42] Procedural law specifies rules of arrest, search and seizure, rights to attorneys, and attorney–client privilege, as well as other "rules of the game."

Tort law—An area of the law that deals with civil acts that cause harm and injury, including libel, slander, assault, trespass, and negligence.

Double jeopardy— Prosecution of a defendant in the same jurisdiction for an offense for which the defendant has already been prosecuted and convicted or acquitted.

Preponderance of the evidence—The burden of proof in a civil trial, which requires that more than 50 percent of the evidence be in the plaintiff's favor.

Beyond a reasonable doubt—The highest level of proof required to win a case; necessary in criminal cases to procure a guilty verdict.

Substantive law— Law that describes which behaviors have been defined as criminal offenses.

Procedural law—Law that specifies how the criminal justice system is allowed to deal with those who break the law or are accused of breaking the law.

Demonstrators gather outside Grand Central Terminal in New York City to protest violent arrests targeting people of color. How much discretion do police have in deciding which laws to enforce?

Procedural laws change with the creation of new case precedents, new laws, or new court opinions. For instance, in the wake of the terrorist attacks on New York City and Washington, D.C., on September 11, 2001, the federal government decided that attorney–client privilege is not absolute and that the police may monitor communications to prevent future terrorist acts.[43] Whether this evidence could be used against an accused terrorist in court is not clear at this time. This question will have to be decided by the courts.

PAUSE AND REVIEW

1. What three criteria determine what behaviors constitute as criminal?
2. How are the criminal law and civil law alike? How are they different?
3. How does the substantive law differ from procedural law?

LEARNING OBJECTIVE 3.6

Distinguish between felonies and misdemeanors and illustrate why the application of these labels is not always consistent.

LEARNING OBJECTIVE 3.7

Justify the need for inchoate offenses.

3.4 Types of Crime

The criminal law has categorized crime according to several different features. For instance, the difference in the seriousness of criminal offenses is captured by the felony versus misdemeanor distinction. Criminal offenses are also differentiated by who commits the behavior, as in the distinction of juvenile status offenses (underage drinking, for instance). Some statutes recognize criminal history in classifications for first-time offenders, career offenders, or sex offenders. In the sections that follow, we will discuss four types of crime: felonies, misdemeanors, inchoate offenses, and infractions.

Felonies

The **felony** is considered the most serious type of criminal offense. Felonies include murder, rape, assault, larceny, arson, and a host of other offenses at the state and federal level. The felony distinction is important because many agencies and corporations deny employment to those convicted of this type of offense. Depending on the jurisdiction, felons may not be allowed to run for public office, own a firearm, or enter certain professions, such as law enforcement. Also, the penalties are often more severe for felonies than for other types of offenses. Incarceration for felonies is usually more than one year, and life imprisonment or capital punishment is specified for some felonies.

Depending on the jurisdiction, felonies are often divided into degrees in order to determine the most appropriate punishment. The most widely known example is that of murder. In 1794, the state of Pennsylvania divided murder into three types: first degree, second degree, and manslaughter. First-degree murder involved premeditation; second-degree murder was a killing that was intentional, but not premeditated or committed during another felony; and manslaughter was a killing for what could be considered a good reason. By the late 19th century, most states had adopted this structure or some variation of it, and it remains in use today for many felonies.[44] For example, robbery may be divided into first-degree or second-degree robbery when the victim or a bystander is injured, if the perpetrator is armed with a deadly weapon, and/or if the perpetrator has an accomplice. The charge may only amount to third-degree robbery if a single perpetrator uses force or a weapon to commit a theft but does no other harm.

Misdemeanors

Misdemeanors are less serious offenses than felonies and are subject to lighter penalties. Usually, the maximum incarceration for a **misdemeanor** is up to one year in jail. Misdemeanants spend their time in county jails or stockades as opposed to state prisons. More often than not, misdemeanants are placed on probation, fined, or required to do some type of community service rather than be incarcerated.

The distinction between felonies and misdemeanors can be confusing. An offense could be categorized as either, depending on the circumstances. Additionally, the prosecutor has wide discretion in deciding which type of offense to charge a defendant with and may, as a result of plea bargaining, reduce the indictment from felony to misdemeanor. In some ways, this distinction gives the prosecutor immense power to coerce plea bargains from a defendant who is afraid of the vast consequences of being convicted as a felon as opposed to a misdemeanant.

When considering the differences between felonies and misdemeanors, it is important to note that a specific behavior may be a felony in one jurisdiction and a misdemeanor in another (or maybe not even a criminal offense at all). Gambling is a good example. Nevada has many types of legal gambling, whereas other states outlaw many types of gambling. For example, Georgia had no legalized gambling until the state decided that the revenue was so attractive that it instituted its own lottery system while continuing to prohibit other types of gambling.

Additionally, the differences between felonies and misdemeanors can be observed in drug laws in which the amount of drugs in possession necessary to be a felony varies widely from state to state. Therefore, although the distinction between a felony and a misdemeanor is important, the actual practice in the application of the label by the criminal justice system is sometimes inconsistent and problematic.

Inchoate Offenses

A crime does not always have to be completed for the offender to be arrested, charged, and punished. To limit the harm caused by crime and to deter individuals from planning and attempting wrongdoing, a category of crimes called **inchoate offenses**

Felony (from Chapter 1)—An offense punishable by a sentence of more than a year in state or federal prison and sometimes by death.

Misdemeanor (from Chapter 1)—A minor criminal offense punishable by a fine and/or jail time for up to one year.

Inchoate offense—An offense composed of acts necessary to commit another offense.

was created. There are three inchoate offenses: attempt, conspiracy, and solicitation. In attempt, an individual tries to break the law; in conspiracy cases, two or more people agree to break the law; and in solicitation, one person encourages another to break the law.[45]

Although conspiracy to commit a criminal offense is often difficult to prove, it is a behavior that legislators have deemed to be so serious that it needs to be discouraged and punished. For example, if Timothy McVeigh, Terry Nichols, and Michael Fortier had been apprehended while collecting the materials and making the plans to bomb the Murrah Federal Building in Oklahoma City in 1995, they could have been charged with inchoate offenses. With the government's focus on preventing acts of terrorism, we can appreciate the need to have conspiracy laws available to incapacitate and deter individuals and groups intent on causing the type of mass destruction in the Oklahoma City bombing and the terrorist attacks on September 11, 2001.

The idea behind inchoate offenses is that the offender should not have to be successful in completing the crime before the criminal justice system can respond. For instance, if law enforcement is aware of a plan to kill the president of the United States, they do not have to wait until the act is completed before they arrest the conspirators.

Infractions

Infraction—In most jurisdictions, a minor civil offense that is not serious enough to warrant curtailing an offender's freedom.

An **infraction** is usually an offense that is not serious enough to warrant curtailing an offender's freedom. For this reason, infractions do not merit jury trials or legal representation provided by the state. Judges decide the case in a bench trial, and the standard of proof is usually the lowest form required for civil procedures, preponderance of evidence. The most common punishment for an infraction is a fine and/or community service. In most jurisdictions, infractions are violations of a local ordinance, a municipal code, or a traffic law. Many states consider infractions to be a matter of civil law, although a few jurisdictions consider some infractions to be criminal.

Exactly what behavior constitutes an infraction varies widely among jurisdictions, and these definitions are specified by state and local legislators. Nationwide, traffic offenses, such as speeding, are likely the most common form of infraction. Some states have even reduced the possession of small amounts of marijuana to the status of an infraction. The exception to the civil nature of infractions is when an offender continues to commit them, and they pile up. For example, a large collection of unpaid parking tickets or speeding tickets may result in the offender being charged with a misdemeanor and serving a short time in jail.

PAUSE AND REVIEW

1. In what ways is a felony different from a misdemeanor?
2. What are the three inchoate offenses?

LEARNING OBJECTIVE 3.8

Outline the elements of a criminal offense.

3.5 Features of Crime

Not all harmful acts are considered criminal offenses. Certainly, many automobile accidents have serious consequences for the victims, but unless the elements necessary for the legal definition of a crime are present, then the accident, no matter how serious, will not be considered by the criminal court. At least some of the following elements must be present in order for any act to be labeled a criminal offense:

1. The criminal act (***actus reus***) (must be present in all offenses)
2. The criminal intent (***mens rea***) (must be present in some offenses)
3. The relationship between *actus reus* and *mens rea* (also called **concurrence**)
4. **Attendant circumstances** (must be present in some offenses)
5. Result (criminal harm; must be present in some offenses)

Together, these elements constitute ***corpus delicti*** or the "body of the crime." This does not mean an actual dead human body, as is found at the scene of a homicide, but rather the aforementioned elements of the crime relevant to the case at hand. Most minor offenses do not require *mens rea*. Offenses composed only of *actus reus* typically require the element of **attendant circumstances**, which are additional conditions that define an offense.

Consider, for example, a case in which a motorist is ticketed for driving 150 miles per hour down a highway. In this instance, the excessive rate of speed is the attendant circumstance, and *mens rea* is not required for the driver to be sanctioned. (See A Closer Look 3.1 for an example of a condition a state may apply to a similar criminal offense.) Serious offenses, however, such as theft, burglary,

Actus reus—"Guilty deed"; the physical action of a criminal offense.

Mens rea—"Guilty mind"; intent or knowledge to break the law.

Concurrence—The coexistence of *actus reus* and *mens rea*.

Corpus delicti—"Body of the crime"; the criminal offense.

Attendant circumstances—Additional conditions that define a given criminal offense.

A CLOSER LOOK 3.1
Watson Murder

Every state organizes its criminal justice system differently. This also holds true for how the states specify degrees of felonies. For example, in the 1980s, the state of California created a type of second-degree murder called a "Watson murder" in an effort to increase the penalties for homicides committed while driving under the influence (DUI).

In January 1979, Robert Watson, after drinking in a Redding, California, bar drove into an intersection at about 1:00 a.m. and struck a car, killing a woman and her 6-year-old daughter. The speed limit was 35 miles-per-hour, and expert testimony estimated that Watson's car was traveling at about 70 miles-per-hour when it hit the victims' car. Watson's blood alcohol content was measured at .23 percent, more than twice the level of legal intoxication.

Watson was charged with second-degree murder and vehicular manslaughter based on the court's finding that Watson acted with implied malice, the concept that ill will can be inferred from certain acts.[46] In this case, the court found that Watson acted with implied malice for three reasons: (1) A person should know the dangers of driving while intoxicated; (2) anyone who drinks alcohol to the point of legal intoxication while knowing that he or she must drive a car is acting with a conscious disregard for others' safety; and, finally, (3) as evidenced by the skid marks, Watson braked his vehicle so hard, he must have been aware that he had created a dangerous situation.[47]

Today, California prosecutors may add a Watson murder charge to any vehicular manslaughter and intoxicated driving charges. To help prosecutors prove the implied malice that is necessary for a Watson murder charge, the state usually gives first-time DUI defendants the "Watson admonishment" that any further intoxicated driving that results in a homicide may bring a second-degree murder charge. The reasoning is that if DUI defendants hear the Watson admonishment, then they cannot be unaware that drunken driving may be fatal; thus, any further DUIs they commit must be done with implied malice.

THINK ABOUT IT
1. Because alcohol affects memory and perception, a person who is heavily intoxicated may not realize that he or she is too intoxicated to drive. How does implied malice apply in this case?

defense, which has become something of an urban legend. In November 1978, former San Francisco city supervisor Dan White shot and killed Mayor George Moscone and supervisor Harvey Milk. White then turned himself over to police. At trial, White's attorneys claimed that White had severe depression before the shooting. A defense psychiatrist mentioned that the health-conscious White had eaten large amounts of junk food during his depression and that this radical change of behavior was a symptom of depression.[64] White's defense was that he was influenced by depression, not that a sugar high made him insane. A jury found White guilty of two counts of voluntary manslaughter, sentencing him to less than 8 years in prison. He served about 5 years, leaving prison in January 1985. He committed suicide that October.[65]

PAUSE AND REVIEW

1. Which six arguments are commonly employed in the defense against a criminal indictment?

FOCUS ON ETHICS   Changing the Substantive Law

Laws are made by elected legislators to reflect their constituents' wishes. In an ideal situation, communities enjoy a broad consensus as to what behaviors should be considered illegal and what the punishments should be for violating the law. However, citizens do not support some laws. These laws are broken regularly and sometimes enforced selectively.

Imagine that you are a state senator and that the majority party leader has told you that because of your hard work and your casting of several key votes, she can fix it with the rest of the party for you to have any law you want added to your state's criminal code. What behavior that is now legal in your state would you choose to make against the law? Does your new law address a significant social problem, or does it simply expose the rest of us to your personal aesthetic tastes, your religious sensitivities, or your individual pet peeves? For example, some people think that anyone smoking in public, even outdoors, should be arrested because of the danger of secondhand smoke.

On the other hand, what law that is currently on the books would you like to see removed? Why do you think this is a bad law, and what would be the social consequences of legalizing this behavior? For instance, if you are concerned with the right of people to choose to use marijuana and decide to repeal the marijuana laws, some unanticipated consequences might accompany this change. More people might use marijuana in unsafe situations, such as while driving. Marijuana might

become more easily available to children, and many people could develop health problems from long-term use.

Think through the possible ramifications of adding or deleting substantive laws. Even though no one would suggest that our system of laws is perfect, we do need to be cautious when we change the law. One of the foundations of a democracy is the confidence of the people in the wisdom and fairness of the law. The criminal justice system cannot maintain the order of society without widespread voluntary social control. Consider how the laws that you would add to the legal code and the laws that you would delete would affect the relationship between citizens and the government.

WHAT DO YOU DO?

1. What law(s) would you add?
2. What law(s) would you delete?
3. Should all new laws be subject to public vote? Why or why not?

For more insight on how someone might respond to such an ethical dilemma, visit Oxford Learning Link at www.oup.com/he/Fuller2e to watch a video that connects this scenario to a real-world situation.

Summary

LEARNING OBJECTIVE **3.1** Frame the development of the U.S. criminal law.	The founders and subsequent generations of Americans chose to implement legal elements from previously established cultures that were consistent with their own values, religions, and economic structures and discarded elements that were not. As a result, U.S. criminal law is a hodgepodge of other societies' attempts to govern conduct through the criminal law and continues to evolve today.
LEARNING OBJECTIVE **3.2** Evaluate the function of each of the four issues that guide precedent.	(1) Predictability: Predictability provides the concept of precedent with a certain level of order. (2) Reliability: Participants in the legal system expect the courts to follow precedent. (3) Efficiency: Participants expect cases to be resolved in a reasonable time. (4) Equality: Similar cases are expected to be treated in a similar fashion.
LEARNING OBJECTIVE **3.3** Identify and define the sources of the criminal law.	**Constitutions:** In democracies, constitutions express the will of the people. In the United States, the federal Constitution governs the nation, and each state also has a constitution that pertains to the citizens and businesses of that state. **Statutes:** Developed from the common law, statutes proscribe criminal behavior. These laws are debated and voted on by legislative bodies and presumably represent the will of the people. **Case law:** Cases decided by judges in state, local, and federal courts are all part of U.S. law. Case law operates under the principle of *stare decisis* (similar cases are treated in a similar way). **Administrative rules:** These rules are developed by federal, state, and local agencies to oversee aspects of commerce and public protection. **Executive orders:** The U.S. president or a state governor issues these directives to government officials and agencies.
LEARNING OBJECTIVE **3.4** Compare and contrast the similarities and differences between criminal law and civil law.	The criminal law specifies the prosecution by the government of a person or people for an act that has been classified as a criminal offense. Civil law governs private rights as opposed to criminal issues. In civil law, the case is between two individuals; in criminal law, the case concerns the defendant and the government. Both civil law and criminal law try to control the behavior of people, and both can impose sanctions. Both overlap in the types of behavior they address, such as personal assault or environmental pollution.
LEARNING OBJECTIVE **3.5** Differentiate between substantive law and procedural law.	Substantive law tells us which behaviors have been defined as criminal offenses. Procedural law specifies how the criminal justice system is allowed to deal with those who break the law.
LEARNING OBJECTIVE **3.6** Distinguish between felonies and misdemeanors and illustrate why the application of these labels is not always consistent.	A felony is a criminal offense that calls for a minimum term of one year or more in state or federal prison. Felonies include murder, rape, assault, larceny, arson, and a host of other offenses at the state and federal level. A misdemeanor is a minor criminal offense (less serious than a felony) punishable by lighter penalties such as a fine and/or jail time for up to one year. An offense may be categorized as either a felony or misdemeanor depending on the circumstances of the offense, the prosecutor's use of discretion, and the laws of the respective jurisdiction.
LEARNING OBJECTIVE **3.7** Justify the need for inchoate offenses.	Inchoate offenses allow law enforcement to deter individuals and groups from causing harm and destruction. An offender should not have to be successful in completing a crime before the criminal justice system can respond.

LEARNING OBJECTIVE **3.8**	1. The criminal act (*actus reus*) (must be present in all offenses)
Outline the elements of a criminal offense.	2. The criminal intent (*mens rea*) (must be present in some offenses) 3. The relationship between *actus reus* and *mens rea* (also called concurrence) 4. Attendant circumstances (must be present in some offenses) 5. Result (criminal harm; must be present in some offenses)
LEARNING OBJECTIVE **3.9** List the six arguments that can be employed in the defense against a criminal indictment.	(1) My client did not do it. (2) My client did it, but my client is not responsible because he or she is insane. (3) My client did it but has a good excuse. (4) My client did it but has a good reason. (5) My client did it but should be acquitted because the police or the prosecutor cheated. (6) My client did it but was influenced by outside forces.

Critical Reflections

1. Which sources of law (the Constitution, case law, statutes) do you think should have precedence in the criminal justice system?

2. Explain how both the civil law and the criminal law are designed to control the behavior of individuals.

3. In your opinion, which of the six criminal defense explanations of criminal responsibility most mitigate an offender's unlawful behavior?

Key Terms

Actus reus **p. 81**
Affirmative defense **p. 84**
Alibi **p. 84**
Attendant circumstances **p. 81**
Beyond a reasonable doubt **p. 77**
Bill of Rights **p. 71**
Case law **p. 74**
Civil law **p. 76**
Code of Hammurabi **p. 68**
Common law **p. 68**
Concurrence **p. 81**
Corpus delicti **p. 81**
Criminal law **p. 75**

Double jeopardy **p. 77**
Entrapment **p. 89**
Felony **p. 78**
Habeas corpus **p. 68**
Inchoate offense **p. 79**
Infancy **p. 87**
Infraction **p. 80**
Insanity defense **p. 84**
Magna Carta **p. 68**
Mens rea **p. 81**
Misdemeanor **p. 79**
Penal code **p. 72**
Precedent **p. 70**

Preponderance of the evidence **p. 77**
Procedural law **p. 77**
Rule of law **p. 64**
Stare decisis **p. 70**
Statute **p. 72**
Statutory law **p. 70**
Statutory rape **p. 88**
Strict liability **p. 83**
Substantive law **p. 77**
Tort law **p. 77**

Notes

1 Maurice Possley, Kwame Ajamu, *National Registry of Exonerations*, www.law.umich.edu/special/exoneration/Pages/casedetail.aspx?caseid=4555. Accessed October 2020.

2 Ibid.

3 Ibid.

4 Ibid.

5 Elahe Izadi, "Ohio Man Exonerated after Spending 27 Years in Prison for a Murder He Didn't Commit," *Washington Post*, December 9, 2014.

6 John Caniglia, "A Free Man: Ricky Jackson to Leave Prison 39 Years after a Boy's Lie Helped Put Him Behind Bars," *Plain Dealer* (Cleveland, Ohio), November 18, 2014. Izadi, "Ohio Man Exonerated."

7 Izadi, "Ohio Man Exonerated."

8 Possley, Kwame Ajamu.

9 Mark Gillispie, "3rd Man Exonerated in 1975 Cleveland Slaying," AP News, December 9, 2014.

10 Aleksandr I. Solzhenitsyn, *The Gulag Archipelago 1918–1956* (New York: HarperCollins, 2002).

11 James Austin and John Irwin, *It's about Time: America's Imprisonment Binge*, 3d ed. (Belmont, Calif.: Wadsworth, 2001).

12 Jeffrey Reiman, *The Rich Get Richer and the Poor Get Prison: Ideology, Class, and Criminal Justice*, 6th ed. (Boston: Allyn & Bacon, 2001).

13 Samuel Walker, *Sense and Nonsense about Crime and Drugs: A Policy Guide*, 4th ed. (Belmont, Calif.: West/ Wadsworth, 1998).

14 National Conference of State Legislatures, www.ncsl.org/research/ elections-and-campaigns/felon-voting-rights.aspx. Accessed October 2020.

15 Jean Chung, Felony Disenfranchisement: A Primer, The Sentencing Project, July 17, 2018, www. sentencingproject.org/publications/ felony-disenfranchisement-a-primer.

16 "Voting Rights for Ex-offenders by State," *Nonprofit Vote*, May 1, 2019, www.nonprofitvote.org/voting-in-your-state/special-circumstances/ voting-as-an-ex-offender.

17 Erik Eckholm, "Kentucky Governor Restores Voting Rights to Thousands of Felons," *New York Times*, November 24, 2015.

18 "Thousands of California Convicts to Regain Voting Rights," *Aljazeera America*, August 4, 2015.

19 Patricia Mazzei, "Florida Gave Ex-Felons the Right to Vote." *New York Times*, May 3, 2019.

20 Lawrence Mower, "Federal judge: Florida Can't Stop Poor Felons from Voting," *Tampa Bay Times*, May 25, 2020.

21 Herbert A. Johnson and Nancy Travis Wolfe, *History of Criminal Justice*, 3d ed. (Cincinnati, Ohio: Anderson, 2003).

22 Ibid.

23 L. W. King, trans., "The Code of Hammurabi," The Avalon Project at Yale Law School, avalon.law.yale. edu/subject_menus/hammenu.asp. Accessed October 2020.

24 Magna Carta, British Library, www. bl.uk/collections/treasures/magna. html. Accessed October 2020.

25 David W. Neubauer and Henry F. Fradella, *America's Courts and the Criminal Justice System* (Belmont, Calif.: Wadsworth Cengage, 2011), 29.

26 Morris L. Cohen, "The Common Law in the American Legal System: The Challenge of Conceptual Research," *Yale Law School Legal Scholarship Repository*, 81, no. 13 (1989). Available at digitalcommons.law.yale.edu/fss_ papers/2950. The Robbins Collection, University of California at Berkeley School of Law, The Common Law and Civil Law Traditions, www.law. berkeley.edu/research/the-robbins-collection/exhibitions/common-law-civil-law-traditions. Accessed October 2020. Joycelyn M. Pollock, *Criminal Law*, 9th ed. (New York: LexisNexis, 2009), 7. Kyle Scott, *Dismantling American Common Law* (Lanham, Md.: Lexington Books, 2007), 16. Oliver Wendell Holmes Jr., *The Common Law* (New Brunswick, N.J.: Transaction Publishers, 2005), xiv.

27 Richard A. Wasserstrom, *The Judicial Decision: Toward a Theory of Legal Justification* (Stanford, Calif.: Stanford University Press, 1961).

28 Lief H. Carter, *Reason in Law*, 4th ed. (New York: HarperCollins, 1994).

29 Karla Castetter, "Chapter 1: Introduction," in *Locating the Law*, 5th ed. (Los Angeles: Southern California Association of Law Libraries, 2011), 1–12.

30 Kermit Hall, *The Magic Mirror: Law in American History* (New York: Oxford University Press, 1991).

31 Charles Rembar, *The Law of the Land: The Evolution of Our Legal System* (New York: Simon & Schuster, 1980).

32 Utah Department of Administrative Services, Division of Administrative Rules, Utah Administrative Code, Title R270. Crime Victim Reparations, Administration, Rule R270-1. Award and Reparation Standards, rules.utah. gov/publicat/code/r270/r270-001.htm. Accessed October 2020.

33 Rules and Regulations of the State of Georgia, Georgia Bureau of Investigation, 92-5-.01, Rules for the limited disclosure and viewing of certain crime scene photographs and videos by bona fide members of the press, rules.sos. state.ga.us/gac/92-5. Available at casetext.com/regulation/georgia-administrative-code/department-92-georgia-bureau-of-investigation/ chapter-92-5-limited-disclosure-of-crime-scene-photographs-and-videos/ rule-92-5-01-rules-of-the-limited-disclosure-and-viewing-of-certain-crime-scene-photographs-and-videos-by-bona-fide-members-of-the-press. Accessed October 2020.

34 Alaine Ginocchio and Kevin L. Doran, *The Boundaries of Executive Authority: Using Executive Orders to Implement Federal Climate Change Policy* (Boulder, Colo.: Center for Energy and Environmental Security, 2008), 5–6. Available at pcap2016.org/ the-boundaries-of-executive-authority-1.

35 John C. Klotter, *Criminal Law*, 6th ed. (Cincinnati, Ohio: Anderson, 2001), 6.

36 Nils Christie, "Conflicts as Property," *British Journal of Criminology* 17 (1977): 1–15.

37 Jennifer Eastman, "A Constitutional Amendment for Victims: The Unexplored Possibility," in *Victimology: A Study of Crime Victims and Their Roles*, eds. Judith M. Sgarzi and Jack McDevitt (Upper Saddle River, N.J.: Prentice Hall, 2003), 333–346.

38 Raymond J. Michalowski, *Order, Law, and Crime: An Introduction to Criminology* (New York: Random House, 1985), 139–141.

39 Frank A. Schubert, *Criminal Law: The Basics* (Los Angeles: Roxbury, 2004), 101–103.

40 Ibid., 10–13.

41 Pamela Manson, "After 7 Years and an Acquittal, Man Is Convicted of Killing Utah Deputy," *Salt Lake Tribune*, February 7, 2017.

42 James R. Acker and David C. Brody, *Criminal Procedure: A Contemporary Perspective* (Gaithersburg, Md.: Aspen, 1999).

43 Philip Shenon, "Lawyers Fear Monitoring in Cases on Terrorism," *New York Times*, April 28, 2008. USA PATRIOT ACT, www.justice.gov/ archive/ll/highlights.htm. Accessed October 2020.

44 Ibid.

45 John Deigh and David Dolinko, eds., *The Oxford Handbook of Philosophy of Criminal Law* (New York: Oxford University Press, 2011), 126.

46 *People v. Watson*, Justia U.S. Law, law. justia.com/cases/california/supreme-court/3d/30/290.html. Accessed October 2020.

47 Jeffrey W. Grass, "Drunk-Driving Murder and People v. Watson: Can Malice Be Implied?" *Southwestern University Law Review* 14 (1984: 477–520).

48 Schubert, *Criminal Law: The Basics*.

49 Ann O'Neill, Theater Shooter Holmes Gets 12 Life Sentences, Plus 3,318 years, CNN, August 27, 2015. Amanda Paulson, "Why James Holmes Insanity Case Is So Unusual for Colorado," *Christian Science Monitor*, April 27, 2015.

50 Michael L. Perlin, "The Insanity Defense: Nine Myths That Will Not Go Away," in *The Insanity Defense: Multidisciplinary Views on Its History, Trends, and Controversies*, ed. Mark D. White (Santa Barbara, Calif.: Praeger, 2017).

51 Ira Mickenberg, "A Pleasant Surprise: The Guilty but Mentally Ill Verdict Has Both Succeeded in Its Own Right and Successfully Preserved the Traditional Role of the Insanity Defense," *University of Cincinnati Law Review* 55 (1987): 954–955 (citing *In re Winship*, 397 U.S. 358, 364 (1970)).

52 Joe Palazzolo, "John Hinckley Case Led to Vast Narrowing of Insanity Defense," *Wall Street Journal*, July 28, 2016.

53 John Q. La Fond and Mary L. Durham, "Cognitive Dissonance: Have Insanity Defense and Civil Commitment Reforms Made a Difference?" *Villanova Law Review* 39 (1994): 95.

54 Kathy McCabe, "N.H. Jurors Face Choice on Insanity Defense," Boston. com, February 28, 2011. Cornell

University Law School, Legal Information Institute, 18 U.S. Code § 17 Insanity Defense, www.law.cornell. edu/uscode/text/18/17. Accessed October 2020.

55 Warren Richey, "Supreme Court Rejects Idaho Case on Prohibiting the Insanity Defense," *Christian Science Monitor*, November 26, 2012.

56 Palazzolo, "John Hinckley Case Led to Vast Narrowing of Insanity Defense."

57 Shawn Boburg, "Would-be Reagan Assassin John Hinckley Jr. Is Freed after 35 Years," *Washington Post*, September 10, 2016.

58 Palazzolo, "John Hinckley Case Led to Vast Narrowing of Insanity Defense."

59 Klotter, *Criminal Law*, 514.

60 CNN, Trayvon Martin Shooting Fast Facts, February 28, 2019, www.cnn.com/2013/06/05/us/ trayvon-martin-shooting-fast-facts.

61 Klotter, *Criminal Law*, 540–542.

62 Federal Bureau of Investigation, ABSCAM, www.fbi.gov/history/ famous-cases/abscam. Accessed October 2020.

63 Jim Newton, "Koon, Powell Get 2½ Years in Prison," *Los Angeles Times*, August 5, 1993.

64 Carol Pogash, "Myth of the 'Twinkie Defense,'" *San Francisco Chronicle*, November 23, 2003. *People* v. *White*, 117 Cal. App. 3d 270, 172 Cal. Rptr. (1981).

65 Ibid.

OXFORD insight study guide
Active Engagement, Deeper Understanding

Learn more with this chapter's digital tools, including the Oxford Insight Study Guide, at www.oup.com/he/Fuller2e.

Chapter 4

The History and Organization of Law Enforcement

FEATURES

Moe Smith (at left in top picture, at right in the bottom one) and Izzy Einstein in their street clothes (top) and in a pair of the disguises they used to infiltrate speakeasies during the 1920s. Would police today use disguises like this to make an arrest?

When the Eighteenth Amendment, which pro-

hibited the manufacture, sale, and transportation of alcohol in the United States, was ratified in January 1919, Isidor "Izzy" Einstein was a postal clerk struggling to raise a family on New York's Lower East Side. Needing a better paying job, he answered an ad for prohibition agents. When he went to apply, the chief agent looked at Izzy, who stood 5' 5" tall and weighed 225 pounds, and said he "wasn't the type." Izzy argued that his regular appearance would "fool people better."[1]

Izzy's strategy worked, and he and his partner Moe Smith became the Bureau of Prohibition's most prolific enforcers. Often, all Izzy had to do was knock on a speakeasy door and ask for a drink. More than once he showed his badge and asked, "Would you like to sell a pint of whiskey to a deserving prohibition agent?" Sometimes he would show up carrying a small barrel of pickles. Izzy explained, "Who'd ever think a fat man with pickles was an agent?"[2]

Izzy and Moe loved to use disguises, once dressing as a husband and wife. They carried legal books into lawyers' speakeasies and wore white coats into a doctors' club near Mount Sinai Hospital.[3] During a bust at a Brooklyn saloon, Izzy stood under a large photograph of himself on the wall that was surrounded by stories of exploits. No one recognized him until he produced a search warrant.[4]

Izzy was so successful that the bureau sent him to make busts in other cities. In Chicago and St. Louis, he found liquor in 21 minutes, in Atlanta, 17 minutes, and in Pittsburgh, 11 minutes. In New Orleans, he made an arrest in 35 seconds after getting into a taxi and asking the driver where the nearest bar was. The driver handed Izzy a bottle.[5]

Honesty was crucial to Izzy's success. He never accepted bribes, never carried a weapon, and many of his arrestees appreciated his cheerful manner.[6] Most, if not all, establishments that sold alcohol were protected by corrupt agents and police officers. That was why so many operated with impunity and why proprietors and bartenders did not believe that an agent like Izzy even existed, much less was going to arrest them.[7] In five years, Izzy and Moe arrested nearly 5,000 people and boasted a 95 percent conviction rate.[8]

THINK ABOUT IT > In what ways did the activities of Izzy Einstein reflect the practices of problem-oriented policing?

4.1 A Brief History of the Police

As long as human beings have lived in large groups, we have needed social control. Much of this control was exerted through informal means, such as censure from families, friends, and other social institutions. However, as social groups became larger and less personally interconnected, formal means became required to deal with situations that did not respond to informal means, such as legal disputes and the control of violent people.

Even though we all realize the necessity of being policed, many of us still harbor some resentment at being controlled. If we have little or no respect for the person controlling our behavior, maybe due to her or his history of being unfair, this resentment may escalate into hostility and resistance. Ultimately, what

LEARNING OBJECTIVE 4.1

Discuss the three enduring features of U.S. policing influenced by English policing.

LEARNING OBJECTIVE 4.2

Describe how the events of September 11, 2001, affected law enforcement.

determines the legitimacy of our own or others' policing behavior is the degree to which it is perceived as fair or just.

The institution of policing is a relatively new phenomenon. Creating agencies devoted solely to maintaining order and apprehending lawbreakers entails a degree of occupational specialization that is available only in highly developed societies. However, like physicians, teachers, and farmers, police officers are needed for communities to function effectively. Although we commonly think of policing as a stable institution built on unchanging tradition, the police are, in fact, subject to rapid social change and constant challenges.[9] Modern policing is the result of a long, uneven development that continues today.

Early Policing in England

The law enforcement function has existed in one form or another for thousands of years. Police in early history usually derived from a military connected with a government or ruler or from the community when citizens created informal groups to protect themselves. In the seventh century BCE, the Roman emperor Augustus created one of the earliest recorded organized police forces. In 17th-century Japan, each town had a military official, the samurai warrior, whose duties included acting as judge and chief of police. In Russia from 1881 to the 1917 revolution, the tsars' Okhrana was a police force that dealt with political terrorism and revolutionary matters.

The form of policing that most directly led to that of modern U.S. policing was the **frankpledge system** in England, which began in Anglo-Saxon England and continued until the 19th century. This system divided a community into tithings, or groups of 10 men who were responsible for the group's conduct and ensured that a member charged with breaking the law would show up in court.

An important office in English policing was that of the shire reeve or sheriff. The sheriff led the shire's (or county's) military forces and judged criminal and civil cases. Later, the sheriff's duties became more restricted, and his job included trying minor criminal offenses, investigating offenses within the shire, and questioning suspects. (The office of sheriff in England continues to this day.)

In the 13th century, the Normans, invaders from France who eventually replaced the Anglo-Saxons as the ruling class of England, updated this system by adding the *comes stabuli*, or **constable**. Constables oversaw the **watch-and-ward system** that guarded the city's or town's gates at night. The actual job of enforcing the law was up to the citizens, who were expected to raise the alarm, or **hue and cry**, and catch people accused of breaking the law. Although the watch system lasted for hundreds of years, it had serious problems. Many citizens resented watchman duty and either refused to do it or did it poorly, and many were too elderly or infirm to do it.

Around 1748, magistrates Henry Fielding and his brother Sir John Fielding created the

Frankpledge system— An early form of English government that divided communities into groups of 10 men who were responsible for the group's conduct and ensured that a member charged with breaking the law appeared in court.

Constable— The head of law enforcement for large districts in early England. In the modern United States, a constable serves areas such as rural townships and is usually elected.

Watch-and-ward system— An early English system overseen by the constable in which a watchman guarded a city's or town's gates at night.

Hue and cry— In early England, the alarm that citizens were required to raise upon the witness or discovery of a criminal offense.

In the 17th century, Samurai warriors performed law enforcement duties in Japan. What other duties were the samurai responsible for?

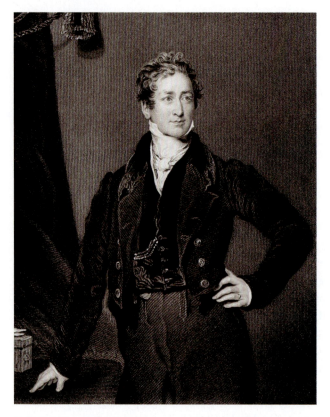

Sir Robert Peel created the first permanent police force in London in 1829. Why was this police force nicknamed the "Bobbies?"

Bow Street Runners—
A police organization created circa 1748 by magistrates and brothers Henry Fielding and Sir John Fielding whose members went on patrol, rather than remaining at a designated post.

Thames River Police—A private police force created by the West India Trading Company in 1798 that represented the first professional, salaried police force in London.

Metropolitan Police Act—Sponsored in 1829 by Sir Robert Peel, it was the first successful bill to create a permanent, public police force.

Bobbies—A slang term for the police force created in 1829 by Sir Robert Peel's Metropolitan Police Act that was derived from the short form of Robert, Bob.

Bow Street Runners in which members were required to patrol specific areas rather than just sit in their watch boxes.[10] In 1798, the West India Trading Company created the first professional, salaried police force in London, the **Thames River Police**. This private police force, formed to prevent thefts from the port, was different from the frankpledge system in that officers patrolled to prevent crime, and officers were salaried and not allowed to accept any other payments. The police force worked so well that two years later the government added it to the public payroll.

Citizens accustomed to a system in which they were basically responsible for themselves were suspicious of a standing police force. However, London's social problems were mounting as a result of poverty and a burgeoning population. In 1829, British statesman Sir Robert Peel convinced the British government to pass the **Metropolitan Police Act**, the first successful bill to create a permanent, public police force. These "new police" carried out preventive patrols, were paid regular salaries, and wore uniforms. The police, who were nicknamed **bobbies** after their founder's nickname, "Bob," adhered to a strict military-type discipline. Although their jurisdiction was limited to London, the bobbies set a new standard of police professionalism.

The English tradition of law enforcement influenced three enduring features of American policing[11]:

1. Limited police authority. As opposed to other European countries, the Anglo-American tradition of policing emphasizes individual rights and liberties.

2. Local control. Law enforcement agencies are, for the most part, local, city, or county institutions. The United States does not have a national police force. We do have many state and federal law enforcement agencies, but they are not like the national police forces found in many parts of the world where control is highly centralized within the government.

3. Fragmented system. The United States has more than 18,000 separate law enforcement agencies, ranging from federal (FBI, Secret Service) to state (highway patrol) to local (city police, county sheriff). These agencies are loosely coordinated, and the state and local agencies have little federal oversight.[12]

Early Policing in the United States

Many differences between the United States and England affected the development of their respective policing styles. One was the lack of a single, coherent philosophy. Whereas the English police were unified under the vision of Sir Robert Peel, local police in the United States formed their own policies and procedures. A second factor was the large and ever-expanding political geography of the United States. As stakes were claimed and territories formed, government and law enforcement followed slowly. This led to the phenomenon of the "Wild West" in the 19th century. The farther the country developed from the cities and seats of

FIGHT BETWEEN THE METROPOLITAN AND MUNICIPAL POLICE.

This 19th-century drawing depicts a fight between the New York Municipal Police, which had been recently dissolved, and its replacement, the Metropolitan Police, which eventually became the New York City Police Department. Why did it take so long for big U.S. cities to create stable police forces?

government on the East Coast, the less controllable it became. A third factor was immigration. The constituency of the United States was (and continues to be) in constant flux, resulting in cities, states, and territories filled with people representing a vast array of cultures and languages. Conversely, the early English police were responsible for a static political and physical geography that had a shared culture and language.

In the United States, informal policing began in Boston in 1631 with the establishment of a night watch. In New York City in the 1650s, when the Dutch settlement was called New Amsterdam, the "schout fiscal" or "sheriff attorney" had such duties as settling disputes and warning the colonists of fire. A group of men called the "Rattle Watch" patrolled at night, carrying loud rattles to raise an alarm if anything was amiss. Policing continued this way for the next two centuries. It was not until 1833 that Philadelphia organized the first dedicated police force, followed by Boston in 1838.[13] The first New York City police agency, the Municipal Police Force, was created in 1845. Their copper star badges were so distinctive that the officers were nicknamed "coppers," which was later shortened to "cops." The modern New York City Police Department formed in 1898 when the state legislature ordered local cities, towns, and villages to consolidate into a single city called New York City and the Police Department of the Greater City of New York absorbed the smaller police agencies.[14]

Another important police force developed in Chicago around 1855. The city's police officers were not trained in the law, and the criminal justice system did not emphasize legal procedure. Chicago police were different from other police organizations in four respects:

1. The police and courts were highly decentralized and often reflected the values of local communities. Community standards rather than legal norms were expected to guide police behavior and check abuses.

2. The police, as part of a larger political system, were a significant resource at the command of local organizations. Police, courts, and prosecutors

3. Criminal justice institutions often operated organized illegal activities, providing the means by which police officers and other officials earned extra income.

4. Police officers and other criminal justice system personnel developed informal systems of operation that reflected what they wanted to do. These informal methods of operation bore, at best, only an indirect relationship to the formal legal system.[15]

The political nature of the Chicago police in the early 20th century resulted in a system in which the police regularly took bribes, solicited votes, harassed the homeless, beat suspects, and assisted gamblers. They also performed many duties that now are normally considered outside the responsibilities of crime control, such as taking injured people to the hospital, mediating family quarrels, rounding up stray dogs, returning lost children to their parents, and removing dead horses from city streets.

The development of professional police departments in large metropolitan areas is important, but it is not the only contributing factor to development of the police in the United States. In rural areas and small towns, particularly in the South and West, the vigilante tradition was part of American life until the early to mid-20th century. Constraints on deviant behavior exercised by churches, schools, and cohesive community life were absent, and the formal system of law enforcement was inadequate. To protect property and social order from rogues and criminals, the elites established vigilante committees.[16] The vigilantes meted out a rough justice that included, but was not limited to, flogging, expulsion, and killing. These actions served not only as punishments, but also as warnings to others that a system of social order existed that everyone was expected to obey.[17]

The Introduction of Police Professionalism

One of the hallmarks of the professionalization of law enforcement over the past century is the degree to which the police mission has become less informal and more legally constrained. At the start of the 20th century, law enforcement in the United States was caught in a web of inefficiency and corruption.[18] The police were a tool of political interests because politicians often recruited the officers. In return, the officers would encourage citizens to vote for some candidates, discourage them from voting for others, and help to rig elections. Police officers and administrators received much of their pay from bribery and payoffs, ignoring some crime in return for payments. Gambling establishments would send officers to collect debts, and the system became so entrenched that payoffs became standardized according to police rank. For example, in New York City in 1900, a patrol officer could earn from $50 to $300 for protecting brothels and gambling establishments. Politicians would often sell particularly lucrative positions, such as police captain.[19]

Politicians and heads of industry realized that maintaining popular support for the existing political and economic system required some changes. One such effort was the 1883 **Pendleton Civil Service Reform Act**. A response to public frustration with incompetence and corruption within the federal government, the act was passed to "regulate and improve the civil service of the United States."[20] The act formed a civil service system that did away with patronage and administered employment and promotions based on merit rather than political

Pendleton Civil Service Reform Act— Law that established federal government positions would be awarded on the basis of merit rather than political affiliation.

Police arrest safe-crackers in a New York City bank in the 1870s. Why were police departments so slow in developing professional behavior?

connections. This legislation shook much of the corruption out of the U.S. civil service bureaucracy, including the country's budding police forces.

The work of August Vollmer, a police chief of Berkeley, California, marks a highlight of the police reform movement. In 1908, Vollmer established formal training for his department's officers. He went on to author the federal **Wickersham Commission report** in 1931, which set the police reform agenda for the rest of the century, and he instituted many modern policies and practices. He was among the first police chiefs to recruit college graduates, and he organized the first police-science courses at the University of California. Many of his students went on to become police chiefs in other cities, where they extended his reform policies. Vollmer's police reform movement, which dominated the law enforcement agenda through the 1960s, focused on six issues:

1. Policing is defined as a profession in which the police serve the entire community on a nonpartisan basis.

2. Policing should be free of political influence.

3. Qualified executives should lead the police. This means that the chiefs of large cities should have some experience running large organizations.

4. The standards for being a police officer should be raised. Law enforcement personnel should be screened for intelligence, health, and moral character. (Although slow in developing, this increase in the quality of personnel resulted in specialized police academies where professional training is required.)

Wickersham Commission report— The 14-volume report published in 1931 and 1932, which was the first comprehensive national study of U.S. crime and law enforcement.

Federal Law Enforcement Agencies

BUREAU OF ALCOHOL, TOBACCO, FIREARMS, AND EXPLOSIVES (ATF)

The Bureau of Alcohol, Tobacco, Firearms, and Explosives is a principal law enforcement agency within the U.S. Department of Justice that enforces federal criminal laws, regulates the firearms and explosives industries, and investigates cases of arson and illegal trafficking of alcohol and tobacco products.

U.S. CUSTOMS AND BORDER PROTECTION

U.S. Customs and Border Protection (CBT) manages, controls, and protects the borders of the United States at and between official ports of entry. Located within the Department of Homeland Security, CBP combines the inspectional workforces and border authorities of U.S. Customs, U.S. Immigration, the Animal and Plant Health Inspection Service, and the U.S. Border Patrol.

DRUG ENFORCEMENT ADMINISTRATION

The Drug Enforcement Administration (DEA), which is organized within the Department of Justice, enforces the controlled-substance laws and regulations of the United States. The agency also manages a national drug intelligence program, seizes assets used in drug trafficking, and enforces laws pertaining to legally produced controlled substances.

FEDERAL BUREAU OF INVESTIGATION

The principal investigative arm of the Department of Justice, the Federal Bureau of Investigation (FBI) investigates major violent and financial crime and interstate crime and assists in terrorism investigations. Areas of investigation include computer-related crimes, cases of public corruption, hate crime, white-collar crime, and organized crime.

U.S. IMMIGRATION AND CUSTOMS ENFORCEMENT

Immigration and Customs Enforcement (ICE) is the largest investigative branch of the Department of Homeland Security. The agency was created in March 2003 by combining the law enforcement arms of the former Immigration and Naturalization Service and the former U.S. Customs Service.

U.S. MARSHALS SERVICE (FEDERAL MARSHALS)

Created in 1789, the U.S. Marshals Service is a federal police agency that protects federal judges and courts and ensures the effective operation of the judicial system. The agency also carries out fugitive investigations, custody and transportation of federal prisoners, security for government witnesses, asset seizures, and serving of court documents. Each of the 94 federal judicial districts has one U.S. Marshal.

U.S. SECRET SERVICE

The U.S. Secret Service protects the president of the United States, as well as other U.S. government officials and visiting officials. The agency also investigates financial fraud and counterfeiting.

Department of Justice—The federal executive agency that handles all criminal prosecutions and civil suits in which the United States has an interest.

Department of the Treasury—The federal executive agency that is responsible for promoting economic prosperity and ensuring the financial security of the United States.

resources dealing with counterfeiting than protecting the president. For a list of the major federal law enforcement agencies, see CJ Reference 4.1.

Although there are about 70 federal law enforcement agencies, the main ones are organized under just three departments: the Department of Justice, the Department of the Treasury, and the Department of Homeland Security.[28]

> Founded in 1870, the **Department of Justice** is responsible for enforcing federal laws. Its primary agencies are the Drug Enforcement Administration (DEA), the Federal Bureau of Investigation (FBI), and the U.S. Marshals.

> The **Department of the Treasury**, established in 1789, primarily enforces the collection of revenue. Its agencies include the Internal Revenue Service (IRS), the U.S. Mint, and the Inspector General.[29]

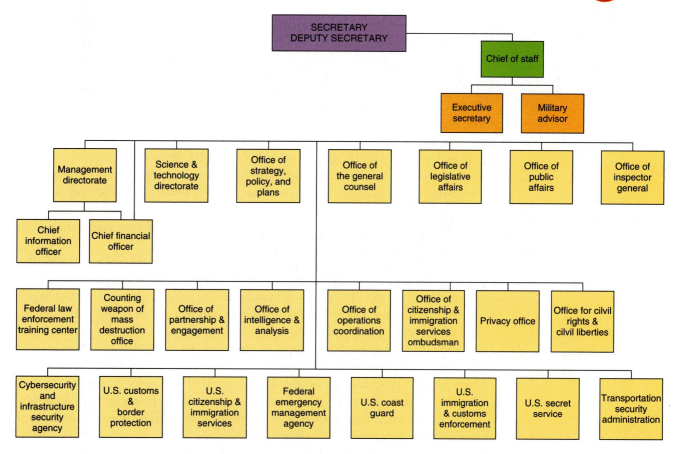

FIGURE 4.1 **Organization of the U.S. Department of Homeland Security** Which agencies within the U.S. Department of Homeland Security are most responsible for immigration enforcement? Which agencies were transferred to Homeland Security because their duties are related to controlling terrorism?

Source: U.S. Department of Homeland Security, Organizational Chart, www.dhs.gov/organizational-chart. Accessed October 2020.

> The **Department of Homeland Security** was created after September 11, 2001 (see Figure 4.1). Under its auspices are several agencies that were transferred in whole or in part to Homeland Security because their duties are related to controlling terrorism. These agencies include U.S. Customs and Border Protection, U.S. Immigration and Customs Enforcement, and the U.S. Secret Service.

Federal officers are among the best paid law enforcement personnel, and competition for these jobs is stiff. Most federal officers train at the Federal Law Enforcement Training Center, which is headquartered in Glynco, Georgia. FBI and DEA agents also take some of their training at their respective academies in Quantico, Virginia. One aspect of this level of law enforcement is the likelihood that employees will be transferred around the country as they advance along their career path. Although there are many federal police agencies, the FBI and Secret Service are the ones that most people associate with federal law enforcement, so we will examine these agencies.

Department of Homeland Security (DHS)—A department of the U.S. government responsible for preventing terrorism and enhancing national security; securing and managing U.S. borders; enforcing and administering U.S. immigration laws; safeguarding and securing U.S. interests on the Internet; and assisting in the federal response to terrorist attacks and natural disasters within the United States.

THE FEDERAL BUREAU OF INVESTIGATION

The FBI has national jurisdiction to investigate federal offenses. The emphasis on which offenses get the most attention has shifted over the years as a result of political considerations and the leadership style of its directors. The FBI began as the Bureau of Investigation in 1908 when President Theodore Roosevelt sent nine Secret Service agents to the Department of Justice to investigate violations of federal law.[30] In the past century, it has grown into a large organization that also assists state and local agencies with expert help in training (FBI National Academy), criminalistics (FBI Crime Laboratory), crime measurement (Uniform Crime Reports), and consultation on difficult cases (Behavior Analysis Unit). Since September 11, 2001, the agency has shifted some of its focus to national security.

THE SECRET SERVICE

After September 11, 2001, the Secret Service was moved from the Treasury Department to the Department of Homeland Security. Its duties—protecting the president and other dignitaries and investigating counterfeiting and financial crimes—remain essentially the same but have been expanded somewhat to provide for defense against terrorism. The Secret Service's original task when it was created in 1865 was to control the proliferation of counterfeit money. Only in 1894 under President Grover Cleveland did the agency begin some protection services.

A year after the assassination of President William McKinley in 1901, the Secret Service began full-time executive protection. In 1913, Congress authorized permanent protection of the president, and in 1917 the president's family began to receive protection. Security was gradually stepped up over the years, owing partly to the 1951 assassination attempt on President Harry S. Truman and the 1963 assassination of President John F. Kennedy. Gradually, the list of protectees came to include major presidential and vice presidential candidates, presidential widows, and visiting heads of state. Today, much of the agency's mission is protecting the country's payment and financial systems from financial and computer-based crimes. Most Secret Service agents spend most of their time on duties other than executive protection.

State Level

In many ways, state law enforcement agencies are overshadowed by local and federal agencies. State agencies have neither the numbers of officers that local agencies have nor the visibility of federal agencies. There are as many variations in how state law enforcement agencies are organized as there are states. Each state

Two Secret Service agents monitor the streets as the presidential motorcade passes. Besides guarding the president, what are some other tasks of the Secret Service?

law enforcement system must be understood on its own terms because no two are exactly alike. This reflects the fact that the United States is a collection of united sovereign governments, with the elected government of each state deciding how that state is administered.

State police forces were developed to keep the peace in rural areas outside cities and towns. State highway patrol units became necessary as automobile usage increased and the state and interstate highway systems were developed.[31] Generally, there are two broad models of state law enforcement: the centralized model and the decentralized model. The centralized model combines investigative and highway patrol functions into one agency. The decentralized model separates these two functions. For example, the state of Georgia has a state highway patrol and an investigative agency, the Georgia Bureau of Investigation.[32] About half of the states have state highway patrols, and half have state police, with the exception of Hawaii, which has no state law enforcement agency.[33] Three western states, Texas, Colorado, and Arizona, have police agencies called "rangers" that are more than a century old and are among the first professional state/territorial law enforcement organizations in the United States. However, the Pennsylvania State Police, created in 1905, is recognized as the first uniformed, professional state police department.

State investigative bureaus have statewide jurisdiction for investigating criminal offenses, such as political corruption, in which local police might not be in a position to investigate their local bosses. State law enforcement agencies also provide services to local law enforcement such as the coordination of multijurisdictional task forces, crime laboratory services, and, when requested, help in investigating offenses. Additionally, most state law enforcement agencies have police training academies that provide the basic instruction that is beyond the capabilities of all but the largest local police forces. Some states also have special agencies that deal with violations of alcoholic beverage or fish and wildlife laws.

Factors that may determine the simplicity or intricacy of a state police system include geography, population density, financial resources, and crime issues. Wealthy states with big cities may have state police agencies with special

This Maryland State Trooper guards the Maryland State Senate chamber on the first day of the legislative session. How do state law enforcement agencies differ from federal ones?

investigation units, community programs, and task forces. States with fewer resources might not have as many programs.

A state's industry or culture can also dictate its programs. For example, New Jersey's Department of Law and Public Safety has a gaming enforcement division to regulate the casino industry, and the Alaska Department of Public Safety has its Fish and Wildlife Protection division. Some states have placed all law enforcement divisions under one organizational umbrella, such as a department of public safety, whereas other states may separate these programs or lodge them within different bureaus of the state government. Given the variety of activities that the state can encompass, those interested in a law enforcement career should investigate opportunities within state agencies.

Local Level

Most of the country's crime is handled by local law enforcement agencies. Each state has a different configuration of political jurisdictions. Cities, counties (or parishes), and multijurisdictional agencies are vested with responsibility in varying ways, depending on the state law. What is most striking about how the criminal justice system is organized is the fact that most law enforcement authority lies at the local level. Many people misunderstand the relationship among the three levels of police, believing that local police answer to state police, who, in turn, answer to federal police. This is not true. Generally, police departments answer to themselves, their communities, and the courts.[34] For a look at the employment distribution among local police departments, sheriff's agencies, and state police agencies, see Figure 4.2.

Much of local police work is especially concerned with order maintenance and problem-solving, such as resolving disputes, finding missing persons and runaways, and dealing with small quality-of-life violations, such as telling the neighbors to turn the music down.[35] In many ways, local policing is where the action is. Each jurisdiction, whether big-city police department, county sheriff's office, or small-town police department, is the first responder to most criminal offenses. Additionally, these agencies have patrol and investigative duties in which they are often the only law enforcement agency involved in the case.

FIGURE 4.2   Number of Sworn and Civilian Employees in State and Local Law Enforcement Agencies Why do local police departments have so many more employees than either sheriffs' offices or state law enforcement agencies (such as state police or highway patrol agencies)?

Source: Shelley S. Hyland and Elizabeth Davis, Local Police Departments, 2016: Personnel, Table 2, (U.S. Department of Justice Office of Justice Programs Bureau of Justice Statistics, 2019), 2. Available at www.bjs.gov/index.cfm?ty=pbdetail&iid=6706.

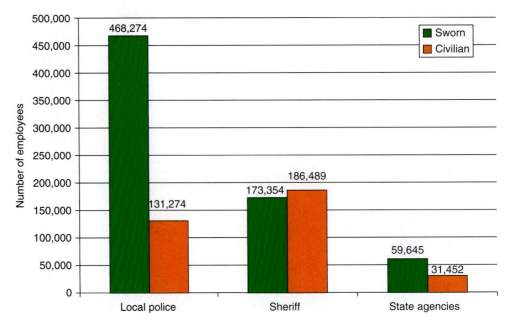

Because local police handle most serious street-level crime, they are the ones we call when we "call the cops."

Most local police forces are operated by municipalities, with a few run by tribal and county governments. The United States has about 12,000 local police departments. The largest local police force in the country is the New York City Police Department. With more than 36,000 full-time officers, it is nearly three times the size of the next largest organization, the Chicago Police Department, which has more than 13,000 sworn officers.[36] (See Figure 4.3 for the 10 largest police departments in the United States.) At the other end of the spectrum, about half of local police departments employ fewer than 10 full-time officers. Not all local police officers are sworn (sworn means that they are certified, have powers of arrest, and have taken an oath to serve and protect the public).[37] Non-sworn department employees work in technical support, administration, as records specialists, evidence specialists, or dispatchers, or in jail.

Local law enforcement agencies perform a range of duties. The most labor-intensive duty is routine patrol, in which officers travel around assigned beats, respond to calls for service, and look for ways to keep the community safe. Some of the time that officers spend on patrol is used to interact with citizens who are not suspected of breaking any law. Officers talk to shopkeepers, watch for traffic infractions, cruise neighborhoods to show citizens they are being served, and investigate anything that looks suspicious or out of place. The business of apprehending suspects constitutes a fraction of the officers' time. Local law enforcement agencies also devote resources and personnel to investigative duties, including homicide, burglary, auto theft, sex offenses, and juveniles. To a lesser degree, their duties may also include animal control, emergency medical service, and civil defense.

Larger departments operate special weapons and tactics (SWAT) and bomb-disposal teams. Along with traditional car patrols, there has been a steady increase

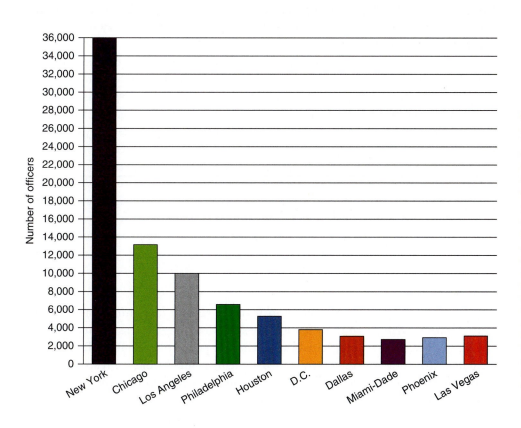

FIGURE 4.3   The 10 Largest Local Police Departments by Total Number of Full-Time Sworn Personnel Why is the New York Police Department so much larger than any other police department in the United States?

Source: Shelley S. Hyland and Elizabeth Davis, Local Police Departments 2016: Personnel, *Appendix Table 1, (Washington, D.C.: Bureau of Justice Statistics, 2019), 14. Available at www.bjs.gov/ index.cfm?ty=pbdetail&iid=6706. Federal Bureau of Investigation,* Crime in the United States, *2019, Table 78: Full-time Law Enforcement Employees by State by City, https://ucr.fbi.gov/ crime-in-the-u.s/2019/crime-in-the-u.s.-2019/topic-pages/ tables/table-78/table-78.xls/view. Accessed October 2020.*

Police officers spend a lot of time interacting with the community. Here, a young girl meets McGruff the Crime Dog, while Roanoke Police Academy recruits look on. How do such interactions help the public understand what their local police departments do?

in bicycle and foot patrols. Large departments may assign officers to special units, such as horseback, bicycle, motorcycle, or boat patrols. Some police officers specialize in specific areas, such as forensic analysis, or in physical or firearms training and instruction. Some departments may ameliorate officer shortages with supplemental and part-time personnel such as sworn reserve officers as well as non-sworn auxiliary officers, community service officers, police aides, and other volunteers. Each agency organizes its investigative duties and personnel according to its problems, resources, and needs, but each of them in some way must ensure that there is an investigative follow-up to reported crime.

Sometimes, law enforcement jurisdictions overlap. A person driving a car too fast within a city's limits may be pulled over and ticketed by a state patrol officer, a sheriff's deputy, or a city police officer. However, with rare exceptions, the state patrol or the county sheriff would unlikely be involved in investigating a homicide committed within a city's limits, which would probably be dealt with by the police agency responsible for that jurisdiction. An example of an exception would be the Atlanta child murders. From July 1979 to May 1981, 29 young black males were murdered in or near Atlanta, Georgia. Although the murders occurred mainly in the city of Atlanta and Fulton County, several agencies joined the investigation, including the local police, the sheriff's office, the Georgia Bureau of Investigation (GBI), and ultimately the FBI. (The federal agency, having no jurisdiction, became involved only by invitation from the local agencies.)

SHERIFF'S OFFICES

Sheriff's offices are the most common form of county law enforcement in the United States, with more than 3,000 offices.[38] Most sheriffs are elected officials and serve counties and municipalities without a police department. Their duties include performing routine patrols, investigating crime (some are responsible for crime lab services such as fingerprint and ballistics testing), executing arrest warrants, serving papers, and providing court security.

Most offices operate at least one jail, and about half provide search and rescue services, as well as SWAT teams. Other services may include bomb disposal, animal control, emergency medical services, and civil defense. A few counties have two sheriff's offices (one for criminal matters and one for civil matters), whereas others have no sheriff's office. In cases in which a city occupies the entire county, as in the case of Miami-Dade, Florida, or several counties, as in the case of New York City, city and county law enforcement may be combined into one department.

REQUIREMENTS TO BECOME A POLICE OFFICER

Once upon a time, the requirements to become a police officer were simple and rather narrow: big, strong, young, healthy, brave, and male. Although some of these requirements still apply, they have been tempered in recent decades by the fact that the most important personal aspect an officer brings to the job is intelligence.[39] Officers, especially those on patrol, must meet specific levels of physical fitness and maintain those fitness levels, as well as maintaining proficiency with firearms. Speaking languages other than English is an asset, and, regardless of the level of service, officers must know how to write reports. Police officers who patrol beats and deal directly with offenses in progress must wear uniforms, whereas investigative officers and detectives do not.

Each department, be it statewide, urban, or rural, has its own requirements for applicants, but these tend to follow similar lines for physical conditioning and ability, age, education, and personal legal history.

> Education. Applicants usually must have at least a high school diploma, and some departments require at least two years of college. Some departments require a college degree.

> Training. Recruits usually attend police academy for about 21 weeks.[40] State and large urban agencies may have their own academies; recruits at small departments may attend a state or regional academy. Recruits learn constitutional and state law as well as local ordinances. They also train in accident investigation, patrol, traffic control, firearms, self-defense, first aid, and emergency response.

> Age, citizenship, physical, and residential qualifications. Applicants must be U.S. citizens and usually must be at least 20 years old. Departments typically have basic requirements for vision, hearing, strength, and agility. For example, a department may require that uncorrected eyesight cannot be weaker than 20/100 in each eye and must be corrected to 20/20 with glasses, contact lenses, or surgery. Some urban departments require officers to live in or near the city limits. For example, the Tallahassee (Florida) Police Department states that at the time of hire, its applicants must live within a 35-mile radius of the city center.[41]

> Personal history. Departments may also extensively investigate their applicants' personal histories. Some agencies have candidates interviewed by a mental health professional, and candidates usually must take lie detector and/or drug tests.

> Disqualifications. An applicant may be automatically disqualified by any of the following: a felony conviction, misdemeanor convictions within the past few years, a specified number of moving violations within the past few years, a dishonorable discharge from the armed forces, convictions for certain offenses (such as domestic violence), or refusal to submit to polygraph, psychological, or drug testing.

Community policing evolved from the 1979 Flint Foot Patrol Program, an experiment in which foot-patrol officers in Flint, Michigan, were assigned to areas that were usually patrolled by car. This type of policing evokes the watchman style, in which the police officer is integrated into the community and has the advantage of being trusted by those being policed.[50] However, community policing is also different from the watchman style because both the police and communities have changed over the years. The watchman style of policing has its limitations, especially in affording equal justice to all citizens. In many cases, the watchman style simply reinforces the privileges of those in power while controlling youth and minorities.

Community policing also has elements in common with the legalistic style of policing in that it strives to treat all citizens equally according to their orientation with the law. However, the legalistic model emphasizes efficiency and exclusivity in the mandate for crime control. This exclusivity comes at a price in terms of distancing the police from their communities. Community policing is viewed as a reform that breaks the monopoly of the police over crime-control activities and brings the citizen back into the equation as an active participant. Community policing is different from both the watchman and legalistic styles in content and scope, and it is worthwhile to consider its history and potential.[51]

The term *community policing* covers many police activities and programs. An exact definition is difficult to provide, but it is fair to say that community policing involves enlisting citizens to help solve law-and-order problems in their own communities.[52] Good policing requires citizen cooperation. If people do not report offenses, do not provide information to the police, and are unwilling to testify in court, then the police cannot effectively control crime. During the civil unrest of the 1960s, the police were forced to do a difficult job in controlling large groups of people. This violence revealed a deep fissure between old and young, workers and hippies, minorities and whites, and also between the police and the communities they served. Many people believed that the police were out of touch with those they served. For this and other reasons, the community policing approach was proposed.[53]

Neighborhood Watch—A community policing program that encourages residents to cooperate in providing security for the neighborhood.

The goal of community policing is ambitious. It involves not only bridging the gap between the police and the citizens but also strengthening the bond among the citizens. A good example of a community-policing style program is **Neighborhood Watch** in which citizens work together to watch over each other's safety and property. Instituted in 1972 by the National Sheriffs' Association, Neighborhood Watch (and, later, other such programs) "put more eyes on the street" to help prevent and report crime and cultivate strong community ties that can help address other neighborhood problems.[54] Another strategy of community policing is the use of foot or bicycle patrol, the goal of which is to foster a close relationship between the police and the public.[55] The patrol car is considered a barrier to communication between police and citizens. Taking the officers out of the cars and placing them in more direct contact with people makes the development of meaningful relationships more likely.

One problem with community policing is that not all communities are alike. Great variation persists among neighborhoods in terms of the socioeconomic, racial, ethnic, and age compositions of the citizens. For example, a middle-class suburb inhabited by white-collar, middle-aged adults and their families and the elderly faces few crime problems compared to a low-income neighborhood populated with transients and drug dealers. It is much easier to institute a Neighborhood Watch program in affluent suburbs where the residents' comings and goings are less frequent and easier to monitor than in low-income neighborhoods where

This Neighborhood Watch sign indicates a crime watch in cooperation with the area police department. What types of community policing efforts have you seen in your neighborhood?

the pattern of social organization and movement is less obvious. Therefore, community policing can be said to work best in the communities that need it least. Nevertheless, studies have suggested that well-planned community policing efforts can achieve at least some of their goals.[56]

Finally, getting the police to concern themselves with order maintenance and community-building can be problematic when many officers view themselves solely as crime-fighters. The inherent tension between the roles of "criminal catcher" and "social worker" may limit the potential for effective community policing.

Problem-Oriented Policing

A strategy related to community policing is **problem-oriented policing**. In many ways, problem-oriented policing can be thought of as simply an aspect of community policing, but it is important enough to be treated as its own topic. We give special attention to problem-oriented policing because it is designed to make more fundamental changes than community policing. Additionally, problem-oriented policing greatly expands the police officer's role from one of reaction to one of proactive problem-solving. It allows police agencies to address crime on a more systemic level than traditional policing.[57]

For example, envision a downtown business district that is experiencing robberies and muggings. In addition to responding to these offenses, a problem-oriented police agency would analyze the causative factors. Included in this analysis might be a crime-mapping effort, which would reveal that the muggings are all in close proximity to a cluster of bars. On surveillance of these bars, the agency discovers that the bars are staying open well past the legal closing time and serving underage patrons. Going into these bars and enforcing the existing liquor laws could affect the robbery and mugging problem. Problem-oriented policing, then, is concerned with identifying and addressing the underlying issues that contribute to crime.[58] Within the scope of the law enforcement mission are many such opportunities that allow the police to do more than simply respond to crime.

Problem-oriented policing—A style of policing that attempts to address the underlying social problems that contribute to crime by integrating research and scientific problem-solving strategies to analyze instances of crime with the goal of developing more effective response strategies.

transgressions are treated more severely than are the transgressions of others. Zero-tolerance policies aimed at reducing crime often result in the unequal treatment of those without power. Given the problems of increased legal judgments against police departments for the behavior of their officers, zero-tolerance policing might be more problematic than beneficial.[71]

For example, in the 2000s, the New York City Police Department and its zero-tolerance efforts were subjected to widespread criticism and intense public protests after some controversial actions. In 2011, the NYPD arrested 50,000 people for possessing small amounts of marijuana, as compared to 1,500 in 1980. New York's state legislature decriminalized possession of 25 grams or less of marijuana in 1977 but deemed its public display a misdemeanor. The NYPD was accused of arresting people for possession after forcing them to "publicly display" the small amounts they carried.[72] For a look at a federal solution to police departments that appear to be abusing their public trust, see A Closer Look 4.1.

A CLOSER LOOK 4.1
Who Polices the Police?

Although it sometimes seems that police departments cannot be held responsible for abusive and violent practices, the federal government does have a remedy for those that continually abuse their communities. The 1994 Violent Crime Control and Law Enforcement Act allows the federal government to sue police departments if they show a "pattern and practice" of using excessive force and/or violating civil rights.[73] The law was passed after the 1991 beating of motorist Rodney King by four Los Angeles Police Department officers and the riots that occurred a year later in response to the officers' acquittal.[74]

To implement change, the government and the police department enter into a "consent decree," a plan that typically includes federal oversight of the department, as well as several reforms.[75] For example, in 2015, after protests over the acquittal of Cleveland, Ohio, police officer Michael Brelo of manslaughter, the city agreed to address what the government called the department's "systemic" use of excessive force.[76] (Brelo had been involved in a 2012 car chase in which he and other officers shot at two unarmed people over one hundred times, which resulted in their deaths.)[77] Included in the Cleveland reforms are:

- prohibition of pistol whipping, "neck holds," warning shots, and firing shots at moving cars;
- prohibition of uses of "retaliatory force" against suspects for fleeing or disrespecting officers;
- prohibition of racial profiling during stops-and-searches;
- training officers in community-policing principles; and
- training officers to deal with individuals with mental health issues.[78]

Police departments that are currently, or have been, under a consent decree include Chicago, Pittsburgh, Los Angeles, Cincinnati, New Orleans, New York City, Detroit, Seattle, Albuquerque, Oakland, California, and Newark, New Jersey.[79]

Police departments do not always enter the arrangement willingly. After nine years of non-compliance by angry veteran officers, a federal judge ordered that the Oakland police department be managed by a receiver, a person who controls a police department until it complies with reforms.[80] For example, in Cincinnati in 2001, the strain between the receiver and the police became so extreme that officers kicked the receiver out of police headquarters. Cincinnati did not come into compliance until 2007.[81] The New York City Police Department was placed under consent decree because its stop-question-and-frisk policy—in which police detain and question, and sometimes search, pedestrians—was deemed unconstitutional owing to the disproportionate number of racially disparate stops-and-frisks. Former New York City Mayor Michael Bloomberg asserted that this practice was necessary and constitutional, but a federal judge disagreed.[82]

Despite the protests, observers say consent decrees work. In 2014, Detroit's 11-year oversight ended after the police department complied with reforms.[83]

THINK ABOUT IT

1. What are some reasonable steps that cities can take to be released from a consent decree?

2. Have there been recent incidents of excessive force by police departments that would qualify a city for intervention by the federal government?

Perhaps the most fundamental problem with zero-tolerance policing is the adversarial relationship it seems to set up between the police and the public. By treating citizens with a heavy hand, the police alienate the very people who could help them solve more serious offenses. When people become angry and defiant, they are more likely to break major laws and less likely to be of assistance to the police.[84]

PAUSE AND REVIEW

1. What are Wilson's three styles of policing?
2. How is community policing different from problem-oriented policing?
3. What are some of the issues associated with zero-tolerance policing?

FOCUS ON ETHICS — Righteous Vengeance?

You are a police officer who is on the trail of a serial child molester who frequents the city's parks. You have a good idea of who it is, but this suspect has been smart enough to elude arrest for over 10 years. This morning you found your suspect dead, lying in a pool of blood with his skull crushed. After a search, you discover in a nearby trash can a baseball bat with the name of the teenaged son of a prominent politician printed on the bat handle. Blood and hair are matted on the bat. You know that this young man was a victim of molestation 10 years ago when this problem first surfaced in the community.

You strongly suspect that the teen killed the molester, but you also believe that the suspect deserved to be killed and that the teen did the community a service. If you hide the bat, there will be no way to trace the offense to this young man whom you think had a good reason to commit this act. If you enter the bat into evidence, the teen could be convicted of murder and sent to prison for a long time. Because you have twin 8-year-old sons, you are happy this perpetrator will no longer prowl the city parks. Can you turn a blind eye to this crime? You know the correct procedure would be

to arrest the teen, but a little voice inside your head is whispering something about a "greater justice," and you are tempted to dispose of the bat.

WHAT DO YOU DO?

1. Dispose of the bat and tell the boy's father so that he can protect you if you are found out and even help you get promoted.
2. Dispose of the bat, and tell no one.
3. Leave the bat where it is. Do your job and make your report, but say nothing about your suspicions. The crime scene techs will know what to do.
4. Tell your chief everything, and let her decide what to do.

For more insight into how someone might respond to such an ethical dilemma, visit Oxford Learning Link at www.oup.com/he/Fuller2e to watch a video that connects this scenario to a real-world situation.

Summary

LEARNING OBJECTIVE **4.1** Discuss the three enduring features of U.S. policing influenced by English policing.	**Limited police authority:** The Anglo-American tradition of policing emphasizes individual rights and liberties. **Local control:** Law enforcement agencies are, for the most part, local, city, or county institutions. **Fragmented system:** The country's law enforcement agencies are loosely coordinated, and the state and local agencies have little federal oversight.

LEARNING OBJECTIVE 4.2 Describe how the events of September 11, 2001, affected law enforcement.	**Role expansion:** In addition to normal duties, police must be on the lookout for suspected terrorists, design contingency plans for catastrophic terrorist events, and be prepared to deal with weapons of mass destruction. **Racial and ethnic profiling:** Law enforcement agencies must ensure that while protecting citizens against terrorism, they do not engage in activities that violate individuals' legal and civil rights. **Immigration enforcement:** Many local law enforcement agencies must periodically investigate the immigration status of suspects and offenders.
LEARNING OBJECTIVE 4.3 Compare and contrast the roles of the federal, state, and local levels of law enforcement and their respective agencies.	The duty of all law enforcement officers is to keep the peace, maintain order, ensure adherence to the law, and investigate when those laws appear to have been broken. Federal law enforcement agencies are special-purpose agencies that have national jurisdiction but concentrate on a specific, limited set of offenses. The Federal Bureau of Investigation is the country's foremost law enforcement agency and deals with most criminal offenses that occur on a national basis. State law enforcement agencies typically consist of state police, state highway patrols, and, sometimes, a state investigative agency. State agencies do not have the numbers of officers that local agencies have or the visibility of federal agencies. No two state law enforcement systems are exactly alike. City and urban police departments, and county police forces (sheriff's offices), make up local law enforcement. These agencies have patrol and investigative duties in which they are often the only law enforcement agency involved in the case because the specific jurisdiction is the first responder to most criminal offenses. Most of the country's crime is handled by local law enforcement. Much local police work is especially concerned with order maintenance and problem solving.
LEARNING OBJECTIVE 4.4 Categorize the advantages and disadvantages of Wilson's three styles of policing.	The watchman style of policing distinguishes between two mandates of policing: order maintenance and law enforcement. The law enforcement mandate is clear-cut: a person either did or did not break the law. Order maintenance may involve issuing warnings or other arrangements rather than outright arrest and extralegal factors such as age, race, appearance, or personal demeanor. The legalistic style concentrates on enforcing the law by writing more tickets, making more arrests, and encouraging victims to sign complaints. Its focus is on treating all citizens alike, but it is impersonal and disinterested. The service style of policing is concerned primarily with service to the community and citizens. Like the legalistic style, it treats all law violations seriously, but the frequent result is not to arrest.
LEARNING OBJECTIVE 4.5 Define problem-oriented policing.	Problem-oriented policing expands the police officer's role from one of reaction to one of proactive problem solving. It allows police agencies to address crime on a more systemic level than traditional policing. Instead of responding to calls for service, problem-oriented officers analyze trouble areas of the community and design tactics to address those problems. Problem-oriented policing also has a crime-prevention mission in that it intervenes when patterns begin to emerge.
LEARNING OBJECTIVE 4.6 Describe zero-tolerance policing and its relationship to the broken-windows perspective.	Zero-tolerance policing is the idea that if every infraction of the law is met with an arrest, fine, or other punishment, offenders will refrain from more grievous activities. An important element of zero-tolerance policing is the broken-windows perspective, which holds that crime follows community neglect. A criticism of zero-tolerance policies is that they often result in the unequal treatment of those without power.

Critical Reflections

1. Would law enforcement activities be more effective if there were simply one national police force? Why or why not? To what extent would an all-inclusive federal police agency be responsive to local customs, sentiments, and cultures?

2. Given the perceived increase of police–citizen conflict that we have seen in recent years, what are the most pressing issues that prevent the police from being effective in enforcing the law and in maintaining citizens' trust? How would you design a research agenda to develop methods for making the police more effective? What programs would you suggest to rebuild trust between the police and the community?

Key Terms

Bobbies **p. 100**
Bow Street Runners **p. 100**
Broken-windows perspective **p. 120**
Community policing **p. 117**
Constable **p. 99**
Department of Homeland Security (DHS) **p. 109**
Department of Justice **p. 108**
Department of the Treasury **p. 108**

Federal Bureau of Investigation (FBI) **p. 107**
Frankpledge system **p. 99**
Hue and cry **p. 99**
Legalistic style **p. 117**
Metropolitan Police Act **p. 100**
Neighborhood Watch **p. 118**
Pendleton Civil Service Reform Act **p. 102**
Problem-oriented policing **p. 119**

Service style **p. 117**
Thames River Police **p. 100**
Watch-and-ward system **p. 99**
Watchman style **p. 117**
White-collar crime **p. 107**
Wickersham Commission report **p. 103**
Zero-tolerance policing **p. 120**

Notes

1 Isidor Einstein, *Prohibition Agent #1* (New York: Frederick A. Stokes Co., 1932).

2 George Pendle, "The Improbable Prohibition Agents Who Outsmarted Speakeasy Owners," History.com, January 16, 2018, www.history.com/news/the-improbable-prohibition-agents-who-outsmarted-speakeasy-owners.

3 Ibid.

4 Karen Abbott, "Prohibition's Premier Hooch Hounds," Smithsonian.com, January 10, 2012.

5 Bureau of Alcohol, Tobacco, Firearms and Explosives, Isador "Izzy" Einstein, www.atf.gov/our-history/isador-izzy-einstein. Accessed October 2020.

6 Greg Veitch, "Izzy and Moe: How the First Prohibition Agent and His Partner Tried to Dry Up Saratoga," *Saratoga Living*, saratogaliving.com/izzy-and-moe-how-the-first-prohibition-agent-and-his-partner-tried-to-dry-up-saratoga. Accessed October 2020.

7 Pendle, "The Improbable Prohibition Agents Who Outsmarted Speakeasy Owners."

8 Abbott, "Prohibition's Premier Hooch Hounds." Pendle, "The Improbable Prohibition Agents Who Outsmarted Speakeasy Owners."

9 Jonathan Rubinstein, *City Police* (New York: Farrar, Straus, & Giroux, 1973).

10 Rubinstein, *City Police*, 6.

11 Samuel Walker and Charles M. Katz, *The Police in America: An Introduction*, 4th ed. (Boston: McGraw-Hill, 2002), 25.

12 Ibid., 25. Walker and Katz provide a good discussion of why history is relevant to understanding the development of the police. They trace the political and social forces that were behind the major reforms of law enforcement.

13 David R. Johnson, *American Law Enforcement: A History* (St. Louis, Mo.: Forum Press, 1981).

14 Raymond W. Kelly, *The History of New York City Police Department*, (New York City: Police Department City of New York), 1993. Online at www.ncjrs.gov/App/Publications/abstract.aspx?ID=145539.

15 Mark H. Haller, "Chicago Cops, 1890–1925," in *Thinking about Police: Contemporary Readings*, ed. Carl B. Klockars (New York: McGraw-Hill, 1983), 87–99.

16 Richard Maxwell Brown, "Vigilante Policing," in *Thinking about Police: Contemporary Readings*, ed. Carl B. Klockars (New York: McGraw-Hill, 1983), 58.

17 Ibid., 57–71.

18 Samuel Walker, *A Critical History of Police Reform* (Lexington, Mass.: Lexington Books, 1977).

19 Dean J. Champion, *Police Misconduct in America: A Reference Handbook* (Santa Barbara, Calif.: ABC-CLIO, 2001), 11–12.

20 Pendleton Act (1883), www.ourdocuments.gov/doc.php?flash=false&&doc=48. Accessed October 2020.

21 Walker and Katz, *Police in America*, 34.

22 Center for Research on Criminal Justice, *The Iron Fist and the Velvet Glove: An Analysis of the U.S. Police* (Berkeley, Calif.: Center for Research on Criminal Justice, 1977), 37.

23 Ibid., 39.

24 Thomas Barker, Ronald D. Hunter, and Jeffery P. Rush, *Police Systems and Practices: An Introduction* (Englewood Cliffs, N.J.: Prentice Hall, 1994), 77.

25 Walker and Katz, *Police in America*, 527–528.

26 Richard Trenholm, "Tim Cook Hits Back at 'Chilling' Order for iPhone 'Backdoor'," CNET, February 17, 2016.

27 Brian A. Reaves, *Census of State and Local Law Enforcement Agencies, 2008* (Washington, D.C.: U.S. Department of Justice Office of Justice Programs Bureau of Justice Statistics, 2011), 2. Available at www.bjs.gov/index.cfm?ty=pbdetail&iid=2216.

28 Connor Brooks, *Federal Law Enforcement Officers, 2016* (Washington, D.C.: U.S. Department of Justice Office of Justice Programs Bureau of Justice Statistics, 2019), 3-4. Available at www.bjs.gov/index.cfm?ty=pbdetail&iid=6708.

29 U.S. Department of the Treasury, home.treasury.gov/about/bureaus. Accessed October 2020.

30 Federal Bureau of Investigation, The Nation Calls, 1908 – 1923, www.fbi.gov/history/brief-history/the-nation-calls. Accessed October 2020.

31 John S. Dempsey and Linda S. Forst, *An Introduction to Policing*, 4th ed. (Belmont, Calif.: Thomson/Wadsworth, 2008), 49.

32 Ibid.

33 Walker and Katz, *Police in America*, 71.

34 Randy L. LaGrange, *Policing American Society* (Chicago: Nelson-Hall, 1993), 54.

35 Samuel Walker and Charles M. Katz, *The Police in America: An Introduction*, 5th ed. (New York: McGraw-Hill, 2005), 231.

36 Federal Bureau of Investigation, Crime in the United States, 2019, Table 78: Full-time Law Enforcement Employees by State by City, https://ucr.fbi.gov/crime-in-the-u.s/2019/crime-in-the-u.s.-2019/topic-pages/tables/table-78/table-78.xls/view. Accessed October 2020.

37 Sworn officers are "police employees who have taken an oath and been given powers by the state to make arrests, use force, and transverse property, in accordance with their duties." Dean J. Champion, *The American Dictionary of Criminal Justice* (Los Angeles: Roxbury, 2001), 132.

38 Connor Brooks, *Sheriffs' Offices, 2016: Personnel* (Washington, D.C.: U.S. Department of Justice Office of Justice Programs Bureau of Justice Statistics, 2019), 2. Available at www.bjs.gov/index.cfm?ty=tp&tid=72.

39 Dempsey and Forst, *An Introduction to Policing*, 49.

40 Brian A. Reaves, *State and Local Law Enforcement Training Academies, 2013* (Washington, D.C.: U.S. Department of Justice Office of Justice Programs Bureau of Justice Statistics, 2016), 4. Available at www.bjs.gov/index.cfm?ty=pbdetail&iid=5684.

41 Tallahassee Police Department, How to Apply to be a Police Officer, www.talgov.com/publicsafety/tpd-employment-po.aspx. Accessed October 2020.

42 Phillip B. Taft Jr., "Policing the New Immigrant Ghettos," in *Thinking about Police: Contemporary Readings*, 2d ed., eds. Carl B. Klockars and Stephen D. Mastrofski (New York: McGraw-Hill, 1991), 307–315.

43 William V. Pelfrey Jr., "Style of Policing Adopted by Rural Police and Deputies: An Analysis of Job Satisfaction and Community Policing," *Policing* 30 (October 1, 2007): 620–636.

44 James Q. Wilson, *Varieties of Police Behavior: The Management of Law and Order in Eight Communities* (New York: Atheneum, 1968).

45 Ibid., 17–34.

46 Ibid., 140–171.

47 Ibid., 172–199.

48 Ibid., 200–226.

49 U.S. Department of Justice, Community Policing Defined. Available at www.hsdl.org/?abstract&did=766797. Accessed October 2020.

50 Robert C. Trojanowicz, Marilyn Steele, and Susan Trojanowicz, *Community Policing: A Taxpayer's Perspective* (East Lansing, Mich.: National Center for Community Policing School of Criminal Justice Michigan State University, 1986).

51 David Alan Sklansky, "Police and Community in Chicago: A Tale of Three Cities," *Law and Society Review* 42 (March 1, 2008): 233–235.

52 Robert Trojanowicz, Victor E. Kappeler, Larry K. Gaines, and Bonnie Bucqueroux, *Community Policing: A Contemporary Perspective*, 2nd ed. (Cincinnati, Ohio: Anderson, 1998).

53 Samuel Walker and Charles M. Katz, *The Police in America: An Introduction*, 4th ed. (Boston: McGraw-Hill, 2002), 202–203. Walker and Katz also stated three other reasons for this change: the police car patrol, the existing use of detectives, and the emphasis on response time. All were found wanting. Additionally, policing was recognized as a complex job that involved more than crime fighting, and citizens were co-producers of police services. Our discussion of these alternative forms of policing is heavily influenced by Chapter 7 of their book.

54 National Neighborhood Watch—a Division of the National Sheriffs' Association,www.nnw.org/about-national-neigborhood-watch. Accessed October 2020. April Pattavina, James M. Byrne, and Luis Garcia, "An Examination of Citizen Involvement in Crime Prevention in High-Risk versus Low- to Moderate-Risk Neighbor-hoods," *Crime and Delinquency* 52 (April 1, 2006): 203–231.

55 Chris Menton, "Bicycle Patrols: An Underutilized Resource," *Policing* 31 (January 1, 2008): 93–108.

56 Wesley Skogan and Susan M. Hartnett, *Community Policing: Chicago Style* (New York: Oxford University Press, 1997).

57 Herman Goldstein, *Problem-Oriented Policing* (New York: McGraw-Hill, 1990).

58 Anthony A. Braga, Glenn L. Pierce, Jack McDevitt, Brenda J. Bond, and Shea Cronin, "The Strategic Prevention of Gun Violence among Gang-Involved Offenders," *Justice Quarterly* 25 (March 1, 2008): 132.

59 Michael D. White, James J. Fyfe, Suzanne P. Campbell, and John S. Goldkamp, "The Police Role in Preventing Homicide: Considering the Impact of Problem-Oriented Policing on the Prevalence of Murder," *Journal of Research in Crime and Delinquency* 40 (May 1, 2003): 194–225.

60 David Weisburd and John E. Eck, "What Can Police Do to Reduce Crime, Disorder, and Fear?" *Annals of the American Academy of Political and Social Science* 593 (May 1, 2004): 42–65.

61 James Q. Wilson and George L. Kelling, "Broken Windows: Police and Neighborhood Safety," *Atlantic Monthly*, March 1982, 29–38.

62 Ibid., 29–38.

63 Benjamin Chesluk, "'Visible Signs of a City out of Control: Community Policing in New York City," *Cultural Anthropology* 19 (May 1, 2004): 250–275.

64 Ibid.

65 Samuel Walker, "Broken Windows and Fractured History: The Use and Misuse of History in Recent Patrol Analysis," in *Critical Issues in Policing: Contemporary Readings*, ed. Roger G. Dunham and Geoffrey P. Alpert (Prospect Heights, Ill.: Waveland Press, 2001), 480–492.

66 D. W. Mills, "Poking Holes in the Theory of 'Broken Windows,'" *Chronicle of Higher Education* (February 9, 2001): A14.

67 Ronald V. Clarke, "Situational Crime Prevention: Its Theoretical Basis and Practical Scope," in *Crime Displacement: The Other Side of Prevention*, ed. Robert P. McNamara (East Rockaway, N.Y.: Cummings & Hathaway, 1994), 38–70.

68 NPR, "Drug Crime Displacement," *All Things Considered*, September 16, 1998.

69 Walker, "Broken Windows and Fractured History," 480–492.

70 Ralph B. Taylor, "Illusion of Order: The False Promise of Broken Windows Policing," *American Journal of Sociology* 111 (March 1, 2006): 1625–1628.

71 Amnesty International, *United States of America: Police Brutality and Excessive Use of Force in the New York City Police Department* (New York: Author, 1996).

72 Brent Staples, "The Human Cost of 'Zero Tolerance'," *New York Times*, April 28, 2012.

73 Joe Domanick, "Police Reform's Best Tool: A Federal Consent Decree," *Crime Report*, July 15, 2014, www.thecrimereport.org/news/articles/2014-07-police-reforms-best-tool-a-federal-consent-decree.

74 Ibid.

75 Ibid.

76 Ben Mathis-Lilley, "Cleveland Police Agree to Extensive Reforms in Deal with Justice Department," *Slate*, May 26, 2015.

77 Brandon Blackwell, "Cleveland Police Officer Michael Brelo Fired over Deadly 2012 Chase, Shooting," Cleveland.com, January 11, 2019. Holly Yan, "Brelo Verdict: Cleveland Officer Acquitted after Shooting Unarmed Couple—Now What?", CNN, May 26, 2015.

78 Mathis-Lilley, "Cleveland Police Agree to Extensive Reforms in Deal with Justice Department."

79 Cheryl Corley, "'The 'Consent Decree Will Make Us Better,' Federal Oversight of Chicago Police Begins," National Public Radio, March 1, 2019.

John Seewer, "How City Police Departments with Consent Decrees Are Faring," Associated Press/U.S. News and World Report, April 4, 2017.

80 Ibid.

81 Saul A. Green and Richard B. Jerome, City of Cincinnati Independent Monitor's Final Report, December 2008. Available at www.cincinnati-oh.gov/police/department-references/department-of-justice-agreement.

82 Domanick, "Police Reform's Best Tool."

83 Elisha Anderson and Robert Allen, "Judge Lifts Federal Monitor's Oversight of Detroit Police," *Detroit Free Press*, August 25, 2014.

84 Lawrence Sherman, "Policing for Crime Prevention," *Preventing Crime: What Works, What Doesn't, What's Promising* (Washington, D.C.: National Institute of Justice, 1998), www.hsdl.org/?abstract&did=804375.

OXFORD
insight study guide
Active Engagement, Deeper Understanding

Learn more with this chapter's digital tools, including the Oxford Insight Study Guide, at www.oup.com/he/Fuller2e.

Chapter 5

Police Organization, Operation, and the Law

Alison P. Taylor in downtown Saginaw, Michigan. Why did the Sixth Circuit Court agree with Taylor that chalking a parked automobile's tires constitutes an unreasonable search?

When Alison

Taylor of Saginaw, Michigan, received her fourteenth parking ticket, she decided to do something about it. She sued the city and its parking enforcement officer, claiming that chalking tires to show a car had stayed too long in a space was an unconstitutional search.[1]

The Fourth Amendment protects "the right of the people to be secure in their persons, houses, papers, and effects, against unreasonable searches and seizures." Chalking car tires may seem like an odd claim as an unreasonable search. However, Taylor and her attorneys based their claim on *United States v. Jones* (2012) in which the U.S. Supreme Court ruled that police violated the Fourth Amendment when they failed to acquire a valid warrant to place a GPS tracker on a car. According to Justice Antonin Scalia, the police committed an unconstitutional search when they placed the GPS device on "private property, for the purpose of obtaining information."[2] Thus, the low-tech chalk mark, placed without a warrant, serves much the same purpose as a GPS tracker in that it marks a car's position in time and space, even if that space is a parking space and the time is all day.

The city of Saginaw argued that tire-chalking should be permitted because the Fourth Amendment precludes only "unreasonable searches." The city contended that tire-chalking is a reasonable search because of the reduced expectation of privacy in an automobile and because the city is providing a "community caretaker function" by ensuring that a few drivers do not hog all the parking spaces in a busy downtown area.

The Sixth Circuit Court disagreed, ruling that the automobile exception does not apply because the police do not have probable cause to believe the parked vehicles are involved in a crime. Additionally, the court found that Saginaw's 2-hour time limit on parking is merely a source of revenue and unnecessary to protect public safety because the public's safety is not at risk.[3]

THINK ABOUT IT > Under what circumstances are warrantless searches permitted by the courts?

LEARNING OBJECTIVE | **5.1**

Recognize how the power of the police is constrained.

5.1 What We Expect of the Police

Law enforcement in a democratic society is accomplished with the greatest care and attention paid to how much authority is granted to the police. Although it may seem that the police simply enforce the legal statutes passed by the legislature, the reality of law enforcement in the United States is much more complicated, and for students of criminal justice, far more interesting. The individual police officer makes dozens of decisions each day that consider the rights of offenders, the opinions of citizens, the demands of supervisors, peer pressure from fellow officers, legal statutes, and the officer's own judgment as he or she decides how to act in what is a highly visible occupation.

One important issue we will consider is police discretion. Discretion is mentioned in other chapters, but we will consider it here in more detail because it is at the core of the police officer's occupation.[4] The Gloucester Police Department's Police Assisted Addiction and Recovery Initiative uses police discretion to refrain from strict enforcement of the law in favor of assisting the community by helping drug addicts get treatment. Without recognition of the problems and issues surrounding the exercise of discretion, a precise understanding of policing is impossible.

In this chapter, we look at how the police are constrained in their efforts to keep order, provide services to citizens, and control crime. These constraints include legislative mandates that limit the power of the police, as well as court opinions that police officers must consider in their duties. By appreciating how the police are controlled by elements both inside and outside their agencies, we can begin to understand why policing is often as much an art as a science.

PAUSE AND REVIEW

1. **What constrains the power of the police?**

5.2 How the Police Are Organized

Police departments vary little in how they are organized. With the exception of some small departments, most departments are structured on a quasi-military template complete with uniforms, ranks, hierarchical chains of command, and centralized decision-making.

A strict hierarchical chain of command accords status and responsibility according to rank, and uniforms display insignia that identify to both insiders and the public the exact social location of the officers. This quasi-military nature has some qualities that make it attractive to police organizations. Egon Bittner, a pioneer in the sociology of policing, identified three reasons why the military model is attractive to law enforcement administrators:[5]

1. Controlling force through discipline. Both the military and the police are in the business of using force, and the occasions for employing physical force are, as Bittner put it, "unpredictably distributed." Personnel must be kept in a disciplined state of alert and preparedness, with reliance on "spit and polish" and obedience to superiors.

2. Professionalization. The introduction of military-like discipline into police agencies in the 1950s and 1960s greatly professionalized departments that had been historically plagued by corruption and political favoritism and influence.

3. An effective model of organization. The police lacked other models of organization. Given that many officers had some sort of military background, it was easy to implement.

The military structure and culture of the police have resulted in some unintended and undesirable consequences. By having such a vast array of rules and regulations, police departments ignore the reality that individual officers must exert a substantial amount of discretion in the everyday performance of their duties. To meet the expectations of the department, a good deal of energy is spent conforming to regulations, and creative and effective decision-making is discouraged. According to Bittner, the police are beset with competing demands to stay out of trouble as far as internal regulations are concerned, while at the same time making arrests that "contain, or can be managed to contain, elements of physical danger."[6]

The analogy of the police as soldiers is inexact and faulty because there is a fundamental difference between how military organizations and police agencies deal with decision-making.[7] In military organizations, important decisions are

LEARNING OBJECTIVE **5.2**

Specify how the job of supervising the police is different from that of supervising the military.

New York City police officers are briefed in a subway station as they prepare to deal with a protest march. Although the military structure and culture of the police require many rules and regulations, individual officers must exert a substantial amount of discretion in the everyday performance of their duties. Can you think of an alternative structure for the police?

made at the top of the chain of command and flow downward. In policing, essential discretion is vested in the judgment of the individual police officer, who determines when an offense has been committed and whether to make an arrest.

Even though the police agency has a hierarchical structure that, on the surface, resembles a military organization, the nature of discretion and the authority for decision-making is actually reversed. Although police administrators can make broad policy and direct their officers' activities to some degree, police officers are dispersed widely, and each officer must decide individually when to invoke the criminal law. Modern communication has made the oversight of officers more efficient, but improved communications cannot mimic the type of organizational oversight that is available in the military.

This is one reason that the selection and training of police officers are so important. They must be able to reason for themselves and interpret a given situation within a time frame that often precludes getting input from superiors. Some crucial differences between the police and the military make supervising the police a different, and in many ways more difficult, job than supervising the military. These differences can be categorized in terms of **discretion**, **visibility**, and **authority**.

Discretion (from Chapter 1)—The power of a criminal justice official to make decisions on issues within legal guidelines.

Visibility—A term that refers to the fact that police work is easily observed by the public and that police are accountable to the public, police supervisors, and legislatures.

Authority—The right and the power to commit an act or order others to commit an act.

1. Discretion. Perhaps the most fundamental difference between law enforcement and the military is the level at which discretion is exercised. In typical military units, the allowance for discretion is highest at the top, and the individual soldier makes few decisions. A consistent and simple pattern of supervision exists in which the generals choose the battlefield strategy. The officers choose which units to commit to battle; the sergeants choose which soldiers will rush the machine-gun nest; and the soldiers do their duty, follow orders, and either succeed, retreat, or die. By contrast, in law enforcement organizations, the most discretion is in the hands of the individual police officer. The chief can set some broad policies, and the supervisors can require the officers to keep them apprised of situations, but the individual officer makes the important decisions. Determining whether a law has been

broken, deciding to make an arrest, and giving advice to citizens are activities that are difficult for the command structure of police departments to control. In effect, each officer exercises a great deal of decision-making authority.

2. Visibility. The public observes police work on a daily basis. Officers must interact with citizens, have their decisions second-guessed by the media, and answer to the chief for any violations of procedure and laws. The military is not quite as exposed to the spotlight of public scrutiny. Battlefields are in other countries; the press is given extremely limited access (especially since the Vietnam War), and anonymity protects soldiers from having their actions judged by the public in all but the most egregious cases.

3. Authority. Military commanders have a great deal more authority over soldiers than police administrators have over police officers. If an officer fails to follow orders, he or she may be disciplined or dismissed. If a soldier fails to follow orders, he or she may be court-martialed. Additionally, many police departments are under collective-bargaining agreements that specify the terms of employment and disciplinary procedures. These collective-bargaining agreements are much more "worker-friendly" than the Uniform Code of Military Justice, which spells out the rights of military personnel.

PAUSE AND REVIEW

1. **Why is the military model an attractive model for organizing police departments?**

5.3 What the Police Do

The job of a police officer involves various activities. Many of these activities are well known and highly visible, such as patrol, whereas others are less obvious but equally vital, such as providing services to crime victims, helping individuals in distress, and answering calls for assistance about real and imagined problems. Police officers are among the first responders to natural disasters, accidents, emergencies, and criminal offenses.[8] To appreciate the complexity and range of activities performed by the police, it is useful to review the major functions of a typical police department.

Patrol

The most visible function of the police is patrol. The police patrol in squad cars or aircraft and on foot, bicycles, horseback, or motorcycle. Police patrol has three primary goals:

> To deter crime. When potential lawbreakers see police officers in the community, they are less likely to break the law. Because potential lawbreakers do not know how close the police are and because they fear that a patrol car could show up at any moment, they can be deterred from spontaneously breaking the law. Although people often break laws without thoughts of getting apprehended by police officers, many other offenses are deterred because of the ever-present threat of an immediate police response.

> To enhance feelings of public safety. Police patrol gives ordinary citizens the confidence to go about their daily routines without fear of being attacked, robbed, or having their homes burglarized. Citizens who have confidence

LEARNING OBJECTIVE **5.3**

Summarize the three primary goals of police patrol.

LEARNING OBJECTIVE **5.4**

Cite examples of extraordinary police duties.

Mounted police stand guard during a Louisiana State University football game. What roles do police officers play during public gatherings?

that the police are nearby are more likely to participate in recreational and civic activities and take advantage of public spaces such as parks and shopping malls. Feelings of security and public safety are essential for the development of meaningful communities where citizens interact with one another based on trust and courtesy rather than suspicion and fear.

> **To make officers available for service.** Think how inefficient and ineffective it would be if the police had to respond to calls for service in outlying areas of the community from a downtown police station. A good deal of time would be lost traveling to crime scenes or other incidents, which would result in suspects leaving the scene, disagreements escalating into serious fights, and even people dying because the police arrived too late. By having officers patrolling assigned beats or sectors of the city, they can be dispatched more quickly to calls for service.[9] Some large cities even have district police stations and storefront precincts that decentralize law enforcement resources. Police patrol not only reduces response time, but also allows officers to become more familiar with a particular section of the city, where they get to know shopkeepers, street people, and local residents. This knowledge enhances the ability of the police to gather intelligence about troublemakers, gangs, and neighborhood bullies, and puts a human face on the police agency because citizens recognize individual police officers.[10]

Patrol officers enjoy facing new and different challenges each day. They are constantly bombarded with requests for services that can be either frivolous or serious. Because the police are first responders, they must assess situations and determine what type of resource should be committed to their resolution. Patrol officers are the public face of government and must deal with a host of situations that many would not consider to be serious police work, such as calls about overflowing sewers, loose dogs, strange smells, and requests to "do something about" the aggressive person on the street corner. When citizens do not know whom to call, or other businesses or services are not available, they call the police.[11]

The police employ several strategies for patrol that vary according to administrative policies, urban geography, and the availability of officers in patrol cars. These strategies are designed to best maximize their patrol functions within a given jurisdiction.

> Single-officer patrol cars. Having single-officer patrol cars disperses more officers over a wider area. Many calls for service, such as responding to traffic accidents, involve mundane and routine activities for which only one officer is normally required.

> Two-officer patrol cars. Many departments staff a patrol car with two officers because of safety concerns. When the police must respond to offenses in progress, gang activity, or domestic violence, it is advisable to have two officers so that they can protect each other.

Police patrol is popular primarily because the time it takes the police officer to get to the scene is assumed to be greatly reduced. However, research has not shown that a quick response time has any effect on the number of offenses solved by police. This is because response time is a more complicated matter than is generally thought. In fact, at least four aspects of response time must be considered:

1. Discovery time. Not all offenses are immediately detected. A great time gap can exist between when the offense is committed and when someone notices it. This is especially true in burglaries in which the home or business owner is away and returns only to discover that his or her house or business has been burglarized. In such cases, it makes little difference how quickly the police were notified because the perpetrator might be miles away by then.

2. Reporting time. People often delay calling the police after discovering an offense. This delay can occur for many reasons, including fear or embarrassment on the part of a victim, poor telephone service in rural areas, or the victim's thinking that he or she can solve the problem without police assistance. When such delays occur, the crime scene can go cold, perpetrators can escape, and witnesses can wander away.

3. Processing time. Once the police are notified, it might take some time for a car to be dispatched. The reasons for this time gap are an inadequate number of dispatchers, antiquated dispatch equipment, and lack of available officers in patrol cars.

4. Travel time. Depending on how patrol cars are dispersed throughout the community, it may take a while for them to get to the crime scene. Often patrol officers are already engaged in incidents in neighboring sections of the city, where they may be supporting other police officers in making arrests, quelling domestic disturbances, or simply taking a break for lunch. Travel time can vary greatly depending on the officers' distance from the crime scene or the difficulty in reaching the crime scene, such as heavy traffic or other delays.[12]

Patrol strategy may be useful for other reasons besides response time. In proactive policing, officers take the initiative to detect and respond to crime rather than reacting to calls for service (reactive policing). In these incidents, a patrol officer may **stop** suspicious individuals or cars and detect lawbreaking. Furthermore, proactive policing allows officers to keep an eye on areas that historically have a high crime rate and to intervene when they see someone breaking the law.[13]

Stop—A temporary detention that legally is a seizure of an individual and must be based on reasonable suspicion.

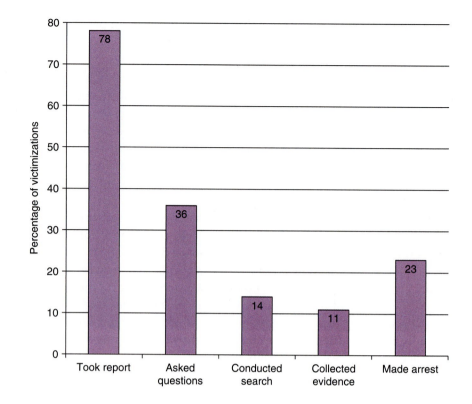

FIGURE 5.1   Police Actions During Initial Response to Domestic Violence Victimizations

These are the actions that police officers took during the initial response to a call involving non-fatal domestic violence from 2006 to 2015. For example, in 78 percent of the victimizations, the police took a report during their initial response. Give some reasons why arrests are made in relatively few non-fatal domestic violence calls.

Source: Brian A. Reaves, Police Response to Domestic Violence, 2006-2015 *(U.S. Department of Justice Office of Justice Programs Bureau of Justice Statistics, 2017), 9. Available at www.bjs.gov/index. cfm?ty=pbdetail&iid=5907.*

can be witnessed at social protests, sporting events, and public celebrations. Police officers are dispatched to contain crowds and ensure that laws are not broken and people are not injured. This type of policing presents special challenges for police agencies because it requires the coordination of many officers. Normally, officers work alone or in pairs and are expected to use a great deal of discretion. In crowd-control situations, officers are required to act more as a military unit in which a commander makes a judgment, and individual officers work as a team to implement it. These situations require special training, coordination between numerous law enforcement agencies, and advanced communications technology.[21]

› Vice. Gambling, recreational drug use, and prostitution are just a few victimless crimes that police officers must deal with.[22] Vice laws vary by jurisdiction: For example, casino gambling is legal in Nevada but not in other states. Vice offenses, many of which are a response to supply-and-demand forces in the marketplace, are extremely difficult for police officers to deter, investigate, and prosecute. Nevertheless, police agencies do not get to select which behaviors are illegal. They are obligated to enforce every law. However, police agencies can decide that certain offenses are less of a priority than others and simply spend less time on them.

› Mental illness. One of the most perplexing problems that police officers must face is dealing with the mentally ill. The police are responsible for keeping the mentally ill from harming themselves and others, while at the same time preserving their constitutional rights. Often, mentally ill people are unable to understand and accept reason and must be physically restrained. Although police officers may have sympathy for a mentally ill individual who is causing problems, the possibility of violence means that officers must always be prepared. Part of the problem is that many communities provide few alternatives for dealing with the mentally ill. Experts agree

A Washington, D.C., police officer leads the crowd in a chant of "Let's go Caps" during the Washington Capitals Stanley Cup Victory Parade on Constitution Avenue in June 2018. What challenges and problems do police face in maintaining order during public celebrations?

that, for the most part, the mentally ill are better treated in the community than in secure institutions, so the laws have specified that many people with mental health problems cannot be locked up. Therefore, it falls to the police to deal with the mentally ill, who are often poor, homeless, or hostile. Police require special training in the laws of dealing with the mentally ill, learning techniques for defusing individuals with a tenuous grasp of reality, and maintaining their own sanity when dealing with dangerous and unreasonable people.[23]

> Juveniles. In addition to enforcing the law, police officers must deal with juveniles who break the law and engage in behaviors that are prohibited because of their age, such as drinking alcohol, skipping school, and running away from home. Additionally, juveniles can commit serious offenses that the police must respond to without knowing the suspect's age. Dealing with juvenile suspects presents several legal, social, and moral dilemmas for police officers. Larger police agencies have officers specially dedicated to dealing with juveniles.[24] Officers may also have to help children who are being neglected by their families, and they may be the first responders to domestic situations in which children are removed from their primary caregivers.

> First response. In times of crisis, such as natural disasters, terrorist attacks, and other types of emergencies, the police not only are among the first officials to arrive on the scene but are also responsible for maintaining order, limiting damage and injury, and ensuring that the situation does not escalate further. This duty as a first responder is taken for granted by society until something goes drastically wrong.

> Use of force. Part of maintaining order is using force, sometimes deadly force. Police use of force is an issue on which reliable statistics are not collected. Thus, actions such as homicides committed by police officers in the line of duty are poorly understood. This subject will be discussed in greater detail in Chapter 6.

Officers often must help children who are being neglected by their families or whose families have placed them in dangerous situations. A boy sits in a car behind his grandmother and her boyfriend, both of whom are unconscious from a drug overdose. A judge later turned over custody of the boy to other family members. What are some other situations in which police officers must deal with juveniles?

PAUSE AND REVIEW

1. **What are the three primary goals of police patrol?**
2. **What happens during investigation?**
3. **Why is traffic enforcement among the most dangerous aspects of police work?**
4. **Name a few examples of extraordinary police duties.**

LEARNING OBJECTIVE | 5.5

Evaluate the positive and negative aspects of police discretion.

LEARNING OBJECTIVE | 5.6

Illustrate the importance of the Fourth Amendment to regulating law enforcement.

Procedural law (from Chapter 3)—Law that specifies how the criminal justice system is allowed to deal with those who break the law.

5.4 The Rules the Police Follow

In Chapter 3, we studied the distinction between substantive law and procedural law. As you will recall, **procedural law** dictates how the government can go about discovering and prosecuting violations of substantive law, or what constitutes criminal offenses. One way to consider procedural law is to think of it as the rules by which the government must play. Some people may think of procedural law as "tying the hands of the police" or "letting criminals go free because of technicalities," but the positive aspects of this control of government actions are extremely valuable in providing for a free and democratic state. Aspects of procedural law were placed in the Constitution because its framers wanted to protect the people from government abuses such as those found in the European monarchies of the time.

Those who work in the criminal justice system sometimes get frustrated by the scope and complexities of procedural law and often test the interpretation with aggressive crime fighting. The law is forever in flux, as new cases are brought before the courts for rulings concerning new technologies, changing community standards, evolving political pressures, and widening constitutional protections to more and more groups of people. Consequently, the law is a living, breathing, changing set of rules that is adjusted to society's demands. However, the law is based on long-held principles that limit just how far it can be stretched, and it dictates that either the underlying values incorporated by the Constitution must be met or the Constitution must be amended.

Police Discretion

The police do not make an arrest every time they are legally authorized to do so. Police officers turn a blind eye to many violations and never engage in full enforcement of the law. If the police attempted to enforce all the laws, at least two bad things would happen. First, the criminal justice system would be swamped by the workload. The wheels of justice would grind to a halt under the weight of a system clogged by many times the number of cases it could reasonably process.[25]

Second, the most serious offenders would be obscured by the sheer mass of cases. The police would not have the time and resources to address the cases that represent the greatest dangers to society. Therefore, it is important to appreciate that the police, both as an organization and as individual officers, decide which laws to enforce, how much to enforce them, when to let some offenses slide, and when to devote attention to truly significant offenses.[26]

These decisions on differential law enforcement are called discretion (see Getting It Right 5.1 for an interesting take on discretion). Decisions to investigate, arrest, charge, and incarcerate are all made by the police in the legitimate performance of their duties. It is important to understand the dynamics that structure these decisions. For example, consider an interstate highway on which the posted speed limit is 55 miles per hour but where traffic generally moves at 70 miles per hour. The police do not enforce the posted limit because to do so would mean ticketing about 90 percent of the drivers. The unstated understanding between the police and the public is that a pattern of non-enforcement is permissible.

In some incidents, the police use their discretion to engage in non-enforcement of the law. It might be fair to argue that the more trivial the offense is, the more likely the police will not practice full enforcement.[27] For instance, laws involving the possession of marijuana have long been subject to less enforcement than those involving heroin or cocaine. Additionally, the police are less likely to arrest two teenagers who fight at school than they are two adults who fight after a traffic accident. The context in which the violation occurs has a great deal to do with whether the police decide to invoke the criminal law.[28]

Although we might agree that the use of police discretion in deciding against full enforcement of the law is desirable, another side of police discretion is troubling. Police discretion also provides an opportunity for selective enforcement.[29] When the police use their judgment in deciding which infractions to pursue, bias,

---

GETTING IT RIGHT 5.1
Problem-Solving Policing

The media often feature attention-getting stories of police brutality and corruption. Occasions of police officers solving situations with imagination, kindness, and empathy, on the other hand, often go unnoticed. For example, in August 2017, Officer Mario Valenti of Skokie, Illinois, was called to the X-Sport Fitness facility to address a complaint that a teenager had been breaking in to play basketball. Vincent Gonzalez, a high school sophomore, could not afford a gym membership and was sneaking in at night to practice. Instead of arresting Gonzalez for trespassing, Officer Valenti

offered to pay $150 for a 3-month membership for Gonzalez. The management of X-Sport was so moved by the gesture that they extended the membership to two years.[30]

THINK ABOUT IT

1. What other options did the police officer have in this situation?

Watch the related video on Oxford Learning Link at www.oup.com/he/Fuller2e.

The police do not make an arrest every time they are legally authorized to do so. This police officer is directing a jaywalking pedestrian to a crosswalk. Why do police officers often refrain from making arrests?

Racial profiling—

Suspicion of illegal activity based on a person's race, ethnicity, or national origin rather than on actual illegal activity or evidence of illegal activity.

discrimination, and individual values may factor into how the law is enforced. When accusations of **racial profiling**, favoritism, corruption, or laziness accompany selective enforcement, the community begins to lose faith in the fairness of the criminal justice system.[31] Yet the police might feel the need to enforce the law selectively as a result of the inconsistencies and unpredictability of the criminal justice system.[32] According to legal scholar Kenneth Culp Davis, selective enforcement raises four questions:

1. Should the police make arrests when they know that prosecutors will not prosecute the defendants or that the court will dismiss the case?

2. Do the police violate full-enforcement legislation when a law is broken in their presence but an arrest is (a) physically impossible, (b) less important than some other urgent duty, or (c) impossible because of limited resources?

3. Does insufficiency of police resources for full enforcement justify a system of enforcement priorities that takes into account all relevant reasons for enforcing or not enforcing? Or must the police indiscriminately try to enforce on any and all occasions, so that what remains unenforced will be so because of limited resources and not policy requirements?

4. Are the police always forbidden to make enforcement decisions on individual grounds?[33]

There are good reasons both for and against selective enforcement of the law. On the one hand, it violates the idea of fair play: that everyone who breaks the law should be treated equally. When the police use discretion to decide whom to arrest, it can appear discriminatory. On the other hand, there might be legitimate reasons to engage in selective enforcement, reasons that result in a community with less overall crime and less damage to citizens and property.[34]

Take the hypothetical case of the vice officer who arrests a drug user and finds out that the offender is responsible for several burglaries to get money to support drug purchases. Although we might reasonably expect that the vice officer would charge the drug user with the burglaries, the officer is also interested in discovering the user's source of the drugs. The vice officer reasons that drying up the source of the drugs will prevent many more drug-related burglaries if there are fewer or no sellers to satisfy the demand for drugs. By encouraging the user to provide information on the seller in exchange for dropping the burglary charges, the vice officer can attempt to clean up the drug trade in that neighborhood. It becomes, then, a value judgment on whether this selective enforcement is justifiable. Certainly, the owner of the burglarized home would want the thief arrested and prosecuted. However, the homeowner might consider it a reasonable compromise to let the burglar go if that person could help eliminate drug sales in the homeowner's community.

Faced with these mixed messages sent by legislators, police administrators, and citizens, police officers must exercise a lot of discretion in deciding which laws to enforce and how fully to enforce them.[35] Certainly, we do not want to give the police full rein to decide how to enforce the law because law enforcement without boundaries is a frightening prospect. While the law limits the actions of the police, it also allows them to exercise discretion on when to apply specific laws to certain situations. Even though we try to control discretion, it will always be a contested area of law enforcement.[36]

The Fourth Amendment

The procedural law that controls the activities of law enforcement is derived from the Fourth Amendment. Although many state laws, court cases, and departmental regulations specify how the police can go about investigation, interrogation, and arrest, all of these rules and regulations must be consistent with the Supreme Court's interpretation of the Fourth Amendment (see CJ Reference 5.1).

Although it constitutes only one sentence, the Fourth Amendment specifies a range of protections from police activity and essentially ensures that citizens are not subject to the arbitrary actions of overzealous police officers. However, the Fourth Amendment does not completely tie the hands of the police. It is subject to interpretation by the courts, and its wording allows justices to include in their rulings their judgment about what the framers of the Constitution intended and what contemporary society demands. For instance, the interpretation of the word *unreasonable* is fraught with difficulty. What is reasonable to one individual may be unreasonable to another. Yet the police must have guidelines to ensure that the cases they present to the prosecutor are not considered unreasonable by the court. To appreciate the intricacies of the Fourth Amendment as a guide for procedural law, we must examine its language in greater detail.

SEARCH

Prosecuting criminal cases depends on information. Many times, the required information is readily available to police officers, but more often, they have to work hard to assemble the evidence necessary to secure a conviction. Suspects,

CJ REFERENCE 5.1
The Fourth Amendment

The right of the people to be secure in their persons, houses, papers, and effects, against unreasonable searches and seizures, shall not be violated, and no Warrants shall issue, but upon probable cause, supported by Oath or affirmation, and particularly describing the place to be searched, and the persons or things to be seized.

especially the guilty ones, do not always cooperate fully with the officers who are investigating them. Suspects might hide, alter, or destroy evidence in their efforts to avoid detection and arrest. The police may **search** the suspect in a reasonable manner, but the court draws a line at the fuzzy concept of unreasonable searches, and the police must be trained in procedural law to judge which is which. A review of some of the concerns of the court is instructive.

Search—An investigation of an area and/or person by a police officer to look for evidence of criminal activity.

> Trespass doctrine. The trespass doctrine defines what constitutes a search. The court says that a search requires physical intrusion into a constitutionally protected area, specified by the Fourth Amendment as persons, houses, papers, and effects. The search of these areas must meet the requirements of the Fourth Amendment as being reasonable. Asking for a handwriting sample is not considered physically intrusive and is thus not a search protected by the Fourth Amendment. However, many people believe the government has no right to demand bodily fluids in its search for evidence because the Fourth Amendment protects our person.[37]

> Privacy doctrine. In 1967, the privacy doctrine essentially replaced the trespass doctrine in *Katz* v. *United States*. This case held that people, not places, are protected from government intrusion whenever they have an expectation of privacy that society recognizes as reasonable. The police have quite a bit of latitude in dealing with citizens on the street and in public places where privacy is usually not expected.[38]

> Plain-view doctrine. The plain-view doctrine maintains that officers have a lawful right to use all their senses (sight, smell, hearing, and touch) to detect evidence of unlawful action. This doctrine also stipulates that such detection of evidence does not constitute a search because the police are not searching when they merely observe their surroundings. Thus, the plain-view doctrine holds that the Fourth Amendment does not protect such gathering of evidence because no search has actually occurred.[39] Three criteria must be met for the discovery of evidence to fall outside the Fourth Amendment's definition of a search: (1) the item must be in plain view of the officer; (2) the officer must lawfully be in the place where he or she discovered the evidence; and (3) the incriminating nature of the evidence must be immediately apparent.[40] Thus, when a police officer pulls a car over for speeding and sees a bag of marijuana on the passenger seat in plain view, the officer can arrest the driver for possession because no search was conducted.[41] (Conversely, if the officer stopped the car because the driver looked suspicious and, without asking the driver's permission, felt under the seat, and found a bag that contained marijuana, the officer's actions would be deemed an illegal search.) As another example, DUI roadblocks, or sobriety checkpoints, are not illegal searches because all cars are stopped. Probable cause is not an issue because no one is singled out for special treatment. The court does not allow law enforcement to use sophisticated technology to enhance their natural senses in discovering evidence in plain view. Thus, the police may use flashlights, binoculars, and even airplanes to look for unlawful activity. In a recent case, the court drew the line at the use of thermal-imaging devices. The police used such a device to measure the heat emitted by special lights used to grow marijuana in a house as **probable cause** to secure a search warrant. The court ruled against the government, contending that such a device was beyond the plain-view doctrine.[42]

Probable cause—A reason based on known facts to think that a law has been broken or that a property is connected to a criminal offense.

> Open-fields doctrine. The right to privacy does not extend to open fields, even if the property is privately owned. For example, the police can arrest

landowners for cultivating marijuana on private land even if the police were trespassing on that land.[43]

> Public places. The Fourth Amendment does not protect individuals from being observed by the police using ordinary senses in public places. Streets, parks, private businesses that are open to the public, and public areas of restrooms are all outside the protection of the plain-view doctrine of the Fourth Amendment.[44]

> Abandoned property. The Fourth Amendment does not extend to abandoned property. Abandonment requires the individual to intend to permanently discard the property. For example, turning your car over to a valet parking attendant would not constitute abandonment because you expect to get your car back. Putting your household trash on the curb to be collected by the garbage service is another matter. Because we cannot expect that our trash will be free from the prying eyes of others, we are careful (or should be) to make sure credit card numbers and other sensitive information are destroyed before they go into the trash.[45]

The legality of law enforcement searches is complex. The Constitution does not say the government cannot search, only that it cannot conduct unreasonable searches. For example, in *Illinois v. Gates* (1983), the U.S. Supreme Court set forth that the probable cause for a search does not demand proof beyond a reasonable doubt. In this case, an anonymous letter to police accused a married couple, Lance and Sue Gates, of buying and selling large amounts of illegal drugs. The police tracked the Gates's activities, obtained a warrant to search their home, and found large quantities of drugs. After their convictions, the Gates appealed to the Supreme Court, stating that because the police could not assess the reliability of the anonymous letter, no basis existed for the search warrant of their home. The Court stated that the "totality of circumstances"—meaning, in this case, how precisely the letter's specifics matched the Gates's activities—and not the letter itself justified the search warrant. The Gates's convictions were upheld.

The Constitution does not say the government cannot search, only that it cannot conduct unreasonable searches. Here, a SWAT team enters a private home in the search for a suspect in the Boston Marathon bombings. Was this search reasonable?

Police officers must understand the parameters of lawful searching to ensure that their cases can withstand constitutional scrutiny. We recognize the necessity for police officers to search for evidence, but we also understand that unreasonable searches are one of the most intrusive features of the criminal justice system. No one likes to have his or her person, home, or "stuff" searched, and the Court has tried to balance the privacy rights of citizens with the needs of law enforcement to collect evidence of crime. The police are restrained in their searches by the requirement that they have a warrant approved by a judge. A valid warrant requires probable cause, a specific description of the persons and places that are going to be searched, and a description of the items that are to be seized. Additionally, the officers must knock and announce their presence and give the occupants a brief time to answer before they enter the house to search.[46]

Two considerations exempt law enforcement from these Fourth Amendment provisions. The first is the problem of officer safety. If the police believe that an armed and dangerous subject is inside a home, should they be required to knock and announce their presence? To do so might invite a hail of gunfire. Second, by knocking and announcing their presence, the police may give suspects an opportunity to destroy evidence. Drugs can be flushed down the toilet, or documents can be burned before the police have time to secure the scene. The Court does not recognize any blanket exception such as a search of a dwelling where drugs might be used and sold, but it does recognize that, on a case-by-case basis, the knock-and-announce rule can be abbreviated.

As a practical concern, obtaining a judge's approval for a search warrant presents difficulties that can hinder a case. It can take a long time to get the warrant, time in which suspects can escape or destroy evidence. Consequently, far more searches are conducted without warrants than with legally secured warrants. The Court has recognized the following four major exceptions to the requirement that officers obtain warrants before conducting a search:

1. Searches incident to arrest. When the police arrest a suspect, it is reasonable, according to the Court, for them to search the suspect for weapons and incriminating evidence. However, in *Chimel v. California* (1969), the U.S. Supreme Court found that an arrest warrant allows only the search of a suspect's person and the immediate vicinity and that any further searches require a warrant.

2. Additionally, the police may search the immediate area under control of the suspect to further ensure their safety and prevent destruction of evidence. The legal issue of what constitutes "under immediate control" of the suspect does not allow the police to extend the search to the whole house. To do this, the police would need to secure a warrant. In the case of an arrest of an individual in an automobile, the area under the offender's control is deemed to be the **grabbable area**, which constitutes the inside of the passenger compartment but not under the hood or in the trunk.

Grabbable area—The area under the control of an individual during an arrest in an automobile.

3. Consent searches. Police officers may conduct a search without a warrant if they obtain the suspect's consent. Individuals may waive their protection against a search as long as the police advise them that they have the right to refuse consent and that if the officers find incriminating evidence, it will be seized and used against them. For a waiver of consent to be considered voluntary, it must be given by a suspect who feels free of coercion, promise, or deception.[47]

4. Exigent-circumstances searches or emergency searches. Sometimes events happen so quickly that it is unreasonable to expect the police to stop and

> ## CASE IN POINT   5.1
>
> ### *Terry v. Ohio* (1968)
>
> ---
>
> #### THE POINT
>
> Police have the right to search suspects to ensure their own safety and the safety of others if they think that suspects are armed.
>
> #### THE CASE
>
> A Cleveland police officer who was in an area that he had patrolled for many years saw two men, John Terry and Richard Chilton, pacing in front of a store and pausing to stare in the window. After each pass, they met and talked on a nearby street corner. They were joined by a third man, who left the group but met them again a few blocks from the store. The officer suspected the men of planning to rob the store. The officer approached the men and identified himself as a policeman. Suspicious, he checked Terry for weapons and felt a gun concealed in his coat pocket, and, in a further search, a gun in Chilton's pocket. Terry and Chilton were eventually convicted of carrying concealed weapons. Terry appealed, the central argument in the case being whether police may search people who are acting suspiciously if they believe a criminal offense is being planned. The Supreme Court upheld Terry's conviction.
>
> #### THINK ABOUT IT
>
> 1. Why were Terry and Chilton not also charged with burglary?

get a search warrant to determine whether there is a danger to their safety, a chance of suspect escape, or the likelihood of the destruction of evidence (see Case in Point 5.1). For instance, if the police chase a suspect into a house, they are not required to get a warrant to search the immediate area, but the search would be limited to the room in which the suspect was caught. The police could not search the whole house.[48]

5. Vehicle searches. Historically, vehicles are exempt from the requirement of a search warrant. A person in a vehicle has a reduced expectation of privacy as compared to someone at home. This does not mean that the police are free to search a vehicle arbitrarily.[49] Probable cause would still be needed, but one's car is not considered as sacred as one's home. Additionally, objects in a car that could conceal items the police have probable cause to suspect, such as a purse, are also subject to a warrantless search.[50]

Procedural law attempts to strike a delicate balance between the rights of individuals to be protected from overzealous police officers and the needs of society to provide those officers with the flexibility and discretion to protect society. Although the Fourth Amendment requirement of a search warrant is highly desirable, it is not practical in all situations in which the safety of an officer or evidence preservation is at issue. Therefore, the court has allowed several exceptions. Other types of searches, called special-needs searches, pose legal issues that result in procedural law continuing to be contested.

SPECIAL-NEEDS SEARCHES

So far, our review of Fourth Amendment issues has dealt with how police officers must handle cases in which a law is believed to have been broken. In some circumstances, searches are allowed in an attempt to prevent crime rather than to catch suspects. This discussion of special-needs searches will demonstrate how the

court, "taking into account all of the circumstances surrounding the encounter, a reasonable passenger would feel free to decline the officers' requests or otherwise terminate the encounter."

STOP-AND-FRISK

From a procedural standpoint, the term **stop-and-frisk** encompasses two distinct behaviors on the part of police officers. The most basic way to think about them is to consider stops as seizures and frisks as searches. To conduct a lawful frisk, the stop must meet the conditions of a lawful seizure. It is useful to consider these actions individually to appreciate how they are related:

Stop-and-frisk—A term that describes two distinct behaviors on the part of law enforcement officers in dealing with suspects. To conduct a lawful frisk, the stop itself must meet the legal conditions of a seizure. A frisk constitutes a search.

Actual-seizure stop—An incident in which police officers physically restrain a person and restrict his or her freedom.

Show-of-authority stop—An incident in which police show a sign of authority (such as flashing a badge), and the suspect submits.

Reasonable-stop standard—A Supreme Court measure that considers constitutionality on whether a reasonable person would feel free to terminate an encounter with law enforcement personnel.

1. Two types of situations in which police officers stop suspects are of concern to the student of the Fourth Amendment. These two situations are **actual-seizure stops** and **show-of-authority stops**. Actual-seizure stops involve police officers physically grabbing a person and restricting his or her freedom. Show-of-authority stops involve the officers showing their authority (such as flashing a badge) and the suspects submitting to it. The Supreme Court uses a **reasonable-stop standard** that considers whether a reasonable person would feel free to terminate the encounter in deciding whether the stop is constitutional. The legality of a stop is highly contextualized and has been codified into procedural law by decisions made in several cases.[59] The courts have ruled on the admissibility of stops in a range of circumstances. Some of the issues the courts have considered are as follows:

   - the role of reasonable suspicion in an officer's decision to stop a suspect;
   - the use of an anonymous tip as a sufficient reason to make a stop;
   - race as an indicator for reasonable suspicion;
   - the use of pre-established profiles as valid reasons to make a stop;
   - the stopping of individuals at international borders; and
   - the constitutionality of roadblocks.

2. Although stop and frisk are closely linked, they are also quite different procedures that the law considers in great detail. Police officers may conduct a legal stop but engage in an illegal search. A frisk involves a light patting of

A woman and children walk past a street mural listing an individual's rights during a stop-and-frisk. How does a stop differ from a frisk?

a suspect's outer clothing with the intent to determine whether a weapon is present. However, if the officer detects contraband (such as drugs) during the frisk, then even though the frisk was initiated to detect weapons, an arrest can be made for drug possession or even intent to sell. At issue is the extent of the frisk. Frisks are considered the least invasive type of search; full body-cavity searches are the most invasive. The court will consider evidence obtained in a frisk only if it is confident that the evidence was discovered by officers conducting the frisk with the intention of detecting weapons to ensure their own safety.[60]

ARRESTS

An arrest is more invasive than a stop. It involves being taken into custody, photographed, fingerprinted, interrogated, and formally charged with a criminal offense. A suspect who is stopped and frisked may be released, but if the case proceeds to an arrest, then a temporary loss of liberty results. Because this loss of liberty can last anywhere from a few hours to a few days, a higher standard of suspicion of guilt is required. Although reasonable suspicion is sufficient for a stop-and-frisk, arrest requires the police officers to have probable cause that the suspect broke the law.

The way in which police arrest suspects is also important. The amount of force used in the arrest should be consistent with maintaining the dignity of the suspect as much as circumstances allow. The Supreme Court has ruled that deadly force is constitutionally unreasonable if it is used simply because the felony suspect is fleeing. In order to use deadly force, the officer must believe the suspect to be a threat to others.

Arrest requires police officers to have probable cause that the suspect broke the law. These officers are arresting a protester after he tried to climb barricades to enter private property. How does an arrest differ from a stop?

The Court also has spoken to the need to have a warrant to arrest someone at home.[61] Although a multitude of circumstances and situations complicate the sanctity-of-the-home concept (such as when the police are chasing a suspect who runs into a residence), these exceptions must be considered in light of the language and intention of the Fourth Amendment's guarantee that people should be secure in their homes. To arrest someone at home, the Court recommends four restrictions:

1. The offense should be a felony. This guards against arbitrary and abusive arrests and ensures that homes are invaded only for serious offenses.

2. The police must knock and announce. This allows the individuals to get dressed and open the door, thus assuring them of some degree of dignity.

3. The arrest should be made in daylight. The fear produced by someone pounding on the door in the middle of the night should be avoided.

4. The police must meet a stringent probable-cause requirement that the suspect is at home. This guards against the police entering the home and frightening others who live there or ransacking the home in their search for the suspect.[62]

Bear in mind that the criteria listed here refer to arrests in homes, not searches.

Interrogation and Confessions

The police may gather information about criminal offenses from the suspects themselves. By questioning suspects, the police can develop the required evidence to charge, prosecute, and convict lawbreakers. Although this sort of interrogation is exactly what we expect of the police, there are limits on exactly what methods can be used and on what types of help the suspects are entitled to.

Upon arrest, the police must give suspects some version of the *Miranda* warning, which is notification of their rights as an arrestee (see Case in Point 5.2). The familiar *Miranda* warning is as much a product of Hollywood as it is the law. The Supreme Court decision provided the content of the warning, but not its wording, which was left up to individual police departments. In 1968, California Attorney General Thomas Lynch asked Deputy State Attorney General Doris Maier and Nevada County District Attorney Harold Berliner to create a simple, easily remembered version. Berliner then printed *Miranda* cards so that all California police officers would have a convenient copy. Soon after, Jack Webb, producer and star of the then-popular television show, *Dragnet*, saw the card and made the *Miranda* warning a regular feature. Thus, the warning that most arrestees hear today was popularized by television. In *Dickerson v. United States* (2000), the Supreme Court stated that police do not have to administer this particular warning.[63]

Even though the police may have good reason to suspect that an individual has broken the law, that person's constitutional rights must be respected in the questioning process.[64] These rights stem from the Fifth, Sixth, and Fourteenth Amendments of the Constitution.

1. Fifth Amendment self-incrimination clause: "No person . . . shall be compelled in any criminal case to be a witness against himself."

2. Sixth Amendment right-to-counsel clause: "In all criminal prosecutions, the accused shall . . . have the assistance of counsel for his defense."

3. Fourteenth Amendment due process clause: "No state shall . . . deprive any person of life, liberty, or property without due process of law."

CASE IN POINT 5.2

Miranda v. Arizona (1966)

THE POINT

Confessions made by suspects who have not been advised of their due process rights cannot be used as evidence.

THE CASE

Ernesto Miranda was arrested in 1963 on suspicion of rape and kidnapping. Police interrogated Miranda for several hours without advising him of his right to an attorney or permitting him to speak with one. Miranda signed a written confession and was later convicted and sentenced to 60 years in prison. Miranda's case, and several others like it, were appealed, and the Supreme Court agreed with their contention that the suspects' right to due process had been violated because they had not been advised of their rights to an attorney or to remain silent. The decision set forth that confessions made by suspects who have not been advised of their due process rights cannot be used as evidence.

The Supreme Court later upheld *Miranda* in *Dickerson v. United States* (2000). In *Dickerson*, the court considered the constitutionality of a statute enacted by Congress in 1968 that states that confessions are admissible if "voluntarily given." The court held that its constitutional decisions may not be overruled by Acts of Congress.

A popular version of the Miranda warning is as follows:

1. You have the right to remain silent.
2. Anything you say can and will be used against you in a court of law.
3. You have the right to an attorney.
4. If you cannot afford an attorney, one will be provided for you.
5. Do you understand each of these rights I have just read to you?
6. With these rights in mind, do you wish to speak to me?

THINK ABOUT IT

1. Is the Miranda warning useful when it comes to protecting suspects' rights, or are the police too intimidating for most suspects to understand the warning as it is read to them and ask for a lawyer? Support your argument.

Defense attorneys and the court use these amendments to oversee how the police conduct interrogations, elicit confessions, and seize evidence. In some cases, the police might violate the law in conducting these activities, and the evidence gathered can be disallowed in court.

PAUSE AND REVIEW

1. What are some reasons to advocate for selective enforcement of the law?
2. In what ways can police discretion negatively affect a community?
3. How does the Fourth Amendment limit the actions of law enforcement?

FOCUS ON ETHICS It's Only Marijuana

You are a police officer in a state that has not yet legalized marijuana. Although the laws are changing across the country, your police department has not formulated any policy instructing its officers to overlook marijuana possession and use. As a police officer, you are constantly called on to use your discretion in deciding when to invoke the criminal law. To be honest, you do not make an arrest every time you have the opportunity because you do not want to spend all your time processing petty cases.

One evening you and your partner are called to a fraternity house on the local university campus after neighbors complained of loud partying at 2:00 a.m. You are admitted into the house by an obviously intoxicated fraternity president who says, "Come on in, ossifers. Look around all you want." As he giggles, you realize two things. First, he has given you permission to conduct a legal search of the house, and second, there is the unmistakable smell of marijuana emanating from both the fraternity house and its president.

As you and your partner conduct a cursory search, you easily find a water pipe, several half-full bags of marijuana, and about a dozen marijuana cigarettes behind the couch, under chairs, and under the rug. You are about to gather all the marijuana to determine whether a felony case can be made when your partner informs you that his wife's little sister, a high school junior, is present but passed out in one of the bedrooms. Your partner begs you to let everyone go with a warning. You are concerned about the number of youths who are engaged in underage drinking and drug use, but your partner is insistent and says, "Hey, it's only marijuana."

WHAT DO YOU DO?

1. Tell your partner that "the law's the law" and arrest everyone in the house on whom you think you can make a good case, including his wife's little sister.
2. Warn everyone to keep the noise down and that if the neighbors complain again and you have to come back, you will institute option 1.
3. Gather up all the marijuana and flush it down the toilet and send everyone home, thus ending the party.

For more insight into how someone might respond to such an ethical dilemma, visit Oxford Learning Link at www.oup.com/he/Fuller2e to watch a video that connects this scenario to a real-world situation.

Summary

LEARNING OBJECTIVE **5.1** Recognize how the power of the police is constrained.	The police are constrained in their efforts to keep order, provide services to citizens, and control crime. These constraints include legislative mandates that limit the power of the police and court opinions that police officers must consider in their duties. The police are controlled by elements both inside and outside their agencies.
LEARNING OBJECTIVE **5.2** Specify how the job of supervising the police is different from that of supervising the military.	**Discretion:** In the military, the greatest allowance for discretion is located at the top of the command chain, but for the police it is with the individual officer. **Visibility:** The activities of the police are more visible to the public than those of the military. **Authority:** Military commanders have more authority over soldiers than police administrators have over police officers.
LEARNING OBJECTIVE **5.3** Summarize the three primary goals of police patrol.	(1) To deter crime. When potential lawbreakers see police officers in the community, they are less likely to break the law. (2) To enhance feelings of public safety. Feelings of security and public safety are essential for the development of meaningful communities. (3) To make officers available for service. By having officers patrolling assigned beats or sectors of a city, they can be dispatched more quickly to calls for service.

LEARNING OBJECTIVE **5.4** Cite examples of extraordinary police duties.	Domestic violence; crowd control; vice; mental illness; dealing with juveniles; first response.	
LEARNING OBJECTIVE **5.5** Evaluate the positive and negative aspects of police discretion.	Allowing the police to decide which laws to enforce, how much to enforce them, and when to let some offenses slide enables police to devote attention and resources to truly significant offenses, thus resulting in safer communities (in terms of less overall crime). If the police attempted to enforce all the laws, the criminal justice system would be swamped by the workload and the most serious offenders would be obscured by the mass of cases. However, police discretion also provides an opportunity for selective enforcement, in which bias, discrimination, and individual values may factor into how the law is enforced. This violation of fair treatment can cause a community to lose faith in the fairness of the criminal justice system.	
LEARNING OBJECTIVE **5.6** Illustrate the importance of the Fourth Amendment to regulating law enforcement.	The procedural law that controls the activities of law enforcement is derived from the Fourth Amendment. It specifies several protections from police activity, including searches, seizures, stops, frisks, arrests, interrogations, and confessions, and it essentially ensures that citizens are not subject to the arbitrary actions of overzealous police officers.	

Critical Reflections

1. **Suggest how police departments could organize themselves and perform if they were not based on a quasi-military model.**

2. **How much discretion should police officers have in deciding what suspects and offenses to pursue? How might police discretion be monitored and evaluated?**

Key Terms

Actual-seizure stop **p. 150**
Authority **p. 132**
Discretion **p. 132**
Grabbable area **p. 146**
Probable cause **p. 144**
Procedural law **p. 140**

Racial profiling **p. 142**
Reasonable-stop standard **p. 150**
Reasonable suspicion **p. 148**
Search **p. 144**
Seizure **p. 149**

Show-of-authority stop **p. 150**
Stop **p. 135**
Stop-and-frisk **p. 150**
Visibility **p. 132**

Notes

1 Jack Denton, "What Does Chalking Tires Have to Do with the Fourth Amendment?" *Pacific Standard*, May 3, 2019, psmag.com/social-justice/what-does-chalking-tires-have-to-do-with-the-fourth-amendment.

2 Campbell Robertson, "Lose the Chalk, Officer: Court Finds Marking Tires of Parked Cars Unconstitutional," *New York Times*, April 25, 2019.

3 *Alison Taylor v. City of Saginaw* (2019).

4 Kenneth Culp Davis, *Police Discretion* (St. Paul, Minn.: West, 1975).

5 Egon Bittner, *The Functions of the Police in Modern Society* (Cambridge, Mass.: Oelgeschlager, Gunn & Hain Publishers, 1980), 53.

6 Samuel Walker and Charles M. Katz, *The Police in America: An Introduction*,

4th ed. (Boston: McGraw-Hill, 2002), 174–175.

7 Peter B. Kraska and Louise J. Cubellis, "Militarizing Mayberry and Beyond: Making Sense of American Paramilitary Policing," *Justice Quarterly* (December 1997): 607–629.

8 Willard M. Oliver, *Homeland Security for Policing* (Upper Saddle River,

N.J.: Pearson Prentice Hall, 2007), 114–116.

9 Larry K. Gaines and Victor E. Kappeler, *Policing in America* (Cincinnati, Ohio: LexisNexis, 2008), 183–185.

10 Walker and Katz, *The Police in America*, 195–196.

11 John S. Dempsey and Linda S. Forst, *An Introduction to Policing*, 4th ed. (Belmont, Calif.: Thomson Wadsworth, 2008), 230.

12 Ibid., 213.

13 Lawrence Sherman, Patrick Gartin, and Michael Buerger, "Hot Spots of Predatory Crime: Routine Activities and the Criminology of Place," *Criminology* 27 (1989): 27–55.

14 George Kelling, *Foot Patrol* (Washington, D.C.: National Institute of Justice, 1987).

15 William B. Sanders, *Detective Work: A Study of Criminal Investigations* (New York: Free Press, 1977).

16 Federal Bureau of Investigation, *Law Enforcement Officers Killed and Assaulted 2019*, Law Enforcement Officers Feloniously Killed, Table 23, ucr.fbi.gov/leoka/2019/topic-pages/tables/table-23.xls

17 H. Laurence Ross, *Confronting Drunk Driving: Social Policy for Saving Lives* (New Haven, Conn.: Yale University Press, 1992).

18 James B. Jacobs, *Drunk Driving: An American Dilemma* (Chicago: University of Chicago Press, 1989).

19 Brian A. Reaves, *Police Response to Domestic Violence, 2006–2015* (U.S. Department of Justice Office of Justice Programs Bureau of Justice Statistics, 2017), 9. Available at www.bjs.gov/index.cfm?ty=pbdetail&iid=5907.

20 Franklyn W. Dunford, David Huizinga, and Delbert S. Elliott, "The Role of Arrest in Domestic Assault: The Omaha Police Experiment," *Criminology* 28 (1990): 183–206.

21 Bittner, "Quasi-Military Organization," 171.

22 Robert F. Meier and Gilbert Geis, *Victimless Crime? Prostitution, Drugs, Homosexuality, Abortion* (Los Angeles: Roxbury, 1997).

23 Judy Hails and Randy Borum, "Police Training and Specialized Approaches to Respond to People with Mental Illness," *Crime and Delinquency* 49 (2003): 52–61.

24 John Fuller, *Juvenile Delinquency: Mainstream and Crosscurrents* (Upper Saddle River, N.J.: Prentice Hall, 2009), 395–429.

25 Arthur Rosett, "Discretion, Severity and Legality in Criminal Justice," in *The Invisible Justice System: Discretion and the Law*, eds. Burton Atkins and Mark Pogrebin (Cincinnati, Ohio: Anderson, 1978), 24–33.

26 Ibid., 25.

27 Albert Reiss Jr., "Discretionary Justice in the United States," in *The Invisible Justice System: Discretion and the Law*, eds. Burton Atkins and Mark Pogrebin (Cincinnati, Ohio: Anderson, 1978), 41–58.

28 Melissa Schaefer Morabito, "Horizons of Context: Understanding the Police Decision to Arrest People with Mental Illness," *Psychiatric Services* 58 (December 1, 2007): 1582–1587.

29 Raymond Goldberg, *Drugs across the Spectrum* (Englewood, Colo.: Morton, 1997), 80.

30 Mike Isaacs, "Teen Thanks Skokie Cop Who Paid for Gym Membership," *Chicago Tribune-Skokie Review*, October 24, 2017.

31 Jerome H. Skolnick and Elliott Currie, *Crisis in American Institutions* (Boston: Little, Brown, 1973). See especially the sections on police and criminal law and corrections.

32 Aleksandar Tomic and Jahn K. Hakes, "Case Dismissed: Police Discretion and Racial Differences in Dismissals of Felony Charges," *American Law and Economics Review* 10 (April 1, 2008): 110–141.

33 Davis, *Police Discretion*, 83.

34 Clearly, the police develop strategies that target high-crime areas or events where crime is likely to appear. The difference between the police presence at a symphony orchestra performance and at a basketball tournament is likely to be significant even though the size of the crowd is the same.

35 Igor Areh, Bojan Dobovsek, and Peter Umek, "Citizens' Opinions of Police Procedures," *Policing* 30 (October 1, 2007): 637–650.

36 American Friends Service Committee, "Discretion," in *The Invisible Justice System: Discretion and the Law*, eds. Burton Atkins and Mark Pogrebin (Cincinnati, Ohio: Anderson, 1978), 35–40. This report argues that discretion should be removed from the criminal justice system so that constitutional protections of due process and equal application of the law will apply to everyone.

37 *Silverman v. United States*, 365 U.S. 505, 81 S. Ct. 679 (1961).

38 "Vehicle Search after Arrest Violated Driver's Rights, Rules Wyoming Supreme Court," *Lawyers USA*, June 2, 2008.

39 "A Bullet Box Observed in Plain View on a Person Gives Probable Cause for Arrest," *Narcotics Law Bulletin*, November 1, 2005, 4.

40 *Horton v. California*, 496 U.S. 128, 136–137 (1990).

41 "After Approaching Robbery Suspect, Police Spot Marijuana and Search Car," *Narcotics Law Bulletin*, May 1, 2003, 7–8.

42 *California v. Ciraolo*, 476 U.S. 207, 106 S.Ct. 1809 (1986). *United States v. White*, 401 U.S. 745, 91 S. Ct. 1122 (1971).

43 *United States v. Dunn*, 480 U.S. 294, 107 S.Ct. 1134 (1987).

44 Carlton Bailey, *Criminal Procedure: Model Problems and Outstanding Answers* (New York: Oxford University Press, 2015), 55–73.

45 *Payton v. New York*, 445 U.S. 573, 100 S.Ct. 1371 (1980). White, Burger, and Rehnquist filed the dissenting opinion.

46 *Stanford v. Texas*, 379 U.S. 476, 85 S.Ct. 506 (1965). *Maryland v. Garrison*, 480 U.S. 79, 107 S.Ct. 1013 (1987). *Wilson v. Arkansas*, 514 U.S. 927, 115 S.Ct. 1914 (1995). *Richards v. Wisconsin*, 520 U.S. 385, 117 S.Ct. 1416 (1997).

47 *Schneckloth v. Bustamonte*, 412 U.S. 218, 93 S.Ct. 2041, (1973). *United States v. Rodney*, 956 F.2d 295, 297 (D.C. Cir. 1992). *Illinois v. Rodriguez*, 497 U.S. 177, 110 S.Ct. 2793 (1990).

48 *United States v. Santana*, 427 U.S. 38, 96 S.Ct. 2406 (1976). *Cupp v. Murphy*, 412 U.S. 291, 93 S.Ct. 2000 (1973); *Ker v. California*, 374 U.S. 23, 83 S.Ct. 1623 (1963).

49 Nicola Persico and Petra E. Todd, "The Hit Rates Test for Racial Bias in Motor-Vehicle Searches," *Justice Quarterly* 25 (March 1, 2008): 37.

50 *Carroll v. United States*, 267 U.S. 132, 45 S.Ct. 280 (1925); *Wyoming v. Houghton*, 526 U.S. 295, 119 S.Ct. 1297 (1999).

51 "Constitutional Law—Fourth Amendment—Ninth Circuit Holds That Destructive Search of Spare Tire at Border Is Constitutional.—*United States v. Cortez-Rocha*, 394 F.3d 1115 (9th Cir. 2005)," *Harvard Law Review* 118 (June 1, 2005): 2921–2928.

52 *United States v. Ramsey*, 431 U.S. 606, 97 S.Ct. 1972 (1977).

53 Michael G. Lenett, "Implied Consent in Airport Searches: A Response to Terrorism, *United States v. Pulido-Baquerizo*, 800 F.2D 899 (9th Cir. 1986)," *American Criminal Law Review* 25 (January 1, 1988): 549–575.

54 *State v. Hunter*, 831 P.2d, 1033 (Utah Ct. App. 1992); *New Jersey v. T.L.O.*, 469 U.S. 325, 105 S.Ct. 733 (1985).

55 "Search and Seizure—Suspicionless Drug Testing," *Harvard Law Review* 103 (December 1, 1989): 591.

56 Michael F. Rosenblum, "Security vs. Privacy: An Emerging Employment Dilemma," *Employee Relations Law Journal*, July 1, 1991, 81.

57 *Hester v. United States*, 265 U.S. 57, 44 S.Ct. 445 (1924). *Abel v. United States*, 362 U.S. 217, 80 S.Ct. 683 (1960). *California v. Greenwood*, 486 U.S. 35, 108 S.Ct. 1625 (1988).

58 Bailey, *Criminal Procedure*, 83–84. *California v. Hodari D.*, 499 U.S. 621, 111 S.Ct. 1547 (1991).

59 *Terry v. Ohio*, 392 U.S. 1, 99 S.Ct. 1868 (1968).

60 *State v. Morrison*, Ohio App. 8 Dist. (1999).

61 David Cole, "The Usual Suspects," *Nation*, July 2–9, 2012, 4–6.

62 New York Civil Liberties Union, Stop-and-Frisk Data.

63 Victor Li, "50-year Story of the Miranda Warning Has the Twists of a Cop Show," *ABA Journal*, August 1, 2016.

64 Craig M. Bradley, "Mixed Messages on the Exclusionary Rule," *Trial*, December 1, 2006, 56–59.

Learn more with this chapter's digital tools, including the Oxford Insight Study Guide, at www.oup.com/he/Fuller2e.

Policing: Innovations and Controversies

FEATURES

This SWAT officer is using a mechanical-arm bomb-disposal robot unit. What other less-than-lethal resources does law enforcement have at its disposal?

CJ REFERENCE 6.1

Police Use of Force

What we know with substantial confidence:

- Police use force infrequently.
- Use of force typically occurs at the lower end of the physical spectrum, involving grabbing, pushing, or shoving.
- Use of force typically occurs when a suspect resists arrest.

What we know with modest confidence:

- Use of force appears to be unrelated to an officer's personal characteristics, such as age, gender, and ethnicity.
- Use of force is more likely to occur when police are dealing with people who are under the influence of alcohol or drugs or are mentally ill.

- A small proportion of officers are disproportionately involved in use-of-force incidents.

What we do not know:

- The incidence of wrongful use of force.
- The effect of differences in police organizations, including administrative policies, hiring, training, discipline, and use of technology on excessive and illegal force.
- Influences of situational characteristics on police use of force and the transactional nature of these events.[13]

We call the police in situations that might require an outside party to mediate or to use force on our behalf because they have been trained and are armed and authorized to do so. However, societal expectations put the police in a precarious position: On one hand, we expect them to use reasonable force when our interests are at stake; on the other hand, we decide what reasonable force is only after the fact. Because the legitimate use of police force depends on the situation's context and because the police must make decisions in the heat of the moment and sometimes under dangerous conditions, determining the lawfulness of the use of force is problematic.[14] This puts the police in a no-win situation. Failure to use appropriate force might risk injury or death to themselves or others. The use of too much force could result in disciplinary action. According to Bittner, we ask police to make a decision requiring the exercise of two conflicting parts of the nature of police work: the police must simultaneously balance their physical prowess with their professional acumen.[15]

The expectation of how much and what type of force an officer will use in a given situation varies according to several factors. Time of day, whether the officer is alone or working with a partner, the size and sex of the suspect, and the environment can influence whether, and how much, force is used. It is recommended that police officers use only the force required to bring order to a situation and no more. This is a highly contingent judgment and one for which considerable variation can be expected. For a look at two landmark cases involving police use of force, see Case in Point 6.1 and 6.2.

CASE IN POINT   6.1

Tennessee v. Garner (1985)

THE POINT

Deadly force may be used only if the suspect poses a threat to the lives of police officers or bystanders.

THE CASE

In 1974, Edward Garner, age 15, and a friend were in a house at night at which the owners were not present. A neighbor reported to police that someone had broken into the home. When the officers arrived, they saw someone running away, shouted warnings to stop, then shot at Garner, who was climbing a fence. The officer said that he was "reasonably sure" that Garner was unarmed but thought that once he got over the fence, he would elude capture. One of the bullets struck Garner in the back of the head, and he died later on the operating table. Because the officers suspected the boys of a felony—burglarizing the house—they believed they were justified in shooting at the boys to stop them.

Garner's father filed suit, claiming that his son's constitutional rights were violated. In 1985, the Supreme Court decided that the use of deadly force was not warranted. Justice Byron White wrote, "It is no doubt unfortunate when a suspect who is in sight escapes, but the fact that the police arrive a little late or are a little slower afoot does not always justify killing the suspect. A police officer may not seize an unarmed, non-dangerous suspect by shooting him dead."

THINK ABOUT IT

1. How did the police officers' actions violate Garner's constitutional rights?

CASE IN POINT 6.2

Graham v. Connor (1989)

THE POINT

The Fourth Amendment's objective reasonableness requirement governs police use of force during an arrest.

THE CASE

In November 1984 in Charlotte, North Carolina, Dethorne Graham, a diabetic, had an insulin reaction while at home. He asked his friend, William Berry, to drive him to a convenience store to buy some juice to stabilize his reaction. At the store, Graham entered and saw several people at the register, Graham did not want to wait, so he quickly returned to Berry's car and asked to go to a friend's house to get some juice. Charlotte police officer M. S. Connor, who had been watching Graham, followed Berry's car and stopped it about a half mile away.

Still experiencing an insulin reaction, Graham exited the car and ran around it twice. Berry and Officer Connor stopped Graham and sat him down on the curb where he passed out. The officers then handcuffed Graham.

Several more officers arrived, and they lifted Graham onto the hood of Berry's car. Graham asked the officers to check his wallet for his diabetic identification, but an officer shoved his head into the car hood and told him to shut up. Another officer remarked that Graham was drunk and should go to jail. The officers then threw Graham headlong into the squad car where Graham sustained multiple injuries, including a broken foot. A friend of Graham's arrived with juice, but the officers would not let him have it.

Officer Connor eventually determined that nothing had happened at the store and took Graham home.

Graham sued the police officers and the City of Charlotte, claiming the officers' excessive use of force violated his Fourteenth Amendment rights. The district court ruled that the police applied force in a good-faith effort to maintain and restore discipline, not maliciously and sadistically to cause harm. Graham appealed, but the Court of Appeals affirmed the decision.

However, the U.S. Supreme Court vacated this judgment, holding that Graham's claims should have been analyzed under the Fourth Amendment's objective reasonableness standard. That is, it must be determined if the officers' actions were reasonable from their point of view with the information they had at the time. The case was remanded to the district court for reconsideration under the Fourth Amendment standard. There, the jury concluded that the police officers' actions were objectively reasonable.

THINK ABOUT IT

1. How does this case differ from *Tennessee v. Garner*? How are they alike? Compare the Court's reasoning in *Tennessee* with its reasoning in *Graham*.

April 12, 2015, police in Baltimore, Maryland, arrested Freddie Gray, a 25-year-old black man, after he ran when he saw police officers. When Gray was caught, he said he had trouble breathing and asked for an inhaler, which police did not provide. Officers then placed Gray in the back of a police van without a seat belt. After a stop during which officers shackled Gray's hands and feet, the van continued. After a couple more stops, during which Gray requested medical help, the van arrived at the police station. There, a medic determined that Gray was no longer breathing, in cardiac arrest, and severely injured. Gray, who had suffered a spine injury, fell into a coma and died on April 19, 2015.[23] Protests and riots spread after Gray's funeral. At least 20 police officers were injured, and 250 people were arrested. Hundreds of businesses were damaged, and vehicles and buildings were burned. Maryland Army National Guard troops were deployed, and a state of emergency was declared in Baltimore. On May 1, 2015, Gray's death was ruled a homicide, and charges were issued against the six officers involved in the incident, including a charge of second-degree murder against the officer driving the van. The state of emergency was lifted five days later.[24] Eventually, all six officers were cleared of state charges, and federal charges were dropped.[25]

Strategies to Control Use of Force

Police departments have traditionally struggled with controlling their officers' discretion and have instituted strategies to ensure that they enforce the law in a fair manner that enhances the safety of themselves and the community. These strategies to evaluate and control police officers' use of force include:

› Training. Police departments have constructed training programs that attempt to develop realistic scenarios in which police officers have an opportunity to consider when and how much force should be used in particular situations.[26]

Many critics of police militarization say police officers should not have the same equipment as the military. Proponents of military gear for police counter that they need such equipment because so many potential assailants are similarly armed. What is your opinion?

> Identifying problem-prone officers. Not every police officer is equally equipped to engage in all forms of policing. Some officers are effective in dealing with the public, whereas others are better at dealing with drug dogs, directing traffic, or working a crime scene. Police records can reveal that some officers have repeated experiences in using force (sometimes excessive). For example, in 2020, Minneapolis police officer Derek Chauvin and three other officers were arrested and charged in connection with the death of George Floyd, who died during an arrest when Chauvin placed his knee on Floyd's neck for almost nine minutes. Chauvin had been the subject of at least 17 misconduct complaints over 20 years.[27]

> Ethics education. The police officer's role is complicated. The officer must often make quick decisions that can have significant consequences not only for the maintenance of public order, but also for the probability of identifying perpetrators of crime and making lawful arrests. Many law enforcement administrators believe that ethics education reinforces officers' adherence to departmental policy and procedures and their ability to resolve moral dilemmas.[28]

Derek Chauvin was charged with second-degree murder and manslaughter in the death of George Floyd, a black man who died after being restrained by him and three other Minneapolis police officers in May 2020.

PAUSE AND REVIEW

1. According to Bittner, what are the restrictions on police use of force, and why are these restrictions considered "essentially meaningless"?

2. How is the excessive use of force by police officers problematic?

6.2 The Militarization of Police

Describe the issues inherent in the militarization of police departments.

Traditionally, major distinctions have been made between the roles of the police and those of the military. Police officers are tasked with serving citizens and protecting them from each other, whereas the military is responsible for protecting citizens from foreign threats. This distinction is somewhat codified by the 1878 Posse Comitatus Act.

Posse comitatus, according to *Black's Law Dictionary*, is "the power or force of the county. The entire population of a county above the age of 15, which a sheriff may summon to his assistance in certain cases as to aid him in keeping the peace, in pursuing and arresting felons, etc."[29] The original intent of the Posse Comitatus Act was to end the use of federal troops to monitor state elections in the former Confederate states.[30] In the 20th century, the act was extended to all domestic services with the enactment of Title 10 U.S. Code, Section 375. The act generally prohibits U.S. military personnel from direct participation in law enforcement.[31]

Congress has enacted exceptions to the act that allow the military to assist civilian law enforcement agencies, such as in enforcing drug laws or suppressing insurrections. The act also allows the president to use federal troops to enforce federal laws when rebellion makes it difficult to enforce the law. Another exception allows for the enforcement of prohibitions regarding nuclear materials or biological or chemical weapons of mass destruction when it is determined that an emergency poses a serious threat and is beyond the capability of civilian law enforcement.[32]

Despite these regulations, there seems to be nothing preventing the police from using military-style tactics and equipment to enforce the law, and the Posse Comitatus Act does not address this concern. As such, the general militarization of the police has been under way for more than two decades.[33]

Posse comitatus—

"The power or force of the county. The entire population of a county above the age of 15, which a sheriff may summon to his assistance in certain cases as to aid him in keeping the peace, in pursuing and arresting felons, etc."[34]

1. The symbolic assailant. Police officers must always be on guard. They are systematically trained and culturally reinforced to consider everyone a potential assailant until they can size up the situation and determine that an individual poses no threat. This is easy for them to do when confronted with a large, drunk, belligerent man wielding a knife. It is less easy when interacting with an elderly woman who seems lost and disoriented. Police officers will not relax until they are confident that the woman poses no harm to herself or others. They cannot assume that she is of no threat until they can independently establish that she is what she seems to be, which is accomplished based on behavioral and contextual clues. The situation of the knife-wielding man, on the other hand, alerts officers to keep their guard up.

2. Danger. Police work can be dangerous (see Figure 6.3). Although death in the line of duty and serious physical injury are relatively infrequent, the possibility of confrontation is always there. Actually, police are drawn to the more dangerous assignments, as a function of both job prestige and excitement.[60] (See A Closer Look 6.1 for why policing is becoming safer.)

3. Social isolation. The public treats police officers differently. Whereas police officers may perceive an individual as a symbolic assailant, the public sees the police officer as a symbolic authority figure. Thus, even when an individual has done nothing wrong, he or she might be wary of an officer because of the perceived power the officer has to detain, question, search, and arrest. Social isolation causes many officers to limit their social interactions to situations in which other officers are around.

4. Solidarity. The combination of danger and social isolation creates a sense of solidarity in the police subculture. An "us against them" mentality exists to cope not only with law violators, but also with the public in general. The police may feel that the public takes them for granted and does not take enough responsibility for helping fight the war against lawbreakers.[64]

The occupational culture of the police, like many other occupational cultures, fosters certain personality characteristics in its practitioners.[65] Danger, authority, potential symbolic assailants, and social isolation are features of the occupation that encourage the construction of the policeman's working personality.

FIGURE 6.3   Federal Law Enforcement Officers Assaulted These four federal law enforcement agencies had the most officers assaulted in 2019. No agents were killed in 2019. Give possible reasons for the greater number of officers assaulted in the Bureau of Indian Affairs.

Source: Federal Bureau of Investigation, Federal Law Enforcement Officers Killed and Assaulted, 2019, *Table 73, ucr. fbi.gov/leoka/2019/topic-pages/ tables/table-73.xls.*

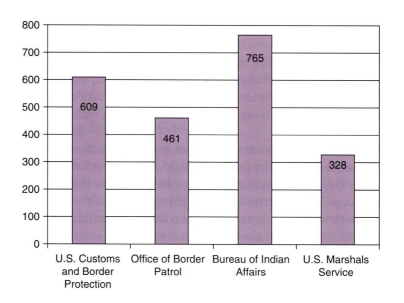

A CLOSER LOOK 6.1
Policing Is Getting Safer

Being a police officer can be dangerous. Police have the highest rate of occupational violent victimization and are behind only taxi drivers in the rate of workplace homicides. Given the occurrence of high-profile police killings in Brooklyn, New York, Dallas, Texas, and Baton Rouge, Louisiana, some observers believe that there is a "war on cops."[61]

However, one study has concluded that policing is not as dangerous as it used to be. Using a comprehensive definition of police deaths that is not limited to felonious assaults and that includes accidents, heart attacks, and duty-related illness, the study found that the overall rate of line-of-duty deaths of police officers has declined by 75 percent and deaths of officers by felonious assault has declined by 80 percent.[62]

Several factors have made policing a safer occupation. First, body armor, which has greatly improved in recent years, is being used more extensively. Second, police training has improved. Deaths from accidental gunfire have dropped by 59 percent, and deaths from aircraft crashes are down 70 percent. As more officers are trained to avoid using force by practicing de-escalation techniques, crisis-intervention methods, and better tactical engagement procedures, modern police have a more sophisticated set of skills to handle potentially violent encounters.[63]

THINK ABOUT IT

1. Can you think of some other policies, techniques, or equipment that could make the work of police officers safer?

This process may have far-reaching implications for the recruitment, training, and control of police officers.[66] For example, how much money and resources should be spent on the selection and training of officers if the very nature of law enforcement occupations instills those individuals with an occupational perspective that dictates how they view the job and respond to suspects and the public?

POLICE UNIONS

Police unions are the official representatives for police officers in collective bargaining with their employers. There is no primary national police union because police departments operate on a local level.[67] Local police unions may be affiliated with national organizations or fraternal orders, such as the Fraternal Order of Police, the International Union of Police Associations (which is affiliated with the American Federation of Labor and Congress of Industrial Organizations, or AFL CIO), the Teamsters, or the American Federation of State, County, and Municipal Employees.[68] Small departments usually do not have unions, but most large urban police departments do. Exactly how many officers belong to unions is unknown.[69]

Police unions influence nearly every aspect of the police officer's job, including management, discipline and accountability, the police subculture, and community relations. Unions may demand higher salaries, improved benefits and working conditions, more participation in setting work schedules, and more protection for employees during disciplinary procedures. Unions have been criticized for resisting more stringent demands on police accountability, especially in use-of-force incidents.[70]

Several states have laws or policies, sometimes called "law enforcement officer bills of rights," that give police officers special employment protections. In other states, union contracts may provide similar protections. Police officers typically have more protections than other government employees, which are fervently defended by unions. According to some observers, such protections sometimes make it more expensive and difficult for supervisors to discipline an officer than the effort is worth.[71] One study of police discipline found that union arbitrators "routinely cut in half" rigorous efforts at discipline.[72] As the nature of police work evolves, the relationship between police unions, supervisors and management, and reformers will likely continue to be tumultuous.

Corruption

Although police corruption has been a significant problem for some agencies at particular times, it is likely not as pervasive as the issues of the policeman's working personality. However, the nature and extent of police corruption are worth our attention because of the constant temptations placed before police officers and because trust in the criminal justice system is one of the cornerstones of a democratic society.[73] The history of policing is replete with examples not only of corruption of individual officers, but also of the widespread, systemic corruption of entire departments and the municipal governments they serve.[74] Unfortunately, no official statistics are kept on the prevalence of police corruption, so it is difficult to estimate how much occurs.

In 1972, the Knapp Commission issued its report on police corruption in New York City. Based on the revelations made by undercover detective Frank Serpico, 19 officers were indicted for accepting payoffs. Subsequent investigations revealed even more violators. In examining this systematic corruption, the Knapp Commission distinguished between two types of corrupt police officers: "meat-eaters" and "grass-eaters." The grass-eaters took bribes but did not solicit them. The meat-eaters actively sought situations that they could exploit for financial gain.[75]

Not all police officers have equal opportunities to engage in corruption. The nature of the department, the community, and the particular assignment all influence how much temptation is placed in the officers' paths or how fertile the situation is for the meat-eater who aggressively seeks situations to exploit. Historically, illegal gambling, prostitution, substance prohibition, and other organized-crime activities have been major sources of police corruption. Presently, because of the war on drugs, tremendous amounts of money are changing hands, putting narcotics officers in positions to engage in corrupt acts. According to scholars Peter K. Manning and Lawrence John Redlinger, narcotics law enforcement can invite police corruption in at least seven ways.

1. Taking bribes. Officers can take bribes in several ways. They can provide advance warning of police raids, or they can take bribes not to arrest those caught using or selling drugs. Additionally, police officers are reported to have testified badly in court in exchange for a bribe.

2. Using drugs. On occasion, police officers might use the very drugs they are mandated to suppress. Additionally, they might use other drugs to stay awake. The incidence of police officers using illegal drugs is probably not as serious a problem today as it might have been a generation ago. Many police agencies require random drug tests of employees, which deters illegal drug use.

3. Buying and selling narcotics. Police might give drugs to addicts to acquire their sworn testimony or to informers to pay them off. Given the limited budgets for operating expenditures such as money to buy drugs for investigations, enterprising narcotics agents might sell drugs to finance operations the department cannot afford. However, these activities are still considered a form of corruption and are not sanctioned by police administrators. Finally, "meat-eating" officers have been known to sell narcotics and use the money for personal gain.[76]

4. Appropriating seized property. Property relevant to a criminal offense must be seized by the police department and held until the case is concluded, at which point the department determines whether to return it to its rightful owner, destroy it, or convert it to government use. The police must scrupulously account for all seized cash, drugs, guns, and automobiles. Although cash used by police to buy drugs is marked and the serial numbers are recorded, the cash seized from drug dealers is subject to theft by the arresting officers. Some of the cash and drugs seized at a crime scene might be diverted before they are officially logged as evidence.

5. Conducting illegal searches and seizures. Police can engage in corrupt misconduct in several ways when initiating searches and seizures on drug suspects. Lying about smelling marijuana or seeing drugs in "plain sight" is one method officers can use to claim probable cause to conduct a search. Officers may plant evidence on a suspect by "flaking," which consists of finding evidence the officer planted on the suspect, or "padding," the practice of adding drugs to a seizure to justify a raise in the charge from misdemeanor to felony. The police can use these practices to entice drug dealers and users to offer bribes of cash or sexual favors for lenient treatment.

6. Protecting informants. Sometimes the police are willing to tolerate a certain level of crime to battle more serious infractions. This becomes a judgment call that can lead to substantial harm to victims, the community, and the reputation of the law enforcement agencies. Both within and between criminal justice agencies there are rivalries, competition, and distrust. The narcotics division might overlook the burglaries of a confidential informant if it is receiving good information that may facilitate the bust of a big drug dealer. A federal agency might hide the offenses of a snitch from a local police department if doing so furthers its agenda. Informants might coax all kinds of rewards, such as money, drugs, or reduced charges, from several agencies at the same time based on the promise of the same information.

7. Using violence. The police might use illegal force in a number of ways that enables them to prosecute or extort lawbreakers. Narcotics officers might use unwarranted violence to cope with drug dealers. They might claim the suspect "went for his gun" and then kill the suspect. They might threaten to tell others in the drug trade that the suspect is an informant, ensuring that person's violent death at the hands of others.[77]

These forms of police behavior all represent some type of corruption. They might sometimes be used to advance the cause of legitimate police work, but because they are illegal, they are of concern to police administrators and police scholars. A department that allows its officers to operate in devious ways inevitably exposes itself to the scandal of corruption and the problems of litigation.[78] Therefore, it seems prudent to consider these types of corruption as pressing issues within law enforcement.

Alcohol Use as a Coping Mechanism

Research has found that the stress of police work is highly related to alcohol abuse. Other coping mechanisms, such as emotional distancing (officers learn to objectify their emotions when faced with dead or injured people, victims, abused children, and so on) and cynicism, were found to be related to alcohol use either directly or indirectly. Studies found that alcohol was used as a method to relieve the inherent stress of police work 20 times as often as cynicism or emotional distancing. In fact, when those methods failed, alcohol use became more likely.[79]

unless officers find ways to cope with the stress in a healthy manner, the job can become overwhelming.[91]

Why would police officers resort to suicide at rates higher than those in most other occupations? The answer lies in the types of stress we have already discussed and in the access the police have to handguns. Firearms are a constant feature in the lives of police officers. About 97 percent of officer suicides involve the officer's own service gun.[92] Police officers are trained in the use of guns, carry them on a daily basis, are prepared emotionally to use guns in the pursuit of lawbreakers, and so have been sufficiently desensitized to the effects of guns.

It is hard to think of any other occupation, including the military, in which guns are such a constant part of the job. In fact, the phrase "he ate his gun," is part of the police lexicon. It is unfair, however, to argue that the gun is solely responsible for police suicide rates. Although firearms are an efficient way to kill oneself, a determined person will find a way regardless of whether there is a convenient gun. It just happens that for police officers, there is always a convenient gun.

PAUSE AND REVIEW

1. What factors, besides stress, influence police officers to turn to alcohol?
2. In what ways do the four key elements of the policeman's working personality contribute to the police subculture?

LEARNING OBJECTIVE 6.5

Argue for and against the use of less-than-lethal weapons.

LEARNING OBJECTIVE 6.6

Define information technology and describe how it may be incorporated into police work.

6.4 Policing and Technology

Many of the recent innovations in law enforcement are related to transparency, citizen safety, and the ability to acquire and store information about law-abiding people, suspects, and offenders. For example, videos posted to the Internet and social media have revealed the controversial treatment of some suspects by police, including beatings and shootings, thus provoking a public call for greater police transparency in their activities. Efforts to control violent individuals and crowds in order to protect citizens have led to the development of less-than-lethal weapons. Finally, the need for increased national security and the desire for citizen safety have led to increased active acquisition of information about U.S. residents. Thus, body-worn cameras for police officers, less-than-lethal weapons, and information technology are new tools that have greatly affected policing in the United States.

Body-Worn Cameras

Body-worn cameras (BWCs) are devices that record interactions between police officers and the public. Officers usually wear the camera on the shoulder lapel or chest so that it can record the scene in front of the officer. Law enforcement can use these recordings to document statements, observations, and other evidence.[93] The main reasons that law enforcement agencies gave for acquiring the cameras were to improve officer safety and the quality of evidence and to reduce civilian complaints and agency liability.[94]

As of 2016, 47 percent of the country's 15,328 general-purpose law enforcement agencies (such as local police departments, most sheriffs' offices, and highway patrols) had BWCs. Of the agencies that had purchased BWCs, 57 percent had distributed the cameras to all the intended officers who were wearing them on a regular basis. About 60 percent of these agencies allowed the officer who wore the camera to access its recordings.[95]

In light of recent police shootings, and given the pace of technological advance in the last two decades, many observers assert that police officers should always wear cameras. One study on body-worn cameras, conducted by the Rialto, California, Police Department, found that equipping officers with cameras reduced use-of-force incidents by 50 percent and complaints against officers by 90 percent.[96] Another study revealed that some law enforcement administrators believe body-worn cameras would be useful for the following reasons:

> Cameras would strengthen police accountability by documenting encounters between officers and the public, as well as provide video evidence for the public.

> Cameras would prevent confrontations by improving officer professionalism and the behavior of the individuals who are being recorded.

> Camera recordings would reveal internal agency problems by disclosing any officer misconduct.

> Camera recordings could be used for training and monitoring, as well as provide evidence for investigations and prosecutions.[97]

However, a 2017 study of Metropolitan Police Department officers in Washington, D.C., arrived at a different conclusion, finding no statistically significant effects on police behavior. The study advised that the use of BWCs would likely not lead to major reductions in the use of force, the number of civilian complaints, or other sweeping changes in officer behavior.[98] Also, in jurisdictions where officers wear cameras, the handling of camera video has become increasingly contentious. States that restrict the public release of body-camera video say doing so could hinder investigations and trials by tainting witnesses and jurors. However, the ACLU asserts that not allowing the release of body-camera video defeats the purpose of recording it in the first place.[99]

Meanwhile, videos of police confrontations, often recorded by bystanders on their mobile phones, continue to be posted on the Internet. Although the Internet contains many portrayals of the police helping people, violent incidents receive the most attention. Thus, the public is demanding more scrutiny of the police and additional

A police officer holds a body-camera video recorder. Why do some police officers turn their cameras off?

TABLE 6.1 Less-Than-Lethal Weaponry

	WEAPON	ERA	USAGE AND EFFECTS
Kinetic impact munitions	Guard rounds	World War II	Copper-clad bullets used by sentries that had fluted cartridges to lessen their impact. Shot with conventional guns, guard rounds were designed not to inflict injury in case a sentry accidentally shot a friendly soldier.[1]
	Rock salt	1930s	During the Great Depression, train guards loaded shotguns with rock salt to keep unauthorized riders off freight trains.[2]
	Teakwood batons	1960s	In Hong Kong, British soldiers fired teakwood batons from flare guns to disperse crowds. The batons were fired at the ground and skipped up to hit targets at the knees. However, a baton was known to have killed at least one person.[3]
	Rubber and plastic bullets, chemical filled "paintballs," beanbags, bird-shot	1970s–current	Fired from low-velocity shotguns and flare guns. Intended to cause pain and bruising with no permanent injury. Some projectiles might contain chemicals to cause stinging and burning on contact. At least one person has died from being struck with a beanbag in the chest. Some projectiles can penetrate the body.[4]
Chemical	CN gas (Mace)	1960s, with limited current use	Both are forms of tear gas. The newer CS is more potent and less toxic than CN. Both types of gas canisters are thrown by hand or fired from a special gun. CN and CS affect primarily the eyes and skin.
	CS gas	current	
	Pepper spray (oleoresin capsicum)	current	Causes a burning sensation in the mucus membranes, eyes, and skin. Usually safe, with few side effects. Originally made with a substance from chili peppers.[5]
	Superlubricants and superadhesives	current	"Goo" that is usually extremely sticky or extremely slippery.
Electroshock and microwave	Taser	current	Uses a compressed-gas cartridge to launch two probes up to 35 feet. The probes have wires that attach to skin and clothing. The Taser can deliver 3,000 volts through about 2 inches of clothing.[6] The shock affects the voluntary nervous system and prevents coordinated activity.[7]
	Stun gun	1980s	The stun gun resembles an electric razor and has to touch the body to deliver a shock. In New York City, several officers and sergeants were charged with using stun guns on suspects during interrogations.[8]
	Active denial technology	developing	Generates and emits microwaves that cause a burning sensation in the skin in both crowds and targeted individuals.[9]
Audio and visual munitions	Flash-bang grenades, the Long Range Acoustic Device, laser blinding devices	current and developing	These "light–sound" devices divert or confuse targets. The Long Range Acoustic Device can make a sound that can inflict an instant headache on anyone within about 1,000 feet.[10] Laser blinding devices use light to temporarily blind or disorient targets.

	WEAPON	ERA	USAGE AND EFFECTS
Mechanical	Entanglements	current	Nets, usually launched by a low-velocity gun or other launch device.
	Water	current	High-pressure streams of water launched from cannons or hoses.

[1] Alan Dobrowolski and Sue Moore, "Less Lethal Weapons and Their Impact on Patient Care," *Topics in Emergency Medicine* 27, no. 1 (January–March 2005): 45.

[2-5] Ibid.

[6] Al Baker, "Tasers Getting More Prominent Role in Crime Fighting in City," *New York Times*, June 15, 2008, late edition, A25.

[7] Dobrowolski and Moore, "Less Lethal Weapons and Their Impact on Patient Care."

[8] Ibid.

[9] "The Future of Crowd Control," *Economist*, December 4, 2004, 11.

[10] Ibid.

The arguments in support of LTL weapons point to the fact that they are not intended to cause fatalities while also protecting police. In many instances throughout the world, police have been outnumbered by rioting crowds and have been barely able to protect themselves, much less the property or the lives of others. Crowd control is a critical issue, especially in urban areas and at public events.

The primary critique of LTL weapons is that, although their use does result in fewer fatalities than the use of firearms, there is the potential for misuse and their adoption as substitutes for "intelligent and professional policing and soldiering."[113] Critics fear that instead of addressing the root of social problems, governments will simply rely on the use of reduced force through police departments and militaries—which are increasingly becoming involved in police-style actions—to control populaces.[114]

DNA Databases

Information technology is technology that helps to manage information by collecting it, storing it, retrieving it, and/or sending it. Several types of technology—not just computers or personal information devices—can be considered information technology. Over the past few decades, local police departments have gradually integrated information technology into their work. One of the most important technological innovations has been the computerized database. Large police departments have their own computer networks. Small departments with lower budgets might hire a private, third-party company to maintain their databases. Some jurisdictions combine their databases or allow other jurisdictions access.[115]

A particularly useful and controversial type of database is the DNA database. DNA, or deoxyribonucleic acid, is the material in living organisms that determines heredity, and nearly every cell in a person's body has the same DNA. This makes DNA especially useful for identifying individuals. Currently, the military keeps DNA records of all in service, and 30 states and the federal government collect DNA from arrestees.[116] Also, under limited circumstances, police may search the databases of private genealogy companies whose clients submit their DNA in order to search for other members of their family tree.[117]

The National DNA Index System (NDIS) grew out of the FBI's Combined DNA Index System (CODIS), a project begun in 1990. All 50 states and the federal government require some types of convicted offenders to provide a DNA sample for inclusion in CODIS and state databases.[118] CODIS has indices for convicted offenders, forensic evidence, arrestees, missing persons, and unidentified human remains. CODIS generates leads in cases in which biological evidence is recovered

compassionate, less aggressive, and less competitive, see their job from a different perspective and hence adopt different policing styles than do men."[129] Advocates for women in policing agree, adding that the aggressive and competitive perspective brought to the street by male police officers is appropriate for only part of the police mission, and a small part at that. The emphasis on crime control must coexist with an emphasis on order maintenance and social support. The mindset brought by women who have been socialized into the roles of caregiving and nurturing significantly expands the nature of the police role.

In summary, the increased participation of women in policing has provided some important sociological lessons. There is more than one way to be a good police officer. According to some studies, the historically male-dominated police culture has been enriched by the inclusion of women, who bring different perspectives to the job. At one time, it was believed that the police subculture shaped recruits into a **policeman's working personality** that was determined by danger, violence, aggression, isolation, and authority. Now the culture appears to be changing as women introduce other values into the policing culture.[130]

Policeman's working personality—The mindset of police who must deal with danger, authority, isolation, and suspicion while appearing to be efficient.

Minorities as Police Officers

The United States has a checkered past in its treatment of minorities, and the criminal justice system has experienced its own stresses in accommodating the inevitable progress of opening occupations to people who have experienced prejudice and discrimination.[131] Historically, law enforcement has not led the way in providing equality to disenfranchised groups. However, some progress has been made, and the rate of improvement has increased with each passing decade.[132]

At times in the distant past, people of color worked as law enforcement officers, though only rarely and discontinuously. People of color were first employed

In 2016, the New York City Police Department changed its uniform policy to allow Sikh officers to wear turbans and grow beards up to an inch long for religious purposes. Relaxing traditional grooming standards is one way that law enforcement can be more welcoming to minorities and create more diverse police departments. What minorities may still be underrepresented in U.S. police departments?

as police officers in New Orleans in 1805. The officers were former African slaves who had won their freedom by serving with the French or Spanish militia, and they acted primarily to keep slaves under control and to catch runaways. These police gradually lost their jobs to whites and did not engage in law enforcement again until after the Civil War.

During Reconstruction, former slaves enjoyed a brief period during which they performed the same type of law enforcement duties as whites. This period of occupational equality was also brief, and soon, as in other aspects of politics, law enforcement was completely dominated by whites. With the exception of tokenism brought on by political patronage in northern cities, police officers of color had few opportunities. Even when they were allowed into the occupation, their roles were greatly limited. People of color were responsible for policing their neighborhoods and were not allowed the full range of duties or to advance into administration.[133]

A new era of opportunity for people of color in all aspects of society began during the civil rights movement in the 1950s and continues today. Led by influential individuals such as Dr. Martin Luther King Jr., the civil rights movement called attention to the problems people of color experienced in the social, economic, legal, and educational arenas. Although far from complete, the civil rights movement has been successful in eliminating much of the institutional racism that had been part of the American social fabric.

Today, police officers of color can be found on virtually every large police force in the country. About 27 percent of local police officers are members of racial or ethnic minorities.[134] Some medium and small departments do not have minorities, but this may have more to do with location and population than with discrimination. Diversity has increased in all population categories since 1987.[135] The law no longer allows police agencies to exclude job candidates based on race.

This march toward equality has not been easy. Many police officers of color were met with hostility when they sought to serve their communities. As police agencies began to integrate, police officers of color faced **double marginality**; that is, not only did their fellow police officers treat them differently, but other people of color also looked upon them with suspicion.[136] In larger cities, with more and more police officers of color, the double marginality issue has decreased. However, when we look at female police officers of color, we see a different type of marginality. These officers feel the dual prejudices against women and minorities as they attempt to develop a place for themselves in law enforcement.[137]

The effects of racism are sometimes difficult to overcome because both whites and minorities must adjust to new ways of thinking about what police officers look like. In policing, the contributions of all Americans make the community not only more tolerant of others but also more supportive of our institutions.

Double marginality— The multiple outsider status of women and minority police officers as a result of being treated differently by their fellow officers.

PAUSE AND REVIEW

1. What are some arguments that have been used to exclude women from policing? What are some criticisms of those arguments?

2. Why do women police officers of color experience double marginality differently than their male counterparts?

FOCUS ON ETHICS — To Trust a Partner

As a new woman police officer, you have sailed through the police academy and in-service training with high marks, and you are excited to be teamed with one of the most popular and respected officers on the force. The two of you work well together. He treats you with respect and increasingly gives you more authority in doing your job. You are developing mutual trust, and you could not be happier with your assignment. However, in the last few weeks you have begun to become concerned about your partner's emotional stability.

When the squad goes out for a drink after the shift, you notice that your partner gets quite drunk. One Saturday night after a particularly stressful shift that included a high-speed chase, shots fired, and the wrestling of a suspect to the ground, your partner confides in you that he is chronically depressed. After several beers, he admits that he and his wife are separating and that his children are the only passion he still has in life. Then the shocker comes. He looks around to make sure no other officers are listening and then tells you he has been having fantasies of "eating his gun." In the academy, they told you to take all talk of suicide seriously, but you are committed to maintaining the trust you have developed with your partner.

WHAT DO YOU DO?

1. Seek advice about your partner's depression from the police psychologist.
2. Try to counsel your partner, and tell no one about his depression.
3. Ask for a new partner.

For more insight on how someone might respond to such an ethical dilemma, visit Oxford Learning Link at *www.oup.com/he/Fuller2e* to watch a video that connects this scenario to a real-world situation.

Summary

LEARNING OBJECTIVE 6.1 Identify some of the problems associated with the excessive use of force by police officers.	Legal liability. Officers who severely injure or kill citizens expose the department and the locality to legal proceedings. Physical injury or death. The use of excessive force may injure or even kill people. Loss of citizen respect. Police officers must have the cooperation of citizens to do their job in an effective and professional way. When they use excessive force, they forfeit that respect. Community reaction. The actions of police officers can generate dissatisfaction and outrage from citizens who engage in public protest, and, in some cases, riotous behavior as a response.
LEARNING OBJECTIVE 6.2 Describe the issues inherent in the militarization of police departments.	The relationship between the police and the community. In many communities, police militarization hinders policing strategies aimed at integrating officers into community life by making police appear unapproachable and alienating citizens. Reorientation of the police identity. Rather than adopting community-oriented policing practices in which officers identify as part of the community, many officers have adopted the military model, which views all citizens as potential violent criminals and promotes fear and intimidation. An increase in private policing. There will likely be more use of paramilitary security around businesses, neighborhoods, and schools.

LEARNING OBJECTIVE **6.3** Identify the major problems associated with police stress and burnout.	The stress of police work is highly related to alcohol abuse. The police officer may experience a change in his or her relationship with a spouse and/or children. Police families experience stress when the officer treats his or her spouse and children like potential suspects. Finally, law enforcement has one of the highest suicide rates of any occupation.
LEARNING OBJECTIVE **6.4** Outline the four key elements of the policeman's working personality.	The symbolic assailant. Officers are systematically trained and culturally reinforced to consider everyone a potential assailant until they can size up the situation and determine that an individual poses no threat. Danger. The possibility of confrontation is always present. Police are drawn to more dangerous assignments as a function of both prestige and excitement. Social isolation. The public treats police officers differently. Whereas police officers may perceive an individual as a symbolic assailant, the public sees the police officer as a symbolic authority figure. Solidarity. The combination of danger and social isolation creates a sense of solidarity in the police subculture. An "us against them" mentality exists to cope with not only law violators, but also the public in general.
LEARNING OBJECTIVE **6.5** Argue for and against the use of less-than-lethal weapons.	Less-than-lethal weapons are not intended to cause fatalities; they also protect police. However, despite the fact that their usage results in fewer fatalities than the use of firearms, there is the potential for misuse.
LEARNING OBJECTIVE **6.6** Define information technology and describe how it may be incorporated into police work.	Information technology is technology that helps to manage information by collecting it, storing it, retrieving it, and/or sending it. Several types of information technology have been incorporated into police work, such as body cameras, in-vehicle computers, automated vehicle license-plate readers, computerized databases, websites, and social media.
LEARNING OBJECTIVE **6.7** Name arguments historically used to exclude women from policing and criticisms of those arguments.	Women are not physically strong enough to be police officers. Critics point out that few police officers can win a fight against young, athletically gifted persons. Police officers must use persuasion to make arrests without fighting, use their weapons when their safety or the safety of others is at risk, and depend on other officers to help subdue suspects, tasks of which women are capable. Women bring different psychological attributes to police work. Advocates for women in policing assert that the aggressive and competitive perspective brought by male police officers is appropriate for only part of the police mission. The emphasis on crime control must coexist with an emphasis on order maintenance and social support. The caregiving and nurturing mindset brought by women significantly expands the nature of the police role.
LEARNING OBJECTIVE **6.8** Define the concept of double marginality.	Double marginality refers to the multiple outsider status experienced by both male and female minority police officers. As police agencies began to integrate, police officers of color were treated differently by their fellow officers and were viewed with suspicion by the people of color they policed.

Critical Reflections

1. How has law enforcement performed relative to other occupations in providing women and minorities equal employment opportunities?

2. What factors govern how much and what type of force an officer will use in a given situation?

3. In what ways is policing a stressful occupation? What strategies can be employed to reduce this stress?

4. How is technology affecting the behavior of law enforcement officers?

Key Terms

Double marginality **p. 187**
Gender **p. 184**

Policeman's working personality **p. 186**

Posse comitatus **p. 167**
Use of force **p. 160**

Notes

1 Clarence Williams, "She Pointed a Gun at Police and Asked to Die," *Washington Post*. February 12, 2018, www.washingtonpost.com/local/public-safety/she-pointed-a-gun-at-police-and-asked-to-be-shot-they-used-drones-to-intercede-instead/2018/02/11/419587c2-0acc-11e8-8890-372e2047c935_story.html.

2 Ibid.

3 Ibid.

4 Ibid.

5 Ibid.

6 For an excellent discussion of how occupations, especially the police, establish their mandates, see Peter K. Manning, "The Police: Mandate, Strategies, and Appearances," in *The Police and Society: Touchstone Readings*, 2d ed., ed. Victor E. Kappeler (Prospect Heights, Ill.: Waveland Press, 1999).

7 International Association of Chiefs of Police, Police Use of Force in America 2001, www.bjs.gov/index.cfm?ty=tp&tid=84, p. 1.

8 Manning, "The Police: Mandate, Strategies, and Appearances," 100–101.

9 Thomas Barker, Ronald D. Hunter, and Jeffery P. Rush, *Police Systems and Practices: An Introduction* (Englewood Cliffs, N.J.: Prentice Hall, 1994). These authors identified three primary roles for law enforcement: crime fighting, order maintenance, and service. They discussed the consequences of the crime-fighter image that they contended is promoted by the public, the media, and the police themselves. These authors said of the crime-fighter image: "in addition to creating

unrealistic expectations about the police's ability to reduce crime, this narrow view prevents an informed analysis of the use of police resources" (p. 102).

10 *Pearson v. Callahan* (2009).

11 Nina Totenberg, " Supreme Court Weighs Qualified Immunity for Police Accused of Misconduct," *National Public Radio*, June 8, 2020.

12 Egon Bittner, *The Functions of the Police in Modern Society* (Cambridge, Mass.: Oelgeschlager, Gunn & Hain, 1980), 37–38.

13 Kenneth Adams, "What We Know about Police Use of Force," in *Use of Force by Police: Overview of National and Local Data*, NCJ 176330 (Washington, D.C.: National Institute of Justice, October 1999).

14 James J. Fyfe, "The Split-Second Syndrome and Other Determinants of Police Violence," in *Critical Issues in Policing: Contemporary Readings*, 4th ed., eds. Roger G. Dunham and Geoffrey P. Alpert (Prospect Heights, Ill.: Waveland Press, 2001), 583–598.

15 Bittner, *The Functions of the Police in Modern Society*.

16 Laurence Miller, "Why Cops Kill: The Psychology of Police Deadly Force Encounters," *Aggression and Violent Behavior* 22 (May 2015): 97–111.

17 Liz Farmer, "Misconduct Is Increasingly a Financial Issue," *Governing*, June 20, 2018, www.governing.com/topics/finance/gov-police-misconduct-growing-financial-issue.html.

18 Duren Banks, Paul Ruddle, Erin Kennedy, and Michael G. Planty, *Arrest-Related Deaths Program Redesign

Study, 2015–16: Preliminary Findings* (U.S. Department of Justice Office of Justice Programs, Bureau of Justice Statistics, 2016), 2.

19 Brad W. Smith and Malcolm D. Holmes. "Police Use of Excessive Force in Minority Communities: A Test of the Minority Threat, Place, and Community Accountability Hypotheses." *Social Problems* 61, no. 1 (February 2014): 83–104.

20 K. M. Lersch, "Police Misconduct and Malpractice: A Critical Analysis of Citizens' Complaints," *Policing: An International Journal of Police Strategies and Management* 21, no. 1 (1998): 80–96.

21 Lynn Langton and Matthew Durose, *Police Behavior during Traffic and Street Stops, 2011* (U.S. Department of Justice Office of Justice Programs Bureau of Justice Statistics, 2013), 1.

22 Sheryl Gay Stolberg, Ron Nixon, Richard A. Oppel Jr., and Stephen Babcock, "Clashes Rock Baltimore after Funeral," *New York Times*, April 28, 2015, A1–A15.

23 CBS News, "Arrest to Death: What Happened to Freddie Gray," May 1, 2015.

24 Krishnadev Calamur, "Maryland Governor Lifts State of Emergency in Baltimore," National Public Radio, May 6, 2015.

25 Rebecca R. Ruiz, "Baltimore Officers Will Face No Federal Charges in Death of Freddie Gray," *New York Times*, September 12, 2017.

26 J. Niehaus, "Realistic Use-of-Force Training: The Technology Is in Place Today for an All-Inclusive Program," *Law and Order* 45, no. 6 (1997): 103–105.

27 Kim Barker and Matt Furber, "Bail Is at Least $1 Million for Ex-Officer Accused of Killing George Floyd," *New York Times*, June 8, 2020. Chao Xiong, "Officers Charged in Floyd Case to Be Tried Together in Hennepin County, Trial Can Be Publicly Livestreamed," *Star-Tribune* (Minneapolis), November 5, 2020.

28 Heather Wyatt-Nichol and George Franks, "Ethics Training in Law Enforcement Agencies," *Public Integrity* 12, no. 1 (2010): 39–50.

29 *Black's Law Dictionary*, Posse Comitatus, thelawdictionary.org/posse-comitatus. Accessed October 2020.

30 RAND Corporation, Preparing the U.S. Army for Homeland Security: Concepts, Issues, and Options, Appendix D: Overview of the Posse Comitatus Act, www.rand.org/pubs/monograph_reports/MR1251.html. Accessed October 2020.

31 U.S. Northern Command, Defending Our Homeland, The Posse Comitatus Act, May 16, 2013, www.northcom.mil/Newsroom/FactSheets/ArticleView/tabid/3999/Article/563993/the-posse-comitatus-act.aspx.

32 Ibid.

33 Peter B. Kraska, "Questioning the Militarization of U.S. Police: Critical Versus Advocacy Scholarship," *Policing and Society* 9, no. 2 (April 1999): 141.

34 *Black's Law Dictionary*, Posse Comitatus.

35 Jamelle Bouie, "The Militarization of the Police," *Slate*, August 13, 2014.

36 Ann Scott Tyson, "With Federal Agents Off the Streets, Portland Protesters Refocus," Christian Science Monitor, August 4, 2020.

37 Abigail R. Hall and Christopher J. Coyne, "The Militarization of U.S. Domestic Policing," *Independent Review* 17, no. 4 (Spring 2013): 485–504.

38 Daryl Meeks, "Police Militarization in Urban Areas: The Obscure War against the Underclass," *Black Scholar* 35, no. 4 (Winter 2006): 33–41.

39 Edward Lawson, Jr., "TRENDS: Police Militarization and the Use of Lethal Force," *Political Research Quarterly* 72 (2019): 177–189.

40 John Murray, "Policing Terrorism: A Threat to Community Policing or Just a Shift in Priorities?" *Police Practice and Research* 6, no. 4 (September 2005): 347–361.

41 Martin Gill, "Senior Police Officers' Perspectives on Private Security: Sceptics, Pragmatists and Embracers," *Policing and Society* 25, no. 3 (2015): 276–293.

42 American Civil Liberties Union, *War Comes Home: The Excessive Militarization of American Policing* (New York: ACLU Foundation, 2014).

43 "Are Federal Programs That Provide Military Equipment to State and Local Police Departments Effective?" *Congressional Digest* 94, no. 2 (February 2015): 10–31.

44 Karena Rahall, "The Green to Blue Pipeline: Defense Contractors and the Police Industrial Complex," *Cardozo Law Review* 36, no. 5 (June 2015): 1785–1835.

45 U.S. Federal News Service, "Cape Coral Police Department's VIN Unit, SWAT Team, Street Crimes Unit Execute Search Warrants on Suspected Marijuana Grow Houses," October 22, 2007.

46 Kraska, "Militarization and Policing—Its Relevance to 21st Century Police." Radley Balko, *Rise of the Warrior Cop: The Militarization of America's Police Forces* (New York: Public Affairs, 2013), 286, as cited in Krena Rahall, "The Green to Blue Pipeline: Defense Contractors and the Police Industrial Complex," *Cardozo Law Review* 36, no. 5 (June 2015): 1785–1835.

47 American Civil Liberties Union, *War Comes Home*, 3, 32.

48 Ibid., 4.

49 Richard K. Lodge, "Police Investigation Details the Night Eurie Stamps Sr. Died," *MetroWest Daily News*, May 1, 2011.

50 John M. Guilfoil, "Officer in Fatal Shooting Will Not Be Charged," Boston.com, March 10, 2011.

51 Norman Miller, "Framingham Police SWAT Team Disbanded," *MetroWest Daily News*, October 5, 2013.

52 Federal Bureau of Investigation, *Law Enforcement Officers Killed and Assaulted, 2003* (Washington, D.C.: U.S. Department of Justice, 2004).

53 Federal Bureau of Investigation, *Law Enforcement Officers Killed and Assaulted 2019*, Law Enforcement Officers Feloniously Killed, Table 23, ucr.fbi.gov/leoka/2019/topic-pages/tables/table-23.xls.

54 "Justice Department Settles Employment Discrimination Lawsuit against the City of Virginia Beach, Virginia Police Department," U.S. Federal News Service, including U.S. State News, April 4, 2006.

55 Judith A. Waters and William Ussery, "Police Stress: History, Contributing Factors, Symptoms, and Interventions," *Policing* 30 (April 1, 2007): 169–188. Akiva M. Liberman, Suzanne R. Best, Thomas J. Metzler, Jeffrey A. Fagan, Daniel S. Weiss, and Charles R. Marmar, "Routine Occupational Stress and Psychological Distress in Police," *Policing: An International Journal of Police Strategies and Management* 25, no. 2 (2002): 421–439.

56 Laurence Miller, *Practical Police Psychology: Stress Management and Crisis Intervention for Law Enforcement* (Springfield, Ill.: Thomas, 2006).

57 Göran Kecklund, Claire Anne Eriksen, and Torbjörn Åkerstedt, "Police Officers' Attitude to Different Shift Systems: Association with Age, Present Shift Schedule, Health and Sleep/Wake Complaints," *Applied Ergonomics* 39 (September 2008): 565.

58 John Von Maanen, "Kinsmen in Repose: Occupational Perspectives of Patrolmen," in *The Police and Society: Touchstone Readings*, 2d ed., ed. Victor E. Kappeler (Prospect Heights, Ill.: Waveland Press, 1999), 221; see also Victor E. Kappeler, Richard D. Sluder, and Geoffrey P. Alpert, "Breeding Deviant Conformity: Police Ideology and Culture," in *The Police and Society: Touchstone Readings*, 239.

59 Jerome H. Skolnick, *Justice without Trial: Law Enforcement in Democratic Society* (New York: Wiley, 1966).

60 Ibid., 47.

61 Heather Mac Donald, *The War on Cops: How the New Attack on Law and Order Makes Everyone Less Safe*, (New York: Encounter Books, 2016).

62 Gisele Galoustian, "It's Safer to Be a Cop in the U.S. Today than 50 Years Ago," Florida Atlantic University, April 4, 2019.

63 Michael D. White, Lisa M. Dario, and John A. Shjarback, "Assessing Dangerousness in Policing: An Analysis of Officer Deaths in the United States, 1970–2016," *Criminology and Public Policy* 18, no. 1 (Feb. 2019): 11–35.

64 Ibid., 42–70.

65 Holly Bannish and Jim Ruiz, "The Antisocial Police Personality: A View from the Inside," *International Journal of Public Administration* 26 (June 1, 2003): 831–881.

66 Michael D. Lyman, *The Police: An Introduction* (Upper Saddle River, N.J.: Prentice Hall, 2002). Lyman provided an excellent discussion on the topic in his chapter "Personal Administration."

67 Kenneth Novak, Gary Cordner, Bradley Smith, and Roy Roberg, *Police & Society* (New York: Oxford University Press, 2017), 153–155.

68 Ibid.

69 Henrick Karoliszyn, "Solidarity in Blue," *Crime Report*, February 22, 2016.

70 Novak et al., *Police & Society*.

71 Catherine L. Fisk and L. Song Richardson, "Police Unions," *George Washington Law Review* 85 (2017): 712–799.

72 Mark Iris, "Police Discipline in Chicago: Arbitration or Arbitrary?" *Journal of Criminal Law and Criminology* 89 (1998): 215, 216.

73 Sanja Kutnjak Ivkovic, "Police (Mis) behavior: A Cross-Cultural Study of Corruption Seriousness," *Policing* 28 (July 1, 2005): 546–566.

74 Lawrence W. Sherman, *Police Corruption: A Sociological Perspective* (Garden City, N.Y.: Anchor Books, 1974). See particularly Sherman's introductory chapter with its important typology of police corruption.

75 Knapp Commission, "An Example of Police Corruption: Knapp Commission Report in New York City," in *Police Deviance*, eds. Thomas Barker and David L. Carter (Cincinnati, Ohio: Pilgrimage, 1986), 28.

76 "Ringleader in Boston Police Corruption Case Sentenced to 26 Years in Prison," U.S. Federal News Service, including U.S. State News, May 16, 2008.

77 Peter K. Manning and Lawrence John Redlinger, "Invitational Edges," in *Thinking about Police: Contemporary Readings*, 2d ed., eds. Carl B. Klockars and Stephen D. Mastrofski (New York: McGraw-Hill, 1991), 398–413.

78 Lee Sullivan, "Drug Unit Corruption: Stopping the Scandal before It Starts," *Sheriff*, January 1, 2008, 27–29.

79 John M. Violanti, James R. Marshall, and Barbara Howe, "Stress, Coping, and Alcohol Use: The Police Connection," *Journal of Police Science and Administration* 13, no. 2 (1985): 106–110.

80 Charles Unkovic and William Brown, "The Drunken Cop," *Police Chief* (April 1978): 29–20.

81 Max T. Raterman, "Substance Abuse and Police Discipline," *Police Department Disciplinary Bulletin* (December 2000): 2–4.

82 Mary J.C. Hageman, "Occupational Stress and Marital Relationships," *Journal of Police Science and Administration* 6, no. 4 (1978): 402–412.

83 Laurence Miller, "Police Families: Stresses, Syndromes, and Solutions," *American Journal of Family Therapy* 35 (January 1, 2007): 21.

84 Clemens Bartollas and Larry D. Hahn, *Policing in America* (Boston: Allyn & Bacon, 1999). 199.

85 Peter E. Maynard and Nancy E. Maynard, "Stress in Police Families: Some Policy Implications," *Journal of Police Science and Administration* 10 (1982): 302–314.

86 Robert Henley Woody, "Family Interventions with Law Enforcement Officers," *American Journal of Family Therapy* 34 (March 1, 2006): 95–103.

87 Julia McKinnell, "Don't Let Their Only Friend Be a Gun," *Maclean's*, June 30, 2008, 59.

88 J. M. Violanti, T. A. Hartley, A. Mnatsakanova, and M. E. Andrew "Police Suicide in Small Departments: A Comparative Analysis," *International Journal of Emergency Mental Health* 14 no. 3 (2012): 157–162.

89 Vera A. Klinoff, Vincent B. Van Hasselt, and Ryan A. Black. "Homicide-Suicide in Police Families: An Analysis of Cases from 2007–2014." *Journal of Forensic Practice* 17, no. 2 (April 2015): 101–116.

90 Mark H. Chae and Douglas J. Boyle, "Police Suicide: Prevalence, Risk, and Protective Factors," *Policing* 36, no. 1 (February 2013): 91–118.

91 John M. Violanti, "Predictors of Police Suicide Ideation," *Suicide and Life-Threatening Behavior* 34 (October 1, 2004): 277–283.

92 Michelle Perin, "Police Suicide," *Law Enforcement Technology* 34, no. 9 (September 2007): 8.

93 Body-Worn Camera Toolkit, Bureau of Justice Assistance, www.bja.gov/bwc/topics-gettingstarted.html. Accessed October 2020.

94 Shelley S. Hyland, *Body-Worn Cameras in Law Enforcement Agencies, 2016* (Washington, D.C.: U.S. Department of Justice Office of Justice Programs Bureau of Justice Statistics, 2018). Available at www.bjs.gov/index.cfm?ty=pbdetail&iid=6426.

95 Ibid.

96 Barak Ariel, William A. Farrar, and Alex Sutherland, "The Effect of Police Body-Worn Cameras on Use of Force and Citizens' Complaints Against the Police: A Randomized Controlled Trial," *Journal of Quantitative Criminology* 31 (2015): 509–535.

97 Lindsay Miller and Jessica Toliver, "Implementing a Body-Worn Camera Program: Recommendations and Lessons Learned," *Community Policing Dispatch* 7, no. 10 (October 2014) 53–66.

98 David Yokum, Anita Ravishankar, and Alexander Coppock, *Evaluating the Effects of Police Body-Worn Cameras: A Randomized Controlled Trial* (Washington, DC: The Lab @ DC, 2017). Available at bwc.thelab.dc.gov.

99 Zusha Elinson, Shibani Mahtani, and Valerie Bauerlein, "Charlotte, Tulsa Highlight Patchwork Approach to Releasing Body Camera Videos," *Wall Street Journal*, September 23, 2016.

100 Miller and Toliver, "Implementing a Body-Worn Camera Program."

101 Chris Bousquet, "Mining Social Media Data for Policing, the Ethical Way," *Government Technology*, April 27, 2018. Eric M. Johnson, "U.S. Cities Push for Local Laws to Oversee Police Surveillance," Reuters, September 21, 2016. Electronic Frontier Foundation, Surveillance Drones, www.eff.org/issues/surveillance-drones. Accessed October 2020.

102 Drew Harwell, "Doorbell-camera Firm Ring Has Partnered with 400 Police Forces, Extending Surveillance Concerns," *Washington Post*, August 28, 2019.

103 Justin Jouvenal, "The New Way Police Are Surveilling You: Calculating Your Threat 'Score'," *Washington Post*, January 10, 2016.

104 Brad Heath, "Police Secretly Track Cellphones to Solve Routine Crimes," *USA Today*, August 24, 2015.

105 Steven D. Seybold, "Somebody's Watching Me: Civilian Oversight of Data-Collection Technologies," *Texas Law Review* 93, no. 4 (March 2015): 1029–1060.

106 Nick Sibilla, "Utah Bans Police From Searching Digital Data Without a Warrant, Closes Fourth Amendment Loophole," *Forbes*, April 16, 2019.

107 Johnson, "U.S. Cities Push for Local Laws to Oversee Police Surveillance."

108 Cyrus Farivar, New California Bill Would Require Local Approval for Stingray Use, *Ars Technica*, April 16, 2015. Seattle, Wash., ordinance 124142 (March 27, 2013).

109 Jason Tashea, "The Rise of the Machines—but with Checks and Balances," *ABA Journal*, June 25, 2019.

110 Stephen Rushin, "The Legislative Response to Mass Police Surveillance," *Brooklyn Law Review* 79, no. 1 (Fall 2013): 1–60.

111 Timothy C. Hardcastle, "What's New in Emergencies, Trauma and Shock?

Pellets, Rubber Bullets, and Shotguns: Less Lethal or Not?" *Journal of Emergencies, Trauma and Shock* 6, no. 3 (2013): 153–154.

112 William P. Bozeman and James E. Winslow, "Medical Aspects of Less Lethal Weapons," *Internet Journal of Rescue and Disaster Medicine* 5, no. 1 (2005).

113 Brian Rappert, "A Framework for the Assessment of Non-Lethal Weapons," *Medicine, Conflict and Survival* 20 (2004): 51.

114 Ibid.

115 Sharon Gaudin, "Pennsylvania Police Use Database as Crime-Fighting Tool," *InformationWeek*, January 19, 2007.

116 Tom Jackman, "FBI Plans 'Rapid DNA' Network for Quick Database Checks on Arrestees," *Washington Post*, December 13, 2018.

117 Jocelyn Kaiser, "New Federal Rules Limit Police Searches of Family Tree DNA Databases," *Science*, September 25, 2019.

118 Office of Justice Programs, National Institute of Justice, DNA Sample Collection from Arrestees.

119 Federal Bureau of Investigation, CODIS brochure, www.fbi.gov/services/laboratory/biometric-analysis/codis. Accessed October 2020.

120 Richard Willing, "DNA 'Near Matches' Spur Privacy Fight," *USA Today*, August 3, 2007, 3A.

121 Ellen Nakashima, "From DNA of Family, a Tool to Make Arrests," *Washington Post*, Met 2d ed., April 21, 2008, A1.

122 Suman Kakar, "Race and Police Officers' Perceptions of Their Job Performance: An Analysis of the Relationship between Police Officers' Race, Education Level, and Job Performance," *Journal of Police and Criminal Psychology* 18 (April 1, 2003): 45.

123 National Center for Women and Policing, "Equality Denied: The Status of Women in Policing: 2000," National Center for Women and Policing, Feminist Majority Foundation, April 2001.

124 Federal Bureau of Investigation, *Crime in the United States,* 2019, Table 74: Full-time Law Enforcement Employees, ucr.fbi.gov/crime-in-the-u.s/2019/crime-in-the-u.s.-2019/topic-pages/tables/table-74. Shelley S. Hyland, *Local Police Departments, 2016: Personnel* (U.S. Department of Justice Office of Justice Programs Bureau of Justice Statistics, 2019), 5. Available at www.bjs.gov/index.cfm?ty=pbdetail&iid=6706.

125 Jody Kasper, "Proven Steps for Recruiting Women," *Law and Order*, December 1, 2006, 63–67.

126 Jerome H. Skolnick, *Justice without Trial: Law Enforcement in Democratic Society*, 3d ed. (New York: Macmillan, 1994), 41–68.

127 Susan E. Martin, "Women Officers on the Move: An Update on Women in Policing," *Critical Issues in Policing: Contemporary Readings*, 4th ed., eds. Roger G. Dunham and Geoffrey P. Alpert (Prospect Heights, Ill.: Waveland Press, 2001), 401–422.

128 John R. Lott Jr., "Does a Helping Hand Put Others at Risk? Affirmative Action, Police Departments, and Crime," *Economic Inquiry* 38 (April 1, 2000): 239–277.

129 Alissa Pollitz Worden, "The Attitudes of Women and Men in Policing: Testing Conventional and Contemporary Wisdom," *Criminology* 31, no. 2 (1993): 203–240.

130 Larry A. Gould and Marie Volbrecht, "Personality Differences between Women Police Recruits, Their Male Counterparts, and the General Female Population," *Journal of Police and Criminal Psychology* 14 (April 1, 1999): 1–18.

131 J. J. Donohue III and Steven D. Levitt, "The Impact of Race on Policing and Arrests," *Journal of Law and Economics* 44 (October 1, 2001): 367–394.

132 Clemens Bartollas and Larry D. Hahn, *Policing in America* (Boston: Allyn & Bacon, 1999). See especially Chapter 12, "The Minority Police Officer," for a discussion of black, Hispanic, American Indian, and homosexual police officers.

133 Ibid.

134 Hyland, *Local Police Departments, 2016: Personnel,* 6.

135 Ibid.

136 Nicholas Alex, *Black in Blue: A Study of the Negro Policeman* (New York: Appleton-Century-Crofts, 1969).

137 Susan E. Martin, "Outsider within the Station House: The Impact of Race and Gender on Black Women Police," *Social Problems* (August 1994): 389.

OXFORD **insight** study guide
Active Engagement, Deeper Understanding

Learn more with this chapter's digital tools, including the Oxford Insight Study Guide, at www.oup.com/he/Fuller2e.

The Role of the Courts

The Courts

Davontae Sanford (center) stands with his mother, Taminko Sanford, during a news conference in Detroit, a day after being released from prison. What sort of recourse should be available for citizens like Sanford whose rights were violated?

In September 2007, 14-year-old Davontae Sanford was arrested

and charged with murdering four people in a Detroit drug house. The night of the murders, police told him during an interrogation that he could go home if he gave them information. Sanford signed a statement saying he and some other youths had planned to rob the house, but that he had changed his mind and not participated.[1]

Police took Sanford home but arrested him the next night. He requested an attorney but was told that he was a "dumb ass" because no lawyers were awake that late. After being pressured into agreeing to a more incriminating statement prepared by police, Sanford was finally read his *Miranda* rights and charged with the murders.[2]

Sanford later recanted the confession in an interview with a psychologist. At trial, on the advice of an attorney who was later disbarred for misconduct, Sanford pleaded guilty to the murders and was sentenced to 37 to 90 years in prison. It was later determined that Sanford had been interrogated without his guardian's consent, a violation of Michigan law, and that a sketch of the crime scene that police said Sanford had drawn had actually been drawn by a deputy police chief.[3]

Days after Sanford's sentencing, police arrested Vincent Smothers for an unrelated murder. Smothers admitted to committing 12 murders-for-hire, including the four that Sanford had confessed to. Smothers says the prosecutor offered him a plea deal for a 50-to-100 year sentence for eight murders if he did not testify in Sanford's legal proceedings about the murders that Sanford had pleaded guilty to.[4] Smothers rejected the deal and pleaded guilty to eight murders without the condition.[5]

Sanford's appellate lawyer tried to withdraw Sanford's guilty plea based on his actual innocence and Smothers's confession, but the motion was denied. The case was remanded to the trial court for expert testimony on confessions in 2013. The prosecution appealed, and in 2014 the Michigan Supreme Court reinstated the trial court ruling that denied Sanford's motion to withdraw his guilty plea. The court held that actual innocence was not a legal basis to withdraw a guilty plea.[6]

When the Michigan Innocence Clinic and Northwestern University's Center on Wrongful Convictions of Youth took Sanford's case, they had his confession analyzed by an expert who determined that the correct aspects of Sanford's confession came from information that the police had fed him. This led to an investigation by Michigan State Police, which concluded that Smothers had indeed committed the murders. A judge vacated Sanford's convictions, and he was released in June 2016. The state of Michigan awarded Sanford $408,356 in compensation.[7]

THINK ABOUT IT > How does Sanford's experience expose the problems of the U.S. court system's adversarial process?

LEARNING OBJECTIVE 7.1

Identify the challenges facing the U.S. court system.

7.1 The Court System in the United States

Often, students of criminal justice are not as interested in the courts as in law enforcement and corrections because working in the court requires legal knowledge. Many students go on to law school and successful careers as attorneys and judges, but to a college freshman, that seems a long time in the future. However, students should consider legal careers because the quality of justice in the United States is determined by the technical expertise, professional acumen, and ethical demeanor of those who work in the courts. Courts are responsible for determining whether a defendant is guilty or not guilty and for deciding on the disposition or sentence for defendants who are found guilty. Such processes occur according to a complex and ever-changing network of laws, personnel, and political pressures. Mistakes can affect the convicted and the victims, as well as reflect badly on the system itself. The courts are besieged on all sides by those who observe an institution in crisis:

> police officers, who complain that offenders are treated too leniently;

> corrections officials, who lack room in their prisons for new inmates and are concerned about the severe sentences that keep inmates incarcerated for many years;

> the public, which sees the courts as an unfathomable machine that fails to provide justice when lawbreakers are released because of technicalities;

> legislatures, which cannot provide the necessary financial resources to handle huge caseloads because tax dollars must be shared among many other government functions, including law enforcement and corrections; and

> offenders and defendants, whether guilty or innocent, as well as victims, who do not believe that the courts dispense justice in a fair manner.[8]

The courts seem to be in a powerful position within the criminal justice system because they make the important determinations of what happens to suspects, defendants, and offenders. However, the courts are actually at the mercy of outside forces. They do not control how they are financed, nor do they control how many cases they receive. They cannot ensure adequate resources to carry out sentences, and because courtrooms are open to the press, the courts cannot control their public image. In many ways, the courts are an institution that takes the blame for deficiencies not of their making.[9]

For instance, when a police officer fails to read a suspect his or her *Miranda* rights or makes a mistake in the chain of custody of crucial evidence, the courts have no choice but to dismiss the case. This can cause the public to believe that the

The courts seem to be powerful, but they are actually at the mercy of many outside forces. Here, police at Quincy (Massachusetts) District Court subdue and handcuff brawlers after a fight spilled out of a courtroom where four teens pleaded not guilty to murder charges stemming from the shooting death of 21-year-old Kyle McManus. What are some of the problems that the courts are subject to?

The Nature of Jurisdiction

Jurisdiction refers to the authority of the court to hear certain cases. The jurisdiction of any court depends on three factors: the seriousness of the case, the location of the offense, and whether the case is being heard for the first time or is on appeal. The three types of jurisdiction are subject-matter jurisdiction, geographic jurisdiction, and hierarchical jurisdiction.[24]

> **Subject-matter jurisdiction**. The nature of the case can determine which court will have jurisdiction. For example, many specialized courts handle only specific types of cases. Drug courts, traffic courts, and juvenile or family courts can be classified by subject-matter jurisdiction. Sometimes the distinction between felonies and misdemeanors will dictate the court to which a case is sent. **Limited-jurisdiction courts**—courts that have jurisdiction only over certain types of cases or subject matter—tend to handle misdemeanors, traffic cases, and low-value civil cases, whereas **general-jurisdiction courts**—courts that may hear all types of cases except for those prohibited by law—typically deal with more serious felonies. Depending on the state, some type of limited jurisdiction court may handle tasks such as issuing warrants, establishing bail, advising defendants of their rights, and setting a preliminary hearing date.

> **Geographic jurisdiction**. The location of an offense dictates which court will hear the case. Therefore, the political boundaries of cities, counties, and states can determine the geographic jurisdiction of a court. Depending on the state, jurisdictions may include courts in several counties that operate under a **circuit court**, which presides over different parts of a judicial district. Aimed at balancing the caseload according to population, a circuit might have one densely populated county or several less populated counties. Military bases and installations, American Indian reservations, and national parks are also subject to geographic jurisdiction. Offenses committed in these locations can be dealt with by courts established especially for the needs of these political structures. For instance, although a homicide committed on a military base may have happened within the jurisdiction of a state circuit court, it also occurred on federal land and thus would be handled by a federal court. Furthermore, if the defendant is military personnel, the case may be handled according to the Uniform Code of Military Justice rather than the federal court system.

> **Hierarchical jurisdiction**. A court's authority to hear a case is based on where the case is located in the system. For example, trial courts and appellate courts (which will be covered in more detail later) hear cases at different points in the system. Trial courts hear cases first, determine guilt, and impose a sentence. If a verdict is appealed, an appellate court reviews the work of the trial court and determines whether the case was handled within the constraints of the Constitution. If it is determined that the trial court judge allowed a mistake to occur, such as the presentation of illegally gathered evidence by the police, the appellate court can overrule the verdict and set aside the sentence. In terms of hierarchy, trial courts are responsible for implementing the substantive law, whereas appellate courts are responsible for ensuring that the trial courts follow procedural law.

These three ways of classifying jurisdiction alert us to the various organizational frameworks that compose our fragmented court system in the United States. As we delve deeper into the nature and structure of federal and state courts and confront the complex and overlapping terminology used to identify courts, it will be useful to remember that each court is classified according to each of these

Jurisdiction—
The authority of the court to hear certain cases.

Subject-matter jurisdiction—The authority of a court to hear a case based on the nature of the case.

Limited-jurisdiction court—A court that has jurisdiction only over certain types of cases or subject matter.

General-jurisdiction court—A court that may hear all types of cases except for those prohibited by law.

Geographic jurisdiction—The authority of a court to hear a case based on the location of the offense.

Circuit court—A court that holds sessions at intervals within different areas of a judicial district.

Hierarchical jurisdiction—The authority of a court to hear a case based on where the case is located in the system.

three measures of jurisdiction. Each court is responsible for handling certain types of cases, according to the geographic location of the offense and according to whether the case is being heard for the first time or is under appeal.

The Structure of the Federal Courts

The U.S. court system is divided into federal and state courts. We can think of this as a dual court system in which each part is further subdivided according to subject matter, geographic, and hierarchical jurisdiction. The federal courts get their power from Article III of the Constitution. Article III, Section 1, creates the U.S. Supreme Court and gives Congress the authority to create the lower federal courts. Thus, federal courts do not have general jurisdiction, as they may only hear cases that fall within the specifications of Article III. Federal courts comprise three main levels: U.S. district courts, U.S. courts of appeals, and the U.S. Supreme Court (for a look at how a case may move through the federal court system, see Figure 7.1).

Federal courts hear the following types of cases:

1. cases in which the U.S. government or one of its officers is a party;

2. cases involving violations of federal law or the Constitution;

3. cases between residents of different states if the dollar amount at issue exceeds $75,000; and

4. cases involving bankruptcy, copyright, patent, and maritime law.[25]

Additionally, state and federal courts may have concurrent jurisdiction. These cases typically involve circumstances in which a resident of one state sues a resident of another state. For the most part, however, the lines between federal and

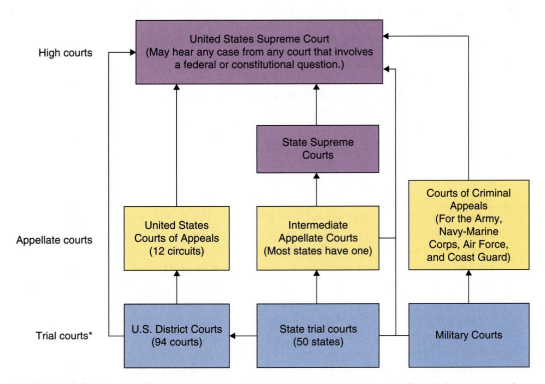

FIGURE 7.1   The Federal and State Court Systems This chart shows how cases may move from the lower courts to the U.S. Supreme Court. The number of cases decreases at each level. The U.S. Supreme Court hears relatively few cases. Why would the number of cases decrease at each level?

The U.S. Courts of Appeals also receive cases from the U.S. Tax Court, the U.S. Court of International Trade, the U.S. Court of Federal Claims, and the U.S. Court of Veterans Appeals.

John Allen Muhammad (in orange) was sentenced to death for the D.C. sniper attacks that resulted in the deaths of 10 people. In this case, why were the lines between federal and state court jurisdictions blurred?

state court jurisdiction are clear except in cases in which the offense violates both federal and state laws. A high-profile example is the 2002 D.C. sniper case, in which the defendants, John Allen Muhammad and Lee Boyd Malvo, killed a federal agent and committed murders in the District of Columbia and other states. There is no law pertaining to such a situation, so the choice of where to prosecute Muhammad and Malvo fell to federal authorities, primarily because the two were in federal custody. After much political wrangling, the state of Virginia was chosen to prosecute the pair first. Both men were convicted. Muhammad was sentenced to death, and Malvo, who was a juvenile at the time of the murders, was sentenced to life in prison.[26] Generally, states may only initiate criminal prosecutions in state courts, and the federal government may only initiate criminal prosecutions in federal court.

Many criminal offenses trigger a federal charge. These include offenses involving drug trafficking, immigration, identity theft, child pornography, child molestation, explosives, offenses committed in federal facilities or on federal property, kidnapping, offenses that cross state lines, bank robbery, **racketeering** (offenses committed with the purpose of promoting an organization or business), organized crime, terrorism, fraud, bribery, extortion, and piracy. Each of the 94 federal judicial districts has a U.S. Marshal. Deputy U.S. Marshals oversee taking into custody suspects charged with a federal offense, including booking, processing and detention, court security, and prisoner transportation.

Once a suspect is charged, he or she goes through a process that is much like the state procedure (described in Chapter 9). The processing of a federal case begins with the 93 U.S. attorneys who are the chief federal law enforcement officers within their districts, and the grand jury.

Federal law enforcement agencies are generally the source of most criminal investigations referred to the U.S. attorneys; however, state and local law enforcement agencies are also sources of referrals. The attorneys, who represent the United States in all criminal prosecutions, determine which cases to prosecute in their district

Racketeering—A federal crime that involves patterns of illegal activity carried out by organized groups that run illegal businesses or break the law in other organized ways.

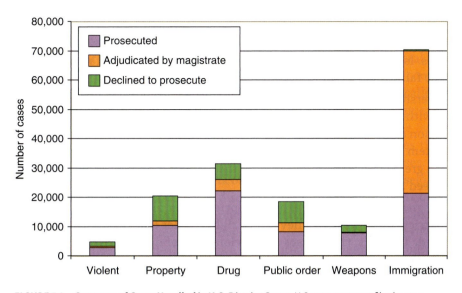

FIGURE 7.2 **Outcome of Cases Handled in U.S. District Court** U.S. attorneys may file charges against defendants in a U.S. district court or decline to prosecute. U.S. magistrates have the authority to adjudicate misdemeanor offenses. Which offenses have the highest percentage prosecuted by U.S. attorneys? Which are mostly adjudicated by a magistrate?

Source: Mark Motivans, Federal Justice Statistics, 2015-2016, Table 4: Outcome and Case Processing Time of Suspects in Matters Concluded (Washington, D.C: U.S. Department of Justice Office of Justice Programs Bureau of Justice Statistics, 2019), 7. Available at www.bjs.gov/index.cfm?ty=pbdetail&iid=6506.

courts (see Figure 7.2 for the outcome of cases). The grand jury reviews the evidence from the U.S. attorney and decides whether it is enough to require a defendant to stand trial. A suspect must be brought before a judicial officer, usually a U.S. magistrate, upon arrest for an initial appearance. If a defendant pleads guilty immediately (90 percent do) and accepts a plea bargain, the court process stops there. If the defendant wishes to go to trial, the case can move from the district courts (trial courts), to the courts of appeals, and, finally, to the U.S. Supreme Court if the Court decides that the case involves a substantial question about the U.S. Constitution or federal law. A more detailed explanation of each type of court follows.[27]

U.S. DISTRICT COURTS

U.S. district courts are trial courts of general jurisdiction that try felony cases involving federal laws and civil cases in which the amount of money in controversy exceeds $75,000. Although civil cases constitute most of the district courts' workload, since 1980 drug and immigration prosecutions have risen significantly and now represent a large percentage of all federal criminal cases (see Figure 7.3).[28]

U.S. district courts are responsible for only a few

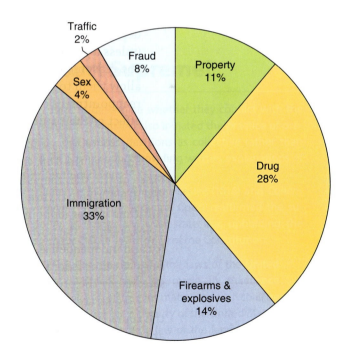

FIGURE 7.3 **U.S. District Courts, Criminal Cases by Offense** Which offenses make up the largest portion of the district courts' workload?

Source: Federal Judicial Caseload Statistics, Table D-2, U.S. District Courts— Criminal Defendants Commenced, by Offense, During the 12-Month Periods Ending March 31, 2015 through 2019. Available at www.uscourts.gov/ statistics/table/d-2/federal-judicial-caseload-statistics/2019/03/31.

types of cases that typically go to court. Most often, these are cases involving a federal question, an issue of diversity of jurisdiction, or a prisoner petition.

Marchers rally for LGBTQ rights outside the U.S. Supreme Court in October 2019 as justices hear arguments in three cases dealing with discrimination in the workplace because of sexual orientation. What process must a case go through in order to be heard by the Supreme Court?

Writ of certiorari— An order from a superior court calling up for review the record of a case from a lower court.

Rule of four—A rule that states that at least four of the nine Supreme Court justices must vote to hear a case.

Amicus curiae—A brief in which someone who is not part of a case gives advice or testimony.

as it involves federal or constitutional law, the typical case involves a "substantial federal question." The Court grants plenary review (meaning that the Court independently examines the issue), with oral arguments by attorneys, in about 80 cases per term. The Court usually deals with about 100 cases without plenary review.[34] The Court does not attempt to serve as a court of last resort for all federal and state cases but instead seeks cases that have broad policy implications for important questions of the day.[35] The Court does have original jurisdiction in cases affecting foreign officials and those in which a state is a party. However, the Court has seldom heard cases involving foreign officials and devotes its original jurisdiction to handling disputes between state governments.[36] In all other cases, the Court has appellate jurisdiction.

The procedure of the Supreme Court is to issue a **writ of certiorari** to a lower court that orders the case records to be sent to the justices so that they can decide whether the case presents the type of questions that should be decided by the Supreme Court. A **rule of four** exists whereby at least four of the nine Supreme Court justices must vote to hear a case.[42] All nine justices then hear the case, unlike the courts of appeals in which a panel of three justices hears a case. When a case is scheduled, attorneys file written arguments, as well as briefs on behalf of other parties called **amicus curiae** ("friend of the court") briefs, which allow an individual or a group that is not party to a case to give advice or testimony.[43] For instance, an organization such as the American Civil Liberties Union or Amnesty International may file an amicus curiae brief in a case involving the death penalty for someone who is mentally disabled.

SPECIALIZED FEDERAL COURTS

Most specialized federal courts hear civil cases.[44] However, a few types of courts hear criminal cases.

The U.S. Court of Appeals for the Armed Forces handles cases of military law in which questions of due process are raised in implementing the Uniform Code of Military Justice. Military justice imposes a broad set of rules and laws on military personnel to which civilians are not subject. Failure to follow orders or showing

Pokagon Tribal Council Chairman Matthew Wesaw speaks during a press conference held to unveil the Pokagon Justice Center in Dowagiac, Michigan. What are some of the functions of the tribal court?

disrespect for an officer are violations of the Uniform Code of Military Justice and can result in punishments that include incarceration or discharge from the armed services. Armed forces personnel are not entitled to all the protections of the Constitution, and the due process afforded to suspected violators of military law is not as extensive as that afforded by civilian courts.[45]

Another specialized federal court that receives many criminal cases is the tribal court. American Indian tribes have a certain level of sovereignty on federal reservations. For example, in many states, American Indians have established casinos on reservations regardless of the approval of state governments. The tribal judicial system revolves around a core of five legal institutions: indigenous forums (also known as traditional courts), Court of Indian Offenses, intertribal courts, the courts of appeals, and tribal courts of general jurisdiction.[46] Tribal law is administered by American Indians and can be imposed in lieu of state law in some circumstances.[47] Especially for issues dealing with traditional American Indian concerns, such as hunting and fishing rights, tribal law can supersede state or federal law. Criminal jurisdiction on Indian lands varies by type of offense, whether the suspect/offender and/or victim is a member of a tribe, and the state in which the alleged offense occurred. Offenses committed on Indian lands are often subject to concurrent jurisdiction among multiple criminal justice agencies. Six states—California, Minnesota (except the Red Lake Reservation), Nebraska, Oregon (except the Warm Springs Reservation), Wisconsin, and Alaska—have mandatory jurisdiction over offenses committed on Indian lands. The following states have optional jurisdiction, either in whole or in part, over Indian lands within their boundaries: Nevada, Idaho, Iowa, Washington, South Dakota, Montana, North Dakota, Arizona, and Utah. In other states, the federal government retains criminal jurisdiction for major offenses committed on Indian lands.[48]

Perhaps one of the most controversial types of federal court is the military commission: "a military court of law traditionally used to try law of war and other offenses. An alien unprivileged enemy belligerent who has engaged in hostilities, or who has purposefully and materially supported hostilities against

GETTING IT RIGHT
Marijuana Convictions Going Up in Smoke

A felony conviction profoundly influences a person's life. The right to vote, eligibility for many occupational licenses, employment for particular jobs, and the ability to secure some types of loans depend on a clean record.

California's Adult Use of Marijuana Act, which went into effect on January 1, 2018, not only legalized and regulated the use of recreational marijuana, but also enabled many people with certain types of marijuana convictions to apply to have their records reduced or eliminated completely. Implementing such a radical reform has been challenging for court officials given the differences in how each of the state's courts, prosecutors' offices, and prisons and jails handle records and other offender data. Inconsistencies in data collection and transparency across these agencies complicate the implementation of criminal justice reforms.[53]

As one California criminal justice official pointed out, it is easy to become entangled in the criminal justice system because criminal justice officials exert all the effort to acquire a conviction. It is much more difficult for a convicted offender to clear a conviction because he or she must take most of the initiative. As a result, many offenders simply do not bother.[54]

To streamline the process, the non-profit organization Code for America developed Clear My Record, an algorithm that analyzes data in court documents to determine which cases are eligible to be cleared. Prosecutors in six counties, including Los Angeles, San Joaquin, and San Francisco, have used the program to clear about 75,000 marijuana-related convictions.[55] The program is also being used in Illinois, which legalized recreational marijuana sales in January 2020.[56]

THINK ABOUT IT

1. Why is expunging marijuana convictions so difficult?

Lower courts—

Sometimes called inferior courts, in reference to their hierarchy. These courts receive their authority and resources from local county or municipal governments.

STATE TRIAL COURTS

State trial courts of limited jurisdiction are usually called **lower courts** or inferior courts. They are so-called simply because of their place on the hierarchical ladder and not because of the quality of justice they dispense. Technically, they are not part of the state court system because in most states the lower courts of limited jurisdiction are not funded by the state but instead receive their authority and resources from local county or municipal governments. These courts handle most cases by either passing sentence or holding preliminary hearings and motions.

Trial courts of limited jurisdiction have a variety of names depending on the state in which they operate. They are called city magistrates, justices of the peace, county courts, or city courts. They handle millions of matters a year, mostly traffic cases, but also misdemeanors, small claims, and the preliminary stages of felony cases. It is in these courts of limited jurisdiction that most citizens come into contact with the court system. The geographic jurisdictions of limited-jurisdiction courts vary by state, having either county jurisdiction or jurisdiction limited to a city or town.

Trial courts of general jurisdiction are referred to as "major trial courts" and are variously named circuit courts, district courts, superior courts, or courts of common pleas. These courts handle major cases in both civil and criminal arenas. State trial courts of general jurisdiction hear most of the serious street-crime cases. Whereas federal courts deal with major white-collar offenders and large-scale drug dealers, state courts handle most cases involving rape, murder, theft, and small-scale drug dealing and drug possession.

Although the state trial court of general jurisdiction is popularly portrayed in the media when there is a jury trial, the bulk of the work of this type of court is

Charles Ray Merritt (left) sits next to his attorney, Rajan Maline, in the San Bernardino (California) Superior Court after being found guilty of the first-degree murder of the McStay family. Merritt was charged in the bludgeoning deaths of his business associate Joseph McStay, McStay's wife, and the couple's two young sons. What types of cases do state trial courts of general jurisdiction handle?

conducted in hallways and judges' chambers, as well as over the telephone and via e-mail as prosecutors and defense attorneys negotiate plea bargains that eliminate the need for a trial.[58] These courts handle various civil cases, including those involving domestic relations, estates, and personal injury. General-jurisdiction trial courts are subdivided into circuits or districts. In some states, a single county serves as the judicial district, but most states have judicial districts composed of several counties.[59]

Finally, state attorneys general are the primary legal authorities of the states, commonwealths, and territories of the United States. Among other duties, they serve as legal counsel to government agencies and legislatures. The powers of attorneys general include the following:

› prosecuting corporations that violate antitrust laws;
› representing state agencies and addressing issues of legislative or administrative constitutionality;
› enforcing environmental laws in most states;
› conducting criminal appeals and state criminal prosecutions;
› running victim compensation programs; and
› bringing civil suits.[60]

STATE INTERMEDIATE COURTS OF APPEALS

Intermediate appellate courts are a relatively recent addition to the U.S. state court system. In 1957, only 13 states had permanent intermediate appellate courts. Currently, 41 states have such courts, which hear all appeals from the lower state courts. Only states with small populations do not have this court level. Intermediate appellate courts often have rotating panels of three or more judges to review cases.[61] Typically, these courts must accept all criminal cases but not necessarily all civil cases. Additionally, appellate courts often review the decisions made by administrative agencies.[62]

In most cases, the decision at the intermediate court of appeals level is the final decision because the state supreme courts, like the U.S. Supreme Court, select only a few cases to consider each year. The exception to this rule is death-penalty cases. In states with capital punishment, the filing of death-penalty appeals in the court of last resort is usually mandatory.[63] There are no jury trials at the appellate level because guilt is not the overriding issue. These courts are more concerned with the conduct of the lower court in providing due process protections for the defendant and ensuring that the judge followed proper procedures.[64]

STATE SUPREME COURTS

Making general statements about state supreme courts is difficult because court systems vary across states. In states that have an intermediate level of courts of appeals, the state supreme court has a discretionary docket, which means it can select the cases it wishes to consider. For sparsely populated states with no intermediate court of appeals, the state supreme court hears appeals from the lower courts. Like the U.S. Supreme Court, the state supreme courts have all the justices hear each case instead of using rotating three-judge panels. All courts of last resort have an odd number of judges, with the most typical arrangement being a seven-judge court, as found in 28 states and Puerto Rico. Sixteen states have five-judge panels, and five have nine-judge panels.

The state supreme court is the court of last resort for all but a few cases that involve issues of constitutional or federal law that the U.S. Supreme Court decides are significant. The state supreme courts also have some authority to discipline lawyers and judges and often serve as a venue for judicial training.[65]

LOCAL AND COMMUNITY COURTS

The nature and organization of local courts across the United States vary widely. Although it is impossible to describe every type of community court here, we will highlight a few of these types of courts to show how they specialize in justice for

Chief Justice of the Oklahoma Supreme Court Noma Gurich, right, administers the oath of office to Dustin P. Rowe, Oklahoma's newest Supreme Court justice. Which is more supreme: a state supreme court or the U.S. Supreme Court?

specific problems. One feature of U.S. government is that it should be close to the people. Therefore, each state has developed its own jurisdictional pattern to allow municipalities, counties, and neighborhoods to structure their local legal systems in a way that is most responsive to citizens' needs. The jurisdictional pattern of each state reflects different geographic features (urban versus rural), types of crime, and resources available to local governments.[66] Here are some types of community courts.

› Drug courts. Many local jurisdictions have adopted the philosophy that minor drug offenses, especially possession, clog the courts with trivial cases and drain resources from more serious offenses. Because drug users who are otherwise respectable citizens and do not pose a threat of violence to the community are usually handled by imposition of a fine or are sent to a treatment program, it is deemed unnecessary to employ the traditional criminal court. Drug courts are specialized or problem-solving courts that can siphon off many cases that are routinely treated more leniently than more serious cases. Drug courts allow the criminal justice system to accomplish several goals. First, the vast numbers of drug offenders can be treated more consistently. Having a court that specializes in low-level drug offenders ensures that cases with similar conditions are assigned similar sanctions. Second, drug-court personnel are more aware of treatment options available in the community.[67] This means that someone who would benefit from counseling or drug treatment is more likely to receive it.[68] Third, it is less expensive and more efficient to deal with low-level drug offenders in the specialized court, thus freeing up the criminal courts for handling more serious offenses.[69]

› Conflict-resolution programs. Many low-level offenses, such as burglaries or street fights, can be more efficiently dealt with by allowing offenders and

Kanawha County Drug Court graduate Anthony Collins hugs his mother following a ceremony that graduated program participants. The ceremony was the 25th graduation to take place since the program began 10 years ago. What is the purpose of community courts?

victims to work out their disputes between themselves and not engaging the formal legal system.[70] Often, all that is required to satisfy victims is an apology, some restitution, and the feeling that offenders are being dealt with seriously. Because many offenders and victims have an ongoing relationship after the settlement of the case, conflict-resolution programs are useful because they can deal with some of the underlying issues that resulted in the offense.[71]

> Family courts. Many jurisdictions have family courts that deal with domestic assault, child abuse, and custody issues. Often, family courts are incorporated into the juvenile court, although in some jurisdictions they are freestanding. The advantage of family courts is that court personnel, including judges, can be more specialized in their knowledge of family dynamics and resources available to solve family problems. Given the focus of this type of court, family court judges are often better able to supervise personnel responsible for investigating child-abuse cases and monitor that the needs of children in their cases are being adequately addressed.

Blood feud—A disagreement whose settlement is based on personal vengeance and physical violence.

> Magistrate courts. Magistrate courts handle minor offenses, preliminary court proceedings, and pre-trial intervention programs, and they establish bail. Many jurisdictions now place the initial arraignment before the magistrate court. The magistrate court keeps minor cases out of the criminal justice system and often diverts them to alternative treatment programs designed to solve the problems that resulted in the offense. By establishing bail, permitting release on recognizance, and considering cases for dismissal, the magistrate court can relieve the local jail of the costly pre-trial incarceration of those suspected of minor offenses.[72]

PAUSE AND REVIEW

1. What are the three types of jurisdiction?
2. How are U.S. district courts different from U.S. courts of appeals?
3. What is the difference between state trial courts of limited jurisdiction and state trial courts of general jurisdiction?
4. How is the structure of the federal courts similar to the structure of state courts? In what ways do the two structures differ?

FOCUS ON ETHICS   Modern-Day Blood Feud

Your little brother had been dating a girl from another school for several months. Recently, during an argument, he got angry and struck her. The next night he was shot and killed in a drive-by shooting on the steps of your parents' home. You are certain your brother's killers are the girl's cousins, but the police have no solid evidence and are not close to making an arrest.

Although you know your brother was no saint, his death has devastated your family, and you believe that, in part, his killing was racially motivated. Your family is Latino, while the girl's cousins are part of a white-supremacy group that has continually harassed people of color in your area. However, the sheriff has commented to reporters that your brother probably deserved what he got and that his office is too busy to expend more resources on this offense unless further evidence turns up.

You have lost faith in the local criminal justice system's ability and motivation to solve your brother's murder and bring his killers to justice. Your grandfather remarks that in his day, if someone was killed, it was the right, if not the obligation, of the family to avenge the death themselves by killing the offender or a member of the offender's family. He looks at you in disgust and implies that you are a coward and a disgrace to the family. Engaging in a **blood feud** would likely lead to more violence and serve as encouragement for the killer's family to seek further revenge, and it could potentially set off a series of reciprocal acts of violence. As a criminal justice major at a local university, you know that modern courts evolved as a means of resolution from a long history of such feuds, skirmishes, and other types of conflicts that often caused more problems than they solved. You also have hopes of one day becoming an FBI agent, but the pull of family honor has you torn, and you want to make sure the killers do not get away with this.

WHAT DO YOU DO?

1. Do nothing. Even though you think the local criminal justice system has failed to properly investigate your brother's murder, there is little you can do that is within the law. Besides, you have your own life and career to think about. Even though your family expects you to seek justice by any means, you are unwilling to continue the cycle of violence started by your hot-headed brother.

2. Uphold your family's honor and retaliate against the cousins of your brother's girlfriend. If the local criminal justice system does not care about your community, it is your duty to seek justice through revenge. If you do not, the Latino community will continue to be victimized by the powerful white majority.

3. Go to the FBI and make a complaint charging that this was a hate crime and that your brother's constitutional rights were violated. If the local criminal justice system refuses to act, make a federal case out of your brother's murder.

For more insight on how someone might respond to such an ethical dilemma, visit Oxford Learning Link at www.oup.com/he/Fuller2e to watch a video that connects this scenario to a real-world situation.

Summary

LEARNING OBJECTIVE **7.1** Identify the challenges facing the U.S. court system.	The court system does not control how it is financed; it does not control how many cases it receives; its financial resources are limited; and it cannot control its public image because proceedings are open to the press. The professional orientation of attorneys requires them to strike the most advantageous deal for their clients, rather than outcomes that may better reflect justice. Outsiders have difficulty understanding court proceedings. Television presentation of justice as entertainment can portray the court system inaccurately.
LEARNING OBJECTIVE **7.2** Outline the importance of the Assize of Clarendon to establishment of the jury.	The Assize of Clarendon was a series of ordinances that established the beginnings of the grand jury system. Twelve men from each jurisdiction informed the king's judges of the most serious offenses committed in each jurisdiction. Gradually, the process evolved from simply identifying and charging wrongdoers to a body that determined whether the evidence was sufficient to detain the accused before trial.
LEARNING OBJECTIVE **7.3** Describe trial by ordeal and its relationship to the jury trial.	There were three main types of trial by ordeal: trial by cold water, trial by hot water, and trial by hot iron (or fire). Trial by ordeal was determined by divine intervention, and priests judged whether God provided a miracle to save the accused. In 1215, the Roman Catholic Church outlawed the practice, which led to development of the jury trial.

LEARNING OBJECTIVE 7.4 Describe the challenges faced by the courts in colonial North America.	Each of the 13 colonies was established under different motivations and conditions; thus systems of government varied widely. England made no effort to develop or enforce standardized practices among the colonies, so courts developed in response to the local economic, political, and social concerns of each colony. Many of the legal protections that existed for defendants in England were absent in the colonies.
LEARNING OBJECTIVE 7.5 Classify the three types of jurisdiction.	Jurisdiction, the court's authority to hear certain cases, depends on three features: 1. The seriousness of the case (subject-matter jurisdiction) 2. The location of the offense (geographic jurisdiction) 3. Whether the case is being heard for the first time or is on appeal (hierarchical jurisdiction)
LEARNING OBJECTIVE 7.6 Outline the structure of the federal courts.	U.S. magistrate courts are the lowest level of the federal court system. U.S. district courts are courts of general jurisdiction that try felony cases involving federal laws and civil cases in which more than $75,000 is at stake. The U.S. courts of appeals consist of 11 district courts, each of which encompasses several states, as well the District of Columbia Circuit, and serve as intermediate courts of appeals. The Supreme Court is at the top of the hierarchical jurisdiction for both the federal and state court systems.
LEARNING OBJECTIVE 7.7 Outline the structure of state courts.	State trial courts of limited jurisdiction (also known as lower or inferior courts) are technically not part of the state court system because, in most states, these courts receive their authority and resources from local county or municipal governments. They handle most cases by either passing sentence or holding preliminary hearings and motions. State intermediate courts of appeals must accept all criminal cases but not necessarily all civil cases, and they often review the decisions made by administrative agencies. In states that have an intermediate level of courts of appeals, the state supreme court can select the cases it wishes to consider. For states with no intermediate court of appeals, the state supreme court hears appeals from the lower courts. Local and community courts vary in nature and organization across the United States according to their own jurisdictional pattern. This allows municipalities, counties, and neighborhoods to structure their legal systems to be most responsive to citizens' needs.

Critical Reflections

1. **Discuss the possible ramifications if the federal government placed all state and local courts under federal jurisdiction.**

2. **In what ways has our concept of courts been influenced by religion, history, and the media?**

3. **In what ways can problem-solving courts actually solve the problems that result in crime?**

Key Terms

Adversarial process **p. 200**

Amicus curiae **p. 210**

Assize of Clarendon **p. 201**

Bench trial **p. 200**

Bill of Rights **p. 203**

Blood feud **p. 218**

Notes

1 Maurice Possley, "Davontae Sanford," National Registry of Exonerations, July 26, 2019, www.law.umich.edu/special/exoneration/Pages/casedetail.aspx?caseid=4913. Lara Bazelon, "The Innocence Deniers," *Slate*, January 10, 2018. George Hunter, "Killing Case in Limbo after Sanford's Release," *Detroit News*, August 29, 2017. George Hunter, "Davontae Sanford Pleads Guilty to Arizona Gunfire Charge," *Detroit News*, October 4, 2018. Associated Press, "Lawyer Accused of Forging Filing Signature Disbarred," *Detroit News*, February 14, 2018.

2 Ibid.

3 Ibid.

4 *Detroit News*, Vincent Smothers 2015 Affidavit to the Court, apps.detroitnews.com/projects/davontae-sanford-road-to-freedom/Vincent-Smothers-Affadavit.htm.

5 Ibid.

6 Possley, "Davontae Sanford." Bazelon, "The Innocence Deniers." Hunter, "Killing Case in Limbo after Sanford's Release." Hunter, "Davontae Sanford Pleads Guilty to Arizona Gunfire Charge." Associated Press "Lawyer Accused of Forging Filing Signature Disbarred."

7 Ibid.

8 Samuel Walker and Charles M. Katz, *The Police in America: An Introduction*, 4th ed. (Boston: McGraw-Hill, 2002), 41. James Austin and John Irwin, *It's About Time: America's Imprisonment Binge*, 3d ed. (Belmont, Calif.: Wadsworth, 2001). Frances Kahn Zemans, "In the Eye of the Beholder: The Relationship between the Public and the Courts," in *Courts and Justice: A Reader*, 2d ed., ed. G. Larry Mays and Peter Gregware (Prospect Heights, Ill.: Waveland Press, 2000), 7–24. David Orrick, "Court Administration in the United States: The On-Going Problems," in *Courts and Justice: A Reader*, 2d ed., eds. G. Larry Mays and Peter Gregware (Prospect Heights, Ill.: Waveland Press, 2000), 207–227. Stuart Nagel, "The Tipped Scales of American Justice," in *The Scales of Justice*, ed. Abraham Blumberg (New York: Transaction, 1970), 31–50.

9 Christopher Smith, *Courts, Politics, and the Judicial Process*, 2d ed. (Chicago: Nelson-Hall, 1997), 4–7.

10 Pamela A. MacLean, "Mixed Signals on Plea Bargains," *National Law Journal*, December 17, 2007, 7.

11 Bryce Lyon, *A Constitutional and Legal History of Medieval England*, 2nd ed. (New York: Norton, 1980), 295.

12 Barbara J. Shapiro, *"Beyond Reasonable Doubt" and "Probable Cause": Historical Perspectives on the Anglo-American Laws of Evidence* (Berkeley: University of California Press, 1991), 47.

13 Ibid., 73.

14 Robert Bartlett, *Trial by Fire and Water: The Medieval Judicial Ordeal* (Oxford, U.K.: Clarendon Press, 1986).

15 Ellen Hochstedler Steury and Nancy Frank, *Criminal Court Process* (Minneapolis/St. Paul, Minnesota: West, 1996), 70–71.

16 Thomas Andrew Green, *Verdict According to Conscience: Perspectives on the English Criminal Jury Trial* (Chicago: University of Chicago Press, 1985).

17 J. H. Baker, *An Introduction to English Legal History*, 3rd ed. (Boston: Butterworths, 1990), 591.

18 Steury and Frank, *Criminal Court Process*, 77.

19 Edwin C. Surrency, "The Courts in the American Colonies," *American Journal of Legal History* 11 (July 1967): 252–276.

20 Ibid., 256.

21 John Ferling, *A Leap in the Dark: The Struggle to Create the American Republic* (New York: Oxford University Press, 2003).

22 Robert Allen Rutland, *The Birth of the Bill of Rights* (Chapel Hill: University of North Carolina Press, 1955).

23 Bruce Ackerman, "The Living Constitution," *Harvard Law Review* 120 (May 1, 2007): 1737–1812.

24 Casey Welch and John Randolph Fuller, *American Criminal Courts* (Waltham, Mass.: Anderson Publishing, 2014), 82–83.

25 United States Department of Justice, Offices of the United States Attorneys, Introduction to the Federal Court System, www.justice.gov/usao/justice-101/federal-courts. Federal Judicial Center, Jurisdiction of the Federal Courts, www.fjc.gov/history/courts/jurisdiction-federal-courts. Accessed October 2020.

26 Sari Horwitz and Michael E. Ruane, "Jurisdictions Vied to Prosecute Pair," *Washington Post*, October 9, 2003.

27 Administrative Office of the U.S. Courts, Criminal Cases, www.uscourts.gov/about-federal-courts/types-cases/criminal-cases. Accessed October 2020.

28 David W. Neubauer, *America's Courts and the Criminal Justice System*, 7th ed. (Belmont, Calif.: Wadsworth, 2002), 68.

29 Larry Kramer, "Diversity Jurisdiction," *Brigham Young University Law Review* (1990): 3–66.

30 United States Courts, Authorized Judgeships, District Courts, www.uscourts.gov/judges-judgeships/authorized-judgeships/chronological-history-authorized-judgeships-district-courts. Accessed October 2020.

31 Christopher E. Smith, "From U.S. Magistrates to U.S. Magistrate Judges: Developments Affecting the Federal District Courts' Lower Tier of Judicial Officers," in *Courts and Justice: A Reader*, 3rd ed., ed. G. Larry Mays and Peter R. Gregware (Long Grove, Ill.: Waveland Press, 2004), 53–66.

32 United States Courts, Court Role and Structure, www.uscourts.gov/about-federal-courts/court-role-and-structure. Accessed October 2020.

33 United States Courts, Chronological History of Authorized Judgeships—Courts of Appeals, www.uscourts.gov/judges-judgeships/authorized-judgeships/chronological-history-authorized-judgeships-courts-appeals. Accessed October 2020.

34 Supreme Court of the United States, The Supreme Court at Work, The Term and Caseload, www.supremecourt.gov/about/courtatwork.aspx. Accessed October 2020.

35 Robert A. Carp, Ronald Stidham, and Kenneth L. Manning, *Judicial Process in America* (Washington, D.C.: CQ Press, 2007). See "The Supreme Court as Policymaker," pp. 28–30.

36 Federal Judicial Center, History of the Federal Judiciary, Original Jurisdiction of the Supreme Court, www.fjc.gov/history/courts/jurisdiction-original-supreme-court. Accessed October 2020.

37 *Marbury* v. *Madison*, 1 Cranch 137 (1803), 55, 56–57, 61.

38 Mary Ann Harrell and Burnett Anderson, *Equal Justice under the Law: The Supreme Court in American Life* (Washington, D.C.: Supreme Court Historical Society, 1982).

39 Mark Tushnet, "*Marbury v. Madison* and the Theory of Judicial Supremacy," in *Greatest Cases in Constitutional Law*, ed. Robert P. George (Princeton, N.J.: Princeton University Press, 2000), 17–54.

40 Laurence H. Tribe, *God Save This Honorable Court: How the Choice of Supreme Court Justices Shapes Our History* (New York: Random House, 1985).

41 Bernard Schwartz, *A History of the Supreme Court* (New York: Oxford University Press, 1993).

42 Eric M. Freedman, "Can Justice Be Served by Appeals of the Dead?" *National Law Journal*, October 19, 1992, 13.

43 Aaron S. Bayer, "Amicus Briefs," *National Law Journal*, February 25, 2008, 15.

44 Lawrence Baum, "Specializing the Federal Courts: Neutral Reforms or Efforts to Shape Judicial Policy?" *Judicature* 74 (1991): 217–224.

45 John R. Crook, "UCMJ Proceedings against U.S. Personnel Accused of Offenses against Civilians in Afghanistan and Iraq," *American Journal of International Law* 101 (July 1, 2007): 663–664.

46 Steven W. Perry, *Tribal Crime Data Collection Activities, 2012* (U.S. Department of Justice Office of Justice Programs Bureau of Justice Statistics, 2012), 11. Available at www.bjs.gov/index.cfm?ty=pbdetail&iid=4493.

47 Judith Resnik, "Multiple Sovereignties: Indian Tribes, States, and the Federal Government," *Judicature* 79 (1995): 118–125.

48 Steven W. Perry, *Tribal Crime Data Collection Activities, 2016* (Washington, D.C.: U.S. Department of Justice Office of Justice Programs Bureau of Justice Statistics, 2016), 1–2. Available at www.bjs.gov/index.cfm?ty=pbdetail&iid=5704.

49 Military Commissions, How Military Commissions Work, www.mc.mil/Aboutus.aspx. Accessed October 2020.

50 Eugene R. Fidell, "The Trouble with Tribunals," *New York Times*, June 13, 2009. Office of Military Commissions, Military Commissions History, www.mc.mil/ABOUTUS/MilitaryCommissionsHistory.aspx. Accessed October 2020.

51 Office of Military Commissions, Comparison of Rules and Procedures in Tribunals That Try Individuals for Alleged War Crimes, www.mc.mil/ABOUTUS/LegalSystemComparison.aspx. Accessed October 2020.

52 United States Courts, Comparing Federal & State Courts, www.uscourts.gov/about-federal-courts/court-role-and-structure/comparing-federal-state-courts. Accessed October 2020.

53 Jill Cowan, "Thousands of Californians Could Get Their Marijuana Convictions Cleared. But It's Complicated," *New York Times*, September 5, 2019. Mikaela Rabinowitz, Robert Weisberg, and Lauren McQueen Pearce, *The California Criminal Justice Data Gap* (Stanford, Calif.: Stanford Law School, 2019). Available at law.stanford.edu/publications/the-california-criminal-justice-data-gap.

54 Ibid.

55 Associated Press/KPIX, "Program to Erase Old Pot Convictions Available to All 58 California Counties," September 5, 2019.

56 Matt Masterson, "Kim Foxx Vacates 1,000 Pot Convictions as Clock Ticks toward Legalization," *WTTW*, December 11, 2019.

57 Ron Malega and Thomas H. Cohen, *State Court Organization, 2011* (Washington, D.C.: U.S. Department of Justice, Bureau of Justice Statistics, 2013). Available at www.bjs.gov/index.cfm?ty=pbdetail&iid=4802.

58 David Bjerk, "Guilt Shall Not Escape or Innocence Suffer? The Limits of Plea Bargaining When Defendant Guilt Is Uncertain," *American Law and Economics Review* 9, no. 2 (October 1, 2007): 305–329.

59 Ibid.

60 The National Association of Attorneys General, What Does an Attorney General Do?, www.naag.org/naag/about_naag/faq/what_does_an_attorney_general_do.php. Accessed October 2020.

61 Bjerk, "Guilt Shall Not Escape or Innocence Suffer?"

62 David B. Rottman and Shauna M. Strickland, *State Court Organization, 2004* (Washington, D.C.: Bureau of Justice Statistics U.S. Department of Justice Office of Justice Programs, 2006), 131.

63 Ibid.

64 Kevin M. Scott, "Understanding Judicial Hierarchy: Reversals and the Behavior of Intermediate Appellate Judges," *Law and Society Review* 40 (March 1, 2006): 163–191.

65 Hope Viner Samborn, "Disbarred—But Not Barred from Work," *ABA Journal* 93 (June 1, 2007): 57.

66 Scott Henson, interview by Eileen Smith, "The Gritty Truth," *Texas Monthly* (February 2008).

67 Patricia Marinelli-Casey, Rachel Gonzales, Maureen Hillhouse, Alfonso Ang, Joan Zweben, and Judith Cohen, "Drug Court Treatment for Methamphetamine Dependence: Treatment Response and Posttreatment Outcomes," *Journal of Substance Abuse Treatment* 34 (March 1, 2008): 242.

68 "Utah Initiative for Offenders Links Treatment, Probation," *Alcoholism and Drug Abuse Weekly*, January 14, 2008, 1.

69 Sharon M. Boles, Nancy K. Young, Toni Moore, and Sharon DiPirro-Beard,

"The Sacramento Dependency Drug Court: Development and Outcomes," *Child Maltreatment* 12 (May 1, 2007): 161–171.

70 Lorig Charkoudian and Carrie Wilson, "Factors Affecting Individuals' Decisions to Use Community Mediation," *Review of Policy Research*, July 1, 2006, 865–886.

71 Jon'a F. Meyer, "'It Is a Gift from the Creator to Keep Us in Harmony': Original (vs. alternative) Dispute Resolution in the Navajo Nation," *International Journal of Public Administration* 25 (November 1, 2002): 1379–1401.

72 Stewart J. D'Alessio and Lisa Stolzenberg, "Unemployment and the Incarceration of Pretrial Defendants," *American Sociological Review* 60 (June 1, 1995): 350.

Learn more with this chapter's digital tools, including the Oxford Insight Study Guide, at www.oup.com/he/Fuller2e.

Chapter 8

The Courtroom Work Group

Shelby Thibodeau speaks with Clifford Williams, left, and his nephew, Nathan Myers, before a hearing to overturn their 1976 murder convictions. What is the function of a conviction integrity review unit?

In May 1976, in Jacksonville, Florida, Jeanette Williams, 30, and her girlfriend, Nina Marshall, 26, were

shot while lying in bed. Williams died, and Marshall was wounded in the neck. Marshall told police that two men, Clifford Williams, 33, (no relation to Jeanette) and his nephew, Nathan Myers, 18, had entered their bedroom and opened fire.[1]

Myers was renting a bedroom in Jeanette Williams's apartment and had been at a party next door. He approached police at the scene and helped identify Jeanette Williams. Marshall, who had staggered outside after being shot, claimed she had seen both Myers and Clifford Williams on the street when she was trying to get to the hospital.[2]

Marshall claimed the two men had entered the bedroom and fired shots over a $100 debt for rent. However, about 40 alibi witnesses said that Clifford Williams and Myers were at the party during the shooting. Despite forensic evidence that pointed to the innocence of Williams and Myers, which included the facts that no gunshot residue was found on their hands and that the shots were fired from outside the apartment and from one gun, not two, police arrested and charged the two men. At trial, the prosecutor told the jury that they need not worry about ballistic tests or gunshot residue because "[w]hen you have an eyewitness, you don't need all that."[3]

Myers was offered a plea deal if he testified against his uncle, but Myers refused. A jury convicted Williams and Myers on Marshall's testimony alone. Myers was sentenced to life in prison. Williams, who had been sentenced to death, later had his sentence commuted to life in prison.[4]

In 2018, Shelley Thibodeau, director of the state's conviction integrity review unit, found evidence that was never presented to the jury and that eventually exonerated Williams and Myers. Thibodeau also discovered that a man who had been in the neighborhood that night, Nathaniel Lawson, told at least five people that he had killed Jeanette Williams.[5]

Williams and Myers, who had spent 43 years in prison, were finally released in 2019. Myers is eligible for compensation from the state up to $2 million, but Williams, because of two prior felony convictions, is barred from compensation under state law. After the hearing, Williams began to cry. "My mother died while I was on death row," he said. "I just wanted to get out and see my kids."[6]

THINK ABOUT IT > Is the prosecutor allowed to ignore evidence that points to the innocence of the accused?

LEARNING
OBJECTIVE **8.1**

Explain what a courtroom work group is.

8.1 The Courtroom Work Group

It may be easy to think of the court as an institution where justice is served in an assembly-line fashion. Individual defendants seem to be reduced to cases and are processed by court officials who appear to display little individual judgment and simply follow legal procedures. This chapter's aim is to humanize the court. Those who work in the courthouse—collectively known as the **courtroom work group**[7]—pursue various personal and institutional agendas and cooperate at many levels to produce an outcome. The courtroom work group is constrained by a range of legal, social, and institutional factors. Only by understanding these factors can we fully appreciate how the court interacts with other components of the criminal justice system.

Consider the opening case of Clifford Williams and Nathan Myers, who were convicted of murder despite physical evidence to the contrary. How did this happen? All their defense attorneys had to do was present the evidence to the jury. But the jury never saw it. The assistant state attorney offered Myers a plea deal if he testified against his uncle, but Myers refused. The two defense attorneys never brought up the evidence and the alibi witnesses. With neither the prosecution nor the defense challenging Nina Marshall's version of events, the prosecution presented the crime as an open-and-shut case, and the jurors accepted it.[8]

"If I had lost a case like that, I might've quit," a former public defender who reviewed the case told the *Florida Times-Union*. "This case stands on its own with the evidence that was available if the defense counsel had used it and had pushed it. This was an easy case."[9]

The criminal court can be volatile. On one hand, the processing of cases may often look like a smoothly functioning system in which defendants are assured the full range of constitutional protections, as well as the guarantee that their voices will be heard. On the other hand, below the surface of public scrutiny, the courtroom can be a chaotic place where the outcome of cases is a matter of negotiation and bargaining.[10]

Some people are alarmed by the reality of courthouse dynamics, which differ vastly from the ideal of impartial justice being dispensed. The notion of attorneys garnering more lenient sentences for obviously guilty defendants violates our image of the courthouse as a place where truth and justice prevail.[11] However, understanding courtroom politics is vital to comprehending the activities of those who comprise the courtroom work group. In this chapter, we will identify the roles and responsibilities of those who handle the vast caseload that passes through the modern courthouse. We will start with the support personnel and then turn to the prosecutor's office and the various types of defense attorneys.

Not all courtrooms are the same. Different levels of jurisdiction (federal, state, and local) and different levels of responsibility (misdemeanors, felonies, and appeals) dictate different working arrangements among the participants in the courtroom work group. The following is a general discussion of the courtroom work group and the typical issues that arise in most courts.

PAUSE AND REVIEW

1. **How does the reality of the courthouse work group differ from common perceptions?**

8.2 The Prosecutor

The prosecutor, sometimes called a district attorney, has, in many ways, the most powerful position in the criminal justice system. The prosecutor functions as the major gatekeeper of the criminal justice process and not only decides which cases are formally defined as criminal offenses, but also argues those cases in court.[12] The prosecutor's position is powerful because the exercise of **discretion**—the authority to decide which cases are inserted into the criminal justice system—rests with this office. With police officers pushing for charges against those whom they arrest, defense attorneys pleading for the best bargain they can get for their clients, and judges wanting to move the docket and bring

Courtroom work group—The judges, prosecutors, defense attorneys, clerks, and bailiffs who work together to move cases through the court system and whose interaction determines the outcome of criminal cases.

LEARNING OBJECTIVE **8.2**

Recognize why the prosecutor is so powerful.

LEARNING OBJECTIVE **8.3**

Outline the five categories of activities that divide the prosecutor's energies.

At Boston's Tufts Medical Center, prosecutor John Pappas, second from left, reads as Judge Michael Bolden, right, takes notes during the arraignment of Bampumim Teixeira (in bed). Teixeira, who was later convicted of murdering two doctors in their home, was wounded in a confrontation with police. Is it surprising that a courtroom workgroup would arraign a suspect in a hospital room?

Discretion (from Chapter 1)—The power of a criminal justice official to make decisions on issues within legal guidelines.

Disposition—The final determination of a case or other matter by a court or other judicial entity.

cases to **disposition** quickly, the prosecutor's power allows him or her to inject personal philosophy and political interests into the justice system.[13] The prosecutor has the discretion to charge the case (or not), to decide what the charge will be, and to dismiss it if he or she so chooses. This pivotal actor has the most influence in plea bargaining.[14]

However, the prosecutor's discretion is not completely unfettered. Even though the prosecuting attorney has sole discretion in deciding which cases to prosecute and which offenses to charge, and in determining what sorts of deals the government will agree to, prosecutorial behavior is limited. During the trial stage, the prosecutor must act within established parameters of procedural law. For instance, if the prosecutor knows of evidence that might show the defendant to be innocent, he or she must share that evidence with the defense attorney.[15] However, defense attorneys are not expected to share evidence of their clients' guilt. The prosecutor must prove the case without the aid of the defense attorney and the defendant. This might seem unfair, but it is important to remember that the prosecutor has the state's resources behind his or her efforts and that the Constitution protects the rights of the accused. Although the prosecutor represents the interests of the state (which includes the victim, police officers, and the ideal of justice), the idea of a free society under the law protects individuals from unrestricted state power.[16]

The Prosecutor at Work

Much of the prosecutor's work is invisible to the public, but this work occupies most of the prosecutor's time and, more important, forms the bulk of activities that determine exactly how justice is dispensed. Five categories of activities divide the prosecutor's energies:[17]

1. Fighting. Prosecutors work to prepare cases for court and possibly for trial. The police officer's efforts must be scrutinized to determine whether the case files are complete and, more important, whether the officer followed the procedural laws in arresting and interrogating the suspect. The prosecutor plans a legal strategy to present the strongest case possible and

to deflect criticism by the defense. The prosecutor must have a good sense of how the judge and jury will react to the case and must consider the psychological and sociological dynamics of witnesses, defendants, and others affected by the cases. In short, the prosecutor must battle to ensure that the state's case is strong, complete, and coherent and satisfies the public's sense of justice.

2. Negotiating. Few cases ever go to trial. Most are **plea-bargained**, meaning that the defense attorney and the prosecutor strike a deal for a plea of guilty or no contest in return for a lighter sentence. Plea bargaining has been the subject of much controversy because it appears to the public as though defendants can escape the full responsibility for their actions. We will discuss plea bargaining in greater detail in Chapter 9, but it is prudent to say here that this practice is vital to the functioning of the criminal justice system. Because some defendants are guilty of the offenses the police charge them with, it is in their interests, as well as the state's, to settle the case as quickly and as economically as possible. The state cannot afford the time and resources required to take every case to a jury trial, and guilty defendants cannot afford to expose themselves to the maximum sentence available under the law. Therefore, a deal is struck in which each party considers the weight of the evidence, the likelihood of a conviction, and the expenses that would be incurred by a trial, and they negotiate a settlement. The prosecutor represents the state and/or the victim in these negotiations and must make several tactical decisions to ensure that the government is getting the best deal possible and that, in a greater sense, justice is being served. Negotiating a plea is an art, and experienced prosecutors must act like poker players, sometimes revealing their evidence and sometimes attempting to bluff the defense attorney into believing that the state's or victim's case is stronger than it actually is.

3. Drafting. The drafting of legal documents is an important function of the prosecutor. Prosecutors must be careful to lay a paper trail of their activities to ensure that cases can be upheld on appeal. Prosecutors must also prepare several documents that enable other actors in the criminal justice system to perform their duties. For instance, the prosecutor drafts the search warrant, specifies which violations of the criminal codes defendants are charged with, and prepares documents that address motions made by the defense. Improperly prepared paperwork can have negative ramifications that include letting guilty suspects escape justice.

4. Counseling. Because the prosecutor occupies such a pivotal position, he or she must contend with the emotional and psychological needs of victims, witnesses, police officers, and other officials who compose the courtroom work group. If a police officer's case is weak, the prosecutor must explain why it cannot be taken to trial, and the police officer must be educated on the specific aspects of the law in which the case was inadequate. Victims may want the maximum penalty available imposed on their assailant, but the prosecutor might be restrained by other factors and must counsel the victim on why the plea bargain was the best outcome possible given the circumstances of the case.[18] Additionally, the prosecutor spends a considerable amount of time advising victims, witnesses, and police officers on how to testify at trial. A poorly prepared witness can be fatal to the state's case, and although the prosecutor will not advise anyone to tell a lie, he or she may advise the witness to answer the defense attorney's questions as succinctly

Plea bargain—A compromise reached by the defendant, the defendant's attorney, and the prosecutor in which the defendant agrees to plead guilty or no contest in return for a reduction of the charges' severity, dismissal of some charges, further information about the offense or about others involved in it, or the prosecutor's agreement to recommend a desired sentence.

Public defenders Diane Howard and Joe Cress stand outside a holding cell where Joseph James DeAngelo is being held during his hearing. The former police officer is suspected of being a serial killer, known as the Golden State Killer or the East Area Rapist, who terrorized California in the 1970s and 1980s. Who pays for the public defender's services?

Not all defense attorneys are equally competent.[35] Many variables divide the successful from the unsuccessful, the ethical from the vile, the connected from the disenfranchised, and the one you want to argue for your life from the one you would not even let contest your parking tickets. These variables are the result of factors such as:

› the law school the attorney attended;
› the law firm the attorney is associated with;
› how long the attorney has worked in a particular jurisdiction;
› how many cases the attorney has previously tried before a particular judge;
› the attorney's relationship and history with the prosecutor;
› whether the attorney is a private attorney or a public defender; and
› whether the attorney has other cases to settle with this prosecutor in the near future.[36]

Given this list of variables that can influence an attorney's effectiveness, the single most important variable may well be how much money has been invested in getting the best representation possible. Although many reasonably priced private attorneys can provide an excellent defense, assembling the witnesses and legal and technical experts and constructing elaborate exhibits can become extremely expensive, and the client foots the bill for the cost of the defense.[37]

To illustrate the power of money, let's look at a high-profile example. In 2000, when Baltimore Ravens linebacker Ray Lewis was tried for murder in Atlanta, Georgia, he was able to provide his defense team with financial resources that most individuals could not muster. When the prosecution produced a witness who claimed he saw Lewis engage in the stabbings following a Super Bowl party in a nightclub, the defense undermined the witness's credibility by producing evidence of past lies. The hostile witness had been convicted of identity theft and running up exorbitant charges on credit cards. In a dramatic and effective courtroom maneuver, the defense attorney asked the witness if he had ever met the individual whose identity he had stolen and whose financial reputation he had besmirched, and then had that individual stand up in court to demonstrate to the jury that the witness had harmed a real person and not simply some abstraction.

Ray Lewis's defense team was able to fly this person across the country from California to Atlanta to stand up in court for 15 seconds to hammer a point about the witness's trustworthiness. The average defendant, who is not a multimillionaire football player, would have been unable to finance such a legal tactic. Prosecutors dropped the murder and aggravated assault charges against Lewis in exchange for his plea of guilty to misdemeanor obstruction of justice charges.

The Defense Attorney and the Courtroom Work Group

Although the defense attorney's first obligation is to provide the best defense possible for the defendant, this duty does not always result in a jury trial in which the truth is revealed and justice is done to the satisfaction of all. Despite the defense attorney's commitment to the interests of the accused, other pressures mediate how aggressively the prosecutor's case is challenged.[38]

Here, Melissa Keeler demonstrates the beating she saw from her apartment window during the murder trial of Baltimore Ravens linebacker Ray Lewis and two other men. Why is it important that a wealthy defendant can provide financial resources for his or her defense that other defendants cannot?

The attorney who engages in criminal defense work on a regular basis becomes part of the courtroom work group. Although ideally the prosecutor's adversary, the defense attorney must develop a working relationship with the group to ensure that the group's goals are achieved. The wheels of justice never turn smoothly, but the obstinate defense attorney who causes them to grind to a halt by contesting and protesting every routine point of law and procedural ruling will quickly find that the judge, prosecutor, court reporter, and others in the courtroom work group will be less flexible and accommodating in their dealings with that attorney and that attorney's clients. An informal system of norms and relationships develops in the courtroom work group to efficiently move the docket and dispose of cases in accordance with expected outcomes.

The dealings of the courtroom work group are best explained by two classic studies of the court conducted by scholars David Sudnow and Abraham Blumberg. Sudnow introduced the concept of **normal crimes**, defined as cases that are considered in the context of how the court handled similar offenses.[39]

Defense attorneys and prosecutors have a good idea about what the sentence will be for a particular offense by considering how that infraction compares to the court's pattern of sentencing. For the offender to receive a more severe or a more lenient sentence than the going rate, the offense's circumstances must be shown to be abnormal. Given this already established norm for sentencing, the defense attorney often encourages the defendant to plead guilty in return for a reduced sentence. When the defense attorney takes a normal crime to trial, the courtroom work group may consider the attorney to be wasting the court's time and resources. Consequently, in the interests of conforming to the expectations of the defense of normal crimes, the defense attorney facilitates the criminal prosecution process rather than zealously advocates for the defendant.

Normal crimes—
Routine cases that are considered in the context of how the court handled similar offenses.

This abdication of the responsibility to protect the defendant's interests might seem wrong, but we will see in the next chapter that plea bargaining is a complex issue. In many ways, the defense attorney is getting the best possible deal for a client when the case is handled as a normal crime.

Part of the client's difficulty in evaluating the contributions of the defense attorney lies in determining what can be attributed to the attorney's expertise and what can be attributed to the courthouse routine. The attorney may be working hard for the client, doing legal research, negotiating strenuously with the prosecutors, and developing treatment plans with probation officers, but the client has limited knowledge of this activity. In fact, according to Blumberg, the dynamics of the courtroom work group help the defense attorney to erect a facade of competence even when the attorney is simply "acting" in an effort to impress the client.

Although Blumberg alerts us to some interesting dynamics of how courtrooms actually operate, we should be cautious about becoming too cynical. All organizations make distinctions between what sociologist Erving Goffman called "front-stage" and "backstage" behavior, in which participants act one way when they are on public display and another when they are surrounded only by trusted co-workers.[40] Courts are no exception, and the defense attorney's dramatics performed for the defendant's benefit do not differ substantially from how judges, prosecutors, or even professors or physicians act when they are attempting to put the best face on their actions. The defense attorney is subject to organizational pressures from the courtroom work group. The defendant must understand that although the defense attorney negotiates with the defendant's best interests in mind, sometimes the best interests of the defense attorney differ from those of the defendant.[41]

The Best Defense: Private Attorney or Public Defender?

The quality of legal defense varies greatly for individuals accused of breaking the law. An attorney's competence might depend on the level of the court, the geographic location, the client's resources, and how state and local governments fund indigent defense efforts. We commonly believe that private attorneys are automatically superior to those provided by the state, but in reality the issue is more complicated than that.[42]

Criminal defense work is not among the most lucrative specializations for private attorneys. Few private attorneys can make a living practicing exclusively, or even primarily, criminal defense law. Many attorneys have more comprehensive practices in which they also practice tort law, family law, or business law.[43] Some of the most expensive and best attorneys confine themselves to specialties such as corporate law and seldom enter a courtroom. As such, a private attorney might not be the best one to represent a drug dealer or someone facing a capital charge of homicide.[44]

However, many successful private attorneys are excellent criminal defenders. Many former prosecutors or public defenders who go into private practice regularly do criminal defense work. In this way, they have an advantage in that they have been part of the criminal court's work group in the past and have already established relationships with the prosecutor's office and the judges. Depending on the private defense attorney's reputation and experience, the cost of representation can be high. Because clients pay for private defense attorneys, the quality of the services rendered is expected to be superior to what is available from a public defender. However, if we can believe Blumberg, the private defense attorney may be likely to extend the case in order to charge a wealthy defendant as much money as possible.[45]

A CLOSER LOOK 8.1
Public Defender Salaries Are Indefensible

The public defender's office in Richmond, Virginia, has trouble keeping attorneys. Over the past three years, 60 percent of their staff has departed for higher-paying jobs elsewhere. The high turnover rate means that clients of the public defender's office are often represented by attorneys who have much less experience than the city's prosecutors.[46]

Pay disparities affect public defenders, as well as the defendants who need their services, throughout the country. In Florida, for example, a recent salary analysis by the state attorney general's office revealed that public defenders earn less than almost any other government attorney in the state.[47] The situation makes the criminal justice process even more precarious for impoverished defendants whose attorneys are overworked, underpaid, and likely not as experienced as prosecutors simply because of the high turnover rate of their positions. In Richmond, Virginia, public defender salaries start at about $50,000 a year, which is almost 40 percent less than the salaries of attorneys who work for the prosecutor's office. The highest paid administrative assistant in the prosecutor's office makes more money than 27 of the 29 attorneys in the public defender's office.[48]

Why such a disparity? Although the state funds both offices at about the same rate, the difference results from unequal local budgetary contributions. In Virginia, most cities and counties augment prosecutors' salaries but do not make similar contributions to public defender offices. For instance, the city of Richmond allots an extra $7 million each year to the salaries and other budgetary needs of the prosecutor's office while contributing nothing to the public defender's office.[49]

Some jurisdictions are trying to rectify the problem. For example, Wisconsin legislators are considering a plan to increase the pay of state public defenders to more closely align with that of state prosecutors.[50] In South Carolina, the Richland County Council recently approved a pay raise for the county's public defenders. According to Council Vice Chairwoman Dalhi Myers, "If you can't retain people who have learned how to do a really good job at what they do, and you are always training new people … and those people are going against very seasoned litigators, then the not-so-well-heeled defendants stand to be in an unfortunate position."[51]

THINK ABOUT IT

1. Why is the disparity between the salaries of public defenders and prosecutors a problem?

Public defenders have a precarious position in the criminal justice system (see A Closer Look 8.1). They are obligated to provide the best defense possible for the defendant, but their salaries may come from any number of sources. The indigent defense systems of 28 states and the District of Columbia are funded completely by the state or mostly by the state with some county funds. The rest of the states depend on county funds exclusively or on county funds, with some additional funds from the state. Several states supplement public defender funding with court fees assessed to indigent defendants who plead guilty or are found guilty.[52]

Because of the large caseloads carried by many public defender offices, the time and resources available are seldom sufficient to provide the extended defense services that the public defender would like.[53] It is difficult to generalize the work of public defenders because of the variation in how they are structured and financed. (For more on the states' obligation to appoint attorneys for indigent defendants, see Case in Point 8.1.)

Each state has its own system for setting up the defense of indigent clients. These systems fall into three broad categories:[54]

> Assigned counsel. In small jurisdictions with limited resources, the judge may assign a practicing member of the bar to represent defendants who lack the financial means to hire a private attorney. There are drawbacks to this

CASE IN POINT 8.1

Argersinger v. Hamlin (1972)

THE POINT

Defendants have the right to an attorney if an offense, regardless of its seriousness, is punishable by incarceration.

THE CASE

Jon Argersinger, an indigent, was charged in Florida with carrying a concealed weapon. With no attorney present, Argersinger was tried by a judge and sentenced to 90 days in jail. The court did not appoint an attorney for Argersinger, which the state supreme court upheld, holding that the right to court-appointed counsel extended only to offenses punishable by more than six months' imprisonment. The U.S. Supreme Court reversed this decision, holding that the right to counsel extended to defendants in any offense for which imprisonment can be imposed.

Scott v. Illinois (1979)

THE POINT

States may incarcerate offenders only if they have been represented by counsel; states are not obliged to appoint counsel for offenders who have not been sentenced to incarceration, even if incarceration is a possible punishment.

THE CASE

Aubrey Scott was convicted of theft by a judge and fined $50, although the maximum penalty was a $500 fine and/ or one year in jail. Citing *Argersinger*, Scott appealed, contending that the Sixth and Fourteenth Amendments required the state to provide him with an attorney. The U.S. Supreme Court affirmed the original opinion and clarified *Argersinger*, holding that offenders could be incarcerated only if they had been represented by counsel. As Scott was not sentenced to incarceration, and could not be because he had not been represented by counsel, the state was not obliged to provide him with counsel.

THINK ABOUT IT

1. What is the main difference between these two cases in terms of incarceration and legal representation?

method of assigning attorneys. A limitation in many jurisdictions is that the judge draws from a pool that consists of attorneys who volunteer.[55] This volunteer pool usually comprises young attorneys developing their courtroom skills or less successful attorneys willing to take the reduced court fee just to make a living. Even in jurisdictions in which all the attorneys are in the selection pool, the defendant might end up with an excellent real estate lawyer who is not familiar with the demands of criminal defense work.

› Contract systems. In a contract system, law firms bid for the business of all indigent defense work. The advantage of this system is that the firm's attorneys quickly become proficient in dealing with the prosecutor and the courtroom work group. Opponents of this system contend that because of the competitive bidding process, the low bidder ends up with a caseload that does not provide enough revenue for the support system of secretaries, investigators, and attorneys that is necessary for a vigorous defense of all cases.

> Public defender. As a result of the decision in *Gideon v. Wainright* (see Case in Point 8.2), the public defender system has been implemented in 49 states and the District of Columbia.[56] Having a full-time public defender staff has several advantages. Attorneys who work in public defender offices quickly gain extensive experience working with the criminal law and become seasoned trial attorneys. Many attorneys like having a public defender office because it relieves their own firms of having to do *pro bono* work that drains their resources. Also, because of the permanence of public defender systems, relationships with other personnel in the criminal justice system have been developed so that the attorneys enter cases at an early stage, usually at the initial hearing.[57]

The image of the public defender is sometimes cast in a negative light when compared to that of private attorneys. This image is, paradoxically, both accurate and misleading. Certainly, someone with sufficient financial resources can hire an attorney who is experienced in criminal law and can provide the best legal defense money can buy.[58] However, many indigent defendants also receive excellent representation from competent, experienced, and dedicated public defenders.

This 1963 photo shows Clarence Earl Gideon after his release from a Panama City, Florida, jail. A unanimous Supreme Court issued its decision in *Gideon v. Wainwright*, declaring that states must provide defendants with "the guiding hand of counsel" to ensure a fair trial. How many states have a public defender system today?

CASE IN POINT 8.2

Gideon v. Wainwright (1963)

THE POINT

Indigent defendants have the right to court-appointed attorneys in felony cases.

THE CASE

In 1961, Clarence Gideon, an impoverished drifter, was charged with breaking and entering a poolroom, a felony under Florida law. Gideon went to court without money or a lawyer and asked the court to appoint counsel for him. The judge told him that counsel was appointed only if the punishment involved the death penalty. The case went to a jury trial in which Gideon defended himself. He was found guilty and sentenced to five years in prison. On appeal, the U.S. Supreme Court overturned his conviction and established that indigent defendants have the right to court-appointed attorneys in felony cases.

THINK ABOUT IT

1. What effect did the *Gideon* decision have on the public defender system?

PAUSE AND REVIEW

1. What variables can influence a defense attorney's effectiveness? Which variable is considered the single most important one and why?

2. Describe the concept of "normal crimes." How does this concept affect the courtroom work group?

LEARNING OBJECTIVE 8.6

List several examples of the duties of judges.

LEARNING OBJECTIVE 8.7

Discuss the three methods of selecting judges.

8.4 The Judge

Judges occupy a unique space in the criminal justice system. On one hand, they are considered the most powerful actors in the system. On the other hand, judges are viewed as impotent referees who must act with neutrality, objectivity, and impartiality. They have neither the prosecutor's extensive power of discretion nor the prestige or salary of a successful defense attorney. The term *judge* encompasses many responsibilities from the local justice of the peace to a Supreme Court justice.

Judges perform several duties. They act as a check and balance to the discretion of zealous prosecutors, as impartial arbiters in the contest between law enforcement and defendants, and as decision-makers in applying punishment or treatment to the guilty. Judges play a role at many points in the criminal justice system, including:

› Signing search warrants. Judges ensure that police officers do not violate suspects' rights against unreasonable searches by reviewing search warrants for evidence of probable cause.

› Informing defendants of charges. The judge informs the defendant of the charges the police officer has filed at the initial-appearance stage.

› Appointing counsel. For indigent defendants, the judge appoints a defense attorney. In many states, this is the public defender who is appointed to that judge's courtroom. In some jurisdictions, the judge appoints a private attorney whose turn it is to provide indigent defense.

› Setting bail. After hearing from the prosecutor who reviews the charges, the defendant's criminal history, and the likelihood that the defendant will appear at subsequent hearings, the judge gives the defense attorney an opportunity to rebut. Then, the judge either sets bail, releases the defendant on recognizance, or orders the defendant confined until trial.

› Taking a plea. At arraignment, the judge informs the defendant of the charges and allows the defendant to enter a plea of guilty, not guilty, or no contest.

› Ruling on motions. The judge rules on motions from the defense and the prosecution concerning the admissibility of evidence. These motions may concern illegal search and seizure issues, the interrogation of suspects, or the use of police lineups.

› Participating in or ruling on plea bargaining. Some judges take an active role in deciding a plea bargain between the defense and the prosecution. Other judges simply approve or disapprove the negotiated decision.

› Presiding at trial. The judge's role in a trial is to ensure that the defendant's due process rights are respected, to rule on the admissibility of evidence, to instruct the jury as to which laws are applicable in the case, and to ensure that all parties, including spectators, conduct themselves properly.

Lila Mubarak stands next to Illinois Judge Gabriel Fuentes after receiving a certificate of naturalization. Judges have many responsibilities besides keeping order in the courtroom. What are some of these responsibilities?

> Sentencing. Although many cases provide clear-cut choices between incarceration and liberty, the alternative options available to most judges are quite limited. Treatment options are scarce, and with prison crowding a serious issue in many states, judges are pressured to find dispositions other than incarceration.

In the next section, we will discuss the methods of judicial selection. More important than the selection method, however, is the question of whether any method produces better judges than other methods.

Judicial Selection: Executive Appointments

At the federal level, judges are nominated by the president and confirmed by the Senate according to their advise-and-consent responsibility as stated in the Constitution. Although in the past this process has been a routine rubber stamp of the president's wishes, recently it has become quite politicized.[59] Controversial appointments are subjected to lengthy Senate hearings in which the nominee is grilled by senators about his or her character, legal history, and views on certain controversial issues that will likely come before the courts. A good deal of screening takes place to find candidates who reflect the president's worldview and yet are not controversial.

For U.S. district court judges, the senators of the state in which the appointment is to be made are commonly consulted as a courtesy. If a senator finds the nominee unacceptable, senators from other states (particularly those in the same party) might vote against the appointment. In this way, senators have both formal and informal influence on the selection of judges in their state. At the state level, the legislature has no comparable advise-and-consent function, so governors have more leeway in the selection of judges. At both levels, the influence of party politics is significant.[60]

Judicial Selection: Election of Judges

In an effort to democratize judicial selection, nearly half of the states elect judges. It is assumed that judges who must run for re-election will conform to the wishes

Candidate Eddie Treviño Jr. won the seat of Cameron County Judge in Brownsville, Texas, in November 2016. What other ways are judges selected?

Missouri Bar Plan—A form of judicial selection in which a nominating commission presents a list of candidates to the governor, who decides on a candidate. After a year in office, voters decide on whether to retain the judge. Judges must run for such re-election each term. Also called merit selection.

of the people rather than the dictates of the elite.[61] For the most part, the campaigns for judgeships have low visibility, and voters have little knowledge about the qualifications or temperament of the candidates. For this reason, incumbent judges have a distinct advantage over challengers, especially when the title "judge" is printed next to their names on the ballot. Some elections are hotly contested, especially seats on the state supreme court.[62]

Judicial Selection: Merit Selection

In an effort to remove politics from the judicial selection process, court reformers have adopted a system called merit selection or, as it is sometimes known, the **Missouri Bar Plan**. In this process, a judicial nominating commission comprising lawyers and laypeople presents a short list of qualified candidates (usually three) to the governor, who makes the final decision. Judges are then required to face the voters after a short period of time (one year). Instead of running against another candidate, the vote is simply on whether the judge should be retained in office. Judges must stand for re-election each term, but they are seldom removed because they essentially have no opponents, and the voters seldom know of reasons why they should be removed.[63]

Each method of selecting judges has its merits. When judges are elected, they are considered more accountable to the voters and more likely to represent the interests of the average citizen rather than those of the elite of the legal profession. This admirable philosophy is pitted against the alternative of the appointment of judges, where, presumably free from catering to the voters, the judge can enjoy judicial independence and rule on the merits of the case.

Perhaps the most important and notable change in the judicial selection process is the increase in the number of women and minorities appointed to the bench. The profile of the judge as a white male is being radically changed without affecting other background characteristics such as judicial education. As more women go to law school and work their way up the ranks of prosecutors' offices and law firms, more of them are being elected or appointed as judges. To a large extent, the same can be said for minorities, but because of the under-representation of black lawyers, there are fewer black judges. More minorities are on the bench in states in which judges are appointed than in states in which judges are elected.[64]

PAUSE AND REVIEW

1. List five examples of judges' duties.
2. What are the three methods of selecting judges?
3. How many states elect judges?

8.5 The Participants

LEARNING OBJECTIVE **8.8**

Describe the two primary court functions that probation officers perform.

LEARNING OBJECTIVE **8.9**

Characterize the tasks of law enforcement, court support staff, corrections, and the public.

Although a certain adversarial atmosphere is present in the courtroom, those in the courtroom work group also exhibit a high level of cooperation.[65] The participants working in the courthouse, and, ultimately, in the courtroom, all come from disparate backgrounds, agencies, and ideologies. As in the criminal justice system in general, those who work in the courthouse have different funding sources, constituents, responsibilities, and goals. These people who sometimes seem to be working at cross purposes—for example, the prosecutor and the defense attorney have competing agendas regarding defendants—are in many other ways cooperating to move cases in a timely manner.[66] Consequently, there is a certain level of expectation of how each case will be settled based on the going rate. In sociological terms, a routinization of work occurs whereby everyone (except the defendant) has a good idea about the outcome of the case. Nevertheless, each actor has a vested interest in seeing cases resolved according to his or her particular social and legal location within the courthouse. Let's review this variety of courthouse actors and the duties they perform in the courtroom.

Law Enforcement

Various types of law enforcement officers interact daily within the courtroom work group. First is the courthouse security officer, who is responsible for protecting everyone in the courthouse.[67] A second type of law enforcement officer working in the courthouse is the sheriff's deputy, who transports prisoners to and from jail. The courthouse usually has a holding pen where deputies keep prisoners until they are required in the courtroom. The **bailiff** is a court officer responsible for maintaining order in the courtroom.[68] In some jurisdictions, a bailiff works in a specific judge's courtroom. In other jurisdictions, bailiffs rotate from courtroom to courtroom as needed. Additionally, the constant parade of law enforcement

Bailiff—Court officer responsible for executing writs and processes, making arrests, and keeping order in the court.

Two bailiffs escort a man from a courtroom. Besides attorneys and judges, who are some of the other essential courtroom actors?

LEARNING OBJECTIVE **8.8** Describe the two primary court functions that probation officers perform.	Probation officers interview offenders and write pre-sentence investigation reports in which they review the case and make sentencing recommendations to the judge. Probation officers also supervise offenders on probation to ensure that they follow the judge's orders and obey the law.
LEARNING OBJECTIVE **8.9** Characterize the tasks of law enforcement, court support staff, corrections, and the public.	**Law enforcement:** Courthouse security officers protect everyone in the courthouse. Sheriff's deputies transport prisoners and monitor them until they are required in the courtroom. Bailiffs maintain order in the courtroom. A senior law enforcement officer may coordinate with police agencies to schedule officers for trials. **Court support staff:** Court clerks keep court records and maintain the juror pool. Court reporters transcribe court proceedings. Translators translate testimonies. Court administrators handle administrative tasks. **Corrections:** Probation officers produce pre-sentence investigation reports and supervise offenders on probation. Rehabilitation specialists identify drug and alcohol treatment programs for qualified offenders. **The Public:** Bail agents solicit offenders who cannot afford their bail. Victim–witness program personnel advocate on behalf of victims and introduce victim-impact statements. In juvenile courts, child advocates support the best interests of the child.
LEARNING OBJECTIVE **8.10** Describe the experience of defendants, victims, and witnesses in the context of the courtroom work group.	Due to illiteracy, mental illness, poverty, age, or addiction, defendants often have trouble understanding the workings of the court and may feel powerless. Victims are sometimes diminished because a felony charge pits the defendant against the state and excludes the victim(s). Victims can become disillusioned when their cases are treated in the bureaucratic manner of the court. Witnesses may be inconvenienced by having to show up in court, lose wages at a job, and/or may fear retaliation from a defendant.
LEARNING OBJECTIVE **8.11** Name some services that victim–witness programs provide.	Crisis intervention, follow-up counseling, personal advocacy, employer and landlord intervention, property return, intimidation protection, referral to community resources, court orientation, court transportation and escort, public education, and legislative advocacy.

Critical Reflections

1. Is it fair that the prosecutor has so much power in the court?

2. What benefits do victim–witness programs provide?

3. Which method of judicial selection do you think is the most effective? Which method is used in your state?

Key Terms

Notes

1 Andrew Pantazi, "Jacksonville Men Freed 43 Years after Wrongful Murder Conviction, a First for Florida Conviction Review Unit," March 28, 2019, *Florida Times-Union*. Ken Otterbourg, Hubert Myers, National Registry of Exonerations, April 2019, www.law.umich.edu/special/exoneration/Pages/casedetail.aspx?caseid=5534.

2 Ibid.

3 Ibid.

4 Ibid.

5 Ibid.

6 Ibid.

7 James Eisenstein and Herbert Jacob, *Felony Justice: An Organizational Analysis of Criminal Courts* (Boston: Little, Brown, 1977).

8 Pantazi, "Jacksonville Men Freed 43 Years after Wrongful Murder Conviction, a First for Florida Conviction Review Unit."

9 Ibid.

10 Josh Bowers, "Punishing the Innocent," *University of Pennsylvania Law Review* 156 (May 1, 2008): 1117.

11 Máximo Langer, "Rethinking Plea Bargaining: The Practice and Reform of Prosecutorial Adjudication in American Criminal Procedure," *American Journal of Criminal Law* 33 (July 2006): 223–299.

12 William McDonald, "The Prosecutors' Domain," in *The Prosecutor*, ed. William McDonald (Newbury Park, Calif.: Sage, 1979).

13 Alissa Pollitz Worden, "Policy-making by Prosecutors: The Uses of Discretion in Regulating Plea Bargaining," *Judicature* 73 (1990): 335–340.

14 Talia Fisher, "The Boundaries of Plea Bargaining: Negotiating the Standard of Proof," *Journal of Criminal Law and Criminology* 97 (July 1, 2007): 943–1007.

15 *Brady v. Maryland*, 373 U.S. 83 (1963).

16 Bennett L. Gershman, "Why Prosecutors Misbehave," in *Courts and Justice: A Reader*, 2nd ed., eds. G. Larry Mays and Peter R. Gregware (Long Grove, Ill.: Waveland Press, 1999), 282–292.

17 David W. Neubauer, *America's Courts and the Criminal Justice System*, 7th ed. (Belmont, Calif.: Wadsworth, 2002).

18 Michael Booth, "Victim Need Not Be Told of Plea Bargain," *National Law Journal*, July 16, 2007, 15.

19 Resa Baldas, "Hot-Button Words Are Iced in Court," *National Law Journal*, June 16, 2008, 1.

20 Pamela Utz, "Two Models of Prosecutorial Professionalism," in *The Prosecutor*, ed. William McDonald (Newbury Park, Calif.: Sage, 1979).

21 Joan Jacoby, *The Prosecutors' Charging Decision: A Policy Perspective* (Washington, D.C.: U.S. Department of Justice, 1977).

22 Los Angeles County District Attorney's Office, Office Overview, da.co.la.ca.us/about/office-overview. Accessed October 2020.

23 Griffin Bell, "Appointing United States Attorneys," *Journal of Law and Politics* 9 (1993): 247–256.

24 Rebecca Sudokar, *The Solicitor General: The Politics of Law* (Philadelphia: Temple University Press, 1992).

25 Offices of the United States Attorneys, Mission, www.justice.gov/usao/mission. Accessed October 2020.

26 Bell, "Appointing United States Attorneys."

27 Metro Atlanta Chamber, Metro Atlanta Regional Map, www.metroatlanta-chamber.com/resources/most-popular/map-of-metro-atlanta. Accessed October 2020.

28 "Key Events in State Suits against Tobacco Industry," *CNN*, www.cnn.com/US/9811/16/tobacco.timeline. Accessed October 2020.

29 Neubauer, *America's Courts and the Criminal Justice System*.

30 David Heilbroner, *Rough Justice: Days and Nights of a Young D.A.* (New York: Pantheon, 1990).

31 Neubauer, *America's Courts and the Criminal Justice System*.

32 David Lynch, "The Impropriety of Plea Agreements: A Tale of Two Counties," *Law and Social Inquiry* 19 (1994): 115–136.

33 William J. Price, "Make Sense of Your Client's Story," *Trial*, June 1, 2008, 66.

34 Rodney Uphoff, "The Criminal Defense Lawyer: Zealous Advocate, Double Agent or Beleaguered Dealer?" *Criminal Law Bulletin* 28 (1992): 419–456.

35 Stephen Bright, "Counsel for the Poor: The Death Sentence Not for the Worst Crime, But for the Worst Lawyer," *Yale Law Journal* 103 (1994): 1835–1884.

36 Michael J. McWilliams, "The Erosion of Indigent Rights: Excessive Caseloads Resulting in Ineffective Counsel for Poor," *American Bar Association Journal* 79 (1993): 8.

37 Larry J. Cohen, Patricia P. Sample, and Robert E. Crew Jr., "Assigned Counsel versus Public Defender Systems in Virginia," in *The Defense Counsel*, ed. William F. McDonald (Beverly Hills, Calif.: Sage, 1983).

38 Jerome Skolnick, "Social Control in the Adversary System," *Journal of Conflict Resolution* 11 (1967): 52–70.

39 David Sudnow, "Normal Crimes: Sociological Features of the Penal Code in a Public Defender Office," *Social Problems* 12 (1965): 209–215.

40 Erving Goffman, *The Presentation of Self in Everyday Life* (Garden City, N.Y.: Doubleday Anchor Books, 1959).

41 Brian Sullivan, "Canning Your Client," *ABA Journal* 94 (March 1, 2008): 46–52.

42 Roger Hanson, William Hewitt, and Brian Ostrom, "Are the Critical Indigent Defense Counsel Correct?" *State Court Journal* (Summer 1992): 20–29.

43 Carroll Seron, *The Business of Practicing Law: The Work Lives of Solo and Small-Firm Attorneys* (Philadelphia: Temple University Press, 1996).

44 Bright, "Counsel for the Poor."

45 Abraham S. Blumberg, "The Practice of Law as a Confidence Game," *Law and Society Review* (June 1, 1967): 15–39. "The real key to understanding the role of a defense counsel in a criminal case is to be found in the area of the fixing of the fee to be charged and its collection. The problem of fixing and collecting the fee tends to influence to a significant degree the criminal court process itself, and not just the relationship between the lawyer and his client" (p. 24).

46 Ned Oliver, "Most Public Defenders in Richmond Make Less Than a Secretary in the Prosecutor's Office," *Virginia Mercury*, September 30, 2019.

47 Andrew Pantazi, "Paying for Justice: Public Defenders and Prosecutors Flee for Better Salaries," February 23, 2018, *Florida Times-Union* (Jacksonville).

48 Oliver, "Most Public Defenders in Richmond Make Less Than a Secretary in the Prosecutor's Office."

49 Ibid.

50 Laurel White, "Lawmakers Consider Pay Bump for Wisconsin Public Defenders," *Superior Telegram* (Duluth, Minn.) November 5, 2019.

51 Chris Trainor, "Richland County Hikes Pay for Public Defenders," June 18, 2019, *Post and Courier/Free Times* (Columbia, S.C.).

52 Suzanne M. Strong, *State-Administered Indigent Defense Systems, 2013* (Washington, D.C.: U.S. Department of Justice Office of Justice Programs Bureau of Justice Statistics, 2016), 1. Available at, www.bjs.gov/index.cfm?ty=pbdetail&iid=5826. Julia O'Donoghue, "Inadequate Representation: No More Money Expected for Public Defenders," NOLA.com, April 18, 2016. Tim Lockette, "Lawyers on Layaway," *Anniston Star*, September 28, 2013.

53 McWilliams, "Erosion of Indigent Rights."

54 Alissa Pollitz Worden, "Privatizing Due Process: Issues in the Comparison of Assigned Counsel, Public Defender, and Contracted Indigent Defense Systems," *Justice Systems Journal* 14 (1991): 390–418.

55 Gail S. Goodman, R. S. Edelstein, E. B. Mitchell, and J. E. Myers, "A Comparison of Types of Attorney Representation for Children in California Juvenile Court Dependency Cases," *Child Abuse and Neglect* 32 (April 1, 2008): 497.

56 Lynn Langton and Donald J. Farole, Jr., *Public Defender Offices, 2007 Statistical Tables* (Washington, D.C.: U.S. Department of Justice Office of Justice Programs, 2010), 1. Available at bjs.ojp.usdoj.gov/index.cfm?ty=pbdetail&iid=1758.

57 Neubauer, *America's Courts and the Criminal Justice System*, 179–182.

58 Arye Rattner, Hagit Turjeman, and Gideon Fishman, "Public versus Private Defense: Can Money Buy Justice?" *Journal of Criminal Justice* 36 (March 1, 2008): 43.

59 Sheldon Goldman and Elliot Slotnick, "Clinton's Second Term Judiciary: Picking Judges under Fire," *Judicature* 82 (1999): 264–285.

60 Terry B. Friedman, "The Politicization of the Judiciary," *Judicature* 82 (July 1, 1998): 6–7.

61 Paul Brace and Brent D. Boyea, "State Public Opinion, the Death Penalty, and the Practice of Electing Judges" *American Journal of Political Science* 52 (April 1, 2008): 360–372.

62 Philip Dubois, *From Ballot to Bench: Judicial Elections and the Quest for Accountability* (Austin: University of Texas Press, 1980).

63 Ibid., 205.

64 Kathryn Fahnestock and Maurice Geiger, "We All Get Along Here: Case Flow in Rural Courts," *Judicature* 76 (1993): 258–263.

65 Blumberg, "The Practice of Law as a Confidence Game."

66 Sudnow, "Normal Crimes."

67 "Review Cites 8 Steps to Boost Court Security," *Crime Control Digest*, March 24, 2006, 4.

68 N. Gary Holten and Lawson L. Lamar, *The Criminal Courts: Structures, Personnel, and Processes* (New York: McGraw-Hill, 1991), 109–110.

69 Stacey Laskin, "Dramatic Drop in Court Reporters Causes Alarm," *National Law Journal* (July 23, 2007): 6.

70 Ibid., 111–112.

71 John Rosecrance, "Maintaining the Myth of Individualized Justice: Probation Pre-sentence Reports," *Justice Quarterly* 5 (1988): 235–256.

72 Gary A. Rabe and Dean J. Champion, *Criminal Courts: Structure, Process, and Issues* (Upper Saddle River, N.J.: Prentice Hall, 2002). Chapter 7 presents an excellent review of pre-trial procedures.

73 Jennifer Eno Louden, Jennifer L. Skeem, Jacqueline Camp, and Elizabeth Christensen, "Supervising Probationers with Mental Disorder: How Do Agencies Respond to Violations?" *Criminal Justice and Behavior* 35 (July 1, 2008): 832.

74 Ronald Burns, Patrick Kinkade, and Matthew C. Leone, "Bounty Hunters: A Look behind the Hype," *Policing* 28 (January 1, 2005): 118–138.

75 Patricia Resick, "The Trauma of Rape and the Criminal Justice System," *Justice System Journal* 9 (1984): 52–61.

76 Ira Schwartz, *Justice for Juveniles: Rethinking the Best Interests of the Child* (New York: Lexington Books, 1989).

77 Robert Davis and Barbara Smith, "The Effects of Victim Impact Statements on Sentencing Decisions: A Test in an Urban Setting," *Justice Quarterly* 11 (1994): 453–469.

78 Fahnestock and Geiger, "We All Get Along Here."

79 Marvin Free, *African Americans and the Criminal Justice System* (New York: Garland, 1997).

80 Arthur Rosett and Donald R. Cressey, *Justice by Consent: Plea Bargains in the American Courthouse* (New York: Lippincott, 1976).

81 John Irwin, *The Jail: Managing the Underclass in American Society* (Berkeley: University of California Press, 1985).

82 J. Dyer, *The Perpetual Incarceration Machine: How America Profits from Crime* (Boulder, Colo.: Westview, 1999).

83 Andrew Karnsen, *Crime Victims: An Introduction to Victimology*, 4th ed. (Belmont, Calif.: Wadsworth, 2001).

84 Emma Schwartz, "Giving Crime Victims More of Their Say: A Federal Law Has Created Tensions in the Legal

System," *U.S. News & World Report*, December 24, 2007, 28.

85 Candace McCoy, *Politics and Plea Bargaining: Victims' Rights in California* (Philadelphia: University of Pennsylvania Press, 1993).

86 Kerry Healey, *Victim and Witness Intimidation: New Developments and*

Emerging Responses (Washington, D.C.: National Institute of Justice, 1995).

87 Peter Finn and Beverley Lee, *Establishing and Expanding Victim-Witness Assistance Programs* (Washington, D.C.: National Institute of Justice, 1988).

88 William G. Doerner and Steven P. Lab, *Victimology* (Cincinnati, Ohio: Anderson, 1995), 53–54.

89 Elizabeth Connick and Robert Davis, "Examining the Problems of Witness Intimidation," *Judicature* 66 (1983): 438–447.

Learn more with this chapter's digital tools, including the Oxford Insight Study Guide, at www.oup.com/he/Fuller2e.

Chapter 9

The Disposition: Plea Bargaining, Trial, and Sentencing

OUTLINE

9.1 THE CRIMINAL COURT PROCESS 256

9.2 PRE-TRIAL RELEASE DECISIONS 257

9.3 THE PLEA BARGAIN 259

Issues That Affect Plea Bargaining
Types of Plea Bargains
Should Plea Bargaining Be Abolished?

9.4 THE TRIAL 266

The Pre-trial Phase
  Pre-trial Motions
Opening Arguments
The Prosecution's Presentation of Witnesses and
  Evidence
The Case Goes to the Jury
The Defense Doesn't Rest
Appeal

9.5 SENTENCING 279

Indeterminate Sentencing
Determinate Sentencing
Mandatory Minimum Sentences

SUMMARY 285

FEATURES

CJ REFERENCE 9.1
What Are Grand Juries and How
Do They Work? *p. 269*

CJ REFERENCE 9.2
The Exclusionary Rule *p. 270*

CASE IN POINT 9.1
Batson v. Kentucky (1986) *p. 276*

GETTING IT RIGHT 9.1
The Role of the Prosecutor and
Conviction Review Units *p. 279*

FOCUS ON ETHICS
Letting the Big Ones
  Get Away *p. 285*

Former Pennsylvania State University assistant football coach Jerry Sandusky arrives at the courthouse to be re-sentenced after an appeals court found that mandatory-minimum sentences had been improperly applied against him. What is the purpose of mandatory-minimum sentences?

In 2012,

Jerry Sandusky, a former assistant football coach at Pennsylvania State University, was sentenced to a mandatory minimum of 30 to 60 years in prison for sexually molesting boys. Sandusky, then age 68, was convicted on 45 counts of child sexual abuse that he perpetrated over 15 years, targeting victims through his youth charity, The Second Mile.[1]

In 2015, a Pennsylvania Superior Court deemed mandatory minimum sentences unconstitutional, citing the 2013 U.S. Supreme Court case, *Alleyne v. United States*.[2] According to *Alleyne*, the jury in the *Sandusky* case had to find, beyond a reasonable doubt, an aggravating factor that merited a mandatory minimum sentence. In Sandusky's case, this factor would have been that the victims were under the age of 16. At the time, the jury was not required to do this because *Alleyne* was decided after Sandusky's trial. However, the *Alleyne* ruling was applied to Sandusky's case because it was handed down before Sandusky's direct appeal was finished.[3]

In 2019, the Pennsylvania Superior Court ordered the lower court to re-sentence Sandusky.[4] Sandusky, who has maintained his innocence, also applied for a new trial but was denied, and the original 30- to 60-year sentence was re-imposed.[5]

In 2019, a federal judge also overturned the misdemeanor child endangerment conviction of Graham Spanier, 70, the former president of Pennsylvania State University. In March 2017, Spanier was convicted of not going to the police when he learned that Sandusky was seen abusing a boy in a campus locker room shower. The judge wrote that Spanier was improperly charged under a 2007 law for events that occurred in 2001, when he had learned of the complaint about Sandusky. According to the judge, prosecutors should have used a 1995 version of the law, which was applicable at the time of the 2001 incident.[6]

THINK ABOUT IT > Why has the *Sandusky* case continued for so long?

LEARNING OBJECTIVE **9.1**

Summarize how sentencing disparities may negatively influence popular opinion about the criminal justice system.

9.1 The Criminal Court Process

The criminal court process has several important decision points that determine how justice is meted out. These decision points are plea bargaining, trial, and sentencing. In order to appreciate how defendants proceed through the courts to acquittal or conviction, we will consider how each of these decision points affects criminal cases.

The most dramatic and sensational decision point in the criminal justice system is the passing of the sentence. The passing of the sentence is considered to be the result of a deliberation process in which the evidence of the offense, the harm done to society (or other people), and the character of the defendant are weighed and a sentence prescribing a punishment is announced. The road to the disposition of a case is rocky and uncertain. Unlike the image presented by the media, the court's actions are ponderous and fickle, and they often seem unfair. Defendants (even co-defendants) with identical charges, similar records, and equal culpability who appear before the same judge can receive drastically different sentences.[7] For instance, in the case of Jerry Sandusky, nearly eight years after the original sentence, after changes in the sentencing guidelines, and after a request for a new trial was denied, Sandusky was resentenced to his original disposition. Conversely, Graham Spanier's conviction was overturned.

Sentencing disparities among judges, courts, states, or regions of the country all elicit a sense that justice is not uniform.[8] The luck of the draw in determining which judge handles a case or which prosecutor is assigned may mean the difference between incarceration or probation, a long or a short prison sentence, even life or death. This is the inevitable result of funding limitations and political necessity. It is little wonder that many people are wary of the criminal justice process when they see such vast disparities in the outcomes of apparently similar cases.[9]

Despite the fact that court reforms are desired and needed, they are difficult to enact because of the complicated and interdependent nature of the criminal justice system. Reforming one part of the system will have ramifications and unanticipated consequences in other parts of the system. For instance, enacting the popular notion that every offender should serve every day of every sentence would have a profound and negative effect on the prison system. There is not enough prison space to accommodate all the offenders serving all their time.[10] Consequently, the criminal justice system, particularly the courts, must prioritize how to allocate the precious resource of prison beds. Therefore, the process of arriving at the sentence is fraught with difficulties and dissension. This chapter will examine some of the mechanisms that the criminal justice system employs as part of its quest for justice, including the plea bargain, the criminal trial, the concept of defendants' and victims' rights, and finally some of the broader issues concerned with sentencing patterns.

PAUSE AND REVIEW

1. What are the decision points that determine how justice is meted out in the criminal court process?

2. Why are court reforms so difficult to enact?

9.2 Pre-Trial Release Decisions

The criminal justice process often takes a long time. Suspects may be kept in jail if they are dangerous, or they may be released and told to return to court when the system is ready to consider their case.[11] The court must somehow decide which option is appropriate for each suspect. The pre-trial release decision is one of the most important crossroads of the criminal justice system. If innocent people are jailed for months before their cases are heard, then they are being punished unjustly, and if dangerous offenders are released, then they might continue to murder, rape, and rob.[12] Complicating this pre-trial release decision is the overcrowded condition of many jails. Courts have developed several types of systems for making this decision that attempt to ensure that the defendant will appear. These systems all involve some sort of bail/bond alternative:

> Cash bond. The judge sets a bail of a certain amount of money the defendant must give to the court in exchange for release pending trial. If the defendant shows up for the court proceedings, then the entire amount is refunded minus any fees charged by the court. This **cash bond** is meant to ensure that the defendant will come back to prevent losing the money. However, if the bail is too low or a severe punishment is likely, the defendant may flee anyway or "skip bail." The court then issues a warrant for the defendant's arrest, and the defendant forfeits the bail. Although the Eighth Amendment states that "excessive bail shall not be required," it is still difficult for many

LEARNING OBJECTIVE 9.2

Identify alternatives to keeping a suspect in jail.

LEARNING OBJECTIVE 9.3

Contrast the competing values of presumption of innocence and preventive detention in the context of pre-trial release.

Cash bond—A requirement that the entire amount of the bail cost be paid in cash.

defendants to gather a large amount of cash in a short period.[13] Beginning in 1998, pre-trial releases that required bail became more common than non-financial releases, such as release-on-recognizance, because defendants on financial release were more likely to appear in court.[14]

> Property bond. By using a piece of property as collateral, defendants can avoid liquidating their assets to raise a cash bond. **Property bonds** favor the well-off who have equity in property. Defendants who fail to appear before the court forfeit their property.

> Release on recognizance. Defendants accused of minor offenses and who have ties to the community may be **released on recognizance (ROR)**, based on a promise to return to court. ROR programs evaluate how long defendants have lived in the community, how long they have been employed, whether they have family nearby, and other factors in an effort to determine whether they are likely to flee.[15] For example, a South American drug lord who has no local address would probably not be granted ROR. The distinguishing feature of ROR is that the defendant does not need to pay money to be released.

> Surety bond. The most common method for securing bail is a **surety bond**, or the use of a bail agent who promises to pay the defendant's bail if he or she fails to appear for further court proceedings.[16] In exchange for the promise, the defendant pays the bail agent 10 percent of the bail as a fee and may put up some collateral. Thus, if the bail is $10,000, the bail agent makes $1,000. The bail agent does not give the court the bail at that time but must pay if the defendant fails to appear. The bail agent may then hire a bail enforcement agent (or "bounty hunter") to find the defendant and bring him or her back to court. If a bail agent thinks the defendant is likely to flee, the agent may revoke the bond and surrender the defendant to law enforcement.

Pre-trial release is a controversial issue. It must balance two strongly held values: presumption of innocence and preventive detention. On one hand, we believe that someone should not be incarcerated until he or she has been found guilty

Property bond—The use of a piece of property instead of cash as collateral for bail.

Release on recognizance (ROR)—When a defendant pays no money to be released from jail and promises to appear in court when required.

Surety bond—The use of a bail agent who promises to pay the defendant's bail if he or she fails to appear for further court proceedings.

Suspects who cannot afford their bail can use a bail agent to get out of jail while awaiting trial. Suspects who sign a contract with a bail bondsman are considered to be in the bail bondsman's custody. What other types of bail/bond alternatives are there?

by a court of law. However, given the nature of the criminal justice system and the inevitable delays caused by crowded dockets and constitutional guarantees of due process, both the guilty and the innocent could spend months in jail before a trial.[17] If the defendant is found guilty and sentenced to incarceration, the period of time spent in jail awaiting trial is credited toward the sentence. Sometimes the sentence is simply "time served," in which case the defendant is released, having, in effect, served the sentence before the sentence was pronounced. In cases in which the defendant is acquitted or the charges are dropped, the period spent in jail waiting for the courts to process the case is time lost. The defendant, who has suffered the pains of being detained, may feel a sense of injustice.

The issue of presumption of innocence must be weighed against the responsibility of the state to protect society by keeping dangerous people behind bars while the court considers their cases. For example, in a 2002 case in Washington, D.C., two males, an adult and a juvenile, were arrested on suspicion of shooting and killing several people with a high-powered rifle. In what became known as the "D.C. sniper case," the court refused to grant pre-trial release because there was a reasonable fear that one of three bad things could happen.[18] First, because of the seriousness of the offenses, authorities feared that the defendants would attempt to flee the jurisdiction. Second, the defendants could harm more people. Third, given the terror caused by the shootings, it was feared that the defendants might be injured or killed by irate individuals. These concerns are so pronounced in such cases that those who are awaiting trial on murder charges that carry the death penalty are not allowed bail.

Murder defendants, as well as those charged with rape, robbery, burglary, and motor-vehicle theft, are typically the least likely to be released. Other factors affecting release are prior arrests, convictions, and whether the defendant is currently serving probation (the suspension of all or part of a sentence subject to certain conditions) or on parole (the conditional release of an inmate who has partially served a sentence and who remains under the court's control). (Probation and parole will be discussed in detail in Chapter 12.)

There will always be tension between the ideal of "innocent until proven guilty" and the need to protect society from potentially dangerous people. In some situations, it is clear that the defendant is dangerous. In other cases, it is not so clear, and the court must decide whether the suspect can be safely set free before trial. As the criminal justice system struggles with this balancing act, the possibility of class, racial, sex, and gender bias must always be kept in mind.[19] Are impoverished black males being held in preventive detention because they pose a threat or because of a stereotype held by those making the release decision?

PAUSE AND REVIEW

1. What are some alternatives to keeping a suspect in jail?

2. Why is pre-trial release a controversial issue?

9.3 The Plea Bargain

LEARNING OBJECTIVE 9.4

Define plea bargain.

In 2009, Orville Lee Wollard fired a handgun inside his house to scare his daughter's 17-year-old boyfriend who, court documents state, had been abusing her and threatening the family. The bullet struck a wall, and Wollard's daughter and her boyfriend left the house. Wollard, who said he fired the gun in self-defense and in defense of his family, rejected two plea bargains. The first offered three years

> The conviction and sentencing of defendants charged with serious offenses were unaffected, although sentences became more severe for relatively less serious offenses and offenders.[47]

Plea bargaining returned to Alaska in 1993 when the attorney general ended the ban, but forms of it were again abolished in 2014 after the case of Jerry Active.[48] Active had been returned to prison for a few months in 2013 after violating a plea agreement from a 2009 case in which he had been charged with burglary, sexual assault, and sexual abuse of a minor. The day Active was released, he murdered an elderly couple and sexually assaulted their 2-year-old granddaughter.[49]

As students of the criminal justice system, we should realize that the law on the books and the law that is practiced in the courthouse are different. Although we tend to think that the criminal trial is the court system's main activity, in reality, plea bargaining is responsible for the disposition of most cases.[50] As courts are faced with caseloads that outstrip their resources, plea bargaining becomes a useful way to negotiate justice. However, calls for the reform of plea bargaining should not go unheard.[51] By opening the process to victims, police officers, and others who are affected by the sentence, plea bargaining can become a more acceptable tool.[52]

PAUSE AND REVIEW

1. **What are three issues that guide plea bargaining?**
2. **What are the four types of plea-bargaining arrangements?**
3. **What are some criticisms of arguments for the abolition of plea bargaining?**

LEARNING OBJECTIVE 9.7

Outline the steps of the pre-trial phase.

LEARNING OBJECTIVE 9.8

Analyze the role that the standard of reasonable doubt plays in the presentation of witnesses and evidence during the trial process.

9.4 The Trial

Few cases make it to the trial phase because most are settled during plea bargaining (see Figure 9.2 for a review of the criminal justice process). Of the cases that go to trial, few end up in guilty verdicts that allow further processing of the case. Some defendants are acquitted or found not guilty. Sometimes the case is dismissed because the prosecution is unable to present a viable case. Sometimes the case is dismissed because of prosecutorial misconduct that violates the defendant's rights. Regardless, the trial is what most people think about when they imagine justice in the United States. Unfortunately, the media image of U.S. courtrooms is rather distorted. Last-minute confessions on the witness stand by distraught, guilty individuals who are pressured or tricked by a crafty prosecutor do not accurately represent what actually happens in the courtroom. Most of the decisions are made behind the scenes, and excitement and drama in the courtroom are uncommon.

Criminal trials are relatively rare. Which cases make it to trial then? Certainly, we would expect innocent defendants to assert their right to a trial. Additionally, if the defendant does not like the prosecution's deal, the decision may be made to roll the dice. In any event, the trial is a pivotal point in the process because cases that fail to reach a plea bargain set the parameters for how justice is negotiated by the courtroom work group.

A few actions must happen before a trial can occur, two of which were covered in Chapter 1: arrest and booking. Briefly, police make an arrest once they become aware that a criminal offense has been committed and they have enough evidence.

Arrests provide the system with cases. Police may continue to question a suspect after an arrest but must respect the suspect's constitutional rights. The booking process occurs at the police station, where a suspect's name, age, and address are recorded, as well as information on the time, place, and reason for arrest. Usually, a photograph and fingerprints are taken, the suspect's clothing and personal effects are stored, and the suspect is placed in a holding cell until he or she can be questioned further. The rest of the activities occur in the pre-trial and trial phases. Trials follow a specific format that is dictated by law, custom, and the administrative procedures established by the federal government and the states. In general, the trial process is conducted in the following steps:

1. Pre-trial phase
   a. Indictment
   b. Defendant's plea
2. Trial
   a. Prosecution opening statement
   b. Defense opening statement
   c. Witnesses and evidence presented
   d. Defense closing arguments
   e. Prosecution closing arguments
   f. Judge's instructions to jurors about procedures
   g. Judge's instructions to jurors about verdicts
   h. Final verdict
   i. Defendant released if acquitted or sentenced if convicted

The Pre-trial Phase

Several things must happen for a case to proceed through the criminal court process, and cases can be diverted at several points, including during the pre-trial phase, outlined as follows.[53]

> Filing of charges. Law enforcement first presents information about the case and the suspect to the prosecutor, who decides if formal charges will be filed. The suspect must be released if no charges are filed. A prosecutor can also decide to drop the charges later by entering a *nolle prosequi* (Latin for "we shall no longer prosecute"). A *nolle prosequi* must be made after charges are filed but before a plea is entered or a verdict returned. Usually, prosecutors must ask a judge's permission to enter a *nolle prosequi*. The prosecutor's decision to eliminate cases depends on several factors, the first of which is resources. The decision to prosecute depends on personnel, budget, space, and agency priorities. The prosecutor must prioritize cases according to importance and thus may decline to pursue certain ones. The prosecutor might decide that the police have not presented sufficient evidence to ensure successful prosecution or that the police made procedural errors in the arrest that would result in a dismissal. Personal or agency priorities may also influence what types of cases are pursued. For example, political corruption cases might be encouraged or discouraged depending on the party affiliation of the state attorney versus the defendant.

> Initial appearance and preliminary hearing. After arrest, suspects must be brought before a judge within a reasonable time for an initial appearance. The suspect is formally charged with a crime and responds by pleading guilty,

FIGURE 9.2 The Criminal Justice Process These are the basic steps of the criminal justice process. However, not everyone who enters prison is paroled or released. Some offenders are incarcerated for life, whereas others may be sentenced to death. What is the difference between a grand jury indictment and an information?

not guilty, or *nolo contendere* (no contest). Defendants are informed of their rights to bail and to an attorney. The judge or magistrate informs the accused of the charges and decides whether there is probable cause for further detention (i.e., whether the suspect is considered dangerous or likely to flee). A pre-trial release decision can be made at this point; it also might occur at other hearings or be changed further along in the process. Those charged with a misdemeanor may enter a plea immediately. If the plea is guilty, the judge may impose the sentence. For serious offenses, the suspect is asked if he or she has retained counsel (an attorney); if the accused is indigent, counsel is assigned. Defendants charged with felonies usually do not enter pleas at this time. Also, they probably have not been able to consult an attorney before the hearing. At this point, the defendant is scheduled for a preliminary hearing, also known as the preliminary examination or probable cause hearing, where the prosecutor presents evidence to establish probable cause. The exception to this is when the defendant has been indicted by a grand jury, in which probable cause has already been established. In this case, the defendant's first court appearance is at an arraignment similar to the initial appearance.

Bill of indictment—A declaration of the charges against an accused person that is presented to a grand jury to determine whether enough evidence exists for an indictment.

True bill—The decision of a grand jury that sufficient evidence exists to indict an accused person.

No-bill—The decision of a grand jury not to indict an accused person because of insufficient evidence. Also called "no true bill."

Indictment—A written statement of the facts of the offense that is charged against the accused.

Information—A formal, written accusation against a defendant submitted to the court by a prosecutor.

Arraignment (from Chapter 1)—Court appearance in which the defendant is formally charged with a crime and asked to respond by pleading guilty, not guilty, or *nolo contendere*.

> Grand jury. The grand jury hears the prosecutor's evidence and charges against the accused, presented as a **bill of indictment**, and decides if it is sufficient to bring the accused to trial. If the grand jury finds the evidence sufficient, it sends an indictment, a written statement of the facts of the offense charged against the accused, to the court. A grand jury returns a **true bill** if it decides that sufficient evidence exists to indict; if not, a **no-bill** is returned. A prosecutor may still file charges in the event of a no-bill. Prosecutors may also bring further evidence to the same jury or present the original evidence to a second jury. This system also works backward, in a sense. Instead of starting with a suspect and deciding whether to indict, a grand jury may investigate possible criminal activity. If probable cause is found, the grand jury issues an **indictment**, called a grand jury original, naming the suspects. Police then try to arrest the suspects. In some jurisdictions, prosecutors sometimes choose not to use a grand jury and instead file a criminal complaint. (For more on how grand juries work, see CJ Reference 9.1.)

> Indictments and **informations**. Some jurisdictions require grand jury indictments for felony cases. However, an accused may waive the indictment and instead accept an information, a formal, written accusation against a defendant submitted by a prosecutor. Misdemeanor cases and cases when the offense is punishable by one year or less in prison might also proceed by the issuance of an information.[54]

> Arraignment. After an indictment or information has been filed with the trial court, the accused is scheduled for **arraignment**. There, the accused is informed of the charges, advised of his or her rights, and asked to enter a plea. Sometimes the prosecutor and the defendant negotiate a plea bargain, in which the defendant pleads guilty.

> The plea. If the accused pleads guilty or *nolo contendere*, the judge either accepts or rejects the plea. No trial is held if the plea is accepted; the offender is sentenced either at this proceeding or at a later hearing. If the plea is rejected, the case proceeds to trial. For example, a guilty or *nolo* plea would go to trial if the judge believes that the accused is being coerced. If the accused enters a "not guilty" plea, a date is set for the trial, or the accused may request a bench trial (discussed later in this chapter).

CJ REFERENCE 9.1
What Are Grand Juries and How Do They Work?

- Grand jurors are usually selected from the same pool as trial jurors. Unlike trial juries, grand juries are not typically assembled for a specific case, but only for a period of time. The period may last months, but the jurors meet for only a few days each month.
- Grand jury proceedings are private and secret, and witnesses testify against the suspect without the suspect or the suspect's witnesses or suspect's attorney being present. This is to ensure that witnesses may speak freely without fear of retaliation and to protect the suspect's reputation if the jury does not indict. Grand juries do not require a unanimous decision to indict. Depending on the jurisdiction, a two-thirds or three-fourths majority is required. Grand jury investigations often target large, complex drug and conspiracy cases. They are usually not used for minor felonies or misdemeanors.
- The Fifth Amendment requires grand juries to be convened for indictments in federal felony cases. However, the Supreme Court held in *Hurtado v. California* (1884) that the Fifth Amendment grand jury clause does not apply to the states, nor does it violate the Fourteenth Amendment due process clause. Thus, the states are not required to use grand juries. About half the states require a grand jury indictment for felony prosecutions.[55] Only Connecticut and Pennsylvania do not use grand juries for criminal indictments (Connecticut replaced the grand jury with a hearing before a judge). However, both states use grand juries for investigations. Connecticut's grand jury is composed of between one and three judges, whereas Pennsylvania convenes grand juries from regular citizens.[56]
- In some states, grand juries can only investigate offenses that are presented to them by a prosecutor or court. Grand juries in other states can investigate any suspected offense as long as the activity occurs within their jurisdiction. Finally, some state grand juries—sometimes called "special grand juries"—only investigate certain types of offenses, usually drug crime or organized crime. State grand juries may investigate civil matters, the most common of which is the operation and condition of local jails and similar facilities. At the federal level, grand juries investigate criminal activity, especially organized crime. They do not investigate civil matters.

PRE-TRIAL MOTIONS

Prior to the opening statements by the prosecution and the defense, each side can file **pre-trial motions**, which seek to gain the most favorable circumstances for their side and to limit the evidence the other side can present. Often the case

Pre-trial motion—A request made by the prosecutor or defense attorney that the court make a decision on a specific issue before the trial begins.

This courtroom sketch depicts Boston Marathon bomber Dzhokhar Tsarnaev (right) standing before U.S. District Court Judge George O'Toole Jr. in federal court. Judge O'Toole denied Tsarnaev's request for a change of venue. Why might it be in a defendant's interest to be tried in a jurisdiction other than where he or she committed a crime?

is won or lost based on how the judge rules on the pre-trial motions. Some of the more frequent motions include the following:

> **Motion for dismissal of charges.** The defense might ask that the case be dismissed because the prosecution has failed to present a sufficient case that has all the elements necessary to charge the defendant with the offense or because the case has some critical weaknesses. This can happen at the beginning of the trial or at any point along the way. Often, this motion is presented after the prosecution presents its case.

> **Motion for continuance.** This motion delays the trial. Often the defense or prosecution needs more time to prepare the case or to interview newly discovered witnesses. The defense is more likely to be granted such a continuance because the prosecution has an obligation to provide for a speedy trial.

> **Motion for discovery.** The defense has a right to obtain documents and a list of witnesses that the prosecution plans to call.

> **Motion for severance of defendants.** When more than one defendant is charged, each has his or her own defense attorney, who may wish to separate the cases so that each defendant has his or her own trial. This is often done when a conflict of interest exists in which one defendant is more culpable than the other is, or when the testimony of one defendant might incriminate others.

> **Motion for severance of offenses.** Defendants charged with several offenses might ask to be tried separately on all or some of the charges. The judge usually makes this decision.

> **Motion for suppression of evidence.** The defense will attempt to prevent incriminating evidence from being presented during the trial. If the evidence

---

CJ REFERENCE 9.2
The Exclusionary Rule

When a defendant goes free because of a legal technicality, the reason might be the exclusionary rule. Although the exclusionary rule dictates that the police must follow procedural law in the gathering of evidence, the issue is decided in the courts.

The exclusionary rule covers three types of evidence: (1) the identification of suspects, (2) confessions in which *Miranda* rules apply, and (3) searches in which the Fourth Amendment states that "the right of the people to be secure in their persons, houses, papers, and effects against unreasonable search and seizure, shall not be violated."

The Supreme Court adopted the rule for three reasons.

1. If the courts used evidence that was illegally gathered, they would be participating in the violation of the defendant's rights. The courts must respect the rule of law if we are to have confidence in the quality of justice.
2. The exclusionary rule deters law enforcement officers from attempting to break the law. If they know their

evidence will be thrown out of court, they may be less likely to try to circumvent procedural laws.

3. The alternatives to the exclusionary rule are not feasible. Although a defendant might try to sue a law enforcement officer in civil court for damages stemming from police misconduct, this is a cumbersome and expensive process that is unlikely to have the desired effect of encouraging the police to play by the rules.

The prosecutor cannot use illegally obtained evidence. The law allows for the suppression of evidence that violates the exclusionary rule. This is accomplished when the defense attorney files a suppression motion if the defendant was identified in a police line-up that was conducted improperly, gave a confession as a result of police misconduct, or was subjected to an illegal search. The court has allowed some narrow exceptions when the police make mistakes in "good faith."

A fingerprint can tie a defendant to the crime scene. In what ways has scientific evidence become an important factor in some cases?

was gathered illegally or a confession coerced by the police, the judge might rule it inadmissible (see CJ Reference 9.2). The defense might raise due process issues that could result in motions to suppress evidence.

> Motion to determine competency. The defense can request that the judge rule that the defendant is not competent to stand trial. A defendant who cannot assist in the defense and does not understand the purpose and process of the proceedings might be mentally ill or intellectually disabled. Often, the court will order a psychiatrist to examine the defendant.

> Motion for change of venue. In offenses that draw a good deal of media coverage, the defense may claim that finding an impartial jury would be impossible. The court can move the case to another jurisdiction where those in the jury pool would not have heard about the case. Of course, offenses that receive national media coverage make it impossible to assemble a jury pool that has not been exposed to the case.

The prosecution or the defense can present other types of motions, but this list illustrates how motions can be used to a defendant's advantage. These motions set the tone and limits of the trial and are extremely important even if they are not obvious in the process.

Opening Arguments

The prosecution is the first to make an opening argument, explaining why it believes that the defendant is guilty. Evidence is not presented at this time; the prosecution outlines the case and alerts the jury to the types of evidence to come. The goals of the opening statement are to present the defendant as the most likely perpetrator, convince the jury that the case against the defendant is strong, and stress that the prosecution can be trusted to ensure that justice is being pressed in the name of the people. The defense attorney then counters the outline of the case the prosecution has presented. Again, evidence is not presented, but the defense attorney attempts to put a more favorable spin on the prosecution's arguments and assure the jury that once it has seen all the evidence and heard all the facts, it will want to acquit the defendant on all charges.

The Prosecution's Presentation of Witnesses and Evidence

The prosecution begins presenting the case by introducing evidence and witnesses. The goal is to explain thoroughly the defendant's motive for breaking the law and his or her capability for carrying out the action. As the prosecution presents the case, the defense attorney may raise objections to the prosecutor's questions or a witness's answers.[57] The judge rules on these objections by either sustaining or overruling them. The objections can be on points of procedural law or on the competency of a witness to answer a question. For instance, if a police officer claims the defendant was drunk, the defense attorney may object, claiming that the officer could not know for sure that this was the case. The prosecutor may then ask the police officer if a breath test was administered to the defendant and what the result of that test was. Ideally, the process is designed to present the evidence and witness testimony in a factual and fair manner so that the jury can weigh them and reach its own conclusion.

After the prosecution questions a witness, the defense attorney may cross-examine. The right to cross-examine witnesses is derived from the Sixth Amendment and is one of the adversarial features of the trial. The defense attorney tries to **impeach**, or discredit, the witness by asking questions that undermine the prosecution's case. Sometimes the defense attorney can be successful in soliciting information from the prosecution's witness that is favorable to the defendant. Once the defense attorney has cross-examined the witness, the prosecutor may ask additional questions under the right to **redirect examination**. In turn, the defense attorney can ask for a re-cross-examination. Often, this tactic is used later in the trial after other witnesses reveal new evidence. The intent of cross-examining and redirecting is to give each side an equal opportunity to ask questions.

After the state presents its case against the defendant, the defense attorney can ask the judge for a **directed verdict of acquittal**—an order stating that the jury must acquit the accused because the prosecution has failed to present a compelling case documenting the defendant's guilt. Only in the most egregious cases would the judge be likely to make such a ruling. However, it costs the defense nothing

Impeach—The discrediting of a witness.

Redirect examination—The questioning of a witness about issues uncovered during cross-examination.

Directed verdict of acquittal—An order from a trial judge to the jury stating that the jury must acquit the accused because the prosecution has not proved its case.

Willie Cory Godbolt is sworn in before telling a Mississippi court that he did not want to testify on his own behalf in his capital murder trial. Godbolt was tried for the 2017 shooting deaths of eight people. He was found guilty in February 2020. Why are defendants not required to testify at their trial?

to make such a motion. In some cases, the judge might believe the prosecution has failed so miserably to make a logical case that issuing a directed verdict of acquittal would not circumvent justice but would save the court from having to sit through a trial with a foregone conclusion of acquittal.

Once the prosecution concludes the presentation of its evidence and witnesses, the defense may present its own evidence and witnesses. Because the burden of proof rests with the prosecution, the defendant enjoys a presumption of innocence. As such, the defense attorney need only present evidence that raises a reasonable doubt about the defendant's guilt. If the prosecution has a witness from the state crime lab who testified about blood samples or hair fibers, the defense will counter with other scientists to dispute the testimony. If the prosecution presents an eyewitness, the defense may attempt to impeach the testimony by showing that the witness's eyesight or memory is faulty.

After each side has presented its evidence and witnesses, the court allows both sides to present a summation in which they attempt to account for all the facts in a closing argument designed to put the best possible spin on their case. The prosecution gets the last word because of its burden to prove the defendant's guilt **beyond a reasonable doubt**, a legal yardstick that measures the sufficiency of the evidence. The prosecutor does not have to eliminate all doubt; lingering suspicions about the defendant's guilt might remain. New evidence may not be introduced at this stage because the opposing side does not have the opportunity to question it.

Closing arguments can sometimes be flamboyant because the attorneys are not just presenting facts; they are trying to convince the jury that the defendant is a solid citizen or a criminal, sympathetic or disgusting, innocent or guilty. During the closing arguments portrayed on television dramas, culprits often blurt out a confession or the defense attorney brings the jury to tears with a dramatic and heartfelt speech. In reality, the closing arguments are not nearly so theatrical, but they can be extremely interesting and moving.

To convict a defendant, the prosecutor must build a case based on evidence. The reasonable doubt standard works in favor of the defendant, who needs only to raise questions about the quality of the prosecutor's case and does not have to prove anything.

In building the case, the prosecutor uses several different types of evidence. Some evidence is more convincing to the jury than other types, but the prosecutor must weave a convincing pattern that demonstrates that the defendant is guilty as charged. Evidence must conform to a set of rules that ensures that the defendant's rights are respected.[58] For instance, privileged communications between a doctor and patient or lawyer and client are not admissible in court, nor is illegally obtained evidence.[59]

With these and other exceptions, however, the rules of evidence are geared toward obtaining the truth. Evidence is deemed trustworthy when every effort is made to ensure its veracity. For example, original documents are required because copies are too easy to alter. Additionally, young children or those suffering from mental illness might be judged by the court to lack competence, so their testimony would be inadmissible. This is true also for hearsay evidence, secondhand evidence in which someone reports that he or she heard someone say something, because it can be impossible to determine whether someone said what is reported. Other types of evidence, especially scientific evidence, can be discredited when new information is learned. Evidence can be classified in several ways.

> Real evidence. Real evidence consists of objects that can be readily observed. For instance, fingerprints, hair fibers, or blood can all be analyzed and certified by experts. Although opinions about the quality of the evidence or

Beyond a reasonable doubt—(from Chapter 3) The highest level of proof required to win a case; necessary in criminal cases to procure a guilty verdict.

Noah Gaston rests his head in his hands in a Portland, Maine, courtroom in November 2019 after a jury foreman announced a verdict of guilty of murder for Gaston, who fatally shot his wife in their home in 2016. How does Gaston's reaction reflect the consequences of the adversarial process?

the chain of custody might be conflicting, experts can agree upon scientific standards. The courts are turning more and more to science to provide solid real evidence to determine guilt or innocence. Recent examples of death row inmates being released because of DNA evidence is a testament to how science can work both for and against the prosecution.

> Testimony. Testimony consists of statements that witnesses give under oath. Ideally, the prosecution will present witnesses who saw the defendant commit the offense. Lacking eyewitness testimony, the prosecutor might present someone who can place the defendant in the proximity of where the offense was committed at about the same time. Additionally, much real evidence requires expert interpretation. For example, hair fibers do not speak for themselves, so the prosecution must elicit testimony from an expert who is competent to evaluate them in relation to how the prosecutor contends they are connected to the offense.

> Direct evidence. Both real evidence and testimony can be considered direct evidence, which is ascertainable by the five senses: seeing, hearing, smelling, touching, and tasting. For instance, eyewitness testimony is defined as the witness seeing the defendant do something.

> Indirect evidence. Indirect evidence can also be termed "circumstantial evidence." When the prosecution fails to find the "smoking gun," then circumstantial evidence that demonstrates the defendant has bought a gun of the same caliber might be used to help establish the case. With enough circumstantial evidence, the prosecution can build a strong case. However, the defense has an easier time creating doubts with circumstantial evidence than with direct evidence.

The Case Goes to the Jury

Serving on a jury allows average citizens to participate in the criminal justice process in an important way that acts as a check-and-balance against government power. The jury can prevent an overzealous prosecutor from railroading

Pictured with his sons is music producer Weldon Angelos (center), who was sentenced to 55 years in prison as a result of mandatory-minimum sentencing laws for possessing a firearm while selling marijuana. Angelos was released after 12 years. How should mandatory-minimum sentencing laws be reformed?

a defendant. By having a jury comprising 12 citizens (this is the ideal number, but many states allow a jury of six for some types of cases) who consider the defendant's guilt, the dynamics of the courtroom work group are not as dominant as they would be if only criminal justice practitioners decided the cases.

The jury-selection process is a complicated and uncertain procedure that results in juries that might be partial to either the prosecution or the defense. Certainly, each side attempts to influence the jury selection to ensure that its arguments will find a sympathetic ear. The formation of a jury requires several steps.

› Master jury list. Each jurisdiction must develop a list of potential jurors. This list is compiled from voter registration records, driver's license lists, and utility customer lists. The goal is to develop a master jury list that is representative of the community in terms of race, sex, and social class.

› *Venire.* A list of names is randomly selected from the master jury list to form the **venire** or the jury pool. The sheriff's office notifies these individuals by summons to appear at the courthouse for jury duty. Not all citizens who are summoned for jury duty will report. In some jurisdictions, the non-response rate is as high as 20 percent. Furthermore, many citizens request that they be excused from jury duty because of the inconvenience and hardship it imposes. Judges vary widely in their patterns of excusing citizens from jury duty. Juries are selected from this final, reduced jury pool.

Venire—The list or pool from which jurors are chosen.

› *Voir dire.* The prosecutor and the defense attorney have some input into which members of the jury pool wind up on the jury for an actual case. The **voir dire** ("to see, to speak") consists of the questioning of prospective jurors to determine whether they have the necessary qualifications to serve. The questions cover possible previous relationships potential jurors might have had with those involved in the case (e.g., the brother-in-law of the prosecutor would be an inappropriate candidate for the jury), knowledge about the case, attitudes about certain facts that could arise in the trial, and willingness

Voir dire—French for "to see, to speak"; a phrase that refers to the questioning of jurors by a judge and/or attorneys to determine whether individual jurors are appropriate for a particular jury panel.

Determinate Sentencing

The effectiveness of rehabilitation will be discussed in Chapters 11, 12, and 13. For our purposes here, it is sufficient to say that there is widespread concern about its effectiveness and about the public's confidence in the criminal justice system. Although rehabilitation was considered a worthy goal, it was not deemed a sufficient foundation on which to base sentencing decisions.

Legislators decided to pass laws that restricted the discretion that criminal justice decision-makers could exercise in an individual case. Sentencing guidelines were developed that stated that the length of time an inmate would serve would not be determined by the judge or the parole board but by the nature of the offense.[84] Sentencing guidelines forced judges to apply sentences within a narrow range of variability.[85] In 2004, the Supreme Court decided in *Booker* v. *United States* that the federal guidelines violated the Sixth Amendment right to trial by jury because they allowed judges to enhance sentences using facts not reviewed by juries. The Court ruled that the sentencing guidelines in federal courts would be advisory and not mandatory.

In its purest form, a **determinate sentence** gives a fixed sentence to each offender convicted of a particular offense. For example, an armed robbery conviction might call for a 30-year sentence. The judge has no discretion to alter the sentence, regardless of the circumstances of the offense or of the offender. One form of determinate sentencing, the **presumptive sentence**, allows judges limited discretion to consider aggravating circumstances (specifics about the offender or the case that worsen the offense) or mitigating circumstances (specifics about the offender or the case that lessen the severity of the offense) and depart from the guidelines. Some states employ voluntary guidelines, which allow judges the same departures. See Figure 9.3 for an example of a state sentencing guidelines table.

The perceived advantage of the determinate sentence is uniformity. Similar cases are treated in the same manner, and, theoretically, such factors as social class, race, sex, and gender do not affect the sentencing equation.[86] These efforts to remove discretion from the criminal justice system have produced at least three unintended consequences that some consider detrimental to the welfare of offenders and society.

Determinate sentence—A prison term that is determined by law and states a specific period of time to be served.

Presumptive sentence—A sentence that may be adjusted by the judge depending on aggravating or mitigating factors.

1. Determinate sentencing has removed the power to make decisions from those closest to the case. These participants are often in the best position to understand a case's complexities and weigh the conflicting interests of the welfare of society and the offender's punishment.

2. Legislators who espouse determinate sentencing policy are not always sensitive to the limitations of the criminal justice system to bear the demands of long prison sentences for a multitude of inmates. Even the most mundane criminal justice resources, such as prison beds, are limited. The civil and human rights of inmates are infringed upon when prisons are crowded, but criminal justice decision-makers, such as judges and parole board members, have little power to remedy the situation.[87]

3. By limiting the judge's sentencing discretion, determinate sentencing laws may affect the prosecutor's decision as to which charges will be filed, thus shifting power to the prosecution. Defense attorneys unwilling to expose their clients to long determinate sentences are pressured to accept plea bargains to lesser included offenses or in exchange for avoiding the stigma associated with drug or sex-offender convictions. The mandatory

Level	Example	Presumptive sentence range					Suggested maximum probation term range
9	Murder	Life	Life	Life	Life	Life	
8	Manslaughter (voluntary)	96–144 Mos.	108–162 Mos.	120–180 Mos.	144–216 Mos.	204–306 Mos.	3 Years
7	Armed robbery (gun)	60–90 Mos.	68–102 Mos.	84–126 Mos.	108–162 Mos.	160–240 Mos.	
6	Manslaughter (involuntary)	40–60 Mos.	45–67 Mos.	50–75 Mos.	60–90 Mos.	80–120 Mos.	
5	Indecent A&B on child Under 14	12–36 Mos.	24–36 Mos.	36–54 Mos.	48–72 Mos.	60–90 Mos.	2 Years
4	Larceny from a person	0–24 Mos.	3–30 Mos.	6–30 Mos.	20–30 Mos.	24–36 Mos.	
3	A&B DW (no or minor injury)	0–12 Mos.	0–15 Mos.	0–18 Mos.	0–24 Mos.	6–24 Mos.	
2	Assault		0–6 Mos.	0–6 Mos.	0–9 Mos.	0–12 Mos.	1 Year
1	Operating Aft suspended Lic				0–3 Mos.	0–6 Mos.	
0	Lic law violation (not MV) Violation town by-law	IS–0					
	Criminal history scale	A No/minor record	B Moderate record	C Serious record	D Violent or repetitive	E Serious violent	

Sentencing zones

■ Incarceration zone

■ Discretionary zone (incarceration/intermediate sanction)

■ Intermediate sanction zone

■ No supervision, no fines, no fees zone

The numbers in each cell represent the range from which the judge selects the maximum sentence (Not More Than);
The minimum sentence (Not Less Than) is 2/3rds of the maximum sentence and constitutes the initial parole eligibility date.

FIGURE 9.3   Massachusetts Sentencing Grid Which offense/criminal history combinations are in the discretionary zone? Give some possible reasons that the sentencing for these offenses may be either incarceration or intermediate sanctions.

Source: Massachusetts Sentencing Commission, Sentencing Guidelines: Step 5, Chapter 5, April 26, 2019. Available at www.mass.gov/info-details/sentencing-guidelines-step-5-chapter-5.

minimum sentences for these types of offenses provide the prosecutor with tremendous leverage in extracting plea bargains from defendants. Therefore, those in the best position to exercise discretion—the judge and the parole board—often find their hands tied by the determinate sentencing laws.

Mandatory Minimum Sentences

Mandatory minimum sentence—A sentence determined by law that establishes the minimum length of prison time that may be served for an offense.

The **mandatory minimum sentence** is a form of determinate sentencing that addresses certain types of offenses that particularly rankle the public and receive little sympathy from the media or criminal justice practitioners.[88] Typically, mandatory minimum sentencing laws do not allow probation and stipulate incarceration for a specified number of years. Federal mandatory minimum sentences are not sentencing guidelines; thus, they are not subject to the *Booker* decision. Judges typically cannot impose a sentence shorter than the number of years set by Congress for offenses that carry a mandatory minimum.[89] The following are types of offenses that are likely to carry mandatory minimums:

> › Weapons violations. Those who use a gun (or sometimes possess one) while committing a felony will find an additional prison term tacked on to the sentence. This guarantees that the case will not result in a probationary sentence.

> › Repeated drunk driving. In some jurisdictions, those who persist in driving while intoxicated will be sentenced to mandatory prison or jail time.[90]

> › Drug sales and drug kingpin laws. Many jurisdictions, including the federal government, have laws specifying mandatory prison time for the sale of illegal drugs. Some of these laws, aimed at drug kingpins, are especially punitive.

> › Three-strikes laws. Aimed at the habitual offender, these laws result in mandatory incarceration for those who have two prior felonies. Judges are not allowed to consider the circumstances of the present offense and must sentence the offender to a prison term.

> › Truth in sentencing. These laws, which specify that the offender must serve a substantial portion of the sentence before being released, limit the flexibility of the parole board by ensuring that inmates spend most of the original sentence behind bars.

The sentencing decision has become the primary way in which citizens evaluate the quality of justice meted out by the system because it is such a high-profile event. This is unfortunate because sentencing is just one of many decision-making points, and the reliance on this single event obscures the effects of the entire process. Efforts to limit judicial discretion have been frustrated due to the inevitable shift of decision-making power to other points in the system.[91]

PAUSE AND REVIEW

1. What is indeterminate sentencing?
2. What is determinate sentencing?

FOCUS ON ETHICS Letting the Big Ones Get Away

As an assistant prosecutor, you are under orders from the chief prosecutor to rack up drug prosecutions while he campaigns for Congress. You have been successful in putting several large-scale drug dealers behind bars, and you are in line for a promotion based on your success. When the total number of years for offenders' sentences is added up, your record is tied with your only competitor for the promotion. One of your current cases promises to vault you ahead if you can secure a reasonable plea bargain from the defense attorney.

Here's the problem: The drug dealer you have in your sights is clever and connected. He has been charged before with several offenses and has always been able to avoid the law. This time he has been caught with a kilo of cocaine at his girlfriend's house, and you have a perfect case if only she will testify against him. But she refuses to testify; she is pregnant with his child and does not want him to go to prison.

His high-priced defense attorney comes to you with a deal. If you drop the charges, the drug dealer will testify that the cocaine belongs to his girlfriend. Because the girlfriend has shoplifting and fraud convictions from several years ago, the state's mandatory minimum sentence statutes will kick in, and she will go to prison for a 40-year term.

She refuses to cooperate. She does not believe that her boyfriend has offered to roll over on her, and because the cocaine did not belong to her, she believes she will not be prosecuted. Your chief prosecutor wants a big conviction, and this one would ensure your promotion.

WHAT DO YOU DO?
1. Prosecute the girlfriend for the cocaine that was not hers, and send her to prison for 40 years.
2. Dismiss the charges on both of them.
3. Ask the judge to talk to the girlfriend, explaining her options and the likely outcomes.
4. Think of another plan in hopes of bringing justice to this case.

For more insight into how someone might respond to such an ethical dilemma, visit Oxford Learning Link at www.oup.com/he/Fuller2e to watch a video that connects this scenario to a real-world situation.

Summary

LEARNING OBJECTIVE **9.1** Summarize how sentencing disparities may negatively influence popular opinion about the criminal justice system.	Sentencing disparities elicit a sense that justice is not uniform but are the inevitable result of funding limitations and political necessity. Because of plea bargaining, defendants with similar charges, similar records, and equal culpability who appear before the same judge can be sentenced differently. Court reforms are difficult to enact because of the complicated nature of the criminal justice system.
LEARNING OBJECTIVE **9.2** Identify alternatives to keeping a suspect in jail.	**Cash bond:** a certain amount of money set by a judge that the defendant must give to the court in exchange for release pending trial. **Property bond:** use of a piece of property as collateral in exchange for release pending trial. **Release on recognizance:** release of a defendant based on a promise to return to court. **Surety bond:** use of a bail agent, who pays a defendant's bail if he or she fails to appear in court.

LEARNING OBJECTIVE **9.3** Contrast the competing values of presumption of innocence and preventive detention in the context of pre-trial release.	A pre-trial release decision must weigh the issue of presumption of innocence against the state's responsibility to protect society by detaining truly dangerous people in order to prevent possible further harm while the court considers their cases.
LEARNING OBJECTIVE **9.4** Define plea bargain.	A compromise reached by the defendant, the defendant's attorney, and the prosecutor, in which the defendant agrees to plead guilty or no contest in return for a reduction of the charges' severity, dismissal of some charges, further information about the offense or about others involved in it, or the prosecutor's agreement to recommend a desired sentence.
LEARNING OBJECTIVE **9.5** Compare and contrast the types of plea bargaining arrangements.	**Vertical plea:** By pleading guilty or *nolo contendere* to a lesser charge, the defendant can reduce the potential for a harsh sentence. **Horizontal plea:** The defendant pleads guilty to a charge in exchange for other charges being dropped. **Reduced-sentence plea:** The prosecutor and defense attorney, in consultation with the judge, decide on a reduced sentence. **Avoidance-of-stigma plea:** A defendant pleads guilty to a lesser charge in order to avoid a more serious charge that carries a stigma.
LEARNING OBJECTIVE **9.6** Argue for and against the abolition of plea bargaining.	For the abolition of plea bargaining: – It allows offenders to thwart justice. – It often ignores the voices of victims. – The public has less opportunity to comprehend how dispositions are arrived at, causing disillusion. – Some defendants, especially the indigent who cannot afford bail, may plead guilty to crimes they did not commit to get out of jail or avoid risking trial. Against the abolition of plea bargaining: – It is inefficient; the number of cases that defense attorneys are willing to take to trial increases. – The discretion inherent in the process could move to another part of the criminal justice system where it might not be as visible and thus subject to increased abuse or corruption. – Doing so might squeeze the prosecutor out of the process because defense attorneys can attempt to negotiate directly with the judge to secure the best deal for the defendant.
LEARNING OBJECTIVE **9.7** Outline the steps of the pre-trial phase.	1. Filing of charges: Law enforcement agencies present information about the case and the suspect to the prosecutor, who decides if formal charges will be filed. 2. Initial appearance and preliminary hearing: After arrest, suspects are brought before a judge for an initial appearance. The suspect is formally charged and pleads guilty, not guilty, or *nolo contendere*. 3. Grand jury: This jury hears the prosecutor's evidence and decides if it is sufficient to bring the accused to trial. 4. Indictments and informations: Some jurisdictions require grand jury indictments for felony cases. An accused may waive an indictment and accept service of an information. Misdemeanor cases might also proceed by the issuance of an information. 5. Arraignment: The accused is informed of the charges, advised of his or her rights, and asked to enter a plea. 6. The plea: If the accused pleads guilty or *nolo contendere*, the judge either accepts or rejects the plea.

LEARNING OBJECTIVE **9.8** Analyze the role that the standard of reasonable doubt plays in the presentation of witnesses and evidence during the trial process.	The legal standard of "beyond a reasonable doubt" measures the sufficiency of the evidence. The prosecution has the burden of proof but does not have to eliminate all doubt. The defendant enjoys a presumption of innocence, so the defense attorney need only present evidence that raises reasonable doubt about the defendant's guilt. The defense confronts the witnesses and evidence through cross-examination, thus attempting to weaken the prosecution's case and raise a reasonable doubt within the jury about the defendant's guilt.
LEARNING OBJECTIVE **9.9** Distinguish between indeterminate and determinate sentencing and give an example of each.	An indeterminate sentence does not state a specific period of time to be served or date of release. An example is a sentence of "10 years to life" for first-degree murder. A determinate sentence is a prison term that is determined by law and states a specific period to be served. An example is an armed robbery conviction that calls for a 30-year sentence.
LEARNING OBJECTIVE **9.10** Differentiate mandatory minimum sentencing from sentencing guidelines.	A mandatory minimum sentence is a sentence determined by law that establishes the minimum length of prison time that may be served for an offense. Mandatory minimum sentences are not sentencing guidelines, which are a set of rules concerning the sentencing for a specified set of offenses. Judges typically cannot impose a sentence shorter than the number of years set by law for offenses that carry a mandatory minimum.

Critical Reflections

1. Why is the practice of plea bargaining sometimes considered a necessary evil?

2. What is the proper balance between the rights of a criminal defendant and the rights of the victim?

3. Should the discretion involved in criminal sentencing be vested in the hands of the prosecutor, the judge, or the legislature? Why?

Key Terms

Appeal **p. 278**
Arraignment **p. 268**
Bench trial **p. 277**
Beyond a reasonable
    doubt **p. 273**
Bill of indictment **p. 268**
Cash bond **p. 257**
Determinate sentence **p. 282**
Directed verdict of
    acquittal **p. 272**
Hung jury **p. 277**

Impeach **p. 272**
Indeterminate sentence **p. 280**
Indictment **p. 268**
Information **p. 268**
Mandatory minimum
    sentence **p. 284**
No-bill **p. 268**
Nolo contendere **p. 263**
Peremptory challenges **p. 276**
Plea bargain **p. 260**
Presumptive sentence **p. 282**

Pre-trial motion **p. 269**
Property bond **p. 258**
Redirect examination **p. 272**
Release on recognizance
    (ROR) **p. 258**
Sentencing guidelines **p. 280**
Surety bond **p. 258**
True bill **p. 268**
Venire **p. 275**
Voir dire **p. 275**

Notes

1 *CNN*, "Painful Chapter Closes with Sandusky's Conviction for Child Abuse," June 26, 2012.

2 American Civil Liberties Union of Pennsylvania, aclupa.org/sites/default/files/field_documents/

background_information_on_mandatory_minimums.pdf. Accessed January 2020.

3 Paula Reed Ward and Bill Schackner, "Pa. Superior Court Grants Jerry Sandusky New Sentencing Hearing," *Pittsburgh Post-Gazette*, February 5, 2019.

4 Rob Frehse, "PA Court Orders Jerry Sandusky to be Resentenced, Denies His Request for Retrial," *CNN*, February 5, 2019.

5 AP/*Pittsburgh Post-Gazette*, "Jerry Sandusky Resentenced to 30 to 60 Years, Same as Before," November 22, 2019.

6 Billy Witz, "Judge Overturns Conviction of Ex-Penn State President in Sandusky Case," *New York Times*, April 30, 2019. Jon Hurdle and Richard Pérez-Peña, "Former Penn State President Gets Jail Time in Child Molestation Scandal," *New York Times*, June 2, 2017.

7 John Hagan, "Extra-Legal Attributes and Criminal Sentencing: An Assessment of a Sociological Viewpoint," *Law and Society Review* 8 (1974): 357–381.

8 Thomas Austin, "The Influence of Court Location on Types of Criminal Sentences: The Rural-Urban Factor," *Journal of Criminal Justice* 9 (1981): 305–316.

9 Douglas Thomson and Anthony Ragona, "Popular Moderation Versus Governmental Authoritarianism: An Interactionist View of Public Sentiments toward Criminal Sanctions," *Crime and Delinquency* 33 (1987): 337–357.

10 James Austin and John Irwin, *It's About Time: America's Imprisonment Binge*, 3d ed. (Belmont, Calif.: Wadsworth, 1997).

11 John Goldkamp, "Danger and Detention: A Second Generation of Bail Reform," *Journal of Criminal Law and Criminology* 76 (1985): 1–74.

12 Michael Corrado, "Punishment and the Wild Beast of Prey: The Problems of Preventive Detention," *Journal of Criminal Law and Criminology* 86 (1996): 778–814.

13 Michael J. Eason, "Eighth Amendment—Pre-trial Detention: What Will Become of the Innocent?" *Journal of Criminal Law and Criminology* 78 (1988): 1048–1049.

14 Thomas H. Cohen and Brian A. Reaves, *Pre-trial Release of Felony Defendants in State Courts* (Washington, D.C.: U.S. Department of Justice, Bureau of Justice Statistics, 2007), 1. Available at www.bjs.gov/index.cfm?ty=pbdetail&iid=834.

15 Tim Bynum, "Release on Recognizance: Substantive or Superficial Reform?" *Criminology* 20 (1982): 67–82.

16 Mary Toborg, "Bail Bondsmen and Criminal Courts," *Justice System Journal* 8 (1983): 141–156.

17 Keith Hansen, "When Worlds Collide: The Constitutional Politics of *United States v. Salerno*," *American Journal of Criminal Law* 14 (1987): 155–225.

18 Robert Nagel, "The Myth of the General Right to Bail," *Public Interest* 98 (1990): 4–97.

19 Stephen Demuth, "Racial and Ethnic Differences in Pre-trial Release Decisions and Outcomes: A Comparison of Hispanic, Black, and White Felony Arrestees," *Criminology* 41 (August 1, 2003): 873–907.

20 Jason Geary, "A Single Shot, No One Hurt: Why 20 Years?" *Ledger*, June 19, 2009. Steve Bousquet, "The Warning Shot That Condemned Orville Lee Wollard to Prison and Changed Florida," *Tampa Bay Tribune*, February 4, 2016.

21 Arthur Rosett and Donald R. Cressey, *Justice by Consent: Plea Bargains in the American Courthouse* (New York: Lippincott, 1976).

22 Stephanos Bibas, "Designing Plea Bargaining from the Ground Up: Accuracy and Fairness Without Trials as Backstops," *William and Mary Law Review* 57, no. 4 (2016): 1055–1081.

23 National Registry of Exonerations, Guilty Pleas and False Confessions, November 24, 2015. Available at www.law.umich.edu/special/exoneration/Pages/False-Confessions.aspx.

24 Jed S. Rakoff, "Why Innocent People Plead Guilty," *New York Review of Books*, November 20, 2014.

25 Lucian E. Dervan and Vanessa A. Edkins, "The Innocent Defendant's Dilemma: An Innovative Empirical Study of Plea Bargaining's Innocence Problem," *Journal of Criminal Law & Criminology* 103, no. 1 (2013): 1–48. Gregory M. Gilchrist, "Trial Bargaining," *Iowa Law Review* 101 (2016): 609–656.

26 Stephanos Bibas, *The Machinery of Criminal Justice* (New York: Oxford University Press, 2012), xix.

27 Rick Jones, Gerald B. Lefcourt, Barry J. Pollack, Norman L. Reimer, and Kyle O'Dowd, *The Trial Penalty: The Sixth Amendment Right to Trial on the Verge of Extinction and How to Save It* (Washington, D.C.: National Association of Criminal Defense Lawyers, 2018). See endnote 2,

p. 62. Available at www.nacdl.org/Document/TrialPenaltySixthAmendmentRighttoTrialNearExtinct.

28 David W. Neubauer, *America's Courts and the Criminal Justice System*, 7th ed. (Belmont, Calif.: Wadsworth, 2002).

29 Talia Fisher, "The Boundaries of Plea Bargaining: Negotiating the Standard of Proof," *Journal of Criminal Law and Criminology* 97, no.4 (July 1, 2007): 943–1007.

30 B. Grant Stite and Robert H. Chaires, "Plea Bargaining: Ethical Issues and Emerging Perspectives," *Justice Professional* 7 (1993): 69–91.

31 Richard S. Frase, "Comparative Criminal Justice as a Guide to American Law Reform," *California Law Review* 78, no. 3 (May 1990): 539–684. David A. Jones, "Negotiation, Ratification, and Rescission of the Guilty Plea Agreement: A Contractual Analysis and Typology," *Duquesne Law Review* 17, nos. 3 & 4 (1978–1979): 591–632. N. Gary Holten and Lawson L. Lamar, *The Criminal Courts: Structures Personnel and Processes* (New York: McGraw-Hill, 1991), 226–229.

32 Holten and Lamar, *Criminal Courts*.

33 Erving Goffman, *Stigma: Notes on the Management of Spoiled Identity* (New York: Simon and Schuster, 1986).

34 Jeffery T. Ulmer, Megan C. Kurlychek, and John H. Kramer, "Prosecutorial Discretion and the Imposition of Mandatory Minimum Sentences," *Journal of Research in Crime and Delinquency* 44, no. 4 (November 1, 2007): 427.

35 Linda A. Wood and Clare MacMartin, "Constructing Remorse: Judges' Sentencing Decisions in Child Sexual Assault Cases," *Journal of Language and Social Psychology* 26, no. 4 (December 1, 2007): 343.

36 Greg M. Kramer, Melinda Wolbransky, and Kirk Heilbrun," Plea Bargaining Recommendations by Criminal Defense Attorneys: Evidence Strength, Potential Sentence, and Defendant Preference," *Behavioral Sciences and the Law* 25, no. 4 (July1, 2007): 573.

37 Christopher B. Mueller, "'Make Him an Offer He Can't Refuse'— Mezzanatto Waivers as Lynchpin of Prosecutorial Overreach," *Missouri Law Review* 82, no. 4 (2017): 1023–1088.

38 Neubauer, *America's Courts and the Criminal Justice System*.

39 Jay S. Albanese, "Concern about Variation in Criminal Sentences:

A Cyclical History of Reform," *Journal of Criminal Law and Criminology* 75 (1984): 260–271. William Rhodes, *Plea Bargaining: Who Gains? Who Loses?* (Washington, D.C.: Institute for Law and Social Research, 1978).

40 Jay S. Albanese, "Concern about Variation in Criminal Sentences: A Cyclical History of Reform," *Journal of Criminal Law and Criminology* 75 (1984): 260–271.

41 Charlie Gerstein, "Plea Bargaining and the Right to Counsel at Bail Hearings," *Michigan Law Review* 111 (June 2013): 1513–1534.

42 Lynn Mather, *Plea Bargaining or Trial* (Lexington, Mass.: D. C. Heath, 1979).

43 Neubauer, *America's Courts and the Criminal Justice System*.

44 Thomas Church, "Plea Bargains, Concessions and the Courts: Analysis of a Quasi-Experiment," *Law and Society Review* 10 (1976): 377–389.

45 David Lynch, "The Impropriety of Plea Agreements: A Tale of Two Counties," *Law and Social Inquiry* 19 (1994): 115–136.

46 Teresa White Carns and John A. Kruse, "Alaska's Ban on Plea Bargaining Reevaluated," *Judicature* 75 (April 1992): 310–317.

47 Michael L. Rubinstein, Stevens H. Clarke, and Teresa J. White, *The Effect of the Official Prohibition of Plea Bargaining on the Disposition of Felony Cases in Alaska Criminal Courts* (Anchorage: Alaska Judicial Council, 1978), ii–iii.

48 Douglas D. Guidorizzi, "Should We Really Ban Plea Bargaining: The Core Concerns of Plea Bargaining Critics," *Emory Law Journal* 47, no. 2 (Spring 1998): 753–784.

49 Jerzy Shedlock, "Jerry Active, Maintaining Innocence, Sentenced to 359 Years for Murders, Rapes," *Anchorage Daily News*, September 28, 2016.

50 Jon'a F. Meyer and Diana R. Grant, *The Courts in Our Criminal Justice System* (Upper Saddle River, N.J.: Prentice Hall, 2003).

51 Raymond Nimmer and Patricia Krauthaus, "Plea Bargaining Reform in Two Cities," *Justice System Journal* 3 (1977): 6–21.

52 Candace McCoy, *Politics and Plea Bargaining: Victims' Rights in California* (Philadelphia: University of Pennsylvania Press, 1993).

53 Bureau of Justice Statistics, "The Justice System: What Is the Sequence of Events in the Criminal Justice System?" www.bjs.gov/content/justsys.cfm. Accessed January 2020.

54 United States Attorneys' Manual, "When an Information May Be Used," www.justice.gov/usam/criminal-resource-manual-206-when-information-may-be-used. Accessed January 2020.

55 Professors Fagan and Harcourt Provide Facts on Grand Jury Practice in Light of Ferguson Decision, Columbia Law School, https://www.law.columbia.edu/news/archive/professors-fagan-and-harcourt-provide-facts-grand-jury-practice-light-ferguson-decision. Accessed October 2020.

56 Charles Thompson, "What Is a Grand Jury, and How Does It Work?" *Patriot News* (Pennsylvania), January 29, 2019. Christopher Reinhart, Connecticut Grand Juries, www.cga.ct.gov/PS98/rpt\olr/htm/98-R-1101.htm. Accessed January 2020.

57 David A. Bright and Jane Goodman-Delahunty, "Gruesome Evidence and Emotion: Anger, Blame, and Jury Decision-Making," *Law and Human Behavior* 30, no. 2 (April 1, 2006):183–202.

58 Henry J. Abraham, *The Judicial Process*, 7th ed. (New York: Oxford University Press, 1998).

59 Steven Schlesinger, *Exclusionary Injustice: The Problem of Illegally Obtained Evidence* (New York: Marcel Dekker, 1977).

60 Steve Tuholski, "When Facts Don't Fit, Some Jurors Make Up New Facts," *National Law Journal* (February 4, 2008): S3.

61 J. Don Read, Deborah A. Connolly, and Andrew Welsh, "An Archival Analysis of Actual Cases of Historic Child Sexual Abuse: A Comparison of Jury and Bench Trials," *Law and Human Behavior* 30, no. 3 (June 1, 2006): 259–285.

62 Barbara Reskin and Christine Visher, "The Impacts of Evidence and Extralegal Factors in Juror's Decisions," *Law and Society Review* 20 (1986): 423–439.

63 Neubauer, *America's Courts and the Criminal Justice System*.

64 Lincoln Caplan, *The Insanity Defense and the Trial of John W. Hinckley Jr.* (Boston: D. R. Godine, 1984).

65 Michael Freeman and Helen Reece, eds., *Science in Court* (Brookfield, Vt.: Ashgate, 1998).

66 Tom R. Tyler, "Viewing CSI and the Threshold of Guilt: Managing Truth and Justice in Reality and Fiction," *Yale Law Journal* 115, no. 5 (March 1, 2006): 1050–1085.

67 William Brennan, "The Criminal Prosecution: Sporting Events or Quest for Truth?" *Washington University Law Review* (1963): 279–294.

68 John Holloway, "Conviction Review Units: A National Perspective," University of Pennsylvania Law School Penn Law: Legal Scholarship Repository, 2016. Available at scholarship.law.upenn.edu/faculty_scholarship/1614.

69 Dana Carver Boehm, "The New Prosecutor's Dilemma: Prosecutorial Ethics and the Evaluation of Actual Innocence," *Utah Law Review*, no. 3 (May 2014): 613–675. American Bar Association, Rule 3.8: Special Responsibilities of a Prosecutor, www.americanbar.org/groups/professional_responsibility/publications/model_rules_of_professional_conduct/rule_3_8_special_responsibilities_of_a_prosecutor.

70 Holloway, "Conviction Review Units"

71 "Philadelphia District Attorney Exonerates 9 People in 19 Months," *CBS News*, September 3, 2019.

72 Peggy Tobolowsky, "Restitution in the Federal Criminal Justice System," *Judicature* 77 (1993): 90–95. See also Christy Visher, "Incapacitation and Crime Control: Does a 'Lock 'em Up' Strategy Reduce Crime?" *Justice Quarterly* 4 (1987): 513–544.

73 Thomas Arvanites, "Increasing Imprisonment: A Function of Crime or Socioeconomic Factors?" *American Journal of Criminal Justice* 17 (1992): 19–38.

74 Elizabeth Moulds, "Chivalry and Paternalism: Disparities of Treatment in the Criminal Justice System," *Western Political Science Quarterly* 31 (1978): 416–440.

75 U.S. Sentencing Commission, *United States Sentencing Commission Guidelines Manual 2018* (Washington, D.C.: United States Sentencing Commission, 2018), 3. Available at www.ussc.gov/guidelines/2018-guidelines-manual. Tamasak Wicharaya, *Simple Theory, Hard Reality: The Impact of Sentencing Reforms on Courts, Prisons, and Crime* (Albany: State University of New York Press, 1995).

76 John Irwin, *Prisons in Turmoil* (Boston: Little, Brown, 1980). Irwin presents a scathing critique of the indeterminate sentence from a prisoner's point of view.

77 Ibid.

78 William Gaylin, *Partial Justice: A Study of Bias in Sentencing* (New York: Vintage Books, 1974).

79 Irwin, *Prisons in Turmoil*.

80 Steven P. Lab and John T. Whitehead, "From 'Nothing Works' to 'The Appropriate Works': The Latest Stop in the Search for the Secular Grail," *Criminology* 28 (1990): 405–418.

81 John Hagan, "Extra-Legal Attributes and Criminal Sentencing: An Assessment of a Sociological Viewpoint," *Law and Society Review* 8 (1974): 357–381.

82 James B. Jacobs, *Stateville: The Penitentiary in Mass Society* (Chicago: University of Chicago Press, 1977).

83 Francis T. Cullen and Karen B. Gilbert, *Reaffirming Rehabilitation* (Cincinnati: Anderson, 1982).

84 Pamala Griset, *Determinate Sentencing: The Promise and the Reality of Retributive Justice* (Ithaca: State University of New York Press, 1991).

85 Jeffery Ulner, *Social Worlds of Sentencing: Court Communities under Sentencing Guidelines* (Albany: State University of New York Press, 1997).

86 Darrell Steffensmeier, Jeffrey Ulmer, and John Kramer, "The Interaction of Race, Gender, and Age in Criminal Sentencing: The Punishment Cost of Being Young, Black and Male," *Criminology* 36: 763–798.

87 William McDonald, Henry Rossman, and James Cramer, "The Prosecutorial Function and Its Relation to Determinate Sentencing Structures," in *The Prosecutor*, ed. William McDonald (Beverly Hills, Calif.: Sage, 1979).

88 Ibid.

89 Families Against Mandatory Minimums, Sentencing 101. Available at famm.org/our-work/sentencing-reform/sentencing-101. Accessed January 2020.

90 Laurence H. Ross and James Foley, "Judicial Disobedience of the Mandate to Imprison Drunk Drivers," *Law and Society Review* 21 (1987): 315–323.

91 Jeffery T. Ulmer, Megan C. Kurlychek, and John H. Kramer, "Prosecutorial Discretion and the Imposition of Mandatory Minimum Sentences," *Journal of Research in Crime and Delinquency* 44, no. 4 (2007): 427.

OXFORD insight study guide
Active Engagement, Deeper Understanding

Learn more with this chapter's digital tools, including the Oxford Insight Study Guide, at www.oup.com/he/Fuller2e.

PART IV

From Penology to Corrections and Back

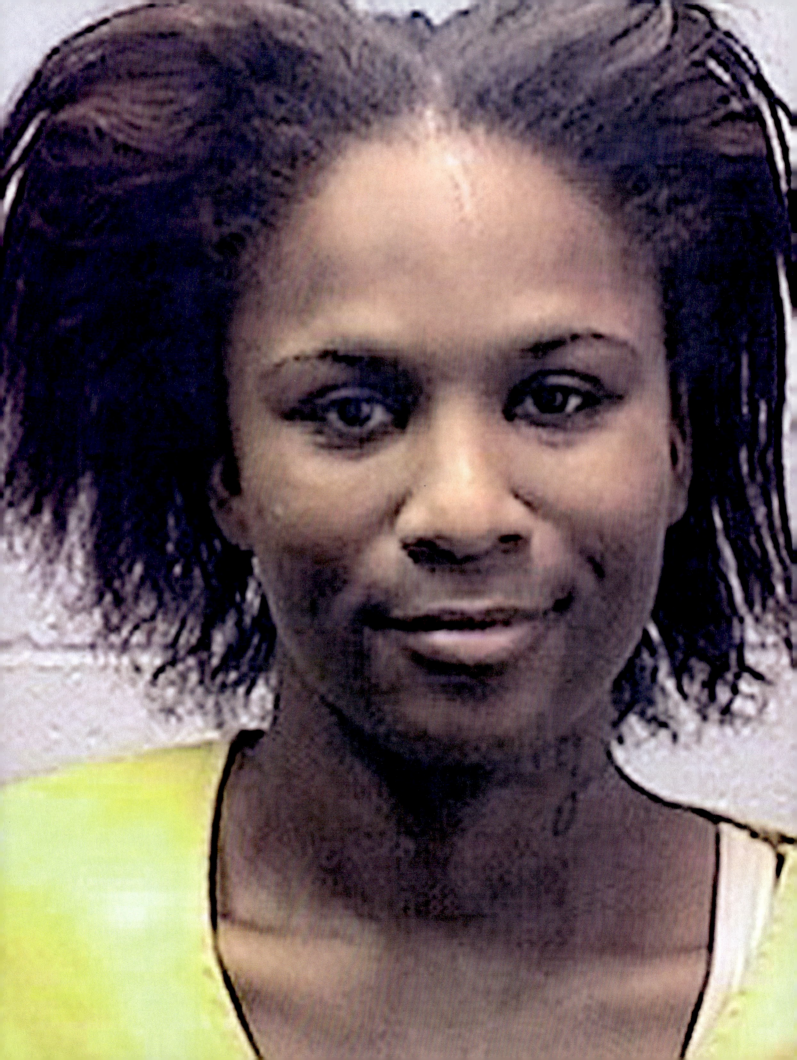

Chapter 10

A Brief History of Prisons and the Death Penalty in the United States

Strawberry Hampton, a transgender woman serving 10 years in Illinois for burglary, was moved from a men's to a women's prison in one of the first cases of its kind in the state. How should prisons deal with transgender inmates?

In 2013,

Miguel Crespo, an inmate serving a life sentence for murder at California's Kern Valley State Prison, told correctional officers that he was going to kill his new cellmate. Nine hours later, officers found Carmen Guerrero, a transgender woman, bound, gagged, and strangled to death in her bunk.[1]

Prosecutors believe Guerrero began working on a transfer request when Crespo was placed in the same cell, writing, "He stated he is not compatible with me. I'm worried to be raped again."[2] During sentencing, Crespo told the judge that he warned prison officials that he was not a homosexual and was not supposed to share a cell with a homosexual.[3] Crespo was sentenced to death.[4]

The unique challenges of transgender inmates have only recently been recognized. For instance, Strawberry Hampton, 27, who identified as female since the age of five, struggled to be recognized as a woman by the Illinois Department of Corrections and to be protected from abuse and discrimination. Before she was transferred to a women's prison, she had been housed in four men's prisons. There, other inmates abused and sexually assaulted her and threatened to rape and kill her, and staff forced her to engage in sex acts with a cellmate. As a result of a lawsuit she filed in 2017, a federal judge ordered training on transgender issues for Illinois correctional staff.[5]

In 2019, transgender inmate Lindsay Saunders-Velez was awarded $170,000 from a lawsuit against the Colorado Department of Corrections after allegedly being raped in a men's prison. Attorneys with the Transgender Law Center filed a lawsuit against the Colorado DOC insisting they improve the treatment of transgender inmates. Lead attorney Paula Greisen argued, "Housing the inmates with men invites sexual predators to victimize the women and that is in fact what is happening."[6]

THINK ABOUT IT > What steps can correctional institutions take to ensure the safety of transgender inmates?

LEARNING OBJECTIVE | **10.1**

Compare and contrast the two prison systems that emerged in the United States during the first half of the 19th century.

LEARNING OBJECTIVE | **10.2**

Describe the three most well-known examples of the Irish System of reform.

10.1 Prisons in the United States

Prison reform efforts in the United States have been aimed at making the institution more effective and humane. Life in prison can be traumatic for any inmate. Historically, this has been especially true for particular groups, including gang members, people with mental illnesses, and people who are homosexual or transgender.[7]

Calls for prison reform are not new, and it is no surprise that an institution designed to restrict freedom dwells at the center of controversy. How can prisons balance the concerns and rights of inmates with the demands of an aggrieved society? We must trace the history of this institution from colonial times to the present, with an eye toward how some well-intended reforms have not worked out as planned.[8]

Control in the Colonies and Early United States: 1770–1860

The North American colonies faced many of the same social control issues as England, but some major differences between the two led to the unique development of American incarceration. Early penal institutions were under local control and mixed various types of offenders; the accused were held with the convicted, civil violators with criminal offenders, and so on.

The idea of incarceration as the sole punishment for convicts took time to develop. Initially, corporal punishment, especially the stocks or whipping, was used in

conjunction with jail to discourage crime. The Pennsylvania Quakers suggested that incarceration and hard labor were preferable to corporal punishment. Pennsylvania's 1786 penal code allowed inmates to work on public projects while chained to cannonballs and dressed in brightly colored clothing. However, because many objected to this public spectacle, hard labor was moved behind the walls of the institution.

Perhaps the most influential early carceral institution in the United States was Philadelphia's Walnut Street Jail. Built in 1773, it demonstrated all the shortcomings of early jails.

> Little attempt was made to reform the criminals. Segregation and classification were hardly known. Rations were poor and irregularly given. Escapes, riots and scenes of debauchery were common. The inmates were . . . offered little employment. Idleness, drunkenness, [shackles], prostitution and gambling were [the] companions of the corrupt keepers. . . . In general, it housed a conglomerate mixture of practices which are strongly denounced by penologists today.[9]

Used as a military prison during the Revolutionary War, the Walnut Street Jail was converted around 1790 into the country's first penitentiary, in which the most hardened convicts were kept in single cells. At this time, the institution's administration was revamped, and a board of inspectors, instead of the sheriff, was given authority over the jail's affairs. Part of the jail's new direction was to ensure that the inmates had meaningful work and steady employment.[10] The innovations at the Walnut Street Jail, now a prison, set the tone for the more formal prisons that were built in the next century.[11]

The first institution to resemble a modern penitentiary was Castle Island in Massachusetts' Boston Harbor. Established by the Massachusetts legislature in 1785, it housed only convicted offenders from the state's various jails.[12] From 1785 to 1798, about 280 prisoners served time on Castle Island, with at least 45 escaping.[13]

LEARNING OBJECTIVE 10.3

Summarize the three ways in which work was deemed beneficial during the early 20th century.

Prisons in the United States

LEARNING OBJECTIVE 10.4

Outline the circumstances that led to the advocacy of rehabilitation as a desirable goal for the field of corrections, as well as its subsequent demise.

This engraving depicts the Walnut Street Jail in Philadelphia, Pennsylvania, circa 1800. What types of offenders were incarcerated in this jail?

Two prison systems emerged in the United States during the first half of the 19th century, which attracted the attention of prison reformers. Both of these systems, the Pennsylvania System and the Auburn (New York) System (the names are based on their initial locations), emphasized regimens of silence and penitence.

THE PENNSYLVANIA SYSTEM

In 1829, the state of Pennsylvania opened a prison on the site of a cherry orchard outside Philadelphia. For years, the Eastern State Penitentiary, called Cherry Hill by locals, was characterized by the **separate-and-silent system**, by which it was reasoned that inmates would reflect on their offenses and reform if they were kept from seeing or talking to one another. By using such extreme procedures as having inmates wear hoods when outside their cells, the Eastern State Penitentiary administration believed it was facilitating the inmates' self-reflection and reform. By keeping the inmates from interacting with each other, the state hoped the inmates would not contaminate each other with antisocial thoughts and behavior. The Pennsylvania System viewed too much labor as interfering with rehabilitative meditation, so inmates did craftwork in their cells.

Kept in solitary confinement, many inmates developed severe mental problems because of the oppressive boredom and lack of human contact. The inmates developed clever means of communicating, such as tapping codes on the water pipes in the cells, but for the most part they were kept as separate as possible by the prison's limited resources.[14] However, as the prison became more crowded, double-celling (having two inmates share a cell) became the norm and isolation was impossible. The separate-and-silent system was costly and soon met its demise, not only because of economics, but also because critics thought keeping anyone in isolation for so long was inhumane.

Separate-and-silent system—A method of penal control pioneered by Philadelphia's Eastern State Penitentiary in which inmates were kept from seeing or talking to one another. This method is comparable to solitary confinement in modern prisons.

This lithograph depicts the Eastern State Penitentiary in Pennsylvania, circa 1855. What problems did the separate-and-silent system of this penitentiary present?

THE AUBURN SYSTEM

The Auburn Prison, opened in 1817 in New York, tried the separate-and-silent system. By 1823 though, it became apparent that this system caused more problems than it solved and that the inmates' mental and physical health issues were more punishing than the administration thought reasonable. Therefore, inmates were locked in separate cells each night but were allowed to eat and work together during the day. They were forbidden to talk to each other, however. This **congregate-and-silent system**, which prohibited face-to-face contact, required inmates to march in lockstep and keep their eyes downcast.[15]

Considerable debate surrounded these two prison systems. On one hand, the Pennsylvania System's supporters touted it as superior because it was easier to control inmates, was more conducive to meditation and repentance, and avoided the cross-contamination inherent when inmates are together. In contrast, proponents of the Auburn model argued that their methods and techniques of incarceration were superior because they were less expensive, could provide better vocational training, and were less harmful to the inmates' mental health. Additionally, the Auburn model used a factory-oriented labor system as opposed to the craft-oriented labor system of the Eastern State Penitentiary. Although neither of these systems was fully copied in other jurisdictions, they did serve as models for other prisons. Reformers adopted aspects of the Pennsylvania and Auburn models and introduced modifications that addressed changing political, economic, and social conditions.[16]

Congregate-and-silent system—A style of penal control pioneered by the Auburn System in which inmates were allowed to eat and work together during the day but were forbidden to speak to each other and were locked alone in their cells at night.

Age of Reform: 1860–1900

At the time that the penitentiary was developed in the United States, the penal practices of other countries influenced U.S. corrections. European countries experimented with techniques designed not only to punish, but also to give inmates a better chance at successfully returning to society upon completing their sentence. This new emphasis on social reintegration, called the Irish System, was tried in the post–Civil War United States. Here, we will focus on the three most well-known examples of the Irish System of reform: those developed by Alexander Maconochie, Sir Walter Crofton, and Zebulon Brockway.

Prisoners at the State Prison at Auburn.

Prisoners marching at the State Penitentiary at Auburn, New York. Why did this prison abandon the separate-and-silent system?

ALEXANDER MACONOCHIE

In 1840, Alexander Maconochie, a retired British naval officer, received command of the Norfolk Island penal colony off the eastern coast of Australia. Here, he developed a system to make inmates trustworthy, honest, and useful to society. This system was based on two fundamental beliefs:

1. Brutality and cruelty debase not only the subject but also the society that deliberately uses or tolerates them for purposes of social control.
2. The treatment of a wrongdoer during his sentence of imprisonment should be designed to make him fit to be released into society again, purged of the tendencies that led him to his offense, and strengthened in his ability to withstand temptation again.[17]

Indeterminate sentence (from Chapter 9)—A prison term that is determined by a parole board and does not state a specific period of time to be served or a date of release.

Marks-of-commendation system—An incarceration philosophy developed by Alexander Maconochie in which inmates earned the right to be released, as well as privileges, goods, and services.

Central to Maconochie's philosophy of incarceration was the **indeterminate sentence** (see Chapter 9), in which the offender would be released when the prison officials believed he was reformed. A **marks-of-commendation system** was instituted in which inmates earned the right to be released. Additionally, privileges, goods, and services could be purchased with marks given for good behavior. The marks system enabled inmates to progress through various stages of social control, the goal of which was to give inmates some control over the pains of incarceration.

Maconochie's rational and systematic implementation earned high praise from prison experts. However, the Norfolk Island system was short-lived. Maconochie returned to England in 1844 and with him went the more humane treatment of inmates on Norfolk Island.

SIR WALTER CROFTON

A decade later, in 1854, Maconochie's progressive ways of treating inmates inspired Sir Walter Crofton, who was appointed director of the Irish prison system. In addition to Maconochie's marks system and the progressive stages of social control, Crofton implemented the concept of a completely open institution in which the inmates could gain experience in trust and avoiding temptation. Crofton is best remembered for instituting an early-release system called "ticket-of-leave," in which inmates were given a conditional release and supervised by local police. Inmates who violated the conditions of their release were returned to prison.[18] (This idea will be more fully discussed in Chapter 12.)

ZEBULON BROCKWAY

The ideas developed by Maconochie and Crofton were instituted by reformer Zebulon Brockway at the reformatory in Elmira, New York, from 1876 to 1900. Brockway used the 500-bed facility to house young men between the ages of 16 and 30 who were first-time offenders. A three-grade program was used in which inmates entered at the second grade. An inmate was promoted to the first grade after six months of good behavior or demoted to the third grade if he failed to conform. Only those who were in the first grade were eligible for release (they were sentenced to an indeterminate term with only the minimum amount of time being fixed). An inmate needed a year of good marks before being eligible for parole. The Elmira Reformatory used volunteers—forerunners of parole officers—to keep track of the released inmates. The important distinction between this accommodation and the Irish ticket-of-leave system is that police officers did not supervise the parolees. The modern separation of law enforcement and correctional activities is an enduring feature of this early program.[19]

Prison reform had its failures as well as successes. It did not progress in an uninterrupted manner from brutality to humane treatment because even reformers such as Zebulon Brockway had some unattractive ideas. For example, corporal punishment was such a regular feature of the Elmira Reformatory that Brockway was nicknamed "Paddler Brockway." In addition, it was difficult to maintain the integrity of the classification system. Designed for young first offenders, the reformatories often housed seasoned offenders, and problems of violence, revolts, rape, smuggling, and arson often arose.[20]

For those who presented significant discipline problems, a form of solitary confinement was used. Brockway called this the "rest cure," but it included being shackled and fed nothing more than bread and water for months at a time. Although such treatment eventually led to the demise of the reform movement, reform has become a recurring theme in corrections. Many of the ideals of the age of reform are at the foundation of modern prison systems. The repeated imperfect implementation of these reforms speaks not to the inadequacy of the reforms but more to the economic, social, and political contexts that invariably frustrate the ideals of prison reformers.

A New Emphasis on Prison Labor: 1900–1930

The idea that work is healthy for both the inmate and society is as old as the prison. Even the Pennsylvania System, which viewed too much labor as interfering with rehabilitative meditation, had inmates do craftwork in their cells. Of particular interest is the degree to which work was viewed as a good thing in itself and when it was viewed as a means to other ends. Work was deemed beneficial in at least three ways:

1. It is a good way to keep inmates occupied. By doing work (sometimes backbreaking work), the inmates have neither the time nor the energy to cause trouble.

2. It has rehabilitative value. Because most prisoners eventually return to society, they benefit from work. They practice good work habits and sometimes learn useful skills.

3. It offsets the cost of incarceration. Inmate labor has been used to construct and maintain prisons, feed inmates, and at times make products that can be sold to other government agencies or even outside society.

The type of prison labor system that authorities choose is always subject to political and technological conditions. Decades ago, in southern states where counties rather than state governments controlled the prisons, the **convict lease system** was used extensively. Partly as a replacement for slave labor, this system allowed major landowners to employ inmates to do backbreaking work at wages that free people would not accept, such as harvesting cotton in Georgia and distilling turpentine in Florida.

By the early 20th century, more than half of the states had adopted state-use laws regarding inmate labor. These laws prevented inmate-made wares from being sold on the open market and only allowed their use by the originating prison or by other state agencies. In 1934, President Franklin D. Roosevelt authorized the establishment of Federal Prison Industries, Inc. (FPI). The FPI system also prohibited the sale of inmate-made wares to the public, restricting sales to the federal government. By 1940, the Ashurst-Sumners Act and its amendment completely prohibited the interstate shipment of nearly all inmate-made wares. In 1977, FPI changed its name to UNICOR.[21] The 1979 Private Sector Prison Industry

Convict lease system—A system in the late 19th and early 20th centuries in which companies and individuals could purchase the labor of prison inmates from state and county governments.

In 1910, this North Carolina convict chain gang lived in wagons, which were moved to different places so that the convicts could work as needed. What types of labor did chain gangs provide for the government?

Enhancement Certification Program eased some of the barriers to interstate shipment of inmate-made wares, allowing certified states to sell items on the open market under certain conditions. These conditions included paying inmates wages comparable with similar jobs outside the prison, collecting funds for a victim assistance program, and only using voluntary inmate labor.[22]

Although thousands of inmates work part- and full-time jobs, most do work to keep the prison running.[23] In many contemporary prisons, the only inmates doing any type of productive labor are those used to maintain the basic needs of the institution.[24] According to activist James Kilgore, who served six and a half years in prison, "[P]urposelessness and excruciating boredom, not overwork, are the dominant features of most prison yards."[25]

Age of Rehabilitation: 1930–1970

Rehabilitating inmates has always been a criminal justice system goal, but not until the 1930s did U.S. prisons acknowledge that rehabilitation was a primary goal. As far back as Maconochie, some advocated the prison's role in reforming individuals, but the state's responsibility for changing inmates' behavior was not widely recognized. Around 1930, several circumstances helped professionalize the field of corrections and allowed progressive reformers to advocate rehabilitation as a desirable and possible goal.[26]

A primary reason why rehabilitation became important at this time was the change in how science regarded illness. This change, in turn, affected how criminologists and correctional practitioners considered criminality. The germ theory of medicine that absolved the sick person of responsibility for contracting an illness spread to corrections. Crime was no longer viewed as a choice made by the offender. The idea that outside influences contribute to criminality led theorists and correctional administrators to speculate on how antisocial behavior is transmitted among individuals. A medical metaphor developed that viewed offenders as "sick," and rehabilitation efforts were dedicated to finding the causes of crime in the biological, psychological, and sociological deficiencies of the individual.[27]

Once the cause was diagnosed, it was a simple matter to prescribe a "cure" of drug or alcohol treatment, family or individual counseling, more education, or anger-management classes. The medical model likened crime to disease and postulated that normal (law-abiding) behavior is within reach of all offenders and that the correctional practitioner can find the optimal treatment.

At the forefront of the effort to prioritize rehabilitation was the establishment of the **Federal Bureau of Prisons** in 1930. This agency eliminated political patronage in filling job vacancies, developed better trained and more professional staff, and greatly improved the conditions of confinement by way of new designs.[28] Prisons were constructed with the goals of facilitating the classification and treatment of offenders. Bureau of Prisons officials were committed to treating offenders as individuals and keeping them occupied in productive activities such as work and education.

Another factor that encouraged rehabilitation was the 1931 Wickersham Commission report, which prescribed a range of criminal justice reforms, including suggestions that rehabilitation be attempted in earnest. The commission documented the failures of prison labor systems and the idleness of inmates in most prisons in its quest to solve the penitentiary's systemic problems. The Wickersham Commission did not present new information, but the fact that it was a governmental fact-finding and policy-suggesting body gave its recommendations a legitimacy that previous reformers lacked.[29]

Although the theoretical foundations of treating offenders were further refined during the mid-20th century, several factors intervened to prevent rehabilitative practices from fully taking hold in prison systems. One of the leading causes was lack of resources. Keeping inmates confined and preventing them from hurting each other, as well as the prison staff, soaked up most of the time, money, and creative energies of prison officials and staff. Treatment programs were considered luxuries in prison systems struggling to maintain minimal custody standards in states that would rather spend their limited tax dollars on education, infrastructure, and health care. In most prisons, the percentage of inmates who received any significant treatment was low. One observer called rehabilitation efforts during this time "token treatment," designed more for public relations purposes than for producing any real change in inmate attitudes and behaviors.[30]

Another reason why the rehabilitation era never fully developed effective methods for changing the lives of inmates and reducing crime was the lack of consensus regarding whether it was or could ever be effective. In a major study of treatment programs published in 1974, the unfortunate consensus was that "nothing works."[31] Even though this conclusion is more complex than initially reported, the correctional community jettisoned rehabilitation as an orienting perspective. Nevertheless, some claim that certain rehabilitative programs work for certain offenders and that although one course of treatment does not work for everyone, rehabilitation is still a worthy and attainable goal.[32]

The final reason why rehabilitation lost favor was the belief of some scholars that the medical model was a flawed metaphor for corrections. To view offenders as "sick" and in need of a "cure" was deemed problematic by many who favored a view that placed responsibility for antisocial behavior squarely on the shoulders of those who chose to violate the law. These scholars believed it was more accurate to think of felons as lazy, unmotivated, poorly socialized, or exploitive. Opponents of the medical model asserted that society did not need to "cure" inmates as much as inmates needed to learn that their unlawful behavior would have negative consequences. Therefore, they called for deterrence rather than rehabilitation.[33]

Federal Bureau of Prisons—Established within the Department of Justice in 1930, a federal agency that manages and regulates all federal penal and correctional institutions.

Retributive Era: 1970s to the Present

The movement away from the rehabilitation philosophy did not occur in a social vacuum. The events of the 1960s brought many changes in how our social institutions operated. A backlash to political protests, reported widespread drug use, relaxation of sexual mores, and general disrespect for authority and tradition manifested in ways that affected the prison.[34]

One example of how events outside the prison found their way inside was the politicization of inmates. As minorities, youth, and women outside prison walls challenged how society treated them, inmates challenged the conditions of their confinement inside the prison.[35] For example, *Hope v. Pelzer* (2002) set guidelines for what constitutes cruel and unusual punishment in prison and the circumstances under which prison officials are liable for the mistreatment of prisoners. In 1995, Alabama inmate Larry Hope was handcuffed to a post for seven hours after fighting with a guard at a work site. Hope filed suit against three corrections officers, but the magistrate judge ruled that the guards were immune to the suit because they were unaware of any constitutional violations of their actions. The U.S. Supreme Court affirmed a lower court's judgment that Hope's treatment violated the Eighth Amendment and also held that the guards were liable for their actions and could be sued.

The courts traditionally had a "hands-off" policy concerning prison operations, but in the 1960s they started to specify exactly which constitutional rights, such as the expectation of privacy, inmates forfeited in prison.[36] This led to major changes in areas such as food and disciplinary procedures. For example, the prison must try to accommodate dietary requirements based on inmates' religious practices. As inmates organized to challenge the conditions of their confinement, a new, racial dimension appeared in the inmates' identity. The Black Panther Party and the Black Muslims agitated to have prisons recognize them as legitimate political organizations within the prison that spoke for minority inmates. The tensions caused by this politicization of inmates made rehabilitation efforts difficult to accomplish. When Black Muslim inmates defined themselves as political prisoners, they became unwilling to adopt the "sick" label of the medical model of rehabilitation and instead contended that society's institutions, particularly prisons, treated individuals

Muslim inmate Steven C. Green prays over his halal meal during lunch at John H. Lilley Correctional Center in Oklahoma. Why did Black Muslim inmates demand to be called political prisoners?

unfairly. For example, in Stateville Prison in Illinois, troublesome Muslim inmates were not allowed to work prison jobs, were denied access to prison recreational and educational activities, and were often placed in segregated cells.

With inmates rebelling against the conditions of their confinement, the courts questioning how prison officials did their jobs, and society losing faith in the promises of rehabilitation, a change in the basic philosophy of incarceration was inevitable. Retribution replaced rehabilitation as the primary goal of the prison. This had significant and widespread implications for how inmates were sentenced and treated in prison.[37] Some of the changes were as follows:

> Determinate sentences. With rehabilitation no longer the prison's main goal, officials were no longer willing to certify when it was safe to return an inmate to society. Therefore, indeterminate sentences were no longer desirable. **Determinate sentences**, or fixed terms of incarceration, were implemented in their place based not on inmates' needs but on the seriousness of their offenses and criminal record. In this way, inmates would be treated for what they did rather than for some perceived deficiency in their psychological makeup or social conditioning.[38]

> Voluntary treatment. With rehabilitation no longer a primary goal of incarceration, treatment services were offered on a voluntary basis because prison administrators believed that treatment was more effective for those who sought it without coercion or conditions. During the rehabilitation era, when inmates participated in treatment to impress a parole board, it was assumed that they were "playing the parole game"; thus, their motivations were suspect.[39] Inmates who entered programs voluntarily were considered more likely to be sincere in their desires to learn new skills, acquire an education, or seek drug treatment. Additionally, there were presumably fewer "jailhouse conversions" when attendance at religious services (previously thought to be indicative of rehabilitative progress) was not considered at parole hearings.

> Abolition of parole. The attempt to eliminate parole as an early-release mechanism is a by-product of a system that abandoned indeterminate sentencing and compulsory treatment. Although this has not been completely accomplished, many critics want inmates to spend their entire sentence behind bars and view parole as "soft on crime." Coupled with a surge in prison crowding, the elimination of parole is problematic, but several states and the federal government have eliminated discretionary parole (when a parole board may conditionally release prisoners based on a statutory or administrative determination of eligibility).[40] Parole's primary function, like that of the prison, has shifted from treatment to supervision.[41]

Determinate sentence (from Chapter 9)—A prison term that is determined by law and states a specific period of time to be served.

The era of retribution may be about to change, however, if not end completely. Correctional budgets cannot afford to allow state and local governments to use mass incarceration as a correctional policy. It might be different if retributive corrections effectively deterred crime, rehabilitated offenders, and gave communities the confidence that justice is being served in a fair and impartial manner. This is not the case, however. One study concluded that, at most, only 12 percent of the reduction in U.S. property crime rates since the 1990s could be attributed to higher incarceration rates.[42] There is no more crime in states with smaller prison populations than in states with larger prison populations.[43] Other studies have similarly concluded that the high incarceration rates of the past few decades did not cause the decrease in crime in the United States. Rather, lower crime rates have had more to do with demographic changes, such as an aging population, income changes, and decreased alcohol consumption.[44]

Many criminal justice system professionals, scholars, and observers agree that a new direction for U.S. corrections is needed. Several reforms have been advocated:

1. Sentences should be proportional to the severity of the crime. Although this idea goes back to the classical school of criminology, the United States has gotten away from proportionality with its use of mandatory sentences, especially "**three-strikes**" sentencing.

2. Incarceration should be used sparingly, utilizing a minimum level of punishment. This value addresses not only mandatory prison sentences, but also the practice of using incarceration for minor offenses that can be addressed in other ways.

3. Penal sanctions should not be so lasting as to permanently restrict a person's citizenship. Once an inmate has "paid his or her dues to society," he or she should be allowed to reintegrate into the community. Former inmates should be allowed to vote, not automatically be denied employment because of their status as former felons, or in other ways be stigmatized and ostracized.

4. The pains of imprisonment should not disproportionately burden any particular group of people, and prisons should equally distribute resources and opportunities to all groups. This would entail examining the processes that have resulted in the mass incarceration of peoples of color, as well as the economically disadvantaged.[45]

Cultivating retribution as the main value of the correctional system is counterproductive, but finding the appropriate balance between addressing crime and protecting the community is difficult. However, despite complications, some legislators are trying to do just that. For example, in 2015, Kentucky's governor issued an executive order granting the right to vote to certain non-violent felons who had completed their sentences. At present, nearly six million former felons are prohibited by their states from voting.[46] Currently, 48 states and the District of Columbia restrict incarcerated felons from voting, and most states restrict the voting rights of felons who are on probation or parole. Several states permanently restrict some

Three strikes—In reference to criminal justice, a term that describes state laws that require an offender's third felony to be punishable by a severe sentence, including life imprisonment.

An inmate at the Cook County Jail in Chicago submits his ballot after voting at a polling place that was opened inside the jail for early voting. The jail is the first in the country to open a polling place to allow inmates to vote. Should incarcerated individuals be allowed to vote?

types of former felons from voting, while others require them to apply for restoration of rights. Felons in Maine and Vermont have always had the right to vote at any point in the system and may do so while incarcerated.[47]

As the push for corrections reform continues, federal and state legislators will likely continue crafting laws that allow judges more leeway in sentencing, replace incarceration with alternative penalties and rehabilitation, and address penal conventions such as solitary confinement.[48] (For an example of how New York City is striving to reform one of its most notorious jails, see A Closer Look 10.1.)

This brief history of U.S. corrections highlights several themes. One is that many correctional practices that seem new and innovative are actually quite old. The ideas of work as useful in reforming individuals, rehabilitation geared to inmates' needs, and the value of keeping inmates busy have all been used in various eras of corrections. What has changed are not the ideas themselves but rather the resources and political will to support those ideas. This raises the question of whether rehabilitation has ever been given an honest chance. No jurisdiction has ever paid more than lip service to the idea of providing the counselors, modern conditions, and aftercare necessary to effectively change the behavior of offenders who have learned to survive by way of a deviant lifestyle. In many ways, it is unrealistic to expect that participating in a few weeks' worth of rehabilitation activities will help an individual overcome a lifetime of poverty, discrimination, lack of education, and drug addiction. Yet often, this is all society can afford in an attempt to change an inmate.

A CLOSER LOOK 10.1
Closing Rikers

Vidal Guzman was 16 when he went to jail on Rikers Island for the first time. When he arrived, a corrections officer told him to "get ready for Gladiator School." Guzman saw two young men hang themselves during his first week. Johnny Perez, who also went to Rikers when he was 16, says, "I've bought drugs from correction officers who've ... told me they're going to put me in solitary if my mother doesn't meet them in a parking lot to pay them."[49]

Rikers Island, the infamous New York City detention complex, sits in the East River on 413 acres between the Bronx and Queens. Consisting of 10 jails, Rikers is currently home to about 7,000 inmates. In October 2019, the New York City Council voted to close the complex by 2026 and move inmates to four new jails situated throughout the city.[50]

Rikers Island has always had an unfortunate reputation. Shortly after New York City purchased the island around 1893, the city began dumping refuse there, increasing the area of the island. After years of complaints about the stench, rats, and persistent trash fires, it was decided that Rikers Island should be used as a prison. Although prisoners had been held on Rikers for years—Confederate soldiers were incarcerated there during the Civil War—the first official prison on Rikers Island opened in 1935. Built on a backfill of garbage and touted as "ultramodern," it was considered a vast improvement over the "medieval cell blocks" of Welfare Island (now Roosevelt Island).[51]

As the decades wore on, Rikers Island became a place where people were detained for years before trial, often longer than their eventual sentences. In 2014, the Office of the United States Attorney in Manhattan issued a report condemning Rikers, alleging it had fostered "a deep-seated culture of violence."[52]

Although few support maintaining Rikers as a correctional institution, the plan to close the complex and the exact nature of what should replace it are still under intense debate. Plans for reform include alternatives to jail for people who cannot make bail, expanding services to people at risk for breaking the law, changing the way the system handles juveniles and the mentally ill, and creating four new borough-based jails.[53] As the politics surrounding the status of Rikers Island unfolds, it will likely inform correctional reform efforts across the country.

THINK ABOUT IT

1. Why has Rikers Island developed a reputation as such an infamous prison?

PAUSE AND REVIEW

1. What are the three most well-known examples of the Irish System?
2. What influences around 1930 helped professionalize the field of corrections?
3. What circumstances led to the rehabilitation era of corrections?

LEARNING OBJECTIVE 10.5

Argue in support of capital punishment.

LEARNING OBJECTIVE 10.6

Argue against capital punishment.

Capital punishment—
The sentence of death for a criminal offense.

10.2 Capital Punishment

Capital punishment is the sentence of death for a criminal offense. This extreme form of social control is highly controversial; individuals and groups voice impassioned opinions on both sides of the issue. Although the cruelty of the death penalty is subject to debate, from a historical point of view this punishment is not unusual. Execution is older than incarceration. Although in this space we cannot consider all the issues and ramifications related to the death penalty, we will briefly examine some of the basic arguments. Easy answers to the issues surrounding the death penalty are elusive. Therefore, the goal of this section is to simply frame the issues.

At the end of 2018, 30 states and the federal government held 2,628 inmates on death row, marking the 18th consecutive year that the number of condemned inmates had decreased. California, Florida, Texas, and Alabama held more than half of all inmates on death row, and 61 inmates were on federal death row.[54] See Figure 10.1 for the number of executions carried out annually in the United States since 1930.

Capital Punishment in Historical Perspective

The concept of killing those who offend societal norms is probably as old as humanity. For example, the first law of the Mesopotamian code of Ur-Nammu, the oldest known legal code, states that, "If a man commits a homicide, they shall kill that man."[55] The reasons for such a stringent punishment include retribution, revenge, and general and specific deterrence. Killing a person can be easier than expending resources on rehabilitation and is a way for the state to show the extent of its power, organization, and control.

The execution chamber at the Utah State Prison. Utah allows for execution by firing squad if the drugs for lethal injection are not available. Bullet holes are visible in the wood panel behind the chair. Is the firing squad a humane method for executing offenders?

FIGURE 10.1 Executions in the United States, 1930–2018 In 1972, the U.S. Supreme Court invalidated capital punishment statutes in several states via *Furman v. Georgia* (1972), bringing about a moratorium on executions. Executions resumed in 1977 when the Court found in *Gregg v. Georgia* (1976), and other cases, that revisions to statutes in several states had addressed the issues of unconstitutionality. However, executions never resumed their peak numbers of the 1930s. Give some possible reasons why there are fewer executions now than in the 1930s.

Source: Tracy L. Snell, Capital Punishment, 2018: Statistical Tables, *Appendix Table 4 (Washington, D.C.: U.S. Department of Justice Office of Justice Programs Bureau of Justice Statistics, 2020),* 23. Available at www.bjs.gov/index. cfm?ty=pbse&sid=1.

Before the 20th century, two major features of the death sentence were spectacle and pain. Spectacle proved to the aggrieved party that justice had been done and assuaged the desire for revenge. It proved that the offender was dead, achieved specific deterrence, and provided a visual aid for general deterrence. Spectacle displayed the blunt power of the state and its willingness to see justice done. It also entertained the masses. In many cases, the last thing the condemned would see would be a jeering crowd.[56] The other feature, pain, was inextricably linked to punishment. The offender was required to hurt while dying and hurt publicly. This satisfied the need for revenge and the desire that the offender be humiliated. Some means of inflicting pain were slow. Others, if the condemned was lucky, were quick.

Over the centuries, authorities killed the condemned using various methods. Often the executions were part of a public spectacle designed to demonstrate the consequences of violating the law. Burning, crucifixion, drowning, boiling, flaying, beheading, impalement, being thrown to the lions, and an endless variety of other gruesome techniques were used to kill people.[57]

Historically, the favored methods of execution in Europe were hanging, beheading, and, one of the most fearsome executions, burning. Many condemned were burned alive; more fortunate ones were burned after being hanged. Burning was considered a punishment that reached beyond death because it meant the body would not receive a proper burial. Only much later in European history did authorities seek to reduce the condemned's suffering. Before the 19th century, death by hanging was carried out as a "short drop": slow strangulation after being either dropped or hoisted a short distance. In the 19th century, British hangmen discovered that a "long drop," letting the offender fall a long distance from a platform, would break the neck and usually bring a quicker death.[58]

In 1792, France popularized the guillotine during the French Revolution. This mechanical device for lopping heads was initially considered humane, being quicker than hanging and less mistake-prone than an executioner wielding an ax or sword. However, concerns grew that a severed head's consciousness might continue for several seconds or even minutes. Numerous experiments were done on severed heads, with reports of faces becoming angry when slapped or the victim's eyes responding to the sound of his or her name.[59] France continued to execute criminal offenders by guillotine until 1977 and finally abolished the death penalty in 1981.

The execution of Louis XVI in Paris, January 21, 1793. Is the guillotine a humane method of execution?

The Search for Humane Execution

The organized call for humane execution in the United States began in the 19th century. Although "long-drop" hangings were supposed to be less painful than "short drops," they were not always carried out properly, resulting in slow, painful deaths. In response, gallows were redesigned. One contraption called the "upright jerker" used weights and pulleys to draw the victim up, snapping the neck. The success of this method depended on the operator's skill and the condition of the machine, and it still sometimes caused lingering asphyxiation rather than a quick death.[60]

Not only have methods of execution changed over time, but the visibility of the practice has changed. Rather than taking place as public ceremonies, American executions are now done behind prison walls, witnessed by only a few corrections staff, family members of the condemned and victim(s), and reporters.[61] The United States' stance on capital punishment continues to fluctuate. In 1972, *Furman* v. *Georgia* set forth a moratorium on the death penalty, but *Gregg* v. *Georgia* (1976) reinstated it (see Case in Point 10.1 and 10.2). Below, we'll examine some of the varying methods of execution that are used in the United States today.

ELECTROCUTION

Thomas Edison insisted in 1887 that the best method of electrical execution was via alternating current. Despite the protests of Edison's rival inventor George Westinghouse, the first electrical execution was performed on William Kemmler using Westinghouse's equipment at New York's Auburn Prison in 1890. Unfortunately, this execution involved more torture than hanging, as electrocution science was poorly understood. Kemmler survived the first 17-second jolt, so the executioners let the second burst go for more than a minute. Blood seeped through the broken capillaries on Kemmler's face as his flesh burned, horrifying witnesses.[62]

Officials continued to experiment with the amounts of electricity and time. Less than a year after Kemmler's execution, four inmates were executed in one day at Sing Sing Prison. By 1937, electrocution was the preferred method of execution by the federal government and many states.

CASE IN POINT 10.1

Furman v. Georgia (1972)

THE POINT

The administration of the death penalty constituted cruel and unusual punishment, not the death penalty itself.

THE CASE

William Furman, a black man, shot and killed a homeowner through a closed door while trying to enter the house at night. Furman, 26, pleaded insanity and was committed to the Georgia Central State Hospital for a psychiatric examination. The staff who examined Furman concluded unanimously that Furman was mentally deficient with "psychotic episodes associated with Convulsive Disorder." They also said that although Furman was not currently psychotic, he also was not capable of helping his attorneys prepare his defense and needed further psychiatric treatment.

Later, the hospital superintendent concluded much the same, except he stated that Furman did indeed know right from wrong and was able to cooperate with his attorneys. Evidence that he was mentally unsound was presented at the trial, but Furman was convicted and sentenced to death. Furman appealed the conviction on the grounds that his Fourteenth Amendment rights were being violated. The Supreme Court concurred, saying that administration of the death penalty in Georgia was racially discriminatory and violated the Eighth and Fourteenth Amendments.

THINK ABOUT IT

1. How did Georgia's administration of the death penalty violate the Eighth and Fourteenth Amendments?

CASE IN POINT 10.2

Gregg v. Georgia (1976)

THE POINT

The Supreme Court effectively reinstated the death penalty, finding that it did not constitute cruel and unusual punishment as long as its implementation was fair.

THE CASE

Troy Gregg was convicted of killing and robbing two men and sentenced to death. Four years earlier in *Furman v. Georgia*, the Supreme Court found the process by which the death penalty was imposed to be cruel and unusual. After *Furman v. Georgia*, the state implemented bifurcated trials, in which guilt or innocence is determined in the first stage, and the penalty is determined in the second. During the penalty phase, the jury is required to consider both mitigating and aggravating circumstances, and if aggravating circumstances are overriding, then the death penalty is to be imposed. The law also prescribed an automatic appeal. Upon appeal, the Supreme Court found all procedures to be correctly followed and ruled that all were constitutional and violated neither the Eighth nor the Fourteenth Amendment. In this case, the Court affirmed that the death penalty itself was not cruel and unusual, as long as its implementation was judged to be fair. Gregg's death sentence was therefore upheld.

THINK ABOUT IT

1. Why was Gregg's death sentence upheld in this case?

GAS

In 1921, the Nevada legislature passed a bill allowing execution by gas. Advocates of gas execution argued that inmates should be asleep when the sentence was carried out, never knowing the exact date and time of their executions. This proved impractical for two major reasons: executions required witnesses, and the inmate would have to live in a special, gas-ready cell for several days. Officials eventually settled on something resembling the modern gas chamber: a chair in a room with a window for spectators. In 1924, Chinese immigrant Gee Jon became the first inmate to die by gas. At least 11 states had gas chambers by 1955.

LETHAL INJECTION

As of 2008, lethal injection has been the standard method of execution in almost all states that have a death penalty, as well as for the military and federal government.[63] A few states (see Table 10.1) have alternatives to lethal injection,

TABLE 10.1   States with Alternative Methods of Execution

STATE(S)	METHOD(S) OF EXECUTION
Alabama, Florida, South Carolina, Virginia	Electrocution or injection. In Alabama, nitrogen hypoxia is an option.
Arizona	People sentenced before Nov. 23, 1992 may choose gas.
Arkansas	Lethal injection. People who committed their offense before July 4, 1983, may choose electrocution.
California, Colorado, Georgia, Idaho, Indiana, Kansas, Kentucky, Louisiana, Montana, Nebraska, Nevada, New Mexico, New York, North Carolina, Ohio, Oregon, Pennsylvania, South Dakota, Texas	Lethal injection. In Kentucky, people sentenced before March 31, 1998, may select electrocution instead. New Mexico authorizes lethal injection for people whose offense occurred prior to July 1, 2009. In South Dakota, anyone sentenced to death before July 1, 2017 may choose to be executed in the manner provided by the state at the time of conviction or sentence.
Delaware, New Hampshire	Lethal injection or hanging. New Hampshire authorizes hanging only if injection cannot be used.
Mississippi	Mississippi authorizes nitrogen hypoxia if injection is unconstitutional; electrocution if lethal injection and nitrogen hypoxia are unconstitutional; and firing squad if other methods are unconstitutional.
Missouri	Lethal injection or gas
Oklahoma	Nitrogen hypoxia if lethal injection is decided to be unconstitutional; electrocution if both lethal injection and nitrogen hypoxia are decided to be unconstitutional; firing squad if all other methods are decided to be unconstitutional
Tennessee	Choice of injection or electrocution for those who committed their offense before December 31, 1998; electrocution if injection is not possible.
Utah	Firing squad if injection is not possible; people who chose firing squad before May 3, 2004, may still be entitled to that method.
Washington	Injection or hanging
Wyoming	Uses gas if injection is unconstitutional.

Source: Tracy L. Snell, Capital Punishment, 2018: Statistical Tables, *Table 4 (Washington, D.C.: Bureau of Justice Statistics, 2020), 9. Available at www.bjs.gov/index.cfm?ty=pbse&sid=1.*

which may either be chosen by inmates or used if lethal injection is ever ruled unconstitutional or the injection drugs become unavailable.

The first execution by lethal injection was performed by the state of Texas in 1982, but the first lethal injection law had been passed in Oklahoma in 1977. At the time, Oklahoma's electric chair needed expensive repairs, and building a gas chamber was even more costly. State Representative Bill Wiseman, with the help of state medical examiner, Dr. Jay Chapman, began to develop methods to administer lethal drugs intravenously. Wiseman and Chapman worked out a two-drug formula and process for lethal injection involving, according to Chapman, "an ultra-short-acting barbiturate in combination with a chemical paralytic." Chapman said later that he did not research drug combinations, only that he knew what was needed from having been under anesthesia himself. Chapman said that he thought lethal injection should involve two drugs, both in individual doses potent enough to kill a human being, "to make sure if one didn't kill . . . the other would." Chapman later added potassium chloride to the cocktail to increase its lethality, warning that improper administration of lethal injections may cause extreme pain in recipients.[64]

Until 2009, the three drugs most frequently used in lethal injection were sodium thiopental as a sedative, pancuronium bromide as a paralytic, and potassium chloride to stop the heart. Experts say that just one of these drugs can kill a human being, but that in any particular execution it is unknown which drug actually causes death.

Today, the supply of some of these drugs has dwindled owing to a European Union ban on the export of pentobarbital and sodium thiopental, and the halt in the production of sodium thiopental by its only U.S. manufacturer, Hospira Pharmaceuticals.[65] In 2016, Pfizer, the last official manufacturer of execution drugs, banned its drugs from being used for executions.[66] States have had to find new drugs, use two or only one of the drugs instead of all three, or adopt different methods of execution.[67] For example, Texas currently uses a single dose of pentobarbital to execute inmates.[68] Some states have used compounding pharmacies—small companies that make limited amounts of medications for specific purposes—to manufacture execution drugs.

Ricky Davis holds up a shirt with the Innocence Project logo after he was released from custody in February 2020. Davis spent 14 years in prison after being wrongly convicted of murder in the stabbing death of his housemate. What factors may lead to an innocent individual being sentenced to death or life in prison?

Given the large caseloads of most prosecutors' offices, little effort is exerted to look at past cases to determine whether mistakes were made. In 1992, attorneys Barry Scheck and Peter Neufeld founded the Innocence Project, a program that initiates new looks at old cases to see whether justice has been served and to free the wrongly convicted. To date, nearly 400 people have been exonerated.[91] By demonstrating that some prisoners are not guilty, the Innocence Project alerts the criminal justice system to the need to re-open some questionable investigations and attempt to find the actual perpetrators.

Is the Death Penalty Dead?

Although capital punishment is politically popular in the United States, there are appeals to discontinue it.[92] Nineteen states and the District of Columbia do not even have the death penalty (see CJ Reference 10.1).[93] Given the questions raised about its effectiveness, fairness, and morality, many people contend that capital punishment is not an enlightened policy. Occasionally, it looks as though the courts will strike down this form of social control, but they seem to be unable to find the constitutional grounds to do so.

In *Ford* v. *Wainwright* and *Atkins* v. *Virginia*, the U.S. Supreme Court limited executions by determining that an offender's mental state must be considered when imposing a death sentence. In *Wainwright* (1986), the Court banned the execution of the insane. In 1974, Alvin Bernard Ford was convicted of murder in Florida and sentenced to death. Although Ford appeared mentally sound during his trial and sentencing, as well as at the time of the offense, his behavior changed while he was on death row. Ford's attorney had him examined by two psychiatrists, both of whom determined that Ford was not competent to undergo execution. The governor appointed three psychiatrists who interviewed Ford and determined that, although he had mental problems, he was fit for execution. Eventually, the U.S. Supreme Court concluded that the Eighth Amendment prohibits the execution of the insane.

In *Atkins* (2002), the U.S. Supreme Court established limits for the execution of the intellectually disabled. In 1996, Daryl Renard Atkins and William Jones abducted Eric Nesbitt at gunpoint, eventually killing him. Jones and Atkins both testified at Atkins's trial. Their descriptions of the incident matched, except that each blamed the other for killing Nesbitt. Atkins's defense relied on one witness, a psychologist who said Atkins was "mildly mentally retarded," a conclusion based, in part, on a standard intelligence test that indicated Atkins had an IQ of 59. The jury found Jones's testimony more articulate and credited Atkins with the murder and sentenced him to death. The U.S. Supreme Court reversed the conviction,

---

CJ REFERENCE 10.1
States/Jurisdictions without a Death Penalty

Alaska	Maine	North Dakota
Connecticut	Maryland	Rhode Island
Delaware	Massachusetts	Vermont
District of Columbia	Michigan	Washington
Hawaii	Minnesota	West Virginia
Illinois	New Jersey	Wisconsin
Iowa	New York	

Source: Tracy L. Snell, Capital Punishment, 2018 – Statistical Tables *(Washington, D.C.: U.S. Department of Justice Office of Justice Programs Bureau of Justice Statistics, 2020), 5. Available at www.bjs.gov/index.cfm?ty=pbdetail&iid=7066.*

holding that executing intellectually disabled offenders violates the cruel and unusual punishments clause in the Eighth Amendment. According to the Court, a "significant number of states" have rejected capital punishment for intellectually disabled offenders, and "the practice is uncommon" even in states that do.

Two primary reasons for limiting executions because of the condemned's mental state are questionable deterrence effects and the condemned's lack of understanding. According to the Supreme Court, executing a mentally ill or intellectually disabled offender will not deter other offenders who have similar incapacities. Also, there are questions about the justice of killing those who do not understand what they are alleged to have done or even that they are being put to death.

However, the Supreme Court has upheld the constitutionality of lethal injection as a form of administering the death penalty.[94] In *Baze v. Rees* (2006), the Court ruled that the possibility that a method of humane execution would be incorrectly administered and hurt the condemned does not violate the Eighth Amendment ban on cruel and unusual punishment. This ruling left the door open for states to continue their capital punishment practices.[95] However, the future promises even more challenges to capital punishment. The Supreme Court is in a pivotal position to decide policy on this issue. Those who are selected to fill vacancies on the Supreme Court are an important factor in whether capital punishment will continue.

PAUSE AND REVIEW

1. **How are specific and general deterrence used as arguments to justify capital punishment?**

2. **Which argument(s) against capital punishment are most compelling to you? Explain your answer.**

3. **Which two cases limited capital punishment based on the offender's mental state?**

FOCUS ON ETHICS   Capital Punishment: Some Immodest Proposals

Almost everyone is dissatisfied with the death penalty for one reason or another. Liberals argue that it is applied in a discriminatory manner and that it fails to act as a deterrent. Conservatives say it is used too sparingly and that the time between crime and execution is too long. Families of victims feel left out of the decision-making process. If we were to redesign whether or how we execute people, what might we do differently? Here are some proposals that would change the face of capital punishment in the United States. How many of them would you vote for?

- Make capital punishment mandatory for all first-degree murders.
- Limit the number and time frame of appeals. The execution would take place one year after sentencing.
- Make executions public. If executions were televised, everyone would have an opportunity to observe what happens. Corporations could potentially sponsor executions.
- Instead of searching for humane ways to kill, permit the criminal justice system to bring back torture.

Offenders would die in painful, protracted, and public ways.

- Allow family members of victims to participate in executions. Victims' families should have a measure of retribution and revenge in the process. Allow a victim's family to initiate a lethal injection, for example.

WHAT DO YOU DO?

1. Are these suggestions extreme? Ask your classmates, family members, and friends what they think. Is there agreement on how offenders should be executed?

2. How far have we come from the times when these proposals were practiced? Are you willing to go back?

For more insight on how someone might respond to such an ethical dilemma, visit Oxford Learning Link at www.oup.com/he/Fuller2e to watch a video that connects this scenario to a real-world situation.

SUMMARY

LEARNING OBJECTIVE **10.1** Compare and contrast the two prison systems that emerged in the United States during the first half of the 19th century.	The Pennsylvania System. The Eastern State Penitentiary was characterized by the separate-and-silent system, keeping inmates from seeing and talking to each other, the goal of which was to prevent the spread of antisocial thoughts and behavior. Solitary confinement caused many inmates to develop severe mental problems because of boredom and lack of human contact. The Auburn System. The Auburn Prison was characterized by the congregate-and-silent system, which locked inmates in separate cells each night but allowed them to eat and work together during the day. This system prohibited face-to-face contact and required inmates to march in lockstep and keep their eyes downcast.
LEARNING OBJECTIVE **10.2** Describe the three most well-known examples of the Irish System of reform.	1. Maconochie's system was based on the ideas that brutality and cruelty debase not only the subject, but also society; and the treatment of a wrongdoer during his sentence of imprisonment should be designed to make him fit to be released into society again. 2. Crofton advocated the concept of a completely open institution in which inmates could gain experience in trust and avoid temptation. Crofton is best remembered for instituting the ticket-of-leave system. 3. Brockway used a three-grade program in which inmates entered at the second grade; an inmate was promoted to the first grade after six months of good behavior or demoted to the third grade if he failed to conform. Only those in the first grade were eligible for release. An inmate needed a year of good marks before being eligible for parole.
LEARNING OBJECTIVE **10.3** Summarize the three ways in which work was deemed beneficial during the early 20th century.	1. Work kept inmates occupied. 2. Work had rehabilitative value. 3. Work offset the cost of incarceration.
LEARNING OBJECTIVE **10.4** Outline the circumstances that led to the advocacy of rehabilitation as a desirable goal for the field of corrections, as well as its subsequent demise.	Changes in how science regarded illness led criminologists and correctional practitioners to adopt the medical model, which compared crime to disease and postulated that law-abiding behavior is within reach of all offenders and that rehabilitation was the optimal treatment. The creation of the Federal Bureau of Prisons in 1930 eliminated political patronage in filling jobs, developed better trained and more professional staff, and improved the conditions of confinement. The 1931 Wickersham Commission report further encouraged rehabilitation and condemned the failures of prison labor systems and the idleness of inmates. However, lack of resources, disagreement regarding its effectiveness, and the medical model's disregard for personal responsibility led to the rise of deterrent and retributive practices in lieu of rehabilitation.
LEARNING OBJECTIVE **10.5** Argue in support of capital punishment.	At the foundation of support for capital punishment is the deterrence argument. An offender is deterred, or prevented, from committing more crimes by being put to death (specific deterrence), which sets an example for society, thus encouraging others to refrain from antisocial behavior (general deterrence). The philosophy of just deserts also asserts that an offender who commits a heinous crime deserves death.

LEARNING OBJECTIVE	**10.6** Argue against capital punishment.	Some people argue against capital punishment for religious and philosophical reasons involving proscriptions against murder. Other critics say deterrence does not work because not everyone considers the risks of punishment; also, deterrence is challenging to validate empirically because it is difficult to measure something that does not happen. Patterns of discrimination in how the death penalty is administered suggest that factors such as race, social class, sex, and gender determine whether the death penalty is applied. Lastly, due to the flaws of the criminal justice process, innocent people are sometimes condemned to death.

Critical Reflections

1. Have correctional policies in the United States become more enlightened and civilized over the past two centuries?

2. What do you see as the future for capital punishment in the United States?

3. Should prisons be responsible for the safety, health, and comfort of inmates?

Key Terms

Capital punishment **p. 306**
Congregate-and-silent system **p. 297**
Convict lease system **p. 299**
Determinate sentence **p. 303**
Federal Bureau of Prisons **p. 301**

General deterrence **p. 312**
Indeterminate sentence **p. 298**
Just deserts **p. 313**
Marks-of-commendation system **p. 298**
Retribution model **p. 313**

Separate-and-silent system **p. 296**
Specific deterrence **p. 312**
Three strikes **p. 304**

Notes

1 *Los Angeles Blade*, "Los Angeles Man Sentenced to Death in 2013 Trans Inmate Murder," December 6, 2019.

2 Miranda Leitsinger, "Transgender Prisoners Say They 'Never Feel Safe.' Could a Proposed Law Help?" *KQED*, January 8, 2020.

3 *Los Angeles Blade*, "Los Angeles Man Sentenced to Death in 2013 Trans Inmate Murder."

4 Leitsinger, "Transgender Prisoners Say They 'Never Feel Safe.'"

5 Angie Leventis Lourgos, "Transgender Inmate Moved to Illinois Women's Prison after Alleging Years of Abuse," *Chicago Tribune*, December 27, 2018.

6 Andrea Dukakis, "Class Action Lawsuit against Colorado Department of Corrections Alleges the Systemic Abuse of Transgender Women Prisoners," *Colorado Public Radio News*, November 22, 2019.

7 Leitsinger, "Transgender Prisoners Say They 'Never Feel Safe.'"

8 David J. Rothman, *The Discovery of the Asylum: Social Order and Disorder in the New Republic* (Boston: Little, Brown, 1990).

9 Rex A. Skidmore, "Penological Pioneering in the Walnut Street Jail, 1789–1799," *Journal of Criminal Law and Criminology* 39, no. 2 (1948): 167–180.

10 Ibid.

11 Harry Elmer Barnes, *The Evolution of Penology in Pennsylvania: A Study in American Social History* (Montclair, N.J.: Patterson Smith, 1968).

12 Phillip L. Reichel, *Corrections: Philosophies, Practices, and Procedures*, 2d ed. (Boston: Allyn & Bacon, 2001), 72.

13 J. Hirsch, *The Rise of the Penitentiary: Prisons and Punishments in Early America* (New Haven, Conn.: Yale University Press, 1992).

14 Barnes, *The Evolution of Penology in Pennsylvania*.

15 Harry Elmer Barnes and Negley K. Teeters, *New Horizons in Criminology*, 3d ed. (Englewood Cliffs, N.J.: Prentice Hall, 1959).

16 Rothman, *The Discovery of the Asylum*.

17 J. V. Barry, *Alexander Maconochie of Norfolk Island* (Melbourne, Australia: Oxford University Press, 1958), 72.

18 Reichel, *Corrections*, 82.

19 Barnes and Teeters, *New Horizons in Criminology*.

20 Thomas G. Blomberg and Karol Lucken, *American Penology: A History of Control* (New York: Aldine de Gruyter, 2000), 76.

21 UNICOR, *Factories with Fences*. Available at www.unicor.gov/ FPIHistory.aspx. Accessed February 2020.

22 William Stone, "Industry, Agriculture, and Education," in *Prisons: Today and*

Tomorrow, ed. Joycelyn M. Pollock (Gaithersburg, Md.: Aspen Publishers, 1997), 116–157.

23 Beth Schwartzapfel, "Modern-Day Slavery in America's Prison Workforce," *American Prospect*, May 28, 2014.

24 John Irwin, *The Warehouse Prison: Disposal of the New Dangerous Class* (Los Angeles: Roxbury, 2005).

25 James Kilgore, "The Myth of Prison Slave Labor Camps in the U.S.," *Counterpunch*, August 9, 2013.

26 Blake McKelvey, *American Prisons: A History of Good Intentions* (Montclair, N.J.: Patterson Smith, 1977).

27 John Irwin, *Prisons in Turmoil* (Boston: Little, Brown, 1980). See especially Chapter 2, "The Correctional Institution."

28 John W. Roberts, "The Federal Bureau of Prisons: Its Mission, Its History, and Its Partnership with Probation and Pretrial Services," *Federal Probation* 61, no. 1 (1997): 53–58.

29 Larry E. Sullivan, *The Prison Reform Movement: Forlorn Hope* (Boston: Twayne, 1990).

30 James B. Jacobs, *Stateville: The Penitentiary in Mass Society* (Chicago: University of Chicago Press, 1977).

31 Robert Martinson, "What Works? Questions and Answers about Prison Reform," *Public Interest* 35 (1974): 22–54.

32 Ted Palmer, "The 'Effectiveness' Issue Today: An Overview," in *The Dilemmas of Corrections: Contemporary Readings*, 4th ed., eds. Kenneth C. Hass and Geoffrey P. Alpert (Prospect Heights, Ill.: Waveland Press, 1999).

33 David Fogel, *We Are Living Proof: The Justice Model for Corrections* (Cincinnati, Ohio: Anderson, 1975).

34 Todd Gitlin, *The Sixties: Years of Hope, Days of Rage* (New York: Bantam Books, 1993).

35 Leo Carroll, *Lawful Order* (New York: Garland, 1998).

36 Jacobs, *Stateville*. See especially Chapter 5, "Intrusion of the Legal System and Interest Groups," pp. 105–137.

37 Irwin, *Prisons in Turmoil*.

38 Pamala Griset, *Determinate Sentencing: The Promise and the Reality of Retributive Justice* (Albany: State University of New York Press, 1991). See also James Austin and John Irwin, *It's About Time: America's Imprisonment Binge*, 3d ed. (Belmont, Calif.: Wadsworth, 2001).

39 Irwin, *Prisons in Turmoil*.

40 Bureau of Justice Statistics, Reentry Trends in the U.S., www.bjs.gov/content/reentry/releases.cfm. Accessed February 2020.

41 Robert Martinson and Judith Wilks, "Save Parole Supervision," in *Correctional Contexts: Contemporary and Classical Readings*, 2d ed., ed. Edward J. Latessa (Los Angeles: Roxbury, 2001), 422–427.

42 Inimai M. Chettiar, Michael Waldman, Nicole Fortier, and Abigail Finkelman, "Solutions: American Leaders Speak Out on Criminal Justice" Brennan Center for Justice, April 27, 2015, www.brennancenter.org/publication/solutions-american-leaders-speak-out-criminal-justice.

43 *Economist*, "Jailhouse Nation," June 20, 2015, www.economist.com/news/leaders/21654619-how-make-americas-penal-system-less-punitive-and-more-effective-jailhouse-nation.

44 Council of Economic Advisors, Economic Perspectives on Incarceration and the Criminal Justice System, April 2016, obamawhitehouse.archives.gov/the-press-office/2016/04/23/cea-report-economic-perspectives-incarceration-and-criminal-justice. Oliver Roeder, Lauren-Brooke Eisen, and Julia Bowling, *What Caused the Crime Decline* (New York: New York University School of Law Brennan Center for Justice, 2015). Available at www.brennancenter.org/publication/what-caused-crime-decline.

45 *Economist*, "Jailhouse Nation."

46 Erik Eckholm, "Kentucky Governor Restores Voting Rights to Thousands of Felons," *New York Times*, November 24, 2015, www.nytimes.com/2015/11/25/us/kentucky-governor-restores-voting-rights-to-thousands-of-felons.html.

47 National Conference of State Legislatures, Felon Voting Rights, October 1, 2020, www.ncsl.org/research/elections-and-campaigns/felon-voting-rights.aspx.

48 Leon Neyfakh, "In Sweeping Speech, Obama Calls for Enfranchising Felons and Limiting Solitary Confinement," *Slate*, July 14, 2015.

49 Rosie Blunt, "Rikers Island: Tales from Inside New York's Notorious Jail," *BBC*, October 20, 2019.

50 Daniel A. Medina, "Rikers 2.0: Inside the Battle to Build Four New Jails in New York City," *Guardian*, December 9, 2019.

51 *New York Times*, "The Treatment of Rebel Prisoners at Riker's Island," December 20, 1863, p. 5. Thomas F. Gilroy, "Mayor Gilroy's Message: His Views upon Various Matters of Public Interest Riker's Island for Penitentiaries," *New York Times*, January 6, 1893, p. 9. *New York Times*, "Riker's Island Secured: Garbage Can Now Be Dumped There by the City," January 28, 1893, p. 9. *New York Times*, "To Improve Riker's Island: A Plan to Employ Convicts and Workhouse," February 18, 1898, p. 9. *New York Times*, "New Prison Ready on Riker's Island: Modern Institution to Receive 500," June 30, 1935.

52 Benjamin Weiser and Michael Schwirtz, "U.S. Inquiry Finds a 'Culture of Violence' against Teenage Inmates at Rikers Island," *New York Times*, August 4, 2014.

53 Jon Schuppe, "New York's Rikers Island Jail Moves Slowly toward Closing," *NBC News*, January 4, 2018.

54 Tracy L. Snell, *Capital Punishment, 2018 – Statistical Tables* (Washington, D.C.: U.S. Department of Justice Office of Justice Programs Bureau of Justice Statistics, 2020), 5. Available at www.bjs.gov/index.cfm?ty=pbdetail&iid=7066.

55 Martha Tobi Roth, *Law Collections from Mesopotamia and Asia Minor* (Atlanta, Ga.: Scholars Press, 1997), 17.

56 George Olyffe, "An Essay Humbly Offer'd, for an Act of Parliament to Prevent Capital Crimes" (London: J. Downing, 1731), 6–7, in *The Death Penalty: An American History*, Stuart Banner (Cambridge, Mass.: Harvard University Press, 2002), 70.

57 Edward Peters, *Torture* (New York: Blackwell, 1985).

58 Robert M. Bohm, *Deathquest: An Introduction to the Theory and Practice of Capital Punishment in the United States* (Cincinnati, Ohio: Anderson, 1999), 73.

59 Alister Kershaw, *A History of the Guillotine* (New York: Barnes & Noble Books, 1993), 81.

60 Stuart Banner, *The Death Penalty: An American History* (Cambridge, Mass.: Harvard University Press, 2002), 171–172.

61 Ibid.

62 Ibid., 186.

63 Death Penalty Information Center, Lethal Injection, deathpenaltyinfo.org/executions/lethal-injection. Accessed October 2020.

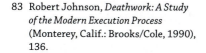

64 Virginia Leigh Hatch and Anthony Walsh, *Capital Punishment: Theory and Practice of the Ultimate Penalty* (New York: Oxford University Press, 2016), 144.

65 *Spiegel Online International*, "Death Penalty Opposition: EU Set to Ban Export of Drug Used in US Executions," December 12, 2011. Jon Stone, "America Is Running Out of Lethal Injection Drugs Because of a European Embargo to End the Death Penalty," *Independent*, March 13, 2015.

66 Erik Eckholm, "Pfizer Blocks the Use of Its Drugs in Executions," *New York Times*, May 13, 2016.

67 Jolie McCullough, "In a Nod to Texas, U.S. Department of Justice Says FDA Can't Regulate Execution Drugs," *Texas Tribune*, May 14, 2019. Robert Barnes, "Supreme Court Upholds Lethal Injection Procedure," *Washington Post*, June 29, 2015. Pam Belluck, "What's in a Lethal Injection 'Cocktail'?" *New York Times*, April 9, 2011.

68 McCullough, "In a Nod to Texas, U.S. Department of Justice Says FDA Can't Regulate Execution Drugs."

69 Samantha Liss, "Centene Says Subsidiary Will No Longer Provide Drugs for Missouri Executions," *St. Louis Post-Dispatch*, February 20, 2018.

70 Associated Press/*Guardian*, "Arizona Tried to Illegally Import Lethal Injection Drug Not Approved in the US," October 23, 2015. Steve Barnes, "Arkansas Buys Lethal Injection Drugs, Aims to End Execution Hiatus," Reuters, August 12, 2015.

71 Mark Berman, "Fourth Arkansas Execution in Eight Days Prompts Questions about Inmate's Movements," *Washington Post*, April 21, 2017.

72 Death Penalty Information Center, State by State Lethal Injection Protocols, deathpenaltyinfo. org/executions/lethal-injection/

state-by-state-lethal-injection-proto-cols. Accessed February 2020.

73 Robert Barnes, "Supreme Court Upholds Lethal Injection Procedure," *Washington Post*, June 29, 2015.

74 Alan Neuhauser, "DOJ Says FDA Has No Right to Regulate Death Penalty Drugs," *Newsweek*, May 15, 2019.

75 Susie Neilson, "Lethal Injection Drugs' Efficacy and Availability for Federal Executions," *National Public Radio*, July 26, 2019.

76 Scott H. Decker and Carol W. Kohfeld, "The Deterrent Effect of Capital Punishment in the Five Most Active Execution States: A Time-Series Analysis," *Criminal Justice Review* 15 (1990): 173–191.

77 Marla Sandys and Edmund F. McGarrell, "Attitudes toward Capital Punishment among Indiana Legislators: Diminished Support in Light of Alternative Sentencing Options," *Justice Quarterly* 11 (1994): 651–677.

78 Robert M. Bohm, "Retribution and Capital Punishment: Toward a Better Understanding of Death Penalty Opinion," *Journal of Criminal Justice* 20 (1992): 227–236.

79 Robert M. Bohm, *Deathquest: An Introduction to the Theory and Practice of Capital Punishment in the United States* (Cincinnati, Ohio: Anderson, 1999). See especially Chapter 5, "General Deterrence and the Death Penalty," 83–101.

80 Alison Tonks, "US States Experiment with Lethal Injections in an Ethical Vacuum," *British Medical Journal* 336 (June 21, 2008): 1401.

81 Oriental Philosophy, Buddhism: The Eightfold Path, philosophy.lander. edu/oriental/eightfold.html. Accessed February 2020.

82 Samuel R. Gross and Robert Mauro, *Death and Discrimination: Racial Disparities in Capital Sentencing* (Boston: Northeastern University Press, 1989).

83 Robert Johnson, *Deathwork: A Study of the Modern Execution Process* (Monterey, Calif.: Brooks/Cole, 1990), 136.

84 Elizabeth Rapaport, "The Death Penalty and Gender Discrimination," in *A Capital Punishment Anthology*, ed. Victor L. Streib (Cincinnati, Ohio: Anderson, 1993), 145–152.

85 Snell, Capital Punishment, 2018, Table 6, p. 12.

86 James R. Acker, "Impose an Immediate Moratorium on Executions," *Criminology and Public Policy* 6 (November 1, 2007): 641.

87 Jeffrey Reiman, *The Rich Get Richer and the Poor Get Prison: Ideology, Class, and Criminal Justice*, 6th ed. (Boston: Allyn & Bacon, 2001).

88 Michael L. Radelet, Hugo Adam Bedau, and Constance E. Putnam, *In Spite of Innocence: Erroneous Convictions in Capital Cases* (Boston: Northeastern University Press, 1992).

89 Scott Shane, "A Death Penalty Fight Comes Home," *New York Times*, February 5, 2013.

90 Stephanie Hanes, "Guilty Plea Closes '84 Case of Rosedale Girl's Murder," *Baltimore Sun*, May 21, 2004. Stephanie Hanes, "'84 Investigation Quick to Overlook the Culprit," *Baltimore Sun*, May 22, 2004.

91 The Innocence Project, www .innocenceproject.org/exonerate. Accessed January 2020.

92 "Amnesty International Calls for End to Death Penalty in United States," *Preview Nation's Health* 38 (June/July 2008): 8.

93 Snell, *Capital Punishment, 2018*, p. 5.

94 Linda Greenhouse, "Justices Uphold Lethal Injection in Kentucky Case," *New York Times*, April 17, 2008, 1.

95 Carmen Gentile, "Florida: Inmate Is Executed," *New York Times*, July 2, 2008, 13.

OXFORD **insight** study guide
Active Engagement, Deeper Understanding

Learn more with this chapter's digital tools, including the Oxford Insight Study Guide, at www.oup.com/he/Fuller2e.

Chapter 11

Prisons and Jails

The Eastern State Penitentiary in Philadelphia. The penitentiary took in its first inmate in 1829 and closed in 1971. What impacts do prisons have on the incarcerated?

John Jay Roach

was dying. Tests had confirmed that he was suffering from liver cancer. Although this disease would be traumatic for anyone, it was especially complicated for Roach because he was serving a 14-year sentence for burglary. Roach, 61, was soon transferred to the hospice unit at the California Medical Facility, a prison in Vacaville that housed 2,300 inmates, including those who are terminally ill. Roach tried to contact his two sisters, but they refused to speak to him.[1]

Roach's wife also had cancer and was living in San Diego. With the help of hospital staff, he requested compassionate release so that he and his wife could "leave this world together." Because Roach's wife was too weak to visit him in prison, the corrections department approved his request. However, a San Diego judge took several days to review the case, and Roach's wife died before he could see her. Soon after, Roach was transferred to a hospice run by the Missionaries of Charity. He died three months later.[2]

THINK ABOUT IT > What are the arguments for and against granting compassionate release?

Define the concept of a total institution as it relates to prisons.

Describe the five pains of imprisonment.

LEARNING OBJECTIVE 11.3

Frame how gangs affect the informal inmate social structure and prison security efforts.

Identify how prison violence and overcrowding are dealt with.

11.1 Prison Life

The field of corrections includes many types of facilities and programs ranging from local jails to federal prisons. Included in this array of correctional efforts are diversion programs, probation and parole programs, and many secure institutions. However, when we think of corrections, usually the first thing that comes to mind are prisons and jails, which remain the centerpiece of the U.S. criminal justice system's attempts to detain, punish, and rehabilitate criminal suspects and offenders. Unfortunately, U.S. prisons and jails are responsible for much more than this. They must deal with inmates who are mentally ill, intellectually and/or physically disabled, and, like John Jay Roach, terminally ill.

This chapter will examine prisons and jails in light of several important issues that illustrate how these institutions affect inmates and correctional workers. We will discuss inmates' social roles and legal rights, the occupation of the correctional officer, the problems and dangers associated with imprisonment, and finally the move to privatize this traditionally public service.

How U.S. Prisons Work

The United States has about 1,800 state and federal correctional institutions.[3] These institutions take a number of forms and have various titles. For example, Texas has a system of facilities called state jails. Other states have correctional facilities or correctional institutions, and many states have rehabilitative facilities, transitional facilities, work camps, boot camps, and inmate medical facilities. Several states have facilities especially for women, and all have one or more youth or juvenile institutions. The number of facilities a state has varies widely. For example, Michigan has 39 state correctional facilities, whereas Delaware has four. Most states fall somewhere in between.[4] As of 2018, state prisons housed more than 1.2 million inmates and federal institutions about 180,00 (see Figure 11.1).[5]

Generally, state prisons have at least three security levels: low, medium, and maximum. However, each state, as well as the federal prison system, has its own

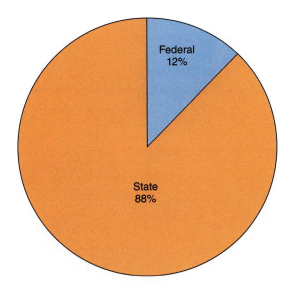

Federal
12%

State
88%

FIGURE 11.1   Number of Inmates Why are there so many more state than federal inmates?

Source: E. Ann Carson, Prisoners in 2018, *Table 1 (Washington, D.C.: U.S. Department of Justice Office of Justice Programs Bureau of Justice Statistics, 2020), 3. Available at www.bjs.gov/index. cfm?ty=pbdetail&iid=6846.*

set of security-level classifications and specifications for each security level. For example, prisons in Georgia have three security classifications: minimum, medium, and close (high security).[6] California designates four security levels. These range from security-level 1 facilities with open dormitories and a low-security perimeter up to security-level 4 facilities that have secure perimeters with armed guards both inside and outside the facility.[7]

Federal prison inmates consist of defendants awaiting trial for federal offenses and offenders who have been convicted of a federal offense. Federal prisons also hold offenders who have been convicted of a felony in the District of Columbia. In special cases, state inmates may be held in a federal prison.[8] The federal government operates five security levels among its 122 prisons (see Figure 11.2 for the percentages of inmates at each security level).

› Minimum-security institutions. Also called federal prison camps, these have dormitory housing, a relatively low staff-to-inmate ratio, and little or no perimeter fencing. Some institutions have a small, minimum-security prison camp next to a larger main facility to provide inmate labor to the main facility and to off-site work programs.

› Low-security institutions. These have fenced perimeters and dormitory or cubicle housing. The staff-to-inmate ratio in these institutions is higher than in minimum-security facilities.

› Medium-security institutions. These have fenced perimeters, often with electronic detection systems, mostly cell-type housing, and a higher staff-to-inmate ratio and greater internal controls than lower security facilities.

› High-security institutions. U.S. penitentiaries have highly secured perimeters with walls or reinforced fences, cell housing, the highest staff-to-inmate ratio, and strict control of inmate movement.

› Administrative facilities. These specialized institutions hold pre-trial detainees; treat inmates with serious or chronic medical problems; and/or hold extremely dangerous, violent, or escape-prone inmates. All administrative facilities, except for the ADMAX (administrative maximum, also called "supermax") facility in Florence, Colorado, can hold inmates in all security categories.[9]

Clinton Correctional Facility is a maximum security state prison located in Dannemora, New York. What are the five federal prison security levels?

Federal correctional complexes are composed of several facilities with different missions and security levels located close to one another. Among other functions, these complexes increase efficiency by sharing services and give staff experience at different security levels. Additionally, the Bureau of Prisons operates four female facilities, all of which are correctional complexes with various security levels.[10]

Every state and the federal government has intake facilities or procedures that classify incoming prisoners by security level, as well as other factors, and sends them to the appropriate facilities. For federal prisoners, the court sends the judgment to the U.S. Marshals who request a prison designation from the Designation and Sentence Computation Center (DSCC) in Grand Prairie, Texas. The DSCC uses data about the judgment and the prisoner to determine the appropriate facility.[11]

FIGURE 11.2   Federal Prison Security Levels Most federal inmates are held at low and medium security levels. Which security category of inmate is held at the administrative level?

Source: Federal Bureau of Prisons, About Our Facilities, www.bop.gov/ about/facilities/federal_prisons.jsp. Accessed February 2020.

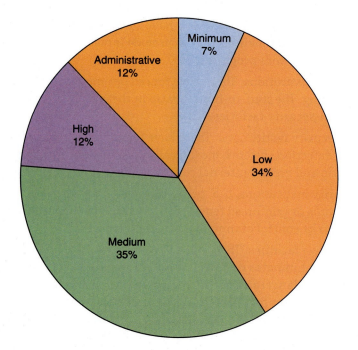

An interesting detail about the federal system is that many prisoners are not taken into custody upon conviction but are allowed to self-surrender. A few weeks after conviction, these prisoners are notified by mail of the institution they must travel to and the date and time they must arrive there. Prisoners usually have about 90 days to turn themselves in.[12] State prisoners are typically taken into custody upon conviction and sent to an intake facility to determine the appropriate facility. Most state intake facilities perform the following functions:

> › identify the prisoner and establish the prisoner's record;
> › interview the prisoner and determine custody level based in part on the severity of the current conviction, history of institutional violence, and escape history;
> › assess the prisoner's medical and mental health;
> › assess the prisoner's security requirements;
> › identify sex offenders, sexual predators, vulnerable inmates, and gang members;
> › assign housing and cells (in some states, the intake facility recommends housing and cell assignments; other states leave this decision to the facility to which the prisoner is sent).[13]

The Pains of Imprisonment

The prison is what sociologist Erving Goffman called a total institution.[14] Much like the military, some religious monasteries, and secure mental health hospitals, the prison is a **total institution**—a closed environment in which every aspect, including the movement and behavior of the people within, is controlled and structured. The inmates' ability to influence the conditions of their confinement is limited, and escape is almost impossible. This total control of inmates' lives, including who their cellmates are, what they eat, and when they can bathe, is designed to help the prison run efficiently, maintain order, and deprive the inmates of the discretion often taken for granted in free society. It is also designed to punish offenders by depriving them of goods and services and relationships with others. Unintentionally, inmates are often deprived of their physical security as well. In an effort to protect society from criminal offenders, the prison places these potentially dangerous people together in a place where they can prey on one another, often in brutal ways.[15]

Total institution—A closed environment in which every aspect, including the movement and behavior of the people within, is controlled and structured.

Although confinement in a small cell may be uncomfortable to many, it is not the worst thing that can happen to a person.[16] Instead, deprivations are largely what define a prisoner's lifestyle. Sociologist and criminologist Gresham Sykes, in his seminal book *The Society of Captives*, argued that maximum-security prisons make incarceration a painful experience by depriving inmates of some basic freedoms, stating that "the modern pains of imprisonment are often defined by society as a humane alternative to the physical brutality and the neglect which constituted the major meaning of imprisonment in the past."[17] Sykes further noted that the pains of imprisonment can be destructive to the psyche and pose profound threats to the inmate's personality and self-worth. Because of deprivation, we have come to believe that incarceration is a sufficient punishment and that physical brutality in the form of corporal punishment is not required to achieve justice. However, this does not mean that inmates do not experience brutality. Sykes described the five **pains of imprisonment** in this way:

Pains of imprisonment—Deprivations that define the punitive nature of imprisonment.

1. Deprivation of liberty. The inmate is confined to an institution and then further confined within that institution. This loss of freedom is the most obvious feature of incarceration, but to adequately understand its effect on the inmate, we must appreciate that not only does it include being restricted to a

small space such as a prison cell but also that this restriction is involuntary. Because friends and family are prohibited from visiting except at limited times, the bonds to loved ones are frayed and sometimes break.[18]

2. Deprivation of goods and services. Inmates do not have access to the food, entertainment, and services that free people routinely enjoy.[19] To be sure, this deprivation is relative, and for some inmates "three hots and a cot" is an improvement over their disadvantaged lives on the outside. Having a dry place to sleep and a government-guaranteed calorie count are things that many in this world would consider an improvement in lifestyle. However, the inmates' perception is subjective, and, according to Sykes, some inmates view the impoverishment that incarceration brings as the prison acting as a tyrant to deprive them of the goods and services they should reasonably have. More often, inmates may see their poverty as a consequence of their behavior and a result of their own inadequacies.

3. Deprivation of heterosexual relationships. Living in a single-sex society such as a prison is stressful. The deprivation of heterosexual activities is one of the most visible and controversial aspects of imprisonment because it sometimes leads to sexual deviation within the prison. Homosexual activities and rape are often associated with incarceration. This is particularly true in male prisons, where, as Sykes contended, the self-concept of men is bound up in their sexuality.[20] Without women to provide feedback for displays of masculinity, the inmates create an atmosphere that is sexually charged and difficult to negotiate. Men do not lose their sex drive when incarcerated; it becomes a type of hypermasculinity that demands that some men be subservient to others.[21] In 2003, Congress enacted the Prison Rape Elimination Act (PREA) to address the problem of sexual abuse of inmates. PREA sets standards for the detection, prevention, reduction, and punishment of prison rape. Federal facilities must comply with PREA standards, and the act awards grants to help state and local governments implement the act's provisions.[22]

4. Deprivation of autonomy. The inability to make decisions about some of the most basic tasks, such as walking from one room to another, is a particularly galling deprivation. Being subject to a bureaucratic staff's rules, whims, and preferences is a humbling experience. Having to ask for everything reduces the inmate to the status of a child. Some inmates argue or bargain with the staff, but their position is so weak that they have little leverage in a well-run prison free of guard corruption.

5. Deprivation of security. This is perhaps the most disturbing pain of imprisonment. Most of those confined to a maximum-security prison have already proven themselves violent, aggressive, and untrustworthy. Having to cope with such cellmates can be an anxious experience, even for those who are violent themselves. There are few places in the prison where one can feel secure. Inmates constantly test each other for physical or emotional weaknesses. Those without the courage or nerve to protect themselves are quickly victimized by others if they cannot find a protector.

These pains of imprisonment define the prison experience. Even in the best-managed prisons, with well-trained guards and adequate resources, these deprivations are present. However, with the exception of being deprived of security, these are not unintended consequences. U.S. prisons are meant to be uncomfortable for inmates. Many people do not feel sorry for inmates who suffer these deprivations.[23] However, these pains of imprisonment are real to inmates, and to understand prison dynamics we must appreciate not only how these deprivations

GETTING IT RIGHT 11.1
Learning a Lesson

Lavonta Bass was eligible for early release from prison but decided not to leave. After spending over a decade locked up for aggravated assault, Bass, 42, had earned his associates degree in prison and wanted his son to see him graduate as valedictorian.[24]

Bass was one of 56 incarcerated students at the East New Jersey State Prison enrolled at either Raritan Valley Community College or Rutgers University as part of the New Jersey Scholarship and Transformative Education in Prison (NJ-STEP) program. According to the Vera Institute of Justice, inmates who receive a postsecondary education while in prison return to their communities with competitive skills and academic qualifications that allow them greater access to jobs and increased earnings.[25]

Research shows that inmates who participate in correctional education have 43 percent lower odds of recidivism than those who do not participate. Furthermore, they are 13 percent more likely to obtain employment once released.[26] For instance, Bard University's Bard Prison Initiative (BPI) reports that 85 percent of its prison alumni are employed within two months of returning home. BPI also supports former inmates by offering logistical support and academic guidance, as well as by organizing paid fellowships and internships that allow formerly incarcerated people to assume leadership positions in areas such as human services, advocacy, and public policy.[27]

THINK ABOUT IT

1. How can society benefit from correctional education for inmates?

Watch the related video on Oxford Learning Link at www.oup.com/he/Fuller2e.

---

affect inmates but also how they cope with this lifestyle. That being said, this does not mean that inmates should not have any opportunities to improve their chances at success once they leave prison (see Getting It Right 11.1).

Prison Gangs

To fully appreciate how the informal inmate social structure of the contemporary prison shapes the lives of inmates and staff, we must consider the effect of prison gangs. Although not all correctional systems have severe gang problems, and not

One of the pains of imprisonment is deprivation. This inmate exercises in a maximum security cell that has been stripped of all possessions, including a mattress, as punishment for various behaviors. What are some other pains of imprisonment?

all gangs are as violent as the ones discussed here, gangs are a concern because without proper vigilance they can form and take partial control of a prison.

Here, we will discuss the California prison gang problem. Although not every inmate is affiliated with a gang, the prison gang problem is most serious in California. The signature feature of the California prison gang structure is that it is based on skin color and ethnicity. Currently, there are at least four major prison gangs:[28]

> Mexican Mafia. The oldest of the prison gangs, the Mexican Mafia, has been traced to the 1950s when a group of Mexican juveniles from Los Angeles was incarcerated together in the Deuel Vocational Institution in Tracy, California. The gang, also called "La Eme," appropriated the number 13 and the letter "M," the 13th letter in the alphabet. They began preying on white and black inmates by extorting and robbing them. They also attacked Mexican inmates from northern California whom they considered to be "farmers." In an effort to destabilize the gang, prison authorities dispersed members to prisons across the state where they recruited other Mexicans. The gang became a vertically integrated organization with considerable power both inside and outside the prison.

> La Nuestra Familia. This Mexican gang draws its members from northern California and is constantly at odds with La Eme. Some of the gang's younger members spun off and created the Northern Structure, which, in addition to feuding with La Eme, has also clashed with the old guard of La Nuestra Familia. Together, La Nuestra Familia and the Northern Structure represent the state's largest prison gang. The gang has a military structure and educates new members about how to identify the enemy and how to resist interrogations. Members who are released must set up "regiments" in their hometowns.

> Black Guerrilla Family. This gang of black inmates originates from the 1960s, when members of the Black Panther Party were incarcerated in California prisons. Back then, the inmates were extremely political and adopted a Marxist rhetoric that cast them as political prisoners of an unjust capitalist state. They espoused revolution, but as the years passed, many became gangsters in their own right, and instead of robbing drug dealers, they became drug dealers. Today the Black Guerrilla Family is composed of black lifers. Younger inmates who join gangs are more likely to be affiliated with inmates who belong to the Bloods or Crips street gangs.

> Aryan Brotherhood. These white gang members employ Ku Klux Klan symbols and Nazi swastikas as evidence of their racial identity. The Aryan Brotherhood is among the most violent and fights hard for its share of prison-yard drug dealing, extortion, and prostitution scams.[29] The Aryan Brotherhood occasionally aligns with La Eme in its ongoing conflict with La Nuestra Familia to the extent of conducting assassinations.

This list of gangs is incomplete because of the changing nature of gang identity and the efforts of prison officials to deal with gangs. Gangs mutate over time, changing their names and leadership, but racial identification is a constant. One may think that the prisons could stop gang activity by isolating leaders, punishing those who display gang insignia, and transferring those who refuse to cooperate. These techniques have been partially successful in the short run, but the diffusion of gang activity to other prisons has complicated efforts at gang control.[30]

It has been somewhat cynically suggested that it is not entirely in the prisons' interests to eliminate gang conflict. Prison officials reportedly keep gangs in a

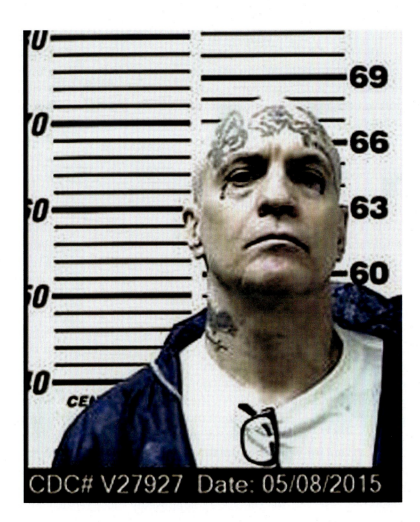

Ronald Yandell is among 16 Aryan Brotherhood prison gang members who were charged with killings and drug smuggling from within California's most secure prisons. What are some other prison gangs?

state of perpetual conflict by allowing rival gang members to use the exercise yard at the same time. At California's Corcoran institution, this practice was routinely a source of amusement for the guards. Not only were rival gang members placed in the same yard, but when the ensuing fight took place, the guards placed bets on which inmate would win.[31]

For the most part, prison officials are forced to make difficult decisions in attempts to stem gang violence. On the one hand, they attempt to segregate inmates who are members of rival gangs and different races to avoid violence. On the other hand, they hope to allow inmates to learn to get along with one another and promote diversity. Prison officials may be accused of discrimination when inmates are racially separated, but when inmates are allowed access to each other and violence ensues, they may be accused of failing to protect the weak. For example, in an effort to reduce the time gang members spent locked in cells without access to rehabilitation programs, California prison officials tried to allow inmates from different gangs to exercise together in the yards. Officials had to end the experiment because gangs would often fight to the point of rioting.[32] One solution has been to build extremely expensive prisons, known as supermax prisons, where all the inmates are separated from one another in a modern version of the separate-and-silent system.[33]

Supermax Prisons

The modern **supermax prison** is based on the federal penitentiary at Marion, Illinois, which the Bureau of Prisons opened six years after Alcatraz closed in 1963.

Supermax prison—An extremely secure type of prison that strictly limits inmate contact with other inmates, correctional staff, and the outside world.

Like Alcatraz, Marion was a high-security institution designed to hold the federal system's most dangerous inmates. As inmate violence at Marion intensified throughout the 1970s, prison administrators added a maximum-level unit to provide for the long-term separation of violent inmates. Marion became the first stand-alone supermax prison in the United States in 1983, when two correctional officers were killed in one day. The prison's administration locked down the facility permanently, confining all inmates in their cells for 23 hours a day. Today Marion is a medium-security institution, and the U.S. Penitentiary Administrative Maximum Facility in Florence, Colorado, serves as the federal supermax prison.

Throughout the 1980s and 1990s, other state institutions assumed the supermax model. Today, several states have at least one supermax prison or a prison with a supermax unit. An excellent example of such an institution is Pelican Bay State Prison, a maximum-security state prison located in Crescent City, California, which recalls the separate-and-silent system utilized in the first prisons in Pennsylvania and Auburn, New York (see Chapter 10).

Constructed in 1989, shortly after the conversion of the federal penitentiary in Marion, Illinois, the Pelican Bay Prison is built to ensure almost total isolation of inmates as well as minimal contact with the staff. The prison itself is such a bleak, stark, and monotonous environment that inmates suffer severe disorientation, depression, and suicidal behavior.[34] High, gray concrete walls surround the exercise yards and totally block out the surrounding national forest. Inmates are confined to their cells with no work, recreation, or contact with anyone other than a cellmate who is equally deprived. When going to the shower (three times a week) or the exercise yard, the inmates are shackled and can move only with the escort of two baton-wielding correctional officers. The prison's security housing unit (SHU)—the term the California prison system uses to designate solitary confinement—is reserved for the state's supposedly most recalcitrant inmates. Until 2015, most of those inmates allegedly belonged to gangs, and the only way out of the unit was to identify other inmates as gang members. However, after an inmate lawsuit, California agreed to end the indefinite isolation of inmates. At one point, more than 500 inmates had been in the unit for more than 10 years.[35] Here is an excerpt from Pelican Bay inmate Gabriel Reyes's account of life in the SHU:

> For the past 16 years, I have spent at least 22½ hours of every day completely isolated within a tiny, windowless cell.... for alleged "gang affiliation." It is a living tomb. I eat alone and exercise alone in a small, dank, cement enclosure known as the "dog-pen." When another prisoner is the subject of a debrief, he is not informed of the content, so he is punished with no means to challenge the accusations.[36]

Pelican Bay Prison is successful in several ways. It keeps the most dangerous offenders securely incapacitated, ensuring both their safety and the safety of the prison staff. This is a significant feat because it usually takes some degree of cooperation from the inmates to run a truly safe prison. Pelican Bay maintains order mechanically by using technology and prison design, giving inmates absolutely no opportunity to assemble outside their cells. For example, Ronald Dean Yandell, a member of the Aryan Brotherhood, spent 15 years in solitary confinement at Pelican Bay. After the inmate lawsuit, Yandell was sent to New Folsom Prison in Sacramento where he had relative freedom. In New Folsom, according to federal investigators, Yandell used a smuggled cell phone to call other members to discuss drug deals and plan murders in an attempt to dominate the state prison system's other white gangs.[37]

The total control of prisons like Pelican Bay comes at a price. This type of prison is costly to operate, demanding a high degree of technology. Keeping an inmate in an SHU is expensive, nearly double the cost of an inmate in the general population. Most states can afford such treatment for only a small percentage of extremely dangerous offenders.[38] For the bulk of the prison population, less expensive prisons, with less control of the inmates, are the norm.

Violence and Overcrowding

The prison is a delicate social system that includes not only inmates but also guards and administrators and, to a lesser extent, the legislators and politicians responsible for funding and personnel decisions. Although inmates are presumed to be powerless in their captivity, they often employ many techniques to address the conditions of their confinement. Inmates may write letters to correctional officials, complain to their congressional representatives, petition the parole board, file briefs in the courts, or simply act out in ways that range from bothersome to seriously violent.

Some of these techniques are more effective than others. The bottom line, however, is that regardless of how frustrated inmates may feel in a correctional institution, they cannot leave. Those of us in society can drop out of school, move out of our parents' houses, quit our jobs, or dump our significant others when we have "had enough." Inmates do not have these options. Being incarcerated means that problems and frustrations can accumulate until a breaking point is reached. This breaking point can be a mental collapse, a fight with a fellow inmate, violence against a guard, or simply retreating from prison life by being so ornery that solitary confinement is required.[39] These are daily occurrences in the prison, and, for the most part, they are handled with established procedures that are understood by all involved.

Occasionally, the inmate's frustrations are shared by others, and the institution's authority is seriously challenged. Inmates acting together can overwhelm the guards and take over the institution in a full-scale prison riot in which people are injured or killed and property is destroyed. Sociologists use the term **collective behavior** to explain how an individual's actions are transmitted into group actions that can go well beyond what any of the individuals in the group intended.[40] This "herd mentality" can cause even law-abiding citizens to engage in destructive actions. (A good example of this mindset is the rioting that sometimes occurs after sports championships.)[41]

In the prison, collective behavior can not only have deadly consequences but also temporarily invert the social structure and shatter the bonds of social control.[42] With the administration no longer controlling the institution, the oppressed become king, the protected become vulnerable, and anyone caught in the middle can become a victim. The prison's most antisocial individuals are, for a limited time, free to wreak havoc.

In 2015, two California institutions experienced several riots. At Folsom Prison in August, about 70 inmates began fighting with "shanks," or inmate-made weapons. The fight resulted in the death of Hugo Pinell, 71, who had been incarcerated for 50 years and was involved in a 1971 escape attempt at San Quentin State Prison that killed three correctional officers and three inmates.[43] In a 2016 riot, an inmate was stabbed by several other inmates and accidentally shot by a correctional officer who was trying to control the incident.[44] Such incidents are often caused by gang or personal rivalries. In a May 2015 incident at the medium-security California State Prison, Solano, inmate Nicholas Rodriguez disappeared during a riot. Officials thought he had escaped until

Collective behavior— A sociological term that describes how an individual's actions are transmitted into group actions that can exceed what any of the individuals in the group intended.

his body was found sawed nearly in half with many of its organs removed, and stuffed in a garbage can near his cell.[45]

Studies on the causes and prevention of prison riots have made it clear that despite many commonalities, each institution has its own limitations, atmosphere, and vulnerabilities.[46] However, scholars point to several reasons for riots and other types of violence among inmates. One study revealed that aggressive inmates committed more assaults in institutions that were overcrowded and had a higher percentage of young inmates.[47] Overcrowding occurs when a facility is holding more people than it is designed for. Some prisons operate dormitories where the beds are so close that inmates can reach out and touch the beds next to them. Over the years, the federal and state governments have continued to build facilities that are crowded as soon as they open. The federal prison population has increased by about 800 percent since 1980, and federal prisons are operating at nearly 40 percent over capacity.[48] Overcrowding is unhealthy and stressful not only for inmates, but also for prison staff and correctional officers. Understaffed facilities with overworked staff endanger everyone within the facility.[49]

In an effort to keep facilities within capacity, some jurisdictions, as well as the federal government, are simply letting some inmates go. In 2014, the U.S. Sentencing Commission altered its sentencing policies for federal offenses, thus qualifying for early release about half of the 100,000 drug offenders in federal prison. In 2019, early release was granted to about 3,000 federal inmates.[50]

One form of early release is the compassionate release of elderly or infirm inmates. Although the federal government, 48 states, and the District of Columbia have laws that permit compassionate release, the law is seldom used. From 2013 to 2017, the Federal Bureau of Prisons approved only 6 percent of the 5,400 applicants.[51] In California, in 2018, 64 inmates applied for compassionate release. Thirteen were granted release after waiting about 70 days for a decision.[52]

Resistance to compassionate release puts prison systems in a precarious situation. Many people, especially victims and their families, believe people convicted of criminal offenses should serve their entire sentences even if they are too ill or infirm to commit any more offenses. Dying in prison, the argument goes, is part of the pains of imprisonment. However, as the prison population ages, the cost of inmate medical

Pictured here is the crowded reception area at the California State Prison in Lancaster. What are some consequences of prison overcrowding?

care becomes exorbitant. Prison systems do not have the funding, personnel, or space to provide adequate care for the terminally ill.[53] For example, Susan Atkins, a follower of Charles Manson who killed five people in 1969, developed terminal brain cancer after 38 years in prison. Her care had already cost the state of California more than $1 million when she applied for compassionate release. Although many people supported Atkins's release, including case prosecutor Vincent Bugliosi, the parole board denied her request. Atkins died in prison in 2009.[54]

PAUSE AND REVIEW

1. **Why are prisons total institutions?**
2. **Name Sykes's five pains of imprisonment.**
3. **What are the pros and cons of operating supermax prisons?**

11.2 Women in Prison

Women's prisons are much like men's prisons. They have the same high-, medium-, and low-security levels with the same security features, such as fences, razor wire, and electronic detection systems (depending on the security level), as men's prisons. The inmates have been convicted of breaking the same criminal laws as men, although far fewer women than men are in prison generally because they commit fewer violent offenses (see Figure 11.3). Some institutions house both men and women in separate facilities.

As of 2017, females made up about 7 percent of the state and federal prisoner population.[55] Regardless of race, female prisoners ages 30 to 34 had the highest rate of imprisonment.[56] The female imprisonment rate was highest in Oklahoma, followed by Kentucky, South Dakota, and Idaho.[57] Although more than twice as many white females as black or Hispanic females were in state and federal prisons, the imprisonment *rate* of black females was almost twice that of white females.[58]

LEARNING OBJECTIVE 11.5

Outline how Elizabeth Fry improved prison conditions for women.

LEARNING OBJECTIVE 11.6

Discuss some of the health issues associated with women's prisons.

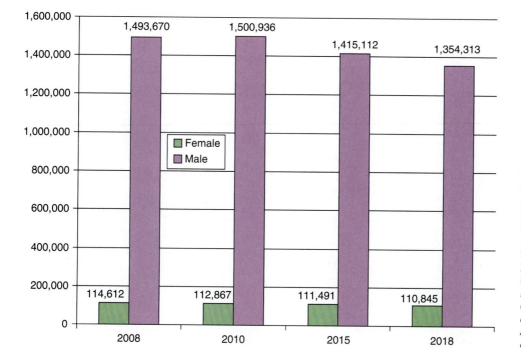

FIGURE 11.3 Male Versus Female Inmates There are far more male than female inmates. Does the male-to-female rate of incarceration remain fairly steady or does it change drastically from year to year?

Source: E. Ann Carson, Prisoners in 2018, Table 1 (Washington, D.C.: U.S. Department of Justice Office of Justice Programs Bureau of Justice Statistics, 2020), 3. Available at www.bjs.gov/index.cfm?ty=pbdetail&iid=6846.

These inmates are receiving instruction in an innovative program that teaches how to translate books into braille. The books will go to schools for the blind across the country. What other vocational skills are taught to female inmates?

Generally, incarcerated women suffer many of the same pains of imprisonment as men. They are likely to have chronic health problems, including mental illness; struggle with drug and/or alcohol addiction; suffer anxiety from missing their families; and lack needed rehabilitation and education. Like men, they are overwhelmingly impoverished, of color, and from disadvantaged backgrounds. Many suffer from post-traumatic stress disorder as a result of abuse earlier in their lives, and the situation only worsens once they are imprisoned. Incarcerated women are likely to have experienced physical or sexual violence at some point in their lives.[76] When a federal review panel investigated the Fluvanna Correctional Center for Women, a maximum-security state prison in Troy, Virginia, one inmate testified that the warden, a woman, would tell correctional officers "that if she took anything and everything from us including our humanity maybe we would not return to prison."[77]

PAUSE AND REVIEW

1. **How did Elizabeth Fry help improve the conditions of women's incarceration?**
2. **What are some health issues women may experience in prison?**

LEARNING OBJECTIVE 11.7

Understand the contributions of the Eighth and Fourteenth Amendments to inmate rights.

Prison Litigation Reform Act— Legislation that restricts litigation by prison inmates based on the conditions of their confinement.

11.3 Courts and the Prison

Should inmates have legal rights while they are incarcerated? This might seem like a silly question. On one hand, inmates are viewed as having forfeited their rights as citizens, and many people believe that one of the consequences of incarceration is that inmates are stripped of the privileges and legal protections that other citizens enjoy. On the other hand, some believe that inmates should not lose all of their rights. In fact, inmates are still protected by the Constitution. Their legal rights, though necessarily attenuated, are not totally restricted. Inmates are only supposed to lose rights consistent with their confinement and the maintenance of institutional safety. Since 1996, the ability of inmates to bring civil rights actions against the government has been hampered by passage of the **Prison Litigation Reform Act** (see CJ Reference 11.1). The law has seen some recent challenges, however, owing to overcrowding and the deplorable conditions of some prisons.

CJ REFERENCE 11.1
The Prison Litigation Reform Act

The 1996 Prison Litigation Reform Act (PLRA) provides a case-management plan for prison inmate civil rights lawsuits.[78] Critics of the act say it makes it more difficult for inmates to file lawsuits, thus curtailing their Eighth Amendment rights by limiting both the means by which those rights can be asserted and the remedies that courts can provide.[79] The PLRA focuses on court practices for processing *in forma pauperis* (as an impoverished person) suits, as most of these inmate suits are filed *pro se* (for oneself). (Scholars have noted that inmates who file *pro se* cases have substantially lower success rates than inmates who have legal representation.[80])

Some PLRA provisions are as follows:

- Inmates must try to resolve their complaints via the prison's grievance procedure and must exhaust all avenues (see Case in Point 11.1).[81]
- A strike is counted for each lawsuit or appeal that is dismissed because a judge decides that it is improper. After three strikes, an inmate cannot file again *in forma pauperis*. The only exception is if the inmate is at risk of imminent serious physical injury.[82]
- Federal courts must screen all inmate suits against government employees and all *in forma pauperis* cases at the beginning of the litigation. Frivolous or malicious cases, cases that fail to state a claim that may be relieved, and cases that seek damages from defendants immune from damages must be dismissed.[83]

CASE IN POINT 11.1

Ross v. Blake (2016)

THE POINT

There is no "special circumstances" exception to the Prison Litigation Reform Act's requirement that plaintiffs exhaust administrative remedies before filing suit.

In 2007, two correctional officers of the Maryland Reception Diagnostic and Classification Center, Michael Ross and James Madigan, restrained inmate Shaidon Blake and punched him several times in the face. Blake reported the incident, and a formal investigation determined that excessive force was used. Blake sued, arguing that the excessive force violated his constitutional rights.

A jury awarded Blake a judgment of $50,000 in the claim against Madigan. Ross, however, contended that Blake had sued without first following the prison's procedures for administrative remedy. Blake stated that he had not sought remedy via the prison's procedures because he thought the prison's investigation satisfied that requirement. The District Court rejected Blake's explanation and dismissed the suit. The Fourth Circuit Court of Appeals reversed, stating that "[t]here are certain 'special circumstances' in which, though administrative remedies may have been available[,] the prisoner's failure to comply with administrative procedural requirements may nevertheless have been justified." The U.S. Supreme Court disagreed and vacated the decision.[84]

Before the 1960s, the courts cultivated a **hands-off doctrine** toward inmates' rights.[85] It was thought that offenders had legal rights granted to them in the arrest and trial phases of the criminal justice process and that incarceration was primarily an administrative matter concerning the internal workings of the prison and not subject to a great degree of judicial oversight. There were a few significant reasons for this hands-off doctrine. First, the decisions made about the conditions of confinement were viewed as a technical matter that judges were not educationally equipped to consider. Second, because of the separation of powers,

Hands-off doctrine—
The judicial attitude toward prisons before the 1960s in which courts did not become involved in prison affairs or inmate rights.

The Eighth and Fourteenth Amendments

EIGHTH AMENDMENT

Excessive bail shall not be required, nor excessive fines imposed, nor cruel and unusual punishments inflicted.

FOURTEENTH AMENDMENT

Section 1.

All persons born or naturalized in the United States, and subject to the jurisdiction thereof, are citizens of the United States and of the state wherein they reside. No state shall make or enforce any law which shall abridge the privileges or immunities of citizens of the United States; nor shall any state deprive any person of life, liberty, or property, without due process of law; nor deny to any person within its jurisdiction the equal protection of the laws.

decisions about prisons were considered a matter for the executive branch of government, not the judicial branch. Third, the public did not really care about what went on in the prison and were content to allow prison administrators wide latitude in the treatment of inmates. Finally, the treatment of inmates was considered a product of privileges rather than legal rights. For these reasons, the courts were historically reluctant to involve themselves with the conditions of confinement.[86]

The social upheavals of the 1960s that advocated for the rights of marginalized groups, such as the civil rights and women's movements, influenced many aspects of society, including the prison. Inmates and those concerned with the welfare of inmates began to petition the courts to address several issues they deemed problematic. For instance, in Stateville Prison in Illinois, Christian inmates were allowed to read the Bible, but Muslim inmates were forbidden to possess the Qur'an.[87] Prison officials were successfully sued in *Cooper v. Pate* (1964), which began a new era in prison litigation by helping to end the judicial hands-off doctrine toward prisons and allowing inmates to sue for civil rights violations. This new interventionism resulted in the courts considering a range of prison issues and fundamentally changed the relationship between the courts and corrections. Inmates found the courts receptive to their complaints about the arbitrary ways in which prisons operated. Prison administrators were forced to treat inmates more uniformly, keep better records, and run their institutions according to well-defined and ascertainable criteria.[88]

From where did the courts draw their authority to enter the realm of inmate rights? Inmates' lawyers turned to the Eighth and Fourteenth Amendments to persuade the courts to reconsider inmates' rights.

Eighth Amendment

As we discussed in Chapter 10, the Eighth Amendment prohibits "cruel and unusual punishments" (see CJ Reference 11.2). However, there is considerable debate as to what should be considered cruel or unusual. The courts have ruled on thousands of cases in which prison administrators were faulted for various policies concerning food, heating, and discipline. Although we cannot discuss all these issues, it has been suggested that the Supreme Court has not provided a clear statement about what constitutes "cruel" or "unusual." Rather, the Court has provided a general statement in which it likens a given situation to that which "amounts to torture, when it is grossly excessive in proportion to the offense for which it is imposed, or that is inherently unfair; or that is unnecessarily degrading, or is shocking or disgusting to people of reasonable sensitivity."[89]

Fourteenth Amendment: Due Process and Equal Protection

The court system has little time to consider cases involving the internal workings of the prison; however, inmates abused by prison officials need somewhere to turn to have their concerns heard. The Fourteenth Amendment states that the due process granted to citizens by the Constitution is also applicable to the states (see CJ Reference 11.2). The concept of incorporation prevents states from restricting rights granted by the federal government. The courts determined in *Wolff v. McDonnell* (1974), which defined the processes required for prison disciplinary proceedings, that inmates are allowed some level of due process.

The equal protection clause of the Fourteenth Amendment addresses racial and sex-based discrimination in the prison. Individuals cannot be treated differently based on their race or because they are male or female.[90] Discrimination that is prohibited in society is similarly not permitted in the correctional institution. Cases that involve religious freedom are also applicable here in that the prison cannot allow certain religions to be practiced while excluding others.[91] Of course, given the multiplicity of religions, there are some limits as to just how far the prison can go in accommodating inmates' needs. For security, economic, and common-sense reasons, not all of the inmates' desired religious requests can be granted. For instance, the prison cannot keep kitchens open 24 hours a day to feed inmates who might have different eating concerns based on religion, nor can prisons cater to the exact dietary restrictions of all religions.[92] Nevertheless, prisons are obligated to make reasonable efforts to address the different legitimate religious needs of many inmates.

Prisons are a unique environment, and the expectations of privacy granted by the Constitution and its amendments are only partially available to inmates. For instance, the standards of privacy in the home do not extend to the prison cell.[93] Although the inmate lives in the cell, there is no constitutional guarantee that it cannot be searched for contraband. The prison has a security imperative to make the institution safe for other inmates and staff that overrides any demand for privacy. Cells may be searched without warning (prior notice would give the inmate time to dispose of drugs, weapons, or other contraband), as may inmates' personal effects, such as books, papers, clothing, and mail.

Inmate Renzee Standberry preaches to fellow Muslim inmates at the Indiana State Prison chapel in Michigan City, Indiana. What efforts are prisons required to make to meet the religious needs of inmates?

The inmate's body is also a point of contention, according to the courts. Under what circumstances, and to what degree, can the inmate's body be searched? The inmate's body has only slightly more protection than does the cell and personal effects. The courts have deemed routine strip and body-cavity searches necessary for the institution's safety.[94] However, body-cavity searches that are abusive, unhygienic, or unreasonably degrading are prohibited. The right to privacy of the body is also a concern when the situation involves male guards and female inmates or female guards and male inmates. It sounds reasonable to prohibit cross-sex supervision of inmates, but the courts consider the matter to be more complex than that. For instance, although modesty and privacy are important concerns, the cost of same-sex guards for the prison might be prohibitive. Additionally, male inmates might object to a homosexual guard watching them shower, or female inmates might feel uncomfortable in the presence of a lesbian guard. The courts have determined that there are simply too many possibilities for potential embarrassment for courts to get involved.

Courts have an additional reason to be reluctant to intervene in sex and gender issues. To prohibit women from supervising male inmates would violate women's rights under Title VII and the equal protection clause.[95] Women cannot be excluded from large parts of the institution and from core duties of the correctional officer simply because of their sex. Certainly, institutions may establish reasonable efforts to diminish cross-sex supervision, but the legitimate demands of institutional security, efficiency, and worker rights all permit this practice.[96]

The courts have also considered the issues of what mail the inmates may receive and with whom and how they can have outside visitation.[97] Prison officials have wide discretion in limiting the mail and publications that inmates can send and receive.[98] The institution must demonstrate how restrictions are consistent with the needs of prison security and efficiency. Mail from those with a personal or professional relationship with the inmate, such as family, lawyers, and clergy, is generally allowed. However, rules concerning visitation vary considerably by institution. Contraband smuggled in by visitors is a constant threat to jails and prisons. Therefore, personal visits may be restricted by separating the visitor and inmate with a glass barrier and having them communicate by telephone. Contact visits, in which inmates and visitors are allowed to touch, have been deemed problematic by the courts and not a constitutional right. There is also no right to conjugal visitation.[99] Such visitation may help maintain the marital bond while the inmate is incarcerated, but it is up to the state to allow this practice, which is usually permitted for only a few inmates.[100]

This warning at the visitor's entrance to the New Hampshire State Prison in Concord alerts visitors to the rules against bringing contraband into the prison. What issues does contraband create for prisons and jails?

11.4 Working in the Prison

LEARNING OBJECTIVE **11.8**

Characterize how occupations within the prison differ from those outside the prison.

Guards, medical technicians, doctors, treatment specialists, administrators, secretaries, and clergy all contribute to the prison dynamic. Most of these occupations are found in free society, but unique demands are placed on those who serve in these positions in prisons. For instance, a secretary in most organizations is encouraged to promote good customer relations. In the prison, the "customer" is the inmate, and secretaries are cautioned to be wary, emotionally distant, and suspicious of every request, motive, and kindness offered by inmates. An occupational environment in which the potential for violence, escape, and duplicity is constant poses many challenges and is not for everyone. Those who work in the prison perform a job that, though important, is not always appreciated.

LEARNING OBJECTIVE **11.9**

Summarize the general functions of prison correctional officers.

By far the most prevalent and problematic of these jobs is that of the correctional officer or guard. Correctional officers keep the institution secure, help maintain the facility, manage inmates, and assist in rehabilitation. Generally, there are seven variations of correctional officer job assignments:[101]

1. Block officers. These officers are responsible for the security of the housing block, which can contain 300 to 400 inmates, and must see that daily work and activities are done in an orderly way. This includes ensuring that inmates are fed, attend medical and rehabilitative treatment programs, are released into the exercise yard at the appropriate time, and get their mail. This is all done in a noisy and hectic environment in which the officer may be surrounded by inmates with varying demands.

2. Work-detail supervisors. Every prison function that requires inmate labor must be supervised by a correctional officer, including managing the commissary (store), laundry, library privileges, and recreational activities. Control of scarce resources may be accompanied by pressures from inmates as well as other correctional officers to stretch the limits of discretion to do favors. Although this gives officers some bargaining power with inmates, it is also a source of tension because the work-detail officers are accountable to the administration for getting the work of the prison done. These officers, who are evaluated on how well they can get felons to do their work, are in a vulnerable position.

3. Industrial shop and school officers. These officers perform security and order-maintenance functions by supervising inmates engaged in work or school activities provided by civilians.

4. Yard officers. The yard is the prison's outdoor recreation area and is the closest thing to the street in the prison environment. The block is the inmate's home, and the school or work assignment keeps the inmate busy, but the yard is where the greatest potential for trouble exists. Yard officers must constantly be alert for signs of trouble.

5. Administrative building assignments. These officers have little inmate contact and perform various administrative functions. They control security gates; handle the storage of weapons; field telephone calls from the outside; and supervise visitations.

6. Wall posts. Some officers watch from a tower what is going on inside the prison yard and on the outside perimeter. This duty is devoid of the anxiety of dealing with inmates at close quarters, but it can be boring. Nevertheless, the position is essential to protect innocent people, especially fellow guards.

7. Relief officers. These officers fill in for other officers who take time off. The job can be stressful because, without a regular post, the officers have not developed working relationships with inmates. Like substitute teachers, these officers are constantly tested by inmates pushing the boundaries of acceptable behavior. Written job descriptions exist for every post in the prison, but the relief officer must quickly learn any of these jobs while simultaneously performing the job for the first time.

Although the exact posting of the correctional officer dictates the type of duties he or she performs, some general functions are performed in every correctional institution. Over the years, bureaucratization has increased the number of specialist guards, but the following general functions are still pertinent to the overall nature of the correctional officers' work:

› Human services. Officers perform many services for inmates, either as a formal part of their duties or because of informal relationships they develop. For example, some inmates may be mentally ill and require extra attention. The three aspects of human-services work are providing goods and services, acting as an advocate, and assisting in inmates' institutional adjustment.

› Order maintenance. Correctional officers maintain the social order in prison by earning the inmates' trust and cooperation. By enforcing rules in a consistent manner, showing inmates respect, and allowing them a certain level of dignity, the correctional officer can help establish an atmosphere in which inmates feel not only secure but also that their world is predictable and

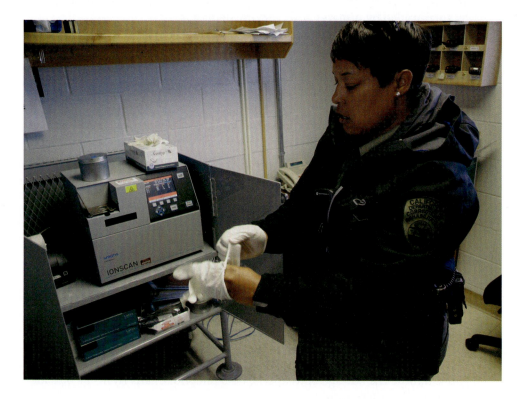

A correctional officer prepares to demonstrate an ion spectrometer that tests for illegal narcotics at Vacaville State Prison in California. What are some types of correctional officer job assignments?

controllable. By maintaining order in subtle ways, as well as with the threat of punishments, the officer can reduce tension in the cell block.

> Security. Security is a passive function in which officers ensure that inmates are not acting out and are kept inside the institution.

> Supervision. Correctional officers supervise inmates who do prison maintenance work. Officers are responsible for seeing that the work is done efficiently and safely.

Correctional officers face many stresses primarily because they are actively engaged in controlling and managing a population held against its will.[102] Stresses include crowding, physical exhaustion, shift work, inmate violence, unsatisfactory relationships with co-workers and/or supervisors, vague institutional goals and policies, and poor organizational support.[103] It is estimated that 37 percent of correctional officers experience job stress, which is higher than the estimated 19–30 percent of the general working population who experience job stress. Stressed correctional officers may lose motivation and become less committed to their jobs. This could lead to actions that compromise the security of the institution and the safety of their co-workers, such as helping an inmate engage in criminal activity either inside or outside the institution.[104]

Stress factors are aggravated for correctional officers who work in overcrowded facilities.[105] In one survey, correctional officers told researchers that overcrowding leads to problems with safety, inmate/inmate violence, inmate/correctional officer violence, and job performance.[106] In particular, these officers noted that inmate/inmate violence increased in the more crowded areas of the institution and that the number of correctional officers had not increased along with the inmate population. As a result, many institutions now have fewer officers supervising more inmates who have become increasingly violent as conditions become more crowded.[107]

Some studies have shown that different types of correctional employees have different levels of job stress. Correctional officers in custodial positions (i.e., those who directly supervise inmates) report more stress than both their supervisors and non-custodial staff.[108] Carceral facilities are strict bureaucratic hierarchies, and the order of command affects relationships between the administration, the correctional officers, and the inmates. In many cases, correctional officers are, as one officer put it, "the meat in the sandwich."[109] That is, correctional officers are at a vulnerable point between the facility administrators, who are responsible for the facility but typically do not have day-to-day contact with the inmates, and the inmates themselves, who have their own needs and desires. Correctional officers must find a way to manage both their employers' expectations and the demands of the often intimidating populations they physically control.[110]

PAUSE AND REVIEW

1. How do occupations within the prison differ from those outside the prison?
2. What are some general functions of prison correctional officers?
3. How might the stresses of being a correctional officer affect job performance?

11.5 For-Profit Prisons

LEARNING OBJECTIVE **11.10**

Argue in support of and against for-profit prisons.

Interest in privatizing prisons for profit began around the mid-1970s, and the first modern for-profit prisons opened in the early 1980s.[111] Several factors that had their roots in the social revolutions of the 1960s contributed to this trend. By the mid-1970s, the United States was reeling from the loss of the Vietnam War, economic recession, gas and oil shortages, major paradigm shifts in civil society, and a skyrocketing crime rate. The government had become unpopular with Americans and probably not without good reason. It had participated in an unpopular war; President Richard Nixon had left office in disgrace, only to be pardoned by his successor President Gerald Ford; and the country seemed to be at the mercy of foreign powers such as the Organization of Petroleum Exporting Countries (OPEC) and Iran's Ayatollah Khomeini. The government, many Americans believed, could no longer do anything right, including run prisons.

As states grappled with growing inmate populations (see Figure 11.4), the idea that for-profit companies could handle inmates more inexpensively and more efficiently grew popular. It was thought that capitalism could solve many problems because an open market would presumably force the providers of any good or service to produce the best value.

Currently, three companies—CoreCivic (formerly Corrections Corporation of America), GEO Group, and Management & Training Corporation (MTC)—are the major providers of for-profit correctional services in the United States:

1. Founded in 1983, CoreCivic is currently the largest provider of for-profit prison services in the United States.[112] The company operates 125 facilities in the United States, including one U.S. Immigration and Customs Enforcement detention center.[113] Its 2019 revenues were $1.83 billion.[114]

2. The GEO Group operates 68 facilities in the United States, as well as facilities in the United Kingdom, Australia, and South Africa.[115] The GEO Group's revenues in 2018 were $2.33 billion.[116]

3. MTC operates 23 correctional facilities (21 in the United States, one in the United Kingdom, and one in Australia), 12 prison and detention medical departments, five U.S. Immigration and Customs Enforcement detention centers, and one probation and parole office.[117] Because MTC is privately held, data on its revenues are not available.[118]

For-profit correctional facilities have met with mixed success, and state and local facilities still take in most inmates. At the end of 2018, for-profit facilities

FIGURE 11.4   Number of Inmates in Custody in State and Federal Prisons and Local Jails Which year did the number of inmates increase the most from the prior year? Decrease the most?

Sources: Joan Mullen, Kenneth Carlson, and Bradford Smith, America's Prisons and Jails, Vol. I Summary and Policy Implications of a National Survey, *Table 1.2 (National Institute of Justice, Washington, D.C.: Government Printing Office, 1980), 17. Tracy L. Snell,* Correctional Populations in the United States, 1993, *Table 1.6 (Washington, D.C.: U.S. Department of Justice Office of Justice Programs Bureau of Justice Statistics, 1995), iii, 8. Lauren E. Glaze,* Correctional Populations in the United States, 2009, *Appendix Table 2 (Washington D.C.: U.S. Department of Justice Office of Justice Programs Bureau of Justice Statistics, 2010), 7. Lauren E. Glaze,* Correctional Populations in the United States, 2010, *Appendix Table 2 (Washington, D.C.: U.S. Department of Justice Office of Justice Programs Bureau of Justice Statistics, 2011), 7. Laura M. Maruschak and Todd D. Minton,* Correctional Populations in the United States, 2017-2018, *Appendix Table 4 (Washington, D.C.: U.S. Department of Justice Office of Justice Programs Bureau of Justice Statistics, 2020), 15. Available at www.bjs.gov/index.cfm?ty=pbse&sid=5.*

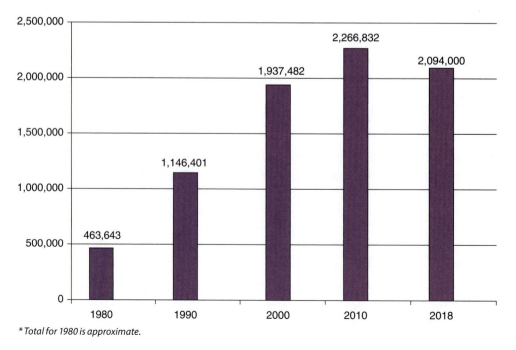

* Total for 1980 is approximate.

held about 8 percent of U.S. prisoners, down 2 percent from the end of 2017.[119] The arguments both for and against for-profit prisons are numerous. The following are some of the arguments used in favor of for-profit prisons:[120]

> Money. Hypothetically, private enterprise can run prisons more cheaply than the government because government agencies have an incentive to grow in order to inflate their budgets. Corporations can operate many prisons across several jurisdictions, which local and state agencies cannot do, allowing for economy of scale. The profit motive of for-profit prisons demands less waste and more suppliers, which allows for-profit facilities to spend money wisely and avoid shortages. Competition with other for-profit prison firms encourages higher quality and lower costs.

> Better employee control. Employees of for-profit enterprises are more easily hired and fired than government employees, who have civil service protections, so for-profit prisons can adjust staff sizes more quickly. Administration and staff have more incentive to do a good job and treat inmates fairly because their jobs are at stake. Furthermore, staff members are less likely to strike because they are more likely to be fired if they do so. In addition, for-profit contractors may save money by paying employees less and providing fewer benefits, as well as promoting more effective personnel management and lower absenteeism and employee turnover.

> Accountability. Stockholders and corporate boards add another layer of review to decision-making but are immune to political pressures.

> Flexibility. For-profit prisons can be built more quickly and cheaply and are designed for more efficient operation. Inmates can also be transferred across jurisdictions, allowing optimum residence levels to be maintained at all facilities.

The arguments against for-profit prisons are as follows:

> Money. The first duty of a for-profit operation is to make a profit. For-profit prisons might cut corners to save money without concern for inmate rights or welfare. If the prison company goes bankrupt or is not making enough money, it can leave a jurisdiction without facilities. For-profit prisons are actually more expensive than government prisons because their profit margins are added to the costs of running the prison.[121]

> Labor. For-profit prisons threaten the jobs, benefits, professionalism, and tenure of public employees, who have less incentive to do a good job because they are less secure and paid less. This increases the risk of strikes and high employee turnover in public facilities.[122]

> Control. Morally speaking, private enterprise should not have the degree of control over human beings that incarceration requires. For-profit prisons might make government prisons more difficult to manage by housing only the best behaved offenders and refusing to incarcerate the difficult ones. Prison corporations might lobby to build more prisons, thus increasing society's dependence on incarceration and weakening the use of alternatives such as parole.

> Accountability. Private corporations are less accountable to the public than those governed by legislatures of elected officials. The layer of managerial involvement created by the existence of stockholders and corporate boards introduces new opportunities for corruption.[123]

Protesters march at a Bank of the West branch in Portland, Oregon. Bank of the West is one of many banks that has dealings with the GEO Group. What are some of the alleged advantages of for-profit prisons?

The final judgment on for-profit prisons remains to be made. The news is rife with their failures: escapes, employee and inmate maltreatment, and riots. As of 2020, California banned for-profit prisons and immigrant detention facilities.[124] Whether they cost less to operate is questionable, and there is little evidence that for-profit prisons do a better job of reducing recidivism.[125]

PAUSE AND REVIEW

1. **What are some arguments supporting for-profit prisons?**
2. **What are some arguments against for-profit prisons?**

LEARNING OBJECTIVE | **11.11**

Explain the two major functions of jails.

Jail—A secure facility that typically holds arrestees, criminal suspects, and inmates serving sentences less than a year.

11.6 Jails

A **jail** is a secure facility that typically holds arrestees, criminal suspects, and inmates serving sentences less than a year. Jails, a fundamental component of the corrections system, are a crucial institution that is connected to the law enforcement, courts, and correctional systems and serve as a major focal point in the administration of justice. Jails are controlled by either the local sheriff or an administrator under the auspices of the county or city.[126] Control of the jail can often be a political issue because it is such an important part of the community, the local criminal justice system, and the local power structure. Where the jail is placed organizationally can have a major effect on how it is funded, who is detained there, and the quality of justice.[127]

As of midyear 2018, 738,400 people were held in jails.[128] Males accounted for 84 percent of inmates. Of all jail inmates, 50 percent were white, 33 percent were black, and 15 percent were Hispanic. Fewer than 3,500 juveniles were held in jails.[129] Alaska, Connecticut, Delaware, Hawaii, Rhode Island, and Vermont combine prisons and jails. Thus, the prison population in these states includes jail inmates, who are typically awaiting trial. In other states, prisons may hold a small number of unsentenced prisoners. At the same time, some states with crowded prisons place some sentenced prisoners in their jails.[130]

CJ REFERENCE 11.3
What Jails Do

- Receive individuals pending arraignment and hold them awaiting trial, conviction, or sentencing
- Re-admit probation, parole, and bail bond violators and absconders
- Temporarily detain juveniles pending transfer to juvenile authorities
- Hold mentally ill persons pending their movement to appropriate mental health facilities

- Hold individuals for the military, for protective custody, for contempt, and for the courts as witnesses
- Release convicted inmates to the community upon completion of sentence
- Transfer inmates to federal, state, or other authorities
- House inmates for federal, state, or other authorities because of crowding of their facilities
- Operate community-based programs as alternatives to incarceration[131]

The jail serves two major functions (see CJ Reference 11.3 for a complete list). First, it holds suspects who have been arrested and are awaiting disposition of their cases. Judges and prosecutors decide whether suspects can be safely released before court hearings, so many people spend short periods behind bars ranging from a few hours to a few weeks. Other offenders spend months behind bars awaiting trial or release. The factors that determine how much time is spent in jail before trial include the gravity of the offense, the offender's reputation and ties to the community, and money.

The jail's second major function is the confinement of misdemeanor offenders who have been sentenced to less than one year of incarceration. In some jurisdictions, these sentenced offenders may serve their time on weekends and live at home during the week while maintaining their employment and family ties. Sentenced offenders often act as trustees and clean the courthouse, mow the grass, shovel sidewalks, or help feed and service the inmates awaiting disposition of their cases.

A local jail can also be connected to a larger local corrections system that includes work-release programs, road crews, stockades, and local probation departments. There is a wide variety of local corrections structures around the country, each with its own concerns, funding issues, and punishment philosophies. For example, former Sheriff Joe Arpaio of Maricopa County, Arizona, was known for his "Tent City," an outdoor jail he set up in 1993 that housed about 2,000 inmates under canvas tarps in the desert in triple-digit temperatures.[132] After Arpaio lost his bid for re-election in 2016, new Sheriff Paul Penzone announced that Tent City would be closed due to its cost inefficiency and ineffectiveness as a crime deterrent.[133]

One of the major issues associated with jails concerns searches. There are no regulations governing the manner in which jails conduct searches as long as they do not unnecessarily humiliate or degrade the inmate. For example, a reasonable search may violate the Fourth Amendment if performed in an unreasonable manner.[134] Recall that not everyone in jail has been convicted of a criminal offense. Some inmates are merely suspects, whereas others are arrestees for minor infractions such as having too many parking tickets. The following is a summary of search policies common to many jails.

› Cell searches. Jail staff can search the cells at any time without the presence of inmates. In *Block v. Rutherford* (1984), the Supreme Court stated that no cause was required for cell searches.

87 Jacobs, *Stateville*, 107.

88 James Bennett, "Who Wants to Be a Warden?" *New England Journal of Prison Law* 1 (1974): 69–79.

89 Reichel, *Corrections*, 522.

90 *Lee v. Washington*, 390 U.S. 333, 88 S.Ct. 994 (1968); *Holt v. Sarver*, 309 F. Supp. 362 (ED Ark. 1970).

91 *Cruz v. Beto*, 405 U.S. 319, 92 S.Ct. 1079 (1972).

92 *Cooper v. Pate*, 378 U.S. 546, 84 S.Ct. 1733 (1964).

93 *Hudson v. Palmer*, 468 U.S. 517, 104 S.Ct. 3194 (1984).

94 *Bell v. Wolfish*, 441 U.S. 520, 99 S.Ct. 1861 (1979).

95 *Grummett v. Rushen*, 587 F.Supp. 913 (1984).

96 *Johnson v. Phelan*, 69 F.3d 144 (1995).

97 *Kentucky Department of Corrections v. Thompson*, 490 U.S. 454, 109 S.Ct. 1904 (1989).

98 *Thornburgh v. Abbot*, 490 U.S. 401, 109 S.Ct. 1874 (1989).

99 *Tarlton v. Clark*, 441 F.2d 384 (1971).

100 Rachel Wyatt, "Male Rape in U.S. Prisons: Are Conjugal Visits the Answer?" *Case Western Reserve Journal of International Law* 37 (March 2006): 579–614.

101 Lucien X. Lombardo, "Guards Imprisoned: Correctional Officers at Work" in *Correctional Contexts: Contemporary and Classical Readings*, ed. Edward J. Latessa et al. (Los Angeles: Roxbury, 2001), 153–167.

102 Caitlin Finney, Erene Stergiopoulos, Jennifer Hensel, Sarah Bonato, and Carolyn S Dewa, "Organizational Stressors Associated with Job Stress and Burnout in Correctional Officers: A Systematic Review," *BMC Public Health* 13, no. 1 (March 2013): 1–13.

103 Finney et al., "Organizational Stressors Associated with Job Stress and Burnout in Correctional Officers." Martin et al., "'They Can Take Us over Any Time They Want'."

104 Finney et al., "Organizational Stressors Associated with Job Stress and Burnout in Correctional Officers." E. G. Lambert, N. L. Hogan, and I. Altheimer, "An Exploratory Examination of the Consequences of Burnout in Terms of Life Satisfaction, Turnover Intent, and Absenteeism among Private Correctional Staff," *Prison Journal* 90, no. 1 (2010): 94–114.

105 Martin et al., "'They Can Take Us over Any Time They Want'."

106 Ibid.

107 Ibid.

108 C. Dowden and C. Tellier, "Predicting Work-related Stress in Correctional Officers: A Meta-analysis," *Journal of Criminal Justice* 32 (2004): 31–47. L. H. Gerstein, C. G. Topp, and G. Correll, "The Role of the Environment and Person When Predicting Burnout among Correctional Personnel," *Criminal Justice and Behavior* 14, no. 3 (1987): 352–369. J. R. Carlson and G. Thomas, "Burnout among Prison Case Workers and Corrections Officers," *Journal of Offender Rehabilitation* 43, no. 3 (2008):19–34. E. A. Paoline, E. Lambert, and N. L. Hogan, "A Calm and Happy Keeper of the Keys: The Impact of ACA Views, Relations with Co-workers, and Policy Views on the Job Stress and Job Satisfaction of Correctional Staff," *Prison Journal* 86, no. 2 (2006):182–205.

109 Finney et al., "Organizational Stressors Associated with Job Stress and Burnout in Correctional Officers." Joseph L. Martin, Bronwen Lichtenstein, Robert B. Jenkot, and David R. Forde, "'They Can Take Us over Any Time They Want': Correctional Officers' Responses to Prison Crowding," *Prison Journal* 92, no. 1 (March 2012): 88–105.

110 Martin et al., "'They Can Take Us over Any Time They Want'."

111 David Shichor, *Punishment for Profit: Private Prisons/Public Concerns* (Thousand Oaks, Calif.: Sage, 1995), 13–14.

112 David Shichor and Michael J. Gilbert, *Privatization in Criminal Justice: Past, Present, and Future* (Cincinnati, Ohio: Anderson, 2001), 209, as quoted in E. Bates, "Prisons for Profit," in *The Dilemmas of Corrections: Contemporary Readings*, 4th ed., eds. Kenneth C. Haas and Geoffrey P. Alpert (Prospect Heights, Ill.: Waveland Press, 1998).

113 CoreCivic, Locations, www.corecivic.com/what-we-do-what-we-dont-do. Accessed February 2020.

114 CoreCivic, Revenue and Earnings Snapshot, ir.corecivic.com/stock-information/fundamentals/snapshot. Accessed February 2020.

115 The Geo Group, Locations, www.geo-group.com/locations. Accessed March 2020.

116 Geo Group, *2018 Annual Report*, p. 3, investors.geogroup.com/FinancialDocs.

117 Management and Training Corp., About Us, www.mtctrains.com/about-us. Accessed March 2020.

118 Timothy Williams and Richard A. Oppel Jr., "Escapes, Riots and Beatings. But States Can't Seem to Ditch Private Prisons," *New York Times*, April 10, 2018.

119 Carson, *Prisoners in 2018*, 27.

120 Charles H. Logan, *Private Prisons: Cons and Pros* (New York: Oxford University Press, 1990), 41–48.

121 Alex Friedmann, "Apples-to-Fish: Public and Private Prison Cost Comparisons," *Fordham Urban Law Journal* 42, no. 2 (December 2014): 503–568.

122 Doris Schartmueller, "People Matter More Than Numbers: Organized Efforts against Prison Privatization in Florida," *Contemporary Justice Review* 17, no. 2 (June 2014): 233–249.

123 Rebecca Cooper, Caroline Heldman, Alissa R. Ackerman, and Victoria A. Farrar-Meyers, "Hidden Corporate Profits in the U.S. Prison System: The Unorthodox Policy-making of the American Legislative Exchange Council," *Contemporary Justice Review* 19, no. 3 (September 2016): 380.

124 Andrea Castillo, "California Bans For-Profit Prisons and Immigrant Detention Facilities," *Los Angeles Times*, October 11, 2019.

125 Ráchael A. Powers, Catherine Kaukinen, and Michelle Jeanis, "An Examination of Recidivism among Inmates Released from a Private Reentry Center and Public Institutions in Colorado," *Prison Journal* 97, no. 5 (2017): 609. Sasha Volokh, "Are Private Prisons Better or Worse Than Public Prisons?" *Washington Post*, February 25, 2014. Andrew L. Spivak and Susan F. Sharp, "Inmate Recidivism as a Measure of Private Prison Performance," *Crime and Delinquency* 54 (July 2008): 482–508.

126 Brandon K. Applegate and Alicia H. Sitren, "The Jail and the Community: Comparing Jails in Rural and Urban Contexts," *Prison Journal* 88 (June 2008): 252–269.

127 Thomas G. Blomberg, "Beyond Metaphors: Penal Reform as Net-Widening," in *Punishment and Social*

Control, eds. Thomas G. Blomberg and Stanley Cohen (New York: Aldine de Gruyter, 1995): 45–61.

128 Zhen Zeng, *Jail Inmates in 2018*, (U.S. Department of Justice Office of Justice Programs Bureau of Justice Statistics, 2020) 1. Available at www.bjs.gov/index. cfm?ty=pbdetail&iid=6826.

129 Ibid., Table 3, p. 5.

130 Ibid., 10.

131 Zeng, *Jail Inmates in 2018*, p. 3.

132 Joe Hagan, "The Long, Lawless Ride of Sheriff Joe," *Rolling Stone* no. 1163 (August 16, 2012): 62–69.

133 Fernanda Santos, "Outdoor Jail, a Vestige of Joe Arpaio's Tenure, Is Closing," *New York Times*, April 4, 2017.

134 "The Fourth Amendment in Jail: Prisoner and Arrestee Rights While in Custody," *Supreme Court Debates* 14, no. 8 (November 2011): 7–15.

135 Tracey Kyckelhahn, *Local Government Corrections Expenditures, FY 2005–2011* (U.S. Department of Justice, Office of Justice Programs, Bureau of Justice Statistics, 2013), 3.

136 Stan C. Proband, "Jail Populations Up—Racial Disproportions Worse," *Overcrowded Times* 4, no. 4 (1993): 4.

137 John Irwin, *The Jail: Managing the Underclass in American Society* (Berkeley: University of California Press, 1985).

138 Michael Welch, "Social Junk, Social Dynamite and the Rabble: Persons with AIDS in Jail," *American Journal of Criminal Justice* 14, no. 1 (1989): 135–147.

139 Bryan Robinson, "Death-Row Inmate Seeks Organ Transplant," ABCNews. com. May 28, 2003. Oregon Live, Oregon Death Row, www.oregonlive. com/pacific-northwest-news/index. ssf/page/oregon_death_row.html. Accessed February 2020.

OXFORD
insight study guide
Active Engagement, Deeper Understanding

Learn more with this chapter's digital tools, including the Oxford Insight Study Guide, at www.oup.com/he/Fuller2e.

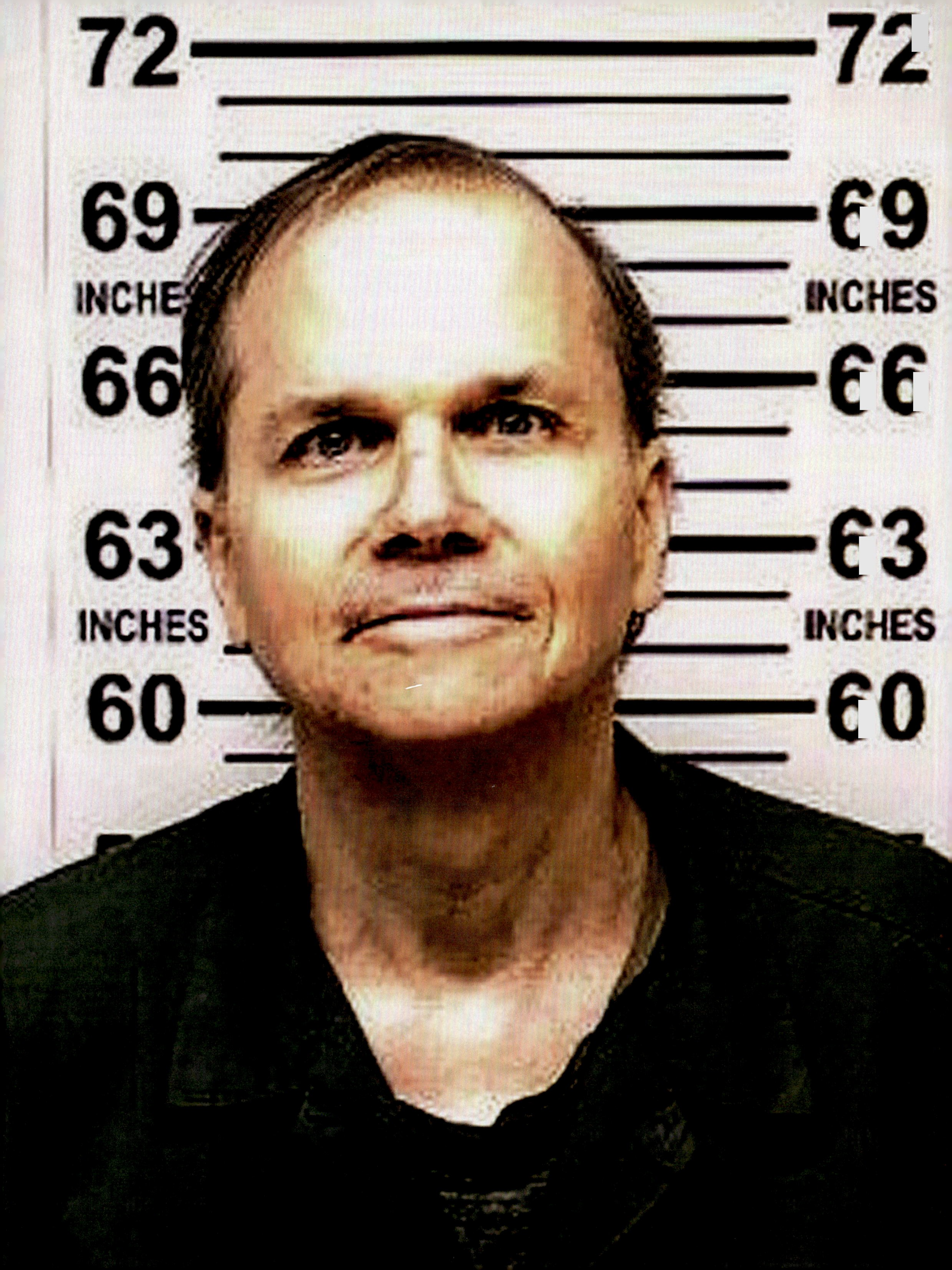
72
72
69
69
INCHES
INCHES
66
66
63
63
INCHES
INCHES
60
60

Community Corrections

Mark David Chapman, who killed John Lennon, told the New York State Board of Parole that he feels "more and more shame" every year for his offense. The board denied his release. Would Chapman have already been paroled if his victim had not been so famous?

In November 2017, Jimmy O'Neal Spencer, 52, was paroled from

prison. Nine months later, he broke into the home of Martha Dell Reliford in Guntersville, Alabama, and bludgeoned her to death. Two other victims, Marie Martin and her 7-year-old grandson, Colton Lee, were found dead in a house across the street.[1]

Spencer had first gone to prison in 1984 for burglary. He attempted to escape and received a 10-year sentence. For a second escape, he received a consecutive 10-year sentence. Spencer was paroled in July 1988 but committed a burglary soon after, for which he was sentenced to life in prison. He escaped in 1993 and was then arrested for another burglary. He received two more consecutive 16-year sentences. Later, he received another 15-year sentence for assaulting an inmate.[2]

According to Madison County District Attorney Rob Broussard, Spencer had gone free because "We only have so much prison space … a decision has to be who we're going to keep and who we'll let go." However, in 2013, Franklin County District Attorney Joey Rushing wrote to the parole board opposing Spencer's release because he was dangerous. A homeowner had to shoot Spencer to stop him during a 1989 burglary.[3]

After his release in 2017, Spencer was assigned to a homeless shelter in Birmingham for six months. He left after three weeks and went to Guntersville, where he got into more trouble with the law, including possession of drug paraphernalia, resisting arrest, and illegal possession of a firearm. His parole was not revoked.[4]

The families of the murder victims were awarded $1 million, the maximum damages available under state law.[5] Jeanette Grantham, director of Victims of Crime and Leniency, questioned how such a serious mistake could be made in freeing a violent career criminal like Spencer. Grantham said, "Paroles of violent offenders are being released by check marks on data driven parole guidelines. Two board members made a couple of check marks and here we are. Regardless of why Spencer was paroled, we know it was a terrible, terrible decision."[6] Spencer was charged with capital murder in August 2018.[7]

THINK ABOUT IT > What are the options for releasing inmates on parole, and how do they affect the criminal justice system?

LEARNING OBJECTIVE 12.1

Outline the assumptions about the nature of crime that lie at the heart of community corrections.

Community corrections—A form of corrections in which criminal offenders are managed in the community instead of in correctional facilities.

12.1 Community Corrections in Context

How does society send a message to offenders while also making the criminal justice response cost effective? Many jurisdictions have implemented **community corrections**, which attempts to not only deter crime but also rehabilitate offenders. This approach involves partially restricting freedoms, imposing fines, and requiring participation in treatment programs. About 6.4 million people are under the supervision of U.S. adult correctional systems. Of those, about 7 in 10 are either on probation or parole.[8]

Although not as visible as prisons, community corrections account for a major portion of the correctional efforts of the criminal justice process.[9] This chapter covers four related community corrections strategies: diversion programs, probation, intermediate sanctions, and parole. In addition, it considers the historical and philosophical underpinnings of attempts to reform and/or incapacitate offenders outside the prison.

Why do we treat and punish some offenders within the community rather than send them all to prison? After all, cases like Jimmy O'Neal Spencer's make the public distrust the criminal justice system. However, the system cannot accommodate all the inmates for the length of time they are sentenced. As new inmates enter prison, others must be released through mechanisms such as parole. It is not affordable or even possible to build enough prisons to house everyone who breaks the law.[10] One of the functions of the criminal justice system is to use prison space primarily for offenders who pose a continued threat.

For the most part, prisons work only in a limited manner. As we have discussed, the criminal justice system has multiple goals: incapacitation, retribution, and to a lesser extent, rehabilitation:

> Incapacitation. Prisons are good at achieving the goal of incapacitation. For the limited time offenders are behind bars, they cannot break any more laws outside the prison. Offenders might break the law within prison by victimizing other inmates or correctional workers, but this depends on how effective the prison is in keeping internal order. In addition, prison gang members may order fellow members to commit offenses on the outside, but the chance of this occurring is likely less than if the offender were free.

> Retribution. The goal of **retribution** is to punish the offender for transgressions of criminal law. Prisons are somewhat successful in accomplishing this goal, but the public is generally unsatisfied when they hear stories about early parole and "country club prisons," a designation often given to federal prisons that incarcerate white-collar offenders.

> Rehabilitation. The goal of rehabilitation might not be met because many inmates become more antisocial during confinement.[11]

> In this sense, prisons might not enhance public safety because they tend to embitter, harden, and alienate inmates. Consequently, efforts are made to limit the deleterious effect of prisons by finding alternatives to incarceration for all but the most dangerous offenders.

Retribution—
Punishment that is considered to be deserved.

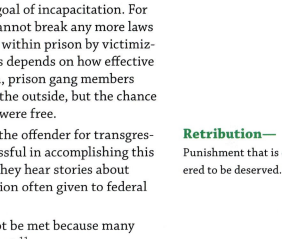

As part of an intensive drug and alcohol rehabilitation program, former prisoners grow and sell produce outside of Larimer County Community Corrections in Fort Collins, Colorado. What other types of community corrections programs do offenders participate in?

At the heart of the community corrections movement are some assumptions about the nature of crime and the benefits of using community resources to address crime. These assumptions include the following:

> Prison is an artificial society. Conformity in prison is not always a good indicator of an inmate's ability to adjust to the free world.

> The prison's total control does little to prepare inmates to take responsibility for their actions.

> The community has resources that are unavailable in the prison, such as drug treatment or work release, which enhance the likelihood of rehabilitation.

> The community can provide support networks to the offender that do not exist in prison. With the help of spouses, parents, children, and clergy who have bonds with an offender, the offender has a greater chance of leading a law-abiding life.

> The offender can contribute to the financial upkeep of his or her family and, if gainfully employed, pay taxes. Additionally, some community corrections programs require offenders to pay the cost of their supervision.

> The state spends less money on offenders in community corrections programs than it does incarcerating them. Prison cells are expensive, and the state can address many more offenders by handling them outside the prison setting.

> The state can accurately identify which offenders are dangerous and need secure incarceration and which ones are safe to release under supervision.

> The number of trained probation and parole officers is sufficient to adequately supervise the offenders selected for community corrections programs.

Is it safe to make these assumptions about the efficacy of community corrections? For the most part, the answer is yes. Millions of offenders have successfully served sentences in community corrections programs during which, in addition to not breaking any more laws, they have completed treatment programs, supported their families, paid taxes, re-entered society, and contributed to the community (see Figure 12.1 for the number of adults who have successfully

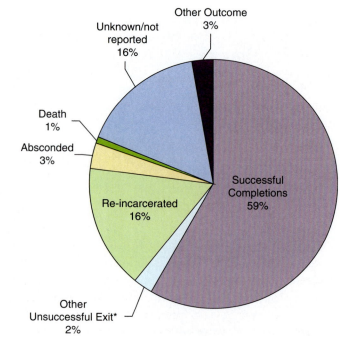

FIGURE 12.1   Adults Leaving Probation Why don't more people successfully complete probation?

This category includes probationers discharged from supervision when they did not complete the conditions of probation or fulfill obligations.

Source: Danielle Kaeble, Probation and Parole in the United States, 2017-2018, *Appendix Table 3 (U.S. Department of Justice Office of Justice Programs Bureau of Justice Statistics, 2020), 18. Available at www.bjs.gov/index. cfm?ty=pbdetail&iid=6986.*

completed probation).[12] Many notable failures have occurred, however, in which offenders have killed, raped, or robbed, causing criminal justice officials to look incompetent and careless. Such instances create tension around the use of community corrections. Despite calls for such radical initiatives as abolishing parole, those who understand the corrections situation in the United States appreciate that early-release mechanisms are necessary.[13] Therefore, community corrections will always be with us. Only the degree to which they are used is controversial. The key concerns are which inmates to release, how many to release, and what level of supervision they should have.

PAUSE AND REVIEW

1. **What are some assumptions about the nature of crime that lie at the heart of community corrections?**

12.2 Diversion

Offenders can be diverted to alternative programs at several points in the criminal justice system. These programs are based on **labeling theory**, which suggests that preventing offenders from developing a criminal self-concept may make them less likely to continue breaking the law. Diversion programs are especially popular when dealing with first-time offenders who have committed relatively minor offenses.[14] Typically, these offenders' charges are held in abeyance (temporarily suspended) while they complete a treatment program or community service or simply stay out of trouble for a specified period.[15] Once the conditions of the diversion program are completed, offenders are released from supervision without a conviction on their record.

Sometimes this brief encounter with the criminal justice system is enough to get the attention of young offenders, who are then successful in avoiding further contact with the law. For many young people who have college aspirations or hope for a career in law, medicine, or teaching, a clean record is crucial. Many prosecutors and judges do not want to spoil the records of young people who commit only minor offenses. They see diversion programs as a way to sort out those who respond immediately from those who will continue to be problems for the criminal justice system.[16]

Although diversion programs limit the number of people who enter the criminal justice system, they are not without critics. Given prison overcrowding and the heavy caseloads that probation officers carry, were it not for diversion programs, the state would dismiss the cases of many first-time offenders who commit minor offenses.[17] Because prosecutors must prioritize what cases to pursue, diversion programs provide an attractive alternative to dropping the charges. However, the overall effect of diversion programs is to widen the net of social control. By **net-widening**, we mean the state controls more and more people who, with one more minor slip-up, could find themselves entangled deeply within the criminal justice system. Some programs have so many conditions and restrictions that clients are almost sure to violate at least some of them. This has been called "stacking the deck." Instead of diverting offenders from the system, some programs, with their multitude of conditions and requirements, actually suck the offender into a deeper quagmire of legal problems.[18] For example, it is one thing to be caught with a misdemeanor quantity of marijuana, but when an offender fails to attend a drug-counseling program or return the diversion officer's phone calls, the resulting revocation of diversion can mean incarceration.[19]

LEARNING OBJECTIVE 12.2

Describe the connection between diversion programs and labeling theory.

Labeling theory— A perspective that considers recidivism to be a consequence, in part, of the negative labels applied to offenders.

Net-widening—A phenomenon through which criminal justice programs pull more clients into the system than would otherwise be involved without the program.

Seattle Police Officer Tom Christenson talks to Gailen Lopton (seated right). After having previously caught Lopton using heroin, instead of incarcerating him, the police offered Lopton the opportunity to participate in a drug rehabilitation program that tries to keep low-level drug offenders out of jail. How do such diversion programs help to curb the number of people entering the criminal justice system?

PAUSE AND REVIEW

1. **What is the connection between diversion programs and labeling theory?**
2. **What are the advantages and disadvantages of diversion programs?**
3. **What is "stacking the deck?"**

LEARNING OBJECTIVE 12.3

Discuss how various actors in the criminal justice system view probation.

LEARNING OBJECTIVE 12.4

Characterize the three universal functions that define the probation officer's occupation.

Probation (from Chapter 1)—The suspension of all or part of a sentence subject to certain conditions and supervision in the community.

12.3 Probation

Probation is a chance for offenders to stay out of prison or jail if they promise to be good. At any given time, there are more probationers than prison inmates or parolees, with state probationers far outnumbering federal probationers (see Figures 12.2 and 12.3). As of 2018, 3,540,000 adults were on probation in the United States.[20] Probationers are not completely free, however. They must agree to certain terms set by a judge, such as performing public-service work, abstaining from alcohol, getting therapy, and reporting regularly to a probation officer.[21] Those who violate these agreements are usually incarcerated for the term for which they were initially eligible. Probation is a widely used sentencing alternative because it accomplishes several positive outcomes. Depending on how one views the criminal justice system, one or more of these outcomes might be more attractive than others. Here, we will consider the practice of probation from the viewpoints of the key actors in the criminal justice system.

> How the offender views probation. To offenders, probation can seem like a relatively good deal. Many offenders embrace the prospect of probation like a lifeline in comparison with facing imprisonment. Probation allows offenders to remain at home and at work. However, probationers do not enjoy the same legal rights as other citizens. Reporting to the probation officer on a weekly or monthly basis; abstaining from alcohol and drugs; and seeking permission to move to a different residence, change jobs, or travel outside the county can cause resentment and alienation.[22] These conditions must be taken seriously

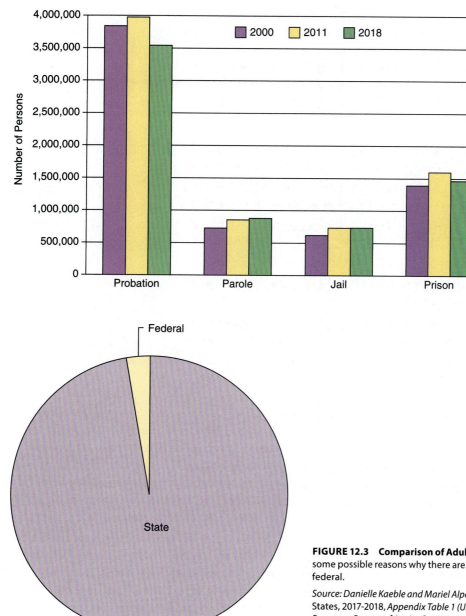

FIGURE 12.2 Persons under Correctional Supervision Why are more people on probation than under any other form of correctional supervision?

Source: Laura M. Maruschak and Todd D. Minton, Correctional Populations in the United States, 2017-2018, *Table 1 (Washington, D.C.: U.S. Department of Justice Office of Justice Programs Bureau of Justice Statistics, 2020), 2. Available at www.bjs.gov/index.cfm?ty=pbdetail&iid=7026.*

FIGURE 12.3 Comparison of Adults on State and Federal Probation Give some possible reasons why there are so many more state probationers than federal.

Source: Danielle Kaeble and Mariel Alper, Probation and Parole in the United States, 2017-2018, *Appendix Table 1 (U.S. Department of Justice Office of Justice Programs Bureau of Justice Statistics, 2020), 14. Available at www.bjs.gov/index.cfm?ty=pbdetail&iid=6986.*

because their violation can bring swift and certain punishment. Revocation may result in receiving the entire prison sentence for which one was initially eligible, despite the time served on probation.

› How the prosecutor views probation. The prosecutor's foremost concern is to win the case positively and efficiently. As discussed in Chapter 8, although often under pressure from the victim(s) to seek prison time, the prosecutor has considerable discretion in fashioning **plea bargains** with defense attorneys.[23] The prosecutor can point to probation as a victory, even though it requires little time or resources. As a plea-bargaining tool, probation allows the prosecutor to avoid costly trials for many cases. Additionally, prosecutors may embrace probation when a case is weak and would likely result in a dismissal if it went to trial.

› How the defense attorney views probation. The defense attorney also views probation as a victory. By keeping the offender out of prison, the defense

Plea bargain (from Chapter 8)—A compromise reached by the defendant, the defendant's attorney, and the prosecutor in which the defendant agrees to plead guilty or no contest in return for a reduction of the charges' severity, dismissal of some charges, further information about the offense or about others involved in it, or the prosecutor's agreement to recommend a desired sentence.

In May 2017, model Dani Mathers (center right), shown here with her attorneys, faced invasion of privacy charges for photographing an elderly woman in a gym locker room and body-shaming her on Snapchat. Mathers pleaded no contest and was sentenced to probation and community service. In what ways does the defense attorney view probation as a victory?

attorney can claim to have preserved the offender's liberty with some reasonable compromises (i.e., the conditions of probation). The defense attorney is not overly concerned with the conditions because, for the most part, they will not hurt the offender and may serve as positive influences. Being required to get more education or counseling does not violate fundamental human rights, and the defense attorney is not likely to object to such requirements.[24]

> **How the judge views probation.** Judges are under tremendous pressure from the public to punish offenders even though prisons are full. Probation allows the judge to impose a sentence that is less expensive than prison and, to some degree at least, satisfies victims and other citizens. The judge can add special conditions such as drug testing, home confinement, and increased supervision. We will discuss these intermediate punishments in greater detail at the end of this chapter.

> **How reformers view probation.** Probation offers the offender a variety of treatment and community-service activities. Community resources such as schools, mental health centers, hospitals, and opportunities for gainful employment cannot be duplicated in prison. If used judiciously, these resources can provide the ingredients for successful rehabilitation and reintegration of the offender. Perhaps probation's major benefit as seen by reformers is the avoidance of the deleterious effects of prison. By avoiding hardened, long-term inmates, the offender may still be able to learn productive work habits and positive social skills.

> **How politicians view probation.** Many politicians adopt a tough-on-crime stance and advocate sending vast numbers of offenders to prison for long sentences. The same politicians, however, do not generally provide the funds needed to build enough prisons, hire enough probation officers, or establish effective community-corrections treatment services. To them, probation is a cheaper way to punish than prison. However, politicians can be expected to condemn probation when some probationer commits a heinous offense while under supervision.

Probation means many things to many people. The emphasis of probation in any given jurisdiction may vacillate between its twin goals of supervision and treatment. Because it is such a fundamental feature of the criminal justice system, however, it will always be used in one form or another.

Probation Officers at Work

The probation officer's job requires a variety of skills, a strong sense of self-worth, and a tolerance for other people not doing what is expected of them. Most probation work is done at the local level, although there are probation officers at the federal level. The probation officer spends time in the courtroom, in the office, and in the field visiting clients where they work and live. Each probation department has standards for monitoring offenders, and each probation officer works out how to accomplish the job's multiple demands. Many probation officers love this work because its discretion and flexibility allow them to use their particular administrative, interpersonal, and investigative strengths to help offenders and protect society. The probation officer's duties are many, but three universal functions define the occupation: investigation, supervision, and service.

INVESTIGATION

The probation officer spends a lot of time gathering information for decision-makers throughout the criminal justice system. The offender's case file contains data gleaned from police reports; prosecutors' files; and interviews with offenders, victims, witnesses, neighbors, teachers, and peers. The most time-consuming and significant report the probation officer writes is the **pre-sentence investigation (PSI)**.[25]

The United States has a bifurcated court process. The first goal of the proceedings is to determine if the defendant is guilty. This is sometimes done by means of a criminal trial, which is used sparingly; most cases are settled through plea bargaining.[26] With plea bargaining, the judge does not have the opportunity to become familiar with either the case or the defendant, so in the second part of the case proceedings, the sentencing, the judge has little information on which to base a sentence. Typically, the judge postpones the sentencing judgment while the

Pre-sentence investigation (PSI)— The report prepared by a probation officer to assist a judge in sentencing; also called a pre-sentence report.

Disgraced ex-Congressman Anthony Weiner had visited his probation officer a day after leaving a halfway house at the conclusion of a 21-month prison sentence for having illegal contact with a 15-year-old girl. Here he is shown leaving a federal courthouse in May 2019. He. What are the three universal functions of a probation officer?

It is unfortunate that the service aspect of the probation officer's job is so limited. Some may argue that rehabilitation is a secondary activity, but evidence suggests that appropriate placement in a decent treatment program can have a positive effect. Although the investigation and supervision aspects of probation will always be the primary focus, the service component may well be the most important one for the long-term behavior change of the offender and ultimately for the protection of society.

For-Profit Probation

For-profit probation—A form of probation supervision that is contracted to for-profit private agencies by the state.

With probation caseloads expanding, many states have found it difficult to provide enough probation officers to adequately supervise everyone who is on probation. As a result, many states use for-profit (also called private) probation services for misdemeanor cases.[38] **For-profit probation** is a contractual agreement between the state government and private companies to supervise misdemeanor probationers. Presumably, these offenders require little in the way of supervision as compared with those convicted of felonies. Relieving state probation officers of this responsibility seems to be a way to focus resources on more serious offenders.

There is considerable debate about the ethical issues of for-profit probation, but it is not unlike the example of for-profit prisons. When traditional government activities are privatized, it is assumed that the service will be less expensive and more effective. To this end, states have developed guidelines and requirements that dictate how for-profit probation agencies supervise misdemeanor cases.[39] These requirements specify such activities as how often the probationers are contacted, the collection of fines and cost-of-supervision fees, and the provision for treatment alternatives, which also may be contracted to for-profit agencies. For-profit probation has many advantages and disadvantages.

ADVANTAGES

> Cost. The cost of supervising individuals on for-profit probation is borne by the probationer.

> Effectiveness. By shifting the burden for misdemeanor offenders to for-profit agencies, state agencies can more effectively supervise and treat more serious felony offenders. Furthermore, misdemeanor offenders experience a greater degree of contact with probation officers, especially considering that the private agency has an incentive to collect cost-of-supervision fees. Most misdemeanor offenders do not require substantial counseling or rigorous supervision, so the high caseloads of these private agencies are not considered problematic.

> Public perception. Under traditional probation, misdemeanor offenders often fall through the cracks. There simply are not enough resources available to provide the type of supervision that the public and crime victims demand. With for-profit probation companies, those convicted of misdemeanors are more likely to face consequences as sentenced.

DISADVANTAGES

> Staff qualifications. Most traditional probation officers are required to have a 4-year university degree and to receive intensive training. Many for-profit agencies, by contrast, have no educational requirement, and for-profit probation agencies offer little or no training. Although many for-profit probation officers are dedicated and effective in their jobs, the lack of standards and guidelines makes this type of arrangement problematic.[40]

Johnny Gibbs helps his disabled father, Mike, into their home in Liberty, Tennessee. Johnny Gibbs has been trying to get a valid driver's license for 20 years, but he cannot afford it. Tennessee suspended his ability to get a license until he turned 21 as punishment for school truancy in 1999. When Gibbs could not pay for traffic violations, he served jail time and probation and went deeper into debt because he had to pay a monthly fee to a private probation company. Why is private probation a controversial issue?

> Profit motive. The primary missions of traditional probation are to protect the public and provide treatment for their clients. The first order of business of for-profit probation companies is to make money. This profit motive can conflict with the basic reasons why misdemeanor probation was established in the first place.

> Ethical concerns. The government has a monopoly on the legitimate use of correctional coercion, and outsourcing it to private agencies may be questionable. A relevant analogy is the employment of mercenaries to fight wars. Public safety is a basic government responsibility, and many believe it should remain in the hands of the government and be accountable to the public.[41]

> Social-class bias. Charging misdemeanor probationers cost-of-supervision fees has a differential effect, depending on individual financial capabilities. Those who have enough money to meet their basic needs might be inconvenienced by the added expense, but those who are unemployed or living paycheck to paycheck may find the cost of freedom more than they can afford. Some agencies charge up to $50 per month for the cost of supervision, which can mean the difference between successfully completing probation or being brought back before the judge on a technical violation.[42]

The use of for-profit probation in the United States will continue to be controversial. As state governments seek to provide services more efficiently without raising taxes, the outsourcing of probation is a tempting strategy.

PAUSE AND REVIEW

1. How do various actors in the criminal justice system view probation?
2. What is a pre-sentence investigation, and what sort of information does it contain?
3. What are the two goals of the supervision function of the probation officer?
4. List some of the advantages and disadvantages of for-profit probation.

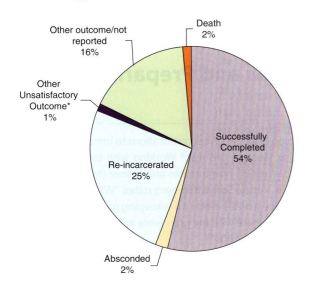

FIGURE 12.4   Adults Completing Parole In your opinion, should the number of parolees who successfully complete their sentences be higher or lower?

* Includes people released to special sentence, as well as closure due to deportation, pending parole institutional hearing, other revocations, other unsuccessful discharges, and early terminations.

Source: Danielle Kaeble and Mariel Alper, Probation and Parole in the United States, 2017-2018, *Appendix Table 7 (U.S. Department of Justice Office of Justice Programs Bureau of Justice Statistics, 2020), 25. Available at www.bjs.gov/index.cfm?ty=pbdetail&iid=6986.*

Master status—A personal status that overwhelms all others.

day (sometimes it is the soup of every day), but a grocery store has dozens of different brands, flavors, and sizes. Moreover, consider the vast array of foods in the store, and the former inmate can experience decision overload. Other concerns have greater consequences. The interpersonal skills needed to survive in prison are not always conducive to getting along with co-workers in society. The necessity of demonstrating a willingness to use violence that can keep one alive in prison is obviously problematic in the workplace, where supervisors and co-workers give and accept criticism without worrying about their physical safety.

2. Weakened social ties. The world that the inmate left behind is not the same as the one he or she returns to. People have moved on with their lives, and the inmate must re-establish social bonds that have been weakened, twisted, or broken by incarceration.[54] Spouses, children, parents, friends, and bosses might act differently and be wary of how the offender has been affected by prison. At its most extreme, these changes in social bonds include divorce or estrangement from spouses and rejection by children. The inmate often comes home to find that someone else has usurped his or her former status as authority figure, breadwinner, and confidant. While in prison, a mother might remember her children in a highly romanticized way, but on release, she may return home to find them hostile, bitter, and attached to a new caretaker. The assumed social location of the inmate that was frozen in time by incarceration thaws out on release and melts into disillusionment, anomie, and alienation.

3. Stigmatization.[55] Sociologist Erving Goffman defines one type of stigma as a "blemish of individual character" and includes imprisonment as one of the stigmas that individuals must carry with them for a lifetime and constantly fight to overcome. This stigma is both legal and social. The legal stigma, depending on the jurisdiction, involves losing the right to vote, to raise children, to hold public employment, to serve on a jury, to hold public office, or to possess a firearm, and it could mean being required to register as a felon. Perhaps the former inmate who concedes that there is a continuous price to pay for crime understands these restrictions. However, the social stigma can be even more frustrating. The stigma of "ex-con" can be as debilitating as that of "convict." For the former inmate who has served a sentence and has paid for his or her offenses, the continuing discrimination and prejudice seem unjust. A fresh start is nearly impossible and carries a **master status** that overwhelms all of his or her positive attributes and accomplishments.[56] Once parents hear that the new boyfriend is a convicted rapist, there may be no convincing them that he has mended his ways, learned his lesson, paid his debt to society, or is in any way a suitable future son-in-law.

Depending on the former inmate's criminal offense, prison experience, and support system outside the prison, he or she will face various challenges upon re-entering society. The stigma associated with being a convicted felon and limited opportunities for employment can hamper a former inmate's efforts to reintegrate into family and society. Leaving prison may relieve former inmates of several problems, but it can also introduce new ones.

Inmate Alan Newby pets Hailey, who is being rehabilitated through the Shelter Pet Obedience Training program at Wildwood Correctional Complex in Kenai, Alaska. The program pairs inmates with abandoned dogs, who later go up for adoption. In what ways does a program such as this prepare inmates for life outside prison?

PAUSE AND REVIEW

1. What is the difference between probation and parole?
2. What three competing principles is the decision to grant parole based on?
3. What three major adjustments stand as obstacles to successful re-entry?

12.5 INTERMEDIATE SANCTIONS

Several other community corrections tactics require examination if we are to truly appreciate how community corrections have developed over the years. Because of prison overcrowding and the heavy caseloads of probation and parole officers, intermediate sanctions have been implemented to make probation and parole more effective, more stringent, and more palatable to the public, who demand that offenders be held accountable for their actions.[57] **Intermediate sanctions** are sentencing alternatives available to the judge who finds regular probation too lenient and prison too severe.[58] With the pressures for parole boards to release inmates early to make room for new offenders, some of these intermediate sanctions are also employed at the parole stage of the criminal justice process.

Intermediate sanctions give the criminal justice system a broader range of mechanisms of social control and enhance the public's perception that crime does not pay. Although some of these newer intermediate sanctions are problematic, critics' concerns are being addressed, and the courts are beginning to recognize that the issue must be resolved. The following is a discussion of some of the more notable intermediate sanctions.

Intensive-Supervision Probation

Intensive-supervision probation (ISP) is simply what probation used to be before the advent of unreasonably high caseloads for probation officers.[59] ISP is

LEARNING OBJECTIVE 12.7

Outline how intensive-supervision probation (ISP) is different from regular probation.

Intermediate sanctions—Sentencing alternatives that are stricter than regular probation but less severe than prison.

Intensive-supervision probation (ISP)—A form of supervision that requires frequent meetings between the client and probation officer.

actually a form of triage in which offenders deemed the most problematic receive extra supervision. Probation officers assigned to these troublesome offenders are given small caseloads and are expected to have more frequent contact with clients.[60] It is believed that if probation officers can concentrate on those who need help or pose a threat to society, then they can recognize emerging problems and intervene quickly. Because it is more structured, ISP differs in several ways from regular probation:

> ISP clients have about four times as much contact with probation officers. More contacts occur at the probationer's home or place of work. Some regular probationers only have to report as little as one or two times a month, and home visits may occur as infrequently as once every six months.

> ISP clients are more likely to be required to participate in electronic home monitoring and random drug and/or alcohol testing.

> Unannounced job-site or home visits are more frequent.

> ISP clients are more likely to be brought before the court for technical violations.

> ISP clients are more likely to be required to maintain full-time employment or vocational training as well as have community-service requirements.

> Curfews are stricter. Some ISP clients must request permission to leave their homes or place of work at any time.

> ISP officers' caseloads are lower, typically 20 or fewer clients, although some might be as high as 40. Regular probation caseloads usually range from 30 to more than 100 probationers per officer.

The focus of the ISP program is up to the individual agency. Some are treatment-oriented, whereas others are more concerned with surveillance. Several tools are available to help the ISP officer detect wrongdoing.

Drug Testing

Rather than relying on behavioral cues or lifestyle changes to detect drug use, the officer can require that clients, on either a routine or random basis, submit a urine sample for analysis.[61] Because one of the conditions of freedom is to refrain from illegal drug use, and because probation and parole are conditional-release practices, the client has a choice of cooperating or going to jail or prison. Most offenders cooperate and retain their liberty, live with their families, hold down a job, and escape the pains of imprisonment.

Submitting a urine sample, though humiliating and insulting, seems a small price to pay for staying out of prison. This is not to say, however, that offenders do not attempt to frustrate the system by masking their drug use. Probationers use several techniques to deceive authorities. These techniques include submitting someone else's urine, eating or drinking various items that mask the presence of drugs, and missing or delaying tests until the drugs in their bodies have been diluted. Probation and parole authorities counter these deceptions by increasing the sophistication of the drug tests (for example, using hair strands instead of urine), surprising the clients with random tests, and closely monitoring the administration of the tests.

House Arrest and Electronic Monitoring

House arrest is an old concept that has appeal today because it allows offenders to maintain family ties, remain employed, pay taxes, and take advantage of community resources such as school and counseling services. It also saves the state the cost of incarceration.[62] Typically, offenders are required to stay home except when they are attending approved activities such as employment, school, treatment programs, or religious services. They are especially restricted during the evening hours, when most offenses take place and when they can expect unannounced calls or visits from their probation officer. Although some citizens are concerned about some home-confined offenders being a danger to the community, for the most part these probationers are selected because they are low-risk individuals and have relatively stable residences in which to be confined.

Electronic monitoring is often used to supplement house arrest but is also used with other programs.[63] Like drug testing, electronic monitoring uses technology to address human concerns.[64] In this case, a device attached to the offender's ankle alerts authorities when it is moved too far from its transmitter. If the offender can slip off the electronic bracelet and leave it next to the transmitter, then he or she is free to roam at will, safe in the knowledge that the probation officer believes he or she is still home. Another limitation of electronic monitoring is that it can only tell the probation officer where the offender is, not what the offender is doing. Offenses such as child abuse, domestic violence, or drug sales could be happening, and the probation officer would not know.

An electronic monitoring innovation that does give corrections officers an idea of what the offender is up to is the Secure Continuous Remote Alcohol Monitoring (SCRAM) device. The SCRAM device measures the amount of alcohol in a person's body through the skin. When alcohol is consumed, ethanol is excreted through perspiration. The device measures alcohol levels by testing the wearer's perspiration and transmitting the data to the monitoring system. This device monitors defendants and convicted offenders for alcohol consumption and sends alerts to community corrections officers when alcohol has been consumed. SCRAM devices are used as a sanction or condition of pretrial release for those who have been charged with or sentenced for driving under the influence or, sometimes, with domestic violence offenses. SCRAM devices help relieve jail crowding and allow clients to remain in the community, drive a car, and remain employed during the course of their sentence or pretrial release period.[65]

In many ways, technological devices may lull us into thinking that offenders are adjusting to their limited freedoms when they are still engaging in serious offenses. Therefore, these tools should be considered merely as supplements to face-to-face supervision rather than as replacements for the traditional probation or parole officer. As technology becomes more sophisticated, so will the methods used to supervise criminal offenders. It is already possible to implant a small transmitter under an offender's skin and use a satellite to track his or her movements.[66] This way, probation officers can tell whether the offender is at home, at work, or at a bar.

Joleen Valencia, who was held past her scheduled parole date while serving a drug-trafficking sentence, looks through her personal scrapbook at a residential re-entry program where she received treatment after her release from prison. New Mexico prison records show that the state has held hundreds of inmates like Valencia past their parole dates under a practice widely known as "in-house parole." Why can this program be called an intermediate sanction?

Fines

The use of fines has been a consistent feature of the U.S. criminal justice system. For some types of offenses, especially some economic offenses such as tax evasion or insider trading, fines are an appropriate sanction.[67] For other types of offenses, the public does not think offenders should be able to "buy" their way out of trouble. Fines are often used in conjunction with other types of sanctions, such as short periods of incarceration.[68]

Fines have several advantages as a criminal sanction. Fines used as an alternative to incarceration not only are less expensive to administer but bring extra money to the criminal justice system's budgets. In fact, many probation systems require their clients to pay cost-of-supervision fines as a condition of probation, thus offsetting a major portion of the expense.[69] Another advantage of fines is the message they send to the public that offenders sometimes do literally pay for their crimes. A large fine levied on a tax cheat or an unscrupulous businessperson gives the public a sense of justice.

The downside of using fines as a criminal sanction involves fairness. For impoverished people who can barely afford to support themselves or their families, adding fines to their sentences places hardship on them that wealthy offenders do not experience. For this reason, in addition to having fixed fines for certain offenses, some countries have instituted a "day fine" system in which the offender is fined in proportion to how much money he or she makes. The fine is based on how much the offender is paid for one day of work, which is then multiplied by the degree of punishment the court wants to administer. Consequently, someone who makes $100,000 a year would pay 10 times the fine of someone who makes $10,000 a year.

Although this fine system may be more equitable than a fixed-fine system, wealth still has its advantages. Someone who makes $10,000 a year has little discretionary money because every dime is used for rent, food, health care, and other necessities. However, offenders making $100,000 a year are more likely to be able to pay a percentage of their income without suffering as much as impoverished offenders.

Shock Probation

Shock probation—The practice of sentencing offenders to prison, allowing them to serve a short time, and then granting them probation without their prior knowledge.

An intermediate sanction that employs fear as a main feature is **shock probation**. In these programs, the probation officer and the judge play a confidence game on the offender. The offender receives a bogus sentence of jail or prison time, and then, after he or she has been incarcerated for 30 to 90 days, the judge converts the sentence to probation.[70] Because offenders think they are going to be imprisoned for a long time, the sudden release is presumed to encourage them to "turn over a new leaf" and start a new life of law-abiding behavior.

There is a certain common-sense appeal to shock probation, but on closer examination, it has some flaws that make it a better public relations tool than corrections program. Incarcerating offenders for 30 to 90 days ruptures any stability they have. They lose their jobs, drop out of school, and sever ties with significant social networks. However, on release after their short stay, they are expected to instantly pick up the pieces of their shattered lives. Shock probation programs may also make the courts look hypocritical and duplicitous and further alienate and label the offender. When used sparingly with carefully selected offenders, this sanction has some corrections value, but for most offenders, probation or a short, planned incarceration is a better option.

Intermediate sanctions include several ways to make sentencing options between probation and prison more effective, severe, and politically popular. These sanctions are driven by a high crime rate with few traditional alternatives, a desire on the part of well-intentioned people to provide more effective community corrections services, and simple economics. If used intelligently, intermediate sanctions provide useful alternatives to incarceration at a low cost and without endangering the community.

Intermediate sanctions, like diversion programs, are susceptible to compromise by the problem of net-widening.[71] Unless their use is monitored closely, intermediate sanctions can be diverted from their intended targets—those who require intense supervision—and used on petty offenders who would normally be released. On one hand, judges want to teach a lesson to vandals, small-time thieves, or first-time drunk drivers and place them in programs that get their attention. On the other hand, because these programs are evaluated constantly and must demonstrate successful **recidivism** rates, judges may select those who are the most likely to complete the sanction successfully. The result is that a greater proportion of citizens are brought under social control by the state, and scarce resources are frittered away on petty offenders instead of being directed at those who pose a genuine threat to society.

Recidivism—

Continuing to break the criminal law and returning to the criminal justice system after being processed for past offenses.

PAUSE AND REVIEW

1. How does intensive-supervision probation differ from regular probation?
2. What are some of the various forms of intermediate sanctions?

FOCUS ON ETHICS   Going Out on a Limb

As a probation officer, you are pretty tough with your clients. However, every once in a while, someone comes along whom you are willing to take a chance on. You have been burned a couple of times before by probationers who promised one thing and did the opposite, but this time you think you have a client who warrants your trust and help.

James is a college freshman and gifted athlete with NFL prospects. He is on scholarship but was implicated in a brawl at a concert where several people were brutally beaten and hospitalized. Although the degree of James's involvement is unclear, his lawyer arranged a plea bargain for probation, with the stipulation that the coach would allow James to remain on scholarship and play that season. Everyone, including you when you did the pre-sentence investigation, believed James was a worthwhile probation risk because of his bright future.

However, as James's probation officer, you suspect that he is developing an entitled attitude and believes that because he is a football star, he need not abide by the conditions of his probation or listen to you when you try to advise him. James is missing classes, not returning your phone calls, has had beer in his dormitory refrigerator even though he is not of drinking age, and violates the court-ordered curfew of midnight on weekends.

You have tried to correct the problem by contacting his coach and advising him of your concerns, but you are finding that the longer the football season goes on, the less anyone—James, his coaches, the judge, or your supervisor—cares about your complaints. Most of the issues are minor technical violations, but you have recently noticed a hostile attitude in James both on the field and off. Today, his girlfriend shows up at your office with a black eye and details about James's violent outbursts, gunplay, and steroids. This weekend is the big game against the cross-state rival, and everyone knows that James must do well for the team to win. However, you are afraid he might not make it to the weekend without hurting somebody unless you take action.

WHAT DO YOU DO?
1. Go to James's dorm room and have a face-to-face, heart-to-heart talk with him.
2. Go to the coach and threaten to get the judge to revoke James's probation before the game if he does not shape up.
3. Express your concerns to the judge and essentially place the issue in her lap, thereby covering yourself.
4. Say nothing until after the game and hope that once the pressure of football is off, James will behave in a more appropriate way.
5. Revoke James's probation. If he does not learn now that he is not above the law, then his behavior may only worsen and land him in real trouble.

For more insight into how someone might respond to such an ethical dilemma, visit Oxford Learning Link at www.oup.com/he/Fuller2e to watch a video that connects this scenario to a real-world situation.

Summary

LEARNING OBJECTIVE **12.1** Outline the assumptions about the nature of crime that lie at the heart of community corrections.	Prison is an artificial society. Conformity in prison is not always a good indicator of inmates' ability to adjust to the free world. The total control of the prison does little to prepare inmates to take responsibility for their actions. The community has resources that are unavailable in the prison, which enhance the likelihood of rehabilitation. The community can provide support networks to offenders that do not exist in prison. Offenders can contribute to the financial upkeep of their families and, if gainfully employed, pay taxes. The state spends less money on offenders in community corrections programs than it does incarcerating them. The state can accurately identify dangerous offenders who need secure incarceration and which offenders are safe to release into the community with supervision. The number of trained probation and parole officers is sufficient to adequately supervise offenders selected for community corrections programs.
LEARNING OBJECTIVE **12.2** Describe the connection between diversion programs and labeling theory.	Offenders can be diverted to alternative (diversion) programs based on labeling theory, which suggests that the more limited the offender's penetration into the criminal justice system, the less likely the offender will be to adopt a criminal self-concept and continue to break the law.
LEARNING OBJECTIVE **12.3** Discuss how various actors in the criminal justice system view probation.	Many offenders embrace probation because it allows them to remain at home, at work, and safe from the pains of imprisonment. The prosecutor, who has the discretion to fashion plea bargains, sees probation as a victory because it requires little time or resources and allows for efficient disposal of cases. The defense attorney views probation as a victory because the offender is kept out of prison and the offender's liberty is preserved with some reasonable compromises (the conditions of probation). Probation allows the judge to impose a sentence that is less expensive than prison and, to some degree, satisfies victims and the public in that the offender did not escape punishment. For criminal justice reformers, probation offers offenders a variety of treatment and community service activities. To politicians, probation is a cheaper way to punish than prison.
LEARNING OBJECTIVE **12.4** Characterize the three universal functions that define the probation officer's occupation.	1. Investigation: The probation officer gathers information for decision makers throughout the criminal justice system. The most time-consuming and significant report that the probation officer writes is the pre-sentence investigation, which assists a judge in sentencing. 2. Supervision: Each probation system has standard conditions that must be met. The probationer must cooperate with the probation officer and follow all lawful instructions. 3. Service: probation officers provide services to offenders who need help, such as finding a job, counseling, or substance abuse treatment.
LEARNING OBJECTIVE **12.5** Differentiate between probation and parole.	Probation is a sentencing option that allows offenders to be placed under community corrections supervision *instead* of going to prison. Parole is a form of early release that happens *after* the offender has served part of the prison sentence. (Probation instead, parole after.)

LEARNING OBJECTIVE **12.6** Summarize the major adjustments that stand as obstacles to successful reentry into society.	1. Prisonization: Life in prison is lived according to rigid rules established by both the administration and the inmate social system. Inmates are not allowed to make decisions, but on release, the magnitude of decisions to be made can be overwhelming. 2. Weakened social ties: The world that the inmate left behind is not the same as the one he or she returns to. Relationships have likely changed, and the inmate must re-establish these bonds. 3. Stigmatization: Imprisonment is a legal and social stigma that individuals must constantly fight to overcome. Legally, this may involve losing the right to vote, parent, hold public employment, serve on a jury, hold public office, or possess a firearm, and might mean registering as a felon. Socially, former inmates often face discrimination and prejudice.
LEARNING OBJECTIVE **12.7** Outline how intensive-supervision probation (ISP) is different from regular probation.	ISP clients have about four times as much contact with probation officers, more unannounced job-site or home visits, and stricter curfews. ISP clients are more likely to be required to participate in electronic home monitoring and random drug and/or alcohol testing, and to maintain full-time employment or vocational training, as well as have community-service requirements. ISP clients are also more likely to be brought before the court for technical violations. ISP officers' caseloads are lighter than those of regular probation officers.

Critical Reflections

1. **Which community resources should correctional agencies partner with in order to best supervise and help released offenders?**

2. **Why is it important to include the community in community corrections?**

3. **What criteria should be employed to determine which offenders are selected for community correctional programs and which should be/remain incarcerated?**

Key Terms

Notes

1 Brian Lawson, "Man Charged in Guntersville Murder Was Paroled in January Despite Life Sentence, DA's 2013 Warning," *WHNT NEWS*, July 27, 2018.

2 Ibid.

3 Ibid.

4 "Guntersville Murder Victims' Families Reach Settlement," *Reporter (Sand Mountain)*. May 24, 2019.

5 Josh Rayburn, "Alabama to Pay $1 Million to Families of Jimmy Spencer Murder Case Victims," *WAAY 31*, May 29, 2019.

6 Carol Robinson, "Why Was Jimmy Spencer Free to Brutally Kill 3 People, Victims' Group Asks." *AL.com*. August 1, 2018.

7 "Guntersville Murder Victims' Families Reach Settlement."

8 Laura M. Maruschak and Todd D. Minton, *Correctional Populations in the United States, 2017-2018*, (Washington, D.C.: U.S. Department of Justice Office of Justice Programs Bureau of Justice Statistics, 2018), 1-2. Available at www.bjs.gov/index.cfm?ty=pbdetail&iid=7026.

9 Belinda Rodgers McCarthy, Bernard J. McCarthy Jr., and Matthew C. Leone,

Community-Based Corrections, 4th ed. (Belmont, Calif.: Wadsworth, 2001).

10 Jane Browning, "Coming to Terms with Prison Growth," *Corrections Today* 69 (October 2007): 18–19.

11 John Irwin, *Prisons in Turmoil* (Boston: Little, Brown, 1980).

12 Francis T. Cullen and Karen E. Gilbert, *Reaffirming Rehabilitation* (Cincinnati, Ohio: Anderson, 1982).

13 Todd R. Clear and Harry R. Dammer, *The Offender in the Community* (Belmont, Calif.: Wadsworth, 2003), 226.

14 Thomas G. Blomberg, "Diversion and Social Control," *Journal of Criminal Law and Criminology* 68 (1977): 274–282.

15 Jeffrey Draine, Amy Blank Wilson, and Wendy Pogorzelski, "Limitations and Potential in Current Research on Services for People with Mental Illness in the Criminal Justice System," *Journal of Offender Rehabilitation* 45 (July 2007): 159–177.

16 Kristie A. Blevins, Francis T. Cullen, and Jody L. Sundt, "The Correctional Orientation of 'Child Savers': Support for Rehabilitation and Custody among Juvenile Correctional Workers," *Journal of Offender Rehabilitation* 45 (July 2007): 47–83.

17 James Austin and Barry Krisberg, "Wider, Stronger, and Different Nets: The Dialectics of Criminal Justice Reform," *Journal of Research in Crime and Delinquency* 18 (1981): 165–196.

18 Thomas G. Blomberg and Karol Lucken, "Stacking the Deck by Piling Up Sanctions: Is Intermediate Punishment Destined to Fail?" *Howard Journal of Criminal Justice* 33, no. 1 (1994): 62–80.

19 Kathy G. Padgett, William D. Bales, and Thomas G. Blomberg, "Under Surveillance: An Empirical Test of the Effectiveness and Consequences of Electronic Monitoring," *Criminology and Public Policy* 5 (February 2006): 61–91.

20 Danielle Kaeble, *Probation and Parole in the United States, 2017-2018* (Washington, D.C.: U.S. Department of Justice Office of Justice Programs Bureau of Justice Statistics, 2020), Table 1, p. 3

21 Heather Barklage, Dane Miller, and Gene Bonham, "Probation Conditions versus Probation Officer Directives: Where the Twain Shall Meet," *Federal Probation* 70, no. 3 (December 2006): 37–41.

22 Ricky N. Bluthenthal, Kara Riehman, Lisa H. Jaycox, and Andrew Morral, "Perspectives on Therapeutic Treatment from Adolescent Probationers," *Journal of Psychoactive Drugs* 38 (December 2006): 461–471.

23 Douglas Thomson, "How Plea Bargaining Shapes Intensive Probation Supervision," *Crime and Delinquency* 36 (1990): 146.

24 Dane C. Miller, Richard D. Sluder, and J. Dennis Laster, "Can Probation Be Revoked When Probationers Do Not Willfully Violate the Terms or Conditions of Probation?" *Federal Probation* 63, no. 1 (June 1999): 23.

25 John Rosecrance, "Maintaining the Myth of Individualized Justice: Probation, Pre-sentence Reports," *Justice Quarterly* 5 (1988): 235–236.

26 David Sudnow, "Normal Crimes: Sociological Features of the Penal Code in a Public Defender Office," *Social Problems* 12 (1965): 255–276.

27 Marilyn West, "A Few Words about Interviewing in Pre-sentence Investigations," in *Correctional Assessment, Casework, and Counseling*, 3d ed., ed. Anthony Walsh (Lanham, Md.: American Correctional Association).

28 Anthony Walsh, ed., *Correctional Assessment, Casework, and Counseling*, 3d ed. (Lanham, Md.: American Correctional Association), 106.

29 Anthony Walsh, "The Role of the Probation Officer in the Sentencing Process: Independent Professional or Judicial Hack?" *Criminal Justice and Behavior* 12 (1985): 289–303.

30 Fay Honey Knapp, "Northwest Treatment Associates: A Comprehensive Community-Based-Evaluation-and-Treatment Program for Adult Sex Offenders," in *Correctional Counseling and Treatment*, 4th ed., ed. Peter C. Kratcoski (Prospect Heights, Ill.: Waveland Press, 2000), 617–633.

31 Fay S. Taxman, "Dealing with Technical Violations," *Corrections Today* 57 (1995): 46–53.

32 Nancy Rodriguez and Vincent J. Webb, "Probation Violations, Revocations, and Imprisonment," *Criminal Justice Policy Review* 18 (March 2007): 3–30.

33 Jeffrey J. Shook and Rosemary C. Sarri, "Structured Decision Making in Juvenile Justice: Judges' and Probation Officers' Perceptions and Use," *Children and Youth Services Review* 29 (October 2007): 1335–1351.

34 Ibid.

35 R. V. Del Carmen and J. A. Pilant, "The Scope of Judicial Immunity for Probation and Parole Officers," *Perspectives* (American Probation and Parole Association) (Summer 1994): 14–21.

36 CNN, "Federal Report Blasts Probation Officers' Handling of Garrido Case," July 9, 2011.

37 Maria L. La Ganga and Shane Goldmacher, "Jaycee Lee Dugard's Family Will Receive $20 Million from California," *Los Angeles Times*, July 2, 2010.

38 Christine S. Schloss and Leanne F. Alarid, "Standards in the Privatization of Probation Services," *Criminal Justice Review* 32 (2007): 233–245.

39 Ibid.

40 Ibid.

41 Celia Perry, Justine Sharrock, and Michael Mechanic, "Probation for Profit," *Mother Jones* (July 2008): 57–58.

42 Ibid.

43 Clear and Dammer, *Offender in the Community*, 182–183.

44 Kaeble, *Probation and Parole in the United States, 2017-2018.*

45 Melinda D. Schlager and Kelly Robbins, "Does Parole Work?—Revisited: Reframing the Discussion of the Impact of Postprison Supervision on Offender Outcome," *Prison Journal* 88 (June 2008): 234–251.

46 Irwin, *Prisons in Turmoil.*

47 Catherine Cuellar, "Investing in Second Chances: An Innovative Program Helps Prison Inmates Make a Fresh Start—and a Business Plan," *Sojourners Magazine* 37 (July 2008): 20–24.

48 Robert C. Davis and Carrie Mulford, "Victim Rights and New Remedies: Finally Getting Victims Their Due," *Journal of Contemporary Criminal Justice* 24 (May 2008): 198–208.

49 Henry Gass, "Chicago Bee Farm Offers Help to Ex-inmates, and a Model for US," *Christian Science Monitor*, October 27, 2015. Parija Kavilanz, "This Chicago Business Trains Former Inmates to Be Beekeepers," *CNN*, May 30, 2019.

50 Jennifer Berry, "Letters from Behind Bars," *Bee Culture: The Magazine of American Beekeeping*, September 28, 2018.

51 Ibid.

52 Gee Atkinson, "Keeping Bees at Lee Correctional," *Bee Culture: The Magazine of American Beekeeping*, March 21, 2017.

53 Donald Clemmer, "The Prison Community," in *Correctional Contexts: Contemporary and Classical Readings*, 2d ed., eds. Edward J. Latessa et al. (Los Angeles: Roxbury, 2001), 83–87.

54 Clear and Dammer, *Offender in the Community*, 213–214.

55 Erving Goffman, *Stigma: Notes on the Management of Spoiled Identity* (Englewood Cliffs, N.J.: Prentice Hall, 1963), 4.

56 D. Stanley Eitzen and Maxine Baca Zinn, *Social Problems*, 6th ed. (Boston: Allyn & Bacon, 1992), 305.

57 Schlager and Robbins, "Does Parole Work?"

58 Norval Morris and Michael Tonry, *Between Prison and Probation: Intermediate Punishments in a Rational Sentencing System* (New York: Oxford University Press, 1990).

59 Joan Petersilia, "Conditions That Permit Intensive Supervision Programs to Survive," *Crime and Delinquency* 36 (1990): 126–145.

60 Joshua Cochran, Daniel Mears, and William Bales, "Assessing the Effectiveness of Correctional Sanctions," *Journal of Quantitative Criminology* 30, no. 2 (June 2014): 317–347.

61 Beau Kilmer, "Does Parolee Drug Testing Influence Employment and Education Outcomes? Evidence from a Randomized Experiment with Noncompliance," *Journal of Quantitative Criminology* 24 (March 2008): 93–123.

62 P. J. Hofer and B. S. Meierhoefer, *Home Confinement: An Evolving Sanction in the Federal Criminal Justice System* (Washington, D.C.: Federal Judicial Center, 1987).

63 Padgett, Bales, and Blomberg, "Under Surveillance."

64 A. K. Schmidt, "Electronic Monitors: Realistically, What Can Be Expected?" *Federal Probation* 55, no. 2 (1991): 47–53.

65 Secure Continuous Remote Alcohol Monitoring (SCRAM) Technology Evaluability Assessment, www.ncjrs. gov/pdffiles1/nij/secure-continuous-remote-alcohol.pdf. Accessed February 2020.

66 What Are Those Microchips That People Put in Their Dogs? Howstuffworks.com, animals. howstuffworks.com/pets/question690.htm. Accessed February 2020.

67 Diana Marszalek, "Jail and Fines Proposed for Theft of Recyclables," *New York Times*, May 25, 2008, p. 2.

68 Sally Hillsman, Barry Mahoney, George Cole, and Bernard Auchter, *Fines as Criminal Sanctions* (Washington, D.C.: National Institute of Justice, 1987).

69 Dale Parent, *Recovering Correctional Costs through Offender Fees* (Washington, D.C.: National Institute of Justice, 1990).

70 Clear and Dammer, *Offenders in the Community*, 255–256.

71 Dale K. Sechrest, "Prison 'Boot Camps' Do Not Measure Up," *Federal Probation* 53, no. 3 (1989): 15–20.

OXFORD
insight study guide
Active Engagement, Deeper Understanding

Learn more with this chapter's digital tools, including the Oxford Insight Study Guide, at www.oup.com/he/Fuller2e.

PART V

Contemporary Issues

A Tucson police officer takes a juvenile into custody. What types of youths enter the juvenile justice system?

> The juvenile justice system seeks to reduce the stigma of deviant behavior. By shielding the names of juveniles from the press, keeping hearings private, and allowing juvenile records to be purged, the juvenile justice system seeks to prevent youths from being labeled "bad kids."

> Having a separate juvenile justice system keeps juveniles apart from adult offenders who might abuse, exploit, or teach them negative behaviors and attitudes.

> By addressing the social, emotional, and educational needs of young offenders, the juvenile justice system seeks to help them gain the necessary skills to become productive members of society.

> The juvenile justice system protects young offenders from receiving the harsh punishments meted out by the criminal justice system.

Those who are dissatisfied with the juvenile justice system critique it for the following reasons:

> Youths who commit serious offenses are treated too leniently. A 17-year-old who commits murder or rape does as much harm to society as a 20-year-old who commits the same offense and arguably deserves to be punished as severely. Many people believe that youths can appreciate the consequences of their unlawful behavior and should be held accountable.

> There are great inconsistencies between the punishments meted out in the juvenile justice system and those meted out in the criminal justice system. For citizens to have confidence in law enforcement and the courts, punishments must be more uniform.

> Juvenile delinquents are not afforded all the due process rights that are available in the criminal justice system. Although the juvenile court is supposed to be working in the youth's best interests, some believe that certain cases are dealt with more harshly because the youth does not have the full protection of the legal rights granted to adults.

TABLE 13.2   Differences between the Adult and Juvenile Justice Systems

ISSUE	ADULT SYSTEM	JUVENILE SYSTEM
Status in Question	The defendant's guilt in breaking a law.	The child's delinquency in breaking a law or committing a status offense.
Searches	Protections exist against unreasonable searches of one's person, home, and possessions.	Protections against unreasonable searches are limited.
Self-Incrimination	Both children and adults are protected.	
Goal of Proceedings	The defendant is assumed innocent until proven guilty.	The best interests of the child, whether guilty or innocent, are paramount.
Nature of Proceedings	Adversarial	Remedial
Arrests	A warrant is required.	Children are not arrested but taken into custody via petition or complaint.
Representation	Both children and adults have the right to an attorney.	
Trials	Open to the public.	Closed hearings. The right to a jury trial does not exist (there are no trials).
Result upon Conviction or Finding of Delinquency	Convicted adults are punished with possible rehabilitation and/or treatment.	Children are protected and rehabilitated.
Treatment	No right to treatment.	Right to treatment.
Release	Via bail or release-on-recognizance (ROR).	Parental or guardian custody.
Public Records	The results of the trial and judgment remain on public record.	Records are sealed and may be destroyed once the child reaches a certain age.
Incarceration	Prison or jail.	Children are held or incarcerated in non-adult facilities.

Finally, juvenile justice cases exhibit many of the features of criminal cases; however, a different vocabulary is used to signify what happens at each stage. As we consider the processing of juvenile cases, we must be aware of these alternative terms (see Table 13.2). Because each state has its own structure and method of processing juvenile cases, the description of the system here will be general and simplified and will highlight common decision points and practices.

Who Enters the Juvenile Justice System?

The modern juvenile justice system is responsible for dealing with many issues affecting children's lives. Managing delinquent behavior is the most visible of these duties, but it is only part of the system's mission. The juvenile justice system is responsible for dealing with the following types of youths:

› Incorrigible youths. Some parents cannot control their children, particularly as they become teenagers and are lured by temptations outside the home. When children disobey their parents, refuse to go to school, leave home for days at a time, or physically abuse their parents and siblings, the court might remove them from their homes and find alternative living arrangements. Sometimes, parents give up on their children and ask the court to take them.

› Dependent youths. When children are abandoned or orphaned, the state becomes responsible for their welfare. Usually, the first option is to place the child with a relative, but if no suitable relative is available, the court will seek a foster home and oversee adoption requests.

› Neglected youths. Some parents are unconcerned, careless, or incapable of providing physical, emotional, and economic care for their children. The juvenile justice system must ensure that neglected children have adequate food, shelter, clothes, and schooling. Sometimes this means working with the parent(s) to monitor the family's living conditions, and sometimes it means moving the child from the home to a more suitable environment.

› Status offenders. Many behaviors are considered legitimate for adults but deviant for children. These are known as **status offenses**. For instance, because of mandatory education laws, children are required to attend school until the age of 16, 17, or 18, depending on the state, whereas there is no such requirement of adults. Underage drinking laws are another example of a status offense. Those under the age of 21 are subject to arrest for consuming alcohol, whereas adults are free to drink as much alcohol as they want as long as they do not violate other laws, such as being drunk in public or driving an automobile while intoxicated. Running away from home, violating curfew, and breaking other age-determined laws make juveniles subject to a range of restrictions that do not affect adults.

› Delinquent youths. Children must obey all the laws that apply to adults, with limited exceptions (for instance, a 15-year-old and a 14-year-old who have sex are treated differently from a 25-year-old who has sex with a 14-year-old). Upon breaking the law, children enter the juvenile justice system, just as adults enter the criminal justice system. However, what happens to youths, once taken into custody, can be quite different. In serious situations, a youth's case might be transferred to adult court (this will be discussed in greater detail later in this chapter).

Although we use multiple methods of assessing crime, such as self-report studies, victimization studies, and official statistics, the actual amount of crime can never be definitively measured. Much crime goes unreported, and a substantial amount of it can never be attributed to any individual or group. When dealing with juvenile delinquency, this inability to accurately comprehend the reality of the crime problem is even more acute. In addition to the many general reasons why people do not report crime, there are other reasons why much juvenile delinquency never finds its way into official statistics or reports, including the following:

› Adults are unaware of the offense. Violence between youths is often unknown to adults who have the ability or desire to report it. Young people might get in a fight after school, and even though the combatants return home bloodied and bruised, they may not tell their parents or guardians the reason. Youths often do not define these conflicts as crime, and they may have good reasons not to make their parents or guardians aware of the problem. Youths who picked the fight may expect little or no sympathy. Consequently, many such activities go unreported.

Status offense—An act that is considered a legal offense only when committed by a juvenile and that can be adjudicated only in a juvenile court.

> Some delinquency and status offending is consensual. Alcohol use, drug use, and sexual activity are all behaviors that would be included in the juvenile delinquency and status-offending picture if they were reported. However, because juveniles often enter into these activities freely, there is little incentive, and great disincentive, to make parents, teachers, or police aware of these transgressions.

> Status offenses are difficult to identify. It is difficult to define exactly when some behaviors become status offenses. For instance, if a 14-year-old runs away from home and is gone for two weeks but reconciles with his or her parents, should this count as running away? At what point does disobeying one's parents become incorrigibility? Additionally, schools have a great deal of discretion, and many have policies that allow them to work with students to keep them attending school before declaring them truant. For this reason, one school district's policy might result in more truancy being recorded than another school district's, although the behavior patterns are similar.

> Adults choose not to report. Adults do not report many minor transgressions by youths because they do not want young people to be subject to the juvenile justice system. To prevent the label or stigma of juvenile delinquency, teachers and police officers often give stern warnings for minor misbehavior in the hope that they were simply youthful transgressions and not indicative of a pattern. According to **labeling theory**, it is often deemed wise to overlook and minimize the deviant behavior of young people so that they are not officially labeled as delinquent and, furthermore, do not think of themselves that way. The idea is to prevent a negative label from becoming a self-fulfilling prophecy.

Labeling theory (from Chapter 12)—A perspective that considers recidivism to be a consequence, in part, of the negative labels applied to offenders.

These reasons explaining why much juvenile delinquency and status offending is not reported should not blind us to the fact that a great deal of it is reported and that it is a substantial problem. Efforts to measure juvenile delinquency have become more sophisticated, and because these measures show some stability in levels and trends, we can make approximations about the seriousness of juvenile delinquency. According to the Uniform Crime Reports, 35,253 people under age 18 were arrested for violent offenses in 2019. Most of these arrests were for aggravated assault, followed by robbery. Relatively few arrests were for murders/non-negligent manslaughter. Most juveniles were arrested for property offenses, with 87,710 arrests. By far, the most common property offense was larceny-theft (see Figure 13.1).[12]

Referral—Similar to a "charge" in the adult system in which an authority, usually the police, parents, or the school, determines that a youth needs intervention from the juvenile court.

We must remember that these figures represent only known offenses and not the actual level of juvenile delinquency. Still, they are useful figures because they give some indication as to the volume of cases the juvenile justice system must handle.

Entering the System

Cases enter the juvenile justice system by a process called **referral**, in which an authority determines that a youth needs intervention from the juvenile court. There are two types of referrals. The first type can come from schools, parents, or child welfare agencies that believe the child is at risk from others, as in cases of child abuse or delinquency. A parent may turn the child over to the juvenile court

This sign is posted on a door at a Philadelphia juvenile holding facility. Are juvenile offenders as dangerous as adults?

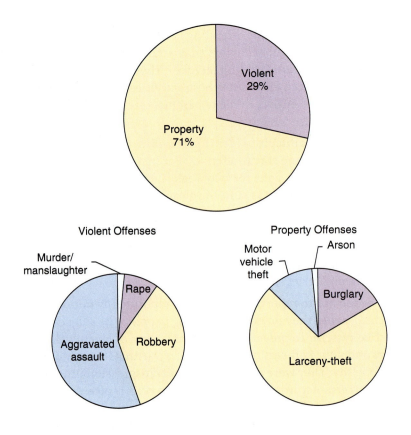

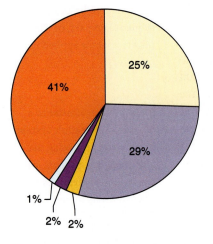

- ☐ Handled within department and released
- ■ Referred to other police agency
- ☐ Referred to welfare agency
- ■ Referred to juvenile court jurisdiction
- ■ Referred to criminal or adult court
- ■ Referred to other authorities

FIGURE 13.2 Police Disposition of Juveniles Taken into Custody What happens to most juveniles taken into custody?

Source: Federal Bureau of Investigation, Uniform Crime Reports: Crime in the United States, 2019, *Table 68, ucr.fbi.gov/crime-in-the-u.s/2019/crime-in-the-u.s.-2019/topic-pages/tables/table-68.*

because he or she cannot provide an adequate home or because the child is incorrigible. A child welfare agency may turn the child over to the court if both parents are incarcerated and no relative is available to care for the youth.

The second type of referral comes from law enforcement. This type of referral is the functional equivalent of an arrest. Depending on the youth's age and the seriousness of the delinquency, the youth's treatment can closely resemble the arrest of an adult, although the process is often different. Based on the philosophy of doing what is best for youths, many large police departments have specialized juvenile units that are familiar with the community resources available to treat youths. As many as one-third of juvenile cases handled by law enforcement are diverted from the juvenile justice system, and the youths are either released or funneled into alternative programs.[13] Of the two types of referrals, the law enforcement referral is the most common by a large margin. For a look at what happens to juveniles taken into police custody, see Figure 13.2.[14]

PRE-HEARING DETENTION

When the police take a youth into custody, they may detain the youth for several hours at the police station in order to obtain general information. During this time, the police may decide to either release or take the youth to a shelter or detention facility until a decision about the case has been made. The rules concerning keeping youths in detention differ from state to state, but the following is typical.

Depending on the jurisdiction, the youth's age determines where he or she is held. For example, for youths under age 12, the jurisdiction may require a judge's decision as to whether the youth may be placed in detention. Youths older than age 12 may be held in detention for up to 36 hours without a court hearing. Law enforcement agencies are discouraged from holding juveniles in adult jails while the case is processed. Federal regulations require that youths be held no longer than six hours in adult jails and that they be kept out of sight and sound of adult inmates. After six hours, youths must be transferred to a juvenile agency that can provide secure detention. Some jurisdictions do not allow particularly young juveniles, such as those under age 15, to be held in adult jails at all.

The rules that determine the pre-hearing treatment of youths differ from state to state. Typical requirements for pre-hearing detention are:

> the youth is accused of an offense against a person;

> an alleged victim requires protection from the youth;

> the youth is believed unlikely to show up for the hearing or will commit another offense upon release;

> the youth is on probation, parole, or release from another charge; or the youth has run away from a court-ordered placement.

For youths in detention, there is usually a time limit, for example, 36 hours from the time of arrest, in which probable cause must be found that the youth committed an offense.

INTAKE

The intake function is a major decision point in the juvenile justice system. An intake officer, who is responsible to the juvenile probation department and/or the juvenile court judge, reviews the case to determine whether evidence is sufficient to prove the allegation against the youth. This review is often in the form of a preliminary hearing in which the youth and his or her parent(s) or guardian(s) are questioned about the youth's understanding of the offending behavior and the willingness and ability of the parent(s) or guardian(s) to correct that behavior. The youth might be released at this point if the evidence is weak; however, the burden of proof is low.[15] Consequently, a finding by the intake officer that sufficient reason exists to move the case forward is enough to keep the case in court.

The intake officer, in conjunction with the probation department, may establish an informal way of handling the case that, if successfully completed, could allow the youth to escape formal processing and the resultant paper trail of legal transgressions.[16] A **consent decree** may be written at this point, in which the youth agrees to some conditions for a specified period of time. These conditions might include restitution to a victim, drug or alcohol counseling, attendance at school, or maintenance of a curfew. Once the youth successfully completes the conditions, the case is dismissed. Because the probation department often monitors these conditions, this procedure is often called **informal probation**. This type of processing allows the case to be diverted from the system without formal charges being filed. If the youth fails to comply with the conditions, the case goes back into the system.[17]

DIVERSION

Diversion, a reform that took root in the 1960s and 1970s, is the effort to deinstitutionalize delinquent and neglected children. Today, rather than incarcerate youths in prison-like reform or training schools, some jurisdictions utilize community correctional practices such as foster homes, halfway houses, and

Consent decree— When the parties to a lawsuit accept a judge's order that is based on an agreement made by them instead of continuing the case through a trial or hearing.

Informal probation— A period during which a juvenile is required to stay out of trouble or make restitution before a case is dropped.

Diversion— The effort to deinstitutionalize delinquent and neglected children.

extended probation-like supervision.[18] By referring youths to programs that address their educational, counseling, and drug treatment needs, diversion seeks to avoid contact between casual offenders and more seriously troubled young people. Jurisdictions use various terms to refer to diversion, including informal processing, adjustment, supervision, proceeding, probation adjustment, deferred prosecution, civil citation, or consent decree.[19] Depending on the jurisdiction, diversion programs may be operated by one or all of the following agencies: law enforcement, the county juvenile probation office, the prosecutor's office, the court, a community-based service agency, public mental health agencies, and private organizations.[20]

Probation is a common method used to divert status offenders or first-time juvenile delinquents from the juvenile court. Some communities use probation to informally monitor at-risk youth and prevent more serious problem behavior.[21] Diversion may also occur at the detention stage or at any of the following pre-adjudication points:

> arrest or apprehension: when law enforcement has contact with a youth;
> intake: when a youth is delivered to an office such as a police department or pretrial detention center that is authorized to book the case;
> petitioning: when the court begins the process leading to adjudication;
> pretrial probation contact: when a court or probation officer interviews a youth and family during the course of formal processing.[22]

Jurisdictions that use diversion programs typically aspire to five major goals:

1. reduce recidivism;
2. avoid labeling;
3. reduce unnecessary social control;
4. provide services; and
5. reduce costs.[23]

Chrystal Carreras stands in front of the Lane County Juvenile Justice Center in Eugene, Oregon. She was one of the first people to graduate from its juvenile drug court. What are the goals of juvenile diversion programs?

Deana Ramsey, principal of the Philadelphia Juvenile Justice Center, speaks about the art that the students have contributed to the school. The school is located inside the city's juvenile detention center, a place where pencils are counted at the end of the day to make sure none have been hidden for potential use as a weapon. What are the benefits of diversion programs?

The goal of reducing recidivism is a typical measure of a program's effectiveness. The goal of avoiding labeling, based on labeling theory, is to prevent young offenders from thinking of themselves as criminals by immersing them in conventional schools, activities, and close contact with their families.[24] The goal of reducing unnecessary social control is to keep youths out of the juvenile justice system, although diversion sometimes has the opposite effect (see the following discussion on net-widening). Diversion programs try to provide services, such as drug treatment or job training, which may not be available in an incarceration environment. By achieving the four prior goals, it is hoped that the fifth, a reduction of costs, will be achieved.

A criticism of diversion is that it is sometimes self-defeating in terms of keeping youths out of the juvenile justice system. Some diversion programs actually pull more youths into the juvenile justice system than would otherwise be involved, a phenomenon called **net-widening** (also discussed in Chapter 12). For example, a correctly functioning diversion program would extract 300 of 1,000 youths processed into the system and divert them to foster homes, rehabilitation programs, and other therapeutic alternatives, such as ranches and camps (discussed later in the chapter). However, a program engaged in net-widening would draw in 300 youths in addition to the 1,000 who are already being processed. Under normal circumstances, these 300 youths might not enter the juvenile justice system at all: their cases would be dropped, and they would be released into the custody of their parents or guardians.[25] In some cases, the youths would only receive a lecture from the police.

Some research indicates that net-widening is pervasive. Many programs, instead of serving the intended non-violent, first-time delinquents who are at risk of more serious delinquency, instead target low-risk youths who would probably be better off not participating in the program at all.

Net-widening (from Chapter 12)—A phenomenon through which criminal justice programs pull more clients into the system than would otherwise be involved without the program.

DETERMINING JURISDICTION

Once an intake officer decides that a case should be processed through the juvenile justice system and not diverted, it is determined whether the case will remain in the juvenile court or be transferred to criminal court. The states have various mechanisms for making this decision (see the Juvenile Waiver section later in this chapter). The prosecutor may file the case in criminal court, or the intake officer may file a petition waiver to transfer the case.[26] The decision is based on two factors: the seriousness of the delinquency and the history and demeanor of the juvenile. Only serious offenses, such as homicide, are bound over (transferred) to criminal court.[27] Most cases involving youths remain under the juvenile court's jurisdiction. If the youth has been before the court many times and has disregarded the authority of the judge and probation staff, waiver to criminal court may be deemed an appropriate way to handle the case. If the youth is not amenable to treatment and continues to break the law while under juvenile court supervision, the prosecutor may decide to kick the case up to criminal court where the protection of society is considered as important as the youth's welfare.[28]

For those who commit minor offenses, a different type of jurisdictional alternative is available in many juvenile justice systems. Teen courts are used to handle non-violent juvenile offenders in the context of having their peers consider their case. In a teen court, the judge, jury, prosecutor, and defense attorney are all other teens who consider the case and pass judgment. It is thought that in the teen court context peer pressure can be used to resolve the case.[29]

ADJUDICATORY HEARING

Within a specified period (this varies by state), an **adjudicatory hearing** is held to determine whether the youth committed the delinquent acts as charged. This hearing is the equivalent of a criminal trial, but it has some important differences. First, the juvenile hearing is a quasi-civil proceeding (not criminal) and therefore may be confidential. Only official and interested parties are allowed in the court. The facts of the case and, most important, the names of juvenile delinquents and victims may be kept from the media. Second, the adjudicatory hearing is conducted by a judge who also acts as the jury. Third, the youth, if guilty, will be adjudicated delinquent, shifting the focus of the case from the delinquent act to the youth's rehabilitation.

Although not an **adversarial process,** the adjudicatory hearing has many of the aspects of a trial. Because of the legal reforms of the 1960s and 1970s, juvenile delinquents enjoy many of the rights afforded adults in the criminal court, including the right to an attorney, the right to confront and cross-examine hostile witnesses, the right to present defense witnesses, and protection against self-incrimination. Furthermore, the standard of proof in an adjudicatory hearing is set at the highest standard: beyond a reasonable doubt. Although youths have the right to an attorney, the youth or his or her parents can waive this right. This makes for a somewhat confusing situation. Attorneys are supposed to exercise independent professional judgment on behalf of their clients, but sometimes the juvenile's best interests conflict with the wishes of the parents, who pay the attorney's fee. At the end of the day, the juvenile's welfare must be balanced with his or her legal rights when the case is processed.

Additionally, the juvenile system has its own terminology, further setting it apart from the adult system. In the adjudicatory hearing (trial), the **petitioner** (prosecutor) will attempt to prove the youth delinquent and in need of **commitment** (incarceration), whereas the **respondent** (defense attorney) challenges the facts of the case.

An interesting controversy surrounding adjudicatory hearings is that in some jurisdictions, juveniles who have been in detention prior to their hearing are brought into court in shackles.[30] Usually, these shackles consist of wrist and ankle

---

Adjudicatory hearing—The process in which a juvenile court determines whether the allegations in a petition are supported by evidence.

Adversarial process (from Chapter 7)—A term describing the manner in which U.S. criminal trial courts operate; a system that requires two sides, a prosecution and a defense.

Petitioner—A person who files a lawsuit; also called a plaintiff.

Commitment—An order by a judge upon conviction or before a trial that sends a person to jail or prison. Also, a judge's order that sends a mentally unstable person to a mental institution.

Respondent—The party who must reply to a petitioner's complaint. Equivalent to a defendant in a lawsuit.

restraints chained at the waist. Many states and jurisdictions have stopped using shackles except in cases in which the youth presents a security risk.[31] One reason for discontinuing the practice is related to labeling theory, which asserts that if a youth is treated like a criminal, then he or she may begin to identify as such and retreat more deeply into a criminal lifestyle.

DISPOSITION

The disposition of the juvenile case is comparable to the handing down of the sentence in criminal court. The disposition can take two paths: **residential placement** (confinement) in a secure facility or referral to probation or a similar non-residential program. (For an example of an unusual disposition, see Getting It Right 13.1.)

As a rule, residential placement is reserved for those adjudicated for the most serious offenses. Residential placement sometimes means being placed in a community halfway house or a foster home. However, residential placement often means the juvenile is sent to a training or reform school that is little different from a prison. Although the youth is confined with other youths, residential placement can, in many ways, be compared to "hard time" in an adult institution.

In some cases, youths can be sentenced to adult facilities in which relatively young adults are confined. Some youths are so advanced in antisocial lifestyles that officials believe that keeping them in juvenile institutions would not provide the proper security and the youths might negatively influence other young offenders.

Some dispositions for juveniles result in sentences in adult prisons. This typically occurs when the juvenile is tried as an adult and thus receives an "adult" sentence. The youths in such cases are usually accused of heinous offenses, which often involve homicide. Until recently, adults who had committed their offenses as youths could be executed, and many states mandated life-without-parole sentencing for juveniles convicted of certain offenses. This is no longer the case, although juveniles may still be tried as adults and serve prison sentences.

A disposition of juvenile probation can be linked to a set of conditions that requires the youth to participate in treatment programs, additional schooling,

Residential placement—Any sentence of a juvenile delinquent to a residential facility where the juvenile is closely monitored.

Boys sit in assigned seats while waiting to go to the gym at the Lucas County Juvenile Detention Center in Toledo, Ohio. What are some of the defining characteristics of residential placement?

GETTING IT RIGHT 13.1
Reading as Punishment

In September 2016, in Loudoun County, Virginia, a boarded-up 19th-century building was spray-painted with graffiti, including the phrases "white power" and "brown power," swastikas, genitalia, and dinosaurs. The building, which students at Loudoun School for the Gifted had raised money to renovate, was the Ashburn Colored School, which had been used during segregation to educate black children.[32]

To Deputy Commonwealth Attorney Alejandra Rueda, the graffiti did not look like the work of white nationalists. Instead, she suspected that the culprits were juveniles. She was right: five males ages 16 and 17, three of whom were minorities, eventually pleaded guilty to the vandalism charges.[33]

Typically, the sentences for this type of vandalism ranged anywhere from probation to community service to incarceration in a juvenile detention facility. However, Rueda had a different sentence in mind. This was the first time any of the teens had been in trouble with the law. She convinced the judge that in lieu of traditional punishment, the teens should be required to read. She provided a list of 35 books, many of which highlight efforts to overcome prejudices and discrimination. The teens were ordered to pick 12, read one a month, and write a book report on each. They also had to write a 3,500-word essay on racial hatred and symbols. Finally, they were required to visit the United States Holocaust Memorial Museum and the National Museum of American History's exhibit on Japanese Americans and internment camps.

Although after two years none of the teens had broken the law again, the sentence was not without controversy. Members of the black community argued that black children would not have received such a lenient sentence. Rueda defended the decision, saying, "Some kids have to be in detention because they are dangerous to society or to themselves, but ... detention can be very traumatic, and that is not the purpose of the criminal justice system when it comes to children."[34]

Here is Rueda's list of 35 books.[35]

The Color Purple, Alice Walker
Native Son, Richard Wright
Exodus, Leon Uris
Mila 18, Leon Uris
Trinity, Leon Uris
My Name is Asher Lev, Chaim Potok
The Chosen, Chaim Potok
The Sun Also Rises, Ernest Hemingway
Night, Elie Wiesel
The Crucible, Arthur Miller
The Kite Runner, Khaled Hosseini
A Thousand Splendid Suns, Khaled Hosseini
Things Falls Apart, Chinua Achebe
The Handmaid's Tale, Margaret Atwood
To Kill a Mockingbird, Harper Lee
I Know Why the Caged Bird Sings, Maya Angelou
The Immortal Life of Henrietta Lacks, Rebecca Skloot
Caleb's Crossing, Geraldine Brooks
Tortilla Curtain, T. C. Boyle
The Bluest Eye, Toni Morrison
A Hope in the Unseen, Ron Suskind
Down These Mean Streets, Piri Thomas
Black Boy, Richard Wright
The Beautiful Struggle, Ta-Nehisi Coates
The Banality of Evil, Hannah Arendt
The Underground Railroad, Colson Whitehead
Reading Lolita in Tehran, Azar Nafisi
The Rape of Nanking, Iris Chang
Infidel, Ayaan Hirsi Ali
The Orphan Master's Son, Adam Johnson
The Help, Kathryn Stockett
Cry, the Beloved Country, Alan Paton
Too Late the Phalarope, Alan Paton
A Dry White Season, André Brink
Ghost Soldiers, Hampton Sides

THINK ABOUT IT

1. If you received this disposition, would you consider it punishment? What if this disposition was given to someone who vandalized something that was important to you?

2. Have you read any of the books from Rueda's list?

Watch the related video on Oxford Learning Link at www.oup.com/he/Fuller2e.

or public service activities.[36] Again, the philosophy of the juvenile justice system is geared toward rehabilitation, but by forcing the youth to engage in multiple activities, he or she may not be able to distinguish between rehabilitation and punishment.[37]

Michelle Carter leaves jail after serving most of a 15-month manslaughter sentence for urging her suicidal boyfriend to kill himself. Carter, who was 17 at the time of her offense, will serve five years of probation. Should Cater have been tried as an adult?

AFTERCARE

To ease the youth's transition from residential treatment back into the community, the court may order some type of aftercare. This can be thought of as similar to the parole function in the criminal court. Aftercare may consist of programs designed to address the youth's problems, including drug or alcohol treatment, counseling, regular school attendance, or employment. The key to aftercare programs is the court's ability to ensure the offender's accountability. If the youth fails to complete the aftercare requirements, another period of confinement may be in store.[38]

Figure 13.3 shows that juveniles can be diverted from the system at many points. However, this does not mean that they are not under some type of control. Cases are held in abeyance (suspended) until youths successfully complete diversion programs or other court requirements. Sometimes this is as easy as not

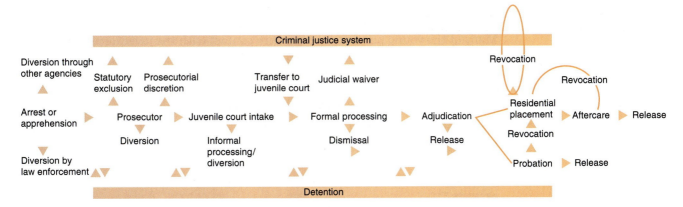

FIGURE 13.3   Juvenile Justice System Case Flow At what point does diversion occur? At what point does revocation occur?

Source: Office of Juvenile Justice and Delinquency Prevention, Statistical Briefing Book Case Flow Diagram (Washington, D.C.: U.S. Department of Justice), http://www.ojjdp.gov/ojstatbb/structure_process/case.html. Accessed November 2020.

getting into trouble for one year. If the court's orders are completed, the case is dismissed, but if the youth violates the law or ignores the directives of the diversion program, he or she will again face a judge who may order more draconian forms of control.

PAUSE AND REVIEW

1. **What are the benefits and critiques of the modern juvenile justice system?**
2. **What types of youths are the juvenile justice system responsible for?**
3. **Why are authorities unable to accurately assess the reality of juvenile delinquency?**
4. **What are the stages of the juvenile justice system?**
5. **What are the major goals of diversion programs, and how does net-widening affect such goals?**

LEARNING OBJECTIVE 13.4

Discuss why belonging to a youth gang is a predictor of chronic delinquency.

LEARNING OBJECTIVE 13.5

Classify the types of public facilities in which youths may be incarcerated.

LEARNING OBJECTIVE 13.6

Defend and criticize the process of waiver to criminal court.

13.2 Issues in Juvenile Justice

Despite the good intentions and concerns of those working in the juvenile justice system, some issues have not been resolved in ways that make youths more controllable or society any safer. In some ways, the juvenile justice system and our society in general have not addressed delinquency comprehensively and effectively. All the institutions that deal with children are partially responsible for this failure. The juvenile justice system is the institution of last resort; therefore, it looks more ineffective than the school, family, or community. If those other institutions were fulfilling their missions more completely, however, there might be fewer delinquent children.

Any real reform of the juvenile justice system must be linked to the way these other institutions interact with law enforcement, the juvenile court, and treatment programs. To a large extent, the solution to effective reform is better funding, but other issues may be more politically feasible than raising taxes and allocating more funds to schools, recreational programs, treatment alternatives, or increasing the number of police officers. To reform the juvenile justice system, the following issues should receive greater scrutiny and consideration.

Chronic Offenders

Many of the young people who come into contact with the juvenile justice system are testing the boundaries of appropriate behavior and seeking to establish their identities. This "kids-will-be-kids" behavior is not what concerns us most because children typically outgrow it.

A small percentage of youth, however, are long-term, chronic, and consistent law violators.[39] According to one landmark study, less than 7 percent of the juvenile population was responsible for 52 percent of all delinquent offenses. Out of a total sample of 10,000 boys, 627 accounted for 71 percent of the homicides, 73 percent of the rapes, 82 percent of the robberies, and 69 percent of the aggravated assaults.[40]

Other findings suggest that going to juvenile court does little to deter youths from further delinquency.[41] Because research has shown that such youths share several factors such as behavior problems, poor grades, drug or alcohol use, family problems (such as criminal parents), abuse or neglect, and patterns of stealing or running away, the solution to chronic delinquency is necessarily complex, broad-based, and expensive.

Gangs

One predictor of chronic delinquency is belonging to a youth gang. The influence of gang ideas is prevalent in popular music, television dramas, and movies, and youths often adopt the style of gangs in clothing, tattoos, and use of gang signs. Graffiti in cities and towns of all sizes throughout the country suggest some level of gang influence.[42]

Regardless of the perceived growth and diffusion of youth gangs, they remain a particular problem in the largest cities, where there are contested neighborhoods, a critical mass of disenfranchised youth, and a long history and tradition of gang activity. For example, in 2016, large metropolitan areas, including Boston and Washington, D.C., dealt with renewed violence from members of Mara Salvatrucha (or MS-13), a Central American gang with roots in Los Angeles, California.[43] Police say the gang has been trying to re-establish itself in the Boston area by recruiting youths in schools, on sports fields, and on playgrounds. To acquire money, MS-13 members typically extort businesses, distribute drugs, and commit robberies.[44] Although large, traditional gangs remain a problem, in some areas small, local gangs cause the most trouble. For instance, in Augusta, Georgia, police officials say that the local gangs are more likely to be violent than the gangs affiliated with traditional, nationwide gangs like the Bloods or Crips because those gangs have more structure and control over their member gangs.[45]

Because there are so many types of youth gangs, it is difficult to construct a general definition other than that they engage in criminal or delinquent activity.[46] Youth gangs are often focused on drug distribution, turf protection, robbery, extortion, or any number of other illegal activities. Many youth gangs are connected to larger, national gangs or gang alliances such as the Folk Nation and the People Nation, which also have adult members. At their most extreme, youth gangs are highly organized, have members who remain active well into their adult years, are connected with prison gangs, and have hundreds of members.

A police officer encourages graduates of the G. R. E. A. T. (Gang Resistance Education and Training) program at the Gilpin Montessori School in Denver, Colorado. Why is belonging to a gang a predictor of chronic delinquency?

Race and ethnicity are another dimension of many gangs.[47] California has Hispanic gangs, black gangs, Asian gangs, and white gangs. This list is misleading, however, because the number and types of gangs can be subdivided in any number of ways. For instance, Asian gangs can be subdivided into Filipino, Chinese, Indochinese (Vietnamese, Cambodian, Laotian, Thai, and Hmong), Korean, Japanese, and Pacific Islander (Samoan, Fijian, Guamanian, and Hawaiian) gangs. There is a constantly shifting loyalty among gangs; sometimes certain ethnic groups will oppose each other one month and then merge to confront another group the following month. The police have established gang units and have recruited officers from many of the nationalities that contribute to the U.S. gang problem.[48]

Race and ethnicity have been shown to be significant factors in how the juvenile justice system deals with youths. Research has shown that white youths consistently receive more lenient treatment from the juvenile justice system.[49] This bias is also evident when dealing with female delinquents.[50]

Although we typically think of the gang problem as being a male issue, research shows that young women are also active in gangs. Previously, female gang activity was thought to be supportive of male gangs, but today, full-fledged female gangs provide many of the functions for their members that make gangs so attractive to males. From a feminist point of view, the social liberation of women and girls has enabled them to become more actively engaged in gang and criminal pursuits.[51] However, we should not make too much of this liberation hypothesis. The opportunity that young women have to form their own gangs does not reflect a greater freedom of choice.

Often, girls and young women are forced to enter gang life to protect themselves in a community that has lost (or never had) social viability. Female gang activity is not a step forward for young women but rather an unintended consequence of so many young men going to training schools and prisons and leaving a void in the drug markets and power relationships on the street. As young women move to fill this void by engaging in gang activity, they are in danger not only of being further victimized by males, but also of victimizing each other and exposing themselves to the juvenile justice system.

Although youth gangs have engaged in crime for a long time, the effect of the drug culture since the 1970s has radically changed the nature of many gangs and greatly increased the amount of lethal behavior associated with gang activity. To some extent, lucrative drug sales have replaced the expressive gang activities of fighting, graffiti, and turf protection. Given the amount of money involved in the drug trade, neighborhood gangs are driven to act more like criminal organizations.[52]

Large, well-established gangs that require adults to run their major vice operations rely on youths to fuel their memberships. Most people who join gangs do so between the ages of 11 and 15, with 15 being the most commonly reported age of gang members. It is also important to understand that most youths leave the gang after a year and that longer tenures in a gang are not as common as may be believed. This is one reason that gangs recruit youths so actively: most will eventually drift away from the gang, leaving relatively few adults to take care of business.[53] However, even if youths do drop out of the gang, the effects of gang membership may be permanent. Compared to youths who never joined a gang, adults who joined a gang during adolescence had poorer outcomes during their adult lives, including higher rates of crime, incarceration, drug abuse, and poor health, as well as lower rates of high school graduation.[54]

According to a La Crosse, Wisconsin, police officer who works with youths on gang prevention, peer perception is an important part of educating young people about gangs. In an interview, the officer stated that youths think that up to half of the students in their classes are gang members, but that nationally only about 7 percent of youths are gang members. When youths learn that gang members are actually a minority and that not "all their friends are doing it," it affects their decisions about joining a gang.[55]

Another view of what makes gangs attractive to some youths comes from Father Gregory Boyle, a Jesuit priest in Los Angeles who runs Homeboy Industries, the largest gang intervention, rehabilitation, and re-entry program in the United States. According to Boyle, "Three types of youths become gang members. One is the kid stuck in despair so bleak that his future doesn't compel him; the second is in so much pain—so damaged that he can't transform his pain so he transmits it; and the third is a mentally ill kid. I've never met a hopeful kid who joined a gang."[56] Boyle advocates providing a sense of hope for young gang members, as well as providing mental health care.

Types and Conditions of Youth Confinement

The types of institutions available for juvenile delinquents vary widely across the United States. However, even when a state has many sentencing options, crowding often means there is no room in the most appropriate type of confinement. As of 2017, more than 40,000 juveniles were committed to some form of incarceration.[57] Juveniles who are convicted in criminal court typically remain in juvenile facilities until they reach their state's age of adulthood, usually between 18 and 21, and then are moved to adult facilities. Generally, three main types of facilities are available in many states.

> Adult prisons. Some young offenders convicted of serious offenses may be kept in adult prisons because of security risks and the harm they may do to other youths. Juveniles are kept separate from adult inmates but are often placed in the most restrictive confinement possible. For many of these dangerous delinquents, this means protective custody in what amounts to solitary confinement.

> Ranches and camps. Ranches and forestry camps enable juvenile delinquents to work outside on public lands. The intent is to provide positive work experiences so that youths can find gainful employment when released. Additionally, by being away from the temptations of urban life and the confines of a training school, the more normal summer camp-like experience of these types of detention is thought to be less stigmatizing and harmful to the youth's self-concept.[58]

> Traditional training schools. These often crowded and understaffed programs are where more serious delinquents are incarcerated for longer periods of time. Some training schools physically resemble adult prisons; others have the appearance of a college campus.[59] Training schools are usually state facilities.[60]

In addition to these types of public institutions are many public and private residential treatment facilities, with juveniles in their mid- to late teens making up most of these placements (see Figure 13.4). Private facilities hold fewer than half as many delinquents as public facilities but more status offenders.[61] These programs offer an alternative to traditional confinement. Although private programs can be expensive, some offer exceptional counseling.

A teenager accused of killing a staff member and injuring another worker at the Turn-About Ranch in Escalante, Utah, carried out the attacks because he wanted to leave. What are the three types of youth confinement institutions in the United States?

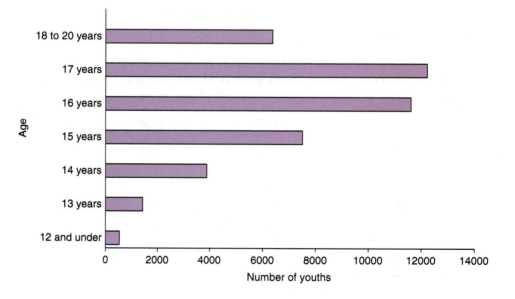

FIGURE 13.4   Juveniles in Residential Placement, by Age Which is the most common age for a youth to be in residential placement?

Source: Melissa Sickmund, T. J. Sladky, Wei Kang, and Charles Puzzanchera, "Easy Access to the Census of Juveniles in Residential Placement," 2019. Available at www.ojjdp.gov/ojstatbb/ezacjrp.

Much like adult prisons and jails, security is an issue at many youth facilities. The level of security varies with the type of facility, but generally, the most secure facilities hold the most troublesome delinquents. Private facilities, which typically house less serious delinquents, are less likely to lock youths in their sleeping rooms than public facilities. Locked doors and gates are often used for juveniles being held for offenses such as homicide, sexual and aggravated assault, robbery, arson, and technical violations. The use of fences, walls, and equipment such as surveillance cameras is common in juvenile facilities. Detention centers and training schools may use razor wire to secure their grounds.[62] One aspect

A 19-year-old transgender woman, who was a resident of a halfway house for juvenile delinquents, says she received death threats from fellow residents. Advocates state that juvenile detention centers in the United States are not equipped to securely house and counsel transgender youths, which increases the likelihood for bullying, assault, depression, and suicide. Why does security remain an issue at many youth facilities?

of security is the facility's ability to protect some youths from themselves. Most youths go to facilities that screen for mental health problems, suicide risk, and substance abuse.[63]

An alternative to prison-style incarceration is the Missouri Model.[64] In 1983, the state of Missouri closed its two training schools in favor of group homes, camps, and small treatment facilities. These facilities maintain security through direct staff supervision rather than fences and surveillance equipment, and they are run by youth specialists rather than correctional guards. Proponents of the Missouri Model say that it results in lower recidivism rates. Despite the success of the Missouri Model, research indicates that youths are best served through home-based interventions rather than out-of-home commitments.[65]

Juvenile Waiver: Treating Children as Adults

One of the outgrowths of the get-tough-on-crime approach has been to treat serious juvenile delinquents as adult offenders. Rather than handling these cases in juvenile courts, these cases are waived to the criminal court, where the protection of society is paramount. It is argued that the most serious juvenile delinquents require a minimum criminal sentence that is not available in juvenile court. All states have provisions for trying juveniles as adults. Some states lower the age for juvenile jurisdiction to 15 or 16 rather than 17 or 18. Other methods by which juveniles may be sent to criminal court are **judicial waiver**, **statutory exclusion**, and **direct filing** (see CJ Reference 13.1).[66]

Critics of the waiver process point out that sending a juvenile to adult court does not always protect the public because the youth may serve only a fraction of the sentence. Additionally, the criminal court might not have the treatment alternatives for young offenders that are available in juvenile court.[67] There is also evidence of racial bias in terms of who is waived to criminal court, with young, black males being disproportionately selected.[68]

The public approves of trying youths as adults in part so that they will receive a criminal disposition. Many people believe that a juvenile who commits a particularly heinous offense should not receive a lenient juvenile disposition such as probation or a sentence to a juvenile institution (although such dispositions are often anything but lenient), but a sentence that fits the crime. These sentences,

Judicial waiver—A form of waiving a juvenile to criminal court in which a judge sends the juvenile to adult court.

Statutory exclusion—Provisions that exclude, without hearing or waiver, juveniles who meet certain age, offense, or past-record criteria from the jurisdiction of the juvenile court.

Direct filing—A form of waiving a juvenile to criminal court in which a prosecutor has the discretion to file charges in either juvenile or criminal court.

CJ REFERENCE 13.1
Waiver to Criminal Court

JUDICIAL WAIVER

A judge sends the juvenile to adult court. The three types of judicial waiver are discretionary, mandatory, and presumptive.

- Discretionary waiver. Transfer of the juvenile to adult court is at the judge's discretion.
- Mandatory waiver. Automatic transfer to criminal court takes place on the basis of the youth's age and the gravity of the offense.
- Presumptive waiver. The burden of proof shifts from the state to the juvenile, who must contest being transferred to adult court.

Some states have "once an adult, always an adult" provisions, which means that once the youth is treated by the court as an adult, that youth will always be considered as an adult in any future proceedings.

DIRECT FILING (CONCURRENT JURISDICTION OR PROSECUTORIAL DISCRETION)

A prosecutor has the discretion to file charges in either juvenile or criminal court.

STATUTORY EXCLUSION

Also called legislative waiver, statutory exclusion comes from a state's legislature and does not require a juvenile court hearing. It automatically excludes some juveniles from juvenile court and sends them directly to adult court. Criteria include age, type of offense, and prior record. Statutory exclusion is used most for particularly heinous offenses, such as murder and aggravated rape. Some states without concurrent jurisdictions may also use statutory exclusion for minor violations such as traffic, fish or game, and local ordinance.

REVERSE WAIVER

Some states have laws that allow juveniles whose cases are filed in criminal court (usually through direct filing) to petition to have them transferred to juvenile court. Not all states allow the reverse waiver in all types of cases. Also, the burden of proof for the reversal may shift to the youth.

which are sometimes mandatory depending on the state, include decades-long prison terms and, until recently, life imprisonment (*Miller v. Alabama* and *Graham v. Florida*) and the death penalty (*Roper v. Simmons*; see Table 13.1 for a summary of these cases). The line of reasoning that the Supreme Court took in *Miller*, *Graham*, and *Roper* was that the Eighth Amendment protection against excessive punishment includes the principle that a punishment should be proportional to both the offender and the offense. In the case of juveniles, their immature ability to reason, their susceptibility to peer pressure, and their inability to choose their parents, living conditions, and school environments are all integral to their status as youths.

PAUSE AND REVIEW

1. Why is belonging to a youth gang a predictor of chronic delinquency?
2. In what types of public facilities may youths be incarcerated?
3. What are some reasons supporting and opposing the process of waiver to criminal court?

FOCUS ON ETHICS   Widening the Net of Social Control

The juvenile court is responsible for safeguarding the welfare of children, including protecting them from abusive or neglectful parents. You are a juvenile court judge who has been struggling with a particularly difficult case involving a 14-year-old boy who continually smokes marijuana, shoplifts, and recently has been running with a local gang and threatening other children with violence.

The experienced caseworker who has been working hard to help this young man tells you that the source of much of the problem is his parents and his family's dynamics. The boy ignores his mother's instructions and argues with his father. You order the family to see a psychologist who specializes in family matters, but the father refuses and contends that the problem is not himself but the "rotten" boy. After several attempts to resolve the situation, you order the boy to be placed in foster care because you believe the father is an unfit parent and a negative influence.

This boy has a 12-year-old brother whose behavior is exemplary. He is an honor student, a star athlete, and an all-around good kid. You order the 12-year-old out of the home as well because the father is recalcitrant and refuses to cooperate with the courts. You think that if he is a poor father for one child, he is probably a poor father for the other and that your duty is to place both boys in foster care for their own well-being.

The 14-year-old seems to be responding well to his new home, but the 12-year-old has now become a problem. He runs away from home, is in danger of being dropped from the honors program because of slipping grades, and refuses to discuss his new problems with the psychologist. You are so angry with the father because of his attitude that you do not want to allow the 12-year-old to return to the home, but you are worried that your actions have resulted in a good kid going bad.

WHAT DO YOU DO?

1. Let the 12-year-old go home and keep pressuring the father to participate in family therapy.
2. Keep both children in foster care until the father cooperates.
3. Return both boys to the home and let the situation run its course. You tried to help, but now it is the father's problem. If his son ends up in prison, it is not your fault.
4. Order the 12-year-old to live with you so that you can show the father that you care about children and are willing to go to great lengths to ensure they are protected.

For more insight into how someone might respond to such an ethical dilemma, visit Oxford Learning Link at www.oup.com/he/Fuller2e to watch a video that connects this scenario to a real-world situation.

Summary

| LEARNING OBJECTIVE **13.1**

Describe the benefits and critiques of the modern juvenile justice system. | Benefits of the juvenile justice system:

• it is supposed to act in the best interests of youths;
• it seeks to reduce the stigma of deviant behavior;
• young offenders are kept apart from adult offenders;
• it seeks to help juvenile delinquents gain the necessary skills to become productive members of society;
• it protects youths from receiving the harsh punishments meted out by the criminal justice system.

Critiques of the juvenile justice system:

• youths who commit serious offenses are treated too leniently;
• many people believe that juveniles should be held accountable for their unlawful behavior;
• the punishments meted out in the juvenile justice system are inconsistent with those meted out in the criminal justice system;
• juvenile delinquents are not afforded all the due-process rights available in the criminal justice system. |

LEARNING OBJECTIVE 13.2 Characterize the types of youths whom the juvenile justice system is responsible for.	**Incorrigible youths:** Some parents cannot control their children, particularly teenagers, who are lured by temptations outside the home. Dependent youths: When children are abandoned or orphaned, the state becomes responsible for their welfare. **Neglected youths:** Some parents are unconcerned, careless, or incapable of providing for their children. **Status offenders:** Many behaviors are considered legitimate for adults but deviant for children (i.e., skipping school, drinking alcohol underage). **Delinquent youths:** Children must obey all the laws that apply to adults, with limited exceptions.
LEARNING OBJECTIVE 13.3 Outline the stages of the juvenile justice system.	**Referral:** Cases enter the juvenile justice system by a referral. Referrals can come from schools, parents, or child welfare agencies that believe the child is at risk from others; referrals can also come from law enforcement agencies. Pre-hearing detention: When the police take a youth into custody, they may detain the youth for several hours in order to obtain information about the youth. **Intake:** An intake officer reviews the case to determine whether evidence is sufficient to prove the allegation. **Diversion:** To deinstitutionalize delinquent and neglected children, some jurisdictions utilize community correctional practices such as foster homes, halfway houses, and extended probation-like supervision. **Determining jurisdiction:** Once an intake officer decides that the case should be processed through the juvenile justice system, it is decided whether the case will remain in the juvenile court or be transferred to criminal court. **Adjudicatory hearing:** A hearing to determine whether the youth committed the delinquent acts as charged. **Disposition:** The disposition (like a sentence) can take two paths: residential placement (confinement) in a secure facility or referral to probation or a similar nonresidential program. **Aftercare:** Programs designed to address the youth's problems, including drug or alcohol treatment, counseling, attending school on a regular basis, or employment.
LEARNING OBJECTIVE 13.4 Discuss why belonging to a youth gang is a predictor of chronic delinquency.	Youth gangs engage in criminal or delinquent activity and are often involved in drug distribution, turf protecting, robbery, extortion, or any number of other illegal activities. Large, well-established gangs that require adults to run their major vice operations rely on youths to fuel their memberships.
LEARNING OBJECTIVE 13.5 Classify the types of public facilities in which youths may be incarcerated.	**Adult prisons:** Some young offenders convicted of serious offenses may be kept here. **Ranches and camps:** These facilities enable delinquents to work outside on public lands. **Traditional training schools:** These schools are where more serious delinquents are incarcerated for longer periods of time.
LEARNING OBJECTIVE 13.6 Defend and criticize the process of waiver to criminal court.	Proponents of the waiver process argue that the most serious juvenile delinquents require a minimum criminal sentence that is not available in juvenile court. Critics of the waiver process assert that sending a juvenile to adult court does not always ensure protection of the public because the youth may serve only a fraction of the sentence imposed by the court. There is also evidence that the waiver process is racially biased.

Critical Reflections

1. Do children really need the same legal protections of the criminal justice system that adults have?

2. Does the juvenile justice system's philosophy of treatment and rehabilitation adequately protect the long-term interests of children?

3. Should age or seriousness of offense determine whether a youth is transferred to the criminal justice system?

Key Terms

Adjudicatory hearing **p. 404**
Adversarial process **p. 404**
Commitment **p. 404**
Consent decree **p. 401**
Direct filing **p. 413**
Diversion **p. 401**
Due process rights **p. 395**

Hearing **p. 393**
Informal probation **p. 401**
Judicial waiver **p. 413**
Juvenile delinquent **p. 393**
Labeling theory **p. 399**
Net-widening **p. 403**
Parens patriae **p. 393**

Petitioner **p. 404**
Referral **p. 399**
Residential placement **p. 405**
Respondent **p. 404**
Status offense **p. 398**
Statutory exclusion **p. 413**

Notes

1 Grace Toohey, "After 55 Years in Prison, Baton Rouge Man Key to Supreme Court Ruling Again Denied Freedom," *Advocate* (Baton Rouge, La.), April 11, 2019.

2 Samantha Michaels, "A 72-Year-Old Juvenile Lifer Won a Landmark Supreme Court Ruling, but Louisiana Won't Let Him Out of Prison," *Mother Jones*, April 12, 2019. *Sentencing Project*, "Louisiana Denies Parole to 72-year-old Henry Montgomery," April 15, 2019.

3 Ashley Nellis, "For Henry Montgomery, A Catch-22," *Marshall Project*, February 28, 2018.

4 *Montgomery v. Louisiana* (2016).

5 Nellis, "For Henry Montgomery, A Catch-22."

6 Michaels, "A 72-Year-Old Juvenile Lifer Won a Landmark Supreme Court Ruling."

7 Nellis, "For Henry Montgomery, A Catch-22." Toohey, "After 55 Years in Prison, Baton Rouge Man Key to Supreme Court Ruling Again Denied Freedom."

8 Michaels, "A 72-Year-Old Juvenile Lifer Won a Landmark Supreme Court Ruling."

9 Donna M. Bishop, "Injustice and Irrationality in Contemporary Youth Policy," *Criminology and Public Policy* 3, no. 4 (November 2004): 633–644.

10 David S. Tanenhaus, "The Evolution of Transfer Out of the Juvenile Court," in *The Changing Borders of Juvenile Justice*, eds. Jeffrey Fagan and Franklin E. Zimring (Chicago: University of Chicago Press, 2000), 15, 31–32.

11 Jodi L. Viljoen, Patricia A. Zapf, and Ronald Roesch, "Adjudicative Competence and Comprehension of Miranda Rights in Adolescent Defendants: A Comparison of Legal Standards," *Behavioral Sciences and the Law* 25, no. 1 (January 2007): 1–19.

12 Federal Bureau of Investigation, *Uniform Crime Reports: Crime in the United States, 2019*, Arrests by Age, Table 38, ucr.fbi. gov/crime-in-the-u.s/2019/crime-in-the-u.s.-2019/topic-pages/tables/table-38.

13 Alexes Harris, "Diverting and Abdicating Judicial Discretion: Cultural, Political, and Procedural Dynamics in California Juvenile Justice," *Law and Society Review* 41, no. 2 (June 2007): 387–428.

14 Federal Bureau of Investigation, *Uniform Crime Reports: Crime in the United States, 2019*, Table 68, ucr.fbi. gov/crime-in-the-u.s/2019/crime-in-the-u.s.-2019/topic-pages/tables/table-68.

15 Douglas C. Dodge, *Due Process Advocacy* (Washington, D.C.: Office of Juvenile Justice and Delinquency Prevention, 1997).

16 Eyitayo Onifade, William Davidson, Sarah Livsey, Garrett Turke, Chris Horton, Jill Malinowski, Dan Atkinson, and Dominique Wimberly, "Risk Assessment: Identifying Patterns of Risk in Young Offenders with the Youth Level of Service/Case Management Inventory," *Journal of Criminal Justice* 36, no. 2 (May 2008): 165–173.

17 James Austin and Barry Krisberg, "Wider, Stronger, and Different Nets: The Dialectics of Criminal Justice Reform," *Journal of Research in Crime and Delinquency* 18, no. 1 (1981): 165–196.

18 Mary Clement, *The Juvenile Justice System: Law and Process* (Boston: Butterworth-Heinemann, 1977).

Chapter 14

Criminal Justice in the Future: Issues and Concerns

Zachary McCoy fell victim to digital surveillance as a result of using an exercise app to track his bicycle rides. Digital surveillance is increasingly becoming a tool of law enforcement agencies. What issues does the increased use of surveillance technology pose for the future of policing?

One day in Gainesville, Florida, Zachary

McCoy, age 30, was notified by Google's legal investigations support team that the police wanted information from his account. Google said it would release his data in seven days unless he blocked the action in court.[1]

Using the case number from the Google e-mail, McCoy searched the police department's website. He discovered that the issue was related to the case of an elderly woman who claimed her home had been burglarized 10 months prior. The woman's house was less than a mile from where McCoy lived. Although he had ridden his bike in her neighborhood, he had never been to her house and did not know her.[2]

McCoy feared he would be arrested if he went to the police. He told his parents about his dilemma, so they spent several thousand dollars of their savings to hire attorney Caleb Kenyon.[3]

Kenyon discovered that the police had used a type of search warrant called a "geofence warrant" to examine mobile data. Their goal was to identify all the mobile devices that had been active within a particular area the day of the alleged burglary. The exercise-tracking application that McCoy used during his bike rides supplied his movements to a Google database called Sensorvault. On the day in question, the data showed that McCoy had ridden his bike past the woman's house three times in one hour.[4]

The data Google gave the police was anonymized, so the police had to ask for McCoy's identity once they became interested in his movements. The e-mail Google sent to McCoy was his only hint that police were investigating him.[5]

Kenyon filed a motion to block the release of any further information about McCoy. Kenyon argued that the warrant was unconstitutional because it allowed police to conduct a sweeping search of many individuals to find one suspect instead of targeting a known suspect. Kenyon then showed the police screenshots of McCoy's Google location history, depicting months of bike rides past the woman's home.[6]

The state attorney's office withdrew the warrant, and police dropped their investigation into McCoy. "I'm glad police were trying to solve [the case]," McCoy told NBC News. "But it just seems like a really broad net for them to cast. How many innocent people do we have to harass?"[7]

THINK ABOUT IT > Should the police be allowed to use information gathered by private companies to watch U.S. citizens? Why or why not?

14.1 The Changing Criminal Justice System

The next generation of criminal justice practitioners—lawyers, judges, police, victim–witness program staff members, and a host of others who work in or with the criminal justice system—will be responsible for determining the nature, tone, and philosophy of how we deal with those who break the law. At an even more important level, however, the next generation of citizens will determine the nature of the substantive law. We may find that tomorrow's rules, mores, customs, expectations, and laws are different from those of today. For example, the experience of Zachary McCoy might have been considered strange 10 years ago, somewhat alarming 20 years ago, and like something out of a science fiction novel 50 years ago. But today, we can understand exactly how it happened. Each generation must deal with new problems and new technologies, making the past a somewhat unreliable guide for policy. This does not mean we should not learn from the past but rather that we should keep an open mind and recognize that criminal justice issues, trends, and technology are always in flux.

PAUSE AND REVIEW

1. How might tomorrow's customs, regulations, and laws differ from today's?

14.2 Technology and Surveillance

One of the most challenging issues in the criminal justice system is the use of surveillance technology to expose the activities of criminals and terrorists. The Bill of Rights, particularly the Fourth Amendment, protects citizens against intrusions into their privacy by the government. This has always been a contentious issue that has engendered a great deal of legal opinion from the courts, which specify just how far the government can go in terms of invading the privacy of citizens while pursuing criminal convictions.[8]

The USA PATRIOT Act

The **USA PATRIOT Act** of 2001 (Uniting and Strengthening America by Providing Appropriate Tools Required to Intercept and Obstruct Terrorism) drastically changed the rules of the relationship between security and privacy. Through legislation drafted in response to the terrorist attacks of September 11, 2001, Congress gave broad authority to the government to do whatever was necessary to prevent further terrorist attacks.

Much of the PATRIOT Act is purely administrative. It allots funds for government agencies to pursue terrorists, permits federal law enforcement to hire more officers and staff, and reinforces federal law against discrimination. However, other parts of the PATRIOT Act reduce judicial oversight of telephone and Internet surveillance. For instance:

Under the PATRIOT Act, federal law enforcement agencies aren't required to determine if a suspect uses or is likely to use a phone before planting a "bug." Under Sections 214 and 216, the federal government is also authorized to sweep the records of Internet Service Providers and network administrators in both private and public sectors, and may monitor and intercept email and cell phone usage without first being required either to have a court order or to report such activities to judicial oversight. The federal government only has to believe that the information is "relevant," and it does not need to show there is a "probable cause," as required under the Fourth Amendment. More important, the federal government can receive such warrants without the courts being allowed to determine if the allegations are truthful.[9]

The PATRIOT Act was forged during an emergency when it was deemed that the government needed these resources on a temporary basis to deal with potential future terrorist attacks. For years, it was politically unpopular to challenge the PATRIOT Act, and it was routinely touted as the "war on terror" continued both abroad and at home. However, the tension between the PATRIOT Act and the Constitution's civil rights guarantees has become more contentious.

LEARNING OBJECTIVE **14.1**

Recognize how surveillance technology conflicts with privacy issues.

LEARNING OBJECTIVE **14.2**

Discuss how the new professionalism in policing will change the nature of police behavior.

USA PATRIOT Act—
A law signed by President George W. Bush on October 26, 2001 in response to the terror attacks of September 11, 2001 that gave the U.S. government broad authority to detect and prevent terrorism.

The NSA's mass surveillance practices stirred up a great deal of opposition from the American public. Why was the agency's collection of the phone records of U.S. citizens so controversial?

USA FREEDOM Act—A law signed by President Barack Obama in 2015 that reauthorized parts of the USA PATRIOT Act but limited the bulk collection of U.S. residents' phone records and Internet data.

In 2015, Congress passed a modification to the PATRIOT Act called the **USA FREEDOM Act** (Uniting and Strengthening America by Fulfilling Rights and Ending Eavesdropping, Dragnet-collection and Online Monitoring) that limits the government's ability to collect information that cannot be directly connected to terrorism. Specifically, the FREEDOM Act limited the National Security Agency's (NSA) practice of collecting every cell phone call and e-mail of all citizens in order to give it the ability to "connect the dots" when it found possible evidence of terrorist activities. Whereas the NSA did not read or hear communications individually, those concerned with privacy believed that the collection of all this data represented a broad overreach of constitutional protections.[10] Although the FREEDOM Act specifies that the government can no longer collect and keep this data, it does allow the government to look at the data that is held by Internet service providers and cell phone companies.[11]

Privacy, Anonymity, and the Police

A key element of privacy is anonymity. It is much easier to guard your privacy if few or no people know who you are. Now, thanks to social media, widespread cell phone use, and the fact that much of our lives are spent online, from banking to shopping to streaming entertainment, protecting one's privacy is increasingly problematic. Technology has made maintaining anonymity and privacy more difficult, with implications for law enforcement and civil rights.

For example, there is a continuous legal scuffle over what personal devices police are allowed to search. In 2019, police in Tampa, Florida, pulled over William Montanez and discovered a marijuana cigarette, a handgun, and two mobile phones in his car. The officers asked for the passcodes to the phones, but Montanez refused, even after the officers obtained a warrant. Montanez's phones remained locked, but he spent 44 days in jail before most of the charges were dropped.[12]

Today, police in some jurisdictions can photograph anyone in a public space and identify that person in detail by uploading the photo to a database or to the Internet. They can see all the publicly available information about that person, including other pictures and personal information scraped from social media and other websites.[13] The power of facial recognition software has many people worried about traditional expectations of basic privacy and anonymity that individuals usually have in public spaces. In 2019, San Francisco banned the use of facial recognition software by law enforcement.

Many jurisdictions have invested in tools to monitor social media. According to a 2016 survey by the International Association of Chiefs of Police and the Urban Institute, more than 70 percent of officers gather information about crime from social media, with many departments using sophisticated data-mining tools.[14] Such capabilities are useful for legitimate policing activities. For example, during the 2015 U.S. Open of Surfing, police in Huntington Beach, California, sought to prevent assaults and other serious offenses by monitoring social media.[15] However, in 2019, it was revealed that FBI employees were caught using a National Security Agency database to spy on relatives and gather information on nearly anyone they wanted to.[16] The same year, a federal judge ruled that the FBI cannot hide whether it uses social media surveillance tools to monitor millions of people in the United States.[17]

The issue of protecting privacy versus allowing for increased exposure for the benefit of law enforcement will continue to be hotly debated. We do not want to hinder the police from preventing and responding to serious crime. However, many people in the United States value their privacy and ability to interact with others without being monitored.

In looking toward the future, it will be necessary to ensure that police departments evolve in their use of technology. Police culture must, above all, maintain its goals of protecting citizens, apprehending offenders, and respecting the rights and dignity of everyone. The task of the criminal justice system is to enforce the law with fairness and concern for the dignity of citizens. However, several factors will continue to create tensions between those who make and enforce the law and those it affects. These include the prevalence of firearms, the widening disparity between socioeconomic classes, and deeply rooted systemic problems in the ways race, sex, and gender continue to divide groups of people. This tension between protecting the public and safeguarding the constitutional and civil rights of individuals is a major challenge of policing.

Pastor Mark Tyler gives testimony on controversial social media posts by officers with the Philadelphia Police Department at a city council meeting. In what other ways do law enforcement officers use or misuse social media technology?

Despite this challenge, much can be done to improve and reform the criminal justice system so that it operates in a manner that is both smarter and more fair. Christopher Stone of the Kennedy School of Government at Harvard University and Jeremy Travis, president of the John Jay College of Criminal Justice, City University of New York, have called for police departments to emphasize four elements of what they call the "new professionalism":[18]

> › Accountability. The police must account for their actions not only to the departmental chain of command, but also to city councils, citizen review boards, state legislators, inspectors general, as well as government auditors and the courts. Police departments must become more transparent in their actions, and individual officers must be expected to be able to defend their behavior. One initiative to increase the accountability of officers is to have them wear body cameras to record their interactions with citizens.

> › Legitimacy. The police must be considered honest brokers in their interactions with citizens. In many communities, the police are viewed as an occupying force or gang. Many citizens have lost their trust and confidence in the police, which makes policing less effective. Police militarization and recent incidents of excessive use of force have weakened the quest to retain legitimacy.

> › Innovation. Future police departments should be willing to evaluate and adopt the positive innovations of other departments. A commitment to innovation means an active investment in personnel and resources in adapting new policies and practices that have proven effective elsewhere.

> › National coherence. True professionalism allows police departments to engage in a national conversation that extends good police practices, as well as knowledge and understanding, across jurisdictions. Officers, supervisors, and executives can then share a set of skills and follow a common set of protocols that have been accepted and proven effective. Conventional wisdom has always held that police officers could be most effective in their home cities, where they had come up through the ranks and appreciated the uniqueness of their communities. A commitment to national coherence suggests that good policing incorporates a universal set of practices and policies that can be effective in jurisdictions across the country.

Policing in the future will certainly incorporate much more technology. However, technology is not the only concern important in developing more efficient, effective, and equitable policing practices. Maintaining the trust of citizens will require that police departments enforce the law in a fair and impartial manner. This legitimacy can be obtained only by having measures of accountability that make the work of police officers transparent to supervisors, politicians, and the general public. This will be an immense task that some departments will undoubtedly perform better than others.

PAUSE AND REVIEW

1. **Which practices authorized by the PATRIOT Act most concern its critics?**
2. **What are the four elements of the "new professionalism?"**

14.3 The High Incarceration Rate

LEARNING
OBJECTIVE **14.3**

Compare the incarceration
rate in the United States
with that of other
countries.

LEARNING
OBJECTIVE **14.4**

Analyze the social cost of
a high incarceration rate
in terms of unintended
consequences.

In the United States, one of the consequences of the war on drugs and the war on crime is that a significant percentage of American citizens are behind bars. Instead of relying on community-based correctional programs for providing a broad range of social and educational services, the criminal justice system has focused primarily on incarceration.

The United States has the largest penal population in the world, with about 2.1 million incarcerated adults (see Figure 14.1).[19] According to a National Academy of Sciences (NAS) study, *The Growth of Incarceration in the United States*, the population of the United States accounts for about 5 percent of the world population, but it incarcerates about 25 percent of the world's prison inmates. With nearly one of every 100 adults in prison or jail, the U.S. incarceration rate is 5 to 10 times higher than that of the rates of western Europe.[20] For a look at the increase in the number of inmates in the United States, see Figure 14.2.

Some observers and scholars argue that the United States' harsh incarceration policy has been effective in reducing crime. It is true that over the past 15 years, crime has decreased in many parts of the country, and many communities are safer than they once were.[21] However, it is difficult to attribute this phenomenon solely to increased incarceration. Several other factors, including economic forces, better target-hardening techniques (such as security cameras and more effective locks), and the stabilization of illegal drug markets, can also be linked to the reduction of crime.[22] In fact, the NAS study cautions against drawing any cause-and-effect relationships between the high incarceration rate and crime reduction, stating that high incarceration may have caused some decrease in crime, but that most research suggests that little, if any, of the decrease in crime was directly related to high incarceration policies.[23]

A significant problem of high incarceration is the unintended consequences it produces. It is difficult, if not impossible, to deprive so many people of their

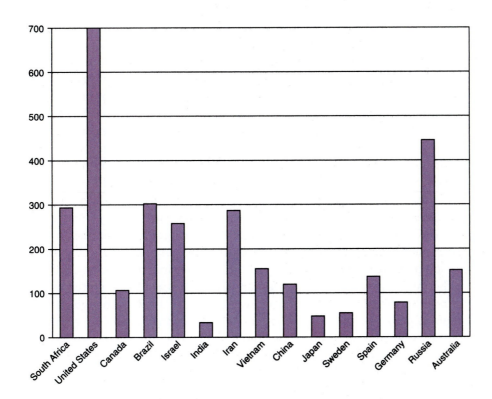

FIGURE 14.1 Incarceration Rates, Selected Countries What are some possible reasons as to why the United States incarcerates so many more of its citizens than other countries?

Source: Roy Walmsley, World Prison Population List, *11th ed. (World Prison Brief, Institute for Criminal Policy Research, 2015). Available at http://www.prisonstudies.org.*

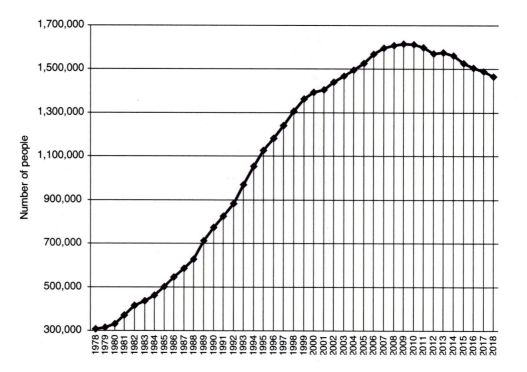

FIGURE 14.2 Inmates Under the Jurisdiction of State or Federal Correctional Authorities This figure shows the increase in the number of people sent to state and federal prisons and jails since 1978. "Jurisdiction" refers to the legal authority of state or federal correctional officials over an inmate regardless of where the inmate is held. Can you give reasons for the steep rise in the number of people incarcerated over the past three decades?

Source: E. Ann Carson and Joseph Mulako-Wangota, Prisoners Under the Jurisdiction of State or Federal Correctional Authorities, *December 31, 1978-2018, Bureau of Justice Statistics. Generated using the Corrections Statistical Analysis Tool at www.bjs.gov/index.cfm?ty=nps, October 2020.*

liberty without creating a ripple effect throughout society. These unintended consequences affect inmates' families; create more effective criminal offenders; disproportionately affect minorities and the impoverished; and damage inmates' physical and mental health, their chances at future employment and fair wages, and their communities. Let's look at these unintended consequences in detail.

Unintended Consequences of High Incarceration

A major unintended consequence of high incarceration rates is that prison does not make many offenders better citizens, but rather accelerates their criminal careers.[24] So much money is spent on the infrastructure of prisons in terms of institutional security, correctional officers, and weapons that fewer resources are allotted to actually changing the inmate's behavior. Because of mandatory-minimum sentence policies, state and federal prisons are packed with offenders serving sentences for relatively minor offenses. Overcrowded prisons mean that fewer resources are available for the rehabilitation and re-entry of inmates into society.[25] It is not surprising that the **recidivism rate** is so high when little is done to adequately prepare inmates for employment and social responsibility.

Recidivism rate—The rate of ex-offenders who commit new offenses and are returned to prison.

According to the NAS report, prison inmates typically come from the most impoverished and disadvantaged constituencies. They are mainly minority men under age 40 who are poorly educated, addicted to drugs and/or alcohol, mentally and/or physically ill, and lacking work training or experience. More than half the U.S. prison population is black or Hispanic. Blacks are incarcerated at about seven times the rate of non-Hispanic whites, and Hispanics are incarcerated at nearly four times the rate of non-Hispanic whites (see Figure 14.3). Although the criminal responsibility of many inmates is real, it is entrenched in the life experiences brought by poverty, illness, addiction, and disadvantage.[26]

The intended and unintended consequences of mass incarceration have been so socially harmful that this policy is coming under scrutiny by both the criminal justice system and society.[27] A review of these consequences reveals that the old tough-on-crime policies have blossomed into new issues and concerns that

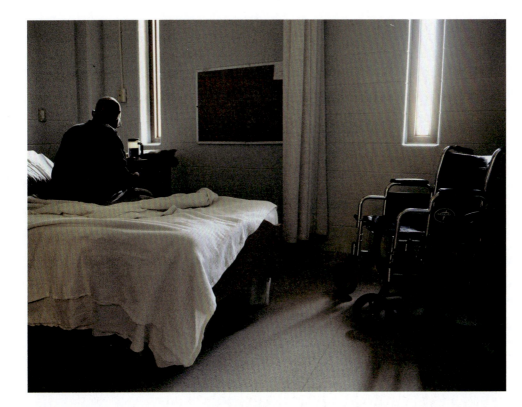

It costs Kentucky $3.3 million a year to care for 50 elderly inmates who cannot take care of themselves, a burden the state is preparing to shift to the federal government. How do changes in sentencing policies in the 1980s and 1990s affect the current aging prison population?

Inmates at the Northern Nevada Correctional Center in Carson City do gardening work in the prison yard. This program is part of an initiative that seeks to prepare inmates for successful reintegration into society when they first enter prison, rather than toward the end of their sentences, the goal of which is to ultimately reduce recidivism. How do high incarceration rates negatively affect recidivism rates?

call into question the over-reliance on jails and prisons to deal with what are essentially problems of impoverishment, mental illness, and drug addiction. Mass incarceration has yet other unintended consequences.

CHILDREN AND FAMILIES

Criminal justice policies that rely on incarceration have limited the ability of an offender's family to effectively raise children. Incarcerated offenders are unable to provide economic support for their families or to supervise and guide their children. Additionally, the children of incarcerated parents tend to have few or inadequate role models and instead often learn how to interact with other people from their peers and the habits they observe in their respective neighborhoods.[28]

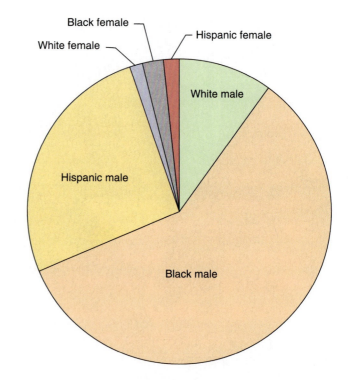

FIGURE 14.3 Rate of Incarceration by Race and Sex In 2018, 2,272 black males per 100,000 regular population ages 18 and over were incarcerated as opposed to 392 white male inmates and 1,018 male Hispanic inmates. How do the male inmate populations compare with the female inmate populations?

Source: E. Ann Carson and Joseph Mulako-Wangota, Estimated imprisonment rate of sentenced prisoners under state and federal jurisdiction, by sex, race, Hispanic origin, and age, December 31, Bureau of Justice Statistics. Available at www.bjs.gov/index.cfm?ty=nps.

Although many children visit their parents in prison, it is common for parents not to want their children to see them behind bars. Children may experience feelings of abandonment, grief, depression, shame, and, in some cases, even guilt over having an incarcerated parent. All too often, a parent's incarceration can lead to a child's eventual delinquency.[29] It is difficult to maintain a healthy relationship with children if incarceration is long term and if the spouse or partner has moved onto another partner. It is difficult for inmates to maintain healthy relationships with their partners, as several factors work against their ability to stay in contact, share feelings, and develop trust.[30] In addition to the emotional strain on the relationship caused by incarceration, there is also an economic effect. Being connected to someone who is in prison can cost a great deal of money in collect telephone calls, travel costs, and sending of money and packages to the inmate. Legal fees can also put a financial strain on the family. Typically, families of inmates also require more public assistance, including food stamps and Temporary Assistance for Needy Families, and studies have found that families of inmates are more likely to experience homelessness.

MENTAL AND PHYSICAL HEALTH

Because jail and prison facilities are so crowded, there is little room in budgets for medical professionals. In the 1970s, the United States released patients from secure mental health facilities where they were not getting the necessary treatment and, in many cases, were being abused. This **deinstitutionalization** was supposed to shift these patients to community-based treatment centers that could better address their needs. Unfortunately, resources were not sufficient to build and staff such treatment centers, and many mentally ill patients found themselves on the street.[31] Today, so many mentally ill and mentally disabled people have been and continue to be incarcerated that the nature of the prison population has shifted from being largely criminal to being significantly mentally ill and mentally disabled, issues the criminal justice system is ill prepared to address.[32]

Additionally, many inmates have serious physical health problems. Prisons and jails are not equipped to deal with infectious and chronic diseases and do

Deinstitutionalization—The policy of removing mentally ill people from public mental-health institutions and closing part or all of those institutions.

An audience watches Utah lawmakers discuss a plan to move the state prison. Why would citizens object to having a new prison built in their community?

not provide adequate dietary and exercise programs to keep inmates healthy.[33] Another concern is aging inmates. Due to shifts in sentencing policy in the 1980s and 1990s, many inmates were sentenced to extremely long prison sentences. As these inmates become elderly, it is obvious that the prison and jail systems are ill equipped to deal with a geriatric population.[34]

The global coronavirus (COVID-19) pandemic of 2020 exposed the hygiene and crowding problems of the country's jails and prisons (see Closer Look 14.1).[35]

A CLOSER LOOK 14.1
Of Prisons and Pandemics

When a chaplain from the Federal Bureau of Prisons called Michael Fleming to ask him if his father's body should be cremated, Fleming was shocked. Fleming's father (also named Michael) was serving 20 years at FCI Terminal Island, a low security federal correctional institution in Los Angeles, for intending to distribute methamphetamine. Fleming had not even known that his father, who was 59 and had pre-existing medical conditions, was sick, nor had he been informed that his father had been sent to a hospital. The chaplain was the first to tell Fleming that his father had died. Fleming only learned that the cause of his father's death was COVID-19 after seeing the news on television.[36]

By the end of April 2020, nearly half of the inmate population at FCI Terminal Island had tested positive for the coronavirus; more than 30 had died and about 600 had recovered.[37] By May 2020, the Federal Bureau of Prisons had tested only 2,700 of its 150,000 inmates for COVID-19. Two thousand of the tests were positive.[38]

Close confinement combined with overcrowded conditions and lack of resources to maintain proper hygiene allowed the virus to flare in prisons.[39] To curb the infection rate, prison officials limited inmate movement, set up tents to increase bed space, and isolated inmates who showed symptoms of the virus. Additionally, state and local institutions authorized the early release of many older, infirm, non-violent, and low-level offenders, as well as those jailed for parole violations, placing them under home confinement or parole.[40]

Unlike people in free society, prisoners cannot effectively control their own spaces. Prison inmates are unable to limit who they come in contact with, making social distancing difficult, acquire personal protective equipment, or access adequate medical care. The COVID-19 pandemic exposed the problematic nature of carceral environments, which will likely continue to be fertile places for any sort of contagious disease.[41]

THINK ABOUT IT

1. How did your state handle the pandemic in prisons and jails?

with disputes and other minor altercations, many of which are rooted in alcohol or drug use, or in mental illness. Sometimes all she needs to do is calm people down. She has some calls involving possible criminal offenses such as burglaries, vehicle thefts, break-ins, robberies, and domestic disputes and the occasional homicide. She explains that most of the officers in her department have similar duties. The exception is about 10 officers who have extensive weapons training and are armed at all times. These officers go on calls that will likely be dangerous. She knows most of the people on her beat, which includes residents and the owners and employees of local businesses. She says that much of her time is devoted to seeing that arrestees who are mentally ill or have substance-abuse problems are referred to the appropriate agencies and to de-escalating tense situations (she is in frequent training for this).

At the end of her talk, she takes questions. You have been reading about the history of policing and ask how her job compares to that of police officers 50 years ago. What does she say, and why?

1. She thinks her job is relatively boring. She would prefer to have been a police officer 50 years ago because it was more exciting then. She would have gotten to carry a weapon and would not have had to use so many strategies to deal with

a situation. She admits to being disappointed that most of the crime she encounters is rooted in substance abuse, mental illness, or poverty, instead of exciting things like bank robberies and car chases.

2. She is largely unsatisfied with her job. To her, a crime is a crime, a criminal is a criminal regardless of the reasons, and all lawbreakers deserve to be arrested. Stealing because you are poor does not make stealing right. It is still against the law to beat up people because you cannot handle alcohol. She wishes she could carry her own gun on the job and is considering going through the year-long training to become an armed officer.

3. She loves her job. She is glad she is not often called on to use force. She says most cases are cleared by referrals to social assistance agencies, which keeps the jail and prison population low. Her knowledge of the community allows her and other officers to remedy many situations before they fester into something that requires force.

For more insight on how someone might respond, visit Oxford Learning Link at www.oup.com/he/Fuller2e to watch a video that connects this scenario to a real-world situation.

Summary

LEARNING OBJECTIVE **14.1** Recognize how surveillance technology has conflicted with privacy issues.		Many people are concerned that the war on terror has resulted in curtailing the privacy rights of citizens. The PATRIOT Act gave broad and sweeping powers to law enforcement to conduct surveillance on individuals' telephone and Internet communications. Although the FREEDOM Act curtails some of the most egregious activities allowed by the PATRIOT Act, critics still claim that the federal government has violated the constitutional protections inherent in the Bill of Rights.
LEARNING OBJECTIVE **14.2** Discuss how the new professionalism in policing will change the nature of police behavior.		The new professionalism will incorporate commitments to accountability, legitimacy, innovation, and national coherence. These commitments will allow future police departments to ensure that the behavior of officers is more transparent and understandable; they have the support of citizens; they utilize the latest tools and techniques that have been proven effective elsewhere; and they operate in a manner consistent with the best practices of exemplary police departments across the country.

LEARNING OBJECTIVE 14.3 Compare the incarceration rate in the United States with that of other countries.	The United States relies on incarceration to a much greater degree than any other country. The U.S. prison population accounts for 25 percent of the world's prison inmates. The U.S. incarceration rate is five times higher than the rates of western European countries.	
LEARNING OBJECTIVE 14.4 Analyze the social cost of a high incarceration rate in terms of unintended consequences.	The high incarceration rate in the United States has a disproportionate effect on minorities and the impoverished. One of the most pressing social causes of the high incarceration rate is the way prisons and jails are used to deal with mental illness and other health problems. A serious problem for the corrections system is aging prison populations. Incarceration seriously inhibits an individual's ability to obtain employment. Incarceration disrupts the bond between spouses, as well as parents and children. The high incarceration rate also affects communities; when incarcerated individuals are released into their neighborhoods, they bring with them a prison mentality that damages the social fabric of the community. Society is affected by the high incarceration rate because individuals are denied their full citizenship rights. Money is diverted from schools, recreational programs, and social programs to build and staff prisons and jails.	
LEARNING OBJECTIVE 14.5 Describe why the term *war* is an inappropriate metaphor for drug policy.	The term *war* implies that society should be ruthless, expedient, prepared to make a sacrifice, and subordinate the individual to the overall goal of winning the war. Traditional wars have an external opponent, but the war on drugs concentrates on U.S. citizens and thus is an inappropriate and inaccurate metaphor.	
LEARNING OBJECTIVE 14.6 Characterize the three types of crime related to drugs.	The three types of crime related to drugs are offenses committed by (1) people who are on drugs; (2) people who need money to buy drugs; and (3) drug dealers.	
LEARNING OBJECTIVE 14.7 Discuss the perceived benefits of legalizing some drugs.	States that have legalized medical marijuana have been able to collect taxes related to marijuana sales. The legalization of some drugs means that fewer police officers are required to police the illegal drug trade, and law enforcement resources can be directed at curbing serious crime. Legalization also helps drug users avoid the stigmatization of being arrested and sanctioned for drug use.	

Critical Reflections

1. **What additional issues do you consider problematic for the future of the criminal justice system? Explain how new laws, improved training, and/or advances in technology may address these issues.**

2. **Develop some alternatives for the high incarceration rate in the United States. How can we better decide which offenders are truly dangerous and which ones can be provided with**

alternative sentencing? How can incarceration be employed in a manner that does not affect minorities so disproportionately?

3. **What type of organizational structure might be employed to minimize excessive use of force? Is there some way to change the police subculture to make it less militaristic and more effective in dealing with crime?**

Key Terms

Notes

1 Jon Schuppe, "Google Tracked His Bike Ride Past a Burglarized Home. That Made Him a Suspect," *NBC News*, March 7, 2020. Jennifer Valentino-DeVries, "Tracking Phones, Google Is a Dragnet for the Police," *New York Times*, April 13, 2019.

2 Ibid.

3 Ibid.

4 Ibid.

5 Ibid.

6 Ibid.

7 Ibid.

8 Randy Barnett, "Why the NSA Data Seizures Are Unconstitutional," *Harvard Journal of Law & Public Policy* 38, no. 1 (Winter 2015): 3–20.

9 Walter M. Brasch, *America's Unpatriotic Acts: The Federal Government's Violation of Constitutional and Civil Rights* (New York: Peter Lang, 10).

10 Charlie Savage, Jonathan Weisman, and Peter Baker, "N.S.A. Collection of Bulk Call Data Is Ruled Illegal," *New York Times*, May 8, 2015, A1–A8.

11 United States House of Representatives Judiciary Committee, H.R. 2048, the USA Freedom Act, www.congress.gov/bill/114th-congress/house-bill/2048. Accessed October 2020.

12 Jon Schuppe, "Give Up Your Password or Go to Jail: Police Push Legal Boundaries to Get into Cellphones," *NBC News*, June 7, 2019.

13 Kashmir Hill, "The Secretive Company That Might End Privacy as We Know It," *New York Times*, January 18, 2020.

14 Chris Bousquet, "Mining Social Media Data for Policing, the Ethical Way," *Government Technology*, April 27, 2018.

15 Ibid.

16 Kieren McCarthy, "Remember the FBI's Promise It Wasn't Abusing the NSA's Data on US Peeps? Well, Guess What …," *Register*, October 8, 2019.

17 Hill, "The Secretive Company That Might End Privacy as We Know It"; Nicholas Iovino, "Judge Rules FBI Cannot Hide Use of Social Media Surveillance Tools," *Courthouse News Service*, November 18, 2019.

18 Christopher Stone and Jeremy Travis, "Toward a New Professionalism in Policing," Harvard Kennedy School, March 2011. Available at www.hks.harvard.edu/criminaljustice/executive_sessions/policing.htm.

19 Roy Walmsley, *World Prison Population List*, 12th ed. (London: Institute for Crime & Justice Policy Research, 2018), 2.

20 Jeremy Travis and Bruce Western, *The Growth of Incarceration in the United States: Exploring Causes and Consequences*, (Washington, D.C.: National Academies Press, 2014).

21 John R. Hipp, "Assessing Crime as a Problem: The Relationship between Residents' Perception of Crime and Official Crime Rates over 25 Years," *Crime and Delinquency* 59, no. 4 (June 2013): 616–648.

22 James M. Byrne, "After the Fall: Assessing the Impact of the Great Prison Experiment on Future Crime Control Policy," *Federal Probation* 77, no. 3 (December 2013): 9–22.

23 Travis and Western, *The Growth of Incarceration in the United States*.

24 Sophie R. Dickson, Devon L.L. Polaschek, and Allanah R. Casey, "Can the Quality of High-risk Violent Prisoners' Release Plans Predict Recidivism Following Intensive Rehabilitation? A Comparison with Risk Assessment Instruments," *Psychology, Crime and Law* 19, no. 4 (May 2013): 371–389.

25 Cassandre Monique Davilmar, "We Tried to Make Them Offer Rehab, but They Said, 'No, No, No!'" Incentivizing Private Prison Reform through the Private Prisoner Rehabilitation Credit," *New York University Law Review* 89, no. 1 (April 2014): 267–292.

26 Travis and Western, *The Growth of Incarceration in the United States*.

27 Michael Tonry, "Remodeling American Sentencing: A Ten-Step Blueprint for Moving Past Mass Incarceration," *Criminology and Public Policy* 13, no. 4 (November 2014): 503–533.

28 Randal D. Day, Alan C. Acock, Stephen J. Bahr, and Joyce A. Arditti, "Incarcerated Fathers Returning Home to Children and Families: Introduction to the Special Issue and a Primer on Doing Research with Men in Prison," *Fathering: A Journal of Theory, Research, and Practice About Men as Fathers* 3, no. 3 (Fall 2005): 183–200.

29 Kristin Turney, "The Intergenerational Consequences of Mass Incarceration: Implications for Children's Co-Residence and Contact with Grandparents," *Social Forces* 93, no. 1 (September 2014): 299–327.

30 Beth M. Huebner, "The Effect of Incarceration on Marriage and Work over the Life Course," *JQ: Justice Quarterly* 22, no. 3 (September 2005): 281–303.

31 Robert Weisberg and Joan Petersilia, "The Dangers of Pyrrhic Victories against Mass Incarceration," *Daedalus* 139, no. 3 (Summer 2010): 124–133.

32 Kristine Artello, "Shifting 'Tough on Crime' to Keeping Kids Out of Jail: Exploring Organizational Adaptability and Sustainability at a Mental Health Agency Serving Adjudicated Children Living with Severe Mental Illness," *Criminal Justice Policy Review* 25, no. 3 (May 2014): 378–396.

33 Meagan Flynn, "Top Doctor at Rikers Island Calls the Jail a 'Public Health Disaster Unfolding Before Our Eyes'," *Washington Post*, March 31, 2020.

34 Heather Habes, "Paying for the Graying: How California Can More Effectively Manage Its Growing Elderly Inmate Population," *Southern California Interdisciplinary Law Journal* 20, no. 2 (January 2011): 395–423.

35 Meagan Flynn, "Top Doctor at Rikers Island Calls the Jail a 'Public Health Disaster Unfolding Before Our Eyes'," *Washington Post*, March 31, 2020.

36 Michael Balsamo, "Over 70% of Tested Inmates in Federal Prisons Have COVID-19," *AP/SFGATE*, April 30, 2020. Richard Winton, "Terminal Island Prison Inmates Have Worst Coronavirus Outbreak in Federal System," *Los Angeles Times*, April 29, 2020.

37 Ibid.

38 Ibid.

39 Ned Parker, Linda So, Brad Heath, and Grant Smith, "Spread of Coronavirus Accelerates in U.S. Jails and Prisons," *Reuters*, March 28, 2020.

40 Alfred Charles, "State Supreme Court Rules Against Inmates Who Wanted Early Release for COVID-19 Threat," *Seattle pi*, April 24, 2020.

41 "Responses to the Covid-19 Pandemic," Prison Policy Initiative, September 11, 2020, www.prisonpolicy.org/virus/virusresponse.html.

42 Haeil Jung, "The Long-Term Impact of Incarceration during the Teens and 20s on the Wages and Employment of Men," *Journal of Offender Rehabilitation* 54, no. 5 (July 2015): 317–337.

43 H. J. Holzer, S. Raphael, and M. Stoll, "Will Employers Hire Former Offenders? Employer Preferences, Background Checks and Their Determinants," in *Imprisoning America: The Racial Effects of Mass Incarceration*, eds. M. Pattillo, D. Weiman, and B. Western (New York: Russell Sage Foundation, 2004), 205–246.

44 D. Pager, B. Western, and N. Sugie, "Sequencing Disadvantage: Barriers to Employment Facing Young Black and White Men with Criminal Records," *Annals of the American Academy of Social and Political Science* 623, no. 1 (2009): 195–213.

45 Mark L. Hatzenbuehler, Katherine Keyes, Ava Hamilton, Monica Uddin, and Sandro Galea, "The Collateral Damage of Mass Incarceration: Risk of Psychiatric Morbidity among Nonincarcerated Residents of High-Incarceration Neighborhoods," *American Journal of Public Health* 105, no. 1 (2015): 138–143.

46 E. Brown, "Expanding Carceral Geographies: Challenging Mass Incarceration and Creating a 'Community Orientation' Towards Juvenile Delinquency," *Geographica Helvetica* 69, no. 5 (December 15, 2014): 377–388.

47 Kayla Martensen, "The Price that US Minority Communities Pay: Mass Incarceration and the Ideologies That Fuel Them," *Contemporary Justice Review* 15, no. 2 (June 2012): 211–222.

48 Kamesha Spates and Carlton Mathis, "Preserving Dignity: Rethinking Voting Rights for U.S. Prisoners, Lessons from South Africa," *Journal of Pan African Studies* 7, no. 6 (October 21, 2014): 84–105.

49 Derecka Purnell, "Examining Disparate Impact Discrimination on Ex-offenders of Color Across Voting, Government Policy and Aid Receipt, Employment, and Housing," *Harvard Journal of African American Public Policy* (January 2013): 1–15.

50 John R. Sutton, "Symbol and Substance: Effects of California's Three Strikes Law on Felony Sentencing," *Law and Society Review* 47, no. 1 (March 2013): 37–72.

51 Charles J. Dunlap Jr., "The Military-Industrial Complex," *Daedalus* 140, no. 3 (Summer 2011): 135–147.

52 Rose M. Brewer and Nancy A. Heitzeg, "The Racialization of Crime and Punishment: Criminal Justice, Color-Blind Racism, and the Political Economy of the Prison Industrial Complex," *American Behavioral Scientist* 51, no. 5 (January 2008): 625–644.

53 Eugene H. Czajkoski, "Drugs and the Warlike Administration of Justice," *Journal of Drug Issues* 20, no. 1 (1990): 125–129.

54 Robert Barnes, "He Sold Drugs and the Police Seized His Car. Does the Constitution Provide Protection?" *Washington Post*, November 27, 2018.

55 *Timbs v. Indiana*, 586 U.S. (2019). Robert Barnes, "Supreme Court Limits Power of States and Localities to Impose Fines, Seize Property," *Washington Post*, February 20, 1019.

56 Emma Anderson, "The Supreme Court Didn't Put the Nail in Civil Asset Forfeiture's Coffin," ACLU, March 15, 2019.

57 David B. Kopel and Trevor Burrus, "Reducing the Drug War's Damage to Government Budgets," *Harvard Journal of Law and Public Policy* 35, no. 3 (Summer 2012): 543–568.

58 David J. Nutt, Leslie A. King, and Lawrence D. Phillips, "Drug Harms in the UK: A Multicriteria Decision Analysis," *Lancet* 376, no. 9752 (November 6, 2010): 1558–1565. Dirk W. Lachenmeier and Jürgen Rehm, "Comparative Risk Assessment of Alcohol, Tobacco, Cannabis and Other Illicit Drugs Using the Margin of Exposure Approach," *Scientific Reports* 5 (2015): 8126. Peter N.S. Hoakena and Sherry H. Stewart, "Drugs of Abuse and the Elicitation of Human Aggressive Behavior," *Addictive Behaviors* 28 (2003): 1533–1554. Robert Gable, "The Toxicity of Recreational Drugs," *American Scientist* 94, no. 3 (2006): 206.

59 Tibor R. Machan, "Drug Prohibition Is Both Wrong and Unworkable," *Think: Philosophy for Everyone* 11, no. 30 (Spring 2012): 85.

60 Jonathan P. Caulkins, Beau Kilmer, Peter H. Reuter, and Greg Midgette, "Cocaine's Fall and Marijuana's Rise: Questions and Insights Based on New Estimates of Consumption and Expenditures in US Drug Markets," *Addiction* 110, no. 5 (May 2015): 728–736.

61 NORML, State Info, norml.org/states. Accessed March 2020.

62 Eric Rosenbaum, "Colorado Passes $1 Billion in Marijuana State Revenue," CNBC, June 12, 2019.

63 Robert G. Morris, Michael TenEyck, J. C. Barnes, and Tomislav V. Kovandzic, "The Effect of Medical Marijuana Laws on Crime: Evidence from State Panel Data, 1990–2006," *PLOS ONE* 9, no. 3 (March 26, 2014): 1–7. Jérôme Adda, Brendon McConnell, and Imran Rasul, "Crime and the Depenalization of Cannabis Possession: Evidence from a Policing Experiment," *Journal of Political Economy* 122, no. 5 (October 2014): 1130–1202.

64 Joseph J. Palamar, Mathew V. Kiang, and Perry N. Halkitis, "Predictors of Stigmatization towards Use of Various Illicit Drugs Among Emerging Adults," *Journal of Psychoactive Drugs* 44, no. 3 (July 2012): 243–251.

65 Nigel Duara, "It's Legal to Smoke Pot in Colorado, but You Can Still Get Fired for It," *Los Angeles Times*, June 15, 2015.

66 Jeffery T. Walker, Ronald G. Burns, Jeffrey Bumgarner, and Michele P. Bratina, "Federal Law Enforcement Careers: Laying the Groundwork," *Journal of Criminal Justice Education* 19, no. 1 (2008): 110–135.

OXFORD
insight study guide
Active Engagement, Deeper Understanding

Learn more with this chapter's digital tools, including the Oxford Insight Study Guide, at www.oup.com/he/Fuller2e

Appendix: **Theories of Crime**

One of the challenges that criminologists face is to develop ideas about crime into systematic theories that clearly spell out perspectives and concepts in ways that can be tested and measured. As criminal justice grows as an academic discipline, criminological theories become more sophisticated and specific. This appendix will help us understand the variety and complexity of criminological theories. By looking at the explanations of crime that have guided the actions of people and the criminal justice system, we can better understand why and how crime remains a significant social problem and continues to demand serious study in the 21st century. By understanding the history of how our ideas about the causes of crime have evolved, we can learn to appreciate the fascinating complexity of the law, the criminal justice system, and other methods of social control.

The Classical School of Criminology

The **classical school of criminology** argues that people freely choose to break the law. The principle of "free will" allows us to consider various courses of action and then select the one we believe is most desirable. If we structure the criminal justice system in such a way that penalties for breaking the law are sufficiently severe, swift, and certain, then people will rationally choose not to break the law.[1]

The classical school of criminology is embodied primarily in the works of Cesare Beccaria (1738–1794) and Jeremy Bentham (1748–1832). Both men were more concerned with reforming the criminal justice system than with understanding why people broke the law or finding the causes of crime.[2]

Cesare Beccaria's ideas about reforming the ways in which society dealt with crime are detailed in his seminal work *On Crimes and Punishments*, published in 1764.[3] In this work, Beccaria presented nine principles concerning crime and the way society responds to lawbreakers. These and other ideas formulated by Beccaria have found their way into many of the principles that guide our criminal justice system today. Beccaria suggested that punishment should only be stringent enough to deter crime. He also advocated the abolition of physical punishment and the death penalty. The presumption of innocence, the right to confront accusers, the right to a speedy trial, and the right not to be required to testify against oneself are all traceable to Beccaria.

According to Jeremy Bentham's theory of **utilitarianism**, people are guided by their desire for pleasure and aversion to pain.[4] To understand the actions of people, we need only understand how they comprehend pleasure and pain. Bentham believed people perform a mental exercise he called the **hedonistic calculus** when considering how to behave. A person attempts to weigh the pleasures that would accrue from breaking the law and the pain that would result if caught. In weighing pleasure and pain, the following are considered:

1. Intensity
2. Duration
3. Certainty or uncertainty
4. Propinquity or remoteness[5]

Classical school of criminology—A set of criminological theories that uses the idea of free will to explain criminal behavior.

Utilitarianism—A theory associated with Jeremy Bentham that states that people will choose not to break the law when the pain of punishment outweighs the benefits of the offense.

Hedonistic calculus—An individual's mental calculation of the personal value of an activity by how much pleasure or pain it will incur.

It is in this consideration of the balance between pleasure and pain that Bentham believed society could affect antisocial behavior.[6] Crime can be prevented by structuring the criminal justice system and the law in such a way that potential offenders can calculate that the pains of crime outweigh the pleasures. Modern sentencing patterns have a high degree of proportionality due to Bentham's ideas. For example, murder can get an offender the death penalty, but stealing a car will not. In Bentham's time, over 200 offenses demanded the death penalty. His work focused on reforming the system by introducing some logic into how, and how much, punishment was meted out.[7]

Bentham's hedonistic calculus is also apparent in the attempt to increase the certainty of punishment. More police officers, better crime-fighting technology, more efficient court systems, and other reforms are aimed at influencing the calculations that potential offenders make. The purpose of increasing the duration of prison sentences (such as life imprisonment) is to discourage severe crime.

The Neoclassical School of Criminology

Neoclassical criminology—A modern interpretation of classical criminology that acknowledges the possibility that human choices are affected by causes external to the will but holds that human beings are ultimately responsible for their choices.

Neoclassical criminology is a modern interpretation of classical criminology that acknowledges the possibility that human choices are affected by causes external to the will but holds that human beings are ultimately responsible for their choices. Neoclassical criminology emphasizes deterrence and retribution. Theoretically, those who are contemplating breaking the law can be deterred if they determine that the costs of committing the offense are higher than the rewards.

The idea behind deterrence is that the more serious a crime, the harsher the punishment. Theories based on deterrence introduce a degree of proportionality into the equation of matching punishments to the amount of harm caused by the offense. That is why people convicted of offenses such as murder may receive capital punishment, whereas those who commit simple assault are more likely to receive probation or a short jail term.

Severity of punishment is not the only aspect of deterrence; the swiftness and certainty of the punishment are also important considerations. Swiftness of punishment in the modern criminal justice system has a limited deterrence effect because the process can take so long. It is not unusual to see individuals executed many years after committing their offenses. The certainty of punishment also has limited utility as a deterrent because the resources to detect all crime are simply not available. Potential offenders, especially those who have been successful in the past, are able to plan their escapades in ways that can greatly limit their detection.

Not all law-breakers are equally adept at assessing the risks and potential rewards of breaking the law. For instance, those who rob a convenience store with a firearm expose themselves to long periods of incarceration for little potential reward. The $300 gained from robbing the store is a poor exchange for a 20-year (or longer) prison sentence if convicted of armed robbery. Several factors may go into this unwise decision, including an elevated opinion of one's confidence and ability, the influence of drugs or alcohol, or a proclivity for thrill-seeking. Many offenders who perform the risk/reward calculus fail to do the math correctly.

Neoclassical theories of criminology provide valuable insights into the factors that potential lawbreakers consider when deciding whether to violate the law and have the potential for policy implications. Rather than attempting to determine why offenders break the law, neoclassical theories allow policymakers to change the situational nature of the criminal act in ways that make crime riskier. Consequently, offenders choose to find other locations and more attractive targets rather than expose themselves to increased chances of apprehension and conviction.[8]

Rational Choice Theory

In criminology, **rational choice theory** is the idea that people consciously weigh the risks against the benefits of their actions, and choose the action they think has the most benefit. Developed by Derek Cornish and Ronald Clarke, rational choice theory seeks to capture the reasoning behind the decision to break the law.[9] Several factors beyond the expected benefits go into this decision. Offenders must also calculate the costs of committing crime, which include not only the potential sanction but also more mundane factors such as the equipment needed, the potential use of violence, and even the distance that the offender must travel to the crime scene.[10]

By understanding how potential lawbreakers think as they decide the costs and benefits of committing a crime, criminal justice policymakers can attempt to deter unlawful behavior by increasing costs. For instance, the severity of an offense is just one cost that can be manipulated by law enforcement. The cost can also be increased by shaming the perpetrator by publishing his or her name in the media, making a target less attractive by maintaining only a limited amount of cash (for example, at a convenience store), or increasing the likelihood of victim resistance (for example, arming a store clerk).[11]

Rational choice theory—The idea that people consciously weigh the risks against the benefits of their actions and choose the action that they think has the most benefit.

Situational Crime Prevention

Situational crime prevention involves making crime less attractive to potential criminals by reducing the physical opportunities to break the law.[12] For example, "target hardening," or securing property by using padlocks, surrounding it with fences, security cameras, and increased lighting may help deter crime. The intent is to convince potential lawbreakers that the costs of physically committing the crime are unreasonably high given the expected potential benefits. When the target is sufficiently protected, potential offenders will presumably move on to more vulnerable targets. Situational crime prevention has been successful in reducing crime in public places, as evinced by the concentrated effort in MacArthur Park in Los Angeles, California. Increased police patrol, enforcement of misdemeanor laws, increased use of security cameras, and the posting of nearly 60 signs in both English and Spanish detailing the rules of appropriate behavior, as well as notices that the police would enforce these rules, are credited with influencing potential offenders to decide that committing a crime in the park is a bad idea.[13]

Situational crime prevention—An idea that involves making crime less attractive to potential criminals by reducing the physical opportunities to break the law.

Routine Activities Theory

Routine activities theory states that crime is most likely to occur when three elements converge: motivated offenders, attractive targets, and the absence of capable guardians (such as police officers). According to the architects of the theory, Lawrence Cohen and Marcus Felson, the first element, motivated offenders, is the least important. The theory assumes that there will always be offenders motivated to break the law, so it is necessary to emphasize the other two elements: attractive targets and capable guardians. By making targets less attractive, that is, more secure, motivated offenders will be less likely to attack. Additionally, potential offenders will be deterred by providing adequate guardianship, such as regular police or security officer patrols.[14]

Routine activities theory—A perspective that states that crime is most likely to occur when these three elements converge: motivated offenders, attractive targets, and the absence of capable guardians.

The Positivist School of Criminology

The classical school of criminology assumes motivation and treats all offenders equally. However, not all offenders are equal. People break the law for different reasons and are not affected by punishment in the same way. The idea that free

Positivist school of criminology—A set of criminological theories that uses scientific techniques to study crime and criminal offenders.

will determines when and how people break the law fails to account for the complex nature of crime and the vast differences among people. There is no way to determine how one exercises free will in deciding to break the law.[15] The **positivist school of criminology**, theories that use scientific techniques to study crime and criminal offenders, is a natural outgrowth of the scientific method. By applying scientific disciplines, criminologists shifted the focus of criminology away from the law and the criminal justice system and toward the offender.[16] By looking to science to help understand patterns of crime, the question became, what factors influence people to break the law?[17]

Biological Theories of Crime

Scientists have long attempted to find a relationship between the body and behavior.[18] Here are some ideas that seek to cast light on the relationship between crime and factors such as heredity, hormones, blood chemistry, and environmental problems including alcohol and drug use.

BIOSOCIAL CRIMINOLOGY

Biosocial criminology utilizes genetic, neuropsychological, environmental, and evolutionary factors to explain crime and antisocial behavior across the life course.[19] The links between genes, hormones, the brain, and behavior are complicated, and scientists are still working out the connections. However, it is important to understand that there is no "crime gene"; that is, there is no single gene, or trait, that makes a person more likely to break the law. Scientists stress that environment deeply affects behavior.

Biosocial criminology—A perspective that utilizes genetic, neuropsychological, environmental, and evolutionary factors to explain crime and antisocial behavior across the life course.

Biosocial criminology is controversial, and the subject must be approached with caution. Some scholars criticize biosocial criminology by pointing out that researchers are trying to use physical traits (genes) to explain a socially defined phenomenon (crime). Another criticism recalls the debate about the focus on street crime versus white-collar and corporate crime. Studies tend to focus on violence, aggression, and impulsivity, all behaviors that are associated with street crime, rather than the more subtle behaviors that may be associated with white-collar and corporate crime. We should be aware that many ethical issues must be considered. At best, we hope to understand the interaction physical factors might have with social and psychological influences and pressures related to criminal behavior.[20]

Genes. The study of the possible effects of genes on antisocial behavior is part of biosocial criminology. A gene is a unit composed of DNA (deoxyribonucleic acid), which contains instructions for coding a protein for a particular function. Genes are the building blocks of our bodies, including our brains. The idea is that genes are partly responsible for behavior because they determine how our brains are constructed. For example, a gene that has been linked to violence regulates the production of an enzyme that controls the amount of the hormone serotonin. People with a version of the gene that produces less of the enzyme tend to be more impulsive and aggressive. Impulsivity and aggression are linked to violence, which in some cases may lead to antisocial behavior.[21] In another example, a study of twins and siblings tried to measure whether having delinquent friends and living in an impoverished neighborhood would cause a gene associated with violent behavior to express itself. The study found that without exposure to the risk factors, the violence-associated genes were not expressed. However, the more social risk factors a child encountered, the more likely genetics would play a role in any violent behavior.[22]

Hormones. The body secretes hormones for several reasons, but one by-product of this activity appears to be alterations in mood and behavior. For instance, a relationship exists between the release of testosterone in males and aggression.[23] A relatively new theory called evolutionary neuroandrogenic theory states that androgens (male sex hormones), primarily testosterone, promote competitive behaviors that may involve harming or victimizing another person. According to the theory, when testosterone levels rise, so does competitive, and often criminal, behavior. The evolutionary purposes of such behavior is to enhance the male ability to acquire resources and thus to attract females, who have evolved to prefer mates who are good at providing resources. According to a study by the theory's proponents, self-reported violent criminality was positively correlated with masculine traits such as high physical strength, high strength of sex drive, deep voice, ample body hair, and penis size.[24] At least one other study supports the idea that prenatal exposure of the brain to high levels of androgens increases the probability of criminal offending later in life; however, much more research is required to establish any firm conclusions.[25]

Brain Structure and Brain Chemistry. Brain chemistry is another area in which researchers are looking for the causes of antisocial behavior. Hormones such as norepinephrine, dopamine, and serotonin are of particular interest to criminologists because they regulate behaviors such as impulsivity, feelings of pleasure, and response to danger.[26] Techniques such as computed tomography (CT), magnetic resonance imaging (MRI), position emission tomography (PET), and single photon emission computed tomography (SPECT) allow researchers to observe how the brain is influenced by injury. This research is still in its early stages, and although there is no consensus about exactly how the brain influences behavior, some evidence suggests that it might eventually prove to be fruitful.

Psychological Theories of Crime

Although it is inadvisable, and maybe impossible, to separate the influences of the body and brain on behavior, criminologists distinguish between biological and psychological theories. Contemporary criminal psychology focuses on how antisocial individuals acquire, display, maintain, and (sometimes) modify their behavior and considers the influence of society, personality, and individual mental processes on behavior.[27] Modern criminal psychology utilizes cognitive and developmental approaches. Cognition refers to the act of thinking, which includes attitudes, beliefs, and values that individuals hold about themselves, other people, and their surroundings. Developmental approaches address individual human development from childhood to adulthood.[28]

BEHAVIORISM

Psychologist B. F. Skinner (1904–1990) theorized that behavior is determined by rewards and punishments. His theory, **behaviorism**, is based on the psychological principle of **operant conditioning**. That is, behavior is more likely to occur when it is rewarded and less likely to occur when it is punished or not rewarded. Operant conditioning is more complicated than it first appears. For example, slot machines are set up to pay on an intermittent schedule. They dispense just enough coins just often enough to keep gamblers pulling the lever. Slot machine designers calculate payoff intervals to encourage more gambling. If the schedule of reinforcement is too long—that is, if the machine does not pay off often enough—then gamblers will stop inserting coins. Like slot-machine

Behaviorism—The assessment of human psychology via the examination of objectively observable and quantifiable actions, as opposed to subjective mental states.

Operant conditioning—The alteration of behavior by rewarding or punishing a subject for a specified action until the subject associates the action with pleasure or pain.

2. Adolescence-limited offenders can be contrasted with the life-course-persistent offender by the absence of problems in childhood and the unlikely continuation of crime into adulthood. Although the offenses of adolescence-limited offenders might be serious, there is little continuity to the patterns of crime they engage in, and there are long periods where they do not break the law at all. Rather than being a way of life, crime for the adolescent-limited offender is episodic and instrumental. This type of offender usually breaks the law infrequently and does so to achieve a specific goal. Adolescence-limited offenders account for most delinquents, and most of them age out of crime and develop into normal productive citizens.

According to Moffitt, adolescence-limited offenders respond to shifting contingencies as they age. With the inevitable progression of chronological age, more legitimate and tangible adult roles become available to adolescents. Adolescence-limited delinquents gradually lose motivation for delinquency as they mature. Moreover, when aging delinquents attain some of the privileges they coveted as teens, the consequences of illegal behavior shift from rewarding to punishing, in their perception. Adolescence-limited delinquents have something to lose by persisting in their antisocial behavior beyond the teen years.[65]

PERSISTENT-OFFENDING AND DESISTANCE-FROM-CRIME THEORY

In the basement of the Harvard Law Library, criminologists John Laub and Robert Sampson found a dataset collected between 1949 and 1963 from 500 delinquent boys by influential criminologists Sheldon and Eleanor Glueck. Laub and Sampson followed up on this data and detailed how those delinquents either persisted in their antisocial orientation or desisted from crime over their life course. Upon tracing some of the subjects' lives until age 70, Laub and Sampson found that some of the subjects continued in a trajectory of crime while others became more involved in society and adopted conventional behaviors. Upon tracking some of the subjects down in late adulthood and old age, Sampson and Laub concluded that almost all of the delinquent boys eventually stopped breaking the law.[66] They found that desisting from crime is typically the result of youths experiencing a turning point in life in which they become connected to conventional society. This change can be summarized as follows:

1. The offenders experienced a structural turning point. This might be in the form of marriage, getting a new job, or joining the military. As the delinquents aged, they had increased opportunities to engage in conventional behavior and become bonded to a lawabiding lifestyle.

2. Conventional lifestyles resulted in greater social control over their lives. When one gets married, it is more difficult to go out "drinking with the boys" or engage in other activities that may present opportunities for crime. A spouse has expectations that must be dealt with, which inevitably curtails any antisocial behavior that took place during bachelorhood. Similarly, when one enters the military, the rules and regulations that must be followed limit the exposure to crime-producing situations. Many of the study's delinquents became bonded to conventional lifestyles in this way.

3. The ex-delinquents' new lifestyles afforded them fewer opportunities to hang out with deviant peers, but more opportunities to engage in pro-social activities, such as going on family outings, going to church, and becoming involved in the community.

4. The new lifestyle required commitment. As one becomes successful in conventional behavior, it is no longer acceptable to participate in activities that put the new lifestyle at risk. Additionally, the new lifestyle provides benefits that replace the social and emotional needs that were addressed by the antisocial lifestyle. For example, for many of the ex-delinquents, holding down a well-paying job meant that they were less willing to do anything that jeopardized that job.

Although the change to conventional activities simply happened to some of the offenders, some of the subjects made conscious choices to change their lifestyle. This idea of agency is particularly important because it suggests that an antisocial lifestyle begun in childhood does not always continue through the life course.

TABLE A.3   Criminological Theories

	NAME/CLASS OF THEORY	THEORY	PRACTICE	THEORISTS
Classical School	**Nine Principles**	Free will and punishment should be based on humane principles.	Promote deterrence through social contract, public education, and legal clarity and equity. Punish proportionally. Eliminate systemic corruption.	Beccaria
	Utilitarianism	People are guided by desire for pleasure and aversion to pain.		Bentham
Neoclassical School	**Rational Choice Theory**	People consciously weigh the risks against the benefits of their actions, and choose the action that they think has the most benefit.	Raise the costs of criminal behavior; shame the perpetrator by publishing his or her name in the media; make targets less attractive by maintaining a limited amount of the desired item (such as cash); increase the likelihood of victim resistance.	Cornish and Clarke
	Situational Crime Prevention	Make crime less attractive to potential criminals by reducing the physical opportunities to break the law.	Target hardening.	Clarke
	Routine Activities Theory	Crime is more likely when offenders are motivated, targets are attractive, and capable guardians are absent.	There will always be motivated offenders. Thus, make targets less attractive and provide adequate guardians.	Cohen and Felson
Positivist School Biological Theories	**Biochemistry**	Hormones, brain structure, and/or brain chemistry may cause criminal behavior.	Provide medication, make diet changes.	
	Biosocial Criminology	Genetics may affect criminal behavior.		

Psychological Theories	**Behaviorism (operant conditioning)**	Behavior is determined by rewards and punishments.	Reward reform, punish continued offensive behavior.	Skinner
	Observational Learning	Cognition, behavior, and environment mutually reinforce each other. Observers, especially children, imitate behavior they see.	Model good behavior.	Bandura
	Moral Development Theory	Human moral development proceeds through stages of moral reasoning. Criminal offenders are stuck at the lower levels of development.	Promote attentive parenting, effective schools, and public programs for children, such as Headstart.	Kohlberg
	Psychopathy	Psychopathy is a specific psychological condition that might or might not co-occur with heinous criminal offending.	For serious offenders, life-long incarceration or commission to a mental institution is common.	Hare
	Antisocial Personality Disorder	APD has much in common with psychopathy except that its definition is marked by behavior, as well as aggression, violence, and irritability.	As those with APD continually break the law, incarceration is common, as are counseling and medication.	
Sociological Theories	**Chicago School**	Social disorganization causes criminal behavior in individuals.	Institute social reform, ensure equal access to societal incentives and norms, improve environments.	Shaw, McKay
	Differential Association Theory	Crime is learned.		Sutherland
	Strain Theory	There is unequal access to societal norms.		Merton
	Social Control Theory	This theory questions why people do not break the law.		Hirschi
	Labeling Theory	Deviants conform to the "deviant" label.		Lemert
Critical Sociological Theories	**Marxism**	Those in power make laws to favor themselves.	Institute social reform, provide minority groups access to more power and decision-making, recognize oppression, allocate group-specific research.	Marx
	Feminism (gender)	Crime study and the criminal justice system are male-dominated and male-oriented.		
	Critical Race Theory	The criminal justice system targets and oppresses people of color.		

Integrated Theories	**Integrated Theory of Delinquent Behavior**	Strain theory, social control, and social learning theories are combined to explain delinquency within the lower and middle classes.	Institute social reform, ensure equal access to societal incentives and norms.	Elliot, Ageton, and Canter
	Interactional Theory of Delinquency	Low social control and exposure to delinquent peers over the course of adolescent development contribute to delinquency and antisocial behavior.		Thornberry
	Control Balance Theory	People seek to correct and balance power differentials in their relationships.		Tittle
Life Course Theories	**Pathway Theory**	Life-course-persistent offenders engage in antisocial behavior for long periods of time, possibly all their lives. Adolescence-limited offenders break the law in adolescence but desist upon adulthood.	Institute social reform, ensure equal access to societal incentives and norms.	Moffitt
	Persistent-Offending and Desistance-from-Crime Theory	As delinquents age, some continue to break the law well into adulthood, while others experience turning points in which they bond to conventional society.		Laub and Sampson

Critical Reflections

1. What is the classical school of criminology?

2. What are the similarities and differences between Beccaria's and Bentham's approaches to crime?

3. What is neoclassical criminology, and what two aspects of crime prevention does it emphasize?

4. Why is the idea of deterrence so important in classical criminology?

5. What is the positivist school of criminology?

6. How are biological and psychological theories of criminology different?

7. How are critical sociological theories of crime different from other sociological theories?

8. How are theories that focus on the offender different from theories that focus on the offense?

9. If most crime is committed by adolescents and young adults, why do some criminologists consider crime across the life course?

10. Can any single criminological theory explain the wide variety of crimes committed in the United States?

Key Terms

Anomie **p.451**
Behaviorism **p.447**
Biosocialcriminology **p.446**

Chicago school **p.451**
Classical school of criminology **p.443**

Critical theory **p.454**
Differential association theory **p.451**

Notes

1   Erline Eide, *Economics of Crime: Deterrence and the Rational Offender* (North Holland, Netherlands: Elsevier, 1994).

2   Philip Jenkins, "Varieties of Enlightenment Criminology," *British Journal of Criminology* 24 (1984): 112–130. José Brunner "Modern Times: Law, Temporality and Happiness in Hobbes, Locke and Bentham," *Theoretical Inquiries in Law* 8, no. 1 (January 1, 2007): 21.

3   Cesare Beccaria, *On Crimes and Punishments,* trans. Henry Paolucci (Indianapolis, Ind.: Bobbs-Merrill, 1764/1963).

4   Jeremy Bentham, "An Introduction to the Principles of Morals and Legislation," in *Classics of Criminology,* 2d ed., ed. Joseph E. Jacoby (Prospect Heights, Ill.: Waveland Press, 1994), 80.

5   Cesare Beccaria, *On Crimes and Punishment* (Indianapolis, Ind.: Bobbs-Merrill, 1963).

6   Frank P. Williams III and Marilyn D. McShane, Criminological Theory, 4th ed. (Upper Saddle River, N.J.: Prentice Hall, 2004), 15–32.

7   Imogene L. Moyer, *Criminological Theories: Traditional and Nontraditional Voices and Themes* (Thousand Oaks, Calif.: Sage, 2001).

8   Ronald L. Simons, Callie H. Burt, Ashley B. Barr, Man-Kit Lei, and Eric Stewart, "Incorporating Routine Activities, Activity Spaces, and Situational Definitions into the Social Schematic Theory of Crime," *Criminology* 52, no. 4 (2014): 655–687.

9   Ronald V. Clarke and Derek B. Cornish, "Rational Choice," in *Explaining Criminals and Crime,* Raymond Paternoster and Rona Bachman (Los Angeles: Roxbury Publishing, 2000), 23–42. Derek B. Cornish and R. V. G. Clarke, *The Reasoning Criminal: Rational Choice*

Perspectives on Offending (New York: Springer-Verlag, 1986), 1.

10 Christophe Vandeviver, Stijn Van Daele, and Tom Vander Beken. "What Makes Long Crime Trips Worth Undertaking? Balancing Costs and Benefits in Burglars' Journey to Crime," *British Journal of Criminology* 55, no. 2 (March 2015): 399–420.

11 Marie Rosenkrantz Lindegaard, Wim Bernasco, and Scott Jacques, "Consequences of Expected and Observed Victim Resistance for Offender Violence during Robbery Events," *Journal of Research in Crime and Delinquency* 52, no. 1 (February 2015): 32–61. See also M. Lyn Exum, Joseph B. Kuhns, Brad Koch, and Chuck Johnson, "An Examination of Situational Crime Prevention Strategies Across Convenience Stores and Fast-Food Restaurants," *Criminal Justice Policy Review* 21, no. 3 (2010): 269–295.

12 Ronald V. Clarke, *Situational Crime Prevention: Successful Case Studies* (Albany, N.Y.: Harrow and Heston, 1997).

13 William H. Sousa and George L. Kelling, "Police and the Reclamation of Public Places: A Study of MacArthur Park in Los Angeles," *International Journal of Police Science and Management* 12, no. 1 (Spring 2010): 41–54.

14 Lawrence E Cohen and Marcus Felson, "Social Change in Crime Rate Trends in Activities Approach," *American Sociological Review* 44 (1979): 588–607.

15 Derek B. Cornish and Ronald V. Clarke, *The Reasoning Criminal: Rational Choice Perspectives on Offending* (New York: Springer, 1986).

16 Charles Darwin, *The Origin of the Species* (Cambridge, Mass.: Harvard University Press, 1859/1964).

17 Deborah W. Denno, "Human Biology and Criminal Responsibility: Free Will or Free Ride," *University of Pennsylvania Law Review* 137 (1988): 615–671.

18 Hans-Ludwig Kroeber "The Historical Debate on Brain and Legal Responsibility—Revisited," *Behavioral Sciences & the Law* 25, no. 2 (March 1, 2007): 251.

19 Kevin M. Beaver and Anthony Walsh, "Biosocial Criminology," in *The Ashgate Research Companion to Biosocial Theories of Crime,* eds. Kevin M. Beaver and Anthony Walsh (Burlington, Vt.: Ashgate Publishing Company, 2011), 3–5.

20 Ty A. Ridenour, "Genetic Epidemiology of Antisocial Behavior," in *Theories of Crime: A Reader,* eds. Claire M. Renzetti, Daniel J. Curran, and Patrick J. Carr (Boston: Allyn and Bacon, 2003), 4–24.

21 Karen Sugden, Louise Arseneault, HonaLee Harrington, Terrie E. Moffitt, Benjamin Williams, and Avshalom Caspi, "Serotonin Transporter Gene Moderates the Development of Emotional Problems among Children Following Bullying Victimization," *Journal of the American Academy of Child & Adolescent Psychiatry* 49, no. 8 (August 2010): 830–840.

22 Kevin M. Beaver, "Environmental Moderators of Genetic Influences on Adolescent Delinquent Involvement and Victimization," *Journal of Adolescent Research* 26, no. 1 (January 2011): 84–114.

23 Alan Booth and D. Wayne Osgood, "The Influence of Testosterone on Deviance in Adulthood: Assessing and Explaining the Relationship," *Criminology* 31, no. 1 (February 1, 1993): 93.

24 Lee Ellis, Shyamal Das, and Hasan Buker, "Androgen-promoted Physiological Traits and Criminality:

A Test of the Evolutionary Neuroandrogenic Theory," *Personality and Individual Differences* 44, no. 3 (February 2008): 699–709.

25 Anthony W. Hoskin and Lee Ellis, "Fetal Testosterone and Criminality: Test of Evolutionary Neuroandrogenic Theory," *Criminology* 53, no. 1 (February 2015): 54–73.

26 Debra Niehoff, "The Biology of Violence," in *Theories of Crime: A Reader*, eds. Claire M. Renzetti, Daniel J. Curran, and Patrick J. Carr (Boston: Allyn and Bacon, 2003), 26–31.

27 Curt R. Bartol and Anne M. Bartol, *Criminal Behavior*, 8th ed. (Upper Saddle River, N.J.: Pearson Prentice Hall, 2008), 6–8.

28 Ibid.

29 G. Terence Wilson, "Behavior Therapy," in *Current Psychotherapies*, 4th ed., eds. Raymond J. Corsini and Danny Wedding (Itasca, Ill.: F. E. Peacock, 1989), 241–282.

30 Michael J. Lillyquist, *Understanding and Changing Criminal Behavior* (Englewood Cliffs, N.J.: Prentice Hall, 1980).

31 G. David Curry and Scott H. Decker, *Confronting Gangs: Crime and Community* (Los Angeles: Roxbury, 1988).

32 Curt R. Bartol and Anne M. Bartol, *Criminal Behavior: A Psychosocial Approach*, 8th ed. (Upper Saddle River, N.J.: Pearson Prentice Hall, 2008), 121–123.

33 C. George Boeree, Albert Bandura, http://webspace.ship.edu/cgboer/bandura.html. Accessed September 2015.

34 Carol Veneziano and Louis Veneziano, "The Relationship Between Deterrence and Moral Reasoning," *Criminal Justice Review* 17, no. 2 (1992): 209–216.

35 William Crain, *Theories of Development*, 5th ed. (Upper Saddle River, N.J.: Prentice-Hall, 2005), 154–158.

36 Eric K. Klein "Dennis the Menace or Billy the Kid: An Analysis of the Role of Transfer to Criminal Court in Juvenile Justice," *The American Criminal Law Review* 35, no. 2 (January 1, 1998): 371–410.

37 Ibid.

38 Geert Jan Stams, Daniel Brugman, Maja Deković, Lenny van Rosmalen, Peter H. van der Laan, and John C. Gibbs, "The Moral Judgment of Juvenile Delinquents: A Meta-Analysis," *Journal of Abnormal Child Psychology* 34, no. 5 (October 1, 2006): 697–713.

39 Robert D. Hare, *Psychopathy: Theory and Research* (New York: Wiley, 1970). Bartol and Bartol, *Criminal Behavior*, 188.

40 John Randolph Fuller, *Juvenile Delinquency: Mainstream and Crosscurrents* (Upper Saddle River, N.J.: Pearson Prentice Hall, 2009), 188.

41 American Psychiatric Association, *Diagnostic and Statistical Manual of Mental Disorders*, 5th ed. (Washington, D.C.: American Psychiatric Association, 2013), 659.

42 Bartol and Bartol, *Criminal Behavior*, 235.

43 Clifford R. Shaw and Henry D. McKay, *Juvenile Delinquency and Urban Areas* (Chicago: University of Chicago Press, 1942).

44 Douglas S. Massey and Nancy A. Denton, *American Apartheid: Segregation and the Making of the Underclass* (Cambridge, Mass.: Harvard University Press, 1993).

45 Edwin H. Sutherland, Donald R. Cressey, and David F. Luckenbill, *Principles of Criminology* (Dix Hills, N.J.: General Hall, 1992).

46 Ross Matsueda, "The Current State of Differential Association Theory," *Crime and Delinquency* 34 (1988): 277–306.

47 Robert K. Merton, "Social Structure and Anomie," *American Sociological Review* 3 (1938): 672–682.

48 Robert Agnew, *Pressured into Crime: An Overview of General Strain Theory* (Los Angeles: Roxbury Publishing, 2006).

49 Lisa Broidy and Robert Agnew, "Gender and Crime: A General Strain Theory Perspective," *Journal of Research in Crime and Delinquency* 34 (1997): 275–306.

50 Robert Agnew, "Pressured into Crime: General Strain Theory," in *Criminological Theory: Past to Present*, eds. Francis T. Cullen and Robert Agnew (New York: Oxford University Press, 2006), 201–209.

51 Travis Hirschi, *Causes of Delinquency* (Berkeley: University of California Press, 1969).

52 Bruce A. Arrigo, ed., *Social Justice/Criminal Justice: The Maturation of Critical Theory in Law, Crime, and Deviance* (Belmont, Calif.: West/Wadsworth, 1999).

53 Karl Marx, *Capital* (New York: International, 1867/1974).

54 [55] Michael J. Lynch and Paul Stretesky, "Marxism and Social Justice: Thinking about Social Justice Eclipsing Criminal Justice," in *Social Justice/Criminal Justice: The Maturation of Critical Theory in Law, Crime, and Deviance*, ed. Bruce A. Arrigo (Belmont, Calif.: West/Wadsworth, 1999), 14–29.

55 [56] Francis T. Cullen, William J. Maakestad, and Gray Cavender, *Corporate Crime under Attack: The Ford Pinto Case and Beyond* (Cincinnati: Andersen, 1987).

56 Sally Simpson, "Feminist Theory, Crime, and Justice," *Criminology* 27 (1989): 605–631.

57 Curran and Renzetti, *Theories of Crime*, 209–228.

58 Gregg Barak, Jeanne M. Flavin, and Paul S. Leighton, *Class, Race, Gender, and Crime: Social Realities of Justice in America* (Los Angeles: Roxbury, 2000).

59 The phrase "We are a nation of laws and not of men" originates from John Adams.

60 Francis T. Cullen, Jon Paul Wright, and Mitchell B. Chamlin, "Social Support and Social Reform: A Progressive Crime Control Agenda," *Crime and Delinquency* 45 (1999): 188–207.

61 Delbert S. Elliott, David Huizinga, and Suzanne S. Ageton, *Explaining Delinquency and Drug Use* (Beverly Hills: Sage, 1985). Delbert S, Elliott, David Huizinga, and Scott Menard, *Multiple Problem Youth: Delinquency, Substance Use, and Mental Health Problems* (New York: Springer-Verlag, 1989).

62 Terence P. Thornberry, "Toward an Interactional Theory of Delinquency," *Criminology* 25, no. 4 (November 1987): 863–892.

63 Ibid.

64 Terrie Moffitt, "Adolescent-Limited and Life-Course Persistent Antisocial Behavior: A Developmental Taxonomy," *Psychological Review* 100 (1993): 674–701.

65 Ibid., 519.

66 John H. Laub and Robert J. Sampson, *Shared Beginnings, Divergent Lives: Delinquent Boys to Age 70* (Cambridge, Mass.: Harvard University Press, 2003).

Glossary

A

Actual-seizure stop An incident in which police officers physically restrain a person and restrict his or her freedom.

Actus reus "Guilty deed"; the physical action of a criminal offense.

Adjudication The action of administering a legal process of judging and pronouncing a judgment.

Adjudicatory hearing The process in which a juvenile court determines whether the allegations in a petition are supported by evidence.

Adversarial process A term describing the manner in which U.S. criminal trial courts operate; a system that requires two sides, a prosecution and a defense.

Affirmative defense A defense in which the defendant must provide evidence that excuses the legal consequences of an act that the defendant has been proven to have committed.

Alibi A defense that involves the defendant(s) claiming not to have been at the scene of a criminal offense when it was committed.

Amicus curiae A brief in which someone who is not part of a case gives advice or testimony.

Appeal A written petition to a higher court to review a lower court's decision for the purpose of convincing the higher court that the lower court's decision was incorrect.

Arraignment Court appearance in which the defendant is formally charged with a crime and asked to respond by pleading guilty, not guilty, or *nolo contendere* (I do not wish to contend).

Arrest When law enforcement detains and holds a criminal suspect or suspects.

Arson Any willful or malicious burning or attempt to burn a dwelling, public building, motor vehicle, aircraft, or personal property of another.

Assize of Clarendon A 12th-century English law that established judicial procedure and the grand jury system.

Attendant circumstances Additional conditions that define a given criminal offense.

Authority The right and the power to commit an act or order others to commit an act.

B

Bail agent An employee of a private, for-profit company that provides money for suspects to be released from jail. Also called a bondsman.

Bailiff Court officer responsible for executing writs and processes, making arrests, and keeping order in the court.

Bench trial A trial in which a defendant waives the right to a jury trial and instead agrees to a trial in which the judge hears and decides the case.

Beyond a reasonable doubt The highest level of proof required to win a case; necessary in criminal cases to procure a guilty verdict.

Bill of indictment A declaration of the charges against an accused person that is presented to a grand jury to determine whether enough evidence exists for an indictment.

Bill of Rights The first 10 amendments to the U.S. Constitution, which guarantee fundamental rights and privileges to citizens.

Blood feud A disagreement whose settlement is based on personal vengeance and physical violence.

Bobbies A slang term for the police force created in 1829 by Sir Robert Peel's Metropolitan Police Act that was derived from the short form of Robert, Bob.

Bow Street Runners A police organization created circa 1748 by magistrates and brothers Henry Fielding and Sir John Fielding whose members went on patrol, rather than remaining at a designated post.

Broken-windows perspective The idea that untended property or deviant behavior will attract crime.

Burglary Breaking into and entering a structure or vehicle with intent to commit a felony or a theft.

C

Capital punishment The sentence of death for a criminal offense.

Case law The published decisions of courts that create new interpretations of the law and can be cited as precedent.

Cash bond A requirement that the entire amount of the bail cost be paid in cash.

Charge Formal statement of the criminal offense the defendant is accused of.

Child advocate An officer appointed by the court to protect the interests of the child and to act as a liaison among the child, the child's family, the court, and any other agency involved with the child.

Circuit court A court that holds sessions at intervals within different areas of a judicial district.

Civil law The law that governs private rights as opposed to the law that governs criminal issues.

Clerk of the court The primary administrative officer of each court who manages non-judicial functions.

Code of Hammurabi An ancient code instituted by Hammurabi, a ruler of Babylonia, dealing with criminal and civil matters.

Collective behavior A sociological term that describes how an individual's actions are transmitted into group actions that can exceed what any of the individuals in the group intended.

Commitment An order by a judge upon conviction or before a trial that sends a person to jail or prison. Also, a judge's order that sends a mentally unstable person to a mental institution.

Common law Laws that are based on customs and general principles and that may be used as precedent or for matters not addressed by statute.

Community corrections A form of corrections in which criminal offenders are managed in the community instead of in correctional facilities.

Community policing A policing strategy that attempts to harness the resources and residents of a given community in stopping crime and maintaining order.

Concurrence The coexistence of *actus reus* and *mens rea*.

Congregate-and-silent system A style of penal control pioneered by the Auburn System in which inmates were allowed to eat and work together during the day but were forbidden to speak to each other and were locked alone in their cells at night.

Consent decree When the parties to a lawsuit accept a judge's order that is based on an agreement made by them instead of continuing the case through a trial or hearing.

Constable The head of law enforcement for large districts in early England. In the modern United States, a constable serves areas such as rural townships and is usually elected.

Convict lease system A system in the late 19th and early 20th centuries in which companies and individuals could purchase the labor of prison inmates from state and county governments.

Corporate crime Offenses committed by a corporation's officers who pursue illegal activity in the corporation's name.

Corpus delicti "Body of the crime"; the criminal offense.

Court administrator An officer responsible for the mechanical necessities of the court, such as scheduling courtrooms, managing case flow, administering personnel, procuring furniture, and preparing budgets.

Court of the Star Chamber An old English court comprising the king's councilors that was separate from common-law courts.

Court reporter A court officer who records and transcribes an official verbatim record of the court's legal proceedings.

Courtroom work group The judges, prosecutors, defense attorneys, clerks, and bailiffs who work together to move cases through the court system and whose interaction determines the outcome of criminal cases.

Criminal Division Part of the U.S. Department of Justice, the Criminal Division develops, enforces, and supervises the application of all federal criminal laws except those assigned to other divisions.

Crime The violation of the laws of a society by a person or a group of people who are subject to the laws of that society.

Crime-control model A model proposed by legal scholar Herbert L. Packer to describe the public's expectation of an efficient criminal justice system.

Crime rate The number of crime index offenses divided by the population of an area, usually given as a rate of crimes per 100,000 people.

Criminal justice A social institution that has the mission of controlling crime by detecting, detaining, adjudicating, and punishing and/or rehabilitating people who break the law.

Criminal law The law specifying the prosecution by the government of a person or people for an act that has been classified as a criminal offense.

D

Dark figure of crime A term describing crime that is unreported and never quantified.

Decriminalization Emendation of laws or statutes to lessen or remove penalties for specific acts subject to criminal prosecution, arrest, and imprisonment.

Deinstitutionalization The policy of removing mentally ill people from public mental-health institutions and closing part or all of those institutions.

Department of Homeland Security (DHS) A department of the U.S. government responsible for preventing terrorism and enhancing national security; securing and managing U.S. borders; enforcing and administering U.S. immigration laws; safeguarding and securing U.S. interests on the Internet; and assisting in the federal response to terrorist attacks and natural disasters within the United States.

Department of Justice The federal executive agency that handles all criminal prosecutions and civil suits in which the United States has an interest.

Department of the Treasury The federal executive agency that is responsible for promoting economic prosperity and ensuring the financial security of the United States.

Determinate sentence A prison term that is determined by law and states a specific period of time to be served.

Direct filing A form of waiving a juvenile to criminal court in which a prosecutor has the discretion to file charges in either juvenile or criminal court.

Directed verdict of acquittal An order from a trial judge to the jury stating that the jury must acquit the accused because the prosecution has not proved its case.

Discretion The power of a criminal justice official to make decisions on issues within legal guidelines.

Disposition The final determination of a case or other matter by a court or other judicial entity.

Diversion The effort to deinstitutionalize delinquent and neglected children.

Docket A schedule of cases in a court.

Double jeopardy Prosecution of a defendant in the same jurisdiction for an offense for which the defendant has already been prosecuted and convicted or acquitted.

Double marginality The multiple outsider status of women and minority police officers as a result of being treated differently by their fellow officers.

Due process model A model proposed by legal scholar Herbert L. Packer to describe the public's expectation of a just and fair criminal justice system.

Due process rights Guarantees by the Fifth, Sixth, and Fourteenth Amendments that establish legal procedures that recognize the protection of an individual's life, liberty, and property.

E

Embezzlement The theft or taking of money or property by a person who is charged by an employer or other authority to be responsible for those assets.

Entrapment The use of extreme means by law enforcement to pressure someone to break the law.

F

Federal Bureau of Investigation (FBI) The main federal law enforcement agency in the United States, which operates under the Department of Justice and deals with domestic crime that crosses state lines, as well as some types of significant crime within the states, such as terrorism.

Federal Bureau of Prisons Established within the Department of Justice in 1930, a federal agency that manages and regulates all federal penal and correctional institutions.

Felony An offense punishable by a sentence of more than a year in state or federal prison and sometimes by death.

For-profit probation A form of probation supervision that is contracted to for-profit private agencies by the state.

Frankpledge system An early form of English government that divided communities into groups of 10 men who were responsible for the group's conduct and ensured that a member charged with breaking the law appeared in court.

G

Gender The socially constructed roles, behaviors, actions, and characteristics that a society considers appropriate for males and females.

General deterrence A method of control in which the punishment of a single offender sets an example for the rest of society.

General-jurisdiction court A court that may hear all types of cases except for those prohibited by law.

Geographic jurisdiction The authority of a court to hear a case based on the location of the offense.

Going rate A term describing how similar cases have been settled by a given set of judges, prosecutors, and attorneys.

Good time The time deducted from an inmate's prison sentence for good behavior.

Grabbable area The area under the control of an individual during an arrest in an automobile.

H

Habeas corpus An order to have a prisoner/detainee brought before the court to determine if it is legal to hold the prisoner/detainee.

Hands-off doctrine The judicial attitude toward prisons before the 1960s in which courts did not become involved in prison affairs or inmate rights.

Hearing A session that takes place without a jury before a judge or magistrate in which evidence and/or arguments are presented to determine some factual or legal issue.

Hierarchy rule When more than one criminal offense is committed in a given incident, but only the offense that is highest on the hierarchy list is reported to the FBI's Uniform Crime Reports.

Hierarchical jurisdiction The authority of a court to hear a case based on where the case is located in the system.

Hue and cry In early England, the alarm that citizens were required to raise upon the witness or discovery of a criminal offense.

Hung jury A jury in a criminal case that is deadlocked or that cannot produce a unanimous verdict.

I

Impeach The discrediting of a witness.

Inchoate offense An offense composed of acts necessary to commit another offense.

Indeterminate sentence A prison term that is determined by a parole board and does not state a specific period of time to be served or a date of release.

Indictment A written statement of the facts of the offense that is charged against the accused.

Infancy In legal terminology, the state of a child who has not yet reached a specific age; almost all states end infancy at age 18.

Informal probation A period during which a juvenile is required to stay out of trouble or make restitution before a case is dropped.

Information A formal, written accusation against a defendant submitted to the court by a prosecutor.

Infraction In most jurisdictions, a minor civil offense that is not serious enough to warrant curtailing an offender's freedom.

Inquest In archaic usage, considered the first type of jury that determined the ownership of land; currently, a type of investigation.

Insanity defense A defense that attempts to give physical or psychological reasons that a defendant cannot comprehend his or her criminal actions, their harm(s), or their punishment.

Intensive-supervision probation (ISP) A form of supervision that requires frequent meetings between the client and probation officer.

Intermediate sanctions Sentencing alternatives that are stricter than regular probation but less severe than prison.

J

Jail A secure facility that typically holds arrestees, criminal suspects, and inmates serving sentences less than a year.

Judicial waiver A form of waiving a juvenile to criminal court in which a judge sends the juvenile to adult court.

Jurisdiction The authority of the court to hear certain cases.

Just deserts A philosophy that states that an offender who commits a heinous crime deserves death.

Justice The administering of a punishment or reward in accordance with morals that a given society considers to be correct.

Juvenile delinquent A person, usually under the age of 18, who is determined to have committed a criminal offense or status offense in states in which a minor is declared to lack responsibility and cannot be sentenced as an adult.

L

Labeling theory A perspective that considers recidivism to be a consequence, in part, of the negative labels applied to offenders.

Larceny A form of theft in which an offender takes possessions that do not belong to him or her with the intent of keeping them.

Legalistic style A mode of policing that emphasizes enforcement of the letter of the law.

Legalization The total removal of legal prohibitions on specific acts that were previously proscribed and punishable by law.

Limited-jurisdiction court A court that has jurisdiction only over certain types of cases or subject matter.

Lower courts Sometimes called inferior courts, in reference to their hierarchy. These courts receive their authority and resources from local county or municipal governments.

M

Magna Carta "Great Charter"; a guarantee of liberties signed by King John of England in 1215 that influenced many modern legal and constitutional principles.

Mandatory minimum sentence A sentence determined by law that establishes the minimum length of prison time that may be served for an offense.

Marks-of-commendation system An incarceration philosophy developed by Alexander Maconochie in which inmates earned the right to be released, as well as privileges, goods, and services.

Mass murder The murder of three or more people in a single incident.

Master status A personal status that overwhelms all others.

Mens rea "Guilty mind"; intent or knowledge to break the law.

Meritorious time Time deducted from an inmate's sentence for doing something special or extra, such as getting a GED.

Metropolitan Police Act Sponsored in 1829 by Sir Robert Peel, it was the first successful bill to create a permanent, public police force.

Misdemeanor A minor criminal offense punishable by a fine and/or jail time for up to one year.

Missouri Bar Plan A form of judicial selection in which a nominating commission presents a list of candidates to the governor, who decides on a candidate. After a year in office, voters decide on whether to retain the judge. Judges must run for such reelection each term. Also called merit selection.

N

National Crime Victimization Survey (NCVS) A survey that is the primary source of information on criminal victimization in the United States and attempts to measure the extent of crime by interviewing crime victims.

National Incident-Based Reporting System (NIBRS) A crime-reporting system in which each separate offense in a crime is described, including data describing the offender(s), victim(s), and property.

Neighborhood Watch A community policing program that encourages residents to cooperate in providing security for the neighborhood.

Net-widening A phenomenon through which criminal justice programs pull more clients into the system than would otherwise be involved without the program.

No-bill The decision of a grand jury not to indict an accused person because of insufficient evidence. Also called "no true bill."

Nolo contendere A plea in which a defendant does not accept or deny responsibility for the charges but agrees to accept punishment. From Latin meaning, "I will not contest."

Normal crimes Routine cases that are considered in the context of how the court handled similar offenses.

P

Pains of imprisonment Deprivations that define the punitive nature of imprisonment.

Parens patriae Latin for "father of the country," the philosophy that the government is the ultimate guardian of all children or disabled adults.

Parole The conditional release of a prison inmate who has served part of a sentence and who remains under the court's control.

Pendleton Civil Service Reform Act Law that established federal government positions would be awarded on the basis of merit rather than political affiliation.

Penal code A code of laws that deals with crimes and the punishments for them.

Peremptory challenges The right of both the prosecution and the defense attorney to have a juror dismissed before trial without stating a reason.

Petitioner A person who files a lawsuit; also called a plaintiff.

Plea bargain A compromise reached by the defendant, the defendant's attorney, and the prosecutor in which the defendant agrees to plead guilty or no contest in return for a reduction of the charges' severity, dismissal of some charges, further information about the offense or about others involved in it, or the prosecutor's agreement to recommend a desired sentence.

Policeman's working personality The mindset of police who must deal with danger, authority, isolation, and suspicion while appearing to be efficient.

Posse comitatus "The power or force of the county. The entire population of a county above the age of 15, which a sheriff may summon to his assistance in certain cases as to aid him in keeping the peace, in pursuing and arresting felons, etc."[i]

Precedent A prior legal decision used as a basis for deciding a later, similar case.

Preponderance of the evidence The burden of proof in a civil trial, which requires that more than 50 percent of the evidence be in the plaintiff's favor.

Pre-sentence investigation (PSI) The report prepared by a probation officer to assist a judge in sentencing; also called a pre-sentence report.

Presumptive sentence A sentence that may be adjusted by the judge depending on aggravating or mitigating factors.

Pre-trial motion A request made by the prosecutor or defense attorney that the court make a decision on a specific issue before the trial begins.

Prison-industrial complex The increased reliance on incarceration, surveillance, and law enforcement in the United States and its relationship to the establishment of for-profit incarceration and probation/parole services, and businesses that supply goods and services to prisons and jails.

Prison Litigation Reform Act Legislation that restricts litigation by prison inmates based on the conditions of their confinement.

Probable cause A reason based on known facts to think that a law has been broken or that a property is connected to a criminal offense.

Probation The suspension of all or part of a sentence subject to certain conditions and supervision in the community.

Problem-oriented policing A style of policing that attempts to address the underlying social problems that contribute to crime by integrating research and scientific problem-solving strategies to analyze instances of crime with the goal of developing more effective response strategies.

Procedural law Law that specifies how the criminal justice system is allowed to deal with those who break the law or are accused of breaking the law.

Property bond The use of a piece of property instead of cash as collateral for bail.

R

Racial profiling Suspicion of illegal activity based on a person's race, ethnicity, or national origin rather than on actual illegal activity or evidence of illegal activity.

Racketeering A federal crime that involves patterns of illegal activity carried out by organized groups that run illegal businesses or break the law in other organized ways.

Rape Sexual activity, usually sexual intercourse, that is forced on another person without his or her consent, usually under threat of harm. Also, sexual activity conducted with a person who is incapable of valid consent.

Reasonable-stop standard A Supreme Court measure that considers constitutionality on whether a reasonable person would feel free to terminate an encounter with law enforcement personnel.

Reasonable suspicion A suspicion based on facts or circumstances that justifies stopping and sometimes searching an individual thought to be involved in illegal activity.

Recidivism Continuing to break the criminal law and returning to the criminal justice system after being processed for past offenses.

Recidivism rate The rate of ex-offenders who commit new offenses and are returned to prison.

Redirect examination The questioning of a witness about issues uncovered during cross-examination.

Referral Similar to a "charge" in the adult system in which an authority, usually the police, parents, or the school, determines that a youth needs intervention from the juvenile court.

Release on recognizance (ROR) When a defendant pays no money to be released from jail and promises to appear in court when required.

Residential placement Any sentence of a juvenile delinquent to a residential facility where the juvenile is closely monitored.

Respondent The party who must reply to a petitioner's complaint. Equivalent to a defendant in a lawsuit.

Retribution Punishment that is considered to be deserved.

Retribution model A style of control in which offenders are punished as severely as possible for a crime and in which rehabilitation is not attempted.

Robbery The taking or attempting to take anything of value from the care, custody, or control of a person or persons by force or threat of force or violence and/or by putting the victim in fear.

Rule of four A rule that states that at least four of the nine Supreme Court justices must vote to hear a case.

Rule of law In the context of criminal justice, the government cannot punish any individual without strict adherence to clear, fair, and defined rules, laws, and procedures.

S

Search An investigation of an area and/or person by a police officer to look for evidence of criminal activity.

Seizure The collecting by police officers of potential evidence in a criminal case.

Self-report study Research in which individuals are asked about criminal offenses they have committed, even those they have never been arrested for or charged with.

Sentencing guidelines A set of rules concerning the sentencing for a specified set of offenses that seek to create uniform sentencing policy by directing the judge to consider certain facts about the offense and the defendant when determining the sentence.

Separate-and-silent system A method of penal control pioneered by Philadelphia's Eastern State Penitentiary in which inmates were kept from seeing or talking to one another. This method is comparable to solitary confinement in modern prisons.

Serial murder The murder of a series of victims during three or more separate events over an extended period of time.

Service style A mode of policing that is concerned primarily with serving the community and citizens.

Sexual assault Sexual contact that is committed without the other party's consent or with a party who is not capable of giving consent.

Shock probation The practice of sentencing offenders to prison, allowing them to serve a short time, and then granting them probation without their prior knowledge.

Show-of-authority stop An incident in which police show a sign of authority (such as flashing a badge), and the suspect submits.

Social control The rules, habits, and customs a society uses to enforce conformity to its norms.

Sociological imagination The idea that we must look beyond the obvious to evaluate how our social location influences how we perceive society.

Specific deterrence A method of control in which an offender is prevented from committing more crimes by either imprisonment or death.

Stare decisis The doctrine under which courts adhere to legal precedent.

State courts General courts and special courts funded and run by each state.

Status offense An act that is considered a legal offense only when committed by a juvenile and that can be adjudicated only in a juvenile court.

Statute A law enacted by a legislature.

Statutory exclusion Provisions that exclude, without hearing or waiver, juveniles who meet certain age, offense, or past-record criteria from the jurisdiction of the juvenile court.

Statutory law The type of law that is enacted by legislatures, as opposed to common law.

Statutory rape Sexual activity conducted with a person who is younger than a specified age or incapable of valid consent because of mental illness, mental handicap, intoxication, unconsciousness, or deception.

Stop A temporary detention that legally is a seizure of an individual and must be based on reasonable suspicion.

Stop-and-frisk A term that describes two distinct behaviors on the part of law enforcement officers in dealing with suspects. To conduct a lawful frisk, the stop itself must meet the legal conditions of a seizure. A frisk constitutes a search.

Street crime Small-scale, personal offenses such as single-victim homicide, rape, robbery, assault, burglary, and vandalism.

Strict liability Responsibility for a criminal offense without intention to break the law.

Subject-matter jurisdiction The authority of a court to hear a case based on the nature of the case.

Substantive law Law that describes which behaviors have been defined as criminal offenses.

Supermax prison An extremely secure type of prison that strictly limits inmate contact with other inmates, correctional staff, and the outside world.

Surety bond The use of a bail agent who promises to pay the defendant's bail if he or she fails to appear for further court proceedings.

T

Terrorism The use or threat of violence against a state or other political entity in order to coerce.

Thames River Police A private police force created by the West India Trading Company in 1798 that represented the first professional, salaried police force in London.

Three strikes In reference to criminal justice, a term that describes state laws that require an offender's third felony to be punishable by a severe sentence, including life imprisonment.

Tort law An area of the law that deals with civil acts that cause harm and injury, including libel, slander, assault, trespass, and negligence.

Total institution A closed environment in which every aspect, including the movement and behavior of the people within, is controlled and structured.

Trial by ordeal An ancient custom in which the accused was required to perform a test that appealed to divine authority to prove guilt or innocence.

True bill The decision of a grand jury that sufficient evidence exists to indict an accused person.

Uniform Crime Reports (UCR) An annual publication by the Federal Bureau of Investigation that uses data from all participating law enforcement agencies in the United States to summarize the incidence and rate of reported crime.

U

U.S. Attorneys The principal litigators of the United States who conduct most of the trial work in which the United States is a party. They prosecute criminal cases brought by the federal government; prosecute and defend civil cases in which the United States is a party; and collect certain types of debts owed to the federal government.

U.S. courts of appeals Intermediate courts that dispose of many appeals before they reach the Supreme Court.

U.S. district courts Courts of general jurisdiction that try felony cases involving federal laws and civil cases involving amounts of money over $75,000.

U.S. Solicitor General The person who determines which cases the federal government will send to the U.S. Supreme Court for review and the positions the government will take before the Court.

U.S. Supreme Court The "court of last resort." The highest court in the United States, established by Article III of the Constitution, hears only appeals, with some exceptions.

USA FREEDOM Act A law signed by President Barack Obama in 2015 that reauthorized parts of the USA PATRIOT Act but limited the bulk collection of U.S. residents' phone records and Internet data.

USA PATRIOT Act A law signed by President George W. Bush on October 26, 2001 in response to the terror attacks of September 11, 2001 that gave the U.S. government broad authority to detect and prevent terrorism.

Use of force "The amount of effort required by police to compel compliance from an unwilling subject," according to the International Association of Chiefs of Police.

V

Venire The list or pool from which jurors are chosen.

Victim "[A] person that has suffered direct physical, emotional, or pecuniary harm as a result of the commission of a crime."[ii]

Victim-impact statement An account given by the victim, the victim's family, or others affected by the offense that expresses the effects of the offense, including economic losses, the extent of physical or psychological injuries, and major life changes.

Victim precipitation A situation in which a crime victim plays an active role in initiating a crime or escalating it.

Victimless crime Behaviors that are deemed undesirable because they offend community standards rather than directly harm people or property.

Visibility A term that refers to the fact that police work is easily observed by the public and that police are accountable to the public, police supervisors, and legislatures.

Voir dire French for "to see, to speak"; a phrase that refers to the questioning of jurors by a judge and/or attorneys to determine whether individual jurors are appropriate for a particular jury panel.

W

War on drugs Governmental policy aimed at reducing the sale and use of illegal drugs.

Watch-and-ward system An early English system overseen by the constable in which a watchman guarded a city's or town's gates at night.

Watchman style A mode of policing that emphasizes the maintenance of order and informal intervention on the part of the police officer rather than strict enforcement of the law.

White-collar crime A nonviolent criminal offense committed during the course of business for financial gain.

Wickersham Commission report The 14-volume report published in 1931 and 1932, which was the first comprehensive national study of U.S. crime and law enforcement.

Writ of certiorari An order from a superior court calling up for review the record of a case from a lower court.

Z

Zero-tolerance policing A form of policing that punishes every infraction of the law, however minor, with an arrest, fine, or other penalty so that offenders will refrain from committing more serious offenses.

Notes

i   *Black's Law Dictionary*, Posse Comitatus.

ii 34 U.S. Code § 20141. Services to victims. See www.law.cornell.edu/uscode/text/34/20141. Accessed June 2019.

Credits

Index

A reference that includes *d* indicates that the term is defined on the page. A *t* indicates that the information may be found in a table, and *f* indicates that the information is located within a feature box.

CLEAR. CURRENT. CONCISE.

Examines the core concepts and fosters the essential critical-thinking and ethical decision-making skills that students need to unravel myths from realities in the criminal justice system.

"*Introduction to Criminal Justice* provides great historical background for all topics, with lots of material for engaging students—even online students. It is well written and has student support in mind."

—**Allan Barnes,**
University of Alaska Anchorage

This is a comprehensive introductory text that enables students to explore and fully understand the foundations of our criminal justice system in the United States."

—**Doug Klutz,**
University of Alabama

ABOUT THE AUTHOR

John Randolph Fuller is Professor Emeritus of Criminology at the University of West Georgia where he taught for more than thirty years. He is the author of several books, including *Criminal Justice: Mainstream and Crosscurrents,* Third Edition (OUP, 2013).

NEW TO THIS EDITION

- **Presents the latest available** research, statistics, and developments

- **Substantially revised** to reflect both changes in the law and the patterns of crime in the United States

- **Features all new chapter-opening vignettes** based on news stories, current events, and cases that capture the attention of students

- **Includes updated and revised examples** that reflect criminal justice issues that have recently gained prominence, and new figures and tables

- **Includes an updated supplements package written by the author,** available on **Oxford Learning Link**

- **A new video package** features fourteen new videos (one per chapter) that help illustrate chapter issues and concepts

- **New "Fast-Class Mini-Lectures"** feature short, five-minute lectures narrated by the author and supported by PowerPoint slides

- **New "Getting It Right"** features highlight instances in which criminal justice practitioners have successfully implemented solutions

- **Updated "A Closer Look"** features address recent issues and controversies

OXFORD
UNIVERSITY PRESS
www.oup.com/us/he

ISBN 978-0-19-750404-8